READING LUKE

Charles H. Talbert

READING LUKE

A LITERARY AND
THEOLOGICAL COMMENTARY
ON THE THIRD GOSPEL

CROSSROAD • NEW YORK

1982

The Crossroad Publishing Company
575 Lexington Avenue, New York, N.Y. 10022

Library of Congress Cataloging in Publication Data

Talbert, Charles H.
Reading Luke.

1. Bible. N.T. Luke—Commentaries.
I. Bible. N.T. Luke. English. II. Title.
BS2595.3.T34   1982   226°.407   82-12737
ISBN 0-8245-0532-8

Acknowledgments

Quotations from the Bible are taken from the Revised Standard Version unless otherwise specified. A quote from the Gospel of the Hebrews comes from *Gospel Parallels* (RSV). Quotations from the early church fathers are from *The Ante-Nicene Fathers*. Citations from Greek and Roman authors are found in the Loeb Classical Library.

To
the memory of Eleanor Mills
Prayer Warrior Extraordinary

CONTENTS

PREFACE

This volume was begun during the spring semester, 1979, when I enjoyed a Reynolds Research Fellowship from Wake Forest University. Its progress has been facilitated by a series of grants from the Graduate Council of Wake Forest University, and by the untiring assistance of Mrs. Anne Francis, secretary to the Department of Religion. That several good friends read all or part of earlier drafts resulted in numerous improvements; the flaws remaining are my responsibility.

Two sources of encouragement deserve special mention. First, I benefitted greatly from the constant stimulation provided both by colleagues in the Society of Biblical Literature's Luke-Acts Seminar which began in 1979 and the earlier Luke-Acts Group, 1973–78, on the one hand, and by my peers in the Catholic Biblical Association's Luke-Acts Task Force, in which I have participated since research for this book began, on the other. Second, the students of Wake Forest University who took my exegetical course on the Gospel of Luke in 1978, 1980, and 1981 have been, in many ways, my teachers. Both colleagues in the professional societies and students in my classes deserve my thanks.

As always, without the support of my wife, Betty, and my children, Caroline and Richard, such an effort would have been impossible.

GETTING READY
TO READ THE GOSPEL

E very reading of a gospel is from a particular angle of vision. It is imperative, therefore, at the outset, to understand the angle assumed in the commentary. The following paragraphs are devoted to this end.

This volume reflects the widespread loss of confidence in the two-source theory that has occurred during the past fifteen years. The anonymous author of the third gospel, a Christian of the second generation and of unknown provenance, who writes on the basis of what the first generation delivered (cf. Heb 2:3–4 for a similar perspective), mentions other reports of the things "fulfilled among us" that were written before his attempt. In the past some have suggested that Mark and Q were among those reports and were used by the evangelist as his primary sources. Since 1963, however, there has been a prolonged assault on the two-document hypothesis. Although the alternatives proposed have not proved convincing, enough difficulties with the priority of Mark and the existence of Q have emerged to render the two-source theory's position as an "assured result" of criticism suspect. It is, therefore, a questionable control on redaction critical work.

> Employing Mark as a control today is about as compelling as using Colossians and Second Thessalonians to describe Paul's theology. It may very well be legitimate to do so, but so many have problems with the procedure that such an assumption narrows considerably the circles with whom one can converse. (C. H. Talbert, "Shifting Sands: The Recent Study of the Gospel of Luke," *Interpretation* 30 [1976]: 393–94)

This commentary will not assume the two-source theory, nor any other source theory, for that matter. Although the movement beyond the study of the Lukan alterations of Mark is both necessary and proper,

1

this does not prevent the comparison of Luke's narrative development with that of the other gospels, including Mark, when they run parallel. This procedure need not assume Luke used any of the other gospels any more than a comparison of Mark and John assumes the former's dependence upon the latter. In this volume comparisons of Luke with other gospels will be made, but without assuming any source theory.

The commentary will investigate the third gospel with a type of redaction criticism heavily influenced by nonbiblical literary criticism.

> From the standpoint of current American redaction criticism, each gospel represents an intricately designed religious universe, with plot and character development, retrospective and prospective devices, linear and concentric patternings, and a continuous line of thematic cross-references and narrative interlockings. The art of interpretation consists in analyzing the complexities of the narrative construction and to comprehend [*sic*] individual parts in connection with the total architecture. (Werner Kelber, "Redaction Criticism: On the Nature and Exposition of the Gospels," *Perspectives in Religious Studies* 6 [1979]: 14)

The thrust of this approach is on understanding large thought units and their relationship to Lukan thought as a whole rather than focusing on the individual pieces of the narrative. Given this approach, the present volume does not follow the word-by-word, phrase-by-phrase, verse-by-verse method of traditional commentaries. Nevertheless, the thrust of this approach is also on the close reading of the text of the gospel itself. Similarly, although the interpreter's dialogue with the gospel is carried on in light of the history of research, this commentary makes little reference to secondary literature. The aim is not to direct one through the maze of scholarship but to make one feel at home in the biblical text itself. The closest parallel to the type of approach attempted here for the third gospel is Part III, "Argument and Structure," of C. H. Dodd's *The Interpretation of the Fourth Gospel* (Cambridge: Cambridge University, 1958).

This book operates from a perspective indebted to genre criticism. Luke-Acts belongs to the ancient biographical tradition. Ancient biographies can be separated into two different categories: literary (e.g., Plutarch's *Lives*) and cultic. Cultic biographies are those produced by and used within religious or semireligious communities, such as philosophical schools, and usually treat the career of the community's

founder as the value norm for devotees and the object of their reverence and worship. Among such lives was a type in which (a) the life of the divine hero was followed by (b) a narrative of successors and selected other disciples. The two components (a + b) were parts of a single work. Such biographies are known both from the later literary collections made of the individual cultic legends (e.g., Diogenes Laertius, *Lives of Eminent Philosophers*) and from fragments of the early and original documents (cf. Ingemar Duering, *Aristotle in the Ancient Biographical Tradition* [Goeteborg: Goeteborgs Universitets Aersskrift, 1957], who has collected the fragments of a pre-Christian biography of Aristotle). The function of such a biography with an a + b pattern in a philosophical school was legitimation. On the one hand, such a biography would legitimate the founder's successors at the time of the document's writing by showing the line of tradition from the founder to them and by showing the continuities between what they did and said and what the founder did and said. On the other hand, this type of biography would legitimate the founder's positions by showing the line of tradition from his time to the time of the document's writing: that the founder really did and said these things can be known with certainty because a line of tradition guarantees it.

Of all the types of literature in antiquity, this variety of biography is most like what one finds in Luke-Acts: that is, the life of the founder of a religious community followed by a narrative about his successors and selected other disciples—both in one work. Here also is a literary genre with some similarity in function to that of Luke-Acts. At least one aim of the Lukan work is to say the true tradition is that which came from Jesus through the Twelve to Paul and from him was passed to the Ephesian elders (Acts 20). This Lukan motif would inevitably function as legitimation in the same twofold way the philosophical biographies did.

This concern for legitimation reflected in the literary genre of Luke-Acts is also found in the preface with which the gospel begins:

> *Since many* have undertaken to *write* a *report* of the things that have been fulfilled among us, as those who were from the beginning eyewitnesses and ministers of the word have delivered them to us, *so also* it seemed to *me* a good thing, since I have followed everything carefully from the first, to *write* an orderly *account* for

you, most excellent Theophilus, so you may have certainty about
the matters of which you have been instructed. (my translation)

The author writes, he says, to give Theophilus certainty (*asphaleian*).
There are at least three major themes running through Luke-Acts
that would contribute to this legitimation: the fulfillment of prophecy,
the occurrence of miracles, and the martyrdom of the hero. Excursus
A treats the first and shows how fulfilled prophecy functioned in antiquity as a legitimation technique. Excursus B takes up the second and
likewise indicates how miracles served in antiquity to give certainty.
The section of this commentary covering 23:26–56 focuses on the legitimating function of martyrdom in Mediterranean antiquity.

The example of Justin Martyr offers evidence of the persuasive power
of fulfilled prophecy, miracle, and martyrdom on behalf of the Christian cause. In two places in his extant writings Justin tells of his conversion to Christianity. (1) In his *Dialogue with Trypho the Jew*, 7,
Justin tells how he walked by the seashore prior to becoming a Christian and met an old man, a Christian, who said to Justin,

> There existed, long before this time, certain men more ancient
> than all those who are esteemed philosophers, both righteous and
> beloved by God, who spoke by the Divine Spirit, and foretold events
> which would take place, and which are now taking place. They
> are called prophets. . . . Their writings are still extant . . . and
> *those events which have happened, and those which are happen-
> ing*, compel you to assent to the utterances made by them, al-
> though, indeed, they were entitled to credit on account of the *mir-
> acles* which they performed.

Here Justin says fulfilled prophecy and miracle were catalysts in his
becoming a Christian. (2) In *II Apology*, 12, Justin again returns to
his conversion:

> For I myself, too, when I was delighting in the doctrines of Plato,
> and heard the Christians slandered, and saw them fearless of death,
> and of all other things which are counted fearful, perceived that it
> was impossible that they could be living in wickedness and plea-
> sure.

As a result of Christian suffering and martyrdom, Justin says (13) that
he, "with all [his] strength strive[s] to be found a Christian."

Taken together, martyrdom, miracle, and fulfilled prophecy were
persuasive to Justin. There is no reason to think Justin was the excep-

tion in his time and place. He and his contemporaries would have heard the evangelist eagerly as he told the story of Jesus and the early church, with emphasis on the martyrdoms of Jesus and Stephen, the miracles of Jesus and the apostles, and the numerous fulfilled prophecies of every sort that dominate the two-volume work. Luke's narrative would have given certainty to Christian and non-Christian alike because it appealed to the persuasiveness of a selfless commitment (martyrdom), of power (miracle), and of being right and having roots (fulfilled prophecy). This narrative of Jesus and the early church is a legitimation document: its story is told with a persuasiveness intended to give certainty.

Certainty was essential if the Lukan biography of Jesus was to serve its practical purpose. Ancient biography, even of a literary type, often aimed at instruction in values (cf. Plutarch, "Cleomenes," 13), which, it was believed, could be most graphically communicated when shown incarnated in living personalities. Hence biographies often became hagiographies. As D. R. Stuart has put it, Aristoxenus' life of Pythagoras and the Pythagoreans consisted of

> preachments in which he sought to glorify the master and the ideals for which the master stood, and to correct the vulgar errors according to which popular belief had deformed the Pythagorean way of life. Thus his treatment . . . had much of the color of a saint's life. (*Epochs of Greek and Roman Biography* [Berkeley: University of California, 1928], pp. 158–59)

The emulation of the hero's way of life was the goal of such biography, but this was not understood as simply a blind and unthinking repetition of acts performed by the great person. Rather one was expected to learn from the hero how to order one's own life. Without necessarily performing the same actions, the reader of such biographies was expected to emulate the values of the hero in his or her own context (A. J. Gossage in *Latin Biography,* ed. T. A. Dorey [London: Routledge & Kegan Paul, 1967], p. 49). If the third gospel is biography, then the work and words of Jesus are narrated with the intent that they be emulated—not in a mechanical way but with imagination and conviction, and not through one's own strength but through the power of the Holy Spirit. That the evangelist repeatedly portrays Jesus as a model for disciples conforms to the preceding assessment of the gospel as a type of ancient biography. From this angle of vision the present commentary unfolds.

For the reader who wants to supplement this volume's approach with the resources of a traditional type of commentary, the following are recommended: Joseph A. Fitzmyer, *The Gospel according to Luke, I– IX* (Anchor 29; Garden City, N.Y.: Doubleday, 1981); I. H. Marshall, *The Gospel of Luke* (New Inter Gk NT Comm; Exeter: Paternoster Press, 1978); and Frederick W. Danker, *Jesus and the New Age according to St. Luke* (St. Louis: Clayton Publishing House, 1977).

MAKING A BEGINNING

1:1–4

G enre studies show that much can be learned about a text first by seeing how it participates in a given genre and secondly by noting how it differs from the genre. This certainly is true of Luke's preface in 1:1–4.

We begin with an examination of the components of ancient prefaces. Although not all are exactly alike, there is a significant number that correspond to one another in remarkable ways. In these prefaces taken from history and biography there are seven components, all or most of which appear regularly. (1) There is often a statement about the author's predecessors, usually about their inadequacies. Diodorus Siculus writes, "A study of my predecessors in this field has inspired me with the strongest feelings of approval for their purpose. At the same time, I hardly feel that the full possibilities of instruction inherent in it have been realized in their works." Philo writes in his *Life of Moses,* "Greek men of letters have refused to treat him as worthy of memory, possibly out of envy, and also because in many cases the ordinances of the legislators of the different states are opposed to his." Luke 1:1 contains this component also: "many have undertaken to compile a narrative." If there is any criticism of his predecessors implied, it is muted. It may very well be that his predecessors encouraged the evangelist to write by their example. If we take *epeidēper* as causal, then "inasmuch as" would mean "because," and Luke would be using the work of previous writers positively to justify his own venture. The absence of explicit critical comments about his predecessors sets Luke apart from most Greco-Roman prefaces.

(2) A preface usually tells the work's subject matter. Polybius writes,

> The events which he has chosen as his subject are sufficiently extraordinary in themselves to arouse and stimulate the interest of every reader, young or old. What mind . . . could feel no curiosity to learn the process by which almost the whole world fell under

7

the undisputed ascendency of Rome within a period of less than
fifty-three years.

Philo, *Life of Moses,* states, "I purpose to write the life of Moses." Luke's
"the things which have been accomplished among us" reflects this
component. In view of the strong emphasis in Luke-Acts on the fulfillment of prophecy (see Excursus A), *peplērophoremenōn* should most
likely be translated "fulfilled" instead of accomplished (cf. also Col 4:17
with 2 Tim 4:5): the things about which his predecessors wrote and
now Luke also (1:3) writes are things which are fulfillments of prophecy.

(3) There is customarily some statement about an author's qualifi-
cations for writing: either knowledge of the subject due to being an
eyewitness, or his having good sources, or having the linguistic ability
to handle the primary materials. Diodorus Siculus writes,

> My home is Agyrium in Sicily, and my intercourse with the Latin-
> speaking settlers in the island has given me a thorough command
> of the Latin language, so that I have been able to derive accurate
> information of all the transactions of the Roman dominion from
> the national records, which have been preserved from an early date.

In his *Life of Moses,* Philo says, "I will . . . tell the story of Moses as
I have learned it, both from the sacred books . . . and from some of
the elders of the nation; for I always interwove what I was told with
what I read, and thus believed myself to have a closer knowledge than
others of his life's history." Luke 1:1–4 tells both about the sources of
the author's material and about his own care in working. The source
of what has been delivered (as tradition—cf. 1 Cor 15:3; 11:23) to us
who live after the first generation (cf. Heb 2:3; Eusebius, *H.E.* 3:39)
is "those who from the beginning were eyewitnesses (cf. Acts 1:21–
22; 10:37; 11:15; 13:31; i.e., the apostles) and ministers of the word"
(cf. Acts 6:4; 26:16; i.e., people like the Seven and Paul). Four terms
characterize the author's description of his care in working. The term
parakolouthēkoti should be translated "investigated" (as in Demos-
thenes, *De Cor.* 53) instead of "followed" as in the RSV: "All things"
in the origins of Christianity have been investigated—"accurately" and
"from the first." The evangelist sets forth his credentials, as was the
Mediterranean custom. One who has read widely in Mediterranean
literature knows, however, that claims of reliability cannot be taken at
face value. Lucian, in his *How To Write History,* 29, complains that

those who have never set foot outside their city begin with such words
as, "Ears are less trustworthy than eyes. I write then what I have seen,
not what I have heard." In spite of claims to historical accuracy in the
letter of Aristeas' preface, what follows is largely fiction. A reader must
evaluate such claims in terms of the accuracy of the narrative which
follows.

(4) A statement of the plan, arrangement, or table of contents of the
work is a normal part of prefaces in antiquity. Diodorus writes,

> My first six volumes contain transactions and legends previous to
> the Trojan War. . . . In the eleven volumes that follow I have
> recorded the general transactions of the world from the Trojan War
> to the death of Alexander; while in the succeeding twenty-three
> volumes I have found room for all transactions between that date
> and the commencement of the Celto-Roman War.

Philo uses a secondary preface to begin the second volume of *Life of
Moses,* and says, "The former treatise dealt with the birth and nurture
of Moses; also with his education and career as a ruler . . . ; also with
the works which he performed . . . ; further with the troubles which
he successfully surmounted. . . . The present treatise is concerned
with matters allied and consequent to these." In 1:3 Luke gives his
plan: it will be an "orderly account," which obviously does not refer to
a chronological scheme of arrangement given the subsequent narrative. That an orderly account need not be chronologically arranged is
evident from Suetonius' statement in his "Life of Augustus," 9: "I shall
now take up its various phases one by one, not in chronological order,
but by classes, to make the account clearer and more intelligible." Furthermore, when Ovid, *Metamorphoses,* 7:520, says he will not ramble
but present things in their order, he means his work will be organized.

(5) A comment about the purpose of the writing was an inevitable
component of an ancient preface. Dionysus of Halicarnassus writes,
"My subject . . . is to eradicate these erroneous suppositions from the
public mind and to implant the truth in their place in treating of the
founders of Rome and of her early institutions and transactions." He
continues, "It is my hope that the discovery of the truth may induce a
proper appreciation of Rome in the minds of my readers." Philo says
in *Life of Moses,* "I hope to bring the story of this greatest and most
perfect of men to the knowledge of such as deserve not to remain in
ignorance of it; for, while the fame of the laws which he left behind

him has traveled throughout the civilized world and reached the ends of the earth, the man himself as he really was is known to few." The third evangelist sets forth his purpose at the beginning of 1:4: "that you have certainty" ("know the truth"). This stated purpose presupposes either doubts about Christianity or perversions of it. If the readers of Luke-Acts were non-Christians, the narrative would be designed to provide what was necessary for them to come to faith. If, as is more probable, the readers were already Christians, the narrative would provide what was necessary either for their certainty so they would remain Christians, or for their proper Christian stance so they would represent what was truly Christian in their lives.

(6) Sometimes the author's name is given. Thucydides' *History* begins, "Thucydides of Athens has written the history of the war between the Peloponnesians and the Athenians." This component is missing from the Lukan preface.

(7) Sometimes the official addressee of the work is named. Josephus, *Against Apion,* writes, "I suppose that, by my books of the Antiquities of the Jews, most excellent Epaphroditus, I have made it evident to those who peruse them, that our Jewish nation is of very great antiquity." The identity of "most excellent Theophilus" is unknown, the Lukan preface telling us only that he has been informed of the things relating to Christian origins. As in Acts 18:25, Rom 2:18, 1 Cor 14:19, Gal 6:6, *katechethes* (informed—vs. 4) may very well refer to Christian instruction of converts. If so the official addressee was a Christian. This need not be the case, however.

Luke 1:1–4 fits nicely into the genre of ancient prefaces, containing six of the seven components widely found in prefaces of histories and biographies. Certain characteristics of ancient prefaces also need to be noted. (1) The style was often highly rhetorical. This is certainly true of 1:1–4. The preface is one sentence which falls into two halves, each with three members or *cola.* The sense of each of the first three members stands in a corresponding relation to the sense of the latter three: (a) "many" in opposition to "also to me"; (b) "to compile a narrative" parallel to "to write an account"; (c) eyewitness tradition echoed in the "certainty" in vs. 4 (cf. Friedrich Blass, *Philology of the Gospels* [Amsterdam: B. R. Grüner, 1969—reprint of 1898 edition], chap. 2). (2) The style was often in marked contrast to that of the rest of the document. This is certainly true for Luke where the excellent Greek of 1:1–4 stands in marked contrast with the semitizing style of 1:5ff. The

exalted style of 1:1–4 simply conforms to cultural expectations for a rhetorical beginning. The same can also be said for 1:5ff. with its semitizing style, as it was a cultural expectation that a narrative would reflect the style of the people described. (3) The length was sometimes out of proportion to the body of the work. This prompted Lucian, in his *How To Write History*, 23, to satirize many prefaces as "the head of a Colossos of Rhodes on the body of a dwarf." The Lukan preface is by contrast a model of brevity. (4) The subjects treated were sometimes quite alien to the contents of the main work. Only a careful reading of the gospel and Acts can determine whether the narrative in fact is aimed at giving certainty or causing one to know the truth as opposed to error. (5) When a writing contained more than one volume or book, a secondary preface was often used (e.g., Philo, *Life of Moses*, II; Josephus, *Against Apion*, has a preface to the whole work at the beginning of Book 1 and a brief recapitulation at the beginning of Book 2. Cf. also *Ant.* 13:1). Acts 1:1–2 functions as such a secondary preface: "In the first book, O Theophilus, I have dealt with all that Jesus began to do and teach. . . ."

When one recognizes that 1:1–4 belongs to the genre of ancient prefaces, while at the same time differing from them in some regards, certain inferences can be made. (1) Regarding genre. Since prefaces were used for many different genres in antiquity, this preface cannot be used to deduce the genre of Luke-Acts. (2) Regarding historicity. Since extravagant claims of accuracy often accompanied fictitious accounts, we cannot determine Luke-Acts' historical accuracy from claims made in the preface. (3) Regarding purpose. Since the topics treated in a preface sometimes differed from those dealt with in the subsequent narrative, the preface's statement about purpose cannot guarantee the aim of what follows. It is, however, worth testing in one's reading of Luke-Acts whether the narrative was written so someone might know the truth about Christian origins. Truth could, of course, be understood either in the sense of accurate information or in the sense of certainty about Christianity.

Luke 1:5—4:15

PROPHECIES
OF FUTURE
GREATNESS

INTRODUCTION

Following the preface of 1:1–4, 1:5—4:15 comprises the first major unit in the third gospel, which is followed by the formal opening of Jesus' public ministry, the frontispiece (4:16–30). Luke 1:5—4:15 depicts the life of Jesus prior to his public career, and constitutes a coherent unit within the gospel. Two strands of evidence make this clear.

The first strand is the literary organization of the unit, which consists of three episodes dealing with John the Baptist and Jesus. Episode One, 1:5–38, involves the annunciations of the births of John and Jesus. The material focusing on John the Baptist (1:5–25) corresponds to that of Jesus' story (1:26–38). Luke 1:39–56 serves as a transition from the two annunciations of Episode One to Episode Two, the narratives about the births and early lives of John and Jesus (1:57—2:52); the section focusing on the Baptist (1:57–80) again corresponds to the material dealing with Jesus (2:1–52). Episode Three, 3:1—4:15, also treats John and Jesus in corresponding ways: 3:1–20 treats the adult ministry of the prophet John; 3:21—4:15 presents the prelude to Jesus' public career. Each of these three episodes is built around a series of correspondences between the story of John and of Jesus which reflects the Lukan artistry; each is concerned to portray Jesus' superiority over John the Baptist. In all three episodes John is depicted as a prophet (1:16–17; 1:76; 3:1–6), not the Messiah (3:15ff.), whereas Jesus is pictured in all three as the Davidic Messiah (1:32–33; 1:69; 2:4, 11; 3:23–38) and Son of God (1:35, 2:49; 3:22). The artistry and the internal coherence argue for the treatment of 1:5—4:15 as a single thought unit in the narrative.

The second strand is the literary genre. In Mediterranean antiquity there was, in biographical writing, a genre constituted by an account of the prepublic career of a great person: in this convention one found an account of the hero's career, before the public activity was begun, which included material on family background, perhaps a reference to

15

a miraculous conception, along with omens and other predictions of future greatness, including childhood prodigies. A representative example of this genre may be found in Suetonius' *Lives of the Twelve Caesars,* in his biography of Augustus.

In the "Life of Augustus" there is one section (94) set aside for "an account of the omens which occurred before he was born, on the very day of his birth, and afterwards." In this unit one finds fourteen omens: (a) portents interpreted by predictions (6 of 14 items) which belong in the same general category as 1:41–45; (b) dreams (3 of 14 items)— e.g., a man dreamed of the savior of the Roman people, then on meeting Augustus for the first time, declared he was the boy about whom he had dreamed (cf. 2:25–35); (c) prophecies (2 of 14 items)—verbal anticipations of the child's greatness and destiny (cf. the prophecies of Luke 1—3); (d) childhood prodigies (2 of 14 items), which claim such childhood exploits were regarded as omens of the youth's destiny (cf. 2:41–51; 4:1–13); (e) reference to a miraculous conception by Apollo (1 of 14 items), though the treatment of Augustus' family belongs to another section of the narrative about his prepublic life. The main thrust of the material in the genre of the prepublic life of a great person was on anticipations of the hero's destiny. It is certainly the case in this example from Suetonius.

In 1:5—4:15 one finds also that the thrust of the material is on anticipations of Jesus' destiny. These anticipations are given in various forms. (1) There are two angelophanies: (a) 1:26–38, the angel Gabriel comes to Mary not only to announce the miraculous conception but also to tell of the child's destiny; (b) 2:8–20, an angel appears to the shepherds in the field announcing the birth of one who will be a savior, Christ the Lord. (2) There are four prophecies: (a) 1:67–79 is a prophecy by Zechariah when he was filled with the Holy Spirit (vs. 67); (b) 2:25–35 gives the prophecy of Simeon, to whom it had been revealed that he should not taste death before he had seen the Lord's Christ (vs. 26); (c) 2:36–38 tells of the prophetess Anna, who spoke of Jesus "to all who were looking for the redemption of Jerusalem" (vs. 38); (d) 3:16–17 gives John the Baptist's messianic preaching, in which he prophecies the coming of the mightier one. (3) Closely related to the series of four prophecies is 1:41–45, which consists of a portent followed by a prophetic interpretation. (4) Luke 3:21–22 has similarities to 1:41–45. It too has a prophetic event followed by a verbal interpretation. The descent of the Holy Spirit in the form of a dove upon

Jesus would be regarded as a prophetic event by Mediterranean readers. The voice from heaven, the *bath qol,* was the interpretation of its
prophetic meaning. (5) Both 2:41–51 and 4:1–13 display the young
Jesus as a prodigy whose wisdom astounds the rabbis and defeats the
devil. (6) The genealogy of 3:23–38 traces Jesus' lineage through David,
through the father of the human race, Adam, to God. When a Greco-
Roman reader confronted 1:5—4:15, it would be recognized as a conventional mode of expression, belonging to the genre of an account of
the prepublic career of a great person. That it fits into a widely-used
genre of biographical writing in Mediterranean antiquity is the second
argument for its being taken as a coherent unit in the gospel.

If 1:5—4:15 belongs to this genre, how does it function in the gospel? The clue is the function of the genre in ancient biography. Suetonius' "Life of Augustus" again offers a representative statement when
we are told,

> Having reached this point, it will not be out of place to add an
> account of the omens which occurred before he was born, on the
> very day of his birth, and afterwards, *from which it was possible
> to anticipate and perceive his future greatness and uninterrupted
> good fortune.* (94) (my italics.)

The genre functioned as a foreshadowing of the character of the public
career of the biographical subject. If this was the purpose of the genre
in the Greco-Roman biographies, this is how a reader/hearer of Luke
would most probably have taken the material of a similar nature in
1:5—4:15. The first section of the gospel, then, should be read as an-
ticipations/prophecies/foreshadowings of the future career of Jesus. This
material would foretell/foreshadow the type of person Jesus would be in
his public ministry, which in Luke's narrative begins at 4:16 (cf. C. H.
Talbert, "Prophecies of Future Greatness: The Contribution of Greco-
Roman Biographies to an Understanding of Luke 1:5—4:15," in *The
Divine Helmsman,* ed. J. L. Crenshaw and Samuel Sandmel [New York:
KTAV, 1980], pp. 129–41). Given this the reader should expect to find
introduced in the section many themes that will be developed later in
Luke-Acts.

JESUS, GOD'S ACT

1:26–38

L uke 1:26–38 is the first half of Episode One (1:5–38), which portrays the annunciations of the births of John the Baptist and Jesus. The two halves closely correspond to one another because the core of both is a theophanic birth announcement like those found in the OT.

In the Jewish scriptures there is a stereotyped pattern for theophanies. When the purpose is to announce a birth (e.g., Genesis 16; 17; Judges 13), the pattern is slightly altered to accommodate this objective. Components of the theophanic birth announcement pattern include: (1) God/the angel appears (Gen 16:7; 17:1; Judg 13:3)—cf. Luke 1:11, 26; (2) the immediate reaction of the person (Gen 17:3)—cf. Luke 1:12, 29; (3) the name of the person (Gen 16:8; 17:5)—cf. Luke 1:13, 28, 30; (4) reassurance (Gen 17:4ff.)—cf. Luke 1:13, 30 (note in Gen 15:1; 21:17; 26:24; 46:3; Judg 6:23, the reassurance is "Fear not."); (5) announcement of the birth (Gen 16:11; 17:16, 19; Judg 13:3)—cf. Luke 1:13, 31; (6) the name to be given (Gen 16:11; 17:19)—cf. Luke 1:13, 31; (7) a prediction of the child's future destiny (Gen 16:12; 17:19, 21; Judg 13:5)—cf. Luke 1:14–17, 32–33; (8) an objection (Gen 17:17–18)—cf. Luke 1:18, 34 (note Gen 15:8, "How am I to know?" and Judg 6:15, "How can I deliver Israel?"); (9) a sign or reassurance (Gen 17:21b; cf. also Gen 15:9, 17; Judg 6:17ff.)—cf. Luke 1:19–20, 35–36; (10) the response (Gen 16:13; cf. also 17:23; 26:25; 35:14; Judg 6:24)—cf. Luke 1:22–23, 38. Luke's two annunciations in 1:5–38 correspond to this stereotyped pattern (cf. G. F. Wood, "The Form and Composition of the Lucan Annunciation Narratives," STD thesis, Catholic Univ of Amer, 1962).

In such a form the emphasis is not on the parent(s), but on the child as the fulfillment of the divine promise. So in 1:26–38, where the birth of Jesus is announced in the typical OT pattern, the emphasis is not on Mary but on Jesus. The christological thrust of Episode One has two foci. The first focus is on Jesus' relation to John the Baptist. The

18

paralleling of the two annunciations conveys continuity between Jesus and John in salvation history. The attempt to establish continuity between Jesus/the church on the one hand and Israel on the other is a major concern of Luke-Acts. It is no surprise to find it foreshadowed here in the links between the annunciations of the births of Elizabeth's son and Mary's son. At the same time the evangelist wants to demonstrate the superiority of Jesus over John. Whereas John will go before the Lord "in the spirit and power of Elijah" (vs. 17), Jesus will "reign over the house of Jacob forever" as the Davidic king (vss. 32–33). Again, since this superiority of Jesus over John is a theme that recurs in the third gospel, it is no surprise to meet the anticipation of it here.

The second focus of Luke's christological concern in this section is on the unusual character of Jesus' conception. Verses 32–33 proclaim he will be the Davidic Messiah, explaining why vs. 31 specified his name would be Jesus ("Yahweh saves"). Verse 35 indicates how this will come to pass: he will be conceived of the Holy Spirit. It is because of his conception by the Holy Spirit that Jesus is Son of God (note the "therefore"). Since Son of God is used for Adam in 3:38, and for the risen Christ in Acts 13:33, this title in Luke-Acts may be employed for one who lives because of God's direct, creative intervention.

It is important to clarify what is not being said here. Luke does not address the issues that arose later in church history, such as (a) *virginitas in partu* (a miraculous birth of the child; i.e., giving birth with Mary's physical organs remaining intact), and (b) *virginitas post partum* (the perpetual virginity of Mary). With Matthew, Luke speaks only of Mary's *virginitas ante partum* (virginity before giving birth; i.e., she conceived Jesus without the involvement of a man): Jesus was miraculously conceived by the Holy Spirit (1:35). It is by virtue of this miraculous conception in the womb of the virgin Mary that Jesus is the Son of God.

The miraculous conception, or virgin birth as it is usually called, has functioned theologically in various ways in Christian history. Three examples illustrate this. (a) In the second century, Ignatius of Antioch confronts a docetic problem. Faced with a denial of Jesus' humanity, Ignatius places most of his emphasis on the birth of Jesus as a sign of his humanity (Eph 7:2; 18:2; Ign Trall 9:1; Ign Smyrn 1:1). The first witness after Matthew and Luke to the virgin birth, then, appeals to Jesus' birth of the virgin Mary as evidence of his real humanity. (b)

Augustine is the source from which a dominant interpretation of Jesus' virgin birth entered medieval Christianity. For Augustine, all people are sinful and need Christ's redemption. We have all inherited original sin which has been passed to us by means of sexual propagation. In order for Christ to be Savior from sin, he must be sinless. For him to be sinless he must not inherit Adam's sin as the rest of us have and do. For this to be so Jesus could not obtain his human nature by means of sexual procreation. Hence the conception by the Holy Spirit is the means by which Jesus avoided the taint of original sin and could be the sinless Savior of all. (c) Protestant Orthodoxy saw the indisputable proof of the truth of Christianity in the miracles of Jesus and in the fulfillment of biblical prophecy in Jesus' career. Understanding the virgin birth as a biological miracle and as the fulfillment of Isa 7:14, these Christians understood the virginal conception as the proof of Jesus' divinity and thereby of the truth of Christianity. Their watchword became, If you deny the virgin birth as a biological miracle, you deny the divinity of Christ (cf. Hans von Campenhausen, *The Virgin Birth in the Theology of the Ancient Church* [Naperville, Ill.: Allenson, 1964], and Thomas Boslooper, *The Virgin Birth* [Philadelphia: Westminster Press, 1962]). Given the various ways the miraculous conception has functioned theologically in Christian history, how does it function for Luke?

To discern the function of the miraculous conception in Lukan thought, it is necessary to note two things. In the first place, the function of the genre of the prepublic career of a famous person to which 1:5—4:15 belongs (see the Introduction to Luke 1:5—4:15) was to answer the question, how are we to explain the hero's later life? In the gospel, as in other Greco-Roman biographies, a miraculous conception story functioned to explain the hero's later greatness: Jesus was what he was because he was divinely begotten.

In the second place, one must be aware of the christology employed by Luke-Acts. Even before Paul three different christologies circulated in the early churches: two-foci, exaltation, and epiphany (cf. R. H. Fuller, *The Foundations of New Testament Christology* [New York: Scribner's, 1965]). Whereas the Gospel of John tells the story of Jesus in terms of an epiphany, Luke-Acts employs an exaltation christology: Jesus in his earthly life is the descendent of David and heir to the promises of the Jewish scriptures. By virtue of his resurrection he is raised to the exalted status of God's Son with power. In the present he

rules from heaven as Lord over all, intervening on behalf of his people to deliver and protect them. A diagram would look like this:

```
                              Son of God with power
              ┌──────────────────────────────────────────
              │  Resurrection
              │
              │
              │
   ───────────┘
        Son of David
```

Exaltation christology functioned to express the church's experience of Jesus Christ in a twofold way: as the present Lord who rules from heaven, and as the historical figure whose story is normative for us. How is it that Christ can function in these two ways? In this schema the explanation for Christ's present reign from heaven is his resurrection from the dead; the explanation for his unique earthly life is his miraculous conception. Christology and genre agree. Jesus' earthly life was what it was because of his miraculous birth.

It was theologically important to begin with the virgin birth because exaltation christology was subject to perversion by those of a legalistic bent. "He was obedient unto death; wherefore God highly exalted him," could easily be understood to say it was Jesus' merit that caused his exaltation. "The Spirit of the Lord is upon me to preach and heal," could be interpreted to mean that because Jesus was more righteous, more prudent, and more wise than anyone else, he was anointed with the Holy Spirit at baptism to carry on God's work. If Jesus' earthly life could be understood in terms of merit, however, then so could the lives of his followers. The result would be the very type of problem Paul opposed in Galatia. In an exaltation schema, then, it was theologically important to begin with a miraculous conception. In that way any interpretation of the earthly life of Jesus and of his followers in terms of merit would be excluded. The greatness of Jesus' life was not a human achievement, but the result of divine intervention. Jesus' career was not the result of the perfection of human striving and effort; only God could produce a life like his. Jesus was God's act. As Luther put it, "Just as God in the beginning of creation made the world out of nothing, so His manner of working continues unchanged" (*Luther's Works*, ed. J. Pelikan [St. Louis: Concordia, 1956], 21:299). If we are to view the miraculous conception of Jesus as Luke viewed it, we must see it as an affirmation of God's grace that excludes all human merit.

MARY, IDEAL BELIEVER AND SOCIAL PARADIGM

1:39–56

L uke 1:39–56 is a transition between Episode One, the annunciations of John and Jesus (1:5–38), and Episode Two, the births
and early lives of the Baptist and Mary's son (1:57—2:52), and consists
of two hymns (vss. 42–45; vss. 46–55) joined by a narrative introduction (vss. 39–41) and conclusion (vs. 56). The first hymn, that of Elizabeth (vss. 42–45), eulogizes Mary as an ideal believer; the second,
Mary's (vss. 46–55), clarifies the links between what God has done for
one individual and what he will do for the structures of society at large.

Elizabeth's hymn has a narrative introduction, vss. 39–41, which
sets the stage for what follows. When Mary visits Elizabeth, Elizabeth's babe leaps in her womb. Here, as in Gen 25: 21–23, the story
of Rebecca's children, the idea is that the movement of the unborn
babe foreshadows his future lot and that of Jesus. The hymn itself
(vss. 41b–45) offers twofold congratulations to Mary ("Blessed are you,"
vs. 42; "Blessed is she," vs. 45). Each expression of congratulations is
followed by the grounds for Mary's being blessed. First, Mary is to be
congratulated because her child will be the Lord (vs. 43), as evidenced
by the unborn babe's leaping for joy in Elizabeth's womb (vs. 44).
Even in the womb John recognizes the messianic Lord. This prenatal
cognition attests the fulfillment of Gabriel's prophecy to Mary in 1:31–
33, 35. Second, Mary is to be congratulated because of her response
to God's word (vs. 45): "Blessed (*makaria*) is she who believed that
there would be a fulfillment of what was spoken to her from the Lord"
(1:45). Mary hears and believes God's word. Here Luke foreshadows
in capsule form his distinctive understanding of Mary which runs
throughout his narrative: Mary is the model disciple.

(1) In 1:38 Mary is depicted as a believer for whom God's word is
enough: "Behold, I am the handmaid of the Lord; let it be to me according to your word." Augustine caught the Lukan intent when he

22

said that Mary, full of faith, conceived Christ first in her heart before conceiving him in her womb (*Sermon* 215:4). Her belief led to an absolute self-surrender to the divine purpose.

(2) Luke 8:19–21, the climax of a unit beginning at 8:1, carries on the same theme. The distinctive Lukan point of view can best be seen when 8:1–21 is compared with its Markan counterpart, Mark 3:19b–35, a unit which begins (vs. 21) and ends (vss. 31–35) with references to Jesus' family. Very likely vs. 21 and vss. 31–35 originally belonged together. In their Markan context they function to indicate that Jesus' family, no less than the scribes who came down from Jerusalem (3:22), do not understand or believe. Consequently, 3:31–35 speaks negatively of Jesus' human family, distinguishing them from his true, eschatological family. This true family is composed of those who do the will of God, which by implication Jesus' natural family does not do. In Luke, however, Jesus' mother and brothers are not outsiders (8:19; Mark 3:31); the controversy context is abandoned by Luke, the parable of the sower (Mark 4:3–8) is moved to the beginning of the unit (8:4–8), and its interpretation (8:11–15) ends with the comment about the good soil being "those who, hearing the word, hold it fast in an honest and good heart, and bring forth fruit with patience" (vs. 15), and 8:21 becomes a commendation of Jesus' natural family for meeting the criterion for inclusion in the eschatological family of God—"My mother and brothers are those who hear the word of God and do it." Mary, in the third gospel, belongs to the good soil, as do Jesus' brothers. (Contrast John 7:1–9 which indicates that Jesus' brothers did not believe in him prior to Easter.)

(3) In 11:27–28, and only in Luke, the physical fact of Mary's motherhood is said to give no special status in Jesus' eyes. Rather than deserving congratulations because her womb bore Jesus and her breasts nourished him, Mary's status is due to her proper response to God's word.

(4) Acts 1:14 shows continuity between the pre- and post-Easter community of Jesus' disciples. Mary's presence indicates her place in the primitive church at the time of Pentecost. The evangelist has thereby portrayed Mary as a "disciple" from the time of Jesus' conception to Pentecost.

(5) The positive picture of Mary and Jesus' natural family in the narrative helps to explain 4:24. Whereas Mark 6:4 has Jesus say about his rejection in Nazareth, "A prophet is not without honor, except in

his own country, and *among his own kin,* and *in his own house,"* 4:24's version simply says, "Truly, I say to you, no prophet is acceptable in his own country." Any note of rejection on the part of Jesus' family is removed; Mary especially stands as a true believer (R. E. Brown et al, *Mary in the New Testament* [Philadelphia: Fortress Press, 1978], and P. J. Bearsley, "Mary the Perfect Disciple: A Paradigm for Mariology," *Theological Studies* 41:461–504 [1980]).

Regarding Mary's significance for the church, the evangelist portrays her as the prototype of the Christian believer: she hears God's word, holds it fast in an honest and good heart (2:19; 2:51), and brings forth fruit with patience. Here foreshadowed in the virgin mother is the Lukan understanding of what it means to be a disciple of Jesus; she hears God's word, believes it, and surrenders herself totally to it: "Let it be to me according to your word" (1:38). If we are to view Mary as Luke did, then we must see her as a model for disciples. This Marian model holds not self-knowledge or insight but self-surrender or abandonment to God's will to be the essence of discipleship.

Verses 46–55 are a hymn of Mary, as the overwhelming weight of textual evidence and the structure of the section demand, and not of Elizabeth, as a few old Latin witnesses claim. The hymn contains two stanzas which praise God for his mercy: vss. 46–50 and vss. 51–55. Verses 49–50 and vss. 54–55 both refer to God's mercy and signal the end of their respective stanzas.

Stanza one of Mary's song speaks of God's mighty act for one woman only: the emphasis is on the gracious initiative of God. The virgin sings of nothing except her low estate (vs. 46) and the grace of God which was upon her far above any merit of hers (vss. 49–50). If Elizabeth's hymn focuses on Mary as a model of faith (vs. 45), Mary's own song of praise focuses its first stanza on God's grace for her, a grace to which she responded in faith.

Stanza two of the Magnificat expands the horizon to speak of God's social revolution through eschatological reversal. In both stanzas God's surprising concern for the lowly is revealed. God's regard for one humble woman becomes the sign of his eschatological act for the world. In the one small event the greater event lies hidden (R. C. Tannehill, "The Magnificat as Poem," *Journal of Biblical Literature* 93:263–75 [1974]). In Luke's understanding God's social revolution, like the conception of Jesus, is not the perfection of the human by human striving

but the result of the divine breaking into history. The reference is eschatological and refers to the Last Day.

The third evangelist here foreshadows his views about the relation between Christ and human culture. On the one hand, it is certainly not Luke's view that there is an identity between God's will for human life and cultural realities. Stanza two of Mary's song proclaims God will ultimately overturn the values and structures of this world's culture. For this evangelist Christ cannot be identified with culture. On the other hand, Luke is no advocate of social action to transform culture, in the sense that we know such action today. Jesus did not go to the top (to Caesar or Pilate) to get things changed, nor did he go to the left (to the Zealots). He went instead to the poor and sinners, offering forgiveness and deliverance, and calling them into a community whose life was to embody God's will. Only God, from Luke's perspective, is able to achieve a just society in the Last Day. In the meantime the evangelist presents Jesus and his church not as having a social ethic for society at large but as trying to have one in their own life together. In the Lukan mind the first duty of the church is to be the church, to be a community which, through the way its members deal with one another, demonstrates to the world what social relations directed by God are. So understood, Jesus and the disciples fulfill their social responsibility not by being one more power block among others but by being an example, a creative minority, a witness to God's mercy. "The church therefore does not fulfill her social responsibility by attacking directly the social structures of society, but by being itself it indirectly has a tremendous significance for the ethical form of society." This statement by a contemporary Christian ethicist accurately reflects the Lukan view (Stanley Hauerwas, "The Nonresistant Church: The Theological Ethics of John Howard Yoder," in *Vision and Virtue* [Notre Dame: Fides Publishers, 1974], p. 212). In Luke-Acts Jesus and his church do not attempt to change society at large by attacking it directly by whatever means—violent or nonviolent—but by subverting its values as they live communally out of God's will before the world (S. Hauerwas, "The Politics of Charity," *Interpretation* 31:262 [1977]). The ultimate transformation of society's structures generally awaits the kingdom of God at the eschaton.

Mary's song reflects her confidence in this ultimate victory of God and the reversal of human values. Following prophetic precedent vss.

51–55 use verbs in a past tense to describe future acts of God. That God has acted for Mary in the present gives such an assurance he will act in the future for the world, this ultimate intervention can be spoken of as though it were already accomplished. This is similar to Rom 8:28–30 where Paul speaks not only of predestination and justification as past but also of the Christians' glorification, a future event, because he is so certain of its reality. To read the Magnificat in terms of Lukan thought, therefore, is to see an individual's (i.e., Mary's) experience of God's grace as prototypical of the way God will ultimately deal with the world at large.

For Luke it is the same God who acts redemptively for an individual and for society at large. It is the same God who acted in the past, who acts in the present, and who will act in the future. If it is the same God, then his acting partakes of the same character: gracious intervention to create anew.

JOHN, PROTOTYPE OF
THE CHRISTIAN EVANGELIST

1:14–17, 57–80; 3:1–20; 7:24–35

The first three passages are from the three episodes of 1:5—4:15; the fourth is from the Galilean ministry (4:16—9:50). Luke 1:14–17 is the prediction about John's future role made by the angel in the context of his birth annunciation in Episode One (1:5–38). Luke 1:57–80 is part of Episode Two (1:57—2:52) and deals with the birth and early life of John the Baptist. It corresponds very closely with the account of Jesus' birth and early life in 2:1–52. The core of 1:57–80 is the Benedictus (1:67–79), the prophecy of Zechariah about John's future role. Luke 3:1–20 also focuses on the Baptist: his person (vss. 1–6), his mission (vss. 7–17), and a summary of the end of his career (vss. 18–20). Luke 7:24–35 gives Jesus' words concerning John in the context of the Galilean ministry. If the first two passages present prophecies about John's future role, the last two offer examples of the fulfillment of those prophecies in John's career and Jesus' assessment of it. Taken together these four units give the Lukan understanding of John the Baptist.

The distinctiveness of this picture of the Baptist can best be seen in the context of the understanding of John in the Gospel of Mark and in the fourth gospel. In Mark John the Baptist is viewed as Elijah who is to come first to restore all things. This can be seen in 1:6 where the Baptist's attire is similar to that of the prophet Elijah (2 Kgs 1:8), and in 9:11–13 where the identification with Elijah is explicitly made. Mark 9:13 also states that John, Elijah *redivivus,* suffered and was martyred, a reference to 6:14–29 (cf. Pseudo-Philo, *Biblical Antiquities* 48:1; Rev 11:4–13, which may enshrine a Jewish tradition). In this way John's fate anticipates that of Jesus. In the fourth gospel, John the Baptist explicitly denies he is the Christ (1:20), or Elijah (1:21), or the prophet (1:21). Nor is he the forerunner, for the Word was before John (1:15, 30). Rather the Baptist is portrayed as a witness (1:7,

27

8, 32, 34), the voice of Isa 40:3 which cried, "Make straight the way of the Lord" (1:23). How is the Baptist portrayed in the third gospel?

Luke 1:14–17, the angel's prophecy to Zechariah, clarifies several things about John. (1) He will be a prophetic figure "filled with the Holy Spirit, even from his mother's womb," who will work in "the spirit and power of Elijah." (2) He will go before the Lord. (3) He will "make ready for the Lord a people prepared."

A hymn attributed to the Spirit-filled Zechariah (1:68–79; esp. vs. 67), makes essentially the same prediction about John in its second stanza. The Benedictus falls into two parts: vss. 68–75, 76–79. Part one is a blessing of God (cf. 2 Cor 1:3–4; Eph 1:3–14). The reasons God is praised are two. First, he has been faithful to his promise to David (cf. 2 Sam 7:11b–16) by raising up a Davidic king (vss. 68b–70; cf. 1:32–33; 2:4). The result of this is Israel's salvation from her enemies (vs. 71). Second, God has also been faithful to his promise to Abraham (Gen 12:1–2, 15; cf. Luke 1:55; Romans 4). This will allow God's people to serve him all of their days without fear (vss. 72–75). In vss. 68–75, then, Jesus is understood as the fulfillment both of God's promise to Abraham and of his promise to David. It is this faithfulness of God to his word that elicits Zechariah's praise (cf. 2 Cor 1:18–20). Part two is a prediction concerning John the Baptist's future work. (1) He will "be called the prophet of the Most High." (2) He will "go before the Lord." (3) He will prepare the way of the Lord (cf. Mal 3:1; 4:5–6). Zechariah's prophecy agrees in its content with that of the angel of the Lord (1:16–17). These prophecies have their fulfillment in the narrative at 3:1–6; 7:26–27.

Luke 3:1–6 begins with an involved system of dating, followed by the statement, "the word of the Lord came to John the son of Zechariah in the wilderness." The style echoes the introductions to the OT prophets (cf. Jeremiah 1). This is followed by an extended quotation from Isa 40:3–5 in 3:4–6. This quotation designates John as the "voice of one crying in the wilderness" which was to precede God's great eschatological deliverance. Thereby Luke is saying that John is a prophet, but not just a prophet: he is the eschatological voice in the wilderness who prepares the way of the Lord (1:76b; 3:4b). Likewise, in 7:26–27, Jesus says the Baptist is a prophet and more: he is the one who will prepare the way.

Taken together what picture of the Baptist do these passages give? John the Baptist is portrayed as the forerunner of the Messiah, who

goes in the spirit and power of Elijah, who is the epitome of the Spirit-filled prophet, mighty in word and deed. The Baptist is not Elijah—hence the description of his garments is omitted at Luke 3:16 because of their association with Elijah—but is merely endowed with the same Spirit and power as Elijah (1:17). John is a prophetic figure (1:76a; 3:1–2, 7:26), the forerunner of the Lord (1:17; 1:76b; 3:4; 7:27), who preaches repentance and forgiveness as a prelude to the coming salvation (1:77; 3:3, 6).

It has been suggested by Walter Wink (*John the Baptist in the Gospel Tradition* [Cambridge: Cambridge University Press, 1968], pp. 113–14) that John the Baptist was used typologically by the church to set forth its conception of its own role in "preparing the way of the Lord." For example, John's suffering as Elijah-incognito in Mark serves as an example to the persecuted Christians in Rome (p. 17); the Baptist in the fourth gospel is "made the normative image of the Christian preacher, apostle and missionary, the perfect prototype of the true evangelist, whose one goal is self-effacement before Christ" (p. 105). In this light it is interesting to note that the Lukan picture of John as a prophetic figure who goes before the Lord preaching repentance and forgiveness as a prelude to the coming salvation looks very much like the picture of Peter and John in Acts 3, especially vss. 19ff.

One way Luke views Christian existence is in prophetic terms. The OT prophets were those on whom the Spirit came, giving them a knowledge both of the secrets of human hearts and of the divine council's decrees. Thus empowered they spoke for God to prepare his people for the Day of the Lord. These prophets provided one category for the evangelist to use in conceptualizing the Christian experience between Pentecost and parousia. Christians were people on whom the Spirit had come. Consequently they prophesied (Acts 2:16–18). Their prophetic word sought the repentance of the people before the Lord's coming (Acts 2:38–39; 3:19–26). The Christian community, then, in Luke's view, is a prophetic community. By its very existence it prepares the way of the Lord by going before him to call people to repentance. If Mary is portrayed as a true believer, John the Baptist is drawn in terms of the true Christian evangelist: in 3:18 John is said to preach the good news to the people.

If John is portrayed as the prototype of the Spirit-filled Christian evangelist, what does he preach and for what does he hope? This model for Christian witnesses preaches Jesus and an ethical life-style. Luke

3:15–17 says the Baptist preached Jesus as the one who would baptize with the Holy Spirit and fire (cf. Acts 2:1ff.); 3:7–9 points to the necessity of bearing fruit (cf. 6:43–45; 13:6–9; 20:9–18). The meaning of this is clarified in 3:10–14: it means the refusal to hoard or to acquire more possessions than are necessary (cf. 12:13–21; 16:19–31). He witnesses so that "all flesh shall see the salvation of God" (3:6). The similarities between John's good news (3:18) and the message both of Jesus and the later church are clear. In his message as well as in the goal and source of his strength, John the Baptist in Luke-Acts functions as the prototype of the Christian evangelist.

GOOD NEWS OF A GREAT JOY

2:1–20

L uke 2:1–20 is a large unit within 2:1–52, the half of Episode Two (1:57—2:52) dealing with Jesus' birth and early life. It is composed of two parts: (a) 2:1–7 is a narrative about Jesus' birth, and (b) 2:8–20 falls into the same annunciation pattern we have encountered in 1:5–25 and 1:26–38. The two parts are joined by certain formal links. On the one hand, there is the recurrence of "the city of David" (2:4, 11) and "swaddling clothes . . . in a manger" (2:7, 12). On the other hand, each participates in a prophecy-fulfillment schema. Luke 2:1–7 speaks of the geographical site of Jesus' birth (the city of David, Bethlehem) and the family from which Jesus came (Joseph was of the house and lineage of David). Both facts are allusions to prophecy; though it is not made explicit by the evangelist, most likely to Mic 5:2:

> But you, O Bethlehem Ephrathah,
> Who are little to be among the clans of Judah,
> From you shall come forth for me
> One who is to be ruler in Israel.

Being born of the lineage of David in the city of David means Jesus is Christ the Lord (2:11). This, of course, fulfills the angelic prophecy made to Mary in 1:32–33: "the Lord God will give to him the throne of his father David." Luke 2:8–20 also is built around a prophecy-fulfillment schema. When the angel appears to the shepherds to announce the birth of a Savior, a sign is given: "You will find a babe wrapped in swaddling cloths and lying in a manger" (vs. 12). This prediction is fulfilled when the shepherds go to Bethlehem and find it as the angel had said (vss. 16, 7). Taken together, 2:1–7 and 2:8–20 function to acclaim the birth of the Davidic Messiah: a Savior, who is Christ the Lord (vs. 11). This, says the angelic messenger, is "good news of a great joy" (vs. 10).

What is good news about Jesus' birth? Why should it be regarded as a great joy? Two items of background information serve as a bridge to

our answers. (1) In the Mediterranean world the birthday of a ruler was sometimes celebrated with a proclamation of the benefits of his birth. An inscription found at Priene, celebrating the birthday of Augustus in 9 B.C., reads in part,

> Providence . . . has brought into the world Augustus and filled him with a hero's soul for the benefit of mankind. A Savior for us and our descendents, he will make wars to cease and order all things well. The epiphany of Caesar has brought to fulfillment past hopes and dreams. (F. Danker, *Jesus and the New Age*, p. 24)

Here Augustus fulfills ancient hopes and brings peace. These benefits are proclaimed on his birthday. (2) In biblical literature heavenly choirs sometimes celebrate future events as though they were already fact (e.g., Rev 5:9–10; 11:17–18; 18:2–3; 19:1–2, 6–8); their song proclaims the benefits that are to ensue: 2:13–14 employs such a heavenly choir. A multitude of heavenly host sing,

> Glory to God in the highest,
> and on earth peace among men with whom he is pleased.
> (vs. 14)

The one who has fulfilled the ancient hopes expressed in the prophecies of scripture is acclaimed as one whose birth will bring glory to God and peace to people on earth. Like Augustus Jesus has on his birthday a proclamation of the benefits of his birth.

Is the peace that Jesus' birth is said to bring the same as that claimed for Augustus? In the Jewish culture from which Christianity came, peace (*shalom* in Hebrew; *eirēnē* in Greek) meant basically wholeness, the normal state of life which corresponds to the will of God. Such wholeness would characterize the basic relations of life: (a) the relation of persons and God, (b) the relation of persons with one another, (c) the relation of persons with the natural world, and (d) one's relation with oneself. This wholeness meant well-being in contrast to evil in any form. It was the gift of God. Given human sin, however, this wholeness was lost. Peace, then, became an eschatological hope (Zech 9:9–10) and the messianic figure the prince of peace (Isa 9:6).

In the NT peace reflects these Jewish roots. It refers, therefore, both to the normal state of life in line with God's will and to the eschatological salvation. As such it involves wholeness in the relation with God (e.g., Rom 5:1; Col 1:20; Eph 2:14, 17), wholeness in the relation of

people with one another (e.g., Mark 9:50; 1 Cor 7:15; Eph 2:14–17; 4:3), wholeness in the relation to the physical world (e.g., Mark 5:34), and wholeness in one's relation with oneself (Rom 8:6; 15:13; Gal 5:22; Phil 4:7; Col 3:15; John 14:27).

Luke-Acts, with one exception, reflects this context. The messianic salvation is described as the way of peace (1:79). Jesus Christ is said to have preached the good news of peace (Acts 10:36). This peace associated with God's acts in Jesus involves recovered wholeness in the relation of a person with God (e.g., Luke 7:50), wholeness in the relation with the physical world (8:48), and wholeness in the relations among persons (e.g., Acts 9:31). The absence of any reference to peace with oneself is not surprising in Luke-Acts both because of the evangelist's focus on the visible and external realities of life, and because the scriptures on which Luke is so dependent have little concern with peace as an inward feeling. For Jesus' birth to be connected with the recovery of peace, therefore, was a matter of great joy, meaning the restoration of wholeness to life in every area: with God, with others, with the physical world. It is this peace about which the heavenly choir sings at 2:14.

For whom is this peace promised? Verse 14 says it is for either "men of good will" or "men of favor" (*anthrōpois eudokias*). The latter translation, which has the better support, means persons upon whom divine favor rests. The gospel mentions two occasions when recipients of divine favor are specified. In the first instance Jesus, after his baptism, is addressed as "my beloved Son, in [whom] I *take delight* (*eudokēsa*): Jesus is the object of divine favor. In the second, 12:32, Jesus says to his disciples, "Fear not, little flock, for it is your Father's *good pleasure* (*eudokēsen*) to give you the kingdom": here Jesus' disciples are the objects of divine favor. Hence, it is among Jesus and his disciples that there is peace among humans. Here is where the wholeness of the basic relations of life is being recovered as a result of Jesus' birth and lordship. This is cause for joy.

This good news, moreover, is for "all the people" (vs. 10), outcast as well as in-group. In Luke's time shepherds were often considered outside the law. Their testimony was considered invalid because of their reputation for dishonesty (b. *Sanhedrin* 25b). Yet it was to such as these the angel announced the good news of the Savior's birth (2:8–11). This can only be regarded as a foreshadowing of the subsequent theme of God's grace shown to sinners which runs throughout Luke.

The messianic Lord is the friend of sinners (e.g., 5:29–32; 7:36–50; 10:30–37; 15:1–2; 17:11–19; 19:1–10). It is to sinners Jesus promises good news (e.g., 18:9–14; 15:11–32). The news that Jesus' birth signals the benefit of peace is intended for all the people. This is cause for great joy.

The angelic choir not only sang about the recovery of wholeness among the disciples of Jesus, a benefit available to all, it also spoke of glory to God being a benefit of Jesus' birth and rule as Lord. Psalm 85:8–9, just as Luke 2:14, connects God's being glorified with peace among his people. How is this to be understood? Since peace is God's gift, it reflects to God's credit that wholeness is being recovered among human beings. The recovery of wholeness in human relationships, which is due to God's acts in Jesus, reflects honor to God. In other words what is good for human beings glorifies God; what glorifies God is good for human beings. Glorifying God and recovering human wholeness are not mutually exclusive: they are an indissoluble whole. When the angels sang of the benefits of Jesus' lordship, they sang both "glory to God" and "peace to men"—one song, heralding a dual benefit of Messiah's birth. That is good news of a great joy.

THE UNREDEEMED FIRSTBORN

2:21–52

Luke 2:21–52 is the second large unit in 2:1–52, the half of Episode Two (1:57—2:52) focusing on Jesus' birth and early life. The events of vss. 21–52 are joined by the theme of obedience to the Jewish law and certain pious customs of the Jews. (1) Luke 2:21 describes Jesus' circumcision on the eighth day in obedience to Lev 12:3. (2) Luke 2:22–24 telescopes at least two traditional Jewish practices prescribed by the law. Verses 22a, 24 reflect the practice of the purification of the mother after childbirth, following the directives of Lev 12:6, 8. That Jesus' mother offered birds for her purification indicates she was poor (cf. Lev 12:8): Jesus came from the poor. Verses 22b, 23, however, echo Exod 13:2, 12, 13, 15 where it is said the firstborn belongs to God and must be redeemed (cf. Mishna, *Bekhoroth,* 8). The actions of Jesus' parents at this point are "according to the custom of the law" (2:27): "And when they had performed everything according to the law of the Lord, they returned to Galilee" (2:39). (3) Luke 2:41 says Jesus' parents went to Jerusalem every year at the feast of the Passover. This was doubtless in obedience to Exod 23:14–17; 34:23; Deut 16:16, which specified that every male was to go to Jerusalem at Passover, Pentecost, and Tabernacles each year. Though the law said nothing about women, some apparently made the pilgrimage in biblical times (1 Sam 1:7; 2:19) and Hillel prescribed that they also should go to Passover. (4) Luke 2:42 indicates that Jesus' trip to Jerusalem was according to custom. This was probably in preparation for his entrance into religious responsibility which, according to *Pirke Aboth* 5:21, came at age thirteen. (5) Luke 2:51 says Jesus "went down with them and came to Nazareth, and was obedient to them." The boy Jesus fulfilled the commandment to honor one's father and mother (Exod 20:12; Deut 5:16). In 2:21–52 the evangelist depicts both Jesus' parents and the young Jesus as obedient to the prescriptions of the law: this thread ties the section together.

The thread of obedience to the law is also theologically important in

2:21–52. Jesus, who as a boy was obedient to the law, came from a family for whom obedience was an unargued assumption of life. In this Jesus' family fulfilled the Jewish ideal which believed the family's functions to include propagating the race, satisfying emotional needs in beneficent ways, and perpetuating religious experience. The third function was stated in a proverb: "Train up a child in the way he should go, and when he is old he will not depart from it" (Prov 22:6). It was in a family whose unargued assumption was obedience to the law that Jesus at twelve personally decided to take on himself the yoke of the kingdom of heaven (vs. 42). His subsequent obedience to his parents (vs. 51) came from a desire consciously committed to do God's will (Eph 6:2–3).

As part of the general context of the obedience by the family of Jesus to the law, we note that the model disciple, Mary, dedicates her child to God. Luke 2:22–24 falls into an AB:B'A' pattern: vss. 22a and 24 (cf. Lev 12:8), which deal with the purification of the mother after childbirth, being A and A'; vss. 22b and 23, which deal with the redemption of the firstborn, being B and B'. The prescription of Exod 13:2 concerning the first-born son was literally fulfilled in the case of Jesus, the firstborn (Luke 2:7), who was not ransomed (Exod 13:13; Num 3:47; 18:16). Contrary to normal custom, Jesus was dedicated to God and remained his property (Bo Reicke, "Jesus, Simeon, and Anna [Luke 2:21–40]," in *Saved By Hope*, ed. J. I. Cook [Grand Rapids: Eerdmans, 1978], pp. 96–108, esp. p. 100). The closest parallel to this emphasis is found in 1 Samuel 1—2, where Hannah gives Samuel, at his birth, to the Lord for as long as the child lives. Consequently, Samuel lives in the presence of Eli at the tent of meeting. If Jesus, in a similar manner, was dedicated to God and not redeemed, he belonged to God permanently. This would explain the reason Jesus would not understand why his parents did not know where to find him in Jerusalem (2:48–49): since he was God's he could be expected to be in his Father's house, as in the case of Samuel. At the plot level of the narrative, the boy Jesus had made a personal identification with the decisions his parents had made about him at his birth. In 2:21–52 family influence and personal decision combined to make the young Jesus what he was.

Luke's twelve-year-old Jesus was not only obedient to God's will, he was also possessed of spiritual discernment beyond what was normal. The story in 2:41–51 about Jesus in the temple depicts the lad as God's

Son (vs. 49) who is characterized by unusual wisdom in understanding the law. The story is enclosed within an inclusion that speaks about Jesus' wisdom (2:40 and 2:52), the centerpiece of its concentric surface structure (Henk J. de Jonge, "Sonship, Wisdom, Infancy: Luke 2:41–51a," *New Testament Studies* 24:317–54 [1978]).

A Mary, Joseph, and Jesus go to Jerusalem (41–42)
  B Jesus stays in Jerusalem, which is not noticed (43)
    C His parents seek and find him (44–46a)
      D *Jesus among the teachers* (46b–47)
    C' His parents, annoyed, reproach him (48)
  B' Jesus' reaction, which is not understood (49–50)
A' Mary, Joseph, and Jesus return to Nazareth (51a)

The centerpiece and the frame agree: Jesus is the wise one. The story portrays Jesus as God's Son who is the wise interpreter of scripture. This is a motif found elsewhere in the narrative of Luke-Acts (e.g., Luke 4:1–13; 4:16–21; 7:26–27; 10:25–28; 20:17–18; 20:37–38; 20:41–44; 24:25–27, 32; 24:44–47). Especially important is Luke 24 where the evangelist depicts the risen Christ as the one who interprets scripture for the disciples and opens their minds to understand its meaning.

Luke's portrayal of the youthful Jesus as a person of unusual discernment, within a section that emphasizes the obedience of both Jesus' family and the lad, is theologically significant. Religious understanding, insight into God's will, develops in the context of religious submission and obedience. The Johannine Jesus says, "If any man's will is to do his will, he shall know whether the teaching is from God or whether I am speaking on my own authority" (John 7:17). This statement can be expanded into a general rule of thumb: the discernment of spiritual truth—God's will—comes only after a willingness to do it, if and when it is known. In the realm of spiritual insight—including an understanding of the religious significance of scripture— one does not know God's will and then decide whether to do it. Rather one wills to be obedient to God's will first and then, and only then, does one discern what it is. Jesus, who as a youth was a precocious interpreter of scripture (God's will), was such only within the context of a conscious acceptance of the yoke of the kingdom of heaven and a personal identification with his parents' dedication of him to God as a baby: discernment followed commitment.

The way the evangelist has spoken about Jesus as a youth is only possible for one who assumes the real humanity of Jesus. (1) "And the child grew and became strong" (vs. 40a); "Jesus increased in stature" (vs 52—cf. 19:3, where the term is used of Zacchaeus who is small of stature). This is the way one talks about someone who has a human body; Heb 2:14 puts it this way: "Since therefore the children share in flesh and blood, he himself likewise partook of the same nature." In Christian history the tendency to deny the truly human body of Jesus has been called Gnosticism. (2) "And Jesus increased [made progress] in wisdom" (vs. 52). This is the way one talks about someone who has a truly human mind. Hebrews implies the same thing: "Therefore he had to be made like his brethren in every respect" (2:17); "one who in every respect has been tempted as we are, yet without sinning" (4:15). Since there is no way Jesus could have been tempted as we are unless he had limited knowledge within the confines of a human mind, as we do, Hebrews joins Luke in affirming Jesus' humanity in the mental sphere. In Christian history the tendency to deny the truly human mind of Jesus has been called Apollinarianism, after Apollinaris, bishop of Laodicea (c. A.D. 390), who held that Jesus had the body and soul of a man but that the reasoning mind in him was the eternal Logos. (3) "Jesus increased in favor with God and man" (vs. 52). This is the type of language one uses for someone who develops both religiously and socially. Hebrews speaks of the same reality: he was made "perfect through suffering" (2:10); "Although he was a Son, he learned obedience through what he suffered" (5:8). This, moreover, is something Jesus shared with Samuel: 1 Sam 2:26 reads, "Now the boy Samuel continued to grow both in stature and in favor with the Lord and with men." It was Marcion in church history who said Christ appeared in Palestine a full-grown man. For Luke Jesus grew and developed: in body, in mind, religiously, and socially: Jesus is truly human. Only thereby can he be the pioneer of salvation, a legitimate model of Christian existence.

SPIRITUAL POWER
FROM ANSWERED PRAYER

Luke 3:21–22, 15–17

L uke 3:21–22, 15–17 comes in the subsection 3:1—4:15, Episode Three in 1:5—4:15: vss. 21–22 are usually referred to as the baptism of Jesus by John; vss. 15–17 give a sample of the Baptist's preaching about the Coming One.

The distinctive Lukan perspective in vss. 21–22 can be seen more clearly if set in the context of the understanding of Jesus' baptism in the other gospels. (1) Matt 3:13–17 contains two verses (14–15) found nowhere else in the canonical tradition and which determine the first evangelist's major emphasis. It appears the evangelist is defending Jesus against the charge that he was a sinner, as evidenced by his submission to John's baptism of repentance for the remission of sins (cf. Matt 3:2, 6, 8). In this Matthew would be struggling with the same type of problem reflected in the Gospel according to the Hebrews (in Jerome, *Against Pelagius,* 3:2):

> The mother of the Lord and his brothers said to him, "John the Baptist baptizes for the forgiveness of sins; let us go and be baptized by him." But he said to them, "In what have I sinned that I should go and be baptized by him? Unless, perhaps, what I have just said is a sin of ignorance."

There is none of this in the Lukan account. (2) According to John 1:31–34 the descent of the Spirit on Jesus—presumably at his baptism—functioned to let the Baptist know Jesus' identity so John could reveal him to Israel. Again there is nothing like this in the third gospel. (3) Mark sees Jesus' baptism with the accompanying descent of the Holy Spirit as an empowering of the Son of God for his battle with Satan and the demonic powers (cf. Mark 3:22–27). The Lukan perspective is closer to Mark 1:9–11 than to either Matthew or John. But although both Luke and Mark see the Spirit's descent in terms of em-

powering, their perspectives are by no means identical. Luke sees Jesus' ministry in terms of the role of the Servant of the Lord in Deutero-Isaiah (cf. 4:16–21), and separates the empowering from the event of baptism while connecting it explicitly with prayer. The details of the Lukan perspective must now be examined.

Luke 3:21–22, which mentions Jesus' baptism only as a backdrop, is a prayer-scene consisting of a vision and an interpretative audition. The evangelist has turned a narrative about Jesus' baptism into an episode of prayer. Luke places great emphasis on the prayer life of Jesus (e.g., 3:21; 5:16; 6:12; 9:18, 28–29; 11:1; 22:32, 39–46; 23:34, 46). It is characteristic of the evangelist to have prayer accompanied by visions and auditions. For example, 9:28–36 mentions that while Jesus was praying, a heavenly apparition occurred—Moses and Elijah appeared—and an interpretative audition followed: "This is my Son" (cf. Acts 10; 12:5ff.; 1:14 plus 2:1ff.; Luke 22:39–46; 1:10ff.).

In 3:21–22, after his baptism and while Jesus is praying, there is a heavenly apparition: the Holy Spirit descends in bodily form as a dove upon him. To Greco-Roman hearers of Luke's narrative this would evoke echoes of the Roman use of the flight of birds of omen to discern the decrees of fate. For example, Plutarch in describing how Numa was chosen king after Romulus tells how Numa insisted that before he assumed the kingship his authority must first be ratified by heaven. So the chief of the augurs turned the veiled head of Numa toward the south, while he, standing behind him with his right hand on his head, prayed aloud and turned his eyes in all directions to observe whatever birds or other omens might be sent from the gods. When the proper birds approached, then Numa put on his royal robes and was received as the "most beloved of the gods." In such a thought-world the Lukan narrative would be viewed as an omen of Jesus' status. Exactly what that status was can be discerned from the bird involved, a dove, and the interpreting voice from heaven.

In Mediterranean antiquity the dove was symbolic of "the beneficence of divinity in love, the loving character of divine life itself" (E. R. Goodenough, *Jewish Symbols in the Greco-Roman Period* [New York: Pantheon Books, 1953—], VIII: 40–41). For the Holy Spirit to come to Jesus in the form of a dove would say to Mediterranean hearers that Jesus was beloved of God. That this is Luke's intent can be seen from the interpretation offered of the event by the voice from heaven: "You are my Son, my beloved, in you I am well pleased." This

is an adaptation of Isa 42:1, in words very near to those found in Matt 12:18. This passage speaks about God's servant on whom God has put his Spirit: God's beloved is given God's Holy Spirit.

The context of 3:21–22 shows that the descent of the Spirit is not the moment at which Jesus becomes Son of God: he was that by virtue of his conception by the Holy Spirit (1:35; cf. 3:23). Rather the post-baptismal gift of the Holy Spirit is interpreted as Jesus' anointing for ministry as God's servant, an equipping of him for his task. Luke 4:16–21, the formal opening of Jesus' ministry in the third gospel, has Jesus read from Isaiah:

> The Spirit of the Lord is upon me,
> because he has anointed me to preach good news to the poor.

Then, after returning the scroll, Jesus sat down and said, "Today this scripture has been fulfilled in your hearing." The reference is, of course, to the baptism-prayer scene with its descent of the Holy Spirit on Jesus (cf. Acts 4:27; 10:38). This depiction of the descent of the Spirit on Jesus as an anointing for ministry is in line with the Lukan under-standing of the Holy Spirit generally as the empowering for ministry (cf. Luke 24:49; Acts 1:8).

A further point is that the Holy Spirit comes in response to prayer. In 3:21–22 the evangelist is interested not in what happened at the baptism but rather what happened after the baptism while Jesus was at prayer. It is a Lukan theme that the Holy Spirit is given in response to prayer (Luke 11:13; Acts 1:14 with 2:1–4; 2:21 with 2:39; 4:23–31; 8:15–17; cf. 22:16), but not necessarily in or through baptism (e.g., Acts 8:14–17; 10:44–48; 19:5–6). Here God's beloved Servant-Son is empowered for the upcoming ministry by the gift of the Spirit in re-sponse to prayer.

It is noteworthy that in the plot of the gospel Jesus found it neces-sary to receive an empowering for ministry before he embarked on his public career. He had been conceived by the Holy Spirit; he had been dedicated to God by his parents as a baby; he had personally identified with his parents' decisions about him and consciously assumed the yoke of the kingdom. Yet none of these could substitute for the nec-essary anointing-empowering given him when he prayed after his bap-tism. What is needed for adequate ministry in the Lukan understand-ing is a prior empowering by God's Spirit. This was true for Jesus and

for his disciples in Acts (cf. Acts 1:8, where the promise is that the apostles will receive power after the Holy Spirit has come upon them, and then they will be witnesses). If this is what is needed, how can it be gotten?

In 3:15–17 vs. 16 points to Jesus as the one who will baptize with the Holy Spirit and with fire. Although the historical John was no Christian preacher and did not identify the Coming One with Jesus, but rather, as vs. 17 indicates, as a heavenly judge who would come at the End Time, the evangelist thinks otherwise. John the Baptist, here in 3:16, speaks of Jesus as the baptizer with the Holy Spirit and fire and understands it in terms of the event in Acts 2:1–4. The Baptist is made to anticipate an event that, from Luke's perspective, had happened and continued to happen (Acts 2:1–4; 4:31; 8:14–17; 10:44–48; 11:15–18; 19:1–7). The empowering of disciples is a gift of the exalted Christ (Acts 2:33).

The same emphasis is implicit in Luke 3:21–22. There is a remarkable correspondence in both content and sequence between the events and persons found in Luke and Acts (see C. H. Talbert, *Literary Patterns, Theological Themes and the Genre of Luke-Acts* [Missoula: Scholars Press, 1974], pp. 15–23). Among these correspondences are the baptism of Jesus followed by prayer and the descent of the Holy Spirit in a physical form, which is paralleled by the prayer of the disciples (Acts 1:14) as they await their baptism in the Holy Spirit which then occurs with accompanying physical manifestations (2:1–13). For Luke the baptism-prayer scene in Jesus' career is prototypical for his disciples' experience. Just as the Holy Spirit had come on Jesus after the baptism of repentance and in response to his prayer to empower him for his work, so the Spirit which the risen Lord has poured out (Acts 2:33) is given to his disciples, after prayer, to empower them for their mission. The one who was anointed by the Holy Spirit in 3:21–22 has become, by virtue of his exaltation, the one who pours out the Spirit, baptizing his followers with the Holy Spirit and fire. It is this baptism which empowers disciples for their ministry.

To what kind of experience is the evangelist referring when he speaks about the baptism of the Holy Spirit and fire? What are the *evidences* of this experience that Luke gives in the Acts of the Apostles? On the one hand, the gift of the Spirit is connected with power to be a witness 1:8; 2:1–42; 4:29–31; 6:10; 9:17–22; passim). It is, moreover, an indispensable power. The disciples are not to venture forth until they

have received the promise (Acts 1:8; Luke 24:49). On the other hand, the presence of the Spirit is often connected with unusual phenomena like speaking in tongues and prophesying (2:4; 10:46; 19:6) when experienced initially, and with miraculous occurrences among those who have had the experience (3; 5:12–16; cf. 5:32; 8:5–7, passim). From Luke's point of view the initial experience sometimes happens before water baptism (10:44–48), sometimes in close proximity with water baptism (19:5–6), and sometimes after water baptism (8:14–17). In the Lukan community the experience could not be reduced to a predictable formula (cf. John 3:8). This is a bit different from Paul who located the experience of the Holy Spirit in its demonstrable effects in the context of proclamation (Gal 3:1–5; 1 Cor 2:1–5; 1 Thes 1:5). Since theology usually follows experience, this would be normal for the apostle who had experienced conversion, call to apostleship, and empowering for ministry as a unity. At the end of the first century people experienced the empowering of the Spirit at various times which explains the variety in Acts. It is also important to be aware that Luke-Acts focuses on the externals of religious experience, like visions, auditions, tongues, miracles. Given this general tendency, when the author speaks about the gift of the Holy Spirit in Acts, he is not talking about the secret inner work of God which convicts and converts, but rather about the moment of the Spirit's release in external manifestations. It was this release of the Spirit, in answer to prayer, sometimes accompanied by unusual phenomena, empowering people for ministry, that Luke called the baptism of the Holy Spirit. Jesus, the one who was himself anointed with the Holy Spirit to empower him for his earthly ministry, now exalted at the right hand of God, is the source of this empowering experience among his followers (Acts 2:33).

VICTORY IN SPIRITUAL WARFARE

4:1–13; 3:23–38; 4:14–15

Luke 3:23–38, 4:1–13, and 4:14–15 belong to Episode Three (3:1— 4:15) of 1:5—4:15. Together with the baptism narrative (3:21– 22), they constitute the Jesus half of the episode which corresponds loosely to the material about John the Baptist in 3:1–20. The baptism, the genealogy, and the temptation are linked formally by the repetition of the expression "Son of God" (3:22; 3:38; 4:3, 9); the baptism, temptation, and concluding summary are formally connected by references to the Holy Spirit (3:22; 4:1; 4:14). If one reads the temptation story aright, therefore, it will be heard in the context of 3:21—4:15.

There are at least three different ways of understanding Jesus' temptations in the NT. (1) In Mark 1:12–13 the temptation functions in an explanatory way. It is the moment at which the bearer of the Spirit bound the strong man so his goods could be plundered (Mark 3:27). The story explains how Jesus in his public ministry could have such power over the demons. (2) When Heb 4:15 speaks of Jesus as "one who in every respect has been tempted as we are, yet without sinning" it is said in the interests of encouragement. To know our great High Priest has been through what we are undergoing and hence is sympathetic with us is a great encouragement to draw near to him with our petitions. (3) In Luke 4:1–13 it functions in an exemplary way: "We may be certain that the story was . . . told for its exemplary features in order to encourage Christians facing temptations and to indicate to them how to recognize and overcome it" (I. H. Marshall, *The Gospel of Luke*, p. 166).

One should note just who is being tempted. The context (3:22) makes it clear that he is the Spirit-empowered Servant of God (cf. Isa 42:1). The empowering by the Holy Spirit does not keep Jesus from being tempted: it enables him to be victorious in the midst of temptation.

The victory Jesus won was, in the first instance, by his wise use of the scriptures (cf. 2:41–51; and 24:25–27). In each of the three temp-

44

tations, Jesus responded to the devil's approach with a quotation from Deuteronomy. In vs. 4 he used Deut 8:3, in vs. 8 he drew on Deut 6:13; and in vs. 12 Jesus employed Deut 6:16. Moreover, he knew the appropriate, as opposed to the satanic, use of scripture, rejecting the devil's interpretation in vss. 10–11 of Ps 91:11–12. The devil, in effect, said to him that the promises of God in scripture applied to anyone, at any time and place, regardless of circumstances, if that person would only claim them. Jesus refused to claim the promise. It was not appropriate for the moment. Discernment was needed to know which particular promise to claim at a given moment. In the third gospel this does not come from dialectical skill in scriptural argument.

Jesus' victory over temptation by means of his correct use of scripture was because of his heavenly resource, the Holy Spirit, the source of his discernment. At 3:21–22 Jesus had been anointed (empowered) by the Spirit for his ministry. In 4:1–2 a literal translation might read, "Jesus, full of the Holy Spirit, returned from the Jordan, and *was being led by the Spirit* in the wilderness for forty days *as he was being tempted by the devil.*" This is significantly different from both Mark 1:12 ("And immediately the Spirit cast him out into the wilderness. And he was in the wilderness forty days being tempted by Satan.") and Matt 4:1 ("Then Jesus was led up into the wilderness by the Spirit to be tempted by the devil."). Unlike the other two evangelists, Luke makes certain the reader knows that during the time Jesus was being tempted, he was being led by the Spirit. Having been empowered by the Spirit, Jesus returns full of the Spirit, and in that power deals with the devil in the wilderness. From the evangelist's perspective, Jesus is victorious in temptation because the empowering of the Holy Spirit enables him to hear scripture's word addressed to his immediate needs.

Luke's point here is very similar to that made by the Pauline school, near the time of the gospel, in Ephesians 6. In the parenetic section of the epistle (chaps. 4—6), toward the end, is an exhortation to put on the whole armor of God that one may be able to stand against the wiles of the devil (6:11). The list of spiritual equipment necessary to emerge victorious from the struggle against the spiritual hosts of wickedness (6:12) is climaxed by the injunction, "And take . . . the sword of the Spirit, which is the word of God" (6:17b). The word of God (which would include the scriptures) is the weapon, but the sword is wielded by the Holy Spirit. We find, then, a similar point being made at the end of the first century by the Pauline school in epistolary form

and by the evangelist in his gospel narrative. Victory in spiritual warfare, for Christ as well as the Christian, comes from a Spirit-enabled hearing and use of the scriptures.

The victory of Jesus over temptation, while exemplary, goes beyond mere example. The one who won the victory was both the second Adam and the culmination of all that God had been doing in the history of Israel. (1) The genealogy speaks of Jesus as the culmination of Israel's history (3:23–38). The link with Abraham (vs. 34) would speak of the continuity of Jesus with God's ancient promises (cf. 1:55; 1:73). The link with David (vs. 31) would serve to legitimate Jesus' claim to the Davidic kingship (cf. 1:27; 1:32; 1:69; 2:4; 3:11). Since Luke's genealogy proceeds from David to his third son, Nathan (2 Sam 5:14; 1 Chr 3:5; 14:4), and from him, through a series of unknown names, to Shealtiel and Zerubbabel and thence again through a series of unknown names to Joseph, it likely links Jesus with the prophets. A minority Jewish tradition erroneously held that David's son Nathan was also the prophet and that the Messiah would descend from this non-royal line (M. D. Johnson, "The Purpose of the Biblical Genealogies with Special Reference to the Setting of the Genealogies of Jesus," Th.D. dissertation, Union Theological Seminary, New York, 1966, pp. 282–95). This descent from David through Nathan, if understood in terms of this particular Jewish tradition, would tie Jesus to the prophetic tradition (cf. 4:24; 9:8; 7:11–17; 24:19; Acts 7:52; 3:22, for Jesus as a prophet). The very location of the genealogy may reinforce its links between Jesus and the prophetic tradition. Just as Moses' genealogy in Exod 6:14–25 comes after his call and just before he begins his mission of leading the tribes out of Egypt, so Jesus' genealogy is found after the ratification of his Sonship by God (3:21–22) and just before the official opening of his Galilean ministry (4:16–30). This would be an appropriate location for one who was viewed as the prophet like Moses (Acts 3:22; 7:52). In many ways then, Jesus was the culmination of Israel's history.

(2) The genealogy also alludes to Jesus as the second Adam. Like many Greco-Roman genealogies which traced a family back to a hero or a god, Luke's line of descent for Jesus runs through seventy-seven names to Adam and through him to God. The genealogy ends with the affirmation that Adam is the Son of God. This conditions the way one understands Jesus as Son of God in 4:3, 9. Just as Adam was Son of

God, that is, a direct creation of God, so is Jesus Son of God, because he too is a direct creation of God (1:35). Read in this way the genealogy evokes the concept of Jesus as the second Adam.

Luke 4:1–13 must be read against the background of Jesus as the culmination of all that God had been doing in the history of Israel and as the second Adam. Unlike Mark 1:12–13, this section uses a long form of Jesus' temptations. Like Matt 4:1–11, the third evangelist's story involves three specific temptations: stones to bread, worshiping the devil, and casting himself off the temple. Luke differs with Matthew, however, on the order of the temptations. Whereas Matthew gives the three temptations in the order bread, pinnacle of the temple, worship Satan, Luke reverses the order of the last two. The explanations which fit best with the immediate context are those that see Jesus' three temptations in terms either of the threefold temptation of Adam and Eve in Gen 3:6 (the tree was good for food, a delight to the eyes, and was desired to make one wise) which is echoed in 1 John 2:16 (lust of the flesh, lust of the eyes, pride of life), or of the temptations of Israel in the wilderness. Psalm 106 gives the temptation of Israel in the same order as in Luke's narrative (food, false worship, putting the Lord to the test), an order also found in 1 Cor 10:6–9. The temptations of Jesus thereby become antitypical of the experience of Israel in the wilderness and of the original pair in the garden: whereas those who came before fell, Jesus, as the second Adam and the true culmination of Israel's heritage, shows the way to victory, reversing Adam's fall and Israel's sin. Thanks to the power of God's Spirit, he has become the first of a new humanity, the leader of the faithful among the people of God. Because he has won the victory and has poured out the Spirit (Acts 2:33), his followers have the possibility of similar victory in their spiritual warfare.

The experience of temptation undergone by Jesus did not deplete his spiritual resources: he emerged with spiritual power. The narrative of the temptation, 4:1–13, is enclosed in an envelope (4:1a, 14): in 4:1a "Jesus full of the Holy Spirit returned"; language echoed in 4:14: "Jesus returned in the power of the Spirit." By means of this stylistic device the evangelist makes clear that the anointed Son, who went through his temptations while being led by the Spirit, emerged from the trials not only victorious over the enemy but also in no way depleted in his spiritual power. With a note of power (4:14) Jesus emerges

from his wilderness struggles and comes into Galilee (4:14–15). The Galilean ministry (4:16—9:50), even more than the wilderness trials (4:1–13), will be the scene of the Spirit's might manifested through the one who is beloved of God.

Luke 4:16—9:50

ANOINTED WITH THE HOLY SPIRIT

INTRODUCTION

The second large unit in the gospel is from 4:16—9:50: before it is 1:5—4:15, the account of the prepublic career of Jesus; at 9:51 a new departure occurs, where Jesus sets his face toward Jerusalem. The material in 4:16—9:50 is held together largely by its *geographical orientation:* at 4:14 Jesus returns to Galilee and, except at 8:20 when he and his disciples cross the lake to the country of the Gerasenes, "which is opposite Galilee," the scene is Galilee. Indications in Matthew and Mark that would otherwise locate Jesus outside Galilee are missing (e.g., Matt 16:13 // Mark 8:27 mentions Caesarea Philippi, but not Luke 9:18; Mark 9:30 says Jesus had passed through Galilee, but not Luke 9:43b). The third evangelist believes the mission to the Gentiles comes after Pentecost. He therefore treats 4:16—9:50 as Jesus' mission to Israel, with one exception. This geographical orientation of the material, however, does not prevent the evangelist from foreshadowing in the events of Jesus' early career the things that were to happen later in church history.

As to the theological function of 4:16—9:50, there are two main concerns in this section of the gospel. In the first place, he wants to speak about one stage of Jesus' way. Two strands of evidence give our clue. (1) By almost unanimous consent of scholars, the speeches of Acts reflect the mind of the author of Luke-Acts. If so, then they should indicate something of the way the evangelist understood Galilee in the life of Jesus. Acts 10:34–43, of all the speeches, contains the most detail relevant to our concerns. This speech, attributed to Peter, speaks of (a) the time of the ministry (after the baptism which John preached—vs. 37; before the ministry elsewhere—vs. 37); (b) the content of the ministry (preaching good news—vs. 36; doing good, healing all who were oppressed by the devil—vs. 38); (c) the basis for this ministry (God anointed Jesus of Nazareth with the Holy Spirit and power—vs. 38); (d) the witnesses of this ministry ("we are witnesses to all that he did"—vs. 39). These basic points found here in one speech are scat-

tered in other speeches in Acts: for example, 13:16–41, a speech attributed to Paul, mentions the time of Jesus' ministry in Galilee ("before his coming John preached a baptism of repentance"—vs. 24) and the witnesses ("those who came up with him from Galilee are now his witnesses"—vs. 31); the prayer of 4:24–30 refers to Jesus' anointing (vs. 27); finally, Peter's speech in 1:15–22 speaks of the witnesses and of the relation of Jesus' ministry to the Baptist's ("One of the men who have accompanied us during all the time that the Lord Jesus went in and out among us, beginning from the baptism of John"—vss. 21–22a).

(2) A second hint as to the meaning of the Galilean ministry of Jesus is the frontispiece to the gospel (4:16–30), which is also the introduction for the Galilean section. In the Lukan version of Jesus' rejection at Nazareth we find two emphases. First, the nature of Jesus' ministry is described. Its content is preaching good news to the poor (vss. 18–19) and setting at liberty those that are oppressed (vs. 18). Its basis is the anointing of Jesus with the Holy Spirit (vs. 18). This much agrees with the picture of the Galilean ministry gained from the speeches of Acts. Second, 4:16–30 describes the results of Jesus' ministry. There is both a rejection of Jesus by his own people and a hint of a wider mission to all kinds of people (vss. 23–24, 25–27). Though the speeches of Acts refer only to Jesus' rejection in connection with Jerusalem, that the evangelist intended this rejection, as well as the hint of a wider mission, to apply to Galilee, may be seen if we note a similar passage, Luke 7:18–30: Jesus' ministry of healing and preaching is rejected by the Jewish leaders, but is accepted by the people and tax collectors (vss. 29–30). Taken together, the speeches of Acts and the frontispiece of the gospel give a reasonably clear sketch of what the evangelist intended to say about this stage of Jesus' career.

The Galilean ministry of Jesus takes place after John the Baptist's work has been completed (3:18–20). It is a period of preaching and healing. Almost from the first there are Galilean witnesses present (4:31—5:11; 6:12ff.; 8:1–3; 9:1–6), the same people who will later view the passion events in Jerusalem. The basis for all Jesus does and says is his anointing with the Spirit of the Lord (3:21–22; 4:16ff.). The portrait of Jesus in this section is of one who is empowered with the Holy Spirit. This empowering divides those Jesus meets into two groups: those who recognize God in Jesus' work and words and those who do not. In 4:16—9:50 the evangelist speaks about one stage of

Jesus' way. In this phase of his career, Jesus is the one who is anointed-empowered by the Holy Spirit and his activity demonstrates the kingly power of God. The accent is on power.

In the second place, Luke also wants to foreshadow in Jesus' career certain facets of the later church's life. The evangelist writes his gospel with the thought in mind of the church and the progress of its mission in Acts: in the ministry of Jesus the later ministry of the church is foreshadowed. One example should suffice. In Luke 7:1–10 is tradition also found in Matt 8:5–13. In Luke's version, vss. 3–6a are distinctive. Thereby it becomes a story of a pious centurion who sends others to secure assistance for him. The point of the tradition as it stands in Luke is the centurion's faith as contrasted with Israel's lack of faith (vs. 9). This tradition, as adapted, is remarkably like the Cornelius episode in Acts 10. It would seem the evangelist has introduced into Jesus' Galilean ministry a character like Cornelius so that Jesus' favorable attitude toward such a man and his faith foreshadows the attitude of the later church toward believing Gentiles. The Spirit-anointed Jesus in Galilee functions as a prototype of the behavior that characterizes the Spirit-empowered disciples in Acts.

The dominant emphasis on the power of Jesus and the subordinate theme of the mission of the gospel to all peoples cannot be missed by an attentive reader of 4:16—9:50. (For a detailed discussion, see C. H. Talbert, "The Lukan Presentation of Jesus' Ministry in Galilee," *Review and Expositor* 64:485–97 [1967].)

FOR THE WHOLE PERSON,
IN THE WHOLE WORLD

4:16–30

L uke 4:16–30 presents the distinctive Lukan form of the rejection of Jesus by his "own country" (Mark 6:1; Matt 13:53) or "Nazareth" (Luke 4:16); Matt 13:53–58 and Mark 6:1–6 relate the incident in much the same way, though they differ on its exact context. In the first gospel the incident ends a collection of seven parables (13:1–52); in the second gospel it completes a cycle of four miracles (4:35—5:43). In both the rejection scene happens well along in the Galilean ministry. Luke, however, tells the story in a long and very different way and places it at the beginning of Jesus' public ministry. This seems awkward in light of 4:23, which assumes 4:31–44. By so locating it, the evangelist indicates that in his story this scene does not simply relate one event among others but has programmatic significance for the whole (cf. Acts 13:13–52, a scene at the beginning of Paul's missionary work that is typical of what repeatedly happened).

The clue to the meaning of 4:16–30 is the unit's literary pattern (H. J. B. Combrink, "The Structure and Significance of Luke 4:16–30," *Neotestamentica* 7:27–47 [1973]). The unit is enclosed in an inclusion: in 4:16a,b, Jesus "came to Nazareth" and "entered into the synagogue"; in 4:30 he was "passing through" the crowd and was "going away." Within the inclusion the passage falls into an AB:A'B' pattern. In A and A', Jesus is speaking a word; in B and B' the crowd is reacting to that word. A, the initial word, deals with the form of Jesus' ministry and is found in 4:16c–21, which falls into two parts: (1) the reading (16c–20) and (2) the teaching (20–21). The reading (16c–20) is itself a symmetrically organized unit:

A He stood up to read (16c)
  B there was given to him (17a)
    C opening the book (17b)
      D Isa 61:1f., plus 58:6 (18–19)

54

C'   closing the book (20a)
B'   he gave it back to the attendant (20b)
A'   he sat down (20c)

(V. E. McEachern, "Dual Witness and Sabbath Motif in Luke," *Canadian Journal of Theology* 12:273 [1966]). Furthermore, the quotation (d) is a combination of Isa 61:1–2; 58:6:

> The Spirit of the Lord is upon me, because he has anointed me (Isa 61)
>   to preach (*euaggelisasthai*) good news to the poor (Isa 61)
>   to proclaim release (*aphesin*) to the captives (Isa 61)
>   and sight to the blind (Isa 61)
>   to set at liberty (*aphesei*) the oppressed (Isa 58:6)
>   to preach (*kēruxai*) the acceptable year of the Lord (Isa 61).

In the teaching (vss. 20–21) Jesus proclaims this scripture has been fulfilled by him. The anointing with the Spirit is, of course, a reference to 3:21–22. In 4:1, 14 the evangelist has taken pains to make clear that the descent of the Holy Spirit at Jesus' baptism was the basis for a continuing endowment with the Spirit. In this way the reader is prepared for the announcement of 4:18 which relates the Spirit to the whole of Jesus' ministry. The Spirit has empowered Jesus to preach the good news of God's salvation (18a, 19) and to announce the healing of the blind (18c).

What does Luke understand "proclaiming release (*aphesin*) to the captives" and "setting at liberty (*aphesei*) the oppressed" to mean? The word *aphesis* in normal Christian use means "forgiveness," and the evangelist elsewhere certainly employs the term in this way (1:77; 3:3; 24:47; Acts 2:38; 5:31; 10:43; 13:38; 26:18). It is therefore possible for the reader to hear this undertone in the word. The term is also used to mean "release from captivity." This is certainly its meaning in the context of Isaiah 61 and 58 and seems to be the dominant intent of Luke 4:18. The material which follows (4:31–41) depicts Jesus as an exorcist and healer and then in 4:43 seems to identify this activity with his preaching the good news of the kingdom. If so, then its use here would refer to Jesus' ministry of physical healing and exorcism. This would fit the general Lukan tendency to think of salvation as encompassing both physical healing and inclusion in the eschatological people of God (e.g., salvation is healing in 8:36, 48; 18:42; Acts 4:9; 14:9; it is inclusion in the eschatological family in 8:12; 13:23; 17:19; 18:26; 19:10; Acts 11:14; 15:1; 16:30). Given this, it seems

correct to understand Luke's view of Jesus' mission, as set forth in 4:18–19, to include preaching, physical healing, and exorcism. This threefold activity, moreover, is portrayed as continuing in the ministry of the disciples in Acts (preaching—e.g., Acts 2:14ff.; 3:12ff.; 10:34ff.; 13:16ff.; healing—e.g., Acts 3:1ff.; 9:33ff.; 9:36ff.; 14:8ff.; exorcism— e.g., Acts 16:16ff; 19:12ff.). It is this threefold form of ministry that the empowering by the Holy Spirit produces both in Jesus and in the disciples: the ministry of Master and disciples alike focuses on the whole person.

In A (4:16c–21), Jesus' word is that the prophecies of Isaiah 61 and 58 are fulfilled in him. The peoples' response, B, is given in two parts. The first part, vs. 22a, is a statement about their reaction: "all spoke well of him, and wondered at the gracious words which proceeded out of his mouth." The second, vs. 22b, is a quotation of their words: "Is this not Joseph's son?" The basic issue is the intent of their response. Do the parts of this verse have the same intent? How are they related? The best option, given what follows, is to read 4:22 so both parts are positive responses. This is a necessity for 22a and is natural for 22b if it is taken to mean, "Is this not a hometown boy?" Such a question would contain within it an implicit demand: since he is "our boy," we can expect great things to be done for us by this Spirit-empowered servant of God. It is this inference from his family connections made by the people of Nazareth that prompts Jesus' second word.

This word, A' (4:23–27), defines the scope of his ministry, and falls into two sections. (1) The first, vs. 23, interprets vs. 22 negatively. In effect Jesus says, "You are making a demand on me as a local boy to set up practice here in Nazareth." (2) The second section, vss. 24–27, is a multifaceted response to this implicit demand. Both proverbial wisdom ("No prophet is acceptable in his own country"—vs. 24) and scripture (vss. 25–26, the widow in the land of Sidon; vs. 27, Naaman the Syrian) argue against their demand. The implication of this response is that the local boy's mission will take him away from his hometown and that God's benefits, promised in Isaiah 61 and 58, are even for the Gentiles (vss. 25–26, 27).

Here, of course, we meet in clear-cut fashion the concern of the evangelist for the universalistic scope of God's salvation in Jesus. It is a theme already heard in the section dealing with the prepublic career of Jesus (2:31–32; 3:6, 23–38). It is found almost immediately after 4:16–30: in 4:43, after a series of exorcisms (4:31–41), Jesus resists

those who would have kept him from leaving them (4:43), saying, "I must preach the good news of the kingdom of God to the other cities also; for I was sent for this purpose." The risen Lord at 24:47 tells his disciples that repentance and forgiveness of sins must be preached in his name to all nations. The commission to go to the end of the earth is repeated in Acts 1:8. The rest of Acts tells the story of the evangelistic mission from Jerusalem to Rome. In Acts 10 it is the Holy Spirit who forces Peter to move to the Gentiles. This mission, however, was already symbolized in the sending of the Seventy (or Seventy-two) by Jesus in Luke 10:1ff. If the form of Jesus' empowered ministry is preaching, healing, and exorcism, the scope of it is universal. In 4:24–27 Jesus says he must bear the good news of the kingdom beyond the confines of those to whom he is most closely related by geographical, cultural, and racial origin.

The reaction of the people to this second word of Jesus, B', is found in 4:28–29: when they heard the word they tried to kill him. "It is not so much that Jesus goes elsewhere because he is rejected as that he is rejected because he announces that it is God's will and his mission to go elsewhere" (R. C. Tannehill, "The Mission of Jesus according to Luke 4:16–30," in *Jesus in Nazareth,* ed. W. Eltester [Berlin: Walter de Gruyter, 1972], p. 62). In being rejected because of his concern for a wider mission, Jesus foreshadows the fate of his disciples in Acts (e.g., 13:44–50; 14:19; 17:4–5; 18:12; 20:3; 22:21; 28:23–29) who sometimes were abused because of a mission to the Gentiles (22:21) and sometimes turned to the Gentiles as a result of rejection by Jews (13:44–50; 28:23–29). This rejection echoes an earlier hint of the same thing in Luke 2:34b. The escape of Jesus (4:30) foreshadows the story in Acts where the gospel triumphantly survived similar acts of hostility and rejection.

To summarize: in 4:16–30 the evangelist gives a programmatic statement of Jesus' ministry—and by extension, the ministry of the church—as one empowered by the Holy Spirit, involving not only preaching but also healing and exorcism, and moving outwards to touch the whole world.

CALLED AND COMMISSIONED

4:31—5:11

This unit falls into two parts: 4:31–44; 5:1–11. (1) The first parallels Mark 1:21–38. Both gospels give (a) an account of an exorcism in Capernaum (Mark 1:21–28; Luke 4:31–37—not in Matthew); (b) the story of the healing of Peter's mother-in-law (Mark 1:29–31; Luke 4:38–39—cf. Matt 8:14–15); (c) a generalizing paragraph about many healings and exorcisms (Mark 1:32–34; Luke 4:40–41—cf. Matt 8:16–17); and (d) a reference to Jesus' departure (Mark 1:35–38; Luke 4:42–43—not in Matthew).

The three Lukan paragraphs dealing with healing are linked together by the verb translated "rebuke" (4:35, 39, 41), thereby enabling the treatment of all three miracle stories as exorcisms or events involving exorcisms. This activity brought Jesus a tremendous following (4:37, 42; 5:1–3). In response to the desire of the people in Capernaum to keep him—as those at Nazareth had wanted to do (4:16–30)—Jesus, as at Nazareth, indicated he was under divine necessity (cf. *dei* in 4:43) to move on. Judging from the context, for Jesus to preach the good news of the kingdom must refer to his exorcisms (cf. 11:20).

(2) The second part of the larger thought unit, 5:1–11, furnishes the clue to the overall intent of 4:31—5:11. One notes first of all its location: whereas in Mark the call of Peter, James, and John comes at 1:16–20, before the exorcism and healings in Capernaum (1:21–34), in Luke the call comes after the series of miracles. This placement serves two functions in the gospel.

On the one hand, Luke's placing the call of the disciples after the series of miracles makes the point that mighty works can be the basis for discipleship. Peter, at least, must have known of Jesus' wondrous powers some time prior to his call (4:38–39). Also, when Peter in 5:5 says, "at your word I will let down the nets," Luke understands this to be based on the authority of Jesus' word already established in 4:31–36. Whereas Mark 1:22 says the people were astonished at Jesus'

teaching "for he taught them as one who had authority, and not as the scribes" (Matt 7:29), Luke 4:31 states they were astonished at his teaching "for his word was with authority." There then follows an exorcism (4:33–35) to demonstrate the authority of Jesus' word to which the people respond: "What is this word? For with authority and power he commands the unclean spirits and they come out" (4:36; Mark 1:27 omits "word" and "and power"). It is this one whose word is powerful and who has healed Simon's mother-in-law by rebuking the fever (4:39) who speaks to Peter in chapter 5 and to whom Peter responds in 5:5: "Master, we toiled all night and took nothing! But at your word I will let down the nets." For the evangelist, Peter's initial response to Jesus is based on a prior knowledge of his power in Capernaum.

"Further, the story within which the call of the first disciples is placed (5:1–11) leaves little room for doubt that they followed Jesus because of his wondrous power. Only after Peter, James, and John see the miraculous catch of fish, are they summoned to follow Jesus" (P. J. Achtemeier, "The Lukan Perspective on the Miracles of Jesus: A Preliminary Sketch," in *Perspectives on Luke-Acts*, ed. C. H. Talbert [Danville, Va.: ABPR, 1978], p. 161). In Luke's schema Peter could respond to Jesus' word to let down the nets on the basis of what he had seen done for others, but his following Jesus came as a result of what he had experienced done for him by Jesus: grace was experienced in and through a miraculous deed done for him. This emphasis on miracle as a catalyst for faith is characteristic of Luke-Acts (e.g., Acts 9:35; 9:42; 13:12; 16:30, 33; 19:17; Luke 8:2; 7:18–23). Of course Luke knew that miracle was ambiguous (Luke 11:14–19) and that non-Christians could also perform mighty works (Acts 8:9–11). Nevertheless, the evangelist shows an unusually positive attitude toward miracle as a means by which faith is created. In 4:31—5:11 he makes very clear that miracle was the catalyst for Peter's response to Jesus.

In order to appreciate Luke's stance, we may compare it with that of Mark and John. The Markan view of miracle is much more negative than Luke's: he not only declares that miracles do not necessarily lead to faith (e.g., 3:19b–35; 4:35—6:6) but also asserts that to confess Jesus as Christ on the basis of his power is only partial vision and must be supplemented by the vision of his cross (e.g., 8:14–21, 22–26, 27–30; 10:46–52). The fourth evangelist has the most inclusive view of miracle in the NT: with Luke he asserts that Jesus' mighty works are sometimes instrumental in peoples' believing in him (4:53; 14:11—

i.e., signs provoke faith); with Mark he knows not everyone believes in Jesus as a result of his miracles (i.e., signs are ambiguous—6:26; 11:46ff.; 9:16, 30, 34). John shows that in order for people to see through the miracle to the sign (i.e., to Jesus' identity) some preliminary faith is sometimes present (2:11; 4:46–54; 20:30–31; 21:6–7), but at other times is not present (2:23; 3:2; 9:ff.; 11:45): when faith is already there the miracles deepen it (2:11; 4:46–54; 20:30–31); when miracles evoke faith or openness to faith, a further development is necessary if Jesus is to be understood properly (e.g., chap. 3; chap. 9). This diversity within the NT reflects the struggles to accord miracle (power) its proper place in the total scheme of things. Although power was one component in the early Christian view of God, it was not the central ingredient: Grace was. The gospels reflect the various struggles within the communities to recognize power as part of who God is and at the same time to set it within a structure in which miracle was subservient to grace and balanced by moral considerations (C. H. Talbert, "The Gospel and the Gospels," *Interpretation*, 33:351–62 [1979]).

On the other hand, Luke's placing the call of the disciples after the series of miracles allows Jesus some ministry and such success (4:37, 40, 42) that he is pressed upon by the people (5:1–3). The call of Peter, James, and John (5:10) functions, then, as Jesus' effort to get some assistance in an overly successful ministry. The same motif is found in Acts 11:19–26 where Barnabas, confronted with enormous success in Antioch, enlists Paul as a helper (cf. also Eph 4:11–12 where, if the punctuation is properly placed, the pastors and teachers function "for the equipment of the saints for the work of ministry"). Success creates the need for helpers (Luke 10:2).

If 5:1–11's location has pointed to the enlistment of the disciples, brought about by Jesus' miraculous activity, as a way for Jesus to deal with his success, the form of the passage confirms what the arrangement implied and gives clues to success for disciples involved in ministry. Confirmation comes when we note that in its present form, 5:1–11 is not so much a call story as it is a commissioning narrative. Call stories (e.g., Mark 1:16–20; 2:14; Luke 5:27–28) involve: (a) Jesus came; (b) he saw the person; (c) he called; (d) the person leaves all and follows him. A commissioning story includes: (a) an introduction describing the circumstances; (b) the confrontation between the commissioner and the one to be commissioned; (c) the commission, in which the recipient is told to undertake a specific task; (d) a protest in

which the person questions in some way the word of the commissioner; (e) a reaction of fear, amazement, unworthiness to the presence of the august commissioner; (f) reassurance to the individual, providing confidence and allaying misgivings; and (g) conclusion, usually involving the beginning of the commissioned one's undertaking the assignment (B. J. Hubbard, "Commissioning Stories in Luke-Acts: A Study of Their Antecedents, Form and Content," *Semeia* 8:103–26 [1977], and "The Role of Commissioning Accounts in Acts," in *Perspectives on Luke-Acts*, pp. 187–98). Examples in Luke-Acts include Luke 24:36–53; Acts 1:1–14; 10:9–23. Luke 5:1–11 fits this form nicely: (a) introduction—5:2; (b) confrontation—5:3; (c) commission—5:4; (d) protest—5:5; (e) reaction—5:8–9; (f) reassurance—5:10b; (g) conclusion—5:11. Although there are overtones of a call story present in vs. 11, the dominant thrust is that of a commissioning of Peter for his role of catching people (i.e., mission). The disciples are commissioned to "go fishing" in order to help Jesus with an overly successful ministry. The merging of call and commissioning in 5:1–11 reflects the view that to be called to be a disciple is at the same time to be commissioned as a fisher.

The use of this commissioning form also speaks about success in a disciple's ministry. The symbolism of the story contrasts the futility of "fishing" with only human resources, with the effectiveness of "fishing" in obedience to Jesus' word. The symbolism of a great catch in response to Jesus' word after a fruitless effort prior to Jesus' command would fit the Lukan view of the church's missionary-evangelistic outreach. It was to be (a) to all nations, but (b) the disciples were to stay in Jerusalem until they were empowered (Luke 24:47; Acts 1:8). The narrative of Acts tells the working out of this principle: after being clothed with power from on high, the first fishing expedition of Peter yielded three thousand converts (Acts 2:41). "Fishing" that results in a large catch is that done in response to Jesus' initiative.

The location of the call-commissioning of Peter in time is important. Luke 5:1–11, unlike John 21:4ff., with which it has marked similarities, is located not after the resurrection but early in Jesus' Galilean ministry. This was because the Lukan view of apostleship demanded an apostle have been with Jesus from the first of his ministry to the time of his ascension (Acts 1:21–22; contrast Paul who thought what was needed was to have seen the risen Lord and received a call—1 Cor 9:1; 15:8–10; Gal 1:16). Peter, Luke was saying by his location of

the episode in time, was a disciple from the first and so had the credentials for apostleship. Theologically, this view of apostleship is significant as it places the church's proclamation under the control of the career of the pre-Easter Jesus as known through his witnesses. The earthly Jesus is the criterion of the true proclamation, the primary check and balance on any ministry done in Jesus' name.

THE DIFFERENCE JESUS MAKES

5:12—6:11

L uke 5:12—6:11 falls into two parts with 5:29–32 functioning as the hinge (i.e., both as the conclusion to 5:12–32 and as the introduction to 5:29—6:11). Here as elsewhere this procedure reflects ancient rules for writing historical narrative (e.g., Lucian of Samosata). The first part tells where Jesus can be found and is a unit analogous to 4:31—5:11. (1) Just as 4:31—5:11 sets in Jesus' prior activity (miracles) the basis for his call of Peter, so 5:12–26 gives in two episodes the kind of person it was who called Levi in 5:27–28. Levi's response (vs. 28) is based on Jesus being one who restores social outcasts to community (5:12–14) and forgives sinners (5:17–26). (2) Just as Jesus' association with Peter pointed toward "catching men" (5:10b), so Jesus' call of Levi resulted in this new disciple's not only leaving everything to follow Jesus (5:28) but also his making a great feast in his house to introduce his associates to Jesus (5:29). In 5:29–32 Jesus is depicted as one who not only restores and forgives an individual but as one who also associates with the many who are in need. (3) Just as in 5:1–11 the great catch being possible only in obedience to Jesus' word foreshadowed the experience of the apostolic church, so 5:29–32 foreshadows the experience of the church after the resurrection which learned to associate with Gentiles who were believed to be unclean by strict Jews (Acts 10:1—11:18—note in 11:18, "Then to the Gentiles also God has granted repentance unto life"). Two Lukan touches in 5:32 make this clear. First, note the perfect tense (*elēlutha*) which means "I have come and my work continues" (Eduardo Arens, *The Elthon-Sayings in the Synoptic Tradition* [Göttingen: Vandenhoeck & Ruprecht, 1976], p. 62). That is, through his church Jesus continues to associate with sinners. Second, note Luke's addition of "to repentance," laying the groundwork even here for Acts 11:18. In all of this Luke's concern has been to show that Jesus is found in fellowship with sinners.

When Jesus says, "Those who are well have no need of a physician,

but those who are sick; I have not come to call the righteous, but sinners to repentance" (5:31–32), he indicates not only where he is to be found but also what credentials are required for his disciples: "The church is the only fellowship in the world where the one requirement for membership is the unworthiness of the candidate" (Robert Munger). Such an understanding of Jesus and his church was strange to Greco-Roman readers. In Origen's *Against Celsus,* 3:59f., Celsus, the pagan critic of Christianity, complains that ordinarily those invited to participate in religious solemnities are the pure who live an honorable life. Christians, however, invite anyone who is a sinner, or foolish, or simple-minded. In short, any unfortunate will be accepted in the kingdom of God. By "sinner" is meant any unjust person, whether thief, or burglar, or poisoner, or sacreligious person, or robber of corpses. Why, says Celsus, if you wanted an assembly of robbers, these are just the kind of people you would call. Origen does not deny the charge but says (3:60–61) Christians extend an invitation to sinners in order to bind up their wounds (id., 7:60). Whereas Plato and the other wise ones of Greece are like physicians who confine their attention to the better classes and despise the common people, Jesus' disciples make provision for the great mass of people. If the Lukan Jesus is to be found in fellowship with sinners, the Lukan view of the church is that of a fellowship composed of social outcasts restored to community, and sinners forgiven by grace who have left all to follow Jesus.

Luke 5:12–32 is also analogous to 4:31—5:11 in focusing on how Jesus reacts to unusual success. If the former section showed him enlisting others to help, this section focuses on his withdrawal to pray. Where is Jesus to be found? He is found not only in fellowship with sinners but also in prayer with God. Jesus in Luke alternates between giving what he has and retreating to be filled, between doing what he sees needs doing and withdrawing to gain fresh vision of what should be done (3:21–22; 6:12; 9:18; 9:28f.; 11:1, passim). In this regard the evangelist depicts Jesus as a model for disciples. A disciple is not above the Lord. Disciples of Jesus will be found where he is: in prayer with God and in fellowship with sinners.

The second part of 5:12—6:11, which deals with the character and justification of a Christian style of life, is 5:29—6:11. This part is in two sections: (1) 5:29–39, a banquet scene with dialogue (cf. 7:36–50; 9:10–17; 10:38–42; 11:37–54; 14:1–24; 19:1–10; 22:4–38; 24:29–32,

41–43); and (2) 6:1–11, two sabbath controversies. The unit is joined by the repetition of key words and phrases: note "eat and drink" in 5:30, 33; "drinking" in 5:39; and three different uses of the verb "to eat" in 6:1, 4. Note also that in 6:6 the evangelist has added "on another sabbath," conforming to the wording of 6:1 ("on a sabbath"), thereby indicating he views 6:6–11 as an extension of the issue raised in 6:1–5.

The form of 5:30—6:11 is shaped by a series of charges about the life-style of Jesus and his followers raised by the Pharisees, together with Jesus' answers. (a) 5:30–32. The charge: With whom you eat and drink is problematic. You associate with the wrong kind of people. Jesus' response: The sick are those who need me (vs. 31), therefore, as host I invite sinners (vs. 32). (b) 5:33–39. The charge: Eating and drinking instead of fasting often and offering prayers is a problem; there is not enough seriousness in the style of life of your disciples. Jesus' response: 1) In 5:34–35 Jesus says fasting in the presence of the proclamation of the good news (cf. 4:18–19) makes no more sense than does fasting at a wedding feast. It is unthinkable. 2) In 5:36–38 is a double parable. A piece of cloth from a new garment is not used to patch an old one because, not having shrunken from being washed, the new cloth would tear on washing, and besides the new would not match the old (vs. 36). Also new wine is not put into old wineskins because it will burst the old, but rather into new skins (vss. 37–38). 3) In 5:39 Jesus says that after tasting something better (the old wine which is aged) no one desires an inferior product (the new wine). The difficulty in interpreting 5:39 is due to our attempt to understand "old" and "new" in the same way in vs. 39 and in vss. 36–38. In vs. 39 "old" should be paraphrased "good" and "new" by "inferior," because here "old" equals what Jesus brings—in contrast to 5:36–38—and "new" is the inferior system of the Pharisees and Baptists. (c) 6:1–11. The charge: When you eat is questionable; your style of life violates the sabbath law of Judaism (6:1–5). This flippant attitude toward the sabbath is also manifest in unnecessary healing on the holy day (6:6–11). Jesus' response: In both instances Jesus appeals to human needs taking precedence over sabbath law. His authority for acting in such a way is that he is the Son of Man (6:5) who sits (22:69) or stands (Acts 7:56) at the right hand of God. He is also an interpreter of the law whose stance is validated by the healing miracle in 6:9–10. Anyone

who does not listen to him will be cut off from the people (Acts 3:22–23). Overall, the section, 5:30–6:11, shows Jesus as a "sign that is spoken against" (2:34).

The basic issue raised in this section has to do with the character and justification of the way of life of Jesus' followers. Luke's view of a disciple is one who has left all to follow Jesus. Attachment to Jesus gives an inner detachment from the world. Yet the disciples' detachment from the world did not express itself in terms of the old outer signs of what it meant to be religious, as the Jewish culture saw it. Two early second century documents tell the story clearly.

(1) The Christian *Epistle to Diognetus*, 5, says:

> For Christians are distinguished from other men neither by country, nor language, *nor the customs* which they observe. For they neither inhabit cities of their own, nor employ a peculiar form of speech, nor lead a life which is marked out by any singularity. But, inhabiting Greek as well as barbarian cities, according as the lot of each of them has been determined, and *following the customs of the natives in respect to clothing, food, and the rest of their ordinary conduct,* they display to us their wonderful and confessedly striking method of life. They dwell in their own countries, but simply as sojourners. As citizens, they share in all things with others, and yet endure all things as if foreigners. Every foreign land is to them as their native country, and every land of their birth as a land of strangers. They pass their days on earth, but they are citizens of heaven. (ANF, 1:26–27)

From this it appears that whereas Christians were detached in spirit from over-absorption in the world, in many ways their way of life was a part of the surrounding culture. This caused the problem for their closest religious kin.

(2) In Justin's *Dialogue with Trypho the Jew*, 10, Trypho is amazed at the Christian's stance in the world:

> But this is what we are most at loss about: that you professing to be pious, and supposing yourselves better than others, *are not in any particular separated from them, and do not alter your mode of living from the nations,* in that you observe no festivals or sabbaths, and do not have the rite of circumcision. (ANF, 1:199)

It appears the orthodox Jew had no problem with the Christians' spirit of detachment from the world, but with the absence of the old distin-

guishing marks that set one off from the general culture, such as observance of the sabbath laws, regular fasts and prayers, and separation from persons who were defiled. The question inevitably would be, Why are you Christians so lax?

The evangelist believed attachment to Jesus brought detachment from the world (5:28—"he left everything . . . and followed him"). At the same time, Jesus' disciples ignored many of the old outer signs of the religiously devout. This did not mean, however, that inner attachment to Jesus and detachment from the world failed to find outer expression in the disciples' involvement with the world. Rather Jesus asserts that *a new inner religious reality demands a new life-style* (5:36–39). The marks of Jesus' followers will not be sabbath observance, fasting and prayers offered, and avoidance of outcasts, but will be joy like that at a wedding (5:33–35) and an overriding concern for human need, spiritual (5:29–32) and physical (6:1–11). Such a way of life has the authority of Jesus behind it.

The apostle Paul had captured this spirit when he wrote to the Romans: "The kingdom of God does not mean food and drink but righteousness and peace and joy in the Holy Spirit" (14:17).

TRANSCENDING THE TIMES

6:12–49

T his section has three major components: (1) 6:12–16, the choice of the Twelve; (2) 6:17–19, the transition from the hills where the Twelve are chosen to the plain where Jesus instructs his disciples; and (3) 6:20–49, the Sermon on the Plain.

In Luke-Acts the apostles are primarily witnesses who guarantee the historical continuity and authenticity of the church's message (Acts 1:21–22): 6:12–16, then, functions to establish an apostolic guarantee for the tradition which follows (6:20–49). In 6:20–49, Luke is saying, we have Jesus' instruction for disciples passed to us by the apostles who were with him (cf. 6:17—"he came down with them"). Note that the list of the apostles' names is repeated in Acts 1:13 and their credentials given in 1:21–22 (they have been with Jesus from the beginning to the Ascension).

Luke 6:17–19 functions in a twofold way. First, the unit delineates the audience for what follows—apostles, a crowd of disciples, and a great multitude of people. Second, it reaffirms the identity of the one who will be delivering the Sermon on the Plain, the Spirit-empowered one (4:18) who speaks of good news (4:18b) and demonstrates it in the healing of diseased bodies and spirits (cf. 4:18c,d,e). With people present to hear and those who will pass on the tradition at hand, the stage is set for the Sermon on the Plain which the evangelist says is directed to Jesus' disciples (6:20), to "those who hear" (6:27).

Although both the Sermon on the Mount in Matthew and the Sermon on the Plain in Luke are built on four blocks of similar material in the same relative order (Matt 5:2–12/Luke 6:20–23; Matt 5:38–48/Luke 6:27–36; Matt 7:1–5/Luke 6:37–38, 41–42; Matt 7:15–27/Luke 6:43–49), the Lukan sermon has a perspective of its own. This point of view can be discerned through a careful analysis of the arrangement of the material in 6:20–49. (The observations on the pattern of 6:20–49 throughout this section are influenced by Robert Morgenthaler, *Die*

Lukanische Geschichtsschreibung als Zeugnis [Zürich: Zwingli Verlag, 1948], 1:81–83.)

The Sermon on the Plain falls into three parts determined by the formulae of introduction: (1) 6:20, "And he lifted up his eyes on his disciples, and said"; (2) 6:27, "But I say to you that hear"; and (3) 6:39, "He also told them a parable." The first part, 6:20–26, contains four beatitudes balanced by four woes. This section offers congratulations and condolences to two kinds of people. The second part, 6:27–38, focuses on the life of love, in four thought units: (a) 6:27–28, a four-member unit—love, do good, bless, pray; (b) 6:29–30, a four-member unit—strikes you, takes away your cloak, begs from you, takes away your goods—followed by a summary, vs. 31; (c) 6:32–35, a four-member unit: the first three—if you love, if you do good, if you lend—are balanced by the fourth—but love, do good, lend—and followed by a summary, vs. 36; and (d) 6:37–38a, a four-member unit: two negatives—judge not, condemn not—balanced by two positives—forgive, give—followed by a summary, vs. 38b. The third part, 6:39–49, is a collection of four parables: vss. 39–40, blind man; vss. 41–42, speck and log; vss. 43–45, trees and fruit; vss. 46–49, two houses. It is concerned with principles that should govern the lives of disciples, such as the proper use of influence. The contrast between the two types of people (6:46–49) at the end of the Sermon echoes the contrast (6:20–26) at the beginning. Taken together the opening and closing contrasts serve as an inclusion around the Sermon as a whole. Any exposition of the passage (6:20–49) must follow the leads Luke has given in the pattern of his arrangement of the material.

The first part of the Sermon on the Plain, 6:20–26, contains four beatitudes and four corresponding woes. Our understanding of the Lukan intent depends first on our grasping the functions of beatitudes and woes in antiquity and second on our perception of the meaning of the key terms used here. (a) Function. The beatitude is a specific genre both in the Greek and Jewish worlds (e.g., Ps 1:1; Prov 8:34; Dan 12:12; Tob 13:14; Ps of Sol 4:23; 17:44; 18:6). Early Christians found it useful (Rom 14:22; Matt 5:3–12; John 20:29; Rev 14:13; 16:15; 22:7). Here in Luke 6 its form consists of *makarios* (blessed) followed by who is blessed and why. The beatitude does not confer a blessing; rather it extols the good fortune accruing to someone for some particular reason. It is not an exhortation to be or to do something; rather it exalts or approves a person on the basis of some good fortune. It may

be paraphrased, "Congratulations to _____ because of _____." It celebrates someone's success.

The beatitudes in the NT are often eschatological: they see the present in the light of the ultimate future. They do not make their judgments on the basis of the appearance of things in the here and now, by present outward success. Instead, the one uttering the beatitude does so from a position within the councils of God and with an awareness of the ultimate outcome of history (as does a prophet, e.g., Jer 23:18, 21–22). The content of the beatitude may be in stark contrast with the painful reality of the present. Paradox is prominent. Congratulations are in order, no matter what the appearances, however, because of what will ultimately be. If the present is radically out of keeping with what will be, the beatitude may signal the reversal of all human values (1:51–53).

The woe is also a set genre in the OT (Isa 5:8–23; 33:1; Amos 5:18; 6:1; Hab 2:6–19), functioning as an expression of pity for those who stand under divine judgment. It bemoans the sad plight of the person(s) in question. Used in an eschatological context, a woe laments the plight of the person designated, whatever appearances are in the present, because of what will ultimately be.

Collections of beatitudes occur (e.g., Sir 25:7–10) and a combination of woes with blessings is not uncommon (e.g., Eccles 10:16–17; Tob 13:12; 1 Enoch 99; 2 Enoch 52). The functions of collections and combinations are the same as those of individual beatitudes and woes. In Luke 6:20–26, therefore, the evangelist is working with a form of communication characteristic of his milieu. In this context both beatitudes and woes are eschatological in cast. They offer congratulations and condolences to people in the present on the basis of what will ultimately be. They celebrate that someone's life is a success or lament that it is a failure because it conforms or does not conform to what life will be like in the New Age.

(b) Meaning of key terms. The crux of the matter is whether or not "poor," "hunger," and "weep," and their counterparts "rich," "full," and "laugh," are to be understood sociologically or religiously. It must be the latter because the gospel canonizes no sociological state. At the same time the religious meaning of the terms often derived from an earlier sociological meaning.

"Congratulations to you poor." The vocabulary of poverty which at first had merely a sociological significance, over the centuries in Is-

rael's history took on a spiritual meaning. In the history of Israel the economically poor observed the spirit of Israel's religion more faithfully than did the affluent elite. They came to be the model of the faithful worshipers: Isa 29:18–19 links the poor and the meek; in Isa 61:1 the Massoretic text's "preach good tidings to the meek" is rendered "to preach to the poor" by the LXX; at Qumran the "poor" were the ones counting worldly goods as nothing (cf. 4QPPs37, 1:8f.; I QH 5:13f.), the devout (cf. *War Scroll*); the Ps of Sol 10:7 mention the pious and the poor in synonymous parallelism (cf. also 5:2, 11; 15:1; 18:2). By the time of Jesus, in a Jewish context, the poor person had become the type of one who is pleasing to God, that is, one who recognizes his total dependence upon God. It was this connotation Matthew aimed to make explicit by his addition of "in spirit" (5:3). That Luke also intended "poor" to carry primarily a religious connotation may be seen from 1:51–53, where in parallelism the "proud and mighty" are equated with the "rich." At the same time the evangelist recognized the "poor" religiously (the powerless who are totally dependent on God) to be oftentimes "poor" economically (cf. 1:45; 2:24). Correspondingly, Luke's lament over the plight of the rich in 6:24, "O the tragedy of you rich people," refers in the first instance to a religious situation. Religiously, the rich are those who trust in their riches (cf. 1 Enoch 94:8–9: "Woe to you, you rich, for you have trusted in your riches.") and ignore God and neighbor (cf. Luke 12:16–21; 16:19–25). Part of the good news the anointed servant preaches to the poor (Luke 4:18) is that those who are powerless and trust wholly in God are to be celebrated as the successful; those who live with the illusion they are self-sufficient are to be lamented as failures. That disciples had difficulty seeing life from this angle is evidenced by the epistle of James near the time of Luke.

"Congratulations to you that hunger now." Again, the term "hunger" has both physical and spiritual connotations in the Jewish traditions. In passages like Ps 132:15; 146:7; Ezek 34:29, the hunger is physical; in Isa 55:1–2; Amos 8:11; Sir 24:21, hunger means also a desire for spiritual satisfaction; in Ps 107:9 and Isa 49:10, the meaning may be either or both. It was the religious connotation that Matthew made explicit by adding "for righteousness" (5:6). That Luke intended the spiritual connotation to be dominant may be seen from 1:51–53 where the hungry are paralleled to the lowly as opposed to the proud. It is those who are unsatisfied spiritually, the hungry who want more than they have, who are to be celebrated. By analogy 6:25's lament

over the "full" must refer to those who are spiritually satisfied, to those unaware that "man shall not live by bread alone" (4:4). The self-sufficient who are spiritually satisfied are to be pitied: "O the tragedy of you that are full."

"Congratulations to you who weep." This is a term used frequently in Luke to express mourning and sorrow of all kinds. Doubtless the fallen structures of life that oppress the defenseless ones are the implied cause of anguish (cf. Ps 126:2, 5–6; Isa 60:2; 61:3; 66:10; 65:16–19; 35:10). "O the tragedy of you that laugh now." The verb translated "laugh" in 6:25b is used in the LXX of an evil kind of laughter which looks down on the fate of enemies and is in danger of becoming boastful and self-satisfied. This nuance may be present here. If so, the lament is over those who are self-satisfied and indifferent to the needs of others (I. H. Marshall, *The Gospel of Luke*, p. 256). Those who suffer under the present structures are to be celebrated; those who revel in those structures are to be pitied.

"Congratulations to those of you who are persecuted." Persecution on account of the Son of Man is to be celebrated. Thereby one joins the goodly company of the prophets who have previously suffered the same fate. It is good company to join. "O the tragedy of you who are popular." To be well spoken of by all in a world that rejects the Son of Man and his followers is lamentable because it places one in the company of the false prophets of old. It is tragic to be in such company. Here one cannot help but hear echoes of Christian trials such as those in Acts 6—7. Note the acting out of the injunction of Luke 6:23 in Acts 5:41.

Why are the poor (powerless), whose only hope is in God, blessed? It is because, trusting only in God, they belong to the sphere of God's rule (vs. 20b). Why, when such people hunger and weep and are persecuted, are they to be congratulated? It is because in God's ultimate victory they will be favored by the structures of the New Age. The type of persons described in 6:20–23 is to be extolled because of what they have now—God himself—and because of what they will ultimately have—support from the structures of life in the kingdom of God. The type of persons described in the woes is to be pitied because, trusting only in what now is, they have nothing more for which to hope (vs. 24b). Like the bad company they keep (6:26—false prophets), they will come up short when God settles the final account (1:51–53).

The second part of the Sermon on the Plain, 6:27–38, contains four

thought units (6:27–28, 29–31, 32–36, 37–38) devoted to an attempt by Jesus to break the pattern of reciprocity in human relations among his disciples. The two initial units belong together in describing love in terms of nonviolence.

The first (6:27–28) establishes a principle: do not reciprocate by returning evil for evil—"Love your enemies, do good to those who hate you, bless those who curse you, pray for those who abuse you." This is a principle also found in Rom 12:14–21 and in 1 Pet 2:18–25 as an integral part of the early church's instructions for Christian living.

The second unit (6:29–31) gives four examples of what it would mean not to return evil for evil (6:29–30) and then concludes with the Golden Rule (6:31). The four examples (strikes, takes away, begs, takes away) of nonviolence are arranged in such a way as to become illustrations of the love of the enemy mentioned in vs. 27. Here we meet Jesus' use of the "focal instance" (for what follows, see R. C. Tannehill, "Tension in Synoptic Sayings and Stories," *Interpretation* 34:142–44[1980]). In a focal instance the situation described is so specific it does not provide a very useful general rule when confined to its literal sense. The specificity is intended to shock the hearers with an extreme command, at striking variance with the way people usually behave in such a situation, to lead the hearer to think beyond the literal meaning of the words and to reflect on the whole pattern of behavior that dominates life. The specific command is not a rule of behavior which can be followed mechanically but is intended to stimulate the imagination to draw out the implications for life as a whole. If no one has struck me on the cheek or taken away my coat, what would a nonviolent response to the violence I experience mean? When the moral imagination is awakened in this way, the words have had their desired effect. Love of the enemy means not returning evil for evil but responding to violence by creative nonviolence. Although the golden rule is not distinctly Christian (Homer, *Odyssey,* 5:188–89; Isocrates, *Nicokles,* 49:1; Seneca, *On Benefits,* 2:1:1; Tobit 4:15; Philo [in Eusebius, *Preparation of the Gospel,* 8:7]; 2 Enoch 61:1; Test Naphtali 1, passim), it is used here (vs. 31) by the evangelist to say one's response to evil treatment should be motivated not by how one is treated but by how one wants to be treated. If one acts as one wants to be treated, one will not be involved in returning evil for evil.

If we are to judge from the narrative in Acts, the evangelist would regard Stephen's martyrdom (7:54–60) as an example of a situation

where a disciple prayed for those who abused him; Paul's response to the Philippian jailer (16:28ff.) would be an example of a Christian's doing good to one who was, on the surface of things, an enemy. It should be noted, however, that Luke apparently had no qualms about advocating the use of legal resources for one's defense against non-Christians when these were available (16:37–39; 22:25–29; 25:10–11). He gives no indication, however, in Acts, that he approved of one Christian's using the law for redress of grievance against another Christian. In this he may have agreed with Paul (1 Cor 6:1–11).

The last two units (6:32–36, 37–38) in the second section of the Sermon on the Plain also belong together in describing love in terms of generosity. The principle is set forth: do not show good will only to reciprocate or just to those who can reciprocate.

In the Hellenistic age of the Mediterranean world the relation between a benefactor and a beneficiary consisted of reciprocal obligations composed of the gratitude of the recipient to the benefactor and a resulting obligation of the benefactor to the beneficiary who had expressed gratitude. The ground rules were as follows: A person showed some kindness to another. In doing this repayment would be expected and the benefaction would be viewed as a loan. That a response of gratitude must be forthcoming influenced one's choice of the recipient of benevolence. A benefactor would help not the poor but the well-to-do because one could expect the recompense of thanksgiving from them. The expression of gratitude that was forthcoming then placed a valid claim for further benefits on the original benefactor (S. C. Mott, "The Power of Giving and Receiving; Reciprocity in Hellenistic Benevolence," in *Current Issues in Biblical and Patristic Interpretation,* ed. G. F. Hawthorne [Grand Rapids: Eerdmans, 1974], pp. 60–72).

The unit 6:32–36 asks three questions ("If you . . . , what credit is that to you? For even sinners. . . ."), then with present imperatives says, "But habitually love your enemies, and habitually do good, and habitually lend expecting nothing in return. . . ." Such generosity transcends the reciprocity principle. The motive for one's transcending that system of doing good is found in 6:35b–36. One shows good will not to reciprocate only and not just to those who can reciprocate because one is acting as the heavenly Father acts. He is kind to the ungrateful and the selfish. One is to be merciful as he is merciful.

The last unit (6:37–38) gives four examples of showing kindness even to the undeserving and then concludes with another motivation

for such behavior: "Judge not, condemn not, forgive, give." Why? "For the measure you give will be the measure you get back" (vs. 38b). If we deny mercy to another we short-circuit God's mercy to us (cf. Matt 18:23–35; 2 Cor 9:6–15).

Luke 6:27–38, then, is a two-pronged attack on reciprocity as a governing principle in human relationships. On the one hand, people should not return evil for evil but rather respond as they would want to be treated: in Luke's mind this means nonviolence in return for violence. On the other hand, people must not restrict their good deeds either to others who have been good to them or to those who can and will be good in return. God shows good will to all and gives abundantly to disciples as they give to others: for Luke this means generosity. A life lived by the principle of reciprocity is too restrictive to express the love to which Jesus has called his disciples.

The call to respond not in kind but out of kind is problematic. How is it possible to respond nonviolently to violence done to us? How is it possible to be generous with those who reject us? Granted the legitimacy of the principle—love your enemies—what resources make it possible? If there are no such resources, what good does it do to lay such a heavy burden on disciples' backs? The narrative gives a clue as to how the evangelist would answer these questions. Jesus' disciples before Pentecost tended to respond in kind (e.g., 9:52–54; 22:49–50); afterward they rejoiced "that they were counted worthy to suffer dishonor for the name" (Acts 5:41). Only God's own powerful presence can enable a person to respond other than in kind; only Pentecost makes Jesus' words anything other than an impossible ideal.

The third and final part of the Sermon on the Plain, 6:39–49, consists of four parables (6:39–40, 41–42, 43–45, 46–49). Just as in 15:3, where the evangelist says Jesus told a parable (singular) and followed the statement with three parables in the remainder of the chapter, so the singular is followed here by four stories (cf. 5:36–38). That he introduces a series with the singular indicates the unity of the parables which follow, insofar as the evangelist is concerned. In chapter 15 Luke told three stories about the lost, its recovery, and the resulting joy. Here the evangelist, in vss. 39–45, is especially concerned with the matter of Christian influence.

Influence is an issue about which Luke speaks elsewhere. In 8:16 he visualizes a Roman-style house in which the lamp is placed in the vestibule to furnish light for those who enter (contrast Matt 5:15 where

a one-room Palestinian house illuminated by the lamp is assumed). The point, in the Lukan context, is that those who have made a right response to the word of God and who belong to the family of God are to be light for those who are entering God's household. The character of those who are already disciples is to illumine the way of the new converts (C. E. Carlston, *The Parables of the Triple Tradition* [Philadelphia: Fortress, 1975], p. 91). Acts reflects the same idea. In 20:17–35 Luke reports a farewell speech of Paul to the Ephesian elders in which Paul says his behavior was a guide to them about the Christian way (vss. 33–35a). In the NT period new Christians learned the meaning of the Christian way from observation of those who were already Jesus' followers. This is why Paul could speak about his converts' imitating him (1 Cor 4:15–17; 11:1; Phil 3:17; 2 Thes 3:7). Christian influence was a matter about which the third evangelist was concerned.

The place of 6:39–45 in the perspective about influence is clarified when we notice the pattern of section. It is ABA'. The central unit (B—vss. 41–42) speaks of the need for the guide to be self-critical and personally transformed before undertaking the tasks of the admonition to and transformation of a fellow disciple. This does not mean that since every disciple is a sinner "he should live and let live and be blind to moral imperfections about him. Such a stance would give the green light to evil and spell the end of mutual admonition in the community" (F. Danker, *Jesus and the New Age*, p. 89). Rather the point is that any effort at improvement of others without taking stock of oneself is ridiculous.

The other two components (A—vss. 39–40; A'—vss. 43–45) function as motivations for the central concern for personal transformation before undertaking to assist others. In vss. 39–40 the motive is that since the pupil can be no better than his teacher, the teacher must not be blind. In order to get the desired result—improvement in the life of the other—one oneself must embody the newness of the Christian way. Verses 43–45 also speak of motivation (cf., *gar*, "for" in vs. 43). Personal transformation in the selfhood of the teacher is essential because what one does and says is only an overflow from who one is. The evangelist is saying the only way those who are already disciples can function as lights in the vestibule of the household of God (8:16) is if their own personal transformation is more basic to them than their role of instructing others (cf. James 3).

The final parable (6:46–49) serves both as the end of section three (6:39–49) and as the conclusion of the entirety of the Sermon on the Plain. Its function (cf. Ezek 13:10–16; Aboth R. Nathan 24) is exhortation. Like Jas 1:21–25 it is concerned with a disciple's doing what has been heard (cf. Matt 7:21–23; John 13:17; 1 John 2:17). Those who do what they hear are stable in times of crisis (Luke 8:15; Psalm 1); not so those who are hearers only (Luke 8:14). The gospel, just as the epistle of James, is concerned that disciples not regard the essence of Christianity as a belief and a confession (you call me, "Lord, Lord") separable from a walk in the world (and not do what I tell you). When the whole self responds totally to the one Lord, the result is an indissoluble union between confession and walk.

JESUS AND OTHER
RELIGIOUS TRADITIONS

7:1–10, 11–17

Luke 7:1–10 (Matt 8:5–13) and 7:11–17 (only in Luke) belong together with 6:20ff. as a prelude to 7:18–23. This is made clear by an examination of several details in 7:18–23. (1) 7:18 (different from Matt 11:12) says the disciples of John told him of "all these things." At first reading one would think "all these things" referred to one or both of the miracles in 7:1–10, 11–17. (2) Although 7:21 (not in Matthew) says Jesus worked miracles before John's disciples, the specific works of 7:21 are not exactly those of 7:22 (same as Matt 11:5). The list of mighty works at 7:22 corresponds with those in Isa 35:5; 61:1, except the Isaiah passages do not refer to lepers being cleansed or to the dead being raised. These two items probably echo the Elijah-Elisha traditions (cf. Luke 4:25–27 with the OT parallels). It is significant that a tradition unique to Luke, 7:11–17, the raising of a dead man, precedes the story of 7:18–23, which refers in vs. 22 to raising the dead. (3) In 7:22, after the references to the mighty works, there is "the poor have good news preached to them." This, of course, was not only what Jesus had announced as his aim (4:18) but what he had explicitly done in 6:20: "Blessed are you poor, for yours is the kingdom of God." This would seem to say that "all these things" of 7:18 would have been understood by the evangelist to include 6:20ff., as well as 7:1–17; that is, what Jesus said as well as what he did.

On what basis should John the Baptist believe? From Luke's perspective the Baptist is offered miracles and the proclamation of good news to the poor which are prophesied in scripture as events of the last days. The data by which John's response is evoked consist of what his disciples had seen and heard (7:22; cf. 1 John 1:3).

This pattern (an eschatological message accompanied by signs and wonders which evoke a response to Jesus) is that which characterizes the Acts of the Apostles (cf. 2; 3—4; 8; 10; 13; 16). From the evan-

gelist's point of view, it is the confrontation with both things seen and things heard that truly raises the issue of Jesus' identity.

Within the larger context the evangelist is especially interested in the story in Luke 7:1–10 where the centurion stands as a type of a believing Gentile. Two strands of evidence combine to make this clear. First, although 7:1–10 recounts the same basic tradition found in Matt 8:5–13 (cf. John 4:46–54), the Lukan form of the healing is expanded by vss. 3–6. Luke's centurion deals with Jesus, not directly as in Matt 8:5–7, but indirectly through two embassies, the first consisting of elders of the Jews and the second of friends. The Jewish embassy speaks to Jesus of the centurion's meritoriousness: "He is worthy to have you do this for him, for he loves our nation, and he built us our synagogue" (7:4–5). Second, this distinctively Lukan section is echoed in Acts 10:1–2: "At Caesarea there was a man named Cornelius, a centurion . . . , a devout man who feared God with all his household, gave alms liber-. ally to the people, and prayed constantly to God." In the overall architectonic scheme of Luke-Acts, in which the events of Acts parallel those in the gospel in content and sequence, these two passages correspond. The evangelist has thereby tied these two episodes together so 7:1–10 functions as a foreshadowing of the conversion of the Gentiles. In other words, the story of the centurion in 7:1–10 gives dominical precedent for the mission to the Gentiles in the narrative of Acts. More precisely, 7:1–10 gives dominical precedent for Peter's actions in Acts 10, just as Luke 8:26–39 gives a warrant for Paul's move outside the bounds of Jewish territory in Acts 13—28. The centurion in 7:1–10 is a type of the believing Gentile in Jewish territory.

The centurion is, moreover, an example of one who has faith in Jesus without having seen him: he deals with Jesus not directly but through two embassies. He represents the Gentiles who "without having seen him . . . love him" (1 Pet 1:8). John reflects the same concern, both in the story of the Greeks who approach Jesus only through the disciples (12:20ff.) and in the beatitude near the end of the gospel: "Blessed are those who have not seen and yet believe" (20:29).

When the elders of the Jews cite the centurion's religious credentials to Jesus and proclaim him worthy (vss. 4–5), we meet another Lukan theme: attitudes toward other religious traditions. At least three points on a spectrum need to be noted. (1) Luke believes Jesus fulfills Judaism. (2) He thinks Jesus judges much of pagan religion. (a) Christianity is entirely opposed to magic; that is, the use of spiritual

power for personal gain (Acts 8:9ff.; 13:6ff.; 19:19). (b) Christianity undermines pagan religion motivated by financial greed (Acts 19:23ff.). (c) Christianity calls for repentance from those who worship the creation rather than the Creator (Acts 17:22ff.; 14:8ff.). (3) The evangelist also believes Jesus completes pagan piety that follows the light it has, worshiping the Creator instead of the creation and engaging in ethical behavior. This posture is stated most explicitly in the speech attributed to Peter in Acts 10:34–35: "Truly I perceive that God shows no partiality, but in every nation any one who fears him and does what is right is acceptable to him." It is this third point that is foreshadowed in Luke 7:1–10. It raises the question of whether or not Luke had either a natural theology (that is, whether one could infer from either the world or from human nature that God is) or a belief in a general revelation (that is, God is at work in all times and places disclosing himself through the world and in every person's depths).

Clarification of Lukan thought on this point depends on a comparison with that of Hellenistic Judaism, Paul, and Justin Martyr. (1) Ancient Judaism had a natural theology of sorts. The Wisdom of Solomon asserts (13:1–9) there is a possibility of an inference being made from the greatness and beauty of created things to God as their Creator (vs. 5); however, the Gentiles have not made this inference (vs. 1). Josephus (*Antiquities* 1:7:1 §154–57) gives another tradition (e.g., Genesis Rabbah 38:13) about Abraham's theistic inference from nature, succeeding where the Gentiles had failed. Philo's *The Migration of Abraham*, 35, also refers to the possibility of a theistic inference being made from the order or rule seen within the human being. In certain circles of ancient Judaism there was a natural theology which held that any human being could, by inference, reason from either nature or the human self to God—though, in fact, some did and some did not.

The author of Luke-Acts has something in common with Hellenistic Judaism. In Acts 14:17, in a speech attributed to Paul and Barnabas in Lystra, we hear that God "did not leave himself without witness, for he did good and gave you from heaven rains and fruitful seasons, satisfying your hearts with food and gladness." There are signs in the natural order which witness to God. Whether or not they have been seen and acknowledged is not mentioned explicitly. The context of the speech, however, vss. 12, 13, 18, seems to indicate that these Gentiles have not attained a knowledge of God. Acts 17:22–31, a speech attributed to Paul, says God the creator made human beings "that they

should seek God, in the hope that they might feel after him and find him" (17:27). Verses 29, 30a, 23, however, seem to indicate that, rather than finding the Creator, the Gentiles have worshiped the creation instead. They did not attain a knowledge of God. These two passages seem very much like Wis 13:1–9. The possibility of a natural knowledge of God is there but it has not been actualized.

The distinctiveness of Acts 10 (and possibly Luke 7:1–10) is that here we find a Gentile who feared God (vs. 2). Cornelius had apparently realized the possibility. It is of those Gentiles who had made the correct inference that Peter speaks in Acts 10:34–35.

This emphasis, however, must be set alongside Acts 4:12 if we are to understand the evangelist correctly. In 4:12 Peter says, "And there is salvation in no one else, for there is no other name under heaven given among men by which we must be saved." So in the Cornelius episode of Acts 10, the Gentile's correct inference via natural theology must be completed by Peter's preaching of Jesus and by the Holy Spirit's falling on Cornelius and his household as a sign of their response in faith. In the theology of Luke-Acts, Jesus is the completion of a correct response made to the witness of God given in the natural order. When in Luke 7:1–10 the centurion is pronounced worthy by the Jews, he is, as noted above, a foreshadowing of the worthy centurion Cornelius of Acts 10 who, in turn, symbolizes a whole class of people in Luke's own time. The evangelist is thinking of virtuous and godly pagans whose following of the light they have has been the preparation for Christ. For such people Christ is the completion of their developing relation to God.

(2) A comparison of Lukan thought with that of Paul is also helpful in clarifying the perspective of Luke-Acts on this matter. In Rom 1:19 the second part of the verse clarifies the first: "For God has manifested it to them" (vs. 19b) shows that the apostle is thinking in terms of a general revelation rather than a natural theology. The media of the revelation are "the things made"; the time of the revelation is "from the creation of the world"; and the content of the revelation is "his eternal power and deity" (1:20). In Rom 1:21 Paul indicates the revelation was actualized, at least to the degree that made humans responsible: "although they knew God they did not honor him as God or give thanks to him." There are some significant differences, then, between the views of Paul and the third evangelist on the matter of the Gentiles' knowledge of God. Luke, like Hellenistic Judaism, talks about a

natural theology instead of a general revelation, about Gentiles who do not worship the creation but acknowledge the Creator.

(3) Justin Martyr forms a final point of comparison. This church father of the first half of the second century believed in a general revelation. He identified the preexistent Son of God with the reason (of the Stoics) of whom the whole human race partakes. There is, then, in Justin's thought, a general revelation to all people, though some distort or pervert it. If anyone lives according to reason, however, that person is a Christian, even if usually thought to be an atheist, as for example, Socrates (*Apology I,* 46:1–4). Yet the general revelation is imperfect and needs to be completed by the special revelation in the incarnation (*Apology II,* 13). Here, as in Paul, the emphasis is on a general revelation. Unlike Paul, Justin thinks the revelation comes not by means of the created order but through the cosmic Christ who enlightens every person. Like the author of Luke-Acts and Paul, Justin thinks God's act in Jesus is necessary to do something left undone without it (cf. also Clement of Alexandria, *Stromateis,* 6).

In their estimation of the religious potential of pagans, Paul is the most pessimistic. There is just enough actualization of general revelation to make all people responsible for their sin. Justin is the most optimistic. Some follow the general revelation, live according to reason, and, like Socrates, can be regarded as Christians even though they live apart from special revelation. Luke stands between these two, in league with Hellenistic Judaism, assessing the possibilities of the pagan religious response to God neither totally positively nor totally negatively, but nuanced. For some pagan religion Jesus is exclusively judge; for other pagan piety Jesus is the completion of the path already taken on the basis of natural theology. Luke 7 and Acts 10 give the evangelist's estimate of the latter position.

How does the evangelist understand the centurion's piety to be completed by Jesus? Though the Jewish elders deem the centurion "worthy" (vs. 4), the second embassy composed of friends of the Gentile makes clear that the man considered himself unworthy (vs. 6). After the confession of his unworthiness, he expresses his absolute trust in Jesus' authoritative word: "Look," he says, "I know from personal experience what the word of a person in authority will do. A word from my superiors makes me act, just as a word from me causes my subordinates to obey. So you just say the word and my servant will be healed" (7:7–8). That Jesus does in fact have authority over the cre-

ated order comes clear in Luke's narrative in 8:22–25. Here Jesus' response is, "I tell you, not even in Israel have I found such faith" (7:9). Whereas the elders of the Jews had pointed to the good works of the centurion, Jesus praised his faith. The story, thereby, presents the centurion as a type of pious Gentile whose relation to God is completed by a confession of his unworthiness before Jesus and by placing his faith in Jesus' authority.

Comparison of 7:1–10 and 5:1–11 shows that Peter, a Jew, and this Gentile come to Jesus in the same way: (a) confession of sin or unworthiness (5:8; 7:6), and (b) trust in Jesus' authority (5:5, 11; 7:7–8). The same theme is put into the mouth of Peter in his speech at the Jerusalem Council (Acts 15), where he says God "made no distinction between us and them, but cleansed their hearts by faith" (Acts 15:9). Also he says, "We believe we shall be saved through the grace of the Lord Jesus, just as they will" (15:11). Paul had made the point earlier in Gal 2:15–16. Whether it is a Jew whose tradition is fulfilled or a pagan whose appropriate response to the light available is completed, the way to Jesus involves some discontinuity with the past (hence the sense of unworthiness or sin) and a submission to a new authority (the lordship of Jesus).

For Luke, Jesus is the ultimate revelation toward which all others point. Whether Jesus is related to other religious traditions primarily as judge or primarily as the fulfillment or completion depends upon the degree of discontinuity or continuity between the other traditions and the revelation in Jesus. Even those religious traditions with the greatest continuity to Jesus still stand before him "unworthy" and in need of submission to his ultimate authority.

CONFIRMED FORGIVENESS

7:36–50, 18–35

L uke 7:36–50 is a story with similarities to that of Jesus' anointing by a woman in Bethany found in Matt 26:6–13 // Mark 14:3–9 // John 12:1–8. In Matthew and Mark it is an unnamed woman, at Bethany, in the house of Simon the leper, who anoints Jesus' head, during the last week of Jesus' life. In the fourth gospel, it is Mary, at Bethany, in the house of Mary, Martha, and Lazarus, who anoints Jesus' feet and wipes them with her hair, at the beginning of the last week of Jesus' life. Here it is an unnamed woman, in Galilee, in the house of Simon the Pharisee, who washes Jesus' feet with her tears and dries them with her hair, who kisses his feet and anoints them, early in the public ministry. The meaning of this distinctive Lukan form of the tradition may be grasped if we concentrate on the context and on the inner organization of the unit.

The context shows that the story in 7:36–50 functions as an illustration of certain issues delineated in vss. 29–35. Immediately preceding 7:36–50 is a large unit of material held together by the focus on John the Baptist in its several parts (7:18–23, 24–28, 29–30, 31–35), the last two parts being linked by a further affinity, a reference to people justifying God: "all the people and the tax collectors justified God" (vs. 29); "wisdom is justified by all her children" (vs. 35—"Wisdom" is a periphrasis for God or for the *boulē tou theou* [purpose of God]. At first sight this use of the verb "to justify" seems strange but Jewish usage shows it is not. In the Psalms of Solomon, *dikaioun* (to justify) does not refer to a human's justification but rather refers to God. God's people justify him; that is, they vindicate the sentence, judgments, and name of God, accepting and acknowledging them to be righteous (2:16; 3:3; 4:9; 8:7, 27). The same usage is found in Ps 51:4: "thou art justified in thy sentence and blameless in thy judgment" (cf. also 2 Esdr 10:16; b. Berakoth 19a). It is this same usage we encounter in Rom 3:4 which cites Ps 51:4, and in 1 Tim 3:16. Both Luke 7:29 (cf. Matt 21:32) and 7:35 (// Matt 11:19) use the verb *dikaioun* in this way.

Here the verb "justified" should be paraphrased "demonstrated or acknowledged to be righteous" (G. Schrenk, *TDNT*, 2:213–15).

In both 7:29 and 7:35, for God to be justified means for him to be acknowledged to be right in the positions taken in the ministries of John and Jesus. It amounts to the acknowledgment of the divine authority of the careers of the Baptist and Mary's son and the acceptance of God's will for one's life as stated by those two (cf. vs. 30). Luke 7:29 says the tax collectors justified God, that is, they accepted the will of God set forth by his servant John, but the Pharisees did not. Luke 7:35 says God's children are those who justify him, that is, accept God's purpose for their lives. Since the will of God set forth in John's ministry was summed up in his "baptism of repentance for the forgiveness of sins" (3:3), for the evangelist to say the Pharisees rejected God's purpose for them is to say they did not repent and did not receive God's forgiveness. Since Jesus came to call sinners to repentance (5:32), to reject him was to miss the acceptance of God that Jesus' presence mediated (5:17–26, 27–32). To justify God was to acknowledge the rightness of his call in John and Jesus and to repent and be forgiven: This the people and the tax collectors did; this the Pharisees and the lawyers did not.

The Pharisee in 7:36 is to be understood as partaking of the character of the Pharisees in 7:29–30. The woman in vss. 37ff., like the tax collectors, had acknowledged God's verdict on her and had received her forgiveness from God. The Pharisee did not accept God's verdict on him and had not received forgiveness in any significant way. The story in 7:36–50, then, is an illustration of those who justified God and of those who did not. In the context it is the overt sinners (the people and tax collectors) who acknowledge the rightness of God's verdict about them stated in the preaching of John and Jesus, repent, and receive forgiveness. The covert sinners (Pharisees and lawyers) do not accept God's will for them, do not repent, and do not receive divine forgiveness. In the illustrative story, "it was a sin of the flesh [Jesus] forgave, a sin of the spirit he reproved" (*Luther's Meditations on the Gospels,* trans. and arranged by R. H. Bainton [Philadelphia: Westminster Press, 1962], p. 49). In Luke's view, everyone, those with covert sins of the spirit as well as those with overt sins of the flesh, stands in need of forgiveness. Luke 7:36–50 tells a story of one who received divine pardon and one who did not.

There are at least two crucial patterns of organization in 7:36–50.

Overall the unit falls into a chiastic pattern. After the introductory statement in 7:36 which serves to locate the events at mealtime in a Pharisee's house, the story has an AB:B'A' pattern.

> A The woman's actions toward Jesus: a display of unusual affection (7:37–38)
> B The Pharisee's negative judgment of Jesus (7:39)
> B' Jesus' response to Simon's appraisal (7:40–47)
> A' Jesus' response to the woman (7:48, 50)

A and A' are action oriented. They focus on the woman's display of affection toward Jesus and on Jesus' confirmation of her forgiveness (vs. 48). B and B' involve explanations to two questions: first, why is the woman known to be forgiven by her display of affection and second, how can Jesus pronounce the confirmation of her forgiveness? These questions will shape the discussion of the passage which follows.

In the East the door of the dining room was left open so the uninvited could pass in and out during the festivities. They were allowed to take seats by the wall, listening to the conversation between the host and guests. When Jesus sat at table with Simon the Pharisee, a woman of the city entered. Instead of sitting by the wall and listening, she lavished her affection on Jesus: (a) she wet his feet with her tears and wiped them with the hair of her head; (b) she kissed his feet; and (c) she anointed his feet with ointment (vss. 37–38). That Jesus permitted the act evoked a negative response from his host (vs. 39).

Verses 39–47 (B and B') comprise what has been called a "Socratic interrogation" and consist of four component parts: (a) question by the opponent (vs. 39); (b) counter-question (vs. 42b); (c) forced answer from the opponent (vs. 43); and (d) refutation of the opponent on the basis of his forced answer (vs. 47). Originating in Hellenistic rhetoric, this form was used by both Jews and Christians in organizing their materials (E. E. Ellis, *The Gospel of Luke* [rev. ed., Greenwood, S.C.: Attic Press, 1974], p. 121).

(a) The Pharisee's unspoken question in 7:39 is cast in the form of an unreal condition in present time; that is, both clauses are regarded as untrue. Jesus, it is assumed, does not know the woman. He, therefore, cannot be a prophet. Note that the story uses this denial by Simon to affirm that Jesus is indeed a prophet; he discerns what the Pharisee is thinking and tells a parable (vss. 41–42a) which ends with

(b) a counter-question: "Now which of them will love him more?" (vs. 42b). (c) Simon's answer is forced: "The one, I suppose, to whom he forgave more" (vs. 43a). (d) Jesus agrees (vs. 43b) and draws an inference (vss. 44–47): "Although, Simon, you did not act discourteously but were correct enough as a host, you did not perform any special acts of hospitality. This woman, however, has lavished affection on me. Why would she do that?" Jesus answers his own question in vs. 47.

There are two possible ways of reading vs. 47. (1) "Because of her conduct her many sins have been forgiven." Here the sinful woman's love is understood as the cause of her forgiveness. (2) "Her many sins have been forgiven, as is evidenced by her conduct." Here the woman's love is viewed as the evidence of her forgiveness. The second reading is linguistically possible (e.g., 1:22; 6:21) and is demanded by the context. The New English Bible's reading is to the point: "And so, I tell you, her great love proves that her many sins have been forgiven; where little has been forgiven, little love is shown." Why is the woman known to be forgiven? The answer is that her display of affection is evidence of it.

After the evangelist tells of Jesus' acts on behalf of needy people, whether physical or spiritual, he often relates the responses he deems appropriate. Sometimes the response is horizontal, an ethical one (e.g., 19:8—"Behold, Lord, the half of my goods I give to the poor; and if I have defrauded anyone of anything, I restore it fourfold."). At other times, the response is vertical, directed not toward other human beings but toward God (e.g., glorified God—5:25–26; 7:16; praised God, 17:18) or, as in the story here, toward Jesus. The evangelist sees the appropriateness of both horizontal (ethical) and vertical (worship) responses to God's forgiveness and healing. In 7:36–50 the emphasis is on lavish affection shown to Jesus as a sign of one's prior salvation (vs. 50), and the absence of that display is regarded as evidence of the lack of an appropriation of forgiveness. Affection and praise lavished on Jesus is an authentic and appropriate evidence of divine forgiveness. Their absence is evidence of unappropriated redemption. Seeing the woman's outburst of love, Jesus said to her, "Your sins are forgiven" (vs. 48).

The question of those at table with Jesus shapes the next phase of the discussion: "Who is this, who even forgives sins?" (vs. 49) How is it that Jesus can pronounce confirmation of the woman's forgiveness? The clue is given in vs. 39, Simon's unspoken negative judgment of Jesus: "If this man were a prophet, he would have known who and

what sort of woman this is who is touching him, for she is a sinner."
Jesus knows the thoughts of Simon's heart and responds to them: the
inference must be that Jesus is a prophet. A prophet is one who knows
not only the minds and hearts of human beings but also the mind of
God (cf. 1 Kgs 22:19ff.).

The third evangelist presents Jesus in prophetic terms on many occasions. In 4:16–30 the motif begins: Jesus is the anointed prophet
who is not accepted in his own country; Luke 7:16 reports the peoples'
response to the raising of the widow's son at Nain was to exclaim, "A
great prophet has arisen among us" (cf. also 13:33; 24:19; Acts 3:22–
23). Here the mark of a prophet is his spiritual discernment and ability
to see beneath the surface of events. Jesus certainly fits this category:
he knows the ultimate outcome of history (6:20–26); he discerns the
thoughts of Simon (7:39ff.); he knows the mind of God about the
woman's sins (7:48). To pronounce the forgiveness of sins because
one knows the mind of God on the matter is a prophetic act (2 Sam
12:13; Isa 40:2; cf. 4QPrNab 1–3:2–4, a fragmentary Aramaic text from
Qumran, where a Jewish exorcist remits the sins of the Babylonian
king, Nabonidus). This is doubtless how the evangelist understood a
similar act of Jesus in 5:17–26. The possibility of Jesus' acting this
way lies in his having been anointed with the Holy Spirit (4:18–19) so
he can "proclaim release to the captives." The fourth gospel depicts
Jesus in the same way: Jesus, on whom the Spirit has descended and
remained (1:32), possesses a knowledge of human hearts (e.g., 1:48;
2:25; 4:17–19, 39). It is of interest to note that Jesus' discernment of
the Samaritan woman's situation elicits the response, "Sir, I perceive
you are a prophet" (4:19). The Johannine Jesus also knows the mind
of the Father (e.g., 5:19–20; 8:28–29).

The spiritual discernment of the anointed Jesus is also a part of the
equipment of the Spirit-baptized disciples in Acts (e.g., 5:3–4; 8:23).
The same is true in the fourth gospel: after the risen Lord has breathed
the Holy Spirit on the disciples (20:22), he can say, "If you forgive the
sins of any, they are forgiven; if you retain the sins of any, they are
retained" (20:23). This is best understood as prophetic confirmation of
what God has done because, being filled with the Spirit, one, like the
prophets of old, knows the mind of God. A similar point is made in
Paul: in 1 Cor 2:10–12, in another connection, the apostle says Christians know the mind of God by means of the Holy Spirit; in 1 Cor 12:8,
speaking of some gifts of the Spirit, he refers to "the utterance of

knowledge." This is almost certainly referring to the type of spiritual discernment that comes from the presence of the Holy Spirit in the life of a prophet, be he Jesus or a Christian. To use Paul's categories, in Luke 7:39–47, 48, we find two words of knowledge uttered by Jesus. By means of the Spirit Jesus discerns both the hearts of people and the mind of God. In exercising this prophetic capacity of spiritual discernment, Luke regards Jesus as prototypical for his disciples (knowledge of the mind of God—Acts 2:14ff.; 13:1–3; 16:9–10; knowledge of the hearts of men and women—Acts 5:1–11; 20:29–30). The empowering presence of God imparts spiritual discernment to the prophetic community of Jesus' disciples, the same discernment manifest in Luke 7:36–50 by Jesus.

THE MINISTRIES OF WOMEN

8:1–21

Luke 8:1–21 is a thought unit consisting of a parable (8:4–8), a request for an explanation of the story by the disciples (8:9–10), and the explanation of the parable (8:11–15), to which have been added an introduction (8:1–3) and two small units which further elucidate the theme of the parable (8:16–18, 19–21). The key terms "hear" (8:8b, 10, 12, 13, 14, 15, 18, 21) and "word" (8:11, 13, 15, 21) act as glue to join the pieces.

The introduction (vss. 1–3) serves to validate the authority of the preaching of the church (which is referred to in the parable and its interpretation (vss. 4–8, 11–15), by showing it was based on the testimony of witnesses who were with Jesus when the kingdom of God was being disclosed (W. C. Robinson, Jr., "On Preaching the Word of God [Luke 8:4–21]," in *Studies in Luke-Acts*, ed. L. E. Keck and J. L. Martyn [Nashville: Abingdon, 1966], p. 136). Those who were "with him" (vss. 1b–2) belong to two groups: (1) the Twelve, and (2) the women. Both groups are designated by the evangelist elsewhere as those who came with him from Galilee (23:49; 23:55; 24:10; Acts 1:11; 13:31). It appears to be Luke's intention to set the Twelve and the women alongside one another as guarantors of the facts of the Christ event.

The evangelist pays special attention to women in his narrative of Jesus and the early church: Luke 1:24ff., Elizabeth (only in Luke); 1:26ff., Mary (only in Luke); 2:36ff., Anna (only in Luke); 4:38ff., Simon's mother-in-law; 7:11ff., the widow at Nain (only in Luke); 7:36ff., the sinful woman (only in Luke); 8:2–3, women who ministered to Jesus and his disciples (only in Luke); 8:43ff., woman with a hemorrhage; 10:38ff., Martha and Mary (only in Luke); 13:10ff., the crippled woman (only in Luke); 15:8–10, the parable of the woman with a lost coin (only in Luke); 18:1–8, parable of the widow (only in Luke); 21:1ff., the widow who gave her all; 23:49, 55, the women at the crucifixion; 24:10–11, 22–23, the women at the tomb; Acts 1:14,

the women and Mary at prayer; 5:1ff., Sapphira; 6:1ff., the widows; 9:36ff., Dorcas; 12:12ff., Mary the mother of Mark and Rhoda; 16:14ff., Lydia; 16:16ff., the slave girl who is healed; 17:12, Greek women of high standing believed; 17:34, Damaris; 18:2, 18, 26, Priscilla; 21:9, Philip's four daughters; 23:16, Paul's sister; 25:13, Bernice.

It is interesting to note how the evangelist frequently sets women alongside men in various ministries. We have already noted the Galilean women alongside the Galilean men as guarantors of the facts of Jesus' career. There are other instances. (1) The women of Luke 8:3 "serve" (*diēkonoun*) just as the men in Acts 6:2 "serve" (*diakonein*) tables. In this matter Luke manifests continuity with early Christianity generally. In Rom 16:1 Phoebe is a deaconess (*diakonon*). 1 Tim 3:8–12 probably refers to deaconesses, not to wives of deacons. Pliny's letter to Trajan early in the second century also mentions deaconnesses. (2) In Luke-Acts women prophesy alongside men (Anna in Luke 2:36–38, adjacent to Simeon in 2:25–35; Acts 2:17–18 says the Spirit has been poured out on all flesh so that "your sons and daughters shall prophesy"; Philip's four daughters who prophesied are mentioned alongside Agabus in Acts 21:9–11). Again Luke possesses continuity with the early church in its practice: e.g., 1 Cor 11:5, from the first century, and Tertullian, *Against Marcion,* 5:8, near A.D. 200. (3) Women are listed alongside the Twelve in prayer before Pentecost in Acts 1:12–14. In the ancient church generally, women engaged in public prayer (e.g., 1 Cor 11:4–5; 1 Tim 2:8–9; *Didascalia Apostolorum* 15:124). (4) Women sometimes have church services in their houses (Acts 12:5, 12; 16:15) just as men do (Acts 18:7). This is a practice also found in Rom 16:3–5 and Philm 1–2. The Cemetery of Priscilla on the Via Salaria in Rome shows that a Christian woman of means could use her house and lands for the service of the church. Again Luke reflects common Christian practice. (5) At least one woman teaches, together with her husband, who is the second named, and the one taught is a male preacher. So Priscilla and Aquila teach Apollos in Acts 18:26. This is a singular reference in the NT. It is in striking discontinuity with 1 Tim 2:12 ("I permit no woman to teach or to have authority over men; she is to keep silent") and possibly with 1 Cor 14:34–35 ("the women should keep silence in the churches. For they are not permitted to speak, but should be subordinate. . . . If there is anything they desire to know, let them ask their husbands at home. For it is shameful for a woman to speak in church"). This may

be a post-Pauline interpolation from the hand of a Paulinist who reflected the same point of view as 1 Tim 2:12. It may just as easily be an integral part of 1 Corinthians and be a reference to Maenadism (ecstatic behavior on the part of women under the influence of an orgiastic deity, like Dionysius), or perhaps to some other type of clamor which was disruptive. This disruptive noise would be prohibited (Richard and Catherine Kroeger, "An Inquiry into Evidence of Maenadism in the Corinthian Congregation," in *SBL 1978 Seminar Papers,* ed. P. J. Achtemeier [Missoula: Scholars Press, 1978], 2:331–38). If 1 Cor 14:34–35 is an interpolation reflecting the posture of 1 Tim 2:12, it is in discontinuity with Luke-Acts. If, however, the passage refers not to women teaching but to disruptive noises of whatever kind, the Corinthian passage is irrelevant to a discussion of women teachers. The difference in Luke's attitude in Acts 18:26 and that of the author of 1 Tim 2:12 is very likely that Priscilla in Acts represents the orthodox Pauline line (cf. Acts 18:1ff.) in Luke's story, whereas women in the Pastorals were the special prey of the heretics (e.g., 2 Tim 3:6–7). A special circumstance dictated the stance taken in the Pastorals. In later Christianity, however, it was the stance of the Pastorals rather than of Luke-Acts that dominated Christian practice. In the Lukan scheme of things, women often functioned side by side with men in Christian ministry, including the ministry of teaching.

The ministry of women in the narrative of Luke-Acts did not cancel their traditional roles in society, though on occasion it did stretch them a bit. They reflect a variety of roles in society. (1) There are single women living with their parents (e.g., Acts 21:8–9, Philip's four unmarried daughters). (2) There is a businesswoman who is apparently without a husband (e.g., Lydia, Acts 16:14–15), though with a household. (3) There is a wife who works with her husband in the family business (e.g., Priscilla who with Aquila was a tentmaker, Acts 18:2–3). (4) There are married women involved in motherhood (e.g., Mary, the model disciple, Luke 2:1ff., 41ff.). In each case, the women disciples used whatever role they occupied as a vehicle for the furtherance of God's will. Their ministries varied just as their roles in society did, but each had a ministry within the context of her particular role.

In some cases the roles defined by society were stretched by the women's ministry. Luke 8:1–3 is a perfect example of this: It was not uncommon for women to support rabbis and their disciples with their own money, property, or foodstuffs (j. Horayot 48a, 1.44; Esther Rab-

bah II, 3; b. Shabbath 62a; b. Berakoth 10b; b. Rabba Kamma 119a), but for a woman to leave home and travel with a rabbi was not only unknown, it was scandalous (Ben Witherington, III, "On the Road with Mary Magdalene, Joanna, Susanna, and Other Disciples—Luke 8: 1–3," *Zeitschrift für neutestamentliche Wissenschaft* 70:243–47 [1979]). Yet the women of 8:1–3, including Joanna, the wife of Chuza, Herod's steward, not only provided for Jesus and his disciples but also accompanied them. Here the social roles were stretched but not shattered. A generation earlier Paul had stood against the shattering of a woman's social role (e.g., 1 Corinthians 7 argues against separating from one's spouse because of one's religious experience, and 11:2–16 speaks against a woman's casting off the symbols of her sexuality in the name of her Christian faith). In Luke's own time the household codes (Col 3:18ff.; Eph 5:21ff.; 1 Pet 3:1ff.) stood for the stability of social roles, though with modifications produced by the leaven of Christian grace, lest Christianity be identified with the disreputable Oriental cults that catered to women and undermined the stability of family life. It would appear that the third evangelist is as positive toward the ministry of women in the church as his social structure would allow. He did not, however, want to undermine the church's chances in Greco-Roman culture by advocating "customs which it is not lawful for us Romans to accept and practice." (Acts 16:21).

In the ancient church there were three ways of ordering the ministry of women: lay ministry (e.g., evangelism, praying and prophesying in church, opening one's home to the church); clerical ministry (e.g., the institution of widow and of deaconness in the third century); and the ministry of the religious (e.g., in the Byzantine world and in the middle ages in the West, it is the nuns who inherit the chief privileges of the earlier widows and deaconnesses: cf. Jean Daniélou, *The Ministry of Women in the Early Church* [London: Faith Press, 1961]). In terms of this threefold structure, one would have to say that Luke viewed the ministry of women as a lay ministry. This, however, is a position determined by the social structures of the world in which the evangelist lived.

Luke 8:4–21 focuses on the matter of responses to the church's proclamation. The unit begins with the parable of the sower (vss. 4–8). In vs. 9 the disciples ask Jesus the meaning of this particular parable, not the parables in general as in Mark 4:10. The interpretation (vss. 11–15) explains that the point has to do with responses to the

"word of God" (Acts 6:7; 12:24; 13:49; 19:20). The question is: why did the gospel find a lasting response in so few? Wrong responses are due to the devil (cf. Luke 22:3), to lack of roots which makes one vulnerable in time of temptation (cf. Luke 22:40, 46; 2 Pet 3:17), and to the cares, riches, and pleasures of life (cf. Acts 5:1–11).

The right response on hearing the word is to "hold it fast in an honest and good heart, and bring forth fruit with patience" (vs. 15; cf. Rom 5:3–4; Heb 6:11–12; 12:1–3, etc.). The distinctive Lukan *en hypomonē*, "with patience," gives the opposite of all wrong responses. It is this "hearing the word of God and doing it" (vs. 21) which characterizes the family of Jesus in Luke-Acts (Luke 1:38, 45; Acts 1:14) and will characterize all Jesus' disciples (Luke 6:47; 10:37; 11:28; cf. Jas 1:22–25).

Those who have made a right response to the word of God, as Jesus' family has done in Luke's narrative, are to be light for those who enter the household of God (vs. 16). As mentioned above, the house assumed is a Roman-style one in which the lamp is placed in the vestibule to furnish light for those who enter. The perseverance of those who are already disciples will illumine the way of new converts.

UNIVERSAL POWER
AND VESTED INTERESTS

8:22—9:6

This section is a single thought unit in the evangelist's scheme, beginning with a distinctive Lukan time reference: "one day" (cf. Mark 4:35; Matt 8:23). This was apparently intended to set all that follows, through 9:6, within the framework of a day. Within these temporal boundaries the material is held together by several interlocking devices. (1) Four miracle stories (8:22–25; 8:26–39; 8:40–42, 49–56; 8:43–48) demonstrate Jesus' power and are followed by 9:1–6, a pericope in which Jesus gives power and authority to the Twelve. (2) The four miracle stories are further linked with 9:1–6 by Jesus leaving a place he is not welcomed (8:37), and telling his disciples about departure from a town that does not receive them (9:5). (3) Key words play a role in joining the four miracle stories. (a) 8:22–25, 26–39 refer to the lake (8:22, 33) and to the boat (8:22, 37). (b) In 8:25, 35, 37, 47 (?), 50, we encounter references to fear. (c) There is a focus on "salvation/being saved" in 8:36, 48, 50. (d) Whereas 8:42, 43 have "twelve years" in common, 8:48, 49 both contain "daughter," 8:48, 50 refer to "faith." Taking our clue from the time reference in 8:22 and the various interlocking devices mentioned, we may regard 8:22—9:6 as a single unit. If so, what point is the evangelist making?

The evangelist focuses on Jesus' gift of his own power to disciples prior to his sending them out to minister. A comparison of the organization of the material in Luke with its arrangement in Matthew and Mark clarifies this intent. (1) In Mark the four miracles in 4:35—5:43 (storm at sea; demoniac healed; hemorrhaging woman; raising of Jairus' daughter) are followed by the rejection of Jesus at Nazareth (6:1–6). The point of this arrangement is that miracles do not necessarily lead to faith. (2) In Matthew the four miracle stories are separated, though they all come in the collection of ten miracle stories to be found in 8—9 (Matt 8:23–27, the storm at sea; 8:28–34, two demoniacs; 9:18–

19, 23–26, the raising of Jairus' daughter; 9:20–22, the woman with a hemorrhage) and in the same relative order as in Mark and Luke. To understand Matthew's intention we must reflect on the way his gospel is organized. The core of the gospel falls into five cycles of material: chapters (a) 3—7; (b) 8—10; (c) 11—13; (d) 14—18; (e) 19—25. Each cycle is divided into what Jesus did, followed by what he said, with a verbal or thematic link in each cycle. In terms of this overall scheme, chapters 8—10 constitute Cycle Two; chapter 10 is what Jesus says (instructions for missionaries) and begins with the statement that Jesus gave the Twelve "authority over unclean spirits, to cast them out, and to heal every disease and every infirmity" (vs. 1). In 10:8 the charge is given to the Twelve: "Heal the sick, raise the dead, cleanse lepers, cast out demons." This teaching follows a narrative section (chaps. 8—9) in which Jesus performs ten miracles including the cleansing of a leper (8:2–4), the healing of all who were sick (8:16), the casting out of demons (8:24–34), and the raising of the dead (9:18–19, 23–25). Also, as Jesus preached the gospel of the kingdom (9:35) so the disciples are charged to do (10:7). The point of this material in the arrangement of the gospel is that Jesus' miracles show he has authority to give to his disciples. Just as in Cycle One (Matthew 3—7) Jesus did not ask his disciples for a righteousness (chaps. 5—7) he had not performed (3:14–15), so in Cycle Two Jesus does not give his missionaries an authority he does not possess.

Luke's arrangement has similarities with both Mark and Matthew. On the one hand, in 8:22–56 the four miracles come together as in Mark 4:35—5:43. On the other hand, Luke's unit of four miracle stories is not followed by the rejection at Nazareth, as in Mark 6:1–6. Rather, like Matthew 10, Luke has the miracles followed by the sending of the Twelve: 9:1–2 says Jesus called the Twelve together and gave them "power and authority over all demons and to cure diseases, and he sent them out to preach the kingdom of God and to heal." The location of the four miracles just prior to the sending of the Twelve seems to say that, like Matthew, the third evangelist aimed to demonstrate the authority Jesus possessed before telling us he gave this power and authority to the Twelve.

This makes an interesting pattern in Luke's picture of the Galilean ministry. In 4:31—5:11 we found four miracles climaxed by the call and commissioning of Peter: the miracles functioned as a catalyst for Peter's response of faith. Now at the end of the Galilean section is

another series of four miracles followed by the sending of the Twelve: the mighty works that precede the commissioning demonstrate the authority of the one who gives power and authority to his emissaries.

Given the nature of Luke-Acts, one would expect to find in the narrative of Acts events corresponding to the miracles in Luke 8:22–56. This we do find: (a) with 8:22–25 compare Acts 27; (b) with 8:26–39 compare Acts 16:16ff.; (c) with 8:40–42, 49–56 compare Acts 9:36–43; and (d) with 8:43–48 compare Acts 5:15; 19:12. In other words, in 8:22—9:6 the evangelist is foreshadowing the experience of the power of the risen Christ in the ministries of his apostles ("sent ones"). The power they have is not theirs but is the power of Jesus (Luke 24:49; Acts 1:8; 3:12, 16; 4:7–12): disciples of Jesus do not minister in their own strength but in the strength of their Lord.

Note also that Jesus called the Twelve together and gave them power and authority (9:1) *before* he sent them to preach and heal (9:2). This also foreshadows the experience of the church in Acts, which was to stay in Jerusalem until clothed with power from on high (Luke 24:49), to witness after the Holy Spirit had come upon it (Acts 1:8): Jesus does not assign a task until he has first equipped those who are to perform it.

Within 8:22—9:6 we focus on one of the miracle stories, 8:26–39, because of its special contribution to the overall emphasis in the larger unit. This story tells of the man who had a legion of demons. The first dimension of meaning in this exorcism story is connected with the textual problem in 8:26. Does Jesus come to the country of the Gerasenes, Gadarenes, or Gergesenes? The best reading is "Gerasenes" (so also for Mark 5:1, though in Matt 8:28 Gadarenes seems the best reading). The difficulty with this is that Gerasenes refers to the inhabitants of Gerasa, modern Jerash, some thirty miles southeast of the Sea of Galilee. Though geographically difficult the reading is theologically important: Gerasa was Gentile territory, as is confirmed by the reference to the herd of swine (8:32). Here for the only time in the gospel Jesus journeys beyond the boundaries of Jewish territory onto pagan soil; his mission reaches to the Gentiles. Here the evangelist sees foreshadowed the future missionary activity of the church that reaches pagans. Salvation is for all people (cf. Luke 2:32; 3:6; 4:25–27; Acts 26:18; note that Luke 9:1–6, like Mark 6:7–13 but unlike Matt 10:5, does not restrict the apostles to Israel). But Luke's point here is more than just the universality of Jesus' concern: it is rather the universal scope of

Jesus' power. That is why a miracle story is used. Jesus has power over demons even in Gentile territory. Furthermore, if the unclean spirits (8:29) which had entered the unclean animals (8:32–33) thought that by driving the herd of swine into the lake they could escape Jesus' power or damage his mission, they were mistaken. The one who cast them out is he who controls the sea also (8:22–25). Again the emphasis is on Jesus' universal power. This is important in the section, 8:22—9:6, because the power of Jesus is given to his "sent ones." The Christian missionaries, then, need fear neither the sea (Acts 27—28) nor the power of the demonic in foreign lands (Acts 16:16ff.; 19:13ff.): Jesus' power is universal.

A second dimension of the story's meaning has to do with the types of response Jesus' universal power evokes. On the one hand, the power of Jesus to heal produces discipleship. This theme is met again in this pericope. Luke alone of the synoptists notes that the cured man was "sitting at the feet of Jesus" (8:35), the posture of a disciple (cf. 10:39; 7:38; 17:16), reinforced by the man's desire to be "with him" (8:38). In some, Jesus' power evokes faith.

On the other hand, there is also present in 8:26–39 the theme of the rejection of Jesus (cf. 2:34–35; 4:28–29; 6:11). When the swine are destroyed by drowning, the herdsmen go into the city and tell what had happened. When the people come and find not only the man well but also the herd gone, they ask Jesus to depart from them (8:37; note 9:5, the rejection of the Twelve). Although the theme that Jesus' rejection is tied to economic motives is not explicitly present in the use of the story by Matthew and Mark, the larger context of Luke-Acts makes it certain this was the third evangelist's intent.

Two stories from Acts illustrate Luke's belief that rejection of Jesus and his representatives often comes from economic motivation. (a) Acts 19:23ff. tells of a certain Demetrius who appealed to the economic motive in stirring up antagonisms against Paul in Ephesus. The author takes pains to emphasize the economic dimensions of the rejection. Verse 24 says the idol-making enterprise "brought no little business to the craftsmen"; vs. 25 has Demetrius say, "Men, you know that from this business we have our wealth"; in vs. 27 Demetrius warns, "There is danger . . . that this trade of ours may come into disrepute." After the uproar ceased Paul departed (20:1). (b) The story in Acts that corresponds most closely to Luke 8:26–39 is found at 16:16ff. Here Paul casts out a spirit of divination from a slave girl who had "brought her

owners much gain by soothsaying" (16:16). The author tells us in vs. 19 that "when her owners saw that their hope of gain was gone, they seized Paul and Silas and dragged them into the market place before the rulers." The result was a beating (vs. 22), imprisonment (vs. 23), and ultimately a request that they leave the city (vs. 39). The language of the request to leave is the same as in Luke 8:37 (Acts 16:39—*ērōtōn apelthein;* Luke 8:37—*ērōtēsen . . . apelthein*). Given the theme of the rejection of Jesus and his gospel because of economic motivations found elsewhere in Luke-Acts, and given the Lukan tendency to foreshadow in the gospel what is treated explicitly in Acts, it is virtually impossible to read 8:26–39 without hearing the evangelist saying the troubles experienced by Christian missionaries because of the economic vested interests threatened by their ministry were already a part of Jesus' career. The one who has universal power is also the one whose rejection is sometimes tied to the threat he poses to economic vested interests. This is both warning and consolation to his followers.

A third dimension of meaning in the exorcism story is linked to the conclusion of the narrative. Matthew ends his exorcism story (8:28–34) with the request for Jesus to leave the neighborhood. Both Mark 5:1–20 and Luke 8:26–39 follow the request for Jesus to depart with a dialogue between Jesus and the healed man. Mark 5:18 suggests the man asked to accompany Jesus as he was getting into the boat. Luke 8:37–39, however, has Jesus leave ("he got into the boat and returned"). Apparently after Jesus' departure in Luke, the healed man who had accompanied him asked "that he might be with him." Jesus, however, sent him away, saying, "Return to your home, and declare how much God has done for you" (vs. 39). Several things emerge from this ending.

(1) The evangelist uses the story as "a paradigm of what conversion involves: the responsibility to evangelize" (I. H. Marshall, *The Gospel of Luke*, p. 341).

(2) The place of the man's witness was in his own home country (vs. 39).

(3) The means of evangelization to be employed by the man was his personal testimony; the content of his witness was his healing by Jesus. The significance of this can be understood only if we recognize the Lukan distinction between two types of disciples or witnesses: those who were "with him" (cf. 8:1) and those who were not (8:38–39).

On the one hand, the evangelist is concerned to emphasize that cer-

tain disciples (the Twelve and the Galilean women) were "with Jesus" from the baptism of John until the time when Jesus was taken into heaven (Acts 1:21–22). In Galilee the witnesses are assembled (Luke 5:1–11; 6:12–16; 8:1–3) and are present with Jesus throughout his ministry, with one exception, 9:1–6. During the absence of the Twelve, however, Luke records nothing about Jesus' deeds or words. The Galileans accompany Jesus to Jerusalem and there see and hear everything: in 23:49 that circle observe the crucifixion and death of Jesus; in 23:55 the burial of Jesus' body was witnessed; in 24:1–11 the same women come to the tomb and do not find the body; in 24:33ff. Jesus appears to the Eleven; and in Acts 1:11 the men witness Jesus' ascension. These Galileans, primarily the Twelve, are those who bear witness to Jesus' resurrection (Acts 1:21–22). In Luke-Acts, then, the Twelve are those who accompanied Jesus from the beginning of his ministry to the ascension. They are the Galileans, the eyewitnesses who have sufficient knowledge of the gospel history and its meaning because they have been with Jesus and heard and seen all things.

In Luke's mind these eyewitnesses control the destiny of the church. This is seen in the theological geography of Acts where Jerusalem controls Christian missions. (a) It is from Jerusalem the universal preaching of the gospel is to begin (Luke 24:47; Acts 1:4, 8). (b) Every new expansion of the church in apostolic times had to receive the approval of Jerusalem (e.g., Acts 8:12, 14–15; 11:1–2, 18, 19–21, 22; 15:2, 12ff.). (c) Paul's entire ministry is given a Jerusalem frame of reference: his conversion is authenticated by the apostles in Jerusalem (9:27ff.); his work at Antioch is undertaken at Barnabas' initiative (11:25f.); his missionary commission is given by a church which was Jerusalem approved (13:1–3); each of his missionary journeys ends at Jerusalem (15:2; 18:22; 21:17); he recognizes the validity of and appeals to the witness of the Twelve (13:31); he refers difficult questions to Jerusalem (15:2), accepts Jerusalem decisions (21:23–26), and appeals to Jerusalem authority (16:5). In sum, Jerusalem controls the mission enterprise in Acts. The meaning of this dominance is closely connected with Jerusalem being, for Luke, the place where the Twelve reside (Acts 1:4; 8:1b; 9:27; 11:1–2; 15:2, 4; 16:4). Jerusalem control is control by the Twelve, which is control by the true facts of gospel history. This is the significance of being "with him." Those who were "with him" guarantee the tradition of Jesus' work and words. It is this

true tradition about Jesus which the evangelist sees as controlling the church's life.

On the other hand, Luke speaks of disciples and witnesses who are not of the Twelve. In Acts Paul represents such people. The Lukan scheme regards Paul as an apostle (Acts 14:14) and teacher of the church, but like the *Epistle of the Apostles* 31, subordinates him to the Twelve. He is a witness to the things in which he has seen the risen Christ (Acts 26:16). In the overall scheme of Luke-Acts, Paul, like the Gerasene man delivered from demons, is a witness to what Jesus Christ had done in his experience but he is not one who was "with him" in the days of his flesh. The Gerasene man was instructed to go home and declare how much God had done for him. He was to bear witness to God's activity in his experience among the Gentiles, a valid missionary enterprise because commissioned by Jesus. Because a person was not with Jesus and the Twelve by no means allows rejection of his ministry (cf. Luke 9:49–50)—both types were commissioned by Jesus, so both are legitimate. Yet those who were "with him" function as a control on those who were not.

The theological issue has to do with the relation between religious experience and tradition. The Gerasene man, like Paul in Acts, symbolizes those Christian witnesses who evangelize from their own experiential religion. Something has happened to them: it is due to Jesus; they invite others to let it happen to them. Luke regards this as authentic evangelistic activity, but at the same time, the criterion by which one may know that a given religious experience is Christian is the authority of the tradition about the earthly career of Jesus. Those who were "with him" are the source of and symbolize that tradition. In Lukan thought there is no cleavage between experience and tradition, between theology and devotion. The two belong together.

THE DARK NIGHT
OF THE "NOT YET"

9:7–50

L uke 9:7–50 marks a crucial turning point in the plot of the gospel
and functions to conclude the Galilean ministry which began with
4:16; it also sets in motion a new departure in the unfolding of God's
plan in the narrative of Luke-Acts. Two questions about Jesus' identity
give focus to the passage as a whole. (1) The first is raised by Herod.
Luke, like Mark but unlike Matthew, follows the pericope of the sending of the Twelve with that of Herod's reaction (Matt 14:1–2; Mark
6:14–16; Luke 9:7–9). In both Matt 14:2 and Mark 6:16 Herod states,
in effect, that Jesus must be John the Baptist raised from the dead.
Luke 9:9, however, is different: Herod says, "John I beheaded; but
who is this?" The Galilean ministry of Jesus as depicted in Luke raises
a christological question: Who is Jesus? (2) The second question about
his identity is raised by Jesus himself. In order to have this question
adjacent to the first, Luke has omitted a major unit of material found
in Mark 6:45—8:26/Matt 14:22—16:12. At the end of his association
with the disciples in Galilee, Jesus asks, "Who do you say that I am?"
(9:20). The material that follows these two questions about Jesus'
identity gives the answer.

In 9:20ff. and 9:28ff. there is an exposition of who Jesus is. He is
the one who, through prayer, moves into a new stage of the spiritual
process, a stage that involves rejection, suffering, and death. He is also
the one who calls his disciples to participation in the same developmental process. The discussion which follows will explore the various
dimensions of this picture.

It is a Lukan concern "to show that prayer is the instrument by
which God has directed the course of holy history, both in the life of
the Son of Man and in the development of the Christian Church" (A.
A. Trites, "The Prayer Motif in Luke-Acts," in *Perspectives on Luke-
Acts,* p. 169). In Acts the narrative begins with the Twelve and others

at prayer (1:14) just prior to the empowering at Pentecost (2:1ff.). The motif of prayer followed by empowering for witness in Jerusalem recurs in 4:31. In Acts 10—11 the prayers of Cornelius and Peter are used by God to include a Gentile household in the eschatological people of God. Acts 13:1–3, moreover, tells how the Gentile mission of Paul grew from a context of prayer: God communicates his will for new departures in his plan to servants while they are at prayer. The same emphasis is found also in the gospel. It is in the context of prayer that Zechariah learns he and Elizabeth will have a son who will go before the Lord "in the spirit and power of Elijah" (1:10, 13, 17). In 3:21–22 Jesus at prayer receives his anointing for ministry and is acknowledged by a heavenly voice as God's beloved. As a result, he begins his Galilean ministry (4:16ff.). Luke 6:12–16 portrays Jesus at prayer before his choice of the Twelve. Given this motif in Luke-Acts it is no surprise to find the evangelist in Luke 9 signaling a new development in Jesus' career by showing Jesus at prayer (9:18ff., 28ff.).

Both references to prayer in 9:18 and 9:28–29 are distinctively Lukan (cf. Matt 16:13 // Mark 8:27; Matt 17:1 // Mark 9:2). Both link Jesus' prayer with his coming suffering. (1) On the one hand, 9:18 says it was "as he was praying alone" that he asked his disciples about his identity. Peter's reply, "You are the Christ of God" (9:18–20), is not followed either by Jesus' praise of Peter (as in Matt 16:17–19) or by Mark's "And he began to teach them" (8:31). Luke joins the command to silence with the prediction of the passion so the command loses importance. He also omits the rebuke of Peter (Matt 16:22–23 and Mark 8:32–33). This concentrates all the attention on Jesus' prediction of the passion (9:22), the fate of Jesus. Implicit within 9:18–22 is that Jesus, while at prayer, came to the realization he must suffer, die, and rise (cf. 24:26, 46; Acts 2:23–24). The anointed one, endued with the power of the Holy Spirit, will enter into his final glory only after rejection, suffering, and death. Furthermore, by putting the passion prediction (9:22) in direct discourse (contra Matt 16:21 // Mark 8:31), Luke makes it a part of the preceding dialogue. It becomes Jesus' prayerful response to Peter's confession.

(2) On the other hand, the transfiguration narrative in 9:28ff. has also been turned into a prayer scene. Typically the evangelist depicts prayer as associated with a heavenly apparition and a divine communication (e.g., 3:21–22; Acts 10—11). In prayer Jesus enters the heavenly world and there is a conversation with two heavenly residents

about his departure (*exodon;* cf. *eisodou* in Acts 13:24). Jesus' exodus is his departure from this world, his ascension, but this transpires through the cross and resurrection. This narrative, like the previous one, makes it explicit that Luke understands Jesus to be convinced through prayer he would die in Jerusalem.

If prayer was the medium through which Jesus came to an awareness of God's will for a new departure in his life, the content of that will involved not immediate exaltation but rather rejection, suffering, death: the one who was anointed with the Spirit would be rejected and killed. There are several significant implications of this picture of Jesus.

In the first place, Luke depicts Jesus' career in developmental terms. This has already been noted at 2:40, 52, in physical, mental, social, and spiritual areas. The focus here is on one who develops in stages of a spiritual process. In the gospel Jesus, in his adult life, passes through three stages: (a) empowering (3:21–22; 4:16ff.); (b) suffering-death (chap. 9ff.); and (c) resurrection-glory (Luke 24). In Luke 9 there is a movement from stage (a) to stage (b), a movement made possible by prayerful discernment.

In the second place, Jesus is one who calls his disciples to participate in the same developmental process through which he lived. Here it is not empowering or glory about which he speaks, but suffering-death. Luke 9:23a ("and he was saying—imperfect tense—to all") continues the dialogue begun at 9:18. After telling of his fate (9:22), as discerned in prayer (9:18), Jesus speaks of the disciples' style of life. For Luke discipleship is a continuing experience, so in 9:23 ("If any man would come after me") the evangelist uses a present infinitive (*erchesthai*—to come) instead of the aorist (*elthein*—v. Matt 16:24; Mark 8:34), the emphasis being on the continuing nature of the relationship. Also Luke adds "daily" to the "take up his cross" of Matt 16:24/Mark 8:34. Whereas Matthew and Mark have in mind the initial act, Luke stresses that the disciple takes up the cross daily, that is, continually. Just as the disciples had been given a share in Jesus' power (Luke 9:1–6), so now they are called to share his death: "If any man would come after me, let him deny himself and take up his cross daily and follow me" (9:23).

How can it be that the Spirit-empowered Jesus must suffer? How can it be that his empowered disciples must share the same experience? The answer lies in the eschatology of main-line first century

Christianity, which combined a "now" and a "not yet" (cf. Paul in 1 Corinthians 4; 15; Philippians 3). The New Age had broken in with the resurrection of Jesus, but the Old Age continues until the parousia. We live in the overlap. To hold these two realities (now—not yet) has always been among the most difficult tasks for Christian life and thought. There is perennially the temptation to allow one to swallow the other: either the emphasis is so focused on the powers of the New Age at work in believers that an eschatological reservation is lost, or the focus is so directed to believers' involvement in the structures and limitations of this life that the power of the Holy Spirit in the midst of weakness is overlooked.

The evangelist, having presented Jesus in his Galilean ministry as a Spirit-empowered conqueror of evil, now is concerned to show that even such a figure is subject to the limitations of this age. He is not immediately and automatically triumphant because of the power of the Spirit unleashed in his life in healing, exorcism, and teaching, but he will be rejected and killed. Only on the other side of this subjection to the limitations of this age will he enter into his final glory. The same limitations apply also to the disciples. Theologically it is necessary to juxtapose "anointed with the Spirit" and "destined to die" because to say less would be to break the delicate balance between the "now" and the "not yet" of Christian existence.

What purpose could such suffering serve for Jesus and for his disciples? In order to answer this question, two items of information are necessary: one from the NT at large and one from Luke. (1) The third evangelist frames Jesus' earthly career within two temptation scenes (4:1–13; 23:35, 36–37, 39). As we have previously seen, the first, 4:1–13, must be read against the background of Jesus both as the culmination of all God had been doing in the history of Israel and as the second Adam, as shown in the genealogy of 3:23–38. The order of the temptations in 4:1–13 echoes not only the threefold temptation of Adam and Eve in Gen 3:6 but also the temptation of Israel in the wilderness as given by Psalm 106: the temptations of Jesus thereby become anti-typical of the experience of Israel in the wilderness and of the original pair in the garden. Whereas those who came before were disobedient, Jesus, as the second Adam and as the true culmination of Israel's heritage, is obedient and thereby has reversed Adam's and Israel's sin. This temptation narrative thus understood has the effect of setting all that follows in Jesus' earthly career under the sign of his obedience.

As will be seen later, a second temptation sequence comes at 23:35, 36–37, 39. It is also a threefold temptation. Jesus spoke of the divine necessity of his death (9:22, 44; 18:31–33); in the garden he surrendered to the divine will even though it meant death (23:39–46); now on the cross he faces the temptation to use divine power for self-preservation (a power he still has—22:51). Three times he is confronted with the demand: "Save yourself" (23:35, 37, 39). That he does not is his obedience unto death, the perfection of his obedience to the Father (cf. 13:32). The Lukan frame around the public ministry of Jesus defines Jesus' career as the way of obedience, even unto death.

(2) In the NT one stream of early Christian thought regarded Jesus' death not only as an atonement for sin and as a defeat of the powers of evil but also as Jesus' ultimate act of obedience or faithfulness to God (e.g., Phil 2:8; Rom 5:18–19): Jesus died rather than sin. In this context Jesus' suffering and death were the arena in which his obedience to God was perfected. Heb 2:10 says God made "the pioneer of their suffering perfect through suffering"; "Although he was a Son, he learned obedience through what he suffered; and being made perfect he became the source of eternal salvation to all who obey him" (5:8–9). Corresponding to this view of Christ's suffering and death was the belief that suffering, and death if necessary, was the arena in which Christians wrestled with sin and, therefore, where they also had their obedience to God developed. 1 Pet 4:1–2 says, "Since therefore Christ suffered in the flesh, arm yourselves with the same thought, for whoever has suffered in the flesh has ceased from sin, so as to live for the rest of the time in the flesh no longer by human passions but by the will of God." Hence the emphasis is on suffering as discipline (Heb 12:7ff.), as a proof (1 Pet 4:12), or a testing (1 Pet 1:6–7) of Christian faith. The NT speaks of a suffering endured by Christ and Christians alike which is the arena in which obedience to God is perfected.

It is in the context of a view of suffering that is integral to the process of spiritual growth that Luke 9 should be understood. Jesus, through prayer, has come to see he is about to enter a new phase of God's plan for him. He is moving beyond the initial stage of empowering-illumination into a dimension of life which, though still empowered, is characterized by rejection (9:22). In this phase he will learn obedience through what he suffers (Heb 5:8–9). His obedience to God in the face of rejection, persecution, suffering, and finally death will signal his victory over sin (1 Pet 4:1–2).

The importance of rejection, persecution, suffering, and the threat of death in the process of spiritual growth is that each entails the possibility of the loss of something which the self either holds dear or is tempted to grasp: one is threatened with the loss of economic security, of status, reputation, or of life itself. Circumstances remove the possibility of one's holding to any of these finite treasures as security, and the suffering of rejection detaches one from these real or potential false gods. That is why the stage of suffering is called purification. One learns obedience to God alone through what is suffered. Rejection or persecution shatters real or potential idols and allows God to draw one to himself alone. This redemptive dimension of suffering would not be possible without the prior stage of empowering or illumination. From the evangelist's perspective only as God lives within is there the potential for suffering to be experienced as purification. The way of Jesus, therefore, was from empowering through suffering to glory.

The Jesus who walked this way also called his disciples to participate in the same developmental process, saying a disciple should "deny himself and take up his cross daily" (9:23). Bearing the burdens of life is an unlikely interpretation because the cross was not a burden but an instrument of death. A condemned person carried it on the way to execution. So to "take up [one's] cross daily" means to live daily as a condemned person, to "deny [one]self." If so, then self-denial means to live the life of a condemned person, one who has been stripped of every form of worldly security, even physical existence. For such a one, there is nothing and no one to whom there can be permanent attachment except the one who goes before carrying his cross. All other attachments have been terminated by the sentence of death, a sentence passed upon oneself.

Luke 9:24–26 consists of three sayings beginning in a similar way: vs. 24—For whoever; vs. 25—For what; vs. 26—For whoever. These verses illumine two benefits of denying oneself, taking up one's cross, and following Jesus. The benefits are given in negative form, as dangers to be avoided. In vss. 24–25 Jesus speaks of a present danger to be avoided by denial of self. One will, by holding to the old self, lose the true self or life (cf. 4:5–8). Self-denial in a Lukan context does not mean the annihilation of one's created individuality and worth, as in some Eastern religions, but it means rather the repudiation of the personality structure that absolutizes the self rather than the Creator, so the good created self (Gen 1:31) can emerge free from the perversions

that have covered it over. It is only when one's idolatrous attachments to the created order are stripped away and the Creator exists as one's ultimate concern that the created self is saved.

In vs. 26 Jesus speaks of a future danger to be avoided by denial of self. The one who responds wrongly to Jesus now will face the eschatological judge whose coming will vindicate Jesus' earthly life and mission. Only a life lived here and now without idolatrous attachments to the created order will be vindicated in the New Age where God is all in all. Both in the present and ultimately, only a life lived as a condemned person yields the meaning the Creator intended. Upon such a way of life the empowered Jesus was now embarking (9:22, 44, 31) and to such a way he called his empowered disciples. Regardless of whether or not a disciple's way involved the physical martyrdom to which Jesus' path led, it was to be lived as a condemned person, as one stripped of all attachments other than to God. Only thereby could the self be purified in the way God desired; only thereby could one's obedience to God be perfected.

Jesus closes his teaching about "rejection-suffering-death-purification" with a reassuring promise: "But I tell you truly, there are some standing here who will not taste death before they see the kingdom of God" (vs. 27). The form of vs. 27 is distinctively Lukan: Matt 16:28 reads, "see the Son of Man coming in his kingdom"; Mark 9:1 says, "see the kingdom of God come with power." Both refer to the parousia. But here Jesus says simply, "see the kingdom of God." In this form the reference must be to the presence of the kingdom seen or experienced within history. Since 17:21 speaks of the kingdom being present in Jesus' ministry, this seems the likely meaning. That context presents Jesus' words about an absolute allegience to him in which every other attachment is stripped away. Now this same Jesus says some who hear his words will indeed experience this kingly rule of God in their lives. This is a word of assurance.

Luke 9:51–19:44

GUIDANCE ON THE WAY

INTRODUCTION

The third major section in this gospel is 9:51—19:44. The first, 1:5—4:15, was an account of the prepublic career of Jesus; the second, 4:16—9:50, a narrative of Jesus' Galilean ministry. This section is within the framework of a journey to Jerusalem (9:51, 53; 13:22, 33; 17:11; 18:31; 19:11, 28, 41, 45), though the geography cannot be satisfactorily traced: in 9:51-53 Jesus passes through Samaria; in 10:38-42 (cf. John 12:1-3) he appears to be on the outskirts of Jerusalem; 13:31-33 locates him either in Galilee or in Perea; 17:11 places him between Samaria and Galilee; he is at Jericho in 18:35—19:10; 19:11 locâtes him near Jerusalem. Today it is widely recognized that this travel section is an editorial framework created by the evangelist.

The arrangement of the journey to Jerusalem is determined by two factors. First, there is an inclusion that holds the entire unit together. The travel section both begins (9:51ff.) and ends (19:28ff.) with a rejection of Jesus (by a village of the Samaritans, 9:52; by Jerusalem, 19:39-44). Second, a chiastic pattern determines the overall arrangement of the material.

A To Jerusalem: rejection in Samaria (9:51ff.)
  B Following Jesus (9:57ff.)
    C How to inherit eternal life (10:25ff.)
      D Prayer (11:1ff.)
        E Signs of the Kingdom (11:14ff.)
          F Conflict with the Pharisees (11:37ff.)
            G Present faithfulness and the future kingdom (12:35ff.)
              H Healing followed by accusation (13:10ff.)
                I Exclusion from messianic banquet/Inclusion (13:18ff.)
                  J Prophets perish in Jerusalem (13:31-33)
                  J' Jerusalem kills the prophets (13:34-35)
                I' Exclusion from messianic banquet/Inclusion (14:7ff.)

                    H' Healing followed by an accusation (14:1ff.)
                    G' Present faithfulness and the future kingdom
                        (16:1ff.)
                    F' Conflict with the Pharisees (16:14ff.)
                    E' Signs of the kingdom (17:11ff.)
                    D' Prayer (18:1ff.)
                    C'+ How to inherit eternal life (18:18ff.)
                    B' Following Jesus (18:35ff.)
                    A' To Jerusalem: rejection by Jerusalem (19:11ff.)

(K. E. Bailey, *Poet and Peasant: A Literary-Cultural Approach to the Parables in Luke* [Grand Rapids: Eerdmans, 1976], pp. 79–82; C. H. Talbert, *Literary Patterns, Theological Themes and the Genre of Luke-Acts* [Missoula: Scholars Press, 1974], pp. 51–56.)

Luke 9:18–50 functions as a prelude to the journey to Jerusalem. Just as the Galilean ministry began (4:16ff.) after Jesus in prayer received his anointing and the attestation of a heavenly voice (3:21–22; cf. 4:18), so the journey to Jerusalem begins (9:51ff.) after Jesus in two sessions of prayer (9:18; 9:28–29) receives his perception of the necessity of suffering (9:22, 31, 44) and the attestation of a heavenly voice (9:35). Since the journey to Jerusalem contains two motifs—(a) Jesus goes to his death, and (b) Jesus instructs the disciples—the material in 9:18ff. supplies the bases for what follows: (a) the necessity of suffering perceived in prayer, and (b) the authority for Jesus' subsequent instruction.

The authority for the instruction of Jesus' disciples is set forth in two paragraphs (9:28–36; 9:37–43a). Apparently in the Lukan account of the Transfiguration the conversation between Jesus, Elijah, and Moses was not overheard by the three who were asleep. In 9:32 *diagrēgorēsantes* could mean either the disciples "kept awake" or "when they came awake," the latter being the more probable. In either case it is to be inferred they were ignorant of the conversation but saw only Jesus' glory (9:32) and were distressed to see the heavenly visitors slipping away from Jesus (*diachōrizesthai* gives the sense "while they were beginning to go away"). Peter's response was an attempt to hold the glory by delaying the departure of Moses and Elijah (9:33). As though in response to the disciples' desire to hold this glory, a cloud overshadows them and a voice comes from the cloud: "This is my Son, my Chosen; listen to him" (9:35; cf. Ps 2:7; Isa 42:1; Deut 18:15): God himself in audible voice declares Jesus' teaching to be authoritative (cf. Acts 3:22–23).

Luke omits the discussion about the coming of Elijah found in Matt 17:9–13; Mark 9:9–13 and places immediately after the Transfiguration the exorcism story of 9:37–43. In so doing he makes the exorcism   — ✓ an integral part of the Transfiguration rather than a postlude. Furthermore, Luke's form of the exorcism story makes it a demonstration of Jesus' authority rather than, as in Matt 17:14–21; Mark 9:14–29, a teaching about the disciples' ministry of healing. In Luke all the stress falls on the authority of Jesus, so 9:37–43 goes together with the voice from heaven (9:35) to reaffirm Jesus' authority prior to his telling his disciples he must be delivered into the hands of men (19:44), before he delivers his *didache* on the way to Jerusalem (9:51—19:44). In this way 9:18ff. functions as a basis for the travel section.

Luke 9:51—19:44 functions theologically in a number of ways. (1) The didactic material given in the context of a journey fits Luke's conception of the life of faith as a pilgrimage, always on the move (cf. Acts 9:2; 19:9, 23; 22:4; 24:14, 22 where the Christian faith is designated "the Way"). This is true for Jesus and for his followers. (2) The journey is to Jerusalem and to Jesus' death. It is in respect of his sufferings that Jesus is described as "going on ahead" of the disciples (19:28). Since it is "through many tribulations that we must enter the kingdom of God" (Acts 14:22), Jesus goes before his disciples as *archēgos* (Acts 3:15; 5:31; Heb 2:10; 12:2), that is, pioneer or leader. (3) Some of the material prefigures the wider mission to be narrated in Acts (e.g., the mission of the Seventy [or Seventy-two] in Luke 10 prefigures the mission of Philip, Barnabas, and Paul in Acts). (4) The presence of the Galileans throughout the travel section furnishes a guarantee for the preservation and continuity of the tradition of Jesus after his ascension. What we are told in 9:51—19:44 has been delivered to us by those who from the beginning were eyewitnesses and ministers of the word (1:1–4).

THE COSTS OF DISCIPLESHIP

9:51—10:24

The first major thought unit in the travel section (9:51—10:24) is linked together by a variety of devices. In 9:52 and 10:1 Jesus sends someone before his face prior to his arrival. This joins 9:51–62 with 10:1ff. The rejection of Jesus by Samaritans (9:52–56) is followed by a threefold dialogue on discipleship (9:57–62), the first of which echoes the Samaritan rejection. In the second and third dialogues (vss. 60, 62), the references to the kingdom of God are Lukan and tie this section together with 10:1ff. where vss. 9, 11 repeat distinctive Lukan references to the kingdom. The unit 10:1–24 is joined by several interlocking devices: vss. 1, 3–4, 16 are linked by the verb "send forth"; vss. 5–7, 8–9, 10–11 by "into whatever [house or city] you enter"; vss. 12, 13–15 by "it will be more tolerable" (on that day or in the judgment); vss. 17–20 are linked by the reference to the return of the Seventy (esp. by the reference to joy in vs. 17 and the twofold "to rejoice" in vs. 20); vss. 21, 22 are joined by their common use of "Father" and "reveal." As a unit, vss. 21–22 are linked to vss. 17–20 by the time reference, "in that same hour," and the mention of Jesus' rejoicing (a different word but the same idea as in vss. 17–20). The concluding unit, vss. 23–24, is tied to what precedes by the introduction in vs. 23 (his disciples) and by the key word "hear" which ties into 10:16. In these ways the evangelist has woven 9:51–10:24 into a unified whole.

The basic pattern of the unit is ABA': 9:52–56 constitutes A; 10:1–24 is A': in both Jesus sends out disciples to prepare for his coming; in both the motif of rejection is present. Luke 9:57–62 constitutes B: here the focus is on the costs of following Jesus. Any discussion of the thought of 9:51–10:24 must take account of the Lukan patterning of the material. Luke 9:52–56 and 10:1–24, therefore, will be treated together and 9:57–62 separately.

A (9:52–56) and A' (10:1–24) point to the Lukan theology of world mission (2:32; 3:6; 4:25–27; 8:26ff.). On the one hand, in 9:52–56 Jesus moves into Samaritan territory. Though he is rejected the story

114

gives a warrant from the life of Jesus for the Christian mission into Samaria in Acts 8. On the other hand, 10:1–24 foreshadows the Gentile mission in Acts 13—28. (a) Luke 10:1, a verse peculiar to this gospel, mentions the Seventy or the Seventy-two others (i.e., besides the Twelve) who are sent two by two. This seems to be Lukan because 22:35, which is addressed to the Twelve, echoes 10:4, seeming to imply that the material in chapter 10 was originally addressed to the Twelve. The textual evidence is very evenly divided between Seventy and Seventy-two. This vacillation of the manuscripts is best explained by Genesis 10 in the Massoretic Text in which the number of the nations of the world is seventy, whereas in the LXX the number is seventy-two. Whatever the original reading, then, the point is the same. The number seventy or seventy-two symbolizes all the nations of the world: the mission is a universal one. (b) Luke 10 includes in its first twenty-four verses much of the material found in Matthew's instructions to the Twelve regarding missionary activity in chapter 10. Luke, however, does not have the saying found in Matt 10:5–6: "Go nowhere among the Gentiles, and enter no town of the Samaritans, but go rather to the lost sheep of the house of Israel." Although the Lukan geography does indicate the mission of the Seventy was within Jewish territory, the omission of the saying allows the number, with its symbolism of all nations, to foreshadow the later Gentile mission. (c) The basic architectural pattern controlling Luke-Acts is the series of correspondences in content and sequence between events in the gospel and those in Acts (C. H. Talbert, *Literary Patterns, Theological Themes and the Genre of Luke-Acts* pp. 15–23). In this parallelism between the two volumes of Luke's work, 10:1ff. comes at just the point to make it correspond with the missionary journeys of Paul to the Gentiles in Acts 13ff. These three strands of evidence, taken together, indicate that Luke intended 10:1ff. to foreshadow the Gentile mission of the church and gives a warrant from the career of Jesus for the Gentile mission of Paul, just as 9:52–56 gives such a warrant for the Samaritan mission of Acts 8. Luke 9:52–56 and 10:1–24 (A and A'), like 4:16–30 at the beginning of the Galilean ministry, focus on the Lukan universalism at the start of the travel narrative: the gospel must be carried to all peoples.

There is a sense in which 9:1–6, 52–56; 10:1ff. belong together as part of a pattern in the gospel. All three speak of Jesus "sending out" disciples. Luke 9:1–6 specifies it was the Twelve who were sent, while

9:52–56 is ambiguous: vs. 52 says he sent out messengers, while vs. 54's reference to James and John would seem to imply the Twelve are involved. In 10:1 the reference is to seventy (or seventy-two) others, the "others" being important. More than just the Twelve are involved in mission; indeed the mission that symbolizes universality is not carried out by the Twelve as such. Here again we see intimations of the narrative in Acts with its distinction between the work of the Twelve and that of others, like Paul. Taken together, 9:1–6, 52–56; 10:1ff. lay the foundation in the earthly life of Jesus for the commission of the risen Christ in Acts 1:8: "You shall be my witnesses in Jerusalem and in all Judea and Samaria and to the end of the earth."

Luke 9:52–56 (A) and 10:1–24 (A') not only present the theology of world mission, they also offer guidelines to govern missionary behavior. On the one hand, both A and A' contain a note of rejection following the theme of universality. Two different responses to this rejection are mentioned. (1) In the Samaritan episode (9:52–56), James and John ask Jesus about the possibility of calling down fire from heaven on those who rejected him, reminiscent of an Elijah episode in 2 Kgs 1:10 (cf. Sir 48:3). Jesus rejects any retaliation against his rejecters. Here is one guideline for dealing with rejection. It is in line with early Christian instruction about disciples' response to offending non-Christians (cf. Rom 12:18–21; 1 Pet 2:20–25; 3:16–17). (2) In the section of the mission of the Seventy (or Seventy-two), the response to rejection is very much that of 9:5. Luke 10:10 instructs the disciples to remove the dust from their feet as an acted parable against those rejecting them (cf. Acts 13:51 where Paul and Barnabas "shook off the dust from their feet" against those in Antioch of Pisidia who responded negatively). This symbolic act declared those who rejected the message had no part in the eschatological people of God. This judgment was to be made, but retaliation was to be foregone.

On the other hand, 10:1–24 contains a number of other guidelines for missionaries, as may be seen when the train of thought is traced. After a universalistic note (10:1) there is a call for prayer that God will supply laborers for the missionary work (vs. 2; cf. Acts 13:1–3). The missionaries are totally dependent on God for their protection (vs. 3) and sustenance (vs. 4a). Their mission is urgent and must not be delayed (vs. 4b; cf. 2 Kgs 4:29). The missionaries are not to have any qualms about subsisting off the generosity of others (cf. 1 Cor 9:4ff.),

but are not to beg from house to house, accepting the hospitality of
one house (vss. 5–7; Acts 16:15; cf. 1 Kgs 17:15; 2 Kgs 4:8). They are
not to worry about the restrictions of the Jewish food laws but are to
eat what is set before them (vs. 8: cf. 1 Cor 10:27). Proclamation of
the kingdom is to be by deed and word (vs. 9; cf. 11:20). Rejection of
the missionaries makes one liable at the judgment (vss. 12, 13–15)
because Jesus is identified with them: rejection of a messenger equals
rejection of Jesus. Furthermore, the closeness of Jesus and the Father
means that rejection of Jesus equals rejection of God (vs. 16: Acts 9:5;
22:7–8; 26:9–11, 14–15). The manifestation of Jesus' power in the work
of the missionaries is testimony to the power of Satan being broken
(vs. 18; with 10:19 cf. Acts 28:1–6; 18:9–10; 27:23–24). The demonstration of power over the demonic, however, is not to be a disciple's
major desire, because an emissary of the Lord can perform mighty
works in his name and still miss the kingdom (cf. Matt 7:22; 1 Cor
9:27). One's primary concern must be for personal salvation (vs. 20;
cf. Exodus 32:32; Ps 69:28; 87:4–6; 139:16; Dan 10:21; 12:1). This is
a warning to the disciples to place less importance on the miraculous.
It is to those who are unlikely candidates that both the divine power
of Jesus's name and the greater importance of having one's name in
the book of life are revealed (vs. 21). It is God who knows who his Son
is and to him the Father has given this authority which the missionaries experience (vs. 22; cf. 3:21–22). Moreover, since it is the Son
who knows the Father, he is the one to make God and his will known
(vs. 22b; cf. 9:35). Finally, Jesus' disciples are to be congratulated because of what they have seen (experienced), namely, the indications
in the missionaries' power over Satan that the time of fulfillment has
come—a time which people of the past were unable to see (experience
[vss. 23–24; cf. 1 Pet 1:10–12]). From such a survey we can see the
evangelist has used this section not only to foreshadow the Gentile
mission of the church, but also to give certain instructions and guidance that would be needed at the time the gospel was written (e.g.,
payment of missionaries; eating of any food set before them; balance
in one's concern for power in ministry and for one's own relationship
with God).

In 9:57–62 (B) the focus is upon the costs of discipleship and consists of a threefold dialogue: a—I will follow you (vss. 57–58); b—follow me (vss. 59–60); a'—I will follow you (vss. 61–62). Here three

would-be disciples misunderstand the nature of the commitment called for by Jesus. To each Jesus states the stringent demands he places on those who would follow him.

In *a* (vss. 57–58) Jesus responds to a man's expression of willingness to follow him wherever he went. Having just been refused hospitality by a Samaritan village (9:53), Jesus tells the man of the consequences of following him: Jesus is homeless; he does not belong to a settled family (cf. Sir 36:24–26 where one who "lodges wherever night finds him" is the unmarried man with no home of his own); to follow Jesus wherever he goes would mean to share the homeless lot of the Son of Man (cf. 18:28–30). To ponder the consequences of discipleship thusly is to raise the question of the man's resolve.

In *b* Jesus takes the initiative and says, "Follow me" (vs. 59a). The response was "Lord, let me first go and bury my father" (vs. 59b). Burial of the dead was a religious duty among the Jews taking precedence over all others. Even priests, who were not normally allowed to touch dead bodies, could do so in the case of close relatives (Lev 21:1–3), so the burial of a father was, to a Jew, the primary duty of filial piety (Tob 4:3; 6:15). An unburied relative apparently was equivalent to the presence of a corpse in the room (b. Berakoth 18a). Since the presence of a corpse defiled a person, it precluded the performance of any other religious rite. Sir 38:16 is intelligible in this context: "My son, let your tears fall for the dead. . . . Lay out his body with the honor due him, and do not neglect his burial." That business, Jesus replied, must look after itself: a disciple must go and proclaim the kingdom of God, because discipleship comes above the highest claims of family and one's duty to it. (Cf. 1 Tim 5:8 where the other side of abandonment to Jesus is spelled out: one is called upon to care for his family.)

In *a'* (vss. 61–62) another says he will follow Jesus, but, like Elisha, only after he has said farewell to those at home (cf. 1 Kgs 19:19–21). Jesus' response is in the form of a proverb (Hesiod, *Works and Days*, 443; Pliny, *Natural History*, 18:19:49): only those who can plow a straight furrow by moving toward a mark without looking away for a moment, no matter what the distraction, are single-minded enough for a disciple's role which calls for perseverance to the end (cf. Phil 3:13; Heb 12:1ff.; Matt 5:8; 13:44–46).

These three dialogues dealing with the costs of discipleship call for an absolute detachment from property and family and for a single-

minded devotion to Jesus that perseveres to the end: "Following him
is not a task which is added to others like working a second job. . . .
It is everything. It is a solemn commitment which forces the disciples-
to-be .to reorder all their other duties" (Robert Karris, *Invitation to
Luke* [Garden City, New York: Image Books, 1977], p. 130). When
disciples go out as missionaries, it is to this type of relationship with
Jesus they are calling their hearers. It is, moreover, to this type of
relationship the missionaries themselves are called.

ON LOVING GOD
AND THE NEIGHBOR

10:25–42

For the evangelist the whole of 10:29–42 is an exposition, in haggadic form and in reverse order, of the two great love commandments of 10:27. The story of the Good Samaritan, vss. 29–37, deals with the meaning of the commandment to love one's neighbor as oneself (vs. 27b); the story of Martha and Mary, vss. 38–42, interprets the injunction to love God with one's whole self (vs. 27a). A discussion of 10:25–42 must deal with both parts of Luke's exposition.

At the level of Lukan theology, the Good Samaritan pericope functions as an interpretation of the command to love one's neighbor. The form of 10:25–37 is that of a *controversy dialogue* with two parallel parts (J. D. Crossan, "Parable and Example in the Teaching of Jesus," *New Testament Studies* 18:285–307 [1972]). Part One, vss. 25–28, has four components: (1) the lawyer's question (vs. 25); (2) Jesus' counter-question (vs. 26); (3) the lawyer's own answer (vs. 27); and (4) Jesus' command (vs. 28). Part Two, vss. 29–37, has the same four components: (1) the lawyer's question (vs. 29); (2) Jesus' counter-question (vss. 30–36); (3) the lawyer's own answer (vs. 37a); and (4) Jesus' command (vs. 37b). The two parts are held together by the key words "neighbor" (vss. 27, 36) and "do" (vss. 25, 28, 37). This form appears distinctly Lukan when a comparison is made with the other synoptics.

On the one hand, 10:25–28 has parallels in Matt 22:34–40 and Mark 12:28–31. (a) Like Matthew, Luke says Jesus' opponent was a lawyer, that he came to test Jesus, and that he addressed him as Teacher. (b) Unlike Matthew or Mark, however, the question put to Jesus (vs. 25) was not about the greatest or first commandment but about how to inherit eternal life (cf. 18:18). (c) More important, in Luke alone Jesus asks the lawyer, "What is written in the law? How do you read?": that is, the counter-question. (d) Also Luke alone has the lawyer, not Jesus, give the answer (vs. 27). (e) Finally, only in Luke does Jesus respond

with an appraisal and a command: "You have answered right; do this and you will live" (vs. 28). Part One of the controversy dialogue depends upon the Lukan distinctions.

On the other hand, 10:29–37 is unique to the gospel. It is generally recognized that the parable of the Good Samaritan is confined to vss. 30–35 and that vss. 29, 36–37 are redactional, due either to Luke or to a pre-Lukan hand that formed the two-part controversy dialogue. It is this redactional material that makes vss. 29–37 fit the controversy dialogue model. Either the evangelist shaped the material in this way or chose this form in preference to another. (Note that Luke omits the Matthew-Mark version of the lawyer's question at the end of his gospel.)

The thrust of the double controversy dialogue can be discerned if we examine first of all the two questions with which its two parts begin and, secondly, the commands with which each part ends. (1) The lawyer asks Jesus, "What shall I do to inherit eternal life?" (vs. 26). Since it is two Jews talking and since it was assumed by Jews that the people of God would inherit the New Age, the import of the question is clear. The lawyer is asking what he as an individual should do to guarantee his place in the people of God who would inherit eternal life: "What do I do to belong to God's people?" Moreover, when the lawyer asks, "Who is my neighbor?" he is wanting to know how he can spot others who belong to God's covenant people. The Jews interpreted "neighbor" in terms of members of the same people or religious community, that is, fellow Jews (cf. Matt 5:43). Even within the Jewish people there was a tendency to exclude certain others from the sphere of neighbor. For example, the Pharisees sometimes excluded the ordinary people of the land and the Qumran Covenanters excluded the "sons of darkness" (1 QS 1:10; 9:21f.). Jews generally excluded Samaritans and foreigners from the category of neighbor. Hence the lawyer's question was basically, "Who belongs to the category of God's people?"

(2) Note that both parts of the controversy dialogue end on the same theme: "do." Verse 29 reads, "do this [present infinitive], and you will live." Verse 37b says, "Go and do likewise" [present infinitive]. The language indicates that the concern is with a certain type of continuing behavior. If the two parts of the dialogue open with questions about who belongs to God's people, they end with commands to behave in a certain way. What is the prescribed way of acting?

Part One has the lawyer give his view about the orientation that

characterized the covenant people of God: Deut 6:5, love God, and Lev 19:18, love your neighbor, are joined in the lawyer's response. Assuming that the Testaments of the Twelve Patriarchs represent pre-Christian Judaism, the two great commandments had already been linked in Jewish thought (T. Issacher 5:2; 7:5; T. Dan 5:3). "You have answered right" (vs. 28a)—Jesus approves of this interpretation of the law—"Do this, and you will live" (vs. 28b; cf. Lev 18:5; Gal 3:12). This accent on doing is in line with the Lukan emphasis on "hearing the word of God and doing it" (cf. 8:21; 6:47; 3:10–14; 1:38). Loving God and loving the neighbor are the signs of covenant loyalty which will guarantee one will live in the New Age with the people of God.

The Lukan transition in vs. 29 (cf. 16:15; 18:19–21) indicates that what follows flows from the need to deal with the lawyer's self-justification: "How can I spot others who belong to God's people so that I can love them?" In response to this question the story of the Good Samaritan is told. After the story Jesus asks, "Which of these three, do you think, proved neighbor to the man who fell among robbers?" (vs. 36); that is, which man acted like one who belonged to the covenant people of God? Which one loved? The answer from the lawyer was inevitable: "The one who showed mercy on him" (vs. 37a). The command of Jesus is the unit's conclusion: "Go and *do* likewise" (vs. 37b).

The Good Samaritan narrative functions at the level of Lukan redaction as an exemplary story. The point is that we should go and do likewise, a commentary on what "loving the neighbor as oneself" really means. It means to act like the Samaritan. The focus Luke gives the parable of the Good Samaritan is not on how Jesus acted but on what Christians of the evangelist's own day should do (Jan Lambrecht, "The Message of the Good Samaritan [Luke 10:25–37]," *Louvain Studies* 5:121–35 [1974]). In the Lukan context this means that people who belong to God's covenant community show love (a) that is not limited by the clean-unclean laws (cf. Acts 10, 15); (b) that does not limit itself to friends but has a universal scope (cf. Luke 2:32; 3:6; 4:25–27; 10:1ff.); and (c) that does not look for recompense (cf. Luke 6:32–36). This, of course, was the way Jesus loved.

In order to deal adequately with 10:25–37, it will be necessary to depart from the procedure normally followed in this commentary. Whereas usually the explanation of a unit is concerned exclusively with what the material meant for Luke, at this point we will treat also the function of the parable of the Good Samaritan in Jesus' *Sitz im*

Leben. Before this can be done a word is necessary about the recent interpretation of parables. (The best summary can be found in Norman Perrin, *Jesus and the Language of the Kingdom* [Philadelphia: Fortress Press, 1976], pp. 89–193.)

The modern study of the parables has shown (1) that the way a parable is used in a gospel is not necessarily the way it originally functioned (so Jeremias), and (2) that a parable may function either to instruct or to provoke: that is, it may be a simile in which the lesser known is clarified by the better known ("the kingdom of God is like") or a metaphor in which two not entirely comparable elements are juxtaposed resulting in a shock to the imagination. The shock forces the listener to make a judgment on the situation in the parable (so Funk, Crossan). It has been on the provocative function of the parables that the most recent interpreters have placed greatest emphasis. The parable of the Good Samaritan makes a fine example.

Detached from its redactional setting in the controversy dialogue, the parable consists of 10:30–35. The dissimilarity of its contents to Judaism and of its form with early Christianity argues for its origins in Jesus' ministry. In order to hear the parable as the original Jewish hearers did, one must recognize: First, Jews despised Samaritans, the descendents of the mixed population which followed Assyria's conquest of Samaria in 722 B.C. (2 Kings 17). Possessors also of a syncretistic religion, the Samaritans opposed the efforts of Ezra and Nehemiah to rebuild Jerusalem and reestablish the sanctuary of Yahweh (Ezra 4:2ff.: Neh 2:19; 4:2ff.), building a rival temple on Mount Gerazim. Josephus (*Antiquities* 11:8:4 §324) says this was during the reign of the last king of Persia (335–30 B.C.) but his story is suspect. This Samaritan temple was razed by John Hyrcanus in 128 B.C. (Josephus, *Antiquities* 13:9:1 §256; *War* 1:2:6 §63)—Josephus says it was in exasperation over the Samaritans' prolonged apostasy and treachery. Pompey liberated them from the Jewish yoke in 63 B.C. Enmity existed between Jews and Samaritans at the time of Christian origins (e.g., John 4:9; Luke 9:52–53), some rabbis even saying acceptance of alms by a Jew from a Samaritan delayed the redemption of Israel. Also a maxim emerged that no Jew need trouble himself to save a Samaritan's life (b. Sanhedrin 57a). In light of the existing tensions, Jewish hearers could be expected to respond negatively to any references to Samaritans.

Second, Jews who were loyal to the scriptures would be concerned

about the laws of cleanness and uncleanness. Among these laws were those which dealt with the uncleanness contracted from touching a dead body (Num 19:11-13, 14-19; Mishna, *Eduyoth*, 8:4). As noted above, priests were exempted from burying even their relatives, except for the nearest of kin—mother, father, son, daughter, brother, virgin sister (Lev 21:1-3). This was because as priests they must avoid uncleanness. The chief priest was not to defile himself even to bury his father and mother (Lev 21:10-11). When, therefore, Jesus' hearers were told the priest and Levite avoided any contact with the man who was half-dead (vs. 30), they would know these religious figures did exactly as they were instructed to do by scripture (G. B. Caird, *The Gospel of St. Luke* [Baltimore: Penguin Books, 1963], p. 148).

The parable makes the despised Samaritan the hero and the Bible-believing-and-obeying priest and Levite the villains. This demands the hearers say what, for them, cannot be said, what is a contradiction in terms: bad (Samaritan) cannot be good; and good (priest and Levite) cannot be bad. If as a hearer one accepts the judgment of the parable, then one's whole world of values is shattered. In this way, the original parable in its setting in Jesus' career aimed not to instruct but rather to challenge, to provoke, to shatter stereotypes. The stereotyper is challenged in his judgments; the usual criteria for evaluating a person's worth are replaced by that of unselfish attention to human need wherever one encounters it. This is provocative. It raises questions about one's caricatures of others and the norms used to identify the good and the bad. It also raises questions about this Jesus who confronts hearers with standards of judgment that are so different from their own. Who is he to overthrow my evaluations of others?

What functioned in Jesus' original setting as a provocation and challenge became in the gospel an exemplary story which teaches disciples how to love their neighbor. This difference in function should not be seen as discontinuity, as though the evangelist were distorting the original material. The same parable which in its address to people commited to other values involved the hearers in such a way they were led to a judgment that was an abrupt reversal of their old world could, on the other side of conversion, function in quite a different way. If one's old world is shattered, a new one must be constructed around one's discipleship to Jesus. "The way the world comes together again through the parables matters just as much as the way its idolatrous security is shattered" (W. A. Beardslee, "Parable Interpretation and the

World Disclosed by the Parable," *Perspectives in Religious Studies* 3:123-39 [1976]). To use the parable of the Good Samaritan as an exemplary story is to allow it to function in the constitution of a new world for those who have already been converted from the old way. To use it as a provocation that shatters the old world of a person is to allow it to function as a catalyst for conversion. It "may turn out to be the case that an alternation between these two types of speech—confirmation and unsettling—is required for communicating the Christian vision" (W. A. Beardslee, "Narrative Form in the New Testament and Process Theology," *Encounter* 36:301-15 [1975]). The parable of the Good Samaritan, then, functions in two ways depending upon whether it is addressed to those whose world and values need shattering or to those whose world needs solidifying. Both are legitimate functions carried out by means of the same form of speech.

The second part of the thought unit, 10:38-42, tells the story of Martha and Mary. If the parable of the Good Samaritan, at the level of Lukan theology, dealt primarily with the meaning of the commandment to love one's neighbor, this episode deals with the meaning of the first commandment. The clue to understanding the role of 10:38–42 in relation to 10:25-28 is the interpretative principle voiced by R. Akiba: "Every section in scripture is explained by the one that stands next to it" (Sifre on Numbers §131). This is reinforced in that 18:18–30 corresponds to 10:25-42 in the chiastic pattern of the travel narrative. Both sections follow the same arrangement: (a) dialogue on the law; (b) love of neighbor; and (c) love of the Lord (Bastian Van Elderen, "Another Look at the Parable of the Good Samaritan," in *Saved by Hope*, pp. 109-19).

Luke 10:38-42 asserts that to love the Lord with all your heart, soul, strength, and mind means to sit at the Lord's (Jesus') feet. To sit at a person's feet was the equivalent of "to study under someone" or "to be a disciple of someone" (cf. Acts 22:3—Paul was raised "at the feet of Gamaliel"). To love God with your whole being, Luke says, is to be a disciple of Jesus. Busyness guarantees nothing; listening to Jesus' words is the crucial point (cf. 5:5). Jesus' response to Martha's agitated request (vs. 40; cf. 12:13; 6:41-42) is plagued by textual problems. The two with the best manuscript support are: (1) "Martha, you are anxious and troubled about many things; one thing is needful"; and (2) "Martha, you are anxious and troubled about many things; few things are needful or one." A final decision is difficult, given the evidence. If

(1) were chosen, the meaning would be that Mary has chosen the one thing that is needful, discipleship, receiving from Jesus rather than trying to be the hostess of the one who came to serve (cf. 22:27). In this case, Mary would be living "by everything that proceeds out of the mouth of the Lord" (Deut 8:3; cf. Luke 4:4; John 6:27). If (2) were chosen, the meaning would be something like, "A couple of olives, or even one, will suffice at present. Mary has the main course already" (F. Danker, *Jesus and the New Age,* p. 133). The good portion would be the "food which endures to eternal life" (John 6:27), which is Jesus' gift to his disciples. With either reading, the point is that loving God means submission to Jesus and receiving from him.

Mary and Martha in this story are a study in contrasts. Mary is characterized by an undivided attention to Jesus himself. She is also one who receives from the Lord. Martha was distracted, not wholly focused on Jesus himself. The reason was her "much serving" (vs. 40). Her desire to work for Jesus distracted her focus on Jesus and prevented her receiving from him what she needed. This study in contrasts holds up Mary as the embodiment of what it means to love God wholly, just as the parable of the Good Samaritan held up the Samaritan as the embodiment of what it means to love one's neighbor.

The thought unit, 10:25–42, consists of an exposition of the two great commandments for disciples. To love one's neighbor means to act like the Samaritan. To love God means to act like Mary. These are the two characteristics of those who belong to the covenant people of God: to receive from the Lord and to give to others. Without the former the latter is either not desired or becomes a burden that produces anger at those who are not doing their part.

PRAYER: FOR WHAT AND WHY?

11:1–13

Luke 11:1–13 is composed of a number of independent traditions: (a) vss. 1–4 (cf. Matt 6:9–13); (b) vss. 5–8 (only in Luke); (c) vss. 9–10 (cf. Matt 7:7–8); and (d) vss. 11–13 (cf. Matt 7:9–11). These traditions are held together not only by the common theme of prayer, but also by a complex series of interlocking devices. (1) Verses 1–4 are linked to what follows in several ways: (a) "And he said to them" (vss. 2, 5), both only in Luke; (b) Father (vss. 2, 11), heavenly Father (vs. 13); (c) bread (vs. 3), loaves (vs. 5), the latter only in Luke. (2) Verses 5–8 are linked to what follows by "I tell you" (vs. 8), "And I tell you" (vs. 9), the latter not being in Matt 7:7. (3) Verses 9–10 are linked with vss. 11–13 by "ask" in vss. 9–10, 11, 12, 13. Clearly the evangelist intended to tie these diverse materials into a single unit dealing with prayer.

In their present form, these verses consist of a request for instruction by a disciple (vs. 1) followed by Jesus' *didache* (vss. 2–13), the content of which deals first of all with what to pray for (vss. 2–4) and then with why one should make a habit of praying (vss. 5–13).

For what should a disciple of Jesus pray? The distinctive Lukan perspective may be grasped only if 11:2–4 is compared with the original form of the Lord's Prayer. Three versions of the prayer are found in early Christianity: Matt 6:9–13; Luke 11:2–4; and *Didache* 8:2. The form in the *Didache* is indebted to that in Matthew, so there are only two basic forms of the prayer preserved by the early church. That in Matthew represents the shape of the prayer as it circulated in Jewish Christianity, that in Luke the shape used by Gentile Christians at the end of the first century. The original form of the prayer appears to have contained the number of petitions in Luke with the language of Matthew being generally more original (Joachim Jeremias, "The Lord's Prayer in Modern Research," *Expository Times* 71:141–46 [1960], and R. E. Brown, "The Pater Noster as an Eschatological Prayer," *New*

Testament Essays [Milwaukee: Bruce, 1965], pp. 217–53). This rule of thumb yields the following result:

> Father:
> Hallowed be thy name;
> Thy kingdom come.
> Give us this day our bread for the morrow;
> And forgive us our debts, as we forgive our debtors;
> And lead us not into temptation, but deliver us from
>   the Evil One.

There is an address followed by two "Thou-petitions" and three "us-petitions."

The two "Thou-petitions" are synonymous parallelism. Since it is disciples who already stand within the kingdom who are praying, to say "Thy kingdom come," would be to ask for the final consummation. The two initial petitions, then, ask God to intervene to bring the New Age to pass. What this would mean for God is that his name would be reverenced and his rule acknowledged.

The first two "us-petitions" view the eschatological victory from the perspective of what it would mean for disciples. The term *epiousion* is difficult because it is so rare. In the third century Origen (*De Oratione* 27:7) said he could find no example of it in other Greek writers. Etymology yields two possible translations: either "daily" (from *epi einai*) or "for the future" (from *epi* plus *ienai*). Jerome said that the Gospel of the Hebrews read it in the latter way, as a reference to the eschatological bread, the manna from heaven, or the food of the messianic banquet. Since the first two petitions are eschatological, it seems preferable to read it in an eschatological manner. Parallel to the petition for the heavenly bread is the prayer for forgiveness, that is, the eschatological forgiveness of sin. The coming of the New Age would mean that God's name would be reverenced and his rule accepted; that disciples would participate in the messianic banquet and their sin be ultimately blotted out.

The last "us-petition" is concerned with the idea of eschatological temptation which is the work of the devil. In the final encounter between God and the Evil One which ushers in God's kingdom, the disciples ask to be sheltered: preserve us from temptation and its source.

The prayer as a whole is the prayer of a community ("Give *us*"; "*our* bread"; "forgive *us*"; "*we* forgive"; "lead *us*"; "deliver *us*") which be-

lieves it has a unique relation to God. The simple *"Abba*-Father" is without analogy in Jewish prayers of the first millennium A.D. This is the way small Jewish children addressed their earthly parents, and to a Jewish mind it would have been irreverent and unthinkable to call God by this familiar word (Joachim Jeremias, *The Central Message of the New Testament* [London: SCM, 1965], pp. 19–21). This unique relation could be described as informal intimacy. In the prayer the community asks for two things: (1) the speedy (cf. "this day") coming of the eschatological kingdom of God with all of its benefits both for God and for the disciples; and (2) protection in the eschatological crisis which precedes the shift of the ages. The historical Jesus taught his disciples to pray for the immediate shift of the ages and for the protection that would guarantee their participation in the New Age. It assumes a single-mindedness that is jarring. The disciples are to pray for one thing essentially: the realization of the ultimate ideal, God's kingdom, the New Age. They are to ask for it to appear immediately. Such a prayer functions provocatively, asking about the ones addressed, why do they not desire this one thing? Why cannot they desire this one thing? What does it say about them that they cannot pray this way? In this sense the prayer calls for a change in the hearers, for the purification of their desires.

The Lukan form of the Lord's Prayer differs from the original not in the number of petitions but in the wording. The place to begin in noting the differences is with the "us-petitions" in vss. 3–4: "Go on giving us day by day our daily bread" (vs. 3). Luke's present tense "go on giving" (Matthew uses the aorist—give today) and the uniquely Lukan "day by day" (cf. 9:23; 19:17; Acts 17:11) control the understanding of this petition. Whatever the qualifying *ton epiousion* may mean elsewhere, here the translation "daily" seems appropriate. The evangelist sees the petition as the disciples' request for God to go on supplying their physical needs day by day. It is not specifically an eschatological prayer in this context. Jesus is telling the disciples, some of whom had been sent out without extra provisions (9:3; 10:4) and had found their needs supplied (22:35), to pray for the provisions they need for the day. Given the Lukan hostility to the accumulation of unneeded possessions (e.g., 12:16–21), one should perhaps understand the evangelist to mean "pray for what you need for the day and for no more."

In vs. 4 the Lukan differences may be a clue to the evangelist's intention. Whereas Matthew uses "debts" as a term for violations of

both the relation to God and the relations of others to us, Luke uses "sins" for our offenses against God. He leaves, however, the debtor language in the second part of the petition. He specifies that we ourselves are continually forgiving all who are indebted to us. If one's understanding of this sentence is determined not by evidence outside the gospel but only by the context, this too may be a part of the Lukan concern with possessions (cf. 6:27–38, especially vss. 34–35, 30). The evangelist may aim for his readers to hear that they should expect God to forgive their sins against him as they continually forgive all of their debtors (understood in terms of "things"). If so, then passing God's forgiveness along to others within the community means something broader than Matthew's context would indicate. In any case, here again the prayer is asking for something within history.

If the petitions in vss. 3, 4a are concerned with the daily life of disciples in this world, it is unlikely that the final petition of vs. 4b should be read as referring to the tribulation just before the eschaton: "Lead us not into temptation" should almost certainly refer to the ordinary temptations of daily life (cf. 4:13; 22:38; Acts 20:19). This would include not only the inward seductions of the devil but also the outward trials which test faith (cf. Sir 2:1ff.; Rom 5:3–5; Jas 1:13). If so, this petition would parallel the Jewish prayer, "Bring me not into the power of sin, nor into the power of guilt, nor into the power of temptation" (b. Berakoth 60b). If the idiom "to enter temptation" means not "to be tempted" but rather "to yield to temptation" and if the negative qualifies the idea of entry, then the petition would be understood as "cause us not to succumb to temptation" (J. Carmignac, *Recherches sur le 'Notre Pere'* [Paris: Letouzey & Ane, 1969], pp. 236–304, 437–45). This would fit the Lukan mind: both Jesus (4:13; 22:28) and his disciples (22:28; Acts 20:19; 14:22) undergo temptations but, empowered by the Holy Spirit, they overcome and do not succumb.

Most likely the first two Lukan petitions should be read in a similar way. While a request for the eschaton should certainly not be excluded, the scope is broad enough to include the disciples' present also. The ancient textual variant in vs. 2b which replaced "hallowed be thy name. Thy kingdom come" with "Let thy Holy Spirit come upon us" (Tertullian, *Against Marcion*, 4:26) reflects the way these two "Thou-petitions" were understood by some. Given 11:13's "the heavenly Father will give the Holy Spirit to those who ask him," the petition calling for the coming of the kingdom was apparently understood

in terms of the gift of the Holy Spirit. Though the textual variant is — ↙
not original, its reading of the passage's intent may be correct. This
can only be decided after an exploration of the relation between the
Spirit and the kingdom in Luke-Acts. (Cf. J. D. G. Dunn, "Spirit and
Kingdom," *Expository Times* 82:36–40 [1970–71]; S. S. Smalley,
"Spirit, Kingdom and Prayer in Luke-Acts," *Novum Testamentum*
15:59–71 [1973]; G. W. H. Lampe, "The Holy Spirit in the Writings of
St. Luke," in *Studies in the Gospels,* ed. D. E. Nineham [Oxford:
Blackwell, 1955], pp. 171–72.)

In Paul the Spirit is the present-ness of the coming kingdom. Where
the Spirit is the kingdom is, so to have the Spirit is to have part in the
kingdom here and now (cf. 1 Cor 4:20; 2 Cor 5:5; Rom 8:23; 14:17).
The same thrust is found in Luke-Acts where the ideas of the power
of the kingdom and the working of the Spirit of God are brought into
a very close relationship. They are in fact virtually identical. In Acts
1:4 the risen Christ speaks with the apostles about the kingdom of God
during his forty days of appearances. At least part of this talk deals
with the baptism in the Holy Spirit (Acts 1:4–5). When the apostles
ask the risen Lord about the kingdom (Acts 1:6), he responds with
words about the Holy Spirit (1:7–8). Luke 12:32 says it is the Father's
good pleasure to give the disciples the kingdom, which parallels 11:13:
the Father will give the Holy Spirit to those who ask him. So when
17:21 says "the kingdom of God is in your midst," Luke means that
the kingdom is present because Jesus is the unique bearer of the Spirit
(1:35; 3:22; 4:18). The kingdom is present in Jesus insofar as he has
the Spirit. In Luke-Acts the presence of the Spirit is the "already" of
the kingdom. Where the Spirit is, there is the kingdom. God's eschatological reign is both mediated and characterized by the Spirit, of whom
Jesus is the carrier *par excellence.* So in the gospel the disciples who
pray, "Thy kingdom come," realize in the pentecostal gift of the Holy
Spirit a partial fulfillment of their prayer. In such an experience they
"see the kingdom of God" before they taste death (9:27). Given this
close identification of the present dimension of the kingdom and the
gift of the Holy Spirit, 11:2, "Thy kingdom come," may be a petition
for the eschaton, but it is also a plea for the gift of the Holy Spirit. The
early variants on the text were, then, at least partially accurate percep-
tions of the Lukan mind.

For what should a disciple pray? In a *Sitz im Leben Jesu* the Lord's
Prayer functions as a call to petition God for an immediate shift of the

ages. The assumptions within the prayer are provocative and shatter all of the hearers' illusions about their devotion to God and his rule. In the context of the third gospel, the model prayer serves a didactic purpose. It gives instruction to disciples about what to pray for in the midst of the on-going historical process: daily bread, forgiveness, victory over temptation, the gift of the Holy Spirit, and the ultimate victory of God. The shift in function in the gospel arises from the lived experience of the church which had continued to exist for fifty or so years. In that time the disciples had found the power unleashed at the resurrection of Jesus—the power that would bring the eschaton to the cosmos—was already at work among the believers. This power was sufficient for all their needs. Out of this experienced reality, they prayed not only for God to bring history to its fulfillment but also for his continued provision of their needs.

Why should a disciple pray? Luke 11:1–13 answers this question not only with the teaching of Jesus (vss. 5–13) but also with his example (vs. 1). On the one hand, it was the example of Jesus that evoked one of his disciples' request, "Lord, teach *us* to pray." A disciple prays because Jesus' example points in that direction. Jesus was a praying activist; from prayer he derived his spiritual power.

On the other hand, Jesus' teaching in 11:5–13 gives a twofold reason for praying. (1) In vss. 5–10 a parable found only in Luke (vss. 5–8) is followed by what amounts to an interpretation (vss. 9–10). The parable's story of a neighbor, who when confronted with a midnight traveler for whom he had no food, shamelessly persisted in his requests to a friend until the friend got up and supplied his needs, has been understood in two very different ways. Some take it to advocate a stormy, unrelenting insistence that persists until God grants the request. Just as the neighbor refused to take "no" for an answer and so had his request met, so also the disciples should persist with God who will eventually respond to shamelessness ("importunity" in the RSV should be "shamelessness" as in NEB). Others, however, take the parable to be a "how much more" story (cf. 18:1–8). If a reluctant friend who does not want to answer a neighbor's request will do so simply because of his neighbor's shamelessness in persisting, how much more will God who is eager and willing answer your prayers. The disciples should pray because God wants to answer. The second interpretation is the more probable because (a) 18:1–8, which is a parallel passage, seems to support this second reading; (b) 11:9–10 makes the point

that one should make a habit of asking, seeking, and knocking because God is certain to answer prayer; (c) 11:11–13 is cast into a "how much more" form; and (d) the first interpretation runs counter to the spirit of Matt 6:7. Viewed in this way, vss. 5–10 function to answer why pray: a disciple prays in the first instance because God will answer.

(2) Luke 11:11–13 gives a second reason why disciples should pray—here again the mode of thought is "how much more." Verses 11–13 differ from their Matthean parallel (7:9–11) in two respects, one important and one insignificant. (a) Luke's two comparisons involve first the fish-serpent and then the egg-scorpion parallels, while Matthew's are first the loaf-stone and then the fish-serpent correspondences. The difference has no major bearing on the meaning. Background information offers the most assistance in understanding the parallels. On the one hand, the fish-serpent parallel is illuminated by there being a type of unclean fish in the Sea of Galilee that can reach five feet in length, crawl on land, and has the appearance of a snake. This eel-like creature is most probably the serpent mentioned here. On the other hand, the egg-scorpion correspondence is clarified when we see that when a scorpion's limbs are closed around it, it is egg-shaped. The point is that even sinful parents will not be cruel enough to give their offspring something positively harmful. If an evil parent will not give hurtful gifts but rather good gifts when asked, how much more will God? (b) Whereas Matt 7:11 says, "how much more will your Father who is in heaven give *good things* to those who ask him," Luke 11:13 reads, "how much more will the heavenly Father give the *Holy Spirit* to those who ask him." Here the difference is major. For the third evangelist the good gift of the heavenly Father is not primarily things, even good things, but the Holy Spirit. After his baptism while Jesus was praying the Holy Spirit descended upon him (3:21–22). In Acts 1:14 the disciples are praying before the pentecostal gift of the Spirit in Acts 2. Indeed, the evangelist would see this promise of Jesus in 11:13 as the basis for Pentecost. What happened there was not only a fulfillment of the promise of the risen Lord (Luke 24:49; Acts 1:4–5, 8) but also of the earthly Jesus. These verses, 11:11–13, furnish a second reason why disciples should make a habit of praying. God will not give anything harmful to those who ask. Above all, he will give himself to those who ask him. If the point in vss. 5–10 is the certainty of God's answer, in vss. 11–13 it is the goodness of the gifts bestowed

by God. With the reference to the gift of the Holy Spirit in vs. 13 to those who ask, the reader returns to the idea with which the larger unit began: "Thy kingdom come" (vs. 2). In the gift of the Spirit the rule of God is present. Furthermore, it is the Father's desire to give the kingdom (12:32).

HEALING IN
BIBLICAL PERSPECTIVE

11:14–36

M uch of the material in 11:14–36 has parallels in the other synoptics but this disparate material has been cast into a unifying pattern: an action of Jesus (vs. 14) leads to a double assault on Jesus (a—vs. 15; b—vs. 16) which is followed by a double reply by Jesus (a'—vss. 17–28; b'—vss. 29–36). Such a pattern of "action-assault-reply" is characteristic of the Lukan narrative (e.g., 5:17–26, where vs. 20 is the action, vs. 21 is the assault, and vss. 22–24 are the reply; 7:36–50, where vss. 37–38 are the action, vs. 39 is the assault, and vss. 40–48 are the reply in two parts; 13:10–17, where vss. 10–13 are the action, vs. 14 is the assault, and vss. 15–16 are the reply; 15:1–32, where vs. 1 is the action, vs. 2 is the assault, and vss. 3–32 are the triple reply; Acts 11:1–17, where vs. 1 is the action, vss. 2–3 are the assault, and vss. 4–17 are the reply). As it stands this unit consists largely of answers to two reactions to Jesus' miracle (vs. 14, only in Luke): (1) the charge that Jesus was a magician (vs. 15), and (2) the demand for a sign to authenticate Jesus' authority (vs. 16, only in Luke).

Luke 11:14, the action of Jesus, reads very much like a summary of a miracle story. As elsewhere (4:39; 6:18; 8:2; 9:6, 1; 10:9, 17; 13:11, 14, 16; Acts 5:16; 10:38; cf. Matt 12:22), the evangelist understands the healing as an exorcism: the man's inability to speak was due to a speechless demon. It is interesting to note that in the gospels the same problem, inability to speak, can be attributed to three different causes: (1) Luke 1:20—Zechariah's inability to speak is due to a divine judgment on his unbelief; (2) Luke 11:14—the man's inability to speak is due to a demon that was dumb; and (3) Mark 7:32—the man's speech impediment is attributed to neither demonic nor divine causation but is apparently assumed to be due to natural causes. This raises the question of the larger biblical perspective on the causes of sickness.

Apparently all three factors mentioned as a cause of dumbness are considered in the Bible as causes of disease generally. (1) There are certainly instances where sickness is directly due to God's punishment of sin (e.g., 2 Sam 12:14–23, esp. vs. 15; 2 Kgs 15:4–5; 1 Cor 11:29–32). (2) In other places sickness is due to Satan (e.g., Job 2:6–7; Luke 13:16; 2 Cor 12:7), though used by God for his purposes. (3) In still other places sickness seems to be due neither to a person's sin nor to Satan's harassment but to the imperfections of the created order (Gen 3:14–19 where the roots are to be found for this view; John 9:2–3; Rom 8:19–23; 1 Cor 15:50; Gal 4:13–14) in which human beings participate. Even godly people, because they are flesh (mortal), get sick (2 Kgs 13:14; Dan 8:27; Gal 4:13; Phil 2:25–30; 2 Tim 4:20).

The cause of the man's distress in 11:14 was having a demon that was dumb. He was not being punished by God for his sinfulness, nor was he the unfortunate victim of a flawed universe: he was in bondage to demonic evil.

If there are multiple causes of sickness in the biblical perspective, there are also multiple avenues to healing. (1) If sickness is due to one's sin, the proper response is repentance, confession, forgiveness (cf. Jas 5:14–16, which seems to be dealing with sickness caused by sin, especially vs. 16a; cf. 1 Cor 11:30–31). (2) If sickness is due to oppression or attack by Satan and his hosts, then two options are offered. In the first place, the demon can be cast out in the name of Jesus Christ (e.g., Acts 16:18; 19:11ff.). Given sin and demonic oppression as possible causes of human illness, one can see why the NT writers regard signs and wonders as following the gospel (e.g., 2 Cor 12:12; Rom 15:18–19). Wherever sin and spiritual oppression are conquered by Jesus, there will inevitably be accompanying healings and deliverances. Often physical and psychological relief are inevitable by-products of Jesus' conquest of evil. They are to be expected. In the second place, ultimately only God can lift Satan's oppression, and sometimes he does not see fit to do so either at once (cf. Job) or ever in this life (cf. 2 Cor 12:7ff.). When this is the case God uses the trouble for some good purpose (2 Cor 12:9; cf. Rom 8:28). (3) If sickness is due to the imperfections in the natural world, then again two options are offered. On the one hand, in both the OT (e.g., 1 Kgs 17:17–24; 2 Kgs 4:32–37; 5:1ff.) and the NT (e.g., the gospels) healing sometimes takes place via a miraculous intervention of God. On the other hand, there is also an understanding of healing through

medicine (e.g., Isa 38:1–5, 21; 1 Tim 5:23; cf. Tobit where medical knowledge comes from God via revelation—e.g., 6:7–8). These two options are rooted in the Bible's understanding of God as both Creator, who has given human beings the capacity to understand the world, and Redeemer, who intervenes, accepts responsibility for both sin and the flaws in his world, and does for us what is beyond the limits of our ability. If God is both Creator and Redeemer, then these two options cannot be played off against one another, as both are a part of who God is and how God acts (cf. Sir 38:1–15). Given the multiple causes of sickness attested to by scripture, it takes discernment to know what is the cause in any given situation, what is the proper avenue of cure, and whether God wishes to heal at spiritual, emotional, and physical levels, all in the here and now, or whether he wishes to save the physical healing until the resurrection.

The means of healing the man's distress in 11:14 was deliverance, the casting out of the unclean spirit by the authoritative word of Jesus. The man was not called upon to repent of his sin, nor was he sent to a doctor for a prescription. He was in bondage to demonic evil, so by power of the Holy Spirit (4:14) Jesus delivered him.

God's miraculous intervention through Jesus to deliver a dumb demoniac leads to a double assault on Jesus. Some said, "He casts out demons by Beelzebul, the prince of demons" (vs. 15). This is the charge that Jesus is a magician: that is, Jesus is accused of using demonic power to achieve his ends. No matter that someone was made well; how Jesus did it is questionable. Jesus' exorcism caused others to test him, seeking from him a sign from heaven (vs. 16): that is, some demanded objective verification of his credentials. No matter that a man was made well; proof is required that this was God's doing. With these two unbelieving reactions to the healing the evangelist demonstrates that Jesus' miraculous deeds do not always evoke faith.

The response to the charge that Jesus' exorcism was due to demonic power is twofold. (1) Verses 17–19 say what the miracle does not mean. It does not mean Jesus is a magician because (a) that would be illogical (vss. 17–18), and (b) it would be inconsistent (vs. 19). It would be illogical because division leads to destruction. Satan, therefore, would not permit rebellion in his own ranks. Furthermore, to accuse Jesus of magic because of his exorcism would be inconsistent since other Jews perform exorcisms without being labeled "servants of Beelzebul" (Acts 19:13ff.; Josephus, *Antiquities* 8:2:5 §45–48; 2:13:3 §286; Tob 6:1–7;

8:1–3). If Jesus' critics are not willing to ascribe other exorcists' work to magic, they cannot so label Jesus.

(2) Verses 20–23 say what Jesus' miracle does mean. If it is ascribed to the "finger of God" (a direct, unmediated act of God, cf. Exod 8:19; 31:18; Deut 9:10; Ps 8:3), it means the kingdom of God has come upon you (vs. 20). This fits with 11:1–13 where kingdom of God and Holy Spirit are virtually synonymous. It means the stronger one (cf. 3:16) has overcome Satan (vss. 21–22). Possession of the defeated one's armor was evidence of the victor's triumph (cf. 2 Sam 2:21 LXX). It is not adequate, however, to cast out a demon if there is no acceptance of the kingdom of God whose power is attested by its expulsion (vss. 24–26). Only God's rule of human life prevents the return of demonic activity, hence those are blessed who "hear the word of God and keep it!" (vss. 27–28). Exorcism, then, is not evidence for Jesus' being a magician but rather for the inbreaking of God's rule in his ministry. In order to benefit permanently from this divine power, however, one must respond properly.

The response of Jesus to the demand for proof that his actions are by God's authority falls into three parts. (1) No sign shall be given to this generation "except the sign of Jonah" (vss. 29–30). Mark 8:11–12 has a similar tradition which says simply, "No sign shall be given to this generation." Matt 12:38–40 more closely parallels Luke: "no sign . . . except the sign of the prophet Jonah (12:39). In Matt 12:40, however, the evangelist inserts a statement peculiar to his gospel explaining his understanding of the sign of the prophet Jonah: "For as Jonah was three days and three nights in the belly of the whale, so will the Son of Man be three days and three nights in the heart of the earth." For Matthew the sign of Jonah is Jesus' crucifixion and resurrection. Luke's view of Jesus' response to the demand for a sign is not that of either Matthew or Mark. He understands the sign of Jonah to be Jonah's call to repentance: "For as Jonah became a sign to the men of Nineveh, so will the Son of Man be to this generation" (vs. 30); for the men of Nineveh "repented at the preaching of Jonah" (vs. 32). The first part of Jesus' reaction to the demand for a sign is to say that the only sign to be given is the prophetic call to repentance.

(2) The second part of the response is found in vss. 31–32: Gentiles will condemn Israel at the judgment because they (the queen of the South and the men of Nineveh) made the appropriate response to the wisdom of Solomon and the preaching of Jonah; Israel, however, fails

to respond properly to something greater than either Solomon or Jonah, namely, the presence of the Holy Spirit in the ministry of Jesus. The notion that the Gentiles would witness against Jews at the judgment was exactly the opposite of Jewish belief (cf. the Christian adaptation of the Jewish belief in 1 Cor 6:2). The second part of Jesus' response to a demand for a sign is to say that Gentiles respond to the call to repentance better than Israel (cf. Acts 13:44–52; 20:23–29; Luke 7:1–10).

(3) The third part of Jesus' response, vss. 33–36, joins three originally unconnected sayings (vss. 33, 34–35, 36) with the catchword "lamp." In this context the unit likens Jesus' ministry to a light that illuminates those who enter a house. There is nothing hidden about the light. Any lack of illumination is due to the recipient. If he or she has a sound eye, light will flood one's whole being. The eye is thought of as a funnel through which light can enter if it is not stoppered. If the eye is not sound (i.e., stoppered), then the self will be dark, unilluminated by the light which shines without (cf. Prov 4:19). Luke's point is that those whose spiritual sight has not been damaged have no need for a sign from heaven (the Gentiles!); the light of God's rule manifest in Jesus' ministry is seen by them clearly. Jesus' ministry is a public light to those entering the kingdom of God (vs. 33). The failure to respond properly is a spiritual analogue to the person whose body is full of darkness because of a diseased or blind eye (vss. 34–35). Hence the call for a sign is a symptom of spiritual blindness.

Rightly understood the power at work in Jesus' healing is God's and is evidence of his rule's presence. Since only one who has experienced God's rule is able to see his kingdom at work (cf. the Greco-Roman principle that it takes like to know like), one who wishes to know whether God is at work in Jesus needs first of all to hear his call to repentance and to respond properly. Unless one has experienced, through repentance, the rule of God in one's life, it will be impossible to recognize its presence in the ministry of Jesus. The presence of God in miracle cannot be recognized by one without God's rule in the individual heart.

POSSESSIONS, PREPAREDNESS, AND REPENTANCE

12:1—13:21

M uch of the material in 12:1—13:21 has parallels elsewhere in the synoptic tradition. Sometimes this material is used quite differently from the way the third evangelist employs it. For example, Matt 10:27 gives a reason for missionaries not to be afraid of opposition, but in Luke 12:3 it is a warning eginst hypocrisy. Or in Luke 12:57–59 the point is to escape the adversary, not to be reconciled with him as in Matt 5:25–26. The third evangelist has taken these diverse materials and has organized them into a two-part unit. Part One is addressed to Jesus' disciples (12:1–53). Jesus speaks first to them (12:1), issuing a call for a Christian response in three areas of life: with regard to persecution (12:1–12), to possessions (12:13–34), and to preparation for the parousia (12:35–48). This charge is climaxed by a paragraph on the divisive effects of Jesus' ministry (12:49–53). Part Two is addressed to the multitudes (12:54—13:21). Jesus, in speaking to them, issues a call for conversion. We find in 12:1—13:21, then, a collection of diverse traditions joined in a framework which may be ascribed to the evangelist. One might think of this large unit as a Christian homily directed first to the disciples (12:1–53) and then to the unbelievers present (12:54—13:21). That non-Christians attended early Christian worship services is clear from 1 Cor 14:23–25.

Part One (12:1–53), which is addressed to the disciples, gives teaching in three areas: (1) on persecution; (2) on possessions; and (3) on being prepared for the parousia. Luke 12:1–12, on persecution, will be discussed in this commentary in connection with 21:12–19. Luke 12:13–34 focuses on a disciple's attitude toward possessions: vss. 13–21 speak to the problem of covetousness, vss. 22–32 to that of anxiety, and vss. 33–34 serve as a general conclusion to the section as a whole. This section is joined to 12:1–12 by the repetition of "multitude" (vss.

140

1, 13), "do not be anxious" (vss. 11, 22), and birds (sparrows in vs. 6, ravens in vs. 24). Verses 13–21, which deal with covetousness, are tied to vss. 22–34, which focus on anxiety, by means of "treasure" (vss. 21, 33, 34), "barns" (vss. 18, 24), and similar statements in vss. 15b and 23.

Luke 12:13–21, which addresses the problem of covetousness, is peculiar to this gospel. This subsection consists of a pronouncement story climaxed with a rebuke of covetousness (vss. 13–15), followed by a parable about the rich fool (vss. 16–21) which expounds the folly of such a covetous attitude. Covetousness was prohibited in the Decalogue (Exod 20:17; Deut 6:21) and was spoken against by the prophets (e.g., Mic 2:2). It was a problem in the church before Luke (e.g., Rom 1:29; Mark 7:22) and at the time of Luke-Acts (e.g., Col 3:5; Eph 5:5; 1 Tim 6:10). In vs. 15a Jesus warns, "Beware of all covetousness." The reason why is set forth in the form of a principle in vs. 15b: "for a man's life does not consist in the abundance of his possessions." Jesus says that what a person is cannot be confused with what a person has.

The parable of the rich fool in vss. 16–21 functions as an exposition of what covetousness is and why such an attitude is folly. Covetousness here is depicted as the accumulation of additional goods by those who already have enough for their needs. It is a craving for more, not because it is needed, but from a desire to hoard. Such striving acts as a means of security and reflects disregard for God and neighbor. That is why both Col 3:5 and Eph 5:5 regard covetousness as idolatry. To trust in one's accumulated wealth as a means of security is folly: "For what does it profit a man if he gains the whole world and loses or forfeits himself?" (Luke 9:25; cf. Sir 11:18–19; Ps 39:6). The accumulation of additional goods when one has enough guarantees not one's security but one's status as idolater. In Luke-Acts the purpose of wealth is found in its being shared.

Luke 12:22–32, which focuses on the problem of anxiety about possessions, falls into two parts (vss. 22–28; vss. 29–32), each with a balanced structure. (1) Verses 22–28, the first part, begin with an injunction: "Do not be anxious about your life, what you shall eat, nor about your body, what you shall put on" (vs. 22). The reason given is, "For life is more than food and the body more than clothing" (vs. 23). An exposition of "food" and "clothing" follows. Verses 24–26 are an exposition of "food." If God feeds the birds, since you are of much greater

value than they, God will feed you too (vs. 24). Besides, anxiety is as ineffective in the area of what you will eat as it is in wanting to add eighteen inches to your height (vss. 25–26). Verses 27–28 are an exposition of "clothing." If God clothes the grass—witness the splendor of the lilies in bloom—since you are more significant, will he not clothe you? (vss. 27–28).

(2) Verses 29–32, the second part of the subsection dealing with anxiety, fall into two balanced units: one telling what to avoid, the other what to seek. In vs. 29 the disciples are told, "Do not seek . . . nor be of anxious mind." Verse 30 gives the reason: "For (*gar*) all the nations of the world seek these things; and your Father knows that you have need of them." In vss. 31–32a the disciples are told, "Instead, seek. . . . Fear not, little flock." Verse 32b gives the reason: "for (*hoti*) it is your Father's good pleasure to give you the kingdom."

In 12:22–32 the disciples are enjoined not to be anxious about food and clothing, the necessities of life, because those who seek God's kingdom (in Luke this includes not only the present experience of the Holy Spirit but also the dwelling with Jesus after death and the ultimate rule of God in the New Age) will find God trustworthy to meet all such needs. Do not be anxious. Trust God. He will provide (Ps 23:1).

Life is God's gift, as are those things that sustain and protect life. For those who trust the power and the goodness of the giver of life, anxiety may abate, the grasping hand may relax, and covetousness be replaced by generosity. Hence the section on possessions is climaxed by 12:33–34, a specific injunction to almsgiving (cf. 11:41; 16:9; 18:22; 19:8; Acts 2:44–45; 4:32–37; 9:36; 10:2, 4, 31; 20:35; 21:24[?]; 24:17). The Jewish practice of almsgiving is echoed in passages like Tob 4:7–11 ("Give alms from your possessions to all who live uprightly," vs. 7) and Sir 3:30 ("almsgiving atones for sin," cf. 29:12). In the Lukan community those with possessions were expected to provide for the poor (vs. 33—cf. Acts 2:44–45; 4:32; 4:34–37; 11:27–30): this was a sign that their treasure was in heaven and their hearts as well (vss. 33–34). The Lukan stance is echoed in 1 Tim 6:17–19. In contrast, covetousness is an indication that God's kingdom is not one's prime pursuit, and anxiety about food and drink an indication that one is unable to trust in God's power and goodness (cf. Gen 3:1–6 where sin is identified with anxious distrust of God's goodness and provision).

Although Jesus believed no one can serve God and money, he called his disciples, in vss. 33–34, to serve God with money.

In 12:35–48 the evangelist turns to the matter of being prepared for the parousia. The sayings in this subsection have a post-Easter perspective. They envisage a situation in which the disciples are awaiting their absent master's return and in which some of the disciples occupy positions of leadership and pastoral responsibility. Within this framework the evangelist first addresses all Christians and then the pastoral leadership. (1) Verses 35–40 enjoin readiness on all Christians. Two parables make the point (vss. 35–38, 39). The first parable tells of servants who are ready for their master's return from a marriage feast and who, upon his return, receive an unheard-of reward: the master serves the servants. What kind of servants receive the reward? Two striking images convey the meaning. "Girded loins" means that the long outer garment is gathered around one's waist so it will not interfere with the most strenuous activity. The verb is a perfect imperative which commands one to be already in a certain state: "Let your loins be already girded"—that is, "Be the kind of servant who never needs to be told to gird them because you always live in this condition." If one is to live with perpetually girded loins, one's lamp is to be continually burning (present imperative). This type of readiness is that which the master rewards. The second parable, the householder and the thief (vs. 39), posits a perpetual watchfulness: though the householder could not stay awake all the time watching for the thief, this never-ending alertness is expected from Jesus' disciples. Verse 40 gives Luke's point: "You also must be ready; for the Son of Man is coming at an hour you do not expect." The readiness enjoined is that which desires to be open to the Master at any moment (vs. 36). All Christians are called to this ready openness.

(2) Verses 41–48 call for faithfulness on the part of those with leadership roles in the Christian community. Peter's question in vs. 41 (only in Luke) provides the opportunity for warnings about the abuse of their positions by church leaders (cf. Acts 20:28ff.; 1 Cor 3:10ff.; 11:21; 1 Tim 4:12–16; 2 Pet 2:1–2, 13). Jesus' parabolic saying is concerned with the situation of a servant who is placed in charge over other servants (vss. 42–43). If he is doing his job when the master comes, he will be blessed (vss. 43–44). If, however, he is irresponsible in his duties he will be punished by the master. A gradation of punish-

ments is given: (a) for active tyranny, death (*dichotomēsei* in vs. 46 means "to cut in two," that is, the dismemberment of a condemned person); (b) for deliberate neglect, a severe beating; and (c) for unintentional neglect, a light beating. This reflects Jewish thought about sins which were unconscious and less culpable than those that were deliberate (cf. Num 15:27–31; Deut 17:12; Ps 19:12–13; b. Baba Bathra 60b). Furthermore, those in positions of leadership, to whom much has been entrusted, will have more expected of them (vs. 48b; cf. Jas 3:1). Christian leaders, then, even more than disciples generally, need to be prepared for the parousia-judgment (cf. 21:34–36; 1 Cor 4:1–5). Readiness for them means their faithfulness in doing the commission given them by the master.

The section addressed to disciples (12:1–53) is climaxed by a paragraph dealing with the divisive effects of Jesus' ministry (12:49–53). The unit is comprised of three originally independent sayings (vss. 49; 50; 51–53), each with a similar form: "I came"; "I have"; "I have come." Taken together, the train of thought is as follows. In vs. 49 Jesus, whom John the Baptist had said would baptize with the Holy Spirit and fire (3:16), looks forward to and longs for that moment. In that time the Spirit, like a burning fire, will accomplish the work of judgment in the hearts of people. But (*de*) Jesus' "baptism" is the precondition for that to happen (vs. 50). The variant in Mark 10:38 shows Jesus' baptism to be his suffering and death. So after his death, the fire will come. This corresponds with the Lukan chronology: Pentecost follows passion. The result of Jesus' coming, the outpouring of the Spirit and fire, and the proclamation of the gospel will be *division*. This theme was anticipated in the birth narratives (2:34–35): "The call for decision is a call for 'division' " (E. E. Ellis, *The Gospel of Luke*, p. 182). From Luke's point of view, the presence of the Holy Spirit in the life and proclamation of the church produces division before it produces unity. Jesus is the great divider.

The second of the two major sections of 12:1—13:21 is addressed to the multitudes (12:54—13:21). This part of the discourse is tied to the first (12:1–53) by the use of "hypocrites" (12:56; 13:15; cf. hypocrisy in 12:1) and the threefold "I tell you" (*legō soi* in 12:59; *legō humin* in 13:3, 5; cf. 12:51, 44, 37, 27, 22, 8, 4) as well as the reference to the multitudes (12:54; 13:17; cf. 12:1, 13). The address to the multitudes is a call for conversion in two parts (12:54–59 and 13:1–21).

The first part, 12:54–59, is a twofold exhortation to interpret the

signs of the times properly (vss. 54–56) and to respond rightly to the challenge of the moment (vss. 57–59). In vss. 54–56 Jesus says the crowds need to be as discerning in their interpretation of the time (that is, the meaning of Jesus' mission) as they are in discerning the weather. To fail to do so will spell disaster (cf. 19:41–44). In vss. 57–59 Jesus says the people need to be as discerning about the realities of God's judgment as they are about settling accounts with a bill collector. In everyday life people wisely settle accounts before they become liable to the jurisdiction of the judge and are thrown into debtor's prison. The same wisdom is called for in the face of the approaching judgment of God (cf. Acts 10:42–43; 17:30–31).

The second part, 13:1–21, gives two significant signs together with their proper interpretation. Luke 13:1–9 raises the question of the meaning of the absence of tragedy in a person's life. "Our lives are going smoothly. As any good Jew knows, trouble is God's punishment for sin, while tranquility is a sign of God's blessing. Our lives are tranquil; there is no disaster. Why then should we repent?" Luke 13:1–9 is a response in three sections to such a position. (1) The first two sections are based upon some recent occurrences in Jerusalem (vss. 1–3, 4–5): the massacre of some Galileans by Pilate (tragedy due to a human cause) and the death of some caused by the fall of the tower of Siloam (tragedy due to a natural cause). Tragedy, says Jesus, is not the measure of one's sinfulness and one's need to repent. Those whose lives are tranquil likewise need to repent. (2) The third section, 13:6–9, is a parable about a fig tree that after three years bore no fruit. Since a fig tree supposedly reached maturity after three years, the probability was that it would not ever bear fruit. The owner wanted it cut down and replaced, but the vinedresser asked for one more year to see if it would bear. The point is that the absence of judgment here and now cannot be construed as a sign of one's righteousness. Rather, if judgment does not strike immediately, it is a sign of God's mercy, not his approval (cf. Acts 14:15–17; 17:30; Rom 2:4ff.; 2 Pet 3:9ff.). One is being given a last chance. Taken together, 13:1–9's three components say that just because people pass through life unscathed by suffering they should not assume that therefore they please God. Tragedy is no sure sign of sinfulness, just as absence of tragedy is no sure sign of righteousness. All alike—those whose lives are tragic and those whose lives are tranquil—are sinners and all alike must repent (change directions in life) before God's judgment does come upon them.

Luke 13:10–21, the healing of the stooped woman, freeing her from the bondage of Satan, is a sign of the presence of God's kingdom (cf. 11:20). Though, like the rising cloud (12:54) or the south wind (12:55), it is seemingly small and insignificant, this single defeat of Satan, like the cloud and wind, signals a certain result—ultimate universal victory over evil (13:18–21).

The challenge to the multitudes is clearly put. Do not misinterpret your freedom from misfortune as a sign of your righteousness: it is God's last opportunity for you to repent. Do not miss the presence of God's rule in Jesus' healings: they are signs pointing to a certain result. Be at least as astute in these matters as you are in your reading of the weather and in your avoiding the judgment of the courts. Repent!

THE RESPONSE
OF ELDER BROTHERS

15:1–32

L uke 15 contains an introduction (vss. 1–3) followed by three parables (vss. 4–7; 8–10; 11–32), two of which are peculiar to the gospel (vss. 8–10; 11–32); the third has a parallel in Matt 18:12–14. The first two parables (vss. 4–7; 8–10) possess a common surface structure: (1) what man/what woman; (2) one sheep lost/one drachma lost; (3) sheep found/coin found; (4) calls friends and neighbors, saying, "Rejoice with me for I have found the lost sheep"/calls friends and neighbors, saying, "Rejoice with me for I have found the lost coin"; (5) Just so, I tell you/Just so, I tell you. The two stories are joined by a simple "or," just as the two parables of 14:28–32 and the two incidents of 13:1–5 were. The three parables are linked together by the key words "joy" (vss. 6–7; 9–10; 23–24, 32), "because the lost is found" (vss. 6; 9; 24; 32), and "repentance" (vss. 7; 10; 18). The entire chapter is joined by an inclusion: the elder son's complaint about the father's receiving the prodigal and giving him a feast (vss. 27–30) echoes the murmuring of the Pharisees and the scribes over Jesus' receiving sinners and eating with them (vss. 1–2).

The chapter is put together with techniques characteristic of the evangelist. (1) The pattern is similar to what we find elsewhere in Luke: an action of Jesus (vs. 1) evokes an assault on him (vs. 2), to which he responds (vss. 3–32)—cf. 13:10–17; 11:37–44, 14–23; 5:29–32, 17–26) (2) Luke 5:36–39 introduces a series of three parabolic sayings with the singular, "He told them a parable also," just as 15:3 does. (3) Luke 13:1–9 has two short, similarly constructed sayings of Jesus followed by a longer parable, just as chapter 15 does. Luke 15, taken as a whole, is a Lukan composition, meant to be read as a unit.

The introduction to the chapter (vss. 1–3) contains two components: the occasion (vss. 1–2) and a transition (vs. 3). The occasion is the Pharisaic criticism of Jesus' association with outcasts ("sinner" has a

connotation that goes beyond our usual moralistic interpretation and involves a disreputable social status). The stance of the Pharisees (5:29ff.; 7:39; 15:1–2) reflects the OT warning about association with evil-doers (Prov 1:15; 2:11–15; 4:14ff.; Psalm 1; Isa 52:11; cf. 2 Cor 6:14–18) which was crystallized in the rabbinic dictum "Let not a man associate with the wicked, not even to bring him to the Law" (Midrash Rabbah on Exodus 18:1 [65a]). In contrast, Jesus eats and drinks with outcasts because "I have not come to call the righteous, but sinners to repentance" (5:32). He enters their houses because "the Son of Man came to seek and save the lost" (19:10). The verb *prosdechomai* (receives) in 15:2 may indicate that here Jesus is hosting sinners, an even more serious offense to a Pharisee than merely eating with them. Given the Pharisaic criticism of his behavior, the transition (vs. 3) tells us that Jesus spoke a parable (consisting of three stories).

The first of these three stories, the parable of the lost sheep (cf. Ezek 34; Ps 119:176), is paralleled in Matt 18:12–14. Luke's point is clarified by a comparison with the Matthean parallel. Matthew 18 is the fourth of five large teaching sections in the first gospel; it is concerned with the relationships of disciples to one another in the church and is addressed specifically to disciples. Verses 12–13 appear as part of a unit, 18:1–14, which deals with "the little ones" in the church (that is, the rank and file disciples who are in constant danger of deception from proud and clever people). The point of the unit is twofold: (1) do not cause a rank and file Christian to sin (vss. 6, 7–9), and (2) if one goes astray, go after him/her (vss. 5, 10–14). Note that in Matt 18:12–13 the sheep is not lost; it *goes astray*. In 18:14, the conclusion, the meaning is that the heavenly Father does not want any *little ones* to perish. In the first gospel, therefore, the parable of the sheep gives directions to disciples for dealing with straying Christians. In Luke, however, the one sheep is *lost* (15:4, 6). Furthermore, the interpretation (vs. 7) appended to the parable (vss. 4–6) makes clear the meaning of "lost." Verse 7 reads, "Just so, I tell you, there will be more joy in heaven over one *sinner* who repents than over ninety-nine righteous persons who need no repentance." The lost in Luke are sinners, the outcasts with whom Jesus eats.

In the Lukan story of the lost sheep, the rejoicing of the shepherd is matched by the rejoicing of friends and neighbors over his having found the lost animal. If his associates join the shepherd in his rejoicing when a lost sheep has been found, how much more should the

Pharisees join heaven in its joy over the repentance of a sinner. Can you join me, says Jesus to his critics, in my rejoicing over the reclamation of any of the outcasts with whom I eat and drink?

The second story, the parable of the lost coin, is little more than an alternative way of saying the same thing. The repetition is for emphasis. Joy over finding the lost coin (not a coin used as an ornament but one that was part of the woman's savings) is the center of concern. The picture of an oriental woman in her house with no windows and a dirt floor lighting a tiny lamp and sweeping until she finds her lost coin climaxes with a conclusion (vs. 10) similar to that of the preceding story: "Just so, I tell you, there is joy before the angels of God over one sinner who repents" (15:10). Taken together the parables of the lost sheep and the lost coin justify Jesus' association with outcasts by appeal to the joy in heaven over the repentance of even one sinner. Those two stories say, You know how you feel if you are a herdsman and you find a lost sheep or if you are a housewife and you recover a lost coin; well, that is how God feels when a sinner repents. You know how your friends and neighbors join you in rejoicing over your find; well, that same kind of communal rejoicing is heaven's response to a sinner's being reclaimed. A question is implicit: Can you share that joy? Will you join with God and heaven's hosts in their rejoicing?

The third story, the parable of the two sons, is perhaps the best known of the gospel parables. This story falls into two parts, the first focusing on the prodigal (vss. 11–24), the second on the elder brother (vss. 25–32). In both parts of the parable the focus is first on the son and then on the father.

In the first part of the story, the portrayal of the prodigal evokes negative feelings. (1) The boy treated his father as if he were dead. According to the laws of property, it was possible for children to receive a division of the father's capital during his lifetime (cf. Sir 33:19–21), but a son had the right of disposal of the property only after the father's death. (2) The prodigal had dissipated his means of caring for his father in case a necessity arose (vss. 18, 21): He had violated the commandment to honor one's father and mother (Exod 20:12; Deut 5:16). (3) He had associated with a Gentile (vss. 15–16) instead of going to the Jewish community for help. He had, moreover, made his living in what for a Jew was a sinful way (feeding pigs). The polite way a Mid-Easterner gets rid of unwanted hangers-on is by assigning them a task he knows they will refuse. Not even this work, which

practically precluded the practice of his religion, got rid of the youth. Here then is a portrait of a despicable youth about whom one's feelings are similar to those of a Pharisee for a tax collector. He was uncouth, unclean, and contemptible.

The portrayal of the father in the first part of the story evokes amazement. (1) The father would be expected to refuse the younger son's request (vs. 12), but instead he grants it. (2) The expected response from the father upon the younger son's return home is mirrored in the prodigal's request: "Treat me as one of your hired servants" (vs. 19). A typical Jewish father might have considered this expedient until the son's reformation had been confirmed. It would, moreover, allow the youth to make reparations required by repentance (cf. Luke 19:8). Instead, the father came out of the house and in a dramatic demonstration showed an unexpected love publicly, even to the point of humiliating himself. The father's actions were without restraint. He ran. Even if he were in a great hurry, for an aged oriental to run would be beneath his dignity. (Sir 19:30 says, "A man's manner of walking tells you what he is.") Yet he ran. The embrace would stop the prodigal from going to his knees. A kiss on the cheek was a sign of reconciliation and forgiveness, the best robe a sign of honor, the ring a sign of authority (cf. Esth 3:10; 8:2; Gen 41:42), the shoes a sign of a free man—slaves went barefoot—and the feast a sign of joy: "Let us eat and make merry; for this my son was dead, and is alive again; he was lost, and is found" (vss. 23–24). Here is the same note of joy over the recovery of the lost that we met in the interpretations of the two earlier parables (15:7, 10). Joy over a recovered sheep or coin is understandable. They are valuable and we benefit from their being found. But the "excessive joy" of the father at the prodigal's return makes no sense. At the very least, one stands puzzled at the father's joy.

Just as in the case of the prodigal, the elder brother in the second part of the story (vss. 25–32) evokes negative feelings. (1) In addressing his father (vs. 29) with no title, he insults him publicly. (2) He accuses his father of rank favoritism (vss. 29–30). (3) He declares he is not part of the family (cf. "my friends" in vs. 29b; "this son of yours" in vs. 30). (4) If, moreover, all that is left belongs to the elder brother, and if he complains about not being able to dispose of it yet as he wants to do, then he also wants the father dead and gone. In other

words, although the elder son has carried out orders (vs. 29b), he has been lawless within the law—not physically but spiritally. If the prodigal was an overt sinner, the elder brother has been a covert one. He is certainly not a lovable figure.

Again in the second part of the parable the father's response is provocative. Reacting to the elder brother's anger, the father goes out (vs. 28) and says, "Son, you are always with me, and all that is mine is yours. It was fitting (*edei*—cf. 2:49; 4:43; 9:22; 13:16, 33; 17:25; 19:5; 22:37; 24:7, 26, 44) to make merry and be glad, for this your brother was dead, and is alive; he was lost, and is found" (vss. 31–32). Given the context the statement should be taken to mean that it was a divine necessity to rejoice over the recovery of the lost (cf. 15:7, 10). Joy is the appropriate (as defined by God's behavior) response to a sinner's repentance.

In taking this stance the third story stands in continuity with the first two. (1) The joy in heaven over a sinner's repentance is greater than a shepherd's happiness over the recovery of a lost sheep (vs. 7). (2) There is joy in heaven over a sinner's repentance just as there is when a woman finds her lost coin (vs. 10). (3) Heaven rejoices over a sinner's reclamation just as the father did over the return of the prodigal, even though it is difficult to accept. In one respect, however, the third story stands in discontinuity with the first two: it remains open. The elder brother's response to the father's joy is not given. Will the elder son accept the father's invitation to rejoice with him over the recovery of the prodigal as the shepherd's friends and the women's neighbors did with them? This is left open for each "elder brother" who hears the parable to decide.

As in all double-edged parables, the emphasis lies in the second half, the climax, which comes to us as a query: Will you share in the communal joy over the prodigal's return? If not, why not? Chapter 15, then, is a threefold statement of God's joy over a sinner's repentance followed by a query: Can you participate in that joy? If not, why not? Can you not rejoice at the efforts to effect a sinner's repentance? If you were able to feel the joy of the shepherd and the woman, why are you unable to feel the joy of the father? Do you get more excited about money and animals than about people (12:15–16; 14:5)? Who are you, in your relation to God and humans, in light of your absence of joy? Why are you not able to participate in the divine necessity to rejoice?

Jesus' response to the assault on his behavior (vs. 2) is to raise a question about his accusers. As has been noted, the conclusion is missing in vs. 32. The hearers must decide their response.

When the parables are used to question the hearers in this way, the christological question is just below the surface. One is forced to ask, "Who is this who professes to know the mind of God?" The Pharisees of vss. 1–2 would not only be forced to ask themselves, "Are we elder brothers?" but also, "What right does Jesus have to make the judgments he does?"

THE USE AND
MISUSE OF WEALTH

16:1–31

The unity of the chapter is apparent first of all from the concern
with possessions that runs through it. The chapter falls into two
parts, 16:1–13 and 16:14–31, each dominated by a parable beginning
"There was a rich man" (vs. 1; vs. 19). The first part is addressed to
disciples (vs. 1), the second to Pharisees (vs. 14—cf. 17:1 where the
audience switches back to disciples).

The first part of chapter 16, vss. 1–13, is composed of a parable with
some interpretations (cf. a similar phenomenon in 18:6ff.). Verse 1a is
a Lukan introduction; vss. 1b–8a give the parable; vs. 8b is one interpretative comment about the story; vs. 9 is a second interpretation;
vss. 10–12 are an elaboration of the second interpretation; vs. 13 is a
conclusion to the second interpretation and its elaboration (vss. 9–12).
These separate pieces are held together by a complex web of interlocking devices. Verse 8a reads, "The master commended the steward of
unrighteousness because he *acted shrewdly*" (*tēs adikias hoti phroni-
mōs epoiēsen*). Each of the italicized words serves as a link with what
follows: (1) vs. 8b says, "for the sons of this world are *shrewder*
(*phronimōteroi*) in their own generation than the sons of light"; (2)
vs. 9 tells the disciples, "*make (poiēsate*) friends for yourselves by means
of the mammon *of unrighteousness* (*tēs adikias*); furthermore, vs. 9's
reference to being received (*dexōntai*) into eternal habitations echoes
the being received (*dexōntai*) into the houses of earthly associates in
16:4); (3) vs. 10's "he who is dishonest (*adikos*) in a very little is dishonest (*adikos*) also in much" echoes the *adikias* (unrighteousness)
of vss. 8a, 9. In addition to these links with vs. 8a, there are other links
between later verses. Verse 11's unrighteous mammon (*adikō ma-
mōna*) ties it to vs. 9. The occurrence of "faithful" links vss. 10 and
12. Verses 11 and 12 are linked by a similar structure: "If you have
not been faithful . . . who . . .?" Verse 13 again uses mammon. By

means of such links the evangelist has constructed a unit from diverse materials in vss. 1–13. He issues a call for Jesus' disciples to be wise in their use of wealth and gives reasons why such wisdom is desirable.

The Lukan call for a wise use of wealth by disciples is located in the parable of the steward (vss. 1b–8a) and its first interpretation (vs. 8b). The parable has provoked much controversy, often unnecessarily. The story is about a man who, when confronted with a crisis, acted shrewdly (cf. 12:57–59). Caught in the act of wasting his master's goods, the steward received notice of the termination of his job. Not strong enough to do manual work and too proud to beg, with prospects of future employment virtually nil, the steward acted to guarantee his future. How? There are two possible ways of reading the remainder of the story that are worthy of attention. (1) Some say that as an agent, he was entitled to a commission. Seeing he was to be dismissed, he decided to forego his commission in order to get the people who would benefit to reciprocate (cf. 6:32) and receive him into their houses when he was unemployed (vs. 4). In this act there was no dishonesty, only prudence to prepare for the future. (2) Others claim the key to the situation is that no one yet knows the steward has been fired. He summons the debtors who therefore assume the entire bill-changing is legitimate. They assume the master authorized the reductions in what they owed and that the steward talked him into it. The steward then delivered the changed accounts to his master. The master looked at them and reflected on his alternatives. Either he could go to the debtors and explain—in which case he would be cursed—or he could be silent, accept the debtors' praise, and allow the clever steward to ride high on the wave of popular enthusiasm. He chose the latter course of action and said to the steward, "You are a wise fellow." Either way the steward acted to guarantee his future by means of his use of the wealth under his control. When the master (the rich man, not Jesus) commended the steward's shrewdness, it was no praise of his original waste. It was rather an acknowledgment that the steward's subsequent actions had wisely guaranteed his future. The first interpretation of the parable (vs. 8b) notes that non-Christians are shrewder in their use of money than are disciples. That is, they, like the dishonest steward, use it to guarantee their future. This serves as a call for disciples of Jesus to act as wisely in their use of the wealth under their control.

What would constitute a wise use of wealth by disciples? Verse 9 explains what is implied in vs. 8b. If a dishonest manager could pro-

vide for his future by a shrewd use of possessions, how much more should the sons of light, by giving alms (unrighteous mammon means worldly wealth, not possessions acquired dishonestly), provide for their future in heaven ("they" is a circumlocution for God; cf. *Mishna,* Yoma 8:9— "He who says, 'I will sin and repent, and sin again and repent,' to him give they no opportunity to repent."). Wise use of money will gain one's welcome in heaven ("eternal habitations"—cf. 1 Enoch 39:4; 2 Esdr 2:11). Verses 10–12 elaborate on this. If disciples have not been faithful in their use of earthly wealth which is on loan from God (*Pirke Abot* III:7), how can they be trusted with the true riches of eternal life? This is one of the few places in the NT where the idea of stewardship is applied to material possessions.

Why is disciples' use of wealth tied to their future in heaven? Verse 13 tells us plainly: One's use of wealth points to whom one serves. Jesus says, "You cannot serve God and mammon." Given this, Christians need to answer the call to manifest a shrewdness in the use of wealth under their control. Affluence in the hands of disciples is to be used sacramentally as a means of expressing love, both to God and to other people who have needs. The church in Acts embodies a proper response to Jesus' call. There was first a spontaneous (Acts 2:44–45; 4:32, 34ff.) and then an organized (Acts 6:1ff.) sharing of wealth within the community to meet needs. Sharing was carried on between congregations some distance from one another (Acts 11:27ff.). This Lukan spirit reflects that of the early church fathers generally. Justin Martyr (*Apology* I, 67) says,

> And they who are well to do, and willing, give what each thinks fit; and what is collected is deposited with the president, who succours the orphans and widows, and those who, through sickness or any other cause, are in want, and those who are in bonds, and the strangers sojourning among us, and in a word, takes care of all who are in need.

Tertullian (*Apology* 39:10) says, "We do not hesitate to share our earthly goods with one another. All things are common among us but our wives." A shrewd use of wealth by disciples would be to use it for meeting the needs of others. Such use signals an end to the worship of money and the existence of one's service of God. It also opens the door to a warm reception by God in heaven.

The second part, 16:14–31, is addressed to the Pharisees (vss. 14–

15), those who held that possession of wealth points to the one whom God loves. The section, which is an attack on the Pharisaic assumptions about wealth, is organized into a two-pronged group of sayings (vss. 14–18), followed by a double-edged parable (vss. 19–31). Verses 19–26 of the parable are an exposition of vss. 14–15, while vss. 27–31 serve as an illustration of vss. 16–18 (E. E. Ellis, *The Gospel of Luke*, p. 201, following a hint by John Calvin). This pattern gives unity to the section.

The first of the double-pronged group of sayings, vss. 14–15, makes two points. (1) Verses 14–15a emphasize that it is not the outer appearance of righteousness and its rewards that counts but what God sees in the heart. The Pharisees scoff at Jesus' statement, "You cannot serve God and mammon" (vs. 13). Given their assumptions, this was predictable. For them tragedy is a sign of God's displeasure; success (e.g., financial prosperity) is evidence of one's righteousness and of God's pleasure. It is no wonder they scoffed at Jesus' "either God or money" stance (cf. 18:24–26 where the disciples, after being told of the difficulty of a rich man's being saved, ask, "Then who can be saved?"). Money for them was a sign, a sure sign, of God's favor and of their place in the kingdom. Their position had roots in their scriptures (e.g., Deut 28:12–13 where wealth and plenty are a sign of God's blessings). Jesus' response to their scoffing was to contrast their outer-public appearance with their inner-private reality (cf. 11:39–41; 18:9–14). (2) In their inner selves they were exalted (that is, self-sufficient, independent of God). This is a stance God hates (vs. 15b). Jesus was speaking out of another strand of OT thought which saw the poor as symbolic of total dependence upon God and the rich as symbolic of independent self-sufficiency. These rich ones oppressed their poor brethren and thereby violated the covenant (Amos 8:4–6), instead of giving alms (Deut 15:11). Jesus' point, therefore, is that prosperity is an ambiguous sign—only a knowledge of the heart can tell for sure whether or not one is righteous.

The first part of the parable of the rich man and Lazarus (vss. 19–25; 26 is a transition) amplifies the two themes of vss. 14–15. (1) The first is that wealth is not necessarily a sign of righteousness. In the parable the rich man who was clothed in purple and fine linen and who feasted sumptuously every day is an example of the misuse of wealth. He neglected the law relating to the poor. Deut 15:4 says there should be no poor person in Israel's midst. So generosity toward the

poor was counted as righteousness (Prov 11:23–24; 21:26; 29:7). It was regarded as a good thing to help the poor and weak through kindness (Prov 14:31; 17:5), loans (Prov 19:17), and liberality (Prov 11:25; 21:26). In Sifre Deuteronomy 116–18, we find a rabbinic commentary on Deut 15:7–11. From vs. 9 of Deuteronomy 15 the lesson is drawn: "Be careful not to refuse charity, for every one who refuses charity is put [by the text] in the same category with idolaters, and he breaks off from him the yoke of Heaven, as it is said, *wicked*, that is, without *yoke*." In the mainline Jewish tradition it was believed one should not withhold needed relief for the poor. In this parable, however, Lazarus received only the leftovers from the table that fell on the ground—what the dogs ate—and was not the object of any significant charity. The rich man, then, was definitely not righteous (cf. 1 John 3:17).

If wealth is no guarantee of one's righteousness, then poverty is no proof of another's evil. This is the only parable of Jesus that names a character. The name, Lazarus (he whom God helps), is symbolic of the beggar's piety. Moreover, ritual uncleanness is no evidence against piety (the unclean dogs who licked his sores rendered him unclean, from a Pharisaic perspective—cf. Luke 10:29–37; Acts 10). A parable that portrayed its hero as an unclean beggar must have been as startling to Pharisaic assumptions (clean plus rich equals righteous) as one that depicted a Samaritan as hero. The first part of the parable, then, illustrates the initial theme of vss. 14–15—prosperity is an ambiguous sign.

(2) The first part of the parable also elaborates the second point of vss. 14–15: God who looks on the heart regards anyone who is proud-exalted as an abomination. The rich man accordingly ended in torment, crying for Abraham to send Lazarus to dip the end of his finger in water to cool his tongue since he was in anguish in the flame. The proud rich man who demonstrated no charity to the poor in this life finds his status reversed in the next. The Lukan God is the opponent of the exalted (self-sufficient who are insensitive to the needs of the poor). Luke 16:19–25 says plainly that the failure to use one's wealth on behalf of the poor in this life leads to torment in the afterlife. The first half of the parable of the rich man and Lazarus, then, illustrates both themes of vss. 14–15.

The second of the group of sayings, vss. 16–18, likewise makes two points. (1) Verse 16 speaks of the inclusiveness of the kingdom. A very different version of the saying is found in Matt 11:12–13. The Lukan

version says that since John the Baptist the kingdom of God has been proclaimed as good news (cf. 4:18; Acts 1:21–22). Two possible consequences of this are worth our attention. (a) Is it that everyone (*pas*— cf. 3:6; 4:25–27; 7:1–10; 8:26ff.) is pressing hard (*biazetai* taken as middle voice means "to overpower by force, to press hard, to act with violence") into it? (b) Or is it that "everyone is expressly invited to come in" (*biazomai* taken as passive voice with the meaning found in the LXX—e.g., Gen 33:11—means "to be begged earnestly, to be urged")? Either way, in the Lukan context the emphasis is on the universality of the kingdom's outreach and the option for everyone to enter it (cf. Acts 13:48; 28:28). (2) Verse 17 (cf. Matt 5:18) affirms the continuing validity of the law (cf. Acts 20:27–28). In this context doubtless the evangelist is thinking of the law that teaches about the care of the poor. One should remember that in the OT laws relating to the care of the poor dealt not only with an individual's giving alms or assistance but also with structural provision for the poor within society at large (e.g., Leviticus 25 equalizes land ownership every fifty years; Deuteronomy 15 gives Hebrew slaves their freedom in the sabbatical year; Ruth 2 indicates the law of gleaning was designed to prevent debilitating poverty among the people of God and the sojourners in the land).

The second part of the parable (vss. 27–31) amplifies the two themes of vss. 16–18. (1) The first theme is that there is a universality in the kingdom's composition. Everyone enters it. This is certainly illustrated by the story of the unclean beggar Lazarus. Who, in this life, would have thought he, of all people, would end in Abraham's bosom and be asked to go to warn the rich man's brothers of their fate? If Lazarus succeeded, the kingdom is certainly inclusive. (2) The second theme is that the law is still in force, in particular that law dealing with the treatment of the poor. In the parable, when the rich man asks father Abraham to send Lazarus to warn his five rich brothers of their destiny unless they change, Abraham answers, "They have Moses and the prophets; let them hear them" (vs. 29). If the law and the prophets do not call the rich to repentance, then even if someone goes to them from the dead it will make no difference. They will not repent. Once again the parable serves to illustrate themes set forth earlier in the chapter (vss. 16–18). Since in double-edged parables the second part receives the emphasis, the evangelist wants to accent the point about

the continuing validity of the law and its teaching on the use of wealth on behalf of the poor.

In Luke 16 the evangelist issues a call and gives a warning. On the one side, he calls for disciples to be as wise as the steward in their use of wealth to guarantee their future. On the other side, he warns that one not assume wealth to be so much a guarantee of one's being approved by God that one neglects the less fortunate, failing to follow the guidance of Moses and the prophets, and thus finds oneself cast out.

THE POSSIBILITY
OF AN IMPOSSIBLE DEMAND

17:1–10

L uke 17:1–10 is a small collection of four independent sayings of Jesus directed to disciples: (1) 17:1–2 (Matt 18:6–7; cf. Mark 9:42); (2) 17:3–4 (Matt 18:15, 21–22); (3) 17:5–6 (Matt 17:20); and (4) 17:7–10 (only in Luke). The collection focuses on two questions: (a) What are disciples called to do? and (b) Are they able to do it? The first two sayings (vss. 1–2, 3–4) answer the initial question, the second two logia (vss. 5–6, 7–10) respond to the latter query.

What does Jesus expect of his disciples in their life together? The answer is given in the first two sayings, which are tied together by their common focus on sin. The first, vss. 1–2, deals with one's offences against others; the second, vss. 3–4, is focused on another's offences, either generally (vs. 3) or against one specifically (vs. 4). (1) Verses 1–2 are a woe pronounced on disciples who cause one of the little ones to stumble (cf. 1 Cor 8:9ff.; 10:32; Rom 14:13–21; 1 John 2:10; Rev 2:14). The issue is Christian influence. That we find material about the perils of influence here, in Matthew 18, in two letters of Paul, in 1 John, and in the Apocalypse indicates the issue was a serious one in early Christianity. Here Jesus holds his disciples responsible for their influence on weaker Christians. (2) Verses 3–4 are a call first to reproof and then to forgiveness of others who sin. Christians' reproof of one another derives from Christ's activity (Acts 10:15; cf. Rev 3:19), as does their forgiveness (Luke 23:34; 22:54–62 with 24:34). In Luke the twofold activity is to be part of the spontaneous life-style of the individual disciple, whereas in Matthew 18 it is a Christian duty ordained in a code of church discipline. Paul, in Acts 15:36–41, may embody reproof but it is unlikely the evangelist regarded him as incarnating forgiveness. The disciples of Jesus are called to a responsible use of their influence and to a limitless forgiveness of those who sin against them who then repent.

160

Are we able to do what is asked of us? The call to cause no little one to stumble and to forgive repentant sinners without limit is so demanding the apostles ask Jesus for more faith (cf. 11:1). Jesus' response is typically oriental in using a vivid and extreme image, which the RSV translates, "If you had faith as a grain of mustard seed, you could say to this sycamine tree [a black mulberry with an extensive root system], 'Be rooted up, and be planted in the sea,' and it would obey you" (vs. 6). The implication derived from this translation is that the apostles do not have faith, but if they had even a little bit it would work wonders. In the Greek text, however, the best reading is, "If you have faith [and the assumption is that you do], you could say to this sycamine tree, 'Be plucked up by the root' . . ." That is, since you have faith, even the minutest amount, the impossible is possible (Nigel Turner, *Grammatical Insights into the New Testament* [Edinburgh: T. & T. Clark, 1966], pp. 51–52). In the RSV translation the point is that if the apostles had the least bit of faith the impossible would be possible. In the second, and correct, reading the point is that the apostles have at least some faith, which is enough to do the impossible.

Further insight into the meaning of 17:6 comes from an examination of the parallels to this saying in Matt 17:20; 21:21 // Mark 11:22–23. These parallels occur in different contexts and have slightly different contents. (a) Matt 17:20 is part of the climax to the healing story that follows the transfiguration in all three synoptic gospels. Whereas Mark 9:29 says the disciples' failure was due to the fact that "this kind cannot be driven out by anything but prayer," and although Luke 9:37–43 does not even deal with the issue of the disciples' failure except by allusion (9:41), Matt 17:20 says the disciples failed "because of your little faith. For truly, I say to you, if you have faith as a grain of mustard seed, you will say to this mountain, 'Move hence to yonder place,' and it will move; and nothing will be impossible to you." (b) Matt 21:21 and Mark 11:22–23 have a similar saying in the context of the cursing of the fig tree. Matthew's connection is explicit. The disciples ask Jesus how the miracle happened. His response is, "Truly, I say to you, if you have faith and never doubt, you will not only do what has been done to the fig tree, but even if you say to this mountain, 'Be taken up and cast into the sea,' it will be done" (cf. Jas 1:6–8).

Luke's use is different from the two uses of the saying in Matthew and the one in Mark in two ways. First, Luke refers to a sycamine tree, not to a mountain. Second, the Lukan context uses the saying to

support the possibility of the disciples' moral behavior (17:1-4), whereas Matthew and Mark use it to explain the success of Jesus' miraculous activity and to promise such success to his disciples. In the case of all three synoptics and both forms of the saying, however, faith is associated with the manifestation of awesome power in the lives of Jesus' disciples, whether it be moral or miraculous.

In order to make sense of the saying, in whatever form, it is necessary to understand what is and what is not meant by faith. (a) It is important to note that "faith is not a magic by which we control God. . . . We cannot use it to back God into a corner and force him to produce a sensational show which will enable us to make the headlines" (Malcolm Tolbert, "Luke," *Broadman Bible Commentary* [Nashville: Broadman Press, 1969], 9:134). In magic one acts to gain control of the spiritual powers so they will do one's bidding. The NT, especially Paul, makes it clear that faith is always a person's response to God's initiative. In Luke 17:11-19, for example, the Samaritan who was healed saw God in the cure effected by Jesus and responded with thanksgiving and praise. Faith is always a human response. (b) It is also important to see faith as a response to God in the context of a relationship; it is personal response to personal initiative. Again, Paul and Luke 17:11-19 speak to this point.

If faith is a disciple's personal response to the personal initiative of God in relationship, then vs. 6 is intelligible in its context. God relates to the sinner with forgiveness (15:11-32). The disciple, a forgiven sinner to whom God has shown and is showing mercy, in faith responds with mercy and forgiveness to those who sin against the disciple (6:35-38; 11:4). In response to the apostles' request for more faith so they would be able to forgive unceasingly, Jesus says, You are living out of a response to God's initiative with you, however limited your response may be. Since God is constantly forgiving you, if you are responding in faith, forgiving without end, though it may seem impossible, is possible to you.

In the version of the logion found in Matthew and Mark, Jesus says that when God has taken the initiative to tell the disciple what God wants to do, an unwavering response of the disciple in that direction results in miracles. If, however, God does not take the initiative in a given situation, it is magic for the disciple to take the initiative and to try to force God's hand by his undoubting belief that God will do what the disciple tells God to do. Faith is not the coercion of God into action

by our believing that he will do our bidding. Rather it is the cooperation with God in the action, which, by his initiative, he has indicated that he wills to perform. For Luke such divine initiative was part of Christians' ongoing religious experience (cf. Acts 4:19–20, 31; 5:19–20, 29; 7:55–60; 8:26, 29; 10:9ff., 44–48; 11:15–17; 13:1–3; 16:6–10.).

The train of thought in 17:1–6 to this point has been: (1) if a disciple is never to cause another to stumble and is always to be forgiving, surely the disciple needs an increase in faith; (2) since the disciple is living out of the response to how God has and does treat him or her, this impossible demand is possible, even with the most minute amount of faith (the assumption is that God's gracious initiative is so generous that even a response to a part of it would result in wonderful behavior in human relationships). Luke believed those who live in faith were able to do what has been asked of them.

If disciples are able to do what is required, they are not able to do more than is required. This point is made in the parable of 17:7–10. Here we meet a man with only one slave, who was forced to do double duty. He worked both as a farm hand (plowing and keeping sheep) and as a domestic servant (preparing supper, serving). After a long day of work, the slave did not expect to be thanked by the master. He had simply done what he had been commanded to do. So, says Jesus, when the disciples "have done all that is commanded" (never being a stumbling block; forgiving unceasingly) they should recognize they have done no more than was commanded. No room is left here for any notion of moral superiority or merit. If, given the enormity of God's gracious initiative, there is even the slightest response of faith on the part of the disciples, the commandments are achievable. Nevertheless, no achievement is ever able to go beyond what is expected.

ESCHATOLOGY, FAITH, AND PROSPERITY

17:11—19:44 (A. 17:11—18:30)

L uke 17:11—19:44 is a long thought unit consisting of a mix of uniquely Lukan traditions together with materials having parallels elsewhere in the synoptic tradition. The pattern of this section is ABCD:A'B'C'D'. (1) 17:11 refers to the movement to Jerusalem; so does 18:31–34. (2) Each reference to the journey to the holy city is followed by a healing story (17:12–19; 18:35–43). The two healings are structurally similar: (a) "Jesus, have mercy" (17:13; 18:38); (b) "your faith has made you well" (17:19; 18:42); (c) give/gave praise to God (17:18, 15; 18:43). The first healing story is two pronged, the second half dealing with salvation; the second healing is followed by another story (19:1–10), related to it by the theme of salvation. (3) After the healings come two sections that deal with eschatology (17:20—18:8; 19:11–27). Both aim to protect against an over-realized eschatology; both focus on the parousia and on the necessary faithful posture of those who wait for the Lord's coming. (4) After these two sections are units that focus on the problem of human response to God. Luke 18:8b raises the problem with which 18:9–30 deals: "When the Son of Man comes, will he find faith on earth?" Luke 18:9–30 contains several traditions that illustrate what it means to be rightly related to God in the here and now. Similarly, 19:27 raises the problem with which 19:28–44 deals: "as for these enemies of mine who did not want me to reign over them. . . ." Two pericopes at 19:28–44 illustrate the rejection of Jesus by Israel. It would seem then that the evangelist has taken a variety of materials and has organized them into a coherent pattern in order to serve his own purposes.

The next section of this book will deal with 18:31—19:44. In this section we will focus on 17:11—18:30, in three stages: (1) 17:11–19; (2) 17:20—18:8; and (3) 18:9–30. Luke 17:11–19 deals with the relation between healing and salvation (Cf. H. D. Betz, "The Cleansing of

the Ten Lepers [Luke 17:11–19]," *Journal of Biblical Literature*
90:314–28 [1971]).

Luke 17:11–19 is a miracle story introduced (vs. 11) by the evangelist's location of the incident between Samaria and Galilee. This is
doubtless to make plausible the reference to the Samaritan in vs. 16.
Its local color is accurate: lepers grouped together (2 Kgs 7:3), avoided
physical contacts with other people (Lev 13:45f.; Num 5:2), but stayed
close to where people lived so they could receive charity. The unusual
feature of the story is that it is a two-part miracle story: vss. 11–14 tell
of the cleansing of ten lepers, while vss. 15–19 follow up the cleansing
of one of them, recounting the Samaritan's conversion. There is a prototype of such a two-part story about the healing and the conversion
of a leper in 2 Kings 5. Naaman the Syrian is healed as he goes and   −✓
washes seven times in the Jordan River in obedience to Elisha's command. When he sees he is healed, he returns to Elisha and confesses
his faith in the God of Israel. The OT story tells how a miracle of
healing is the occasion for the conversion of a foreigner. Luke 17:11–
19, likewise, narrates a miracle of Jesus which serves as a catalyst for
the conversion of the Samaritan. Verse 19 should be translated, "Rise
and go your way; your faith has saved you (*sesōken se*). "Saved" here
does not refer to physical cleansing only. The other nine were healed.
His salvation was linked to the Samaritan's both seeing the giver in
Jesus' gift of healing and responding appropriately. Since in such a
story the climax comes in the second part, Luke's emphasis is on the
faith of the Samaritan. The evangelist is concerned with the attitude
of the person who was cured. The mere experience of being healed
did not save. It was acknowledging what God had done through Jesus
("he fell on his face at Jesus' feet, giving him thanks"—vs. 16) that
enabled him to experience a salvation beyond the physical cure. Healing issues in salvation, Luke is saying, only when God's gracious initiative is recognized and when one's response to that initiative is faith
so that a relationship results.

The evangelist is also saying that often the most unlikely persons
recognize the divine approach and respond appropriately. The leper
who returned after his healing with praise to God and submission to
Jesus was a Samaritan; nine Jews made no such response. The faith
of foreigners is a Lukan concern (e.g., 7:9; 10:25–37; Acts 10–11), as
is the contrast between their faith (cf. Acts 26:16–18 where the Gentiles' eyes are opened) and the unbelief of Jews who are unable to see

God's work in Jesus (cf. Acts 28:26–27 where the Jews do not see). This story, then, foreshadows the rejection of the gospel by the Jews and its enthusiastic reception by foreigners which we see in the narrative of Acts and which was already established at the time Luke-Acts was written.

Luke 17:20—18:8 is a composite passage that deals with three problems of eschatology: (1) the attempt to calculate when the kingdom of God will come; (2) an over-realized eschatology; and (3) the doubt regarding an ultimate, cosmic settling of accounts by God.

The pronouncement story of vss. 20–21 functions as a rejection by Jesus of the attempt to say when the kingdom of God will come. The Pharisees raise the question. The initial part of Jesus' answer indicates that the question assumed the kingdom's coming would be preceded by certain signs. The answer expected would take the form, "The kingdom of God will come when you see such and such taking place." Jesus rejects this assumption, saying instead, "the kingdom of God is in the midst of you" ("within you" though linguistically possible seems inappropriate since Jesus is talking to Pharisees). Luke would understand this to refer to the presence of the Holy Spirit in Jesus' ministry (cf. 11:20; 4:18–19, 1; 3:22). Luke makes two points. (a) Although one may speak about the nearness of the kingdom (e.g., 10:9), it is illegitimate to try to calculate the time of the End (e.g., Acts 1:6–7). This is a rejection of apocalyptic speculation (the attempt to use historical events and natural disasters to determine a blueprint of what is going to happen and when). In his *City of God* (18:53), Augustine spoke to the point:

> In vain, then, do we attempt to compute definitely the years that may remain to this world, when we may hear from the mouth of the Truth (Jesus) that it is not for us to know. . . . But on this subject He puts aside the figures of the calculaters.

The Markan Jesus speaks the same way: "But of that day or that hour no one knows, not even the angels in heaven, nor the Son, but only the Father" (13:32). (b) The only signs of the kingdom proper to look for are those characteristic of the Spirit-empowered ministry of the earthly Jesus (e.g., 4:18–19).

The composite discourse (17:22–37) which follows the pronouncement story of vss. 20–21 functions as protection against an over-realized eschatology. The discourse is linked to the pronouncement story

both formally and logically. Formally, the "Lo, here," and "there" in 17:21 are echoed in "Lo, there," and "Lo, here," in 17:23. Logically, the link relates to the emphasis on the presence of the kingdom. Verses 20–21 speak of the kingdom being present in Jesus' ministry. In vss. 22–23 the disciples, desiring to experience the parousia ("one of the days of the Son of Man" is a Christianization of the Jewish "days of the Messiah" or OT "those days" or "latter days"—that is, the messianic or New Age), are told it is already present (they will say to you, "Lo, there!" or "Lo, here!"). The disciples are not to believe such claims. It would appear from this logical connection that vss. 22–37 are to interpret vss. 20–21 in a way that prevents their being read in terms of an over-realized eschatology. Apparently some in Luke's church were using vss. 20–21 to support the claim that it was possible to experience the eschaton in a secret way in the present. Verses 22–37 guard against such an interpretation by focusing on the nature, the time, and the place of the parousia.

When the disciples hear some say that the parousia is already present in a secret way, not obvious to all, they should not follow them (vss. 22–23). The parousia as an event will not be spatially restricted but will be universal and instantaneous (vs. 24). It will occur after Jesus' passion (vs. 25). It will occur at a time when people are preoccupied with the common ventures of life: eating, drinking, marrying, buying, selling, planting, building (vss. 26–27; 28–30). The proper attitude to have at the parousia is an absolute indifference to all worldly interests. There can be no looking back (vss. 31–33). When it comes the parousia will be a great divider (vss. 34–35). Jesus' response to the disciples' query about where the parousia will take place comes in vs. 37: "It is as senseless to ask for a map of what will happen as it is to ask for a timetable: just as the location of a corpse in the wilderness is obvious from the crowd of circling vultures, so the Son of Man will appear for judgment in an unmistakable manner, and there will be no need to ask where he is" (I. H. Marshall, *The Gospel of Luke*, p. 656).

The evangelist has used an eschatological collection that focuses on the parousia of the Son of Man to prevent an interpretation of vss. 20–21 in terms of an over-realized eschatology. The presence of the kingdom (the Holy Spirit in this instance) in the ministry of Jesus cannot be used to legitimate Christian claims that the parousia has already occurred. The parousia is a future event, cosmic in scope.

The problem of an over-realized eschatology was widespread in early

Christianity. Outside the NT we read of it in numerous sources. (a) Irenaeus, in speaking of those who belong to Simon and Carpocrates, says they hold "that the resurrection from the dead is simply an acquaintance with the truth which they proclaim" (*Against Heresies,* 2:31:2). (b) Irenaeus also says Menander claims that "his disciples obtain the resurrection by being baptized into him" (*Against Heresies,* 1:23:5). (c) Hippolytus reports the Naassenes think that "being born again spiritual" is the resurrection (*Refutation of all Heresies,* 5:3). (d) Hippolytus also claims that the Italian wing of the Valentinians— Heracleon and Ptolemaeus—held a similar position. They regarded the baptism of Jesus as the moment of his resurrection and, correspondingly, the baptism of Christians as the time of their resurrection (*Refutation,* 6:30). (e) In the Gospel of Thomas from Nag Hammadi, in logion 51, the disciples ask Jesus, "When will the new world come?" Jesus answers "What you expect has come, but you know it not." (f) In another Coptic document, *De Resurrectione,* we read, "already you have the resurrection." (g) The Gospel of Philip 121:1–5 says, "Those who say 'They will die first and rise again' are in error. If they do not first receive the resurrection while they live, when they die they will receive nothing." Within the NT a similar problem is echoed in various places. (a) 2 Tim 2:17b–18 is the most explicit statement of the problem: "Among them are Hymenaeus and Philetus, who have swerved from the truth by holding that the resurrection is past already." (b) 1 Cor 4:8 (cf. 15:12ff.) echoes the same view. (c) The same stance is warned against in Phil 3:12–15 (cf. vss. 11, 12, 20) and 2 Thessalonians 2 (cf. vs. 2). The problem with which Luke struggles was widespread in the early church.

The evangelist's response to such an over-realized eschatology is to say first that certain stages or events precede the End, and second that the parousia has a nature different from the experience claimed in the present. A similar response can be found in Tertullian's *On the Resurrection of the Flesh,* 19, and in 1 Cor 15:22ff., Phil 3:12ff., and 2 Thes 2:1ff.

Luke here attempts to prevent a misunderstanding of the experience of the Holy Spirit as the experience of the eschaton. Wherever the experience of the Spirit was identified as the experience of the parousia in early Christianity serious problems resulted: for example, (1) a perfectionism that claimed it was possible for Christians to live sinless lives (1 John 1:8, 10); (2) a spirituality that believed Christians had

transcended their sexuality (1 Cor 7; 11:2–16); (3) a triumphalism that regarded Christian experience as beyond persecution, deprivation, sickness, and weakness (1 Cor 4:8–13; 2 Cor 12:1–10). In the generation before Luke, Paul had stood against such an over-realized eschatology. For the apostle the Christian faith involved the believer in sharing Christ's sufferings as well as his resurrection life (Rom 8:17; 2 Cor 1:5; 4:10; Phil 3:10f.; Col 1:24). The experience of the Spirit for him was an experience of power in weakness (2 Cor 4:7; 12:9ff.; 13:3f.), not of power that transcended and left behind the limitations of this present existence. Luke shares Paul's understanding. Although Luke is especially concerned to emphasize the experience of the power of the Holy Spirit in the lives of Jesus and his followers, it is power experienced within the bounds of this age (cf. 4:18 with 9:21, 44; cf. Acts 2 with 14:22). For Luke, as for Paul, there is a "now" and a "not yet" to Christian existence in the world.

Luke 18:1–8 functions as an exhortation not to lose heart. This pericope is an expansion of the eschatological discourse begun at 17:20: (a) 18:1 indicates that the disciples are still being addressed, and (b) the reference to the Son of Man's coming (18:8) echoes 17:22, 24, 26, 30. Here we confront the problem of doubt about whether the parousia will ever take place and the behavior that such doubt induces (cf. 12:45–46; 2 Pet 3:4ff.; 1 Clem 23:3—24:1; 2 Clem 11:1–7). Is the Son of Man really coming? After all this time can we really believe God will vindicate his people? We have been praying "Thy Kingdom come" for years and nothing has happened. The parable in 18:1–8 was told, says Luke (vs. 1), to encourage the disciples to pray and not lose heart (cf. 21:36). As it stands in its context, the story functions as an encouragement to Christians not to give up hope for the parousia but rather to go on praying "Thy Kingdom come." If a corrupt judge, unconcerned about human need and divine law, would grant an insistent widow justice merely to get rid of her, how much more will God, the righteous judge, speedily vindicate his elect when they cry to him. Pray for the parousia because God is faithful and will vindicate his people.

The pericope also raises a question about those who are plagued with doubt. Will disciples remain faithful until the End (cf. Heb 6:11–12; 10:36–39; 2 Pet 3:11–14; Rev 21:7)? The introduction to the parable (vs. 1) tells how faith is maintained. One does not lose heart because one prays. The maintenance of faith depends on persistence in prayer. This is so because "in prayer we enter into the realm of reality

and see things as they really are, from God's point of view"
(H. A. Williams, *The Simplicity of Prayer* [Philadelphia: Fortress, 1977],
p. 69). "The less we pray, the less we experience life in the Christian
way. We move into another mental world" (J. Neville Ward, *The Use
of Praying* [New York: Oxford University, 1977], p. 141). Hence the
Lukan directive: always pray (cf. Phil 4:6–7).

Luke 18:9–30 is a composite unit that deals with the issue raised by
vs. 8b: "Nevertheless, when the Son of Man comes, will he find faith
on earth?" It illustrates appropriate and inappropriate responses to
God/Jesus in the period before the parousia and falls into two loosely
parallel parts, each part involving both the unmasking of unbelief in
an unlikely situation and the identification of faith in an improbable
person(s).

(1) Luke 18:9–17, the first part, consists of a parable (vss. 9–14)
and a story that illustrates a point of the parable (vss. 15–17). The
parable sets before us two men praying in the temple, a Pharisee (vss.
11–12) and a tax collector (vs. 13). The Pharisee belonged to the most
liberal, pious, and dedicated of Judaism's sects in the first century.
This individual, moreover, went beyond even what was required of a
Pharisee. He fasted twice a week and tithed all that he bought. His
prayer follows Jewish liturgy (cf. Ps 17:3–5). He recognized God as
the source of his lot in life (a point missed by the editorial introduction
of 18:9). He thanks God and does not ask for anything. What fault can
possibly be found with this man or his prayer? He represents the best
in the religion of his time.

The tax collector, on the other hand, was among the most despised
of all of Palestine's inhabitants because of his dishonesty, his disloyalty
to the Jewish people, and his uncleanness (of which his stance shows
he was aware). This individual's prayer also follows Jewish liturgy (cf.
Psalm 51). It is an outburst of despair, a petition for mercy. His situation is indeed hopeless. If he repented, he had to make restitution plus
one-fifth. If he ended his defilement, he lost his livelihood and earned
Roman hostility. This man represents the worst of his times. What
could possibly be right about him? Yet Jesus said, "I tell you, this man
went down to his house justified ("forgiven"—cf. 2 Esdr 12:7 where
"justified" is synonymous with "to be heard in prayer") rather than the
other" (vs. 14a).

The story fits into the general theme of status reversal in the third
gospel. The New Age will overturn the values and structures of the

present evil age. We meet this theme in the birth narratives (1:51–53) and in the Sermon on the Plain (6:20–26). In the travel narrative (9:51—19:44) Jesus' teaching anticipates this eschatological reversal even now in overturning the estimate of what is virtue and what is vice. Consider 10:29–37 (good Samaritan/bad priest and levite); 10:38–42 (good inactive Mary/bad active Martha); 11:37–41 (good unclean/bad clean); 12:13–34 (good poor/bad rich); 14:7–11 (good humble/bad exalted); 15:11–32 (good prodigal/bad elder brother); 16:19–31 (good Lazarus/bad rich man); 18:18–30 (good poor/bad rich). Into this thematic context 18:9–14 fits (good tax collector/ bad Pharisee) as another example of Jesus' reversal of values. How can it be? What is wrong with so obviously good a man as the Pharisee? What can be right about so obviously perverse a person as the publican?

The parable functions first of all as the unmasking of unbelief in an unlikely situation. The introduction (vs. 9) exposes the problem. The parable is told to those who (a) trusted in themselves that they were righteous (self-assured piety) and (b) despised others (spiritual condescension). Such a stance is described by the conclusion (vs. 14) as exalting oneself. This was the plight of the Pharisee. He was self-assured about his righteousness (vs. 12), condescending about his superiority to others (vs. 11). He trusted in what he had done and not done and was proud of who he was. It is such a person whom God humbles.

The Pharisee's posture is unmasked as idolatry. He was usurping the prerogatives of God, which is how the devil acts. To judge is God's prerogative (cf. 1 Cor 4:5), not ours. Proper thanks to God for one's lot in life never involves condescension toward others. Salvation by grace means one can never feel religiously superior to another. Faith never expresses itself as despising others. Spiritual arrogance is presumption, assuming that one stands in God's place, able to judge. It is this exaltation of oneself that God overturns.

The parable functions secondly as the identification of faith in an improbable person. It was the despicable tax collector whose prayer was answered. Why? (a) He trusted not in who he was but in who God was (merciful). (b) He hoped not in what he had but in what he might receive (forgiveness). This stance the conclusion describes as humility (vs. 14).

The same point is made in the very next pericope, 18:15–17. Whereas Mark 9:40 uses this same material as part of a series of traditions giv-

ing teachings about marriage, children, and possessions, Luke uses it as part of a unit describing what is involved in becoming a disciple and being found faithful when the Son of Man comes. Receiving the kingdom of God in a childlike manner in this context refers to humility (cf. Jas 4:6–10; 1 Pet 5:6–10 where humility means submission to God).

If you think God is one who delights in the spiritually superior, then God is not who you think he is. If you think God shuns the despicable sinner who has no one else to turn to, then God is not who you think he is. Why is this so? With the "I tell you" of vs. 14a, Jesus claims to know God's judgments and dares to say what God is like and how he acts. He claims to know the mind of God.

(2) Luke 18:18–30, the second part of vss. 9–30, consists of a recognition story (vss. 18–23) and a dialogue between Jesus and his disciples (vss. 24–30). The two components give an example of one who was exalted before God and of some who were humbled before him. The recognition story (a narrative in which a person recognizes something about himself he did not know before) unmasks the ruler's unbelief. A ruler inquires of Jesus about what style of life would place him among the people of God who will inherit the New Age. Following the spirit of Deut 30:15–20, Jesus refers to the commandments. When the ruler professes to have kept them since childhood, Jesus says, "One thing you still lack. Sell all that you have and distribute to the poor, and you will have treasure in heaven; and come, follow me" (vs. 22). From this the ruler learned something about himself he did not formerly know. He learned he was an idolater. Though he attempted to worship God and mammon at the same time, when the test was put to him he saw that his wealth was really his god. "Jesus always requires from one just that earthly security upon which one would lean" (E. E. Ellis, *The Gospel of Luke*, p. 217). He did not really keep the first and greatest commandment so his lack of faith was exposed. Jesus' response was that it would be impossible for a rich man to enter the kingdom were it not for God's grace (vss. 24–27).

The dialogue between Jesus and his auditors (vss. 24–30) identifies as faith a life detached from idolatrous relationships and attached to Jesus. Peter says the disciples have fulfilled the calling the ruler refused: "Lo, we have left our homes and followed you" (vs. 28; cf. 5:11, 28). It is this detachment from everything and every relationship for the sake of the kingdom that constitutes the humility (submission to

God) the Son of Man at his parousia recognizes as faith (cf. 9:57–62; 14:25–33). The one who has left family for the sake of the kingdom will receive more back in this life (vs. 30), perhaps a reference to the new family in the church. The principle is that one gives everything to God and then receives back from him what he wants to give. Luke, unlike Mark 10:30 and Matt 19:29, does not promise wealth but only community ("house" in vs. 29 refers to family; "wife, brothers, parents, children" to the various parts of the family). The evangelist does not connect prosperity with piety in any kind of necessary cause and effect relationship (cf. Acts 11:27–30; 24:17). For him the pious are often poor (Luke 2:24; 14:21; 16:19ff.). This raises the issue of the larger biblical perspective about wealth and poverty.

There is a variety of attitudes towards wealth and poverty in the OT. (a) In some circles affluence was connected with righteousness and poverty with wickedness: for example, in the Deuteronomic theology (Deut 28:12ff.; 8:7–10; 26:1–9) and in some Wisdom circles (Prov 6:6–11; 10:4; 28:19). (b) In other circles affluence was associated with evil, while the poor could be regarded as the righteous whom God vindicates: for example, in the prophetic writings (Amos 8:4ff.; Mic 2:1–5; Jer 5:28) and in some Wisdom circles (Prov 28:6; Sir 10:21–23). (c) In still other circles the ideal was neither poverty nor wealth—because each was subject to perversion—but for just enough to meet one's needs (Prov 30:7–9). There is, then, no one viewpoint.

There is a neutral attitude towards wealth and possessions in the NT: neither prosperity nor poverty is a value. This stance is intelligible given its theological context. Though affluence was God's intention in creation (that is, apart from sin, cf. the garden of Eden) and is his intention in the New Age beyond the resurrection (cf. Matt 8:11–12, or any description of the messianic banquet), in the present time affluence and poverty are both affected by the fallenness of the creation. God's objective is now first and foremost to free his creation from its sin (idolatry and injustice). Hence there is no guarantee of affluence to a believer in this life. (3 John 2 does not refer to financial prosperity any more than John 10:10 does. Mark 10:29–30 probably refers to what is available to the Christian from the resources of the Christian community. Paul speaks in Phil 4:10–13 of poverty and plenty as matters of indifference.) Rather God uses poverty and plenty for his ends and our good (that is, ultimate salvation—Rom 8:28). If it takes a miracle of abundance to communicate with us, he will do it; if it takes a bare

subsistence to heal us of some imperfection, he will see to it; if he sees we can handle plenty, then it is his will we share with the less fortunate. In the NT, then, there are two main concerns regarding possessions: first, that the individual's heart be right, that there be no idolatrous attachments to things; second, that the structures of life in the community of faith reflect the values of the faith. At no point does the NT claim prosperity is guaranteed to believers in the here and now—that would be to fall into an over-realized eschatology.

ON BEING PART
OF THE PEOPLE OF GOD

17:11—19:44 (B. 18:31—19:44)

L uke 18:31—19:44 is the second part of a balanced longer section that begins at 17:11. Each part begins with a reference to Jesus' movement towards Jerusalem, followed by a healing story, then an eschatological section, and finally a passage focusing on the problem of the human responses to God.

After the notice of Jesus' movement towards Jerusalem (18:31-34), are two stories (18:35-43; 19:1-10) connected with Jericho (18:35; 19:1), dealing with the salvation Jesus brings (18:42—sesōken se, it has saved you; 19:9–sōtēria, salvation), which focus on the importance of the human response in the appropriation of Jesus' gifts (18:43; 19:8). The two stories function as paradigms of what conversion entails. The first, 18:35-43, has parallels in the synoptic tradition in Matt 20:29-34 (two blind men) and Mark 10:46-52 (blind Bartemaeus). Common to all three versions is the request of the blind one(s): "Son of David, have mercy on me/us," and "Let me/us receive my/our sight." This is what is desired from Jesus. Jesus answers this request by healing the blindness. The healing evidently opened the door to a perception of yet another problem because, as a result of the healing, he/they followed Jesus. Here Jesus' answer to one question on one level led to awareness of another issue on another level to which Jesus also could supply a solution. Jesus took him/them where he was/they were, and brought him/them to where he/they needed to be. The crucial difference between Luke's version of the story and that of Matthew and Mark comes at 18:43 // Matt 20:34 // Mark 10:52. Matthew reads, "and immediately they received their sight and followed him." Mark reads, "And immediately he received his sight and followed him on the way." Luke reads, "And immediately he received his sight and followed him, glorifying God." This Lukan distinction is similar to the reaction of the cleansed leper in 17:15, 18 (cf. 7:16). The human response to the

175

healing and to conversion is vertical, that is, praise to God (cf. 7:36–50). The meeting of a physical need led to a spiritual conversion and produced an outpouring of praise. Here is one paradigm of conversion then and now.

The second paradigm of what conversion entails is found in 19:1–10. This is a conflict story (Jesus' act, vss. 1–6, meets with criticism, vs. 7, to which Jesus responds, vss. 9–10) which has many similarities to the narrative of the call of Levi in Luke 5 (in both Jesus is going somewhere; there is a tax collector; Jesus issues an invitation; a positive response is given; Jesus then enters the tax collector's house; an objection is brought; Jesus responds, justifying his behavior; an "I came" saying is appended). Verse 8, on first reading, presents a problem. It interrrupts the sequence between vs. 7 where the people murmur because "he has gone in to be the guest of a man who is a sinner," and vs. 9b where Jesus responds (to the people about Zacchaeus): "Today salvation has come to this house, since he also is a son of Abraham." Verse 8, further, seems characteristically Lukan: "Lord" and "repentance" (cf. 5:32). It appears the evangelist added vs. 8 to a story from the tradition. The story originally told of table fellowship between Jesus and Zacchaeus in which Zacchaeus' joyful reception of Jesus signaled his being a son of Abraham (cf. 7:36–50). By the addition of vs. 8, the evangelist spelled out the appropriate response to the grace Jesus brought to this rich tax collector through their table fellowship. It was a horizontal one. Zacchaeus said, "Behold Lord, the half of my goods I give to the poor; and if I have defrauded any one at anything, I restore it fourfold." In the OT, when a defrauder confessed and made a voluntary restitution, the amount stolen plus a fifth was sufficient (Lev 6:5; Num 5:7). When a man was compelled to make reparation for a deliberate act of robbery, if the animal was alive he must pay double, but if dead or sold he must pay fourfold or fivefold (Exod 22:1, 3b–4; 2 Sam 12:6). Zacchaeus was willing to treat his wrong acts as belonging to the latter category. This action demonstrated a new attitude toward wealth. What was impossible with man had become possible with God (18:27). In vs. 9 Jesus pronounces the reality of salvation in Zacchaeus' life as demonstrated by the tax collector's response in vs. 8 (cf. 7:36–50). He really was what his name said he was, a righteous or pure one.

If one remembers that the traditions about the historical Jesus have been shaped by the church's experience with the risen Lord, it will

enable one to read this edited conflict story in a new way as a paradigm of what conversion entails. (a) The pericope shows how Jesus draws a person (vss. 1–4): "The Lord often . . . inspires in men a blind feeling which brings them to Him although He is still hidden and unknown. . . . He does not disappoint them but in time reveals Himself to them" (*Calvin's Commentaries: A Harmony of the Gospels,* trans. T. H. L. Parker [Grand Rapids: Eerdmans, 1972], 2:281). There was something about Jesus that drew Zacchaeus to climb the sycamore for a glimpse of one who was as yet unknown.

(b) The story also says Jesus comes in to a person (vss. 5–7). The risen Christ in Rev 3:20 verbalizes the reality: "Behold, I stand at the door and knock; if anyone hears my voice and opens the door, I will come in to him and eat with him, and he with me." The language of indwelling is widespread in Paul (e.g., Gal 2:20; Col 1:27) and the fourth gospel (e.g., 14:23; 15:5). When Jesus came into the sinner Zacchaeus' house, he brought forgiveness.

(c) The passage, in addition, says Jesus confirms the person (vss. 8–9), giving assurance of the reality of what has transpired in the secret of the human soul. This assurance rests on two things: a transformed life (vs. 8) and the witness of Jesus (vs. 9). The author of 1 John says he wrote "that you may know that you have eternal life" (5:13). He appeals to the same two bases. On the one hand, there is the evidence of a transformed life: "we know we have passed out of death into life, because we love the brethren" (3:14; cf. 4:12b). On the other hand, there is the inner witness: "By this we know that we abide in him and he in us, because he has given us his own Spirit" (4:13; cf. 3:24b; cf. Rom 8:15–17; 2 Cor 1:22). The third evangelist, in this story of the earthly Jesus, is echoing the same postresurrection reality. Here is a second paradigm of what conversion entails.

Luke 19:11–27 consists of at least three components: (1) vss. 11–12a (through "He said therefore") which are Lukan transitional and introductory material; (2) a parable about a man going away and leaving his affairs in the hands of three servants (// Matt. 25:14–30); and (3) a political parable in vss. 12, 14, 15a, 27, and possibly with fragments in 17b and 19b (F. D. Weinart, "The Parable of the Throne Claimant [Luke 19:12, 14–15a, 27] Reconsidered," *Catholic Biblical Quarterly,* 39:505–14 [1977]). These components are joined together into an allegory of salvation history, making three points.

(1) Here, as in 17:22ff., the evangelist wants to protect against an

over-realized eschatology. The introduction indicates that "because he was near to Jerusalem, they supposed that the kingdom of God was to appear immediately." The allegory which follows says the End is not yet. First Jesus goes away to receive kingly power (cf. Acts 1:11; 2:36); later he will return (cf. Acts 3:20–21). Why would Luke stress a point obvious to his readers after Easter? If one views 19:11 as a reflection of problems in Luke's church, then it may be that some disciples were regarding the events in Jerusalem (Jesus' resurrection and ascension) as the parousia. In response the evangelist is saying, "not yet." There is a difference between the resurrection/ascension and the parousia (and, by inference, between one's dying and rising with Christ on the one hand, and one's resurrection on the other).

(2) The major focus of the allegory is on the accountability of the three servants upon the nobleman's return (vss. 15b–26). Here Luke is addressing the question, what is the responsibility of Jesus' servants in the interim between the ascension and the parousia (cf. 12:35–48)? They are expected to be faithful to their commission. Faithful servants are those who are productive, who make the most of what they have been given. They will receive a reward. Not everyone has the same resources with which to work: that difference is taken into account. The unproductive servant, however, will be punished. Luke, though, has nothing like Matt 25:30: "And cast the worthless servant into the outer darkness; there men will weep and gnash their teeth." Like Paul in 1 Cor 3:10–15, the third evangelist seems to think the unfaithful servant's work will be burned up, but "he himself will be saved." The judgment at the parousia for disciples will focus not on whether they make it into the kingdom but whether or not they receive a commendation and reward.

(3) Though Luke does not discuss the ultimate punishment of the third servant, he does speak about the destiny of those who refused to have the nobleman reign over them (vss. 14, 27). It is probable that in vs. 14 the story is making use of contemporary events. In 4 B.C. Archelaus went to Rome to obtain the kingdom which his father, Herod the Great, had left him. The Jews revolted and sent an embassy of fifty to oppose him at Rome (Josephus, *Antiquities,* 17:8:1 § 188; 17:9:3 § 222; 17:11:4 § 317; *War,* 2:6:1, 3 § 80, 93). Luke's allegory uses these current events to speak about the Jewish (and unbelieving Gentile?) rejection of Jesus' kingship (cf. 23:2, 36–37). The result at the parousia for those who rejected Jesus' sovereignty will be judgment (vs. 27:

cf. 12:8–9; Acts 17:30–31): "As for these enemies of mine, who did not want me to reign over them, bring them here and slay them before me" (vs. 27). Verse 27 sets the stage for the rejection of Jesus by Jerusalem which is the major focus of 19:29–44.

Luke 19:29–44 contains a record of three events: (1) Jesus' ride on a colt which evokes an ovation (vss. 29–38 // Matt 21:1–9 // Mark 11:1–10); (2) the Pharisees' protest (vss. 39–40 // Matt 21:15–16); and (3) the lament over Jerusalem (vss. 41–44). The first and second of these units are joined by the term "disciples" (vss. 37, 39); the first and third by "peace" (vss. 40, 44).

(1) In 19:29–38 Jesus approaches Jerusalem as the peaceable king. The tradition of Jesus' ride on a colt is set at the Mount of Olives (19:29). This location may echo Zech 14:4 and thus have eschatological overtones. In Luke, given 19:11–27 and 17:22ff., this must not be thought of in terms of the eschaton. Furthermore, the ride on a colt (only an animal that had never been used as a beast of burden was suitable for sacred purposes—Num 19:2; 1 Sam 6:7) most likely echoes Zech 9:9 (Matt 21:5 and John 12:15 make it explicit). Jesus comes not in war but in peace (cf. 2:1–20). A number of distinctive Lukan traits tells us the author's special concerns. (a) In Luke there are no branches (Matt 21:8 // Mark 11:8 // John 12:13). Since the branches had nationalistic overtones (2 Mac 10:7), the omission serves to emphasize the absence of any revolutionary element in Jesus' movement. (b) So, even if the disciples call Jesus "King" (vs. 38—probably to pick up 19:12, 15), it would not justify the charges of 23:2. (c) In Luke the disciples set Jesus on the colt (vs. 35—Matt 21:7 // Mark 11:7 // John 12:14 say Jesus sat on the animal). The evangelist is saying the disciples were acclaiming Jesus king: Jesus does not claim kingship for himself. (d) In Luke it is the disciples (not the crowds as in Matt 21:9 // John 12:12) who give Jesus the ovation. They understand something of his identity (8:9–10) because of the mighty works they had seen (cf. 18:43; 7:16), though they still do not understand the necessity of suffering (18:34; 24:25–27). The ride on the colt in the third gospel sets Jesus forth as the peaceable king who is recognized as such by his disciples (cf. 20:21–26; 23:2–4). In Jesus God had come calling on Jerusalem (19:44).

We may think of time either in terms of duration or of content: for example, (a) duration—chronological time that can be measured on a clock or a calendar; (b) content—the character of the time, that which

fills the moment, so the time of planting or meal time. The latter kind of time confronts us with an opportunity and demands of us a response. In 19:44 Jesus speaks of "the time of your visitation." He means that in his ministry God had come calling, had visited his people (cf. 7:16). The content of the time of Jesus' career was a divine visitation (17:21; 11:20; 10:9). The visit of God in the ministry of Jesus was recognized by his disciples who set him on the colt (vs. 35).

(2) The protest of the Pharisees in 19:39–40 (only in Luke) speaks of the rejection of the peaceable king by the Jewish leadership (cf. Acts 13:27). (3) The lament over the city in 19:41–44 (cf. Isa 29:3; Ps 137:9) ties the destruction of Jerusalem to the Jewish rejection of Jesus (cf. 13:34–35; 21:20, 21, 24; 23:27–31). The tragedy is that Jerusalem did not know the time of her visitation by God (vs. 44; cf. 1:78; 7:16). God had come calling but his visit had gone unrecognized. It is as though the Lukan community after A.D. 70 was saying that when the Jewish people rejected the peaceable king, they opted for Zealot violence which resulted in the destruction of the city of peace (cf. 23:18–19, 25). This point raises the larger question of how the evangelist regards Israel.

The Lukan estimation of Israel may be summarized in five steps. (1) Before Israel's refusal of the gospel, Luke regards her as a reality existing on two levels: first, as a historical people defined by race and nationality, the Jewish nation (e.g., 7:5; 23:2; Acts 10:22; 24:10, 17; 26:4; 28:19); and second, as the people of God (e.g., 1:68; 2:32; 7:16; Acts 7:34; 13:17).

(2) The evangelist makes much of the Jewish rejection of Jesus and the Christian message (e.g., 2:34; 4:28–29; 13:34; 19:14, 39, 44; 20:13–16; 23:102, 18–19, 23; 24:20; Acts 4:1–2, 17–18; 5:17–18, 40; 7:58; 13:45; 14:19; 17:5–9, 13; 18:5–6, 12–17; 19:8–9; 20:3; 21:27–30). At the same time Luke makes it clear that the earliest believers were Jewish (Acts 1:13–14, 21) and that there were many Jewish converts to Christianity (Acts 2:41, 47; 4:4; 5:14; 6:7; 13:43; 17:4, 12; 21:20) both in Jerusalem and elsewhere. Hence Luke shows the Christian movement divided Israel into two groups: the repentant and the unrepentant (2:34–35). Israel has not rejected the gospel but has become divided over the issue.

(3) In the Lukan perspective the repentant portion of the Jewish nation is Israel, the people of God. It is to and for these believing Jews the promises have been fulfilled. This restored Israel is the presuppo-

sition of all the missionary work to the Gentiles (Acts 15:15–18). God first rebuilds and restores Israel and then, as a result, the Gentiles seek the Lord. The unrepentant portion of the nation, however, has forfeited its membership in the people of God (Acts 3:23). A formal statement of rejection of the unrepentant portion of the Jewish nation is delivered three times, once in each main area of missionary activity. Acts 13:46 has Paul and Barnabas say to the unbelieving Jews in Antioch of Pisidia, "It was necessary that the word of God should be spoken first to you. Since you thrust it from you, and judge yourselves unworthy of eternal life, behold, we turn to the Gentiles." In Acts 18:6, in Corinth, when the unbelieving Jews opposed him, Paul says, "Your blood be upon your heads. I am innocent. From now on I will go to the Gentiles." Finally, in Acts 28:25–28 Paul says to the unbelieving Jews, "Let it be known to you then that this salvation of God has been sent to the Gentiles; they will listen."

(4) It is incorrect to say that for Luke it is only when the Jews have rejected the gospel that the way is open to Gentiles. It is equally incorrect to say that only when Israel has accepted the gospel that the way to the Gentiles is opened. Both, however, are parts of the total view of Luke. That is, both Acts 15:15–18 on the one hand, and Acts 13:46, 18:6, and 28:25–28 on the other, are parts of the total perspective of the evangelist. In the first place, the Jewish Christian community in Jerusalem, as the restored Israel, is the means through which salvation comes to the Gentiles (Acts 15:15–18), who are incorporated into believing Israel. They are, however, incorporated without circumcision and the law, without first becoming proselytes (Acts 15). In the second place, the explanation as to why the Lukan church feels no obligation to evangelize the national-racial entity of Israel is that these unrepentant ones have excluded themselves from Israel, the people of God (Acts 13:46; 18:6; 28:25–28). Hence, in Luke's view, by the end of Acts the people of God is no longer a race or a nation but those who believe (Luke 20:9–18). The unbelieving Jews remain a historical people who experience the fall of Jerusalem and the destruction of the temple (13:35a; 19:41–44; 21:20–24; 23:28–31), but they do not belong to Israel, the people of God. The destruction of the temple and the holy city, moreover, are understood as the consequence of the rejection of Jesus by the racial-national Israel. (Cf. Eusebius, *Ecclesiastical History*, 3:5:3–6, for an explicit statement of this Christian point of view. For an analogous interpretion of a historical disaster as result-

ing from the martyrdom of an innocent man, see Josephus' statement about the destruction of Herod's army as a just punishment for his treatment of John the Baptist in *Antiquities,* 18:5:2 § 116–19.)

(5) The question whether Luke, like Paul in Romans 9–11, envisioned a final conversion of the entire Jewish people prior to the parousia, prompted by the inclusion of the Gentiles in the people of God, is debatable. Most scholars think the Lukan Paul of Acts 28:25–28, unlike the historical Paul of Romans 11, seems resigned to a Gentile church. A few scholars think Luke, like Paul in Rom 11:20, looked forward to a time when the Jews as a people would be reinstated (e.g., A. W. Wainwright, "Luke and the Restoration of the Kingdom to Israel," *Expository Times* 89:76–79 [1977]). Acts 1:6; Luke 21:24, 28; 22:28–30 are about the only supports for this stance. There is enough question about these texts, however, to make it improbable that the Gentile Christian community from which Luke-Acts came expected the final conversion of the nation as a whole before the parousia. The evangelist would not have ruled out the conversion of any individual Jew, but as far as the direction of the church's mission was concerned, it was to Gentiles. In this Luke is akin to Justin Martyr who believed that in the second century a remnant of Jews were still being saved by conversion to Christianity (*Dialogue with Trypho,* 32;55;64). These Jewish Christians, who lived within the church, Justin allowed to practice the law (*Dialogue,* 47:2).

The Lukan position with reference to Israel may be summed up in three propositions: first, Christianity is completed Judaism; second, the nation-race no longer is synonymous with the people of God—there is no future hope for the nation as such; third, one becomes a part of God's people by individual decision for Jesus.

Luke 19:45–24:53

MARTYRDOM
AND VINDICATION

INTRODUCTION

The fourth major section of the gospel is 19:45—24:53, the narrative of the last events in Jerusalem. In order to gain some perspective about how the evangelist views this section, we look first at its pattern, then at how this period is seen in the speeches of Acts, and finally at the correspondences between this last period of Jesus' earthly career in the gospel and the corresponding period in Paul's career in Acts.

(1) Luke 19:45—24:53 falls into two large sections: 19:45—21:38, Jesus' teaching in the temple, and 22:1—24:53, the Passion itself. The first large division is held together not only by its location in the temple but also by an inclusion, 19:47 and 21:37. Luke locates more of this material in the temple than do the other synoptic writers. For example, Luke 21's apocalyptic speech occurs in the temple, whereas Mark 13 locates it outside. The temple functions in Luke's section as a site for Jesus' teaching. By suppressing the temple cleansing—for the most part—and by inserting vs. 47 in chapter 19, Luke has caused the plot of the rulers to be a response to Jesus' teaching in the temple, and not to its cleansing. This fits: later Luke omits the charge that Jesus said he would destroy the temple.

The second large division is the Passion proper. (a) In the gospel the Passion of Jesus is portrayed as the supreme assault of Satan (22:3, 31, 53). (b) Throughout there is a pro-Roman and an anti-Sanhedrin thrust. Whereas Jesus' answers before the Sanhedrin were to exclusively religious issues, the Jewish leaders distort his replies and in their report to Pilate use a political charge. Pilate, however, is not able to discover enough evidence either in the Jewish charges or in Jesus' answers to proceed with a criminal trial. The shaming of Jesus is transferred from Pilate to the half-Jew Herod and his Jewish guard. Pilate is prepared to let Jesus go with a warning (*paideusas*, 23:22, being the lightest form of Roman beating; contrast Mark 15:51b's *phragellosas*, the most severe whipping). In 23:47 the centurion pro-

185

nounces the final verdict for Rome: he is innocent. This pro-Roman sentiment was not likely to persuade some Roman that the Christians were innocent but was likely designed to persuade Christians that Roman justice was advantageous to them (P. W. Walaskay, "The Trial and Death of Jesus in the Gospel of Luke," *Journal of Biblical Literature* 94:81–93 [1975]). (c) In the Passion narrative there is an effort to minimize the failure of the Eleven. Luke has shaped the material so it is a "promise of ultimate victory after passing failure, especially for Peter," rather than of complete collapse as in Mark (R. H. Lightfoot, *History and Interpretation in the Gospels* [New York: Harper & Brothers, 1934], 174–75). (d) Luke locates all of the resurrection appearances in Jerusalem, in contrast to the other gospels.

(2) Since the speeches of Acts are most likely Lukan compositions, it is helpful to examine them to see what emphases they contain about Jesus' days in Jerusalem. Their focus is on Jesus' death and resurrection. Nothing is said about his teaching in the temple. About his death we hear: (a) Jesus could not be charged with anything deserving death (12:28); (b) the Jews delivered him up (2:23; 3:13; 13:28); (c) the Jews asked Pilate to kill him (3:13; 13:28); (d) Herod was involved against Jesus (4:27); (e) instead of Jesus the Jews asked for a murderer (3:14); (f) Jesus was laid in a tomb (13:29); (g) these events were in accord with prophecy (13:27; 3:18).

About his resurrection, the speeches say, (a) God raised Jesus (2:24; 5:30; 10:39–40; 13:30); (b) God made him manifest (10:39–40), or he appeared (13:31) to Galileans (13:31), witnesses who ate and drank with him after the resurrection (10:39–40); (c) the resurrection is in fulfillment of prophecy (2:25–28). One recognizes immediately that the references to Herod and to witnesses eating and drinking with Jesus after the resurrection are peculiar to Luke-Acts.

(3) The remarkable correspondences both in content and sequence between the events and persons found in Luke and those in Acts constitute the primary architectonic pattern in Luke-Acts (C. H. Talbert, *Literary Patterns*, pp. 15ff.). This pattern of correspondences is especially clear in the final sections of both Luke and Acts. The following examples are representative:

19:37 Jesus receives a good reception and the people praise God for the works they have seen.	21:17–20a Paul receives a good reception and God is glorified for the things done among the Gentiles.

19:45–48	Jesus goes into the temple. He has a friendly attitude toward it.	21:26	Paul goes into the temple. He has a friendly attitude toward it.
20:27–39	The Sadducees do not believe in the resurrection. The scribes support Jesus.	23:6–9	The Sadducees do not believe in the resurrection. The scribes support Paul.
22:19a	At a meal, Jesus takes bread, gives thanks, and breaks it.	27:35	Paul has a meal in which he takes bread, gives thanks, and breaks it.
22:54	A mob seizes Jesus.	21:30	A mob seizes Paul.
22:63–64	Jesus is slapped by the priest's assistants.	23:2	Paul is slapped at the high priest's command.
22:26; 23:1; 23:8; 23:13	The four trials of Jesus (Sanhedrin; Pilate; Herod; Pilate).	Chps. 23; 24; 25; 26	The four trials of Paul (Sanhedrin; Felix; Festus; Herod Agrippa).

Some of the details in the trials of Jesus in the gospel and of Paul in Acts correspond:

23:4, 14, 22	Three times Pilate declares Jesus innocent.	23:9; 25:25; 26:31	Three men, Lysias, Festus, and Agrippa, declare Paul innocent.
23:6–12	Pilate sends Jesus to Herod for questioning.	25:13– 26:32	Herod hears Paul with the permission of Festus.
23:16, 22	Pilate says he will release Jesus.	26:32	Herod says, "This man could have been released."
23:18	The Jews cry, "Away with this man."	21:36	The Jews cry, "Away with him."
23:47	A centurion has a favorable opinion of Jesus.	27:3	A centurion has a favorable impression of Paul.

These correspondences function in the interests of the Lukan belief that Jesus is the pioneer or leader (*archēgos*) of the Christian Way. His career is, then, prototypical for his followers. Throughout the Passion one should be alert to the recurring emphasis on Jesus as the model for Christian existence.

TESTED IN THE TEMPLE

Luke 19:45—21:38 (A. 19:45—21:4);
2:1-7; 11:37-54; 14:1-24

L uke 19:45—21:38 constitutes a large thought unit in the gospel, 19:47 ("he was teaching daily in the temple") and 21:37 ("every day he was teaching in the temple") functioning as an inclusion to hold the material together. In 19:45-46 Jesus enters not the city but the temple. The temple functions in this section as the site for Jesus' teaching (cf. 2:41-51), which teaching serves as a confrontation between God's accredited agent and the Jewish people. The outcome is the rejection of God's messenger (cf. 4:16-30; Acts 3—4; 5:12-42; 13:13-52; 18:1-11) which issues in God's judgment on those who have rejected Jesus. The teaching in the environs of the temple falls into two parts: (1) 19:45—21:4, and (2) 21:5-38. In this chapter, the focus will be on the former part.

Luke 19:45—21:4 has, for the most part, parallels in the other synoptics. All of this material, however, has been shaped to fit Luke's "teaching in the temple" motif.

In 19:45—20:18 the material has become a warning to the leaders of religious establishments. Four points are made in the warning. (1) God will not allow the religious leadership of his people to fail to nourish the flock. The entry into the temple (19:45-46) functions to indict the religious leadership for allowing the temple's purpose to be perverted (cf. Isa 56:7; Jer 7:11). Jesus' act and word testify that the religious establishment has not been faithful to its charge to nourish God's people.

(2) When the sheep are not fed, others may be expected to come to remedy the deficiency. Jesus' teaching in the temple daily (19:47a) appears to be in response to the failure of the Jewish leaders.

(3) There follows a predictable twofold response by the religious establishment (20:1-19). The leaders question the reformer's authority: "Tell us by what authority you do these things, or who it is who gave you this authority" (vs. 2). When such a challenge is put to him, Jesus responds with a question of his own: "Was the baptism of John from

188

heaven or from men" (vs. 4)? That is to say, "Can you recognize God's presence anywhere else than in the official structures?" The people are able to recognize it (vs. 6b). There is also the temptation characteristic of every bureaucracy, including the religious ones, to forget to whom the vineyard belongs. Jesus tells the people (note the contrast between the favor of the people, 19:48, and the opposition of the leaders, 20:19) a parable directed against the religious leadership. The story is actually another allegory of salvation history as Luke sees it (cf. 14:16–24; 19:11–27). Time after time the tenants (the religious bureaucracy) fail to recognize God's authority in his prophets (e.g., John the Baptist—20:4–7) and have repeatedly expressed hostility to God's messengers (13:34; Acts 7:52). Now they have rejected even the beloved Son (3:22; Acts 7:53): "This is the heir; let us kill him, that the inheritance may be ours" (vs. 14). The allegory implies that the bureaucracy recognized him but rejected him because they were unwilling to relinquish control over the vineyard to its rightful owner. They had ceased to be stewards of another's property and had begun to seek to function as owners in their own right.

(4) Such a rejection of the Son results in an overthrow of the established leadership. The allegory says that for rejecting God's Son, the tenants will be severely punished: "He will come and destroy those tenants, and give the vineyard to others" (20:16; cf. 19:27). This is not a reference to the destruction of Jerusalem and to the shift of the good news to the Gentiles. It is an attack on the religious bureaucracy (vs. 19) and says that because of their rejection of Jesus, their positions as caretakers of God's people are cancelled and in their place others are appointed (in the Lukan context, the apostles—22:28–30; Acts 1:15–26). One's response to the beloved Son is absolutely decisive: "Every one who falls on that stone will be broken to pieces; but when it falls on any one it will crush him" (vs. 18). This verse, which is peculiar to Luke, is a statement similar to that of the rabbi cited in Midrash Rabbah on Esth 3:6: "Should the stone fall on the crock, woe to the crock. Should the crock fall on the stone, woe to the crock. In either case, woe to the crock" (cf. Luke 2:34; 12:8–9; Acts 4:12). One's place in the religious establishment hinges on one's acquiescence in the claims of the beloved Son as owner of the vineyard. This is the criterion by which every religious establishment is judged by God.

The first attempt to discredit Jesus having failed, a second effort was made at 20:20–26, so they could "deliver him up to the authority and

jurisdiction of the governor" (vs. 20; cf. 18:32). At issue here is the attitude toward the state advocated by Jesus. Our appreciation of vss. 20–26 is enhanced if we first look at some background material from the rest of the gospel. Luke 2:1–7 is crucial, with the data relevant to our purposes related to the census in vs. 2. There are two possible translations of this sentence. (1) The usual way is to render it, "This was the first enrollment, when Quirinius was governor of Syria" (RSV). If one translates in this fashion, there is a problem of chronology. Quirinius did not become governor until A.D. 6. At that time he conducted a census together with Coponius, the procurator of Judea. This innovation was widely resented and led to a Zealot uprising under Judas the Galilean (Josephus, *Antiquities,* 18:1:1, 6 § 4–10, 23–25). The difficulty is that 1:5 locates the annunciation of John the Baptist's birth in the days of Herod, king of the Jews, presumably Herod the Great who died in 4 B.C. Since Luke 1:26 locates the annunciation of Jesus' birth in the sixth month of Elizabeth's pregnancy, presumably Jesus too would be born under Herod the Great, as Matthew 1—2 also claims. This makes a discrepancy in dating of a minimum of ten years (4 B.C.– A.D. 6). If so, then the evangelist has made an error, whether unconsciously or purposefully (Horst Moehring, "The Census as an Apologetic Device," in *Studies in the New Testament and Early Christian Literature,* ed. D. E. Aune [Leiden: Brill, 1972], pp. 144–60). (2) An alternate translation of vs. 2 is offered by Nigel Turner (*Grammatical Insights into the New Testament* [Edinburgh: T. &. T. Clark, 1966], pp. 23–24), who observes that the Greek of the period often used "first" when "former" or "prior" would have been more grammatical. If so, then it would be possible to translate, "This enrollment was before Quirinius was governor of Syria," or "This enrollment was prior to (the enrollment) when Quirinius was governor of Syria" (cf. John 5:36; 1 Cor 1:25 for similar compressions). If this reading is adopted, there is no chronological error on Luke's part. Then the question would be, Why would the evangelist have wanted to refer to Quirinius and possibly his census?

Which ever of the two translations one accepts, the reason for Luke's reference to Quirinius is obvious. His census was the occasion for a rebellion led by Judas of Galilee, from which came the Zealot movement. That Acts 5:37 mentions Judas the Galilean's revolt in connection with the census indicates the associations that were in the evangelist's mind when he mentioned a census and Quirinius together in

Luke 2:2. The actions of Judas apparently were part of a general pattern of rebelliousness among Galileans. Returned to the Jewish state by the Hasmoneans, the Galileans after 63 B.C. aimed to reestablish the Hasmonean state. There were instances of rebelliousness under Ezekias (47 B.C.), in the uprising of Antigonus (40–37 B.C.), at the death of Herod (4 B.C.), in Judas' opposition to the census (A.D. 6), under the Roman procurators, and in the Jewish revolt of A.D. 66–74 (F. Loftus, "The Anti-Roman Revolts of the Jews and the Galileans," *Jewish Quarterly Review* 68:78–98 [1977]). For Luke to depict the Galilean family of Jesus doing its civic duty would be significant. Joseph, like Jesus and his later followers, was obedient to Roman rule. Jesus' family did not participate in the Galilean spirit of rebellion that oftentimes brought recrimination from Roman officials (cf. 13:1–2).

The one who was born a peaceable king (2:1–20) entered Jerusalem on the same note. Jesus came riding on a colt (a sign of peace), with no nationalistic trappings (the absence of the branches), amid the acclamation of his disciples: "Peace in the heavens and glory in the highest." Furthermore, Jesus' entrance into the temple (19:45–46) is told by the evangelist in a way that eliminates almost all details of violence. It is against this background that one must read 20:20–26. In A.D. 6 Judas of Galilee (Josephus, *Antiquities,* 18:1:6 § 23–25; 20:5:2 § 102) had denounced the payment of taxes to Caesar as treason against God. Now the spies ask Jesus, "Is it lawful (that is, scriptural) for us to give tribute to Caesar or not?" No matter how he answers, they think, he will offend someone. Asking for a coin, Jesus inquired about whose image was on it. When his opponents said, "Caesar's," he said, "Then render to Caesar the things that are Caesar's, and to God the things that are God's." In this context, the logion points in two directions.

(1) The saying affirms the sovereignty of God. From Luke's point of view the authority of the political realm belongs to God who then delivers it to whom he wishes (cf. 4:6—"for it has been delivered to me," that is, by God). A ruler who does not give glory to God but rather usurps God's prerogatives is subject to God's judgment (cf. Acts 12:20–23). A disciple, when confronted with the choice, must obey God rather than humans (Acts 4:19–20; 5:29). From the evangelist's perspective there are not two realms, Caesar's and God's, but rather only one, God's. The only areas in which Caesar can expect allegiance from Jesus' disciples are those in which his patterns are in conformity with God's desired patterns. That the Roman officials in Acts provided protection

for the preachers of the gospel doubtless accounts for the positive portrayal they receive from the evangelist (cf. Acts 13:7, 12; 16:35–39;
18:12–17; 19:35–41; 21:31–39; 22:25–26; 23:19–24, 31–32; 27:42–
43).

(2) The logion speaks a word of assurance about Christian political
intentions. It is very difficult not to see vss. 24–25 as affirming the
payment of taxes. Give Caesar his money. Those who use Caesar's
money will have to pay Caesar's taxes (cf. Rom 13:6–7). The evangelist would see this saying as falsifying the Jewish charge that Jesus
was "forbidding us to give tribute to Caesar" (23:2). Jesus was not
hostile to the state as such. Within the context of total submission to
God, Jesus advocated submission to the state. Given Roman protection
of the church from mob violence, both Gentile and Jewish in origin
(e.g., Acts 18—19), in the early years of the Christian movement, it is
no surprise that many Christians heard this emphasis primarily (Rom
13:1–7; 1 Tim 2:1–2; Tit 3:1–2; 1 Pet 2:13; 1 Clement 61; Pol Phil
12:3; Justin, *Apology I*, 17:3; Tertullian, *Apology*, 30). The attitude of
loyalty and moderation toward Rome largely characterized the church
through the second century. Yet faced with emperor worship and the
persecution which followed Christian reluctance to participate in it,
the author of Revelation developed his resistance to the state from the
former point: "Render to God the things that are God's."

This passage raises a larger question: what kind of political and social stance does Luke attribute to Jesus? A recent book, *Jesus, Politics,
and Society* (Maryknoll, N.Y.: Orbis Books, 1978), by Richard Cassidy,
portrays the Lukan Jesus as a Gandhi-like figure advocating nonviolent resistance. Cassidy works with three possibilities: (a) nonresistance (where people refrain not only from physical violence but also
from directly confronting those responsible for existing ills; they identify with those suffering from such evils; they offer no defense if they
themselves are subjected to violence by those who have power; their
hope is that their example will eventuate in changes in the attitudes
and actions of others); (b) nonviolent resistance (where people avoid
violence to persons but confront in a nonviolent way those responsible
for existing social ills; their hope is that the challenge will serve to
create a dialogue which may eventually result in a favorable change of
behavior); and (c) violent resistance.

These or similar stances had their representatives among the Jewish
population at the time of Christian origins. (a) The Zealots were the

advocates of armed revolution against Rome. (b) Josephus gives two examples of nonviolent resistance in Jesus' time. The first is found in *Antiquities* 18:3:1 § 261–309 and *War* 2:9:3 § 184–203, an account of a five day sit-in to protest Pilate's introduction of images into Jerusalem. When threatened with death if they did not end their protest, the Jews cast themselves on the ground and bared their throats, declaring they gladly welcomed death rather than violate their law. The protest caused Pilate to remove the offensive images from the city. The second is found in *Antiquities* 18:8 § 244–72 and *War* 2:10 § 184–98, and tells of the action of the Jews who left fields untilled in the sowing season for more than a month. The protest prevented Caligula's statue being erected in the temple. (c) Although during the Hasmonean rule at least some of the Pharisees functioned as a political party, from the rise of Herod the Great until the end of the first Jewish revolt against Rome, the Pharisees seem to have moved from direct political involvement to an attitude of indifference regarding rulers and the forms under which they ruled. It seems likely that the Pharisees did not oppose Roman rule in Judea. Their concern was with the proper ordering of the life of God's people according to the law.

The Lukan Jesus' portrayal is more complex than Cassidy's description allows. Three components must be recognized in Luke's picture of Jesus' social and political posture. (a) Although Jesus shows no deference towards political rulers (e.g., 13:31–33), this does not mean he is involved, Gandhi-like, in a nonviolent resistance to them. Like the Pharisees Jesus manifests an indifference to the political rulers. For someone who believed that all power and authority resided with God and all history unfolded according to his purpose, such rulers were of little consequence. Since the rulers shared no common assumptions that would facilitate dialogue with Jesus, he opted for silence in their presence. (b) Toward the Jewish structures, however, Jesus showed no indifference. Here he was involved in nonviolent resistance. Confrontation between Jesus and the Jewish leaders was frequent (e.g., 5:12—6:11; 11:37-54; 13:10–17; 14:1–24; 16:14–15; 19:47—20:47). Only at 19:45 is there any hint of possible violence, but the evangelist has so shaped the cleansing story that it becomes merely Jesus' entry into the site of his subsequent teaching (19:47—21:38). Moreover, 22:49–51 has Jesus explicitly reject violence against Jewish authority. Nonviolent confrontation aimed at dialogue and change of behavior seems the best description of Jesus' stance toward the Jewish struc-

tures (the people of God). This was doubtless because Jesus and the Jews shared common assumptions about God and about religious values. With such people dialogue could be profitable. (c) Jesus' primary vehicle for social change was the structure of life in the community of his disciples. Among his disciples Jesus sought a revolutionary change in social attitudes. They were to live in the present in light of God's reversal of all human values in the eschaton. Such a stance, of course, was regarded by some as "turning the world upside down" (Acts 17:6). By embodying structures of social relationships to reflect the new life in the Spirit under the lordship of Jesus, the Christian community functions in the larger society as an agent of social change.

The third attempt to discredit Jesus as a teacher came from the Sadducees, who denied the resurrection (cf. Acts 23:8; Josephus, *Antiquities*, 18:14 § 16–17; *War*, 2:8:14 § 164–65). Posing resurrection riddles was a favorite way for Sadducees to torment Pharisees. For example, they might ask whether or not those who will allegedly be resurrected will require ritual cleansing since they were in contact with a corpse (b. Niddah 70b). Or they inevitably inquired where in the Pentateuch Moses taught resurrection from the dead, since they accepted only those five books as scripture. Luke 20:27ff. reflects just such a Sadducean ploy. The problem they pose is based on Deut 25:5–10, the law of levirate marriage. If a brother died childless, a surviving brother was to take the widow and beget children for his dead brother. The firstborn of such a union was to bear the name of the deceased (cf. Gen 38:8; Ruth 3—4). Though the law of levirate marriage was not enforced in the time of Jesus, the question was raised to show that since resurrection would imply polyandry, which was unacceptable, it was excluded by the law of Moses.

Jesus' answer is twofold. (1) In vss. 37–38 he says the inference drawn by the Sadducees from their posed problem is inaccurate because it does not reckon with the continuing nature of the relationship between God and his people. The form of Jesus' answer resembles rabbinic argument. In the Talmud (e.g., b. Sanhedrin 90b–91a), we read again and again the question, "How is resurrection derived from the Torah?" The rabbis appealed to numerous passages for support (e.g., Num 18:28; 15:31; Exod 6:4; 15:1; Deut 31:16). In one first century example sectarians asked R. Gamaliel, "Whence do we know that the Holy One will raise the dead?" Gamaliel appealed to Deut 31:16, Isa 26:19, and Cant 7:9, all to no avail. They were not satisfied

until he quoted Deut 11:21, "Which the Lord swore unto your fathers to give to them," and pointed out that the text said not "to you" but "to them." Since the promise could only be fulfilled by the patriarch's resurrection, resurrection is derived from the Torah (Pentateuch). Luke 20:37–38 follows this type of rabbinic argument, appealing to Exod 3:6, which called the Lord the God of Abraham, Isaac, and Jacob. Since Yahweh is not God of the dead but of the living, the patriarchs must either be in some sense alive or they will be raised. The meaning is basically that when God has a relationship with someone, that relationship is not terminated by death: God will not allow an ∮nemy of his, death, to destroy that which means so much to him (cf. Rom 8:35—39).

(2) In vss. 34–36 (considerably longer than Matt 22:30 // Mark 12:25) Jesus says the problem posed is inappropriate because it does not take into account the difference between life on earth and life beyond the resurrection. Human life in this world is mortal, and our sexuality guarantees the survival of the human race. Beyond the resurrection, however, people do not die, so the type of sexual unions appropriate in this life do not apply (cf. 2 Baruch 51:10; 1 Enoch 104:4, 6; 1 QSb 4:24–28; 1 QH 3:21ff.; 6:13). (Given this line of reasoning, if the Corinthians believed they had already been raised from the dead—1 Cor 4:8—then their attitudes toward marriage are understandable—1 Corinthians 7.) The one who knows the mind of God therefore knows what life in the other world will be like (cf. Luke 6:20–26; 13:28–29; 16:19–31).

The scribal commendation of Jesus (vs. 39) that follows the discomfiture of the Sadducees becomes the occasion for a twofold critique: (a) of scribal theology (vss. 41–44), and (b) of the scribal way of life (20:45–47; 21:1–4). The critique of their theology is addressed to the scribes (vs. 41, cf. vs. 39); the critique of their way of life is addressed to the disciples (20:45). (a) Luke 20:41–44 poses a puzzle for the scribes very much in the same manner the Sadducees had presented Jesus with a riddle. The pericope assumes first that "the Lord" is God, that "my Lord" equals the Messiah, and that David is the author of the psalm (vs. 42); and second, that, according to oriental mores, a son did not surpass his father. Given assumption two, how could the Messiah be David's son (vs. 44)? David would not address a son of his as Lord. No answer to the riddle is given, but Luke's readers would have their own answer. The one who is David's son (1:69; 2:4; 3:23–38) became

David's Lord by virtue of his resurrection-ascension-exaltation (Acts 2:34–36; 13:22–23, 33–37).

(b) The critique of the scribal way of life echoes, in part, earlier attacks on the Pharisees, scribes, and lawyers (11:37–54; 14:1–24). In order to gain perspective it will be helpful to examine these earlier passages briefly. Luke 11:37–54 is a meal setting (vs. 37) in which there are two parallel units:

Provocation by Jesus (vs. 38)	Provocation by Jesus (vs. 45)
Response by the Pharisee (vs. 38)	Response by the lawyer (vs. 45)
Three woes on the Pharisees (vss. 39–44)	Three woes on the lawyers (vss. 46–52)

It closes with a statement about the scribes' and Pharisees' conspiracy against Jesus (11:53–54).

The passage functions as an expose of the disparity between outer appearance and inner reality in the life-style of Pharisees and lawyers. Two excerpts give the thrust of the meaning: "Now you Pharisees cleanse the outside of the cup and of the dish, but inside you are full of extortion and wickedness. You fools! Did not he who made the outside make the inside also?" (vss. 39–40); "Woe to you! for you are like graves which are not seen, and men walk over them without knowing it" (vs. 44).

Luke 14:1–24 is set at dinner in a Pharisee's house. The dinner scene is a literary device (cf. Plato, *Symposium;* Esther; Ep Artist § 182–294; Plutarch, *Nine Books of Table Talk*) to provide a unified setting for four separate traditions (14:1–6, 7–11, 12–14, 15–24). These four traditions fall into a clear chiastic pattern:

> A   Unconcern about others (humans) while giving an appearance
>   of being religious (14:1–6)
>   B   Self-seeking as a guest (14:7–11)
>   B'   Self-seeking as a host (14:12–14)
> A'   Unconcern about others (God) while giving the appearance of
>   being religious (14:15–24)

This passage also functions as an expose of the disparity between outer appearance and inner reality. The first tradition (vss. 1–6) assumes the Pharisee and his guests were opposed to healing the man

with dropsy on the sabbath. Jesus' behavior and words expose their callous unconcern for the man even while they profess to protect the rituals of religion. Something in vs. 5 has fallen into an artificially constructed well (*phrear;* Exod 21:33 shows such accidents were by no means uncommon). The best textual tradition reads, "son or ox." Jesus asks, "Which of you, having a son or even an ox that has fallen into a well, will not immediately pull him out on a sabbath day?" Would this have been the case? Jewish attitudes toward assistance on the sabbath varied. At Qumran it was taught that a person could be pulled from a pit so long as no implements were used, but an animal could not be lifted out on the sabbath (CD 11:13-17). In the Talmud (b. Shabbath 128b) two rulings are given: the mild ruling allows helping an animal out of a pit; the harsh one allows only the provision of fodder to it. It would seem, then, that even the most severe opinion would allow human beings to be pulled out even on the sabbath, though there was a difference of opinion about animals. Luke 14:5 assumes the Pharisees allow both people and animals to be pulled out on the sabbath. Jesus' argument runs from the lesser to the greater: if pulling an animal or a son out of a pit on the sabbath is permitted by Jewish logic, then how much more should a man in the pit of illness be extricated from his plight. The effect of the argument is to expose the callousness of the Pharisees, who have an appearance of being religious (keeping the sabbath) but are unconcerned about people in need.

The second and third traditions (vss. 7-11; 12-14) expose the self-seeking of the people at the meal. Verses 7-11 begin with the note that the guests were seeking the places of honor at the dinner (vs. 7). The prescription of Jesus ("go and sit in the lowest place") is based on the way God acts: "Every one who exalts himself will be humbled, and he who humbles himself will be exalted" (vs. 11; cf. 1:48, 52; 3:5; 18:14; 6:20-26). Verses 12-14 assume the host has invited only those who could benefit him in the future: his self-seeking as a host is exposed. Jesus' prescription ("invite the poor, the maimed, the lame, the blind") is based on the way God will act: "You will be repaid at the resurrection of the just" (vs. 14).

The fourth tradition (vss. 15-24) opens with a pious utterance by one of those present: "Blessed is he who shall eat bread in the kingdom of God" (vs. 15). The allegory of Jesus given in response exposes the hollowness of the words. It follows the outline of salvation history presented in the narrative of Luke-Acts. The many in Israel had been

invited to the messianic banquet through God's messengers (the prophets). When the time for the banquet came, God sent his servant (Jesus—Acts 4:27; 3:26; and his disciples) to say, "Come," but when the announcement was made, those invited refused because they were preoccupied with the common ventures of life (cf. Luke 17:26–30). Faced with refusal by the Jewish leaders, the Lord turned first to the outcasts among the Jews (cf. 15:1–2), then to the Gentiles. The pious profession of vs. 15 masks the unconcern which such a one had for God and his kingdom. The allegory exposes the disparity between profession and practice. It is as though Jesus looks through spectacles that allow him to penetrate the outer appearance and lay bare the inner reality of one's life. It is against this background one may turn to 20:45ff.

In 20:45–47 Jesus critiques the scribal way of life. In their outer appearance they are ostentatiously religious. Yet the reality of their situation is stated in vs. 47a: "who devour widows' houses" (that is, by taking them as pledges for debts which cannot be paid). This is the disparity between outer profession and inner reality of which the disciples are to beware (vs. 45–46a). What the disciples are to emulate is found in 21:1–4. Since it was not possible under Jewish law to offer less than two mites, the widow was making the smallest offering possible. Yet she is praised by Jesus above the rich (like the scribes). For Jesus "what matters is not the amount that one gives but the amount that one keeps for oneself" (I. H. Marshall, *The Gospel of Luke*, p. 750). Beware the scribes! Emulate the widow! The latter is whole; the former are hollow.

With this, the first part of Jesus' teaching in the temple ends. Challenged by many, he was overcome by none.

ON PERSECUTION
AND PERSEVERANCE

19:45—21:38 (B. 21:5–38);
12:1–12; 14:26–35

M uch of the material in 21:5–38 has parallels in the other synoptics, but the evangelist has shaped the total unit to reflect
his own conceptions. For example, whereas Matt 24:1–3 and Mark
13:1–4 locate the discussion outside the temple on the Mount of Olives
and specify the disciples (Matthew) or four named disciples (Mark) as
the auditors of the discourse, Luke keeps Jesus inside the temple and
makes the teaching public (20:45; 21:37–38). If, as the contents indicate (21:12–19), at least part of the teaching is intended for disciples,
they are instructed in the hearing of all the people. Luke 21:5–26,
thereby, functions as the second part of the public teaching of Jesus
in the temple in Jerusalem (19:45—21:38).

The occasion for the teaching in Luke 21 is an admiring remark
made by someone about the adornments of the temple (vs. 5). In response (cf. 14:15) Jesus utters a prophetic oracle: "As for these things
which you see, the days will come when there shall not be left here
one stone upon another that will not be thrown down" (vs. 6). This
echoes the prophecy of the destruction of the temple by Micah (3:12)
and Jeremiah (7; 22:5) in earlier times. The oracle prompts two questions: "when will this be, and what will be the sign that this is about
to take place?" (vs. 7). The questions are answered in an apocalyptic
discourse (vss. 8–36) which sets the fate of the temple in a much
larger context, concerned with other issues. The dialogue falls into the
following pattern:

A The time of the eschaton, warning not to be misled (vss. 8–9)
B Political upheavals (vs. 10)
C Cosmic disturbances (vs. 11)
D The time of testimony (which comes before all this)
(vss. 12–19)

199

B' Political upheavals (of which the fall of Jerusalem is a part) (vss. 20–24)
    C' Cosmic disturbances (vss. 25–26)
A' The time of the eschaton, warning to be ready (vss. 27–36).

If we arrange the items into an ordered series, it would run as follows: (1) a time of testimony (vs. 12a indicates this period comes *before* all the rest); (2) the emergence of false messiahs; (3) political upheavals (including the fall of Jerusalem); (4) cosmic disturbances; and (5) the coming of the Son of Man. From this apocalyptic timetable we can extract the Lukan answers to the two questions raised in vs. 7. When will the temple be destroyed? It will occur as part of the political disturbances prior to the End. What will be the sign when this is about to take place? The sign will be when you see Jerusalem surrounded by armies (vs. 20). Though it was the oracle about the temple's destruction that prompted the questions which evoked the discourse, the evangelist's concerns are broader in this chapter than the fall of Jerusalem and the temple's demise (though the fall and the demise are a part of the recurrent theme in Luke: 13:31–35; 19:28–44; 23:26–31).

Two primary concerns, in addition to the destruction of Jerusalem, are evident in Luke 21: (1) persecution, which is the time of testimony (vss. 12–19), and (2) perseverance or readiness for the Son of Man's coming (vss. 34–36).

Proper appreciation of Luke's treatment of persecution requires looking first of all at an earlier passage that also dealt with this problem: 12:1–12, which serves as background for the examination of 21:12–19. In 12:1–12 the combination of sayings is so ordered that its message is directed to the church's life after the resurrection of Jesus. (1) The section begins with a warning against hypocrisy, that is, not being on the inside what one appears to be on the outside (vs. 1). Such a life is futile because at some point (in a time of persecution?) it will be exposed (vss. 2–3). (2) The disciple should not acquiesce because of a fear of those whose ultimate power is their ability to kill only the body (vs. 4). Rather they should fear God who has power over one's destiny after death (vs. 5). Gehenna, originally a valley near Jerusalem where children were sacrificed to Molech (Jer 7:31–32), was, after Josiah's reform, turned into a garbage dump (2 Kgs 23:10), and ultimately became a symbol of punishment reserved for God's enemies (Rev 14:7–13; cf. Mark 9:43–48; 1 Pet 4:17–19). This one who has power over

your ultimate destiny cares for you. Do not fear your persecutors (vss. 6–7). (3) One's ultimate destiny depends upon the relation to Jesus: "Everyone who acknowledges me before men, the Son of Man also will acknowledge before the angels of God; but he who denies me before men will be denied before the angels of God" (vss. 8–9). The only way to avoid a contradiction between this principle and the qualification in vs. 10 is by understanding the crucial difference in the Lukan mind between the period of Jesus, in which only he enjoys the abiding presence of the Holy Spirit, and the period of the church when the promised Spirit is bestowed on the disciples. The general principle of vss. 8–9 may be qualified by saying that hostility to or denial of the earthly Jesus is forgiveable—so Peter who denied Jesus (22:54ff.) was forgiven by the risen Lord (24:34) and the Jewish people who acted in ignorance are offered a second chance after Jesus' resurrection (Acts 3:14–15, 17, 19, 26; 5:30–31). After the resurrection of Jesus reviling the Holy Spirit is not forgiveable (vs. 10). For the unbelievers rejecting the Christian message is resisting the Holy Spirit (Acts 7:51; cf. 28:25–28). The disciples, who are the evangelist's primary concern here, would be rejecting the Spirit's inspiration when, required to testify before persecutors, they would, in direct opposition to the Spirit's influence deny Christ (vss. 11–12; cf. 21:14–15; Acts 4:8, 19–20; 5:30). By denying Christ the disciples deny the Holy Spirit within and blaspheme the only one who can mediate God's forgiveness. This Lukan exhortation to stand firm in the face of persecution functions as the background for 21:12–19.

The chronology of the events described in 21:8–19 does not coincide with the order of their appearance in the text where a warning not to be misled by false messiahs and other signs into thinking the End has arrived (vss. 8–9), and references to political upheavals (vs. 10) and cosmic disturbances (vs. 11) precede the section on persecution (vss. 12–19). Chronologically, however, the persecutions precede the other items (cf. vs. 12a—*pro de toutōn pantōn*, "but before all these things"): that is, in the interim before the eschaton the disciples will experience persecution (cf. 6:22–23; 8:13; 12:11; Acts 4—5; 12; 16; 18; 21).

The persecution will be of two types (cf. Luke 12:11): Christians will be brought before Jewish synagogue courts (vs. 12a), and they will be brought to trial before kings and governors (vs. 12b). This, of course, is exactly the case in the narrative of Acts (e.g., 4—5; 9:1 for Jewish arrests; 24; 25—26 for trial before governor and king). That the ac-

count in Acts conforms to historical reality, at least in the case of Paul, may be seen from 2 Cor 11:23ff. Such a moment of persecution from church and state is "a time for you to bear testimony" (vs. 13).

In this time of testimony the disciples need have no anxiety about what to say, "for I will give you a mouth and wisdom, which none of your adversaries will be able to withstand or contradict" (vs. 15). A similar promise was given in Luke 12:11–12, with the Holy Spirit teaching the disciples what ought to be said. Luke 21:15's "I will give you" may be designed to echo Exod 4:15. Again the promise is fulfilled in Acts (4:8–13; 6:10, "But they could not withstand the wisdom and the Spirit with which he spoke.").

The persecution will find even one's closest family and friends as betrayers (vs. 16a), which gives impact to the logion in 14:26 (cf. Acts 21:27; 22:1; 23:12—kinsmen). Persecution for some will result in death (cf. Acts 7:58–60; 12:1–2). Martyrdom is a real possibility for Jesus' disciples. Given this, how can the distinctively Lukan saying in vs. 18 ("But not a hair of your head will perish") be understood? Are we take vs. 16 as referring to only a few martyrs and vs. 18 as referring to the safety of the church as a whole? Or does vs. 16 refer to the threat to the bodies of the disciples and vs. 18 to the safety of their essential being? Because of 12:4ff. the latter seems the better option. Though they kill the body, that is all they can do: God preserves the life. Knowing this, the disciples' endurance (faithfulness to the end) gains them their lives (since 14:14 and 21:35 point to Luke's belief in resurrection only of the righteous, this would mean "resurrection lives"). In the early church endurance was a key quality encouraged in Christians who faced persecution (cf. Heb 10:32–39; Rev 2:2; 21:7–8; Jas 1:2–4; Rom 5:3–4).

The second of the evangelist's primary concerns in Luke 21 is the perseverance of the disciples, their readiness for the Son of Man's coming (vss. 34–36). Proper appreciation of what Jesus is saying in this chapter depends upon seeing it against the background of what has been said earlier in the gospel. In 14:25–35 Jesus addresses the multitudes who have been given an invitation to the table of God (14:23) in such a way as to discourage hasty enthusiasm. Perseverance depends upon counting the cost before one embarks upon the Way. Luke 14:26–35 says one should do this because the demands of discipleship are rigorous, and it is tragic not to be able to follow through on what has been begun. (1) Verses 26–27 give two parallel sayings

about the demands of discipleship. Both sayings end with the refrain, "it is not possible to be my disciple." (a) The "hating" of one's family and one's own life in vs. 26 is a Semitic way of expressing absolute and total detachment. When disciples are confronted with a conflict of loyalty, they will give priority to the commitment to Jesus (9:59–62; 18:28–30; cf. Deut 33:9). (b) Verse 27 is basically the same logion as 9:23. The bearing of one's cross is an expansion of the idea of hating one's own life in vs. 26. When one is confronted with a conflict between his or her commitment to Jesus and his or her own unredeemed desires, the unredeemed self is treated as dead and one's commitment to Jesus reigns supreme: "Discipleship is not periodic volunteer work on one's own terms and at one's convenience" (Robert J. Karris, *Gospel of St. Luke* [Chicago: Franciscan Herald Press, 1974], p. 59). Absolute detachment from all else and total commitment to Jesus are what is demanded of disciples. Given this rigorous demand it would be advisable to count the cost before accepting the invitation to the messianic banquet.

(2) Three sayings speak to the tragedy of not being able to follow through on what one has begun. (a) In vss. 28–30 this tragedy is expressed in terms of embarrassment. Be like the farmer who sits down first and counts the cost of building a tower to guard his vineyard against marauders at harvest season. He does this to avoid the embarrassment of not being able to finish what he has started. (b) In vss. 31–32 it is stated in terms of subjection to a foreign king. Be like the king who sits down first and reckons his chances of winning before venturing forth into battle against a foe who cannot be beaten. He does this to avoid subjection to an alien rule. (c) In vss. 34–35a the tragedy is discussed in terms of discarded salt. Salt in Palestine was obtained by evaporation from the Dead Sea. Since the water of the Dead Sea contained many substances evaporation produced a mixture of crystals of salt and gypsum or carnallite. The mixture would taste salty even though it was not pure salt. If, however, in the process the salt crystals were dissolved, what was left might appear to be salt but would have no salty taste. This residue would serve no useful purpose and so would be thrown away. Though Matt 5:13 addresses a form of this saying to disciples, Luke uses it to speak to a group of would-be disciples (the multitudes—vs. 25). He says, "Count the cost before you accept the invitation because to fail to persevere is to be as useless as tasteless salt and to be subject to the same judgment."

The evangelist has arranged the materials of 14:25–35 to set forth the demands of discipleship, call for sober calculation of what is involved before setting out on the Christian Way, and tell of the tragedy involved in failure to finish what one has begun. Perseverance is essential for disciples. If 14:25–35 addressed this word about perseverance to would-be disciples, 21:34–36 speaks to those who are already disciples. The accent on perseverance is the same, however.

Luke's concern for the readiness of Christians (vss. 34–36) is set in the context of an apocalyptic scheme: (1) political upheavals, of which the fall of Jerusalem is one part (vss. 20–24); (2) cosmic disturbances (vss. 25–26); (3) the coming of the Son of Man in a cloud (9:34; Acts 1:9): "Now when these things begin to take place, look up and raise your heads, because your redemption is drawing near" (vs. 28). For the Lukan church, that looked back on the destruction of Jerusalem and lived in a world with cosmic signs aplenty, all that would be left in this apocalyptic timetable would be the coming of the Son of Man. Luke's readers should know that just as the fresh foliage in spring signals the coming of summer, so the disasters and cosmic disturbances signal the nearness of the End (vss. 29–31). Since the evangelist believed that all had taken place in the apocalyptic scheme except the Son of Man's coming, the End was near. In light of this, the simplest way to read vs. 32 is that Luke believed the End would come before "this generation" (that is, his own) passed away (of course, IQpHab 2:7; 7:2, indicates the "last generation" could mean "several lifetimes"). In this belief Luke was one with most of the early church (e.g., 1 Thes 4:15; 1 Cor 15:51–52; Mark 9:1; Heb 10:25, 37; 1 Pet 4:7; Jas 5:8–9; Rev 22:7, 12, 20). Luke 21:33 is the basis for believing vs. 32: "Heaven and earth will pass away, but my words will not pass away."

In the context of this statement of the impending coming of the Son of Man (the cosmic judge), the evangelist exhorts his readers to watch (be prepared) at all times (cf. 12:35–40; 18:8). Being prepared means two things in this passage. On the one hand it means to pray (vs. 36b; cf. 11:4b; 22:40, 46). In Luke's mind prayer was the opposite of losing heart (18:1). It signaled intense persistence. On the other hand being prepared means allowing nothing to distract one from his or her primary concern (vs. 34). Two dangers are cited as of special importance: (a) sensuality (here "dissipation and drunkenness"—cf. 8:14; 12:45–46; Rom 13:11–14), and (b) preoccupation with the cares of this life

(cf. 8:14; 14:15–24; 17:26–27, 28–30). Persevere! Be prepared! It is certain everyone will have to render an account to the cosmic judge (vs. 35; cf. 19:11–27; Acts 17:31; Rev 20:11–13; 1 Pet 4:5; Rom 2:5–11; 14:12; Matt 12:36; Jude 14–15).

MEALTIME FAREWELLS

22:1—23:56 (A. 22:1–38)

Much of the material in 22:1–38 has at least loose parallels in the other synoptics but the overall impact of the material is distinctly Lukan. The setting shifts from the temple where Jesus taught daily (19:45—21:38) to the city. The battle between Jesus and the Jewish leadership moves from the intellectual sphere (chap. 20) to a plot to capture Jesus in the absence of the multitude (22:1–6). Satan joins the fray (22:3) and the Passover season (22:1) becomes the hour of the power of darkness (22:53). Satan manipulates Judas by means of the latter's attachment to money (22:5; Acts 1:18a; John 12:4–6).

Luke 22:7–38 is arranged as a supper scene in two parts: the preparation (vss. 7–13), and the meal itself which functions as the occasion for a farewell speech (vss. 14–38). (1) In the preparation scene Jesus takes the initiative, sending Peter and John to prepare the meal. A prophecy by Jesus tells them how to find the place where the group will eat. When they enter the city they will confront a man carrying a jar of water (an unusual thing because women normally carried water jars). This man will lead them to a spot where a room would be available: "And they went, and found it as he had told them; and they prepared the passover" (cf. 19:32). The fulfillment of Jesus' words so exactly in this instance would instill confidence in Luke's hearers that the predictions of Jesus which dominate vss. 14–38 would be fulfilled. (Deut 18:22 gives as a way to recognize a false prophet that his predictions do not come true.)

(2) The interpretation of the meal itself depends first of all upon how the textual question of vss. 19b–20 is settled. The Western Text omits the words, " 'which is given for you. Do this in remembrance of me.' And likewise the cup after supper, saying, 'This cup which is poured out for you is the new covenant in my blood.' " These words are included by most other manuscript evidence. The external evidence for the longer text is overwhelming. The weakness in its claim to originality is in accounting for the origin of the shorter text. Until about

1950 there was widespread scholarly agreement in favor of accepting the shorter form. Since then P⁷⁵ (the Bodmer papyrus of Luke dating from about A.D. 200) has strengthened the argument in favor of the longer text, which will be accepted here.

The meal itself consists of two sets of sayings about eating and drinking (vss. 15–18, 19–20). (a) In the first set there are two parallel sayings.

1) I have earnestly desired to eat this passover with you before I suffer; *for I tell you I shall not eat it until* it is fulfilled in the *kingdom of God.* (vss. 15–16)

2) Take this [cup] and divide it among yourselves; *for I tell you that from now on I shall not drink* of the fruit of the vine *until* the *kingdom of God* comes. (vss. 17–18)

These verses are specifically linked to the Passover (vs. 15): Jesus says he will eat no more Passovers until the kingdom of God comes. The sayings are, therefore, oriented to the future. If we had only vs. 16, one would inevitably understand the reference to be to the messianic banquet (cf. 13:29; 14:15). Verse 18, however, is sufficiently general that it could be fulfilled in the references to postresurrection appearances where Jesus ate and drank with disciples (24:41–42; Acts 1:4; 10:41; cf. Luke 9:27). Both postresurrection appearances and the postparousia banquet are probably involved. Repeatedly in the gospel Jesus has warned his disciples of his approaching fate (9:33, 44; 12:50; 13:32–33; 17:25; 18:32–33). Now he tells them the time has come. He will depart this life, an exodus (9:31) to be accomplished at the season that celebrated the Exodus from Egypt (Exodus 12).

In this context vss. 15–18 function in the interests of the farewell speech to come in vss. 19–38. In the farewell speeches characteristic of Jewish and Christian materials certain factors are constant: a hero figure knows he is going to die (cf. 2 Pet 1:15 where the apostle describes his death as an exodus); he gathers his primary community together and gives a farewell speech with two standard components— there is first a prediction of what will happen after he is gone and then there is an exhortation about how to behave after his departure. The evangelist has turned the meal into a farewell speech setting. In 22:15–18 Jesus says he is about to die; vss. 19–38 give the predictions and exhortations of the speech proper; vss. 7–13 lend credibility to the pre-

dictions by showing a prophecy of Jesus in another regard fulfilled to
the letter. The desire to use a farewell speech, therefore, determines
the shape of his material in 22:7–38. The distinctively Lukan words at
the Last Supper (vss. 15–18) are included and placed first to allow
Jesus to say he is about to die just before he gives his last words to the
apostles. They are not eucharistic as such. In their Lukan context they
are Jesus' prediction of impending death.

(b) In vss. 19–20, the second set of parallel sayings, we find two
more items.

> 1) And he took bread, and when he had given thanks he broke it
> and gave it to them, saying, "This is my body which is given
> for you. Do this in remembrance of me." (vs. 19)

> 2) And likewise the cup after supper, saying, "This cup which is
> poured out for you is the new covenant in my blood." (vs. 20)

These verses are not explicitly linked to the Passover. Here Jesus asks
his disciples to repeat the meal in his personal memory (vs. 19) and
says his death is the seal of the new covenant (vs. 20). The orientation
is to the past. The similarities to the Pauline tradition of the Lord's
Supper in 1 Cor 11:23–25 are striking.

What is the view of Jesus' death reflected in these words? Three
expressions need analysis if we are to arrive at an adequate answer:
"new covenant," "in my blood," and "given for you." In the first place,
Jesus speaks of a new covenant related to his death. The reference is
to Jer 31:31–34 where Yahweh declares he will make a new covenant
with Israel: "I will put my law within them, and I will write it upon
their hearts" (vs. 33). A similar kind of promise is found in Ezek 36:26–
27, though the expression "new covenant" is missing: "A new heart I
will give you, and a new spirit I will put within you. . . . And I will
put my spirit within you, and cause you to walk in my statutes and be
careful to observe my ordinances." In 2 Cor 3:3, 6 is a Pauline appropriation of the thought of Jeremiah 31:

> You show that you are a letter from Christ . . . written not with
> ink but with the Spirit of the living God, not on tablets of stone
> but on tablets of human hearts. (vs. 3)

> God . . . has qualified us to be ministers of a new covenant, not
> in a written code but in the Spirit; for the written code kills, but
> the Spirit gives life. (vs. 6)

Jeremiah saw the new covenant as involving an urge from the inside to be faithful to the relationship with God in contrast to the old command from the outside. Paul specified that the urge from the inside came from the Spirit. Luke 22:20 uses this new covenant mentality.

The necessity for a new covenant lay in the sinfulness of God's creatures (v., Jer 17:9—, "The heart is deceitful above all things, and desperately corrupt"). In the new covenant God himself assumes responsibility for enabling one "to will and to do his good pleasure" (Phil 2:13). The new covenant prophesied by Jeremiah and Ezekiel and spoken about by Paul and the Lukan Jesus is new in the sense that God now assumes responsibility for enabling humans to relate faithfully to him.

In the second place, Jesus says the new covenant is sealed by his blood, which echoes the covenant ceremony of Exod 24:3–8 where Moses, after throwing the blood on the people, said, "Behold the blood of the covenant which the Lord has made with you" (vs. 8). Jesus says his coming death will seal the new covenant in the heart so that there would be an urge from within to obey God. In Lukan theology, as in Pauline, the instrument of this inner power is the Holy Spirit. In the emptying of the cup Jesus saw the promise of a new relation to God, one controlled by the Holy Spirit within the disciple which would be sealed by his death. If the death of Jesus is in any way to be regarded as sacrificial in Luke-Acts, it is as a sacrifice that seals a covenant (cf. Gen 15:8–21; 17): it is not an atonement for sin.

In the third place, the expression "which is given for you" in the saying over the bread should not be understood in terms of an atoning sacrifice. Although "given" (*didomenon*) can be used with reference to sacrifice (e.g., Exod 30:14; Lev 22:14), it can also be used for martyrdom (Isa 53:10). The same is true of "for you" (*huper*), which can be used of a martyr's actions (2 Mac 7:9; 8:21; 4 Mac 1:8, 10) as well as of a sacrificial offering (Lev 5:7; 6:23). Since the dominant thrust of Luke's understanding of Jesus' death is that of martyrdom, it seems preferable to understand the language here in those terms as well. Here we are told that Jesus' martyrdom would have beneficial effects for the disciples—exactly what was said in the remarks about a new covenant.

Taken as a whole the words of Jesus over the bread and wine in 22:19–20 speak of Jesus' death as a martyrdom which seals the new covenant characterized by life in the Spirit. Jesus asks that this death

be memorialized in a repeated meal observed by his disciples. The foundational event in the community's life must not be forgotten.

Viewed in their immediate context vss. 19–20 function as part of the farewell speech form into which the evangelist has cast his material: in vss. 15–18 Jesus predicts his imminent death; in vss. 19–20 he predicts that it will seal the new covenant and exhorts his apostles to repeat it as a memorial to him. The other components in vss. 21–38 function similarly.

Luke 22:21–23 functions as a prediction. Someone at the table with Jesus will betray him. Luke, unlike Matt 26:21–25 // Mark 14: 18–21, locates this prediction of betrayal (Ps 41:9) after the meal, thereby saying it is possible to eat with Jesus and still betray him. Similar points are made in 1 Corinthians 10 and John 13, indicating this was a serious problem in early Christianity (cf. A. Vööbus, *The Prelude to the Lukan Passion Narrative* [Stockholm: Este, 1968], p. 24). Presence at the Lord's table is no guarantee against apostasy. The meal possesses no magical powers. Here is a warning for Luke's community about a danger for which to be alert.

Luke 22:24–27 functions as exhortation. Luke, unlike Matt 20:25–28 // Mark 10:42–45, has the disciples' dispute over greatness not on the way to Jerusalem but after supper with Jesus, thereby saying it is possible for disciples to eat with Jesus and still be involved in strife among themselves because of their desire for places of status (cf. 1 Cor 3:1–4; 12—14; John 13; Matt 23:1–11; again, this points up a real problem in the early church). The correction for this strife is located in the reversal of values so characteristic of Luke: "let the greatest among you become as the youngest, and the leader as the one who serves." The basis for this reversal is the example of Jesus: "I am among you as one who serves." This passage presupposes a community with leaders who are overly impressed with their authority (cf. 12:41–48). Here is another warning for Luke's church. The supper guarantees neither a lasting vertical relationship nor a harmonious horizontal one.

Following the two warnings Jesus gives two promises to comfort his disciples. The first, 22:28–30, is prediction. The apostles who have continued with Jesus in his trials will participate both in the messianic banquet (cf. 13:28–29; 14:15) and in the last judgment (cf. Matt 19:28; 1 Cor 6:2, 3): Jesus promises ultimate vindication for those who walk his way.

Luke 22:31–34, the second promise, functions as both prediction

and exhortation. Jesus predicts the satanic attack on the disciples (the "you" is plural in vs. 31; cf. Job 1—2; Zech 3:1–3) and assures Peter of his intercession on his behalf (the "you" is singular in vs. 32; cf. John 17:15; Rom 8:34; Heb 7:25). He predicts the threefold denial that is coming so soon. Peter's slip is not regarded by Luke as apostasy. Operating from his confidence that Peter will repent, Jesus exhorts him to strengthen his brethren when he is able. Satan tries to secure the apostasy of Jesus' disciples, but Jesus' prayer protects them. This can only be seen as a foreshadowing of the risen Lord's heavenly intercession for his saints. It is a comforting promise.

Luke 22:35–38, an exhortation based on a prediction, closes the farewell speech. The prediction is that now the conditions of the Lord's passion ("he was reckoned with transgressors," that is, treated as a criminal—23:39ff.) apply to his followers. The peaceful conditions of the first missions (9:1ff.; 10:1ff.) no longer apply. Since this is so, there is an exhortation: be ready for hardship and self-sacrifice, a part of Jesus' Way (cf. Luke 9). Its purpose is the refinement of one's faith. 1 Pet 1:6–7 puts it well: "Now for a little while you may have to suffer various trials, so that the genuineness of your faith, more precious than gold which though perishable is tested by fire, may redound to praise and glory and honor at the revelation of Jesus Christ." Failing to grasp the point, the disciples take Jesus' words literally and produce two swords. Frustrated, Jesus breaks off the conversation: "Enough of this."

The farewell speech of 22:14–38 relates that Jesus' disciples need warnings about the dangers of apostasy, strife, denial, and persecution as part of the lives of those who eat at Jesus' table. Disciples receive not only exhortation to right behavior but also assurances. Jesus' death has sealed a new relation with God through the Spirit; he is praying for his own; and he promises his disciples ultimate vindication with him.

A MODEL FOR MARTYRS

22:1—23:56 (B. 22:39—23:25)

Luke 22:39—23:25 has parallels for much of its material in the other synoptics; again, however, the shape of the material is distinctively Lukan. The distinctive thrust of this section is best understood against the background of the Lukan view of Jesus' death as a martyrdom which is a model for his disciples. First, two things need to be said about Jesus' death. On the one hand, in contrast to other NT witnesses (like Paul e.g., 1 Cor 15:3; 2 Cor 5:21; Rom 3:25, and Matthew e.g., 26:28), Luke avoids any connection between Jesus' death and the forgiveness of sins. (a) In the speeches of Acts both Peter (2:38; 3:19; 5:31; 10:43) and Paul (13:38; 17:30; 26:18) preach the forgiveness of sins as the risen Christ directed (Luke 24:47). Yet neither combines the forgiveness of sins with the death of Jesus on the cross. (b) In contrast to Mark 10:45 ("For the Son of man also came . . . to give his life as a ransom for many"), Luke 22:27b ("I am among you as one who serves") avoids any mention of an atoning death. (c) In 22:37 (Isa 53:12) and Acts 8:32–33 (Isa 53:7–8), although Isaiah 53 is quoted, there is no mention of the sacrificial death of the servant. (d) In Luke-Acts, neither baptism (Acts 2:38, 41; 8:12, 13, 16; 8:37–39; 9:18; 10:47–48; 16:15; 19:5; 22:16) nor the Lord's Supper (Luke 22:16–20; 24:30ff.; 24:41ff.; Acts 2:42–46; 20:7, 11; 27:35) is connected with Jesus' atoning death (contrast Rom 6:3ff. and 1 Cor. 11:23ff.). In Luke-Acts forgiveness of sins flows from the earthly Jesus, especially at mealtime (Luke 19:7f.; 15:1ff.; 5:29–32), and after the resurrection from the exalted Lord (Acts 3:28; 4:11; 5:31—"God exalted him at his right hand as Leader and Savior, to give repentance to Israel and forgiveness of sins.").

On the other hand, Luke portrays the death of Jesus as a martyrdom, the unjust murder of an innocent man by the established powers due to the pressure of the Jewish leaders. (a) Jesus is innocent of the charges against him (23:4, 14, 15, 22, 41, 47). (b) He is delivered by the Jewish chief priests and scribes (Luke 22:66; 23:1–2, 10, 13, 18,

21, 23, 24; cf. Acts 5:27, 30; 13:27) and executed by Gentiles (Luke 23:34; Acts 4:27). (c) His death is parallel to the sufferings of the prophets of old at the hands of the Jews (Luke 13:33; Acts 7:52— "which of the prophets did not your fathers persecute? And they killed those who announced beforehand the coming of the Righteous One, whom you have now betrayed and murdered"). So Jesus stands at the end of a long line of martyrs. (d) Like the martyrs in 2 Mac 7:2, 11; 4 Mac 6:1; 10:23, Jesus is silent before his accusers (Luke 23:9). As in the Martyrdom of Isaiah, Jesus' martyrdom is due to the devil (Luke 22:3, 53). As in the case of the martyrs slain by Herod (Josephus, *Antiquities,* 17:6:2–4 § 167), there is an eclipse at Jesus' death (Luke 23:45). (e) His demeanor in his martyrdom leads to the conversion of one of the thieves crucified with him (Luke 23:40–43). (f) Jesus' martyr death is a fulfillment of OT prophecies (Luke 23:25–27, 46; Acts 13:27–29), a part of God's plan (Acts 2:23).

Secondly, the martyrdom of Jesus is viewed as a model for his disciples. This becomes clear when we note that the story of Stephen's death in Acts parallels that of Jesus in the gospel. (a) Both are tried before the Council (Luke 22:66f.; Acts 6:12f.). (b) Both die a martyr's death. (c) Acts 7:59, "Lord Jesus, receive my spirit," echoes Luke 23:46, "Father, into thy hands I commit my spirit." (d) Acts 7:60, "Lord, do not hold this sin against them," echoes Luke 23:34, "Father, forgive them; for they do not know what they are doing." (e) Both stories contain a Son of Man saying: Luke 22:69; Acts 7:56. This is remarkable since Acts 7:56 is the only occurrence of the title Son of Man outside the gospels and on any lips except those of Jesus. (f) Both men's deaths issue in evangelistic results (Luke 23:39–43; Acts 8:1ff.; 11:19ff.). Moreover, the story of Stephen's martyrdom fulfills Jesus' words: Luke 21:12–19, especially vs. 16 ("some of you they will put to death"; cf. also 12:1–12). The deaths of both Jesus and Stephen are portrayed as martyrdoms in Luke-Acts, the former being the model for the latter.

It is against the backdrop of the Lukan view of Jesus' death as a martyrdom which serves as a model for his followers that one reads 22:39—23:25. This passage pictures Jesus, on the way to martrydom, as an example for his community. There are a number of facets to the example offered. (1) Luke 22:39–46, the first of two episodes set on the Mount of Olives, portrays Jesus as an example in his use of prayer as protection against the temptation to lapse. The evangelist has shaped

the prayer scene for his own ends. First, he specifies that the disciples "followed him" (vs. 39). There is not the effort in Luke to put distance between Jesus and the disciples that we find in Matthew and Mark. They are with him in his trials (23:28; Acts 14:22). For the evangelist the apostles' perseverance is as important as their being present throughout Jesus' career for their testimony's reliability after Easter. Second, Luke frames the account of Jesus' prayer with an exhortation to those who follow him "to pray that you may not enter into temptation" (vss. 40, 46; cf. 11:4—"enter into" means "succumb to"). The present imperative has durative force: "go on praying." Prayer is the weapon of a disciple as well as his master in the face of satanic attack in an hour of darkness (21:36; 18:7–8). This framing device gives the story a parenetic function: Jesus is teaching his disciples to pray in the face of trouble and attack (cf. Acts 4:23–31). This command is given in the context of the problem of the disciples' lapsing (Luke 22:22, 32, 34, 54–62). Third, the evangelist uses Jesus as a model of the praying Christian. Verses 43–44, absent in the other synoptics, are textually questionable. In spite of the strong evidence for their omission, however, there is equally strong internal evidence for their inclusion. It is, for example, a Lukan tendency to have prayer followed by some type of heavenly manifestation (e.g., Luke 3:21–22; 9:28–31; Acts 10:1–7). Also, the best parallels for a strengthening angel are in Dan 10:18–19 and Genesis Rabbah 44, words to or about the potential martyrs of the Maccabean period, and the best parallels for the themes of sweat and blood are in the story of Eleazer's martyrdom in 4 Mac 6:6, 11; 7:8. The use of these two items fits with the overall tendency in Luke to depict Jesus as a martyr. It seems preferable to include the verses. Jesus prays and an angel from heaven appears to strengthen him so he can pray more intensely. Here Jesus is no more forsaken by his Father than he is by his disciples. Heaven sends a strengthening angel to equip him for his martyrdom. Jesus carries out his own admonition to pray in times of crisis (cf. Acts 14:23–31; 12:1ff; 16:25ff.). By teaching and by example Jesus instructs disciples about how potential martyrs face the power of darkness (J. Warren Holleran, *The Synoptic Gethsemane* [Rome: Universita Gregoriana Editrice, 1973], chaps. 3, 6, 7). Finally, the content of the prayer is submission: "not my will, but thine, be done." Temptation to lapse is overcome by the intense prayer of surrender (cf. Eph 6:18; Col 4:2). Jesus' prayer is the disciples' model.

(2) The second episode, 22:47–53, also presents Jesus as teacher and model for his community. In this version of the arrest, two related variations from the other synoptics point to the evangelist's intent. (a) In vs. 49, when Jesus' disciples see what is about to happen, they ask, "Lord, shall we strike with the sword?" (b) Then in vs. 51, after one of the disciples had cut off the right ear of the high priest's slave, Jesus responds, "No more of this." Then he touches the ear and heals it. By means of these two episodes Jesus is presented as one who does not sanction physical violence as a means of escaping from martyrdom: violence as self-defense is renounced.

(3) In 22:54—23:25, the trials of Jesus, are several more examples in which Jesus serves as a model for his community in a time of crisis. In contrast to Matthew and Mark, who have three trials (Sanhedrin at night; Sanhedrin in the morning; Pilate), Luke has four (22:66—Sanhedrin, 23:1—Pilate; 23:8—Herod; 23:13–Pilate), probably to parallel the four trials of Paul in Acts (Acts 23—Sanhedrin; 24—Felix; 25—Festus; 26—Herod Agrippa). (a) Though Luke has Jesus taken to the high priest's house at night after his arrest (vs. 54), there is no nighttime trial. As the reader waits for daybreak, the denial of Peter is described (vss. 54b–62). Satan is sifting Peter (22:31), but a distinctive Lukan look by Jesus (vs. 61a) brings tears of repentance (vs. 62; though omitted by some, this verse is supported by such strong external evidence it should be included). Here the martyr, Jesus, is concerned to return straying disciples to the fold (22:32). Even in times of personal crisis, Jesus is concerned for others. In this he is a model for his community. He also is one whose faithfulness evokes our own (cf. 1 Tim 6:13–14).

(b) Though Jesus was submissive to the Father's will (22:42), he did not seek martyrdom. The trials make this clear. When day came Jesus was brought before the Council (22:66) briefly in what appears to be a preliminary investigation. The case against him was based solely on what Jesus himself said. There were no false witnesses as in Matt 26:60 // Mark 14:56–57. The issue was his identity: Are you the Christ? Are you the Son of God? There was no mention of the destruction of the temple as in Matt 26:61 // Mark 14:58. Jesus' answers were evasive: the first (vss. 68–69) said that though the Jewish leadership would not believe, God would vindicate his servant (cf. Acts 2:33–36; 5:31; 7:56); the second simply said, "That is what you say" (vs. 70). In his evasiveness Jesus acted in accord with general cultural norms. Mar-

tyrdom was not to be sought. Pagan teachers like Seneca (*Epistle* 24:25) said, "Above all, . . . avoid the weakness which has taken possession of many—the lust for death." Jewish teachers denounced overeagerness for martyrdom as self-annihilation (Genesis Rabbah 82) and argued that under duress evasion was acceptable. Early Christians reflected the same stance: the *Martrydom of Polycarp,* 4, stated, "we do not approve those who give themselves up, for the gospel does not teach us to do so"; the *Acts of St. Cyprian* put it, "our discipline forbids anyone to surrender voluntarily." Jesus had no lust for death, was not bent on self-annihilation, but submitted to his Father's will. If that led to martyrdom, so be it. In this he functions as a pattern for his disciples.

(c) The Jewish Council in Luke does not condemn Jesus to death as in Matt 26:66 // Mark 14:64; they bring him to Pilate for the second trial (23:1). In 23:1–5 the Jewish leaders register their charges against Jesus. They have nothing to do with the previous examination, but are specifically political: 1) perverting the nation; 2) forbidding payment of taxes to Caesar; and 3) claiming to be a king (vs. 2). Of course, Luke intends the reader to see the charges as false (cf. 19:41–44 where Jesus is for peace; 20:21–25 where taxes are not prohibited; 22:67–70 where his answers are ambiguous about his identity). In being the object of false witness Jesus' experience is prototypical for his followers. It was the question of kingship that would most concern a Roman official (cf. Acts 17:7–8). So Pilate asks, "Are you the king of the Jews?" Jesus' answer (vs. 3) is the same as that given to the Sanhedrin (22:70): he is evasive. Pilate's evaluation is different from the Council's: "I find no crime in this man." The Jewish leadership is insistent: "He stirs up the people, teaching . . . from Galilee even to this place." Mention of Galilee is part of their propaganda against Jesus because Galilee was a hot-bed of revolutionary activity. By implication they bear false witness against Jesus. It is something with which Jesus' disciples will have to live.

(d) When Pilate learned that Jesus was a Galilean, he sent him to Herod, who happened to be in Jerusalem then (vss. 6–7) and who was eager to see Jesus (cf. 9:9). The third trial of Jesus, before Herod (vss. 6–12), is peculiar to Luke. It serves three possible functions. 1) It provides a second official witness to Jesus' innocence and so satisfies the demands of Deut 19:15. This seems indisputable in light of 23:14–15. Jesus is not guilty of sedition. The two officials agree on that. 2) It

may serve to fulfill Ps 2:1ff. quoted in Acts 4:25–26 and in vs. 27 of that chapter is applied specifically to Herod and Pontius Pilate who collaborated to kill Jesus. It seems better to say, however, that the gospel regards Herod and Pilate favorably because of their judgment on Jesus' innocence, while Acts 4 regards them hostilely as involved in Jesus' death. 3) Like Ephesians, where Christ's death is the reconciliation of human hostility, particularly of the division between Jew and Gentile, 23:12 may indicate that the Jewish ruler (Herod) was reconciled to the Gentile (Pilate) on the very day of the shedding of Jesus' blood (John Drury, *Tradition and Design in Luke's Gospel* [Atlanta: John Knox, 1976], pp. 16–17). Though this third option is possible, it is not explicit in the Lukan scheme. The primary function of 23:6–12 seems to lie in the first explanation, Luke's preoccupation with the innocence of Jesus. Here again, he is a model for disciples: "For it is better to suffer for doing right, if that should be God's will, than for doing wrong. For Christ also died . . . the righteous for the unrighteous" (1 Pet 3:17–18).

(e) The emphasis on the innocence of Jesus is continued in the fourth and final trial (23:13–25), where Pilate appears more as an advocate who pleads Jesus' case than as a judge presiding over an official hearing: "I did not find this man guilty . . . neither did Herod. . . . I will therefore chastise him and release him" (vss. 14–16). The chastisement was a light beating accompanied by a severe warning (cf. Acts 16:22–24; 22:24). Pilate was saying in effect that he would give Jesus a suspended sentence. The opponents of Jesus, which now include the people along with the chief priests and rulers (23:13—but not the Pharisees), all cry out for Jesus' death and Barabbas' release (vs. 18). This is part of the irony of the gospel story: those who sought Jesus' death because of his alleged sedition called for the release of one guilty of an insurrection started in the city and of murder (vs. 19). Pilate tries once more to release Jesus: "I have found in him no crime deserving death" (vs. 22). "But they were urgent, demanding with loud cries that he should be crucified. And their voices prevailed" (vs. 23)—Pilate released Barabbas the insurrectionist and delivered Jesus to their will. The impression made by the trials as a whole is that an innocent man has been condemned, and Jesus goes to his death a martyr.

In this story of Jesus' progress toward death, his disciples are intended to see certain things relating to their lives as well. Although innocent, Christians may be given over to the will of their opponents

with their vindication coming only after suffering (Acts 16:19–39) or death (Acts 7). At such a time it is important that the Christians have prayed and continue to do so in order to escape the temptation to lapse (22:39–46). Martyrdom is not to be sought, but neither is violence to be used to escape. The disciples may expect false witness to be borne against them. Note the irony: that with which one is charged is often that of which one's accusers are guilty. In such times of crisis Jesus is one's model.

INNOCENT AND OBEDIENT

22:1—23:56 (C. 23:26–56a)

While the material in 23:26–56a has parallels in the other synoptics, for the most part, its overall purpose is quite different. The clue to the distinctive Lukan development of the material is found in the very first pericope of the unit, vs. 26, the reference to Simon of Cyrene. The evangelist has shaped this statement so Simon carries the cross "behind Jesus." Thereby the pericope not only speaks about the nature of discipleship (cf. 9:23; 14:27—taking the cross and following Jesus), but also about who Jesus is (*archēgos*, pioneer, leader, one who goes before and opens the way for others to follow—cf. 19:28; Acts 3:15; 5:31; also Heb 2:10; 12:2). Jesus has gone before the disciples (19:28); they are to follow after him in the way he has opened. Simon is a symbol for disciples who share Jesus' trials (22:28). The NT sometimes refers to Jesus as an example (e.g., John 13:15; 1 Pet 2:21), as does this book; whenever this is done the term is intended in the sense of this leader-follower pattern. This picture of Jesus sets the stage for what follows.

In vss. 32–56 Jesus' way is described in terms of both horizontal and vertical relationships. In his horizontal relations with others Jesus' innocence is accented. In his vertical relationship with the Father, Jesus' obedience is highlighted. Though these threads often run together in the narrative, one does not truly perceive Jesus' way unless both are seen. The one who as a lad "increased . . . in favor with God and man" (2:52) now ends his career with the emphasis on just those two relationships. The implication throughout is that the one so described is intended to function as a model for the disciples who follow him. The pattern can be anticipated as one reads the following paragraphs.

Luke 23:32–43 records Jesus' crucifixion among the transgressors (22:37), together with a variety of responses to the event. Several components of the narrative stand out. (1) Although vs. 34a, "And Jesus said, 'Father, forgive them, for they know not what they do,'" is omitted by many manuscripts, it is almost certainly a legitimate part of the

text. The language and thought are Lukan (Father—10:21; 11:2; 22:42; 23:46; forgive because of ignorance—Acts 3:17; 13:27; intercede for executioners—Acts 7:60). Also sayings of Jesus are found in each main section of the crucifixion narrative (23:28–31, 43, 46). If one were missing here the pattern would be disturbed. It could have been omitted because either it was believed to have conflicted with vss. 28–31 or it was thought that the events of A.D. 66–70 showed it was not answered. The prayer seems to echo Isa 53:12: "he . . . made intercession for the transgressors." In so doing Jesus was modeling what he had taught (6:27–28; 17:14): he not only taught God's will but was also obedient to it.

(2) The responses of the rulers (vs. 35), the soldiers (vss. 36–37), and one of the criminals crucified with him (vs. 39) combine to form a threefold temptation of the crucified Jesus much like the earlier threefold temptation in the wilderness (4:1–13): "If you are the Christ, the king, save yourself." Though Jesus' power was still with him (22:51), as in the wilderness, he refused to use it for himself even to save his life. This episode needs to be set in the context of the overall development of Jesus' career. The temptation in the wilderness (4:1–13) followed his empowering by the Holy Spirit after his baptism and in response to his prayer (3:21–22; cf. 4:16–21). Then the question was whether or not Jesus would use the divine power for his own benefit, for his self-aggrandisement, or for the advancement of his cause. By a Spirit-directed use of scripture Jesus overcame the temptation. Thereafter his power was used for the benefit of others. The temptation on the cross (23:35–39) comes near the climax of Jesus' career which began at 9:18. Since then Jesus has been walking the way of rejection, suffering, and now death. It is a way that perfects his obedience to God by stripping him of every possible idolatrous attachment. Now at the end, hanging on the cross, his life ebbing away, the same question is raised again: Will you use the divine power with which you are endowed for self-preservation? The final attachment in this world to which one is tempted to cling in an idolatrous way is life itself, mere continuance of physical existence: "If you are the Christ, the king, save yourself." The crucified criminal adds, "and us" (vs. 39). The crucified Jesus will not cling even to physical existence and thereby make it an idolatrous attachment. He is obedient unto death (Phil 2:8). He is willing to die rather than sin (i.e., be an idolator). In this his obedience is perfected (Heb 5:8–9; 1 Pet 4:1–2).

(3) The second criminal crucified with Jesus responded differently, he accepted his punishment as justified, an expression of penitence if taken in a Jewish context (vss. 41–42), pronounced Jesus innocent (vs. 41b), and said, "Jesus, remember me when you come in your kingly power" (vs. 42). The plea is to be acknowledged by Jesus at the parousia (9:26; 12:8–9; 18:8b; 19:15; 21:27, 36b), but Jesus responded, "Truly, I say to you, today you will be with me in Paradise" (vs. 43), promising immediate bliss. Paradise originally meant a garden or park such as a king would possess. In intertestamental Judaism it was used of the realm reserved for the righteous dead (Levi 18:10). In 2 Cor 12:4; Rev 2:7 it refers to the realm of bliss in heaven. Luke would regard it as being synonymous with being "in Abraham's bosom" (16:22). He has an interest in individual eschatology, that is, in what happens to a person at death (e.g., 12:4–5, 16–21; 16:19–31; 23:43; Acts 7:55–60), a concern with roots in ancient Judaism. The Apocalypse of Abraham 21 says the righteous dead proceed straight to Paradise where they enjoy heavenly fruits and blessedness, while the wicked dead go immediately to the underworld. 1 Enoch (60:8, 23; 61:12; 70:4) indicates the righteous already dwell in the garden of life. Paul apparently accepted this notion (e.g., 2 Cor 5:8; Phil 1:23), as does Luke-Acts. The exchange indicates that the martyrdom of Jesus performed an evangelistic function which is best understood against the background of ancient thinking about martyrdom.

Any appreciation for the Lukan understanding of Jesus' martyrdom must come from a knowledge of pagan, Jewish, and early Christian attitudes towards martyrdom. With pagans, on the one hand, martyrdom was regarded positively in many circles in antiquity. (a) It was a commonplace that true philosophers lived their doctrine as well as expounded it. The philosopher's word alone, unaccompanied by the act, was regarded as invalid (e.g., Seneca, *Epistle*, 52:8–9; Dio Chrysostom, *Discourse*, 70:6). Some very harsh things were said about philosophers' sincerity—or lack of it—in antiquity. Josephus (*Against Apion*, 1:8) exaggerated when he said no Greek philosopher would ever die for his philosophy. The same sentiments are found, however, in Lucian (*The Fisherman*, 31): "in their life and actions . . . they contradicted their outward appearance and reversed [philosophy's] practice." Epictetus (*Discourses*, 1:29:56) says, "what, then, is the thing lacking now? The man . . . to bear witness to the arguments by his acts." Seneca (*Epistle*, 23:15) joins the chorus: "there is a very disgraceful

charge often brought against our school—that we deal with the words, and not the deeds, of philosophy." In view of this cyncism about philosophers' sincerity, sometimes only the willingness to die or actual death could validate a philosopher's profession.

The *Life of Secundus the Silent Philosopher* furnishes an example of a philosopher's sealing his profession with his willingness to die. Secundus, because of an incident that had caused his mother's suicide, put a ban on himself, resolving not to say anything for the rest of his life—having chosen the Pythagorean way of life. The Emperor Hadrian arrived in Athens and sent for Secundus to test him. When Secundus refused to speak, Hadrian sent him off with the executioner with instructions that if he did speak his head should be cut off; if he did not speak, he should be returned to the Emperor. When he was returned to Hadrian after having been willing to die for his vow of silence, Secundus was allowed to write answers to the twenty questions asked by the Emperor—which answers were then put in the sacred library. His willingness to die had validated his philosophy.

(b) The sealing of one's profession in death as a martyr sometimes issued in furthering the cause of the philosopher. Plato's *Apology* tells the story of Socrates' death. In chapter 39 Socrates says, "I would fain prophesy to you; for I am about to die, and that is the time when men are gifted with prophetic power. And I prophesy to you who are my murderers, that immediately after my death punishment far heavier than you have inflicted upon me will surely await you." What is meant in the context is that there will be more accusers than there are now: his position vindicated by death, Socrates' disciples will attack the Athenians as never before.

On the other hand, Greco-Roman teachers warned that martyrdom does not provide certain results; it may win some but not necessarily others (Lucian, *Peregrinus*, 13; Marcus Aurelius, 11:3:2). Above all, as noted above, martyrdom that was sought was regarded as lust for death and was not persuasive (Seneca, *Epistle*, 24:25).

The view of martyrdom in ancient Judaism had similarities to the Greco-Roman stance though there were also differences. On the one side, there was a positive attitude toward martyrdom. (a) Two streams of thought ran parallel. One stream spoke of the prophets dying as martyrs at the hands of God's people (e.g., *Lives of the Prophets; Martyrdom of Isaiah;* cf. also Matt 23:31–39; Heb 11:36ff.; 1 Thes 2:15; Mark 12:1–12). The emphasis is on the sinfulness of God's people (cf.

Luke 13:33–34; Acts 7:52). The other stream spoke of the faithful among God's people dying as martyrs at the hands of the Gentiles. Here, as in Greco-Roman paganism, it was believed the true prophet sealed the truth of his testimony with death. In 4 Maccabees 7 the aged scribe Eleazer refused to eat swine's flesh as demanded by the Syrians or even to pretend to eat it (cf. 2 Mac 6:18ff.). Instead he endured willingly the scourge, the rack, and the flame (2 Mac 7:4). 4 Mac 7:15 cries out, "O life faithful to the Law and perfected by the seal of death."

(b) Sometimes the martyr's actions made converts to Judaism. One tradition (b. Abodah Zarah, 18a) tells of Rabbi Hanina ben Teradion who, in the time of Hadrian, was arrested for teaching Torah to groups. As a punishment he was burned to death. After watching, the executioner then threw himself into the fire, whereupon a *bath qol* exclaimed, "Rabbi Haninah and the executioner have been assigned to the world to come."

On the other hand, as we have seen, Jewish teachers give the same types of cautions about martyrdom found in Greco-Roman paganism: martyrdom is no guarantee of another's conversion (e.g., 2 Mac 6:29). Above all, overeagerness for martyrdom is denounced as self-annihilation (e.g., Genesis Rabbah 82).

Ancient Christianity was deeply indebted to both pagan and Jewish views about martyrdom. On the one hand, there was a positive attitude towards martyrdom. Like pagans and Jews, most Chrisitans believed the truth of their profession must be sealed in blood if it came to that (e.g., Revelation; Justin, *Apology II,* 12). Only some Gnostics refused to undergo martyrdom (e.g., Irenaeus, *Against Heresies,* 1:24:3–6—Basilides; Tertullian, *Against All Heresies,* 1—Basilides). Christians, even more than pagans and Jews, believed martyrdom had "evangelistic" benefits: it helped to spread the gospel. Justin, *Dialogue,* 110, says, "the more we are persecuted, the more do others in ever-increasing numbers embrace the faith." Tertullian, *Apology,* 50, agrees: "we conquer in dying. . . . The oftener we are mown down by you, the more in number we grow; the blood of Christians is seed." The Epistle to Diognetus 6:9 says, "Christians when they are punished increase the more in number every day." In 7:7–8, it proclaims, "Can you not see them thrown to wild beasts, to make them deny their Lord, and yet not overcome? Do you not see that the more of them are punished, the more numerous the others become?" Lactantius (d. c. A.D. 325), *Di-*

vine Institutes, 5:19, says, "It is right reason, then, to defend religion by patience or death in which faith is preserved and is pleasing to God himself, and it adds authority to religion."

On the other hand, Christians also shared the pagan and Jewish reservations about martyrdom: martyrdom, while very persuasive, was certainly not a proof. (Cf. *The Acts of the Christian Martyrs,* ed. H. Musurillo [Oxford: Clarendon Press, 1972], passim.) Overeagerness for martyrdom was denounced (e.g., *Martyrdom of Polycarp,* 4). Not only did such a lust for death violate the Christian belief that life belonged to God, it also detracted from the persuasiveness of the act.

The narrative of Jesus' death in the third gospel comes alive against this background: Jesus did not die because of a lust for death (cf. 22:42); he sought to avoid it, if God would permit it. In dying he legitimated his profession as he sealed it with his blood. He was absolutely sincere in his stance. This legitimation is evidenced in the conversion of the criminal on the cross: Jesus' martyrdom had such evangelistic benefits (cf. Acts 8:1, 4; 11:19ff. for the evangelistic benefits of Stephen's martyrdom). Such a death is persuasive because it testifies to a selfless commitment.

That the one who was converted was a crucified criminal means that this story fits into the motif of Jesus' mediating forgiveness to the outcasts of society (5:29ff.; 7:36ff.; 15:1–2; 18:9–14; 19:1–10). That the conversion and its confirmation by Jesus come before Jesus dies means that this story fits into the theme that it is the Jesus who lives— whether in his earthly life or after his resurrection, e.g., Acts 5:31— who grants forgiveness. Though the evangelist has no doctrine of forgiveness being made available through the death of Jesus, as do Paul and others, he does see forgiveness mediated by the Jesus who lived and who lives. The death of Jesus in Luke-Acts is his rejection by the leaders of Israel. The Passion narrative in the gospel is basically a rejection story, very much like the stories about Stephen and Paul in Acts. Jesus dies as a martyr and his blood does seal a new covenant (22:20), but it is not an atoning sacrifice.

(4) Luke 23:44–56 tells of Jesus' death and burial. Several facts stand out in the account of Jesus' death (vss. 44–49). (a) From noon until three o'clock there was darkness (cf. Amos 8:9). In the Greco-Roman mentality events with cosmic significance were attested by cosmic signs (e.g., Lucan, *Civil War,* 7:199–200, says that at the battle of Pharsalia the "sorrowing deity in heaven gave notice of the battle by the dimness and obscurity of the sun"). This was a time of the power of darkness

(22:53). (b) When Jesus dies, it is with the uniquely Lukan words, "Father, into thy hands I commit my spirit" (vs. 46), an echo of Ps 31:5. Absent are the words, "My God, my God, why hast thou forsaken me?" (Matt 27:46 // Mark 15:34). Jesus dies quietly, full of trust, a model for Christian martyrs to follow (Acts 7:59). This calm assurance in God at the moment of his death was enough to convince the centurion of Jesus' innocence. Unlike Matt 27:54 // Mark 15:39, who have the centurion say, "Truly this man was the Son of God," Luke's guard says, "Certainly this man was innocent" (vs. 47—*dikaios*). Whereas in the other synoptics the centurion was a christologist, in Luke he is an apologist. (c) Verse 49 proclaims that the Galileans witness Jesus' death. These people who will be present throughout the Passion events to guarantee their facticity (cf. 23:55; 24:10; 24:33ff.; Acts 1:11) are those "with Jesus" who will function as a control for what develops after the resurrection. Here we have it affirmed: Jesus really died.

Luke's account of the burial of Jesus by Joseph of Arimathea (vss. 50–56) has two significant variations from the story in Matthew and Mark furnishing clues to its main function in the gospel. First, in vs. 51, Luke says Joseph "had not consented to their purpose and deed." In other words, Joseph was a member of the Sanhedrin who thought Jesus was innocent. The declaration of Jesus' innocence has been a dominant thread in Luke 23: (a) Pilate—vs. 4; (b) Herod—vs. 15; (c) Pilate—vs. 14; (d) Pilate—vs. 22; (e) one of the crucified criminals— vs. 41; (f) the centurion—vs. 47; and now (g) Joseph of Arimathea— vs. 51—becomes Luke's final human witness to the innocence of Jesus. Second, in vs. 55, the evangelist not only indicates that some women saw where Jesus was buried but also specifies that they were those who had come with him from Galilee (cf. 8:1–3) and that they saw how his body was laid. In the Jerusalem events the evangelist is concerned to establish the corporeality of the one who dies, is buried, is raised, and ascends—hence the reference to Jesus' body. Luke is concerned to guarantee both the corporeality of the church's Lord and the continuity between the one who dies in Jerusalem and the one who worked in Galilee by having the Galileans present as witnesses to the Jerusalem events. Theologically this means that the one who was empowered is the one who dies. The death, moreover, is a real one. It was through the suffering of these things that Jesus' obedience was perfected. It was only on the other side of these sufferings that the empowered one entered into glory.

VICTORY,
PRESENCE, AND MISSION

23:56b—24:53; 9:10–17

Luke 24 is, with one exception, composed of materials not found elsewhere in the synoptic tradition. The chapter consists of five major events (two empty tomb episodes; two major appearances; Jesus' departure) located in Jerusalem or its environs, which transpire on one long day (early morning on the first day of the week, 24:1; that same day, 24:13; that same hour, 24:33; then, 24:50). When one notes the Galilean orientation of the appearances in Matt 28:7, 10, 16–20; Mark 16:7; John 21, this exclusive focus on Jerusalem is seen as distinctive (cf. 24:47–49; Acts 1:4). The chapter as a whole is held together by an inclusion (23:56b; 24:53), both the introductory and concluding statements averring that Jesus' disciples are loyal, pious Jews (cf. 2:21ff.; Acts 3:1ff.; 5:12). There are at least three overriding functions of the resurrection chapter.

The first overriding function is to state the nature of Jesus' victory over death. The evangelist's view can only be grasped if seen in the context of early Christian understanding of Jesus' resurrection and the Lukan understanding of Jesus as a prototype of Christian existence. On the one hand, in earliest Christianity the resurrection of Jesus encompassed three different realities: (1) Jesus' victory over death; (2) his removal from human time and space into another dimension (that of God); and (3) his new function as cosmic Lord.

In Luke-Acts the unity of these three realities is broken and they become three separate events on a chronological time line. (1) The resurrection of Jesus is reduced to the reality of his victory over death. (2) The ascension becomes Jesus' removal to heaven. (3) The exaltation designates the moment of Jesus' new status as Lord and Christ. It may be said that this division of a unity into its parts, when done by Luke, is for "the sake of analysis": by taking the different pieces of a whole individually, the evangelist can focus on the meaning of each

without distraction. This means, however, that in Luke-Acts the resurrection of Jesus refers only to Jesus' victory over death.

On the other hand, Jesus functions as a prototype of Christian existence. As we have seen, he is the pioneer who goes before, opening the Way for his disciples to follow. His existence, then, is a model for what his followers may expect. Given this, if Luke speaks about the nature of Jesus' victory over death, it must be taken as a comment about the nature of the victory over death for which Christians hope also. Against this double background we may investigate the resurrection traditions of Luke 24.

Both the first empty tomb tradition and the second appearance story witness to the corporeality of the risen Christ. (1) Luke 24:1–11 tells of the women finding the tomb empty (cf. Matt 28:1–10 // Mark 16:1–8), and has some emphases all its own. First, the evangelist emphasizes the priority of the women's own experience over the angels' words. Luke contrasts what the women found (the stone rolled away) with what they did not find (the body of Jesus). The focus on the absence of the body refers back to the women's observance of how Jesus' body was laid in the tomb (23:55). It is also echoed in a Lukan notice in the Emmaus account (24:23, "did not find his body"). The two angels' words (Luke 9:30; Acts 1:10) simply interpret the empirical data: "Why do you seek the living among the dead?[peculiar to Luke] He is not here but has risen" (24:5). Whatever the nature of Jesus' victory over death was, it involved the absence of his body from the tomb.

Such an assertion is buttressed in three ways by Luke. First, he mentions by name (vs. 10) the women who witnessed the absence of the body of Jesus, echoing the named ones at 8:1–3. This serves to link the Jerusalem witnesses to the career of Jesus from the very first— the same Galileans witnessed his burial in 23:55 and his crucifixion in 23:49 (cf. Acts 1:22; 10:37–41). These women told the disciples, the Eleven and "all the rest" (vs. 9; cf. 24:33), referring to those who were present so as to be qualified to be apostles (Acts 1:15–26) (J. Plevnik, "The Eleven and Those with Them according to Luke," *Catholic Biblical Quarterly* 40:205–11 [1978]): Galilean witnesses attest the absence of the body of Jesus from the tomb. Second, 24:12, if original, offers another empty tomb episode. The trend of recent research is to accept this verse as integral to the gospel (J. E. Alsup, *The Post-Resurrection Appearance Stories of the Gospel Tradition* [Stuttgart: Calver Verlag, 1975], p. 103): the style is Lukan, vs. 24 appears to be a

cross-reference to vs. 12. It could have been omitted because it was thought to contradict vs. 34, but if it is accepted as part of the original text, then vs. 12 would function as a second witness to support the testimony of the women in 24:1–11 (cf. Num 35:30; Deut 17:6f.; 19:15; b. Sotah 2b; b. Sanhedrin 37b; b. Baba Bathra 31b; CD 9:16—10:3; Luke 23:1–16; 24:4; 2:25–38). The evangelist produces two sets of witnesses to the empty tomb (cf. 24:22–24). Given Jewish assumptions, the witness of the men would have been needed: Josephus (*Antiquities*, 4:8:15§219) says, "From women let not evidence be accepted, because of the levity and temerity of their sex" (cf. Mishna, *Rosh Hashana*, 1:8). In order to be persuasive in a Jewish context, the second episode was necessary to buttress the first. Third, 24:12 also aims to discredit any theory about the theft of the body as an explanation for the absence of Jesus' body: "He saw the linen cloths by themselves" (cf. Matt 28:11ff.; John 20:1ff. for similar concerns). In these three ways this gospel supports the tradition of the absence of Jesus' body from the tomb; it is a part of Luke's way of celebrating Jesus' victory over death.

(2) Luke 24:36–43 tells of an appearance of Jesus to the Eleven in Jerusalem; this also functions to establish the corporeality of the risen Christ (cf. 1 John 1:1; John 20:24–29). When Jesus appeared the disciples supposed they saw a spirit. The story combats such a belief with physical proof of two kinds: First, Jesus says, "See my hands and feet, that it is I myself; handle me, and see; for a spirit has not flesh and bones as you see that I have" (vs. 39; cf. 1 John 1:1–2); then he said to them, "Have you anything here to eat?" Luke adds, "They gave him a piece of broiled fish, and he took it and ate before them" (vss. 41–43; cf. Acts 1:4; 10:41). The significance of this action for the Jewish mind is clear: angels do not eat (e.g., Tob 12:19; Josephus, *Antiquities*, 1:9:2§197; Philo, *On Abraham*, 118). Only human beings eat. For Luke the risen Lord, no less than the pre-Easter Jesus, was flesh and bones, corporeal, truly human. The risen Jesus not only eats, he also can be seen (presumably even the wounds in his hands and feet) and touched.

These two stories say the same thing about the nature of Jesus' victory over death: it is not to be understood as an escape from this perishable frame but as a transformation of it; it is not to be understood as a transformation into a purely spiritual, angelic being, because Jesus remained flesh and bones, though immortal and not limited by

time and space (24:31); it is no more the immortality of the soul while his body decayed than it is the survival of his shade (a pale shadow of the life on earth, cf. 1 Sam 28:8ff.). These views are presupposed in Paul's discussion of the Christians' resurrection in 1 Corinthians 15: "With what kind of body do they come?" (vs. 35b). Luke's answer is very much the same as Paul's, except he does not give an analytical answer, but gives his reply in the form of a narrative of the risen Christ who is understood as the prototype of Christian existence. In Luke 24 one sees the nature of Jesus' victory over death: it is the same victory for which his disciples hope (1 John 3:2).

The second overriding function of Luke 24 is to clarify the nature of the Eucharist, at least for the Lukan community. Proper appreciation of this appearance story comes only when we set it against the larger background of Jesus' meals in Luke-Acts. Jesus is frequently involved in meals: (1) with sinners (5:29–32; 15:1–2; 19:5–7); (2) with Pharisees (7:36–50; 11:37ff.; 14:1ff.); (3) with disciples (22:19–20; 24:30; 24:41–43; Acts 1:4—the term is literally "to take salt with someone" but the Latin, Syriac, and Coptic translations read, "to eat together"; Acts 10:41); (4) with the multitudes and disciples (9:11–17). Three of the meals in which the earthly and risen Jesus is involved mention the breaking of bread (9:11–17; 22:19–20; 24:30).

The first of these, Luke 9:10–17, echoes earlier elements in the narrative. In 1:53 Mary sings in celebration of the miraculous conception of Jesus and of the recognition of him as Lord by Elizabeth and by the yet unborn John: "He has filled the hungry with good things." This is doubtless the equivalent of the prophetic perfect in Hebrew, an utterance of such certainty that its content can be spoken of as already having happened. In 6:21 Jesus says, "Blessed are you that hunger now, for you shall be satisfied." Luke 9:10–17 picks up this theme and portrays Jesus as the one who satisfies the hungry, feeding them through his apostles.

That the symbolism of Jesus as the one who satisfies the hungry was intended by the evangelist is shown by Luke's location of the incident. While Matt 14:13 // Mark 6:31 locate the feeding in a lonely place (cf. Luke 9:12), Luke specifies Bethsaida, a main city of Philip's tetrarchy, located on the northern end of the lake across the Jordan from Herod's jurisdiction. Like the reference to the land of the Gerasenes (8:26), this location is geographically awkward because the feeding story demands a lonely place (9:12) rather than an urban area, but

the use of the name Bethsaida is for its symbolic value—the name means "place of satisfaction." Luke 9:17 reinforces the point when it tells us that as a result of the feeding "all were satisfied." Again, Jesus is the one who satisfies the hungry.

In Acts we hear that the church was involved in breaking bread (2:42; 2:46; 20:7; 27:33–36—all but the last text in the setting of Christian worship). Since there are evidences of cultic meals in early Christianity with only bread and no mention of wine (e.g., Acts of John 106–10; Acts of Thomas 27, 49–50, 133), or with bread and salt (e.g., Pseudo-Clementines, *Recognitions* 4; *Homilies* 14:7), this seems to be the Lukan terminology for the Eucharist in Acts (P. H. Menoud, "The Acts of the Apostles and the Eucharist," in *Jesus Christ and the Faith,* trans. E. M. Paul [Pittsburgh: Pickwick Press, 1978], 84–106). If so, then for Luke's community the Eucharist is the cultic extension of the multiplication of the loaves and of the Last Supper, the continuation of the fellowship meals Jesus had with his disciples during his earthly life, done as a memorial of Jesus the martyr in obedience to his command (22:19). Such meals doubtless anticipated the messianic banquet (13:29; 14:15). It is in this context that 24:13–33, a resurrection appearance at mealtime where ritual actions are repeated, is to be understood. This story functions as a bridge between the meals of the earthly Jesus and the breaking of bread in the narrative of Acts.

In 24:30 the risen Christ "took bread and blessed, and broke it, and gave it to them." This action also echoes previous meals (9:16; 22:19). Although earlier they had been kept from recognizing him (vs. 16), now the disciples' eyes are opened and they do recognize him (vs. 31a; cf. Heb 6:4 where "enlightened" is an image of conversion; Mark 10:46–52; John 9). The table fellowship which was interrupted by Jesus' death is here resumed at the risen Jesus' initiative. Hereafter, the disciples will go on doing this in remembrance of him (22:19). That the evangelist wanted his readers to recognize the eucharistic overtones seems confirmed by the ending of the unit in vs. 35: "Then they told what had happened on the road, and how he was known to them in the breaking of the bread." This incident, moreover, is but one of several occasions when the risen Jesus ate with his followers (Acts 1:4; 10:41). This story not only serves as a bridge between the meals the earthly Jesus had with his disciples and the later church's Eucharist, it also says that at such meals the presence of the risen Lord was

known: Jesus is alive and one place of his recognition is at the breaking of the bread.

The distinctiveness of this understanding of the Eucharist may be seen when it is compared with that of the fourth gospel and of Paul. In the fourth gospel the Eucharist is the cultic extension of the incarnation: through its physical elements one experiences contact with the divine world just as one did through the flesh of Jesus in the days of his incarnation (cf. John 6). In Paul the Lord's Supper is the moment in which one remembers (identifies with, participates in) Jesus' death much as the Israelites-Jews remembered (participated in) the events of the Exodus at their Passover meal (cf. 1 Corinthians 11). Luke sees the Supper as the extension of the meals with the earthly Jesus and in anticipation of the messianic banquet, a meal at which one experiences the presence of Christ as the disciples did after the resurrection.

The third overriding function of Luke 24 is to underscore the mission command of the risen Christ. Three components deserve attention. (1) The command itself is found in 24:46–48: "Thus it is written, that the Christ should suffer and on the third day rise from the dead, and that repentance and forgiveness of sins should be preached in his name to all nations, beginning from Jerusalem. You are witnesses of these things." The evangelist thinks that after Jesus' resurrection his trial is reopened and fresh evidence is presented by the apostles to get the Jews to change their verdict. The new evidence is the event of Jesus' resurrection. The condemnation of Christ had been done in ignorance (Acts 3:17; 13:27), but in raising Jesus God showed the Jews they had made a mistake: they had crucified the Christ (Acts 2:36). Now, however, the Jews are given a chance to change their minds, to repent (2:38; 3:19; 5:31). If they do not, then they themselves will be cut off from the people of God (Acts 3:22–23). The witnesses are to press for this decision (Allison Trites, *The New Testament Concept of Witness* [Cambridge: Cambridge University Press, 1977], 129–30). What is to begin in Jerusalem, however, is to be carried to all nations (cf. Acts 1:8).

(2) The authority for the mission command is twofold. On the one hand, the one who gives it speaks a compelling word. Twice in this chapter there is a reference to words spoken by the pre-Easter Jesus which have been fulfilled in the events of the Passion-resurrection. In vs. 6 the angels say, "Remember how he told you, *while he was still*

in Galilee, that the Son of Man must be delivered into the hands of sinful men, and be crucified, and on the third day rise." The reference is to the predictions in 9:22, 44 (cf. 17:25; 18:32–33). What Jesus prophesied has been fulfilled. In vs. 44 is a similar motif: "These are my words which I spoke to you, *while I was still with you,* that everything written about me . . . must be fulfilled." The events of Luke 22–24 have fulfilled Jesus' prophetic words. In the Lukan world, as we have noted, both pagans and Jews believed that the fulfillment of prophecy legitimated authority. Hence, if Jesus' words have been fulfilled, he is a true prophet who speaks with authority. This is the one who gives the mission command. On the other hand, vss. 46–47 not only indicate that the Christ's Passion is a fulfillment of scripture but so is the mission to Israel and the nations: the authoritative writings reinforce the mission command, understood as a divine necessity. This twofold emphasis upon the fulfillment of prophecy serves to give the authority for the new outreach by the disciples. Matt 28:16–20, the great commission, also gives a mission directive and underscores it with authority but in a different way: the Matthean Jesus says, "All authority has been given to me." By virtue of his resurrection-exaltation he rules over the cosmos. In Luke-Acts the exaltation comes later (Acts 2:36), so here the risen Christ appeals to the authority of fulfilled prophecy for his missionary directive.

(3) Jesus does not just give his mission command and then leave its accomplishment to his followers. He makes two provisions for his witnesses. On the one hand, the witnesses are to stay in Jerusalem until they are "clothed with power from on high" (24:49; cf. Acts 1:4–5; 1:8; 2:1ff.). Part of the reason for this rests in the Lukan belief that a valid testimony to Christ requires two prominent witnesses, in accordance with Deut 19:15, namely, the witness of the apostles and the witness of the Holy Spirit (cf. Acts 5:32—"we are witnesses to these things, and so is the Holy Spirit"). In part it is due to the belief that God has the initiative in salvation history so that what human beings do must be done in response to the divine leading and empowering. The gift of the Holy Spirit supplies that power and leading. The pentecostal gift of the Spirit is Jesus' first provision for his followers who are given a missionary directive. In Lukan theology this is prototypical: there is no evangelistic outreach without a prior empowering.

On the other hand, Jesus does not leave his disciples until he has put them under the protection of God. Luke 24:5–53 is a departure

scene that takes place at night of the same Easter day. The evangelist often describes the departure of supernatural beings (1:38; 2:15; 9:33; 24:31, Acts 10:7; 12:10). This was a common motif among both pagan (Euripides, *Orestia*, 1496; Virgil, *Aeneid*, 9:657) and Jewish peoples (Gen 17:22; 35:13; Judg 6:21; 13:20; Tob 12:20f.; 2 Mac 3:34). Luke uses the typical departure motif to speak of Jesus' ascension into heaven: "He parted from them and was carried up into heaven" (vs. 51a). The inclusion of the words "and was carried up into heaven" is supported by the manuscript evidence, by Acts 1:2's recapitulation of what has been described in the gospel, and by the long ending of Mark (16:19f.), which seems to reflect a knowledge of the longer text here in Luke. Jesus did not leave his followers, however, until he first had blessed them: "While he blessed them, he parted from them" (vs. 51a). This act of blessing is like that of the high priest, Simon, in Sir 50:19–20. With a priestly act the risen Jesus puts his disciples under the protection of God before he leaves them (cf. Matt 28:20, "and lo, I am with you to the end of the Age; John 17:9–19). Just as the gospel began with the ministry of the priest Zechariah, so it ends with Jesus acting as priest for his flock (cf. Heb 2:17; 3:1; 6:19–20).

EXCURSUS A:
THE FULFILLMENT OF
PROPHECY IN LUKE-ACTS

The theme of the fulfillment of prophecy plays a major role in the Lukan narrative. Prophecy is understood in the sense of a prediction of things to come. Fulfillment means what was predicted has happened or is believed to have happened. Fulfilled prophecy in the Lukan narrative comes from three types of sources: (1) from the Jewish scriptures; (2) from a living prophet; (3) from a heavenly being. We will examine examples in each of these categories.

(1) OT prophecy. Two examples should suffice. (a) 4:16–21 says Jesus went into the synagogue at Nazareth, read from Isa 61:1–2; 58:6, and then said, "Today this scripture has been fulfilled in your hearing." The prophecy of Isaiah has been fulfilled in the narrative about Jesus' ministry. (b) Acts 13: 16–41 reports a speech by Paul in the synagogue at Antioch of Pisidia. Verse 23 says of David's posterity, "God has brought to Israel a Savior, Jesus, *as he promised*." Verses 27, 29 continue the theme: "For those who live in Jerusalem and their rulers, because they did not recognize him nor understand the utterances of the prophets which are read every sabbath, fulfilled these by condemning him" (vs. 27). "And when they had fulfilled all that was written of him, they took him down from the tree . . ." (vs. 29). Verses 32–33 give the climax: "And we bring you the good news that what God promised to the fathers, this he fulfilled to us their children by raising Jesus; as also it is written in the second psalm. . . ." These two examples show Luke believed the career of Jesus fulfilled the prophecies of the Jewish scriptures.

(2) Prophecy of a living prophet. (a) Sometimes the living prophet is Jewish. For example, in 1:67–79 Zechariah prophesies. Part of what he says is about the future of his son, John the Baptist: "And you,

child, will be called the *prophet* of the Most High; for you will go before the Lord to *prepare his ways*" (vs. 76). Jesus asks, "What then did you go out to see? A *prophet?*" and answers, "Yes, I tell you, and more than a prophet. This is he of whom it is written, 'Behold, I send my messenger before thy face, who shall *prepare thy way* before thee' " (7:26–27). (b) At other times the living prophet is the earthly Jesus. Numerous examples present themselves. In 9:22, 44; 18:31–33 Jesus predicts his passion, which is fulfilled in the narrative of Luke 22—24. Jesus prophecies in 11:13 that the Father will give the Holy Spirit to those who ask him: this is fulfilled in the narrative of Acts 2:1ff. In 13:35b Jesus says the Jews will not see him until they say, "Blessed is he who comes in the name of the Lord," a prediction fulfilled at 19:38. Jesus says in 19:29–31 his disciples will find the desired colt in an opposite village and tells them what will be asked of them and how to answer: vss. 32–34 tell the fulfillment of his words. Luke 21:15 predicts that when the disciples are called upon to give testimony, they will be given "wisdom, which none of your adversaries will be able to withstand or contradict": This is fulfilled in the episode of Stephen in Acts 6:10. In 22:10–12 Jesus tells the disciples how to find the room where they will celebrate the Passover: it happened as he had told them in vs. 13. Jesus predicts Peter's denial (22:34), a prophecy fulfilled in 22:54–61. (c) On still other occasions the living prophet is a Christian. In Acts 11:27–28a Agabus predicts a famine: we hear that it occurred in vs. 28b. In Acts 21:10–11 Agabus predicts that Paul will be bound by the Jews and this is fulfilled in the narrative which follows. Paul predicts in Acts 27:22, 34 that no lives will be lost because of the storm at sea: vs. 44 says all escaped to land.

(3) Prophecy of a heavenly being. (a) Sometimes it is an angel who prophesies. In 1:13 the angel of the Lord tells Zechariah he will have a son: this prediction is fulfilled at 1:57, 63. An angel in 1:26–27, 31 tells Mary she will bear a son: in the narrative of 2:7, 21 this is fulfilled. In 2:8–12 the angel tells the shepherds they will find the babe wrapped in swaddling clothes and lying in a manger: they find this in 2:15–16. Acts 27:23–24 has an angel appear to Paul and tell him he will survive the storm at sea and will stand before Caesar: Paul escapes from the sea and ultimately arrives in Rome. (b) At other times the risen Christ makes predictions. In Luke 24:49 and Acts 1:4–5 he promises the gift of the Spirit, which is granted in Acts 2. He tells the disciples in Acts 1:8 that after their empowering they will be witnesses

to the ends of the earth: the rest of the narrative of Acts, of course, shows this to be true. In Acts 18:9–10 the Lord appears to Paul in a vision to promise him protection in Corinth: Acts 18:12–17 shows the fulfillment of this prophecy.

Whether it is a prophecy made in the OT by a living prophet or by a heavenly being, the evangelist takes pains to show its fulfillment in the course of his narrative. The question arises as to how this motif would have been understood by Luke's readers. In order to answer it is necessary to explore briefly the functions of prophecy in the Mediterranean world, both pagan and Jewish.

The notion that a divine necessity controls human history, shaping the course of its events, was a widespread belief in Mediterranean antiquity. (a) Polybius (b. 208 B.C.) realized early in his career that Roman power was irresistable. As a Stoic he believed the Roman order was part of a divine providence that ruled the world. This belief was expounded in his *Histories*. In I:4:1–2 he says, "Fortune (*hē tychē*) having guided almost all the affairs of the world in one direction and having forced them to incline towards one and the same end, a historian should bring before his readers under one synoptical view the operations by which she has accomplished her general purpose." (b) Josephus shared in this cultural belief, but as a Jew viewed the divine necessity as deriving from the personal will of a god who is a living person, not a neutral force. So, in *Antiquities* 10:8:2–33, 42, he tells of Jeremiah's prophecy of the fall of Jerusalem being fulfilled and says these events manifest the nature of God, "which foretells all which must (*dei*) take place, duly at the appointed hour." Pagan and Hellenistic Jew alike thought of history as unfolding according to a divine necessity or compulsion which could be expressed in terms of *dei* or *deon esti*. It was in these terms that Luke's language about the *dei* of events would have been understood (cf. 2:49; 4:43; 12:12; 13:14; 15:32; 18:1; 19:5; 22:7, 37).

The concept of history's fulfilling of oracles, whether written or oral, was also a cultural commonplace. Three examples from the pagan world will give a feel for this. (a) Lucian's *Alexander the False Prophet* tells of one Alexander who wanted to start a new religion. As a first step, he and a companion went to Chalcedon and buried bronze tablets which stated that in the near future Asclepios and his father, Apollo, would migrate to Pontus. These tablets were found and the people began building a temple. Alexander then went to Abonutichus, dressed

as Perseus, declaiming an oracle which said he was a scion of Perseus. A Sibylline prophecy of his activity was then produced. As a result of one oral and two written prophecies, the stage was set—a new religion could emerge. (b) Suetonius' "Life of Vespasian" contains a section of omens which prophecy his ascendency to emperor. Among them are references not only to Josephus' declaration that he would soon be released by the same man who would then be emperor, but also to antique vases discovered by soothsayers which had on them an alleged image of Vespasian. (c) Apuleius' *Golden Ass* moves to its climax with Lucius trapped in the form of a donkey as a result of his experimentation with magic. Despairing over his plight, he cries to Isis to save him. The goddess appears by night and gives an oracle (11:7), which the next day Lucius follows exactly: he eats the roses that are part of the procession in Isis' honor and is miraculously changed back into a human being. Having been saved from his fate, Lucius is initiated into the Isis cult and says, "I was not deceived by the promise made to me" (11:13). In all three of these pagan examples the fulfillment of the oracle legitimates the religious or political authority of the person to whom the prophecy referred or of the god who gave it. In the strict sense this is proof-from-prophecy: what happened was in line with what the divine realm had revealed prior to the fact.

Three Jewish examples should also suffice. (a) The deuteronomic history (Deuteronomy through 2 Kings) uses the device of prophecy and fulfillment. For example, in Deuteronomy 28 Moses says that if Israel does not keep the covenant and obey the commandments, she will go away into exile (vss. 25, 36–37). In 2 Kings 17 the northern kingdom falls to the Assyrians and the Israelites are taken into bondage: The exile was because of Israel's sins (vs. 7); what was done was "as the Lord spoke by all his servants the prophets" (vs. 23). In 2 Kings 25 the southern kingdom is taken away into Babylonian exile: Moses' prophecy in Deuteronomy 28 is shown to have been fulfilled in the subsequent narrative of 2 Kings. This, in effect, legitimates the other things Moses said in Deuteronomy about how Israel should live. (b) At Qumran was a religious community that believed its own history was the fulfillment of the prophecies of the scriptures. In the commentaries on Isaiah, Micah, Psalm 37, and especially Habakkuk, are statements of the community's position. When it interprets the prophets and the Psalms as prophecies which are fulfilled in the wickedness of Qumran's enemies and in the righteousness of Qumran's covenanters,

it is not only saying that the time of fulfillment has come, but also that it is the heir of the promises to Israel, the true people of God. This is in effect an argument for the continuity of the community with Israel of old. (c) Josephus, *Antiquities,* uses the motif of prophecy and its fulfillment as evidence for the providence of God (2:16:5 § 333): in 8:4:2 § 109–10 the fulfillment of David's prophecy makes clear the providence of God; in 1:11:7 § 278–81 the fulfillment of Daniel's prophecies of the destruction of Jerusalem by Antiochus Epiphanes and the Romans is said to demonstrate God's providence (against the Epicureans). The pattern of prophecy-fulfillment in the history of Israel constitutes evidence for belief in a providential God. The providence of God, moreover, consists primarily in his rewarding virtue and punishing vice (H. W. Attridge, *The Interpretation of Biblical History in the Antiquitates Judaicae of Flavious Josephus* [Missoula: Scholars, 1976]).

The Mediterranean mind-set which viewed history as the fulfillment of oracles also held that an oracle could be misunderstood as well as understood. The very act of misunderstanding could be the means by which the prophecy was fulfilled. Herodotus' *History* is a storehouse of examples, with the classic example being his story of Croesus who, after acknowledging the Delphic oracle to be the only true place of divination, asked if he should send an army against the Persians. The oracle replied that if he should send an army, he would destroy a great empire. Mistaking the meaning of the oracle, Croesus went to war against the Perisans and lost. Sending his chains to Delphi, Croesus asked if it were the manner of the Greek gods to be thankless. The priestess replied that the oracle was right. Croesus should have asked whether the god spoke of Croesus' or Cyrus' empire: "But he understood not that which was spoken, nor made further inquiry; wherefore now let him blame himself" (1:91). When Croesus received the answer he confessed the sin was not the god's but his own. The similarity of this way of thinking to Acts 13:27 would not be lost on Luke's original hearers: "those who live in Jerusalem and their rulers, because they did not understand the utterances of the prophets which are read every sabbath, fulfilled these by condemning him." Whether Luke's community was composed of former Jews or pagans—or both— his original readers would have found no surprises in the theme of history's course being determined by the fulfillment of oracles/ prophecies.

The functions of a prophecy-fulfillment theme in the Mediterranean world match remarkably well with what we find in Luke-Acts. (a) As the pagan evidence showed prophecy made by a person or about a person, when fulfilled, legitimated the individual's religious or political status. It could evoke conversion to the one whose promise was kept. It is in this way that some prophetic utterances are used in Luke-Acts (e.g., prophecy made by Jesus, when fulfilled, legitimates his author- ity—Luke 9:22/Luke 22—24; 11:13/Acts 2; 12:11–12/Acts 5:29; prophecy made about Jesus, when fulfilled, legitimates him—Luke 1:31/1:42; 2:7/2:21). (b) As the evidence from the deuteronomic his- tory showed, a prophetic promise, when fulfilled, can serve to legiti- mate the other things the prophet has said. When Jesus predicts the destruction of the temple (13:35a; 21:6) and the capture of Jerusalem by the Gentiles (19:43–44; 21:20–24; 23:28–31) and Luke's readers know of the events of A.D. 70, or when the risen Lord predicts the Gentile mission (Luke 24:47; Acts 1:8) and his readers are told of the progress of the gospel to Rome, these fulfilled words function to give authority to the other things Jesus said, like his parenetic sayings in 9:51—19:44. (c) As the evidence from Qumran showed, the claim that one's particular history and that of one's founder fulfilled the proph- ecies of the scriptures argues not only for the arrival of the eschaton but also for one's continuity with the history of Israel. As the heirs of the promises, Christians are the true descendents of Israel of old: the speech in Acts 13:16–41 seems especially emphatic in this regard. The argument emphasizes the continuity between Jesus and the history of ancient Israel, as well as showing his death and resurrection were in accord with the divine will. What we have not yet made clear, how- ever, is exactly how such an argument on behalf of continuity would have been heard by Greek-speaking people, whether Jews or pagans.

It was a cultural commonplace in the Hellenistic age for a people to try to trace its own origins back to the remotest antiquity (e.g., Jose- phus, *Against Apion*, 2:152; Diodorus, 1:44:4; 1:96:2). This was in large measure due to the Greek belief that what was most ancient was most valuable. The Jews copied the practice (note the parallels be- tween Josephus' *Antiquities* and the *Roman Antiquities* of Dionysius of Halicarnasus) and claimed their writings were the oldest. It was in terms of such a belief that the early Christian apologists and antiher- etical writers often built their arguments. Tertullian, for example, in his *Apology* (21), claims, "Our religion is supported by the writings of

the Jews, the oldest which exist." In *Against Marcion* (5:19) he says, "I am accustomed, in my prescription against all heresies, to fix my compendious criterion of truth in the testimony of time; claiming priority therein as our rule, and alleging lateness to be the characteristic of every heresy." Continuity between Christians and Israel and between the events of Jesus' career and the OT prophecies was important because it allowed Christians to appeal to the argument from antiquity, which would allow Greek-speaking Christians to feel not the least bit inferior to pagans with their cultural and religious claims allegedly rooted in antiquity.

(d) The evidence from Josephus showed the motif of prophecy-fulfillment in the history of Israel was used to provide evidence for the providence of God in human affairs—that is, that a personal God acts to reward virtue and punish vice. The promises that no harm would come to Paul (Acts 18:9–10; 27:23–24) and their fulfillment fit into this function: God cares for his own who work as missionaries. In Luke-Acts, therefore, the prophecy-fulfillment schema functions very much as it does in its Mediterranean milieu.

In 1:1–4 the evangelist speaks about the "things which have been accomplished/fulfilled among us." Given the importance of the theme of the fulfillment of prophecy in the two-volume work, it seems almost certain that the translation should be "fulfilled among us." The story of Jesus and the early church is one that fulfills the various prophecies made by the Jewish scriptures, by living prophets, and by heavenly beings. Insofar as the Christian story fulfilled the prophecies of the scriptures, it would be about those who had ancient roots. Insofar as it told of the fulfillment of the prophecies of Jesus and Christian prophets, it would depict them as being right. Taken together, having roots and being right would be highly persuasive. It would contribute to the certainty the evangelist wants to give Theophilus (vs. 4). The theme of the fulfillment of prophecy, then, would seem to be a legitimation device in the Lukan narrative, just as it was in Mediterranean antiquity generally.

EXCURSUS B:
MIRACLE IN LUKE-ACTS
AND IN THE LUKAN MILIEU

A n appreciation of the Lukan attitude toward miracle is closely
tied to an understanding of the attitudes toward miracle in the
Lukan milieu: pagan, Jewish, and Christian.

(1) Pagan attitudes toward miracle range from very positive to very
negative depending upon the context/circle in which an opinion is expressed. (a) In some circles the principle was fully accepted that miracle proved divinity. For example, Philostratus in the *Life of Apollonius,* 7:38, tells how, when Apollonius was in prison because of
Domitian, to show his freedom to his companion Damis, he took his
leg out of its shackles. Having done this, he then put his leg back
again. At that moment, Damis said, he first understood clearly that
Apollonius' nature was godlike and more than human. Again, Suetonius in his "Life of Vespasian," 7:2, tells us that Vespasian as yet lacked
prestige and a certain divinity, since he was an unexpected and newly-
made emperor. These, however, were soon given to him. In Alexandria
two miracles were performed. Vespasian healed a man who was blind
and a man who was lame was made to walk.

Since miracle had the power to prove deity, it was one means of
winning converts to various religious cults. Ovid, *Metamorphoses,*
3:695ff., has a priest of Dionysius named Acoetes tell how he became
a follower of the god when an epiphany was disclosed in a miraculous
event. Philostratus, *Heroicus,* describes a conversion of a Phoenician
trader brought about by a vinetender's telling what the hero had done
for him. Apuleius, *Metamorphoses,* 11, says Lucius was changed back
from a donkey to a human being by a miracle effected by Isis. As a
result he became a devotee of the goddess and was initiated into her
cult.

It was also likely that miracle was a means of encouraging the devotion of the adherents of a cult. Strabo (c. 801) tells that stories of miracles were collected for the Serapeum at Canopus. This would seem to be for the purpose of reinforcing those who were adherents of this religion.

(b) There were other circles, however, that discredited miracle. Lucian is a prime example. In his *Lovers of Lies* members of various philosophical schools are mocked for their desire to tell tales of wonder. Lucian professes himself baffled by the puzzle: why do serious people have an interest in lies about miracles? For Lucian, magic and miracle had become identical. In *Alexander the False Prophet* Lucian tells of a cult's origin via miracle and other things like fulfilled prophecy. The entire account, however, is told to discredit the oracle and its founder. Philostratus' *Life of Apollonius of Tyana* gives further evidence, being written to defend the philosopher against the charge of being a magician because he had worked miracles. In such circles as these, therefore, miracle was no proof; it was a problem.

(2) Jewish attitudes toward miracle show the same mixed reaction found in pagan circles. (a) In the period of Christian origins, miracle was widely regarded by Jews as the divine legitimation of a position, a person, or of God himself. In the first place, miracle was believed to legitimate the word or position of a prophet or rabbi. Sifre Deut 18:19 states that if a prophet who starts to prophesy gives evidence by signs and miracles, he is to be heeded; if not, he is not to be followed. This anonymous saying is early because a discussion between Jose ha-Gelili and Akiba presupposes the existence of such a statement (b. Sanh 90a; Sifre Deut 13:3). Josephus, *Antiquities*, 2:12:3 §280, reports God gave Moses three signs (rod became a serpent; leprous hand; water turned to blood) and said, "Make use of those signs, in order to obtain belief among all men, that you are sent by me and do all things according to my commands." The same motif is also found elsewhere in Josephus (e.g., *Ant.* 9:2:1 §23; 10:2:1 §28; 20:5:1 §168). In b. Ta'anith 23a, there is a tradition about the first century Honi who was effective in praying for rain. Once when there was a drought the people asked Honi to pray. He prayed and no rain fell. Then he drew a circle and stood within it and exclaimed before God, "I swear that I will not move from here until Thou hast mercy on Thy children." When it only dripped, he told God vehemently that this was not what he had asked. When it then rained so hard as to do damage, he strongly told God

that he had asked for rain of blessing not for rain to destroy life. When the normal rain continued so long that flooding became a problem, Honi again strongly told God it was time for the rain to stop. Immediately the clouds dispersed and the sun came out. Thereupon Simeon b. Shetah said, "Were it not that you are Honi, I would have placed you under the ban. But what shall I do to you who acts petulantly before God and He grants your desire?" Simeon's response means Honi's behavior should be rejected but since Honi's prayer produced the miracle of rain, his behavior was legitimated. This story shows that in the time of Honi the Circle Drawer matters of behavior toward God were settled by miracle. This is supported: a *bath qol* or voice from heaven was decisive in settling halakic questions in favor of Beth Hillel and against Beth Shammai at Jamnia not long after A.D. 70 (Alexander Guttmann, "The Significance of Miracles for Talmudic Judaism," *Hebrew Union College Annual,* 20 [1947]: 363–406, especially 369–71).

In the second place, miracle was believed to prove one's innocence or righteousness. In j. Berakoth 5:1 we hear that once when Rabbi Haninah b. Dosa was praying he was bitten by a snake but did not interrupt his prayer. Not only did the rabbi not feel the bite but also the snake was later found dead at the entrance to its den. The righteousness of the rabbi was vindicated by his immunity to a poisonous snakebite. In b. Baba Mezia 58b–59, after the excommunication of R. Eliezer, R. Gamaliel was traveling in a ship. When a huge wave arose to drown him, he said, "It appears to me that this is on account of none but R. Eliezer ben Hyrcannus." Thereupon he arose and cried, "Sovereign of the Universe, Thou knowest that I have not acted for my honor, nor for the honor of my paternal house, but for Thine, so that differences may not multiply in Israel." At that the raging sea subsided. Here the miracle of the sea's subsiding vindicates the rabbi's innocence.

The significance of deliverance from snakebite and storm at sea can only be understood if one is aware of the general cultural background. It was a common belief, pagan and Jewish, that divine forces in cooperation with nature (especially storms at sea) and the animal kingdom (especially snakes) punish wickedness. Homer, *Odyssey,* 12:127–41, 259–446, tells how Odysseus' crew were all destroyed in a shipwreck because they had slaughtered Helios' sacred cattle. Chariton's novel (3:3:10; 3:3:18; 3:4:9–10) also attests the belief that the polluted are drowned at sea while the just are delivered. An epitaph of Statyllus

Flaccus tells how the ship-wrecked sailor who had just escaped from
the storm and raging sea lay stranded, naked, and destitute on a sandy
beach in Lydia. Suddenly a poisonous snake bit him and killed him.
The epitaph concludes, "Why did he struggle against the sea? He could
not escape the lot that awaited him on the land" (H. Conzelmann, *Die
Apostelgeschichte* [Tübingen: Mohr, 1963], p. 147). In the Tosefta,
Sanhedrin 8:3, R. Simeon ben Shetah (c. 80 B.C.) said he saw a man
with a sword running after a fellow. The two ran into a deserted building. When Simeon entered he found the one slain and the other with
the sword dripping blood: "But he who knows the thoughts, he exacts
vengeance from the guilty; for the murderer did not stir from the place
before a serpent bit him so that he died." So certain was such punishment believed to be that in some circumstances the absence of destruction by storm or snakebite could be adduced as proof of innocence. The Athenian orator Antiphon (480–411 B.C.) wrote a speech
for a client, one Helion, who on a sea journey was accused of murder.
The speech says that although retribution comes on the guilty and
those associated with him, "in my case the opposite is true on every
count. For all those with whom I have sailed have enjoyed good voy-
ages. I claim all this as great proof of the charge that the plaintiffs
have accused me falsely" (G. B. Miles and G. Trompf, "Luke and Antiphon: The Theology of Acts 27–28 in the Light of Pagan Beliefs about
Divine Retribution, Pollution, and Shipwreck," *Harvard Theological
Review*, 69:259–67, esp. p. 262 [1976]). For a rabbi to escape death
after the bite of a poisonous snake or in the midst of a storm at sea
testifies to his innocence or righteousness (cf. Paul, Acts 27–28).

In the third place, miracle was believed sometimes to be effective in
gaining acknowledgment of the superiority of Israel's God. In 2 Kgs 5:
15–19 Naaman the Syrian who had been healed of leprosy confesses
his belief in Israel's God and asks indulgence as he is forced to go into
the temple of the god of his land. In 2 Mac 3:35–39 Heliodorus makes
a confession of the Jewish God's supremacy after experiencing a miracle.

(b) There was reluctance in many circles of Judaism after the end
of the first century A.D., however, to allow miracle any legitimating
power. The crucial point in time when miracle was disallowed as the
authentication of a position in matters of *halakah* is recounted in b.
Baba Mezia 58b–59b. In the period of the second generation of Tan-
naim, (A.D. 90–130) there was a debate between R. Eliezer and R.

Joshua which was resolved against Eliezer. This was done in spite of miracles supporting R. Eliezer's position (the uprooting of the carob tree; water flowing backwards; a *bath qol*) because the Torah had already been given on Sinai. In the following Tannaitic generation, the third, the principle "one should not mention miracles" makes its appearance. This was largely aimed at the miracles of rising Christianity. Furthermore, B. J. Bamberger's *Proselytism in the Talmudic Period* [reprint ed., New York: KTAV 1968] gives no examples of proselytes being made via miracle. In Judaism, therefore, after A.D. 100 miracle did not function as legitimation, as it had before.

(3) The ancient church also manifests a mixed attitude toward miracle. (a) On the one hand, many believed miracles were still happening in the life of the church (Justin, *Apology II*, 6; Irenaeus, *Against Heresies*, 2:48–49; 2:31:2; 2:32:4; Tertullian, *Apology*, 23; Origen, *Against Celsus*, 1:2:46; 3:24; Eusebius, *Church History*, 5:7; Augustine, *City of God*, 22:8; *Sermon*, 322). Further, miracles had or have an evangelistic-legitimating function (Quadratus [according to Eusebius, *HE*, 4:3:2]; Acts of Paul; Arnobius 2:12; Marcion [according to Tertullian, *Against Marcion*, 3:2–3]; Abgar legend [related by Eusebius, *HE*, 1:13]; Origen, *Against Celsus*, 1:46; Eusebius, *Church History*, 2:32).

(b) On the other hand, others believed miracles belonged to the first age of the church as a necessary prop to the rise of faith but were now unnecessary (John Chrysostom, *Homily in Matt* 12:2; 14:3; *Homily in John* 12:3; *Homily in 1 Cor* 6:2). Many believed miracles were either a problem or proved nothing: Theophilus of Antioch (*To Autolycus* 1:13) says if he were to provide an example of a man raised from the dead and alive, his adversary would not believe it. Furthermore, Jewish/pagan attacks on Christian miracles contended: 1) Christian miracles were no more remarkable than the wonders ascribed to other gods and heroes; 2) Christian miracle stories were fictitious; 3) Christian miracles were due to magic (G. W. H. Lampe, "Miracles and Early Christian Apologetic," in *Miracle*, ed. C. F. D. Moule [London: Mowbray, 1965], pp. 205–18). Considering these problems, it is not surprising some Christians made little use of miracle to legitimate their position.

In light of this sketch of the Lukan milieu it becomes possible to say something about Luke's attitude toward the role of miracle in Christian faith. (a) Luke-Acts has perhaps the most positive attitude toward

miracle among the gospels. In the first place, as our discussion of 4:31—5:11 has shown, the evangelist believes miracle has an evangelistic function. It evokes faith (cf. also Acts 5:12–16; 8:6–7, 12; 9:32–35, 36–42; 13:6–12; 16:16–34; 19:11–20). In the second place, Luke believes miracle legitimates one's position or words. Acts 2:22 says Jesus was "attested to you by God with mighty works and wonders and signs which God did through him in your midst." This seems the case in passages like Luke 7:11–17, 18–23. Passages like 6:6–11 seem to settle the legal question of sabbath observance via miracle (cf. Honi's experience). In Acts 15:12 miracle plays a role in the church's decision about the inclusion of the Gentiles. In the third place, miracle, for Luke, establishes one's innocence or righteousness. In Acts 2:32–36; 3:14–15, the raising of Jesus from the dead vindicates him over against those who have rejected him. In Acts 27–28, Paul's deliverance from shipwreck and from snakebite attest his innocence.

(b) At the same time Luke is positive about miracle, he also is far from naive about its value. First, the evangelist, like pagan and Jewish critics of miracle, knows miracle is no proof that compels conversion (cf. 6:6–11; 8:26–39; 11:14ff.; Acts 4:16–21; 14:8–18; 16:16ff.). Second, miracle by itself is not an adequate guide. It needs to be supported by the OT and by Jesus' words (Acts 15:12, 13–19; 11:15–16; Luke 9:1–6; 10:9, 17–19). Third, miracle needs to be distinguished from magic by the good character of those who work miracles. Note that Luke 4:1–13 shows Jesus from the first as not self-indulgent or power hungry. The same point is made again in 23:35–39 in a threefold temptation echoing 4:1–13. Neither does Jesus use his miraculous power to harm anyone or anything. Plato (*Rep.* II:364) speaks of wandering soothsayers who promise to punish enemies in this world; certain Jews would like Honi to destroy their enemies and kill him when he will not; Apollonius of Tyana (*Life* 3:7) defends himself against the charge of being a magician by saying he does not harm people—it is surely significant that Luke omits the cursing of the fig tree. In Acts Peter is shown to be hostile to a magician who was motivated by gain (8:18–19). Paul also is shown to be hostile to a magician (13:6ff.) and to magic (19:18–19). Moreover, he is portrayed as not greedy (18:3; 20:33–35). Fourth, to have experienced a miracle, Luke believes, is not the same thing as having faith, being healed is not the same as being saved (Luke 17:11–19). Finally, in terms of priorities, having miraculous powers is secondary in importance to having experienced conversion (10:20).

JIM CRAMER'S
REAL MONEY

SANE INVESTING

in an

INSANE WORLD

JAMES J. CRAMER

Simon & Schuster

New York   London   Toronto   Sydney

SIMON & SCHUSTER
Rockefeller Center
1230 Avenue of the Americas
New York, NY 10020

Copyright © 2005 by J. J. Cramer & Co.
All rights reserved,
including the right of reproduction
in whole or in part in any form.

SIMON & SCHUSTER and colophon are registered trademarks
of Simon & Schuster, Inc.

For information about special discounts for bulk purchases,
please contact Simon & Schuster Special Sales:
1-800-456-6798 or business@simonandschuster.com

Designed by Elliott Beard

Manufactured in the United States of America

10   9   8   7   6   5   4   3

Library of Congress Control Number: 2005042499

ISBN 0-7432-2489-2

ACKNOWLEDGMENTS

I want you to be rich. Really rich. That's my goal. I don't want you to just do better. And I don't want you to try to make ends meet. I know I can help you get there. I've made too many other people rich for me to think that I won't do it with you.

I got rich using commonsense principles, not elite precepts and training, and I know you can, too. The arithmetic you need to know to navigate the stock market is fifth-grade math. I know it because I help a fifth grader every night with her numbers.

When I wrote *Confessions of a Street Addict,* I used to go into Amazon to read the reviews until my wife decided they were driving me nuts. What I found were people who loved the story of my life but were disappointed that I didn't tell how I made my money.

That's what this book is for. I tell everything. In fact, I'm debating, as I write this, whether to go back to managing money using the same rules and principles I outline here, because I am so certain that they work.

But before you get to it, I want you to know who was instrumental in helping me explain how I really made those millions of dollars. First, my wife, Karen, who figured so prominently in *Confessions,* has to again take center stage here. She is a testament to the non–Ivy League nature of what I am about to write, as she spent more time

breaking me of Harvard habits than celebrating them when we worked together at Cramer & Company.

My father, Ken, is instrumental in my analysis as he spent countless days when I was growing up and then long after explaining the power of the business and inventory cycles. He understood it intuitively. I had to learn it. I would be remiss in not thanking his late mother and father, two fabulous businesspeople, long since passed, who instilled an ethic that was both indelible and hardwired by the time it got to me. My late mom, Louise, never got to see me reemerge as a writer. Since she cared about the "soul" more than the money, she'd be happy how things turned out.

While I am celebrating family, I have learned a tremendous amount about business and winning in the markets from my brother-in-law, Todd Mason, who may be the smartest man on the planet, aside from his obvious intelligence in marrying my sister Nan.

In my work life, I have so many to thank, so many who have taught me the right way to do things, but let's start with Bill Gruver and Richard Menschel, two deacons who once ruled Goldman Sachs's equity side. I'll add Marty Peretz, who first gave me money to manage and then insisted that I make it grow at a pace that exceeded every-body else's. Thanks, Marty!

Of late, I want to send kudos to Will Gabrielski and David Peltier of TheStreet.com as well as David Morrow, the editor-in-chief of TheStreet.com, for helping along the manuscript, and, of course, the larger-than-life Tom Clarke, the CEO of TheStreet.com, who must next run money because he has the patience and the fortitude to do so.

I can't go without a thanks to my friends at CNBC, the fabulous Susan Krakower, Larry Kudlow, Matt Quayle, Linda Sittenfeld, Donna Vislocky, Andrew Conti, Christine Dooley, and, of course, Bob Fas-bender, who helped turn me into an alleged TV star. My friends at WOR deserve equal gratz: Mike Figliola, my producer, and the great folks who work with Rick Buckley there, including Joe Billota, Bob Bruno, and Maurice Tunick. I want to thank Cheryl Winer, too, as I

would never have discovered radio without her persistence that I belong in that great medium.

I want to thank all of those professionals who keep me out of trouble—my agents Suzanne Gluck and Henry Reisch and my lawyers Eric Seiler and Bruce Birenboim. The last guy deserves my undying love because I would have long since given up any public life without his counsel.

And of course to David Rosenthal and Bob Bender, my publisher and editor, who really get me and whom I love very much and would die before I'd disappoint.

Lastly, I want to thank Cece and Emma, who put up with countless weekends without me as I toiled over this book, and who remind me, constantly, of what really matters: family. No matter how rich you get, it can't come near the joys of fatherhood and a loving family.

*To my fabulous daughters, Emma and Cece Cramer,
two little savers whom I love so much*

CONTENTS

JIM CRAMER'S
REAL MONEY

THE ART

of

INVESTING

For years, investors have tried to slog through how-to books about investing and trading, hoping to glean some wisdom that can make them wealthy. For years, writers have churned out these investment texts with an eye toward either dry, academic theory or lightweight analysis that would not hold up under even the mildest professional scrutiny. There's nothing in between, nothing to satisfy your craving for making large amounts of money through common sense and a modest investment of time, homework, and inclination.

A total stock market junkie, I have either been bored to tears by these tomes or recognized that they are the works of charlatans who couldn't make you a dime. Most investing books, like most of the mutual fund managers out there, would probably do worse for you in the stock market than if you just picked a portfolio of the Standard & Poor's benchmark 500 stocks. The books are bought because they are easy to read, easy to practice how-to volumes written by individuals who tend never to have managed money or to have made big money personally in the stock market. How many of these writers started

with nothing and made boatloads simply by buying the right stocks and selling or avoiding the wrong ones? Their texts are formulaic and arcane or simplistic and overpromising. The authors don't have the benefit of a lifetime's worth of stock picking. They don't teach you what can go wrong as well as right.

Those books are not *this* book. This book understands not just the nuts and bolts of investing, but the psychology and humanity of investing. This book is the distillation of everything I have learned, every important rule, every smart move, every edge I have ever been able to garner to make huge amounts of money in the market. In this book I tell you everything that made me rich and everything that could have made me poor. In this book I give you the secrets of how great wealth stays wealthy, secrets I have been taught by thirty-eight of the wealthiest families in the world—the families for whom I managed money for twenty years. I made hundreds of millions of dollars for myself and my investors. I love the process of making money. I love talking about it, writing about it, and most of all, doing it. I know losing and winning; in my best year I lost $300 million, but in that same year, I *made* $450 million, netting $150 million for the good guys.

In many ways, though, I don't think of this book as a financial book or as a how-to-invest book or a how-to-trade book. As a nationally syndicated talk show host and the creator of a company, TheStreet .com, where I have interacted with literally hundreds of thousands of investors, I know what you do wrong more than you do right. I know your financial weaknesses better than anyone managing money today, maybe better than anyone on Earth, including yourself. I know what you can't figure out. I know what causes you to lose money and what causes you to sell low and buy high. Most important, I know why you stray, why you can't consistently make money, and why you might consistently lose money by buying stocks. I know what will get you on course for a lifetime's worth of successful investing, not just a quick gain to your wallet. I know this because I hear every day from dozens of grateful investors in phone calls to my show or in e-mails to

TheStreet.com who tell me that I have changed their lives, made them money in the market for the first time, and kept them from losing money that they would have certainly given back without my instruction. I coach them every day, and what I coach them from is my own internal playbook, developed over twenty-five years of making great returns in good *and bad* markets, a playbook that, until now, was only in my head. Now it is in your hands.

In that sense, I think of this book more like a financial diet-for-life book, not a money book. Heck, I've written the first diet book of investing! I have pioneered ways to make the game of investing come alive so that you are interested enough, and stay interested enough, to last on my regimen to riches. I have spent a lifetime trying to explain the process of investing in English, using analogies to sports, to movies, to battles, to anything I can find that makes the stock market more simple and clear for you. I can't have you get frustrated or fed up or scared of your own money. Then you'll just run off to someone who doesn't care as much about your money as you do and wants to make money *from* you, not *for* you. I want you in charge of your finances, I want you to be your own guru, and I want you to like the process enough to take control, even if that means injecting some fun and speculation into the process to keep you in the game.

Most financial books are so arid and ascetic, and so unaware of your weaknesses, that they have no more value to you than if I blithely said, "Eat right and get plenty of exercise." That's just poppycock. That doesn't grab you. That's not going to make you thin; that kind of financial advice isn't going to make you wealthy. That's just going to make you lose interest and give up or surrender your hard-earned assets to someone who can use you for commission or high-fee fodder. You'll capitulate during the bear phases, you'll sell at the bottom, first chance you get. You will be defeated by every decline in the market, and there will be tons of them. You will be like so many broken investors of the 2000–2003 bear market, shunning IRAs, avoiding their 401(k)s, or not taking advantage of any of the myriad opportunities

even the worst markets offer. I know I can coach you through the hard parts and help you navigate them successfully. I can help you complete the big-money voyage.

I know you. I know you want to speculate. I know you want to make some outsized gains. I know you will ride your losses if you aren't careful, and I know you will succumb to the junk food of finance, penny stocks and the like, if you are left to your own devices. That's why, in my regimen, I build in speculation, similar to the way that good-tasting beef is built into the Atkins diet. I insist that you do some speculation as part of your investing menu. I insist that a portion of your assets be devoted to pure speculation. That way you can be truly diversified, own some solid blue chips, some good dividend yielders from many groups and yet still have that lottery ticket that can't hurt you and can make you rich in a quick stroke. I recognize that the true balance, the true diversification, includes owning some riskier assets that could just pan out huge.

Remember, the biggest return generators of our life, the Home Depots, the Best Buys, the Comcasts, were incredibly risky, if not considered outright dangerous, just when you had to buy them aggressively. These were the stocks that turned thousands into millions but would have been avoided by conventional investors because they were too dicey. Other times, particularly after brutal sell-offs or when you have proprietary hunches you know you have to act on, call options— again something considered too risky by conventional wisdom— might be the most prudent *and conservative* strategy, particularly for the younger of you just starting out investing, but even for older folks who intend on working for a living for many years and have that paycheck to fall back on. I know for some this is heresy, I know there are well-respected pundits who will shudder at someone not taking the party line, someone not trashing speculation and all it stands for. But those pundits aren't living in the real world. In fact, they exist only on the sidelines, as critics who know little of the true investing process or hate speculation so much they would spurn 100 points of gain if it meant owning something that might not exist ten years from now,

even if the prospects short-term for the stock, if not the company, are simply too bright to ignore. For them, I say feel free to criticize my views, but don't deny that sometimes the easiest money is made in the dumbest if not the most speculative of wagers.

Just as important, I show you what *not* to buy, what can ruin your portfolio, what kind of stocks are in what I call "The Danger Zone," guaranteed to wreck whatever profits your other stocks might create for you. I teach you tricks that the other books don't know to keep those winners on and the losers off.

Throughout this book, I tell you things your brokers don't want you to know and your financial advisers are praying you never find out about how Wall Street *really* works. I expose concerns and flaws that your mutual funds keep you in the dark about, lest you wise up to their underperforming ways. I tell you what you need to know to be confident and in control of your most important asset, your money. And I do it gleefully, and with passion, because I have made Wall Street work for me, not against me, all my life. I can be your coach and your captain, revving you up and ensuring we go the distance together to riches.

This book approaches the process of investing the way a successful diet book approaches the process of losing weight. I know that to keep you on a diet that can make you big money over time I have to keep you interested, keep you captivated. I need you to stay on it in order to stay in the game, the equity game. I need you to like the equity (stock) regimen. Why equities? Because every academic study shows that in any twenty-year period in history, no asset—not gold, not real estate, not bonds, not cash—outperforms high-quality equities that can pay good dividends. In fact, holding stocks that pay good dividends over time will allow you to make more money from the dividend accumulation than you can ever hope to make in bonds, the chief investment alternative to stocks, even when the dividend seems much smaller *now* than the coupon (interest) of the current crop of fixed-income alternatives. Of course, the problem with that simple statement is that most people buy low-quality equities that will never pay good divi-

dends or they hold on to high-quality dividend payers that become low-quality disasters without dividends. That's the bad fat in the financial diet and I can excise it for you before it gets into your veins. That's what happened to so many of you in the stock bubble that was pricked in 2000; that's why many of you have given up or are willing to invest in mutual funds that charge high fees for subpar service *and* performance. I know that if I can keep you in the good stocks, you will benefit from the unassailable logic of owning outperforming assets without the high commissions and loads that the traditional broker and mutual funds ply.

I also recognize, and will get you to recognize, that you can change course, that you can *sell* when the stocks you thought might get you there fail to generate that success. Sure you might pick Yahoo! in its infancy, or eBay, but in doing that you might also buy a CMGI or a Webvan, to name a walking zombie and a deceased piece of business. But nowhere in the canons of investing does it say you have to hold the bad ones once they start turning sour. I will show you the warning signs to sell the bad ones in a "field bet" where you pick out an emerging technology or an emerging group and ride out the winners by financing them with what remains of the losers.

Many of you know instinctively that you don't need expensive helpers, either brokers or mutual funds, right now and you will have the courage to jettison them by the time you are finished reading. I can't tell you how many times *each day* I speak to people with great common sense, on *Jim Cramer's RealMoney,* my national radio show, who want to do things right themselves and are talked out of reasonable courses of action by highly paid professionals. I can be your second opinion that gives you the confidence to make better decisions on your own.

But if after you read this book you still need financial advisers because of constraints of time and temperament, I will give you the tools you need to be sure they will obey your wishes and not abuse you as they might others who are less informed of the real ways of Wall Street.

This book works this way: If I can make you money legally, using speculation, who the heck cares if we do it with nonacademic methods, because making as much money as possible in a short period of time is the goal. And I promise I can get you to hold on to those gains once you have them. You should no more care that it is done speculatively than you should care that your diet works with the unorthodox inclusion of beef and cheese. You should also not care if some of the stocks you buy are not meant for the long term but are there simply to capture the current fancy, the fad of the moment. Again, because I encourage selling, this method is not only *not* reckless, but also prudent even while it allows you to capture outsized gains.

Just because my book makes the process of making money compelling, even enjoyable, doesn't mean that it's simple and can be done by everyone. I can get you started but my methods take some time and some effort and, most important, some discipline. You will be rewarded if you follow them, perhaps with riches beyond what you dreamed of, but not if you don't do the homework, not if you don't pay attention, and not if you break any of the rules that *must* be followed—and there are many of them. Homework—boring, basic homework—breeds the conviction that sometimes you need to buy more, to double down instead of cutting and running. It has to be done as a prerequisite to any purchase. That's right: In here there are no five easy steps to follow, no quick and dirty foolproof methods, no painless paths to financial independence. There's a complicated and rigorous diet that must be followed if you are going to become rich and stay rich through stocks.

Don't panic, though, at the notion of hard work to augment your capital. Nothing in this book is intellectually above the ken of my thirteen-year-old, and none of the processes of elimination and stock picking require more than the simple arithmetic precepts that no longer stump my ten-year-old. Some percentages, some division, some multiplication, that's as tough as it gets. I know how to teach and coach the financial diet. I know what it takes to keep you on it. I give you all of the safe stuff that you have to have to keep yourself trim and

wealthy, but I also give you the secrets, the stuff that I have learned that I believe will make you incredibly wealthy if you simply stay on the plan. I know it can work because I did it.

Lately, no doubt because of the devastating bear market that ended in 2003, the fashion among financial writers and television journalists is to say the investment process is hopeless, that no one can actually attempt to make you money. It's the collective throwing up of the hands! The thinking goes, Nobody can beat the market so just join an index fund and *be* the market. These cynics and negativists believe that all information is so perfect that you can't possibly pick stocks better than anyone else. Or that nobody has the tools and the skills to triumph over the market for the long run. Just give up and accept the mediocrity of the averages themselves, regardless of whether they gain or lose money. These postbubble diatribes fill a bookcase of mine at home. They are well reasoned and assume that only colossal amounts of luck separate the long-term winners from the losers. If you don't have the luck, if you approach investing from skill, you can't win.

I would love to be so cynical as to believe those negatives. I would love to believe them because then we could stop right here and I could tell you to forget about using your time and managing your money, that it is all for naught, that your money is like a potted plant, put it in the corner, give it some sunlight and water, and maybe it will grow. Or maybe it won't. So what? The naysayers want you to read a gardening book about finance, for heaven's sake! But then I start thinking what would happen if I had said that to myself twenty-five years ago when I started to invest with a few hundred dollars to my name and piles of credit card bills, fresh out of college. What would have happened to me, hundreds of millions of dollars ago, if I had listened to those who told me that what I wanted to do—make a huge amount of money quickly with a small amount of money—was impossible? Would I, too, have just given up and said, "You know, it's a waste of time this stock market business?" Would I have said, "I know I will never get rich with the market, so what's the point of trying?" What would have happened if I had listened to those who said that without a degree

from a major business school, I could never understand enough to make lots of money? What would have happened if I had paid attention to those who told me that common sense doesn't apply to stocks? I guess someone else would have made all of that money.

Instead, I didn't listen. I built my own way to riches, a way that kept me enthralled and intrigued by the market, without ever letting it beat me or knock the enthusiasm out of me. I used methods that weren't from a business school but from the street—common sense and liberal arts, not calculus and abstruse portfolio theory. Sometimes I think, Maybe I'm just a walk-on player who successfully navigated the NFL of riches. If that's the case, I know I can teach you to walk on and win, too, provided that you have the desire and the perspicacity to see it all through.

When I wrote *Confessions of a Street Addict,* my book about my career as a professional investor, I told a lot about the trials and tribulations of someone who loves the market with every breath he takes. But I didn't give away any of the trading and investing secrets that enabled me to retire at an early age to read, write, and talk about investing, to get others interested in taking control of their money. Some critics who bought the book found it wanting because I didn't say *how* I got rich and instead focused on the saga of it all.

This time around those who wanted the insights behind my hedge fund or for the money I manage now, my personal money, won't be disappointed. This time I give you the diet that I developed to stay on a regimen to riches.

Is it for everybody? Let's put it this way, it is for every one of the 92 million Americans who own stocks, and it is certainly for all 55 million Americans who have been forced to become their own portfolio managers, tasked with running their 401(k)s and their IRAs. It is definitely *the* primer if we are given control, as I think we will soon be, of our own Social Security accounts. That mammoth task requires a book like this if only to ensure that you aren't ripped off by the myriad financial sorts who can't wait to get their hands on your retirement money.

Of course, not everyone will be up to the methods I outline, so I have written the book "in the alternative," meaning that if you can't be your own best manager, you can be the best client and the best customer for someone else who helps you. But if you get into it, and I *know* I can get you into it, I think you can beat *every single manager out there* simply because you will have all of the tools and the rules, the ins and the outs. Unlike fund managers, you will not be flooded with new money if you are successful, or need to hit the road to drum up new clients as so many brokers must do to stay in business. The individual investor's edge—from not having to report daily to not having to have to promote endlessly to being able to take taxable gains when *you* want to—makes it imperative that you give it a try. Think of it like this, you are solely in charge of your performance—your gains and when to take them, your losses and when they can help you at tax time. You are focused not on the time-consuming task of asset gathering or commission generating, but on the actual wealth creation and preservation tasks that are often secondary at the big financial institutions we know so well and try so hard to respect. This book also works for every age and for every amount, no matter how small, down to about $2,500 (with an option to use an exchange-traded fund or a mutual fund for those with less money to work with). I started with a couple of hundred bucks. I refuse to be dissuaded by the idea that any amount is "too little" with which to start. Too many brokers don't want to help clients who don't have big money to start. I have no such constraints. In fact, one of the reasons why I retired from my hedge fund, where I worked only for wealthy individuals, was that I couldn't help ordinary people who needed my help *much more* than the clients I catered to. My clients were already rich; I could only move them up the Forbes 400 list. I want to help you *become* rich, a far more noble goal. I want to coach and educate you because I know that our country does absolutely nothing to help people understand stocks and bonds and corporate finance. I know we presume a level of knowledge about money that is unjustified, given that we are taught nothing beyond how to balance a checkbook, and even that we're not so hot at.

My task is simple: make the game compelling enough for you to stay on the diet that I know has catapulted me from a struggling writer making $15,000 a year to someone who never has to work again and does so only because I find the challenge of getting others to invest well to be the mission I believe I was put on earth to accomplish. So, get ready for some financial exercise; get ready for a satisfying investing diet for all who crave big returns without big risk.

1

STAYING
in the
GAME

If you look through my wallet, you will find all the things that everyone carries: license, credit cards, pictures of my wife and kids, and some cash. But if you look deeper, in some of the crannies, you'll find two things no one else has: my first pay stub, a tattered, faded beauty from the *Tallahassee Democrat* newspaper from September 1977, and a snippet of a portfolio run from the lowest day of my life, October 8, 1998.

I keep these talismans with me wherever I go, because they remind me why I got into stocks and why I had to stay in stocks no matter what, because the opportunities are too great *not* to be in them. The $178.82 I made that first week as a general assignment reporter in Tallahassee serves as a reminder to me that a paycheck is almost never enough to make a decent living on *and* to save up for the necessities of later life. That torn and bedraggled stub, with its $30 in overtime and oversized take by the federal government, keeps me honest and reminds me where I am from, how I never want to go back there, and how hard work at your job isn't enough to make you rich. You have to

invest to make that happen. If you invest well you should almost always be beating the return you get on your day job.

The other smudged rectangle of paper in my wallet, the one that obscures the right-hand corner of my wife's picture, bears a series of cryptic numbers: 190,259,865; 281,175,544; and 90,915,674. The last number has a big black minus sign right after it. That's a cutout from my daily portfolio run on the most disastrous day my hedge fund ever had, October 8, 1998, a day when I was down $90,915,674—that's right, more than $90 million on the $281 million that I was supposed to be managing. I had "lost" almost half the money under my management in a series of bets in the stock market that hadn't yet paid off, to put a positive spin on an unmitigated decline. At that moment, everyone—my investors, my employees, the press, the public—*everyone* had written me off, except for my wife, whom I had worked with for so many years and who knew never to count me out. "You've had it, Cramer, you are gone," the collective brokerage chorus told me.

Not two months before I had been on the cover of *Money* magazine as the greatest trader of the era. Now I was wondering whether I could survive the year. With just two months left, I had to find a way at least to make back that $90 million if I wanted to stay in a business that I had thought I was born for. Most hedge funds don't come back from those kinds of titanic losses.

Using the very same techniques and tactics I will describe here, I methodically made back all of the money I had lost to date that year, and by December I had returned to a slim profit for the year. I finished up 2 percent, a $110 million comeback in less than three months. I averaged $1.4 million in profits every single day. Yet I still waived my management fee of $2 million because I didn't think I deserved a penny given how I had almost broken the bank. I still don't think I deserve to get paid for a comeback, because I dug my own hole by not following my disciplines and my rules, by succumbing to a lack of diversification and to inflexibility, those two assassins of capital.

That snapshot of how close I came to failure reminds me how important it is to stay investing and trading stocks *no matter what* be-

cause they are just too lucrative to stay away from for any long period of time. It also serves to remind me of how humbling this business is and how important it is to adjust course, for I had been sloppy and blind to a changing market during that catastrophic year. Had I not been flexible and willing to change strategies, I would never have come back.

In the very next year after my near-cataclysmic debacle, I made more than $100 million. The following year I made $150 million, again using the same rules and techniques I will describe here. I had plenty of help in the $100 million year: the market was terrific, easy, almost straight up. But in 2000, the biggest year, the $150 million year, the market peaked and crashed, yet I still profited supremely because you don't need the market to go up to make money. The fact that almost every mutual fund lost money in my biggest year is not a statement about my stock-picking prowess but evidence that if you are disciplined, use common sense, and take advantage of all the devices and tools out there, you can profit no matter what. Or, as I say at the end of my radio show every day, "There's always a bull market somewhere" that you can make profits from.

But you have to stay in that game to find that bull market. In the end, when all else fails, "Stay in the game" is the only mantra that's worth repeating. It keeps you from picking stocks that can wipe you out. It keeps you from speculating on situations that are worthless. It keeps you from borrowing a lot of money, known as margining, and hoping that stocks will make a magical move upward. It keeps you from wallowing in worthless penny stocks. It keeps you from trying to make a killing in tech. And it stops you from averaging down on bad stocks, because stocks aren't like parents when you get lost at the mall; they don't always come back. Staying in the game is the ultimate lesson. How do I know this? Because it is what I have done. I have been able to make big money when big money could be made because I didn't get discouraged or fed up or desperate when times got tough. I didn't do anything illegal or silly or unethical to stay in the game because I knew that when the game eventually turned, I would be there

to pounce on what was to be gained. Staying in the game makes sense rationally and empirically because, over the long term, we know stocks outperform all asset classes. The reason more people don't get rich with stocks, though, is that people can't seem to stay in long enough to win. They get bored, tired, frustrated, defeated, or reckless. They get discouraged. They get beaten by the unnerving and jarring and humbling process not of investing but investing *successfully*.

My methods are designed to keep you from getting discouraged and quitting. Staying in the game is key, it is everything, and if you can't stay in the game then you have failed. And I have failed. I can't let that happen.

But before I take too much credit for the system and methodology I used to keep me making money, I have to give credit where it is due, to my wife, Karen, the woman the Street called the Trading Goddess for her manner and her proficiency in managing money and barking orders to dozens of brokers and traders. Karen was a professional institutional trader before I met her. She was responsible for taking me to the next level. She took a kid who had an eye for spotting undervalued and overvalued stocks, then she grafted on a set of rules, all of which are included in this book, that have seen me through the darkest hours and allowed me to outperform even when I don't have a great set of stocks on hand. She is like a master card player who can turn a good hand into a great one with a couple of tosses and a keen sense of what's in the deck. In fact, on the day that my portfolio "run" dripped with $90 million in red ink, she had to return to the office to reinstill the rules and disciplines that I had forgotten in the three years since she had retired. She again drilled them into my head, so they now tumble out here almost by rote.

Mrs. Cramer's Rules, the Rules of the Trading Goddess, make up a large portion of this book. Like me, Karen had no formal business school or accounting training. Like me, she lived from paycheck to paycheck until she found her true calling, making money in the stock market from scratch. Unlike me, she had no fundamental knowledge of how business worked or how to read a balance sheet or how inter-

est rates control what you will ultimately pay for a stock. She always regarded those skills as overrated. What she understood was discipline and skepticism: the discipline to cut losses and run winners, and the skepticism to see through the hype that surrounds us on Wall Street. She understood better than anyone I have ever met that stocks are just pieces of paper representing shares of companies and no more than that. She knew that you could have conviction about where stocks could go and how high they could go, but it was only discipline that saved you when things didn't work out the way you thought, and she knew that things don't work out the way you think they will far more often than you would like to believe. Sure, the pieces of paper we trade are linked, albeit loosely, to the underlying entities that issued them, but in her eyes it was always important to recognize that everyone, from the media to veteran Wall Streeters, places too much importance on this linkage, which is frequently severed by rumors, by larger market forces, and, of course, by short-term imbalances in supply and demand—all of which can be gamed effectively. Occasionally stock prices are linked irrationally to the high side, as in Japan in 1988–89 or in this country in 2000, and just as occasionally they are linked to the low side, as in September 1982, when the great bull market began; in October 1987, after the stock market crash; and in October 2002, the most recent important bottom that is restoring wealth through equity appreciation in this country. Karen taught me to spot these tops and bottoms, formidable skills that I know I can teach you. I spend considerable time fleshing out those top- and bottom-calling skills in this text so you can do the same without me.

The Trading Goddess also taught me the difference between investing and trading, and how not to confuse them. Karen was—and I remain—an opportunist, one who is not bound by any particular investing philosophy beyond the need to adjust to the vicissitudes of a turbulent market so you are not knocked out of the business before the good times return. Callers and e-mailers are always asking me if I am a trader or an investor. I always respond the same way: what a stupid and false dichotomy.

In the interest of putting this question to rest forever, let me tell you up front why the trader/investor distinction makes no sense. This is not pro football, where you play offense or defense, where specialized skill sets predominate and no one is a generalist. Managing your own money is like playing hockey, where everybody has an opportunity to defend and to score and everybody is expected to take that opportunity. Sometimes stocks are making radical moves in days, as they did in the 1999–2000 period, and you have to capture those moves. If you frowned on those opportunities because they were too "trading oriented" or because you only like to buy "value," you might have missed some huge profits. If you stayed dogmatic, dug in your heels, and insisted on owning overvalued stocks that had already made great moves, you could give it all back. Both of these so-called "strengths" are actually weaknesses, inflexible weaknesses that will doom you to substantial losses at various points in the cycle.

Critics of mine dwell on my bullishness in December 1999 and January and February of 2000, the peak of the last bull market, or the bubble, as some insist on calling it. But the leaps stocks were making in that contained time span have not been and may never be replicated again. In that market the goal was to make those trading gains and go home, as I did with my March 15, 2000, RealMoney.com piece saying to take things off the table, four days after the exact top in the NASDAQ. Rather than feeling guilty about some who stayed in too long, I prided myself in recognizing that the market had changed for the worse in the spring of 2000, after the greatest run of all time, and you had to switch direction, no matter what your previous pronouncements and beliefs had been. You had to stay flexible to be conservative, to be prudent, to be commonsensical and keep your gains. Wall Street gibberish about being "in for the long term" or "only interested in stocks that trade for less than their growth rate or their book value" is just plain recklessness. You have to be willing to change your mind and your direction. Nowhere in the commandments of investing is it written "One shall not change one's mind even if it may be wrong." Businesses change, they become good, they go bad. Markets

change, they become good, they go bad. You can't be blind to those changes without losing money or risking being blown out of the game. But you must swear to stay in no matter what. It's not flip-flopping if you like WorldCom when the business is good and hate it when the business goes bad, even though I was accused mightily of flip-flopping, for example, when I tossed aside WorldCom in the $80s after owning it for more than five years. Had I not "flip-flopped" and booted the stock to kingdom come, I might have lost everything I had made in that stock and then some. You must roll with the punches of investing, bobbing and weaving when the underlying businesses falter or fade.

We all like to think of ourselves as conservative investors, but one of the Trading Goddess's most endearing and enduring traits is to recognize when buying, instead of staying in cash, is a conservative strategy and when holding, instead of selling, is the riskiest strategy of all. We'll explore in another section the arsenal of both short- and long-term tools and of using the downside of the market to make money, because, again, that can be the most conservative style available.

Most important, the Trading Goddess taught me to be unemotional and commonsensical about the direction of stock prices. While sports analogies help the business come alive, we can't root for stocks and stick with the home team. There is no home team. While dogma may pay in politics, it's a killer in stocks. While religion is important, hope and prayer are best left elsewhere when it comes to your money. They aren't valid here. While science has made tremendous strides in hundreds of areas of life, the stock market is not a science. It is just a humbling collection of pricing decisions involving the supply of equities and a level of demand mitigated by greed and fear, two animalistic, psychological components. Those who try to quantify it, measure it, and use mathematical formulas to tame it will in the end be chewed up and eaten by it, as the biggest gang of Nobels under one roof, Long-Term Capital Management, a moronically reckless hedge fund, showed when it lost billions and went belly-up in 1998. There are forces and emotions that determine how markets function that are

not susceptible to academic logic. Often to figure out how that market is valuing things we have to go outside the balance sheet and income statements, because the emotions of the market can blind you if you are constrained by those. If we simply limit the debate over how stocks get valued to price-to-earnings multiples or price-to-book valuations (don't freak out, I'll explain those, too, in a way that you will at last understand), the market will often seem completely and utterly full of baloney and impossible to understand. But I will teach you how to make sense of all the markets we have seen, how to understand the underlying patterns, and how to know when to avoid stocks or to short them, and to know when the sages and pundits simply can't be trusted when they say, "Stay away, the market's too dangerous." In still another section of the book I will present my biggest mistakes, with hysterical and humbling simplicity, so you will never make them. As I like to say, I've made every mistake in the book, so you don't have to make any. I am your laboratory. I have done the failed experiments and can show you the results that will keep you from doing them. I detail them here in ways that will make you remember when you are about to make similar costly errors so you stop before the red ink cascades through your portfolio.

Yes, stocks are pieces of paper, but they can be bought and sold with a level of emotionless precision that I can prep you for that will work in any kind of market. Broom the dogma, cultivate the discipline, open your eyes, and let's check out the basics in a way that contains—heck, that busts—all the Genuine Wall Street Gibberish that clouds so many minds trying to fathom why stocks go up or down every day.

2

┌   ┐

GETTING STARTED

the

RIGHT WAY

└   ┘

The proliferation of investment information has never been greater. We have tons of people telling us what to do. We have lots of experts telling us how to get started and what you need to know before you buy and sell. Yet they presume a level of knowledge that most of us simply don't have. Unfortunately, plenty of novices immediately get clobbered making amateurish mistakes because they don't understand the basics. These mistakes make neophyte investors feel that the game is rigged against them or that they will never succeed on a regular basis. Many of you got started during an era when everything worked, when the economy was strong, interest rates were low, and stocks went up pretty much every day. Homework was anathema to profits because it kept you out of the most promising short-term situations. That level of perfection had been previously unheard of and is unheard of again. Now people feel that things are simply unfathomable. I think the opposite is true: Stocks can be fathomed, but you need the basics, and the basics weren't taught during the heyday of the late 1990s when so many got into buying and selling

stocks. And they certainly aren't taught at any level of school in this country.

I know there is always frustration out there among the first-timers because many of you e-mail me or call me at my radio show, *Jim Cramer's RealMoney,* and ask me if I used to lose money regularly when I started. In fact, many of the millions of people who got their start in equities during the boom, bubble, and burst of the late 1990s to 2000 are convinced that the business is a sucker's game and that you might as well just turn it over to someone who is a professional.

But we are a profession without standards. The media, always so eager to tout any manager regardless of credentials, particularly if he is a good talker, never let you know that most of the "professionals" out there are rank amateurs themselves, often with much less experience at handling money and much more experience in sales than you. The astounding progression of individuals who first got clobbered by buying any old piece of trash online and then tendered their money to mutual fund charlatans, who then sold them out to wealthy hedge funds, is enough to make anyone throw his hands up in disgust about the process. You see why individuals reach the conclusion that handling money well in any fashion is simply impossible. The individual has experienced a fleecing that I wouldn't wish on the most shaggy of sheep in the dead of summer.

First, let's clear up a couple of misperceptions about the business of investing. I always thought the buying and accumulating of stocks looked easy. But once I started, I learned about the hazards of commissions, about the changing nature of markets, and the vagaries of the brokerage business. I learned that it seemed impossible to know enough to buy or sell anything right. No one could ever know enough to pull the trigger with any confidence; the task was too daunting.

And of course, when I started, I lost money. Big money. I would go on colossal losing streaks where literally everything I bought went down. I experienced tremendous ups and downs that were psychologically debilitating; often I just wanted to return to the confines of whatever paycheck I was drawing and learn to be content with that in-

come. But I always believed that stocks could be mastered if someone would just show me the landscape, if someone would explain to me the real pitfalls and give me the real rules, not the ones that I read in books or heard about on TV or saw in articles about the market. I call what I knew the Mistaken Basics. They are why, in part, I come to Praise Speculation, Not Damn It.

Part of the reason that I failed so dramatically when I first bought stocks is that I, like everyone else who has ever bought a stock, believed in conventional wisdom about stocks. In fact, I can sum up the doctrine I foolishly believed in with three rules:

1. Buy and hold because that's how you make the most money.

2. Trading is always wrong, owning is always right.

3. Speculation is the height of evil.

I guess it is only fitting in a book written by a successful investing iconoclast that the first thing we do is demolish these three shibboleths. They are blights on the investing landscape, idols that must be smashed before we go a step further. So, let's do it.

First, the concept of buy and hold is a beautiful thing because it presumes a level of ease and a level of perfection that we should all strive for. What could be better than a philosophy bedrocked in patience and conviction? Unfortunately that level of conviction about pieces of paper—all that stocks really are, and don't you ever forget it—is impossible. Patience, while a virtue, can turn into a vice when you sit there and watch a good company go bad and hold on to its stock anyway under the guise of prudence. I can say with confidence that an unmodified program of buying and holding stocks will definitely smash your nest egg worse than a McDonald's cook whipping up a fresh batch of Egg McMuffins. Buying and holding is actually a bizarre misinterpretation of the long-term data that I have quoted about why you need to stay in the game. Given that no asset class has beaten equities over any twenty-year cycle, it is natural to assume that if you buy stocks and hold them you get to beat all other asset classes.

However, the foremost academic on this particular issue, Jeremy Siegel, a Wharton professor, blanches visibly when he hears the distillation of his work interpreted as a recommendation to buy and hold stocks. Siegel's work shows that if you buy and hold *good quality stocks that often pay dividends,* you get the benefit of the cycle. In fact, the dividend portion is the reason why stocks outperform bonds, and not vice versa. Take it away, and you fail to win. Just buying and holding any old stocks, Siegel will tell you, can be a ticket to the poorhouse.

That's why on *Jim Cramer's RealMoney,* I have changed the superficial buy-and-hold mantra to the more arduous "buy and homework" doctrine, meaning that the real homework begins after you have bought a stock. Just buying and holding Sunbeam, Enron, WorldCom, Dome Petroleum, and Lucent, each at one time the most heavily traded stock of its era, was a recipe for certain disaster. Homework, or the spadework that I describe to you in my chapter on what constitutes homework, would have gotten you out of all of these stocks before the damage and the rot set in. Again, not buy and hold, but buy and homework. If you are going to make big money in the market, only with homework can you be sure that your stocks qualify as good quality stocks that can pay a dividend.

Second, the idea that trading is somehow evil is ingrained in most individuals almost from the moment they begin to invest. Stubborn adherence to this point of view has led to more big losses than any other strategy I know. Trading, meaning the rapid or short-term buying and selling of stocks, is something that can prove to be entirely necessary if you are to be prudent and lock in gains when the market takes stocks past their logical extremes, which happens quite frequently in every generation of stocks. If you chose to never sell because, say, you are afraid of the tax man, or because you despise paying commissions, you need to get your head examined. When I got into this business, it made some sense *not* to sell. It would routinely cost you several hundred dollars in commission to trade more than a couple of hundred shares. When combined with the spread, the difference between the bid and asked, for all but the most liquid or heavily

traded stocks, a diminution of return was almost a given. A quarter of a point of spread, $200 in commissions, and gigantic taxable gains might have turned a substantial gain into a moderate loss on a trade. But that was then, this is now; we are in a whole different ballgame. Taxes these days are incredibly low even on short-term gains, because ordinary tax rates are much lower than they used to be. Trades that would have cost hundreds of dollars in commissions will now be done for about seven dollars by any discount broker. The liquidity of almost all stocks is pretty terrific since the advent of decimalization, where stocks trade in penny increments. You no longer get nicked for quarters and halves on the buy and sell. Pennies, just pennies separate almost all of the places you can buy and sell stocks. They just don't eat into the profit anymore. You can't use them as an excuse not to take a profit. In fact you have to be a fool not to sell to lock in at least some of a big gain these days lest it be taken away. The old bias against trading, however, remains as people simply don't know how little friction there is between the buy and sell these days.

Finally, the bias against speculation has taken on mythic proportions. I don't know of a soul besides me who thinks that speculating can be a handy tool on the road to riches. Yet I know that all of my biggest gains, my largest wins, came from pure speculation, which I define as making a calculated bet with a limited amount of capital that turns into a monster home run. I believe that speculation is not only healthy and terrific, but is vital to true diversification. You must be diversified to stay in the game when things go bad. (More, later, about how diversification is the only free lunch in the business.) But diversification without speculation is stultifying and can mean the difference between your losing interest—which is unforgivable—and your paying attention. Speculating, particularly when you are younger, is not only prudent, it is *essential* to making it so you don't have to be totally dependent on that darned paycheck to become rich. I believe in my heart and in my head that if I had never speculated I would be working as a lawyer right now, perhaps proofreading some indenture somewhere in the middle of the night trying desperately to stay awake

as others made the money. You've got to build in speculation as part of diversification. It is a crucial component.

I play a game called "Am I Diversified?" every week on my radio program. I ask people to read to me their five largest holdings. When they have done it they have to ask me whether they are diversified. I feel so strongly about this notion that I have taken to asking why people don't have one stock bet that could make them significant amounts in a short time. I want to see speculation for a portion of even an older individual's portfolio, albeit only a name or two—a small percentage—to keep you interested. Given the nature of the potential losses I don't want someone who will need the money for retirement to speculate with more than a fifth of his portfolio. You have to make taking a chance a part of your arsenal. I know this prospeculation view runs counter to anything you have ever heard or read, but this is how I made it big in the market, this is why I was able to beat the market even when I was just starting out both as an investor-hobbyist and then as a professional at Goldman Sachs before I went off on my hedge fund. Of course a portfolio of nothing but speculation is like a diet of nothing but bacon and cheese; it will kill you. But speculation in moderation is no different from enjoying some so-called fattening foods in an endless bid to stay on the healthier regimen. The current wisdom, though, is either buy and hold whatever strikes your fancy as solid, even if it isn't, or turn everything over to someone who doesn't care as much as you do about either capital preservation (no defense) or capital appreciation (no offense).

Understand that I love to invest. I love to buy and do homework. I have owned some high-quality stocks for years and years and years. Yet I always do the homework still. And I always speculate when I am able to speculate, either through the use of options (which I'll explain later) or through the use of small-dollar acorns that I think can grow to be tall oaks or, even better, to be taken over by larger oaks long before they go through the slow process of growing up.

I know that academics and those market professionals who believe that stocks are priced perfectly don't believe that you can make large

amounts with small investments in a short period of time. They think such situations don't exist or that they are flukes, luck. Because they don't believe in them and because you often search for them and fail, the tendency, the belief, becomes ingrained that there is no quick way to make big money.

Let me give you an example of a situation I stumbled on in my younger stock-picking days—an example of what some would say was just rank speculation but I say was a legitimate opportunity—that might show you why I believe in speculating wisely. This opportunity came when I was younger and had almost no money to speak of, precisely the time to speculate the heaviest because you have your whole work life to make the money back if things don't pan out.

At Harvard Law School, I managed in my spare time to work for Alan Dershowitz, helping to get the supremely guilty—at least in my view—Claus von Bulow acquitted on procedural grounds. The job paid well, more than eight dollars an hour. Despite being phenomenally bored with my law school classes—to this day I regard them as pure torture—I made it my business to go every day. I would check in on the markets every hour via the phone booths located outside the classrooms, usually reserved for homesick kids calling their mothers after a particularly brutal grilling or exam. That spring, 1984, the oil patch had heated up. Getty Petroleum had just gotten a bid. I had made some money speculating in some call options, which for a little money provide the right to be able to capture the upside above a particular level of stock, in the Conoco battle the previous year and in Sinclair Oil, another target, not long after. I had small positions— several hundred dollars' worth of money I had saved from the Dershowitz chores—in both oils and was drawn to the group. At this point I was also managing a pool of money for my friend Marty Peretz, who had found me via my answering machine. I had such a hot hand picking stocks while attending classes that I began recommending a stock a week on my machine. Only later, in my third year at law school, did I discover that such a touting system was a violation of the 1940 Investment Advisor Act, but I hadn't taken that class yet, so who

knew? Marty tried to reach me to write a positive book review for the *New Republic*, which he owned and edited, on behalf of a mutual friend, Jim Stewart, a terrific author, and got discouraged when I never called him back. After three straight weeks where he said I had made more money for him than any other person alive in the thirty years he'd been buying and selling stocks, he handed me a check for $500,000 over a cup of joe at the Coffee Connection. I ran his money side by side with my little pool of cash. I told Marty that I thought our next big hit would be Gulf Oil; it just seemed too logical. I purchased us small amounts of Gulf call options (again, the right to make money if a stock reaches a certain level). I had decided early on that call options, if you can handle their risk, were the ideal method of speculation for a small investor because the downside was limited and the upside was bountiful. (More on how calls work and how to master them later in the advanced section of the book.)

One day, while I was in class, Chevron launched a bid for Gulf Oil. I was gleeful after I called in and discovered I had had my first big hit. I had been discouraged when I had initially lost money for Marty, but this Gulf Oil deal put me in the black with him. I wanted to give his money back and just trade for myself—I hated the responsibility of running other peoples' money and still do! But Marty wouldn't hear of it. Now we were back where we started, and I was feeling better about myself.

That spring I had been taking Antitrust with the giant of antitrust, the late Phil Areeda. Most of law school was a valueless blur, but this guy was a master. I still recall his classes, among the few I took seriously, because he was a great teacher. We were working on a unit on Standard Oil and the origins of antitrust law. I always sat in the back and said nothing. If I was ever called on, I always passed, lest I look like an idiot. But I was taking it all in. I thought, You know something, this guy Areeda knows what the heck he's talking about. Most of the professors were a bunch of left-wing, dogmatic blowhards. But Areeda was in the game.

Right after the announcement of the bid, and the concomitant

move up of Gulf, the oil giant's stock started slipping. One day during a break in class, I checked in with my broker, Joe McCarthy from Fidelity, and heard the disturbing news that Gulf had fallen back almost to where we had first bought the calls, on chatter that the government was definitely going to block the Gulf-Socal (as it was called then) merger. I was so distraught I didn't even notice that the break was over and I slunk back into class late, several minutes after intermission had ended.

It was obvious that I was tardy. Areeda hated that. He was too much of a gentleman and I was not enough of a scholar not to feel bad about coming in after class had started. At the conclusion of the class, I went up to him to apologize for my slothfulness. Areeda knew I was one of those students who couldn't care less about law school, but he knew I was interested in business. I took a chance. I said, "Professor, I was late because I own Gulf Oil and my broker says that the deal won't go through."

He looked me in the eye and he said something I would never forget: "It's a done deal." I looked at him the way a man looks at the piece of glass he just found in his backyard that he now realizes is a diamond. I said to him that I had real money riding on this one. Was Justice going to block the deal?

"Not a chance," he said. He knew the players. He knew Reagan's people wouldn't block it.

I asked him again.

He said he didn't have any more time to waste. If I had done my homework, which I obviously had not, I would have known that the decision was in the bag. I left the class and bet the farm for me and for Marty on Gulf Oil, wagering just about every penny I had in the bank, some $2,000 at the time.

Justice approved the deal soon after and I made a fortune for Marty and enough for myself to pay for law school and college (I still owed substantial amounts from college) and emerge from school free and clear. Two thousand dollars turned into twenty-five thousand just like that. And an indebted student who expected to labor for years to free

himself of that indenture was freed before he graduated. I had speculated and I had succeeded.

Would I endorse this view if you called me on my radio show or
met with me privately for a consultation? Yes, if you were young
enough that you could afford to lose it all and still make it back. No, if
you were older and speculating the same percentage of assets I did,
which was just about everything. I want you to speculate, but as you
get older, you don't have the rest of your life to make the money back
from the paycheck side of the ledger, so, naturally, you have to scale
back and take smaller risks. But as a small percentage of assets and
with a hunch like I had with Gulf, absolutely. These kinds of informed
bets are the best kind of investments, because the risk, the downside, is
limited, and the reward, the upside, is monumental. I know, I know,
you won't always have the insight of some Harvard antitrust professor, but these kinds of home runs, while not as frequent as singles, do
get hit every day in this business.

Why is this kind of short-term thinking so antithetical to most investors? How did we get brainwashed into buy and hold forever? I
think that the literature on the topic is very much responsible for the
misapprehensions about speculation, buying and holding, and trading. All investing literature has one thing in common: It refuses to
admit that great investing, long-term or short-term, has much in
common not with science or mathematics, but with *gambling*! There,
I said it. We are wagering on the direction of stocks, both long and
short. We are wagering in a way that we hope will allow a little bit of
money to grow into something huge. We are betting that we can evaluate merchandise and figure out which can win, which places, which
shows, and which loses. We want more winners than losers; if we get
more winners than losers we will grow rich. Once you admit that it is
wagering, and that you have to monitor the jockey (the manager) as
well as the horse (the company) as well as the track (the stock market),
then you can make some sense of what you are up against and know
which rules do and don't apply.

That's why it is no coincidence that (until now) I always recom-

mended one text to those trying to figure out how to beat the market. One book, besides this one, that can change your view of investing forever. It's not *Reminiscences of a Stock Operator* by legendary trader Jesse Livermore (written under the pseudonym Ed Lefèvre), even though that's a real hoot. Nor is it something by value investor Benjamin Graham, nor the Peter Lynch books, which are excellent, nor the Bill O'Neill books, although I would come to like them later.

In fact, it is not a stock book at all. It's *Picking Winners* by Andy Beyer, the premier horse-racing columnist in the country, who until recently penned a column for the *Washington Post*. Yep, a handicapping book. Because the two, horse-race betting and stock betting, are so alike that the wagering rules he lays out apply to both. Beyer excels in handicapping horses; I excel in handicapping stocks. Beyer's main lessons, besides the basic need to be a good speculator, are vital for you to understand, and I will give you a variety of ways to master them. They seem simple, but in the reality of stocks, it will take plenty of practice and homework for you to use and maintain them:

1. If you learn from mistakes you will not repeat them.

2. Only go to tracks where there aren't a lot of good players so you can clean up. (The analogy here is only to invest in stocks where the research and information flow aren't perfect and lots of minds aren't already trying to figure it out.)

3. Only bet on situations where you have total conviction. Leave the rest to others; you don't have to play. You don't have to invest in everything that comes down the pike.

Now, let's analyze how these three rules apply to stocks. First, amateurs must realize that much time must be spent doing homework (I will show you what homework entails) and learning the stocks you own. Approach it like a job. Investing can be a hobby, but trading can't. Even Mrs. Cramer, who is a fabulous trader, has failed miserably as a part-time trader, although her investing skills are still top of the heap.

Second, while you can't be an expert on everything, you can learn a few stocks well and profit handily from those. I will show you where to find them, but you still have to do the homework when you get them.

Most of all, recognize that you have to have an edge, something different that you can bring to the party. I will show you some methods you can use to gain an edge in your investments, using commonsensical approaches to the businesses around you.

To get there, you must have a basic understanding of what stocks are, how stocks work, and why they go up and down. You have to know how they work before I can give you the rules, show you the mistakes, and explain the best ways to find the best stocks, and, finally, how to speculate in ways that could make you rich without a lot of money, both basic and advanced methods. Only then can you make the wagers, both short- and long-term, that fit the rules that Beyer outlines. Only then can we benefit from his handicapping wisdom.

We assume so much in this business, we who own and trade stocks. We assume that you understand what a stock is, what it represents, and how stocks figure into the capital structure. Those are blithe assumptions. I know this because I have seen people confuse shares of a stock with something that is almost tangible, something that is palpable, and that misconception leads to a level of certainty and lack of accurate skepticism that can betray you in a heartbeat. So let's take a second to explain where stocks come from and where they fit into the investment picture. Those who have been investing for years should still pay heed because you may assume certain things, too, that may not be true.

First of all, all companies need money, especially companies that are trying to grow. They can get money in a couple of ways. They can go to the bank as we go to a bank to get a loan such as a mortgage. The collateral for the loan might be the inflow of cash the company expects (the receivables) or it might be the worth of the company itself. A company can issue debt, or bonds, that it pays interest on over time, and then, when the debt is due, it pays back the principal.

If the owners of the company are willing, or if some of the owners

want to get money out of the company, the company can issue common stock shares in the enterprise. A company's capital structure can be made up of shares that are issued to the public and bonds that are issued to the public.

We all assume that the common stock the company issues represents the real ownership of the company. We proudly talk about how we own shares in the company and are therefore somehow "owners" of the company, as if we were all members of some grand club that owns the clubhouse. The first thing I want to do is disabuse you of that entitlement. When you own stock, you do have a fractional interest in the company if there is no other element in the capital structure, that is, if there is no debt. But beyond the danish and O.J. that you might get if you attend the annual meeting, owning stock itself entitles you to nothing. Worse, if the company has debt, the debt holders are senior to you and have more power than you. I call these folks the bond bullies. As long as the company is doing well, the bond bullies behave themselves and let the stockholders run the company. However, if the company loses a lot of money, to the point where it can't pay the interest on the bonds, the bond bullies take over. I stress this because in the period from 2000 to 2003, many common stock shareholders were wiped out and bond holders took over companies. The common stock shareholders in many cases did not know what hit them. They thought they owned the company. So, remember, you only own it when things are good. When things go bad, you don't own anything but the piece of paper that the common stock is printed on, and you probably don't even have that because almost all stocks these days are held electronically, with no certificates issued.

The saving grace of stocks is that they can only go to zero. Don't laugh, I've owned some stocks that were so bad that it was a blessing they stopped at zero. Each share of common stock is theoretically worth something, a fractional share of ownership. But if you go to the company to redeem your shares to cash out of your ownership, the company will tell you that while it issued the shares, it won't take them back from you. Companies aren't department stores of shares. You

have to sell those shares to someone else. In fact, the company can issue more shares at any given time to dilute your ownership in the enterprise. It can also buy back those shares if it wants in the open market, if it chooses to shrink the number of shares outstanding.

Why do people own stock if the company won't take it back? Why is it worth anything? I know people who have traded stocks for years and years who have never asked themselves that, yet it's a tremendous leap of faith to understand why an electronic entry of shares that can't be taken back to the company is worth anything at all.

The answer is really twofold: There is an enterprise value to the whole company that can be bought or sold and can grow over time from the retained earnings of the company, and there is an income stream (known as dividends) that can come from the shares when the company is prosperous. If you own a stock that pays a dividend you could be getting both the income stream and the value of an appreciating stock. Most companies, however, don't start out as dividend payers. Many other companies have no intention of paying a dividend because they want to reinvest earnings to grow the company and don't want to return any capital to the shareholders.

Why are we given this opportunity to participate in the welfare of a public company? Why do companies go public, or sell shares to investors? What is the stock made of and what determines its price? Let's look at it through one situation I know well, one that is somewhat typical of the process, although each company, of course, is different from others in its own way. Let's look at TheStreet.com, a publicly traded company that I own a ton of shares in. Marty Peretz and I started the company in 1996 by putting in $100,000 every month. It didn't begin to generate any revenue until 1997, but then advertising on the Web took off like a rocket and we needed money both to pay people and to expand. The money we needed was beyond what Marty and I could afford. Frankly, while we were growing revenues, or sales, nicely, we were losing money hand over fist. We had no profits, which are sales minus expenses and the cost of the goods sold, but we had two revenue streams, subscription and advertising, and we had a brand,

which had some amorphous value. When we had burned through all of the money that Marty and I were willing to invest we had to raise money from other individuals, known as venture capitalists. They gave us money not because they were our buddies—far from it—but because they hoped to get more than their money back when the company was sold to another company or if it went public. We were in it to build the company, they were in it for the payoff. That's a fairly typical situation for young, growing companies.

After we burned through the venture capitalists' money, we raised money from a couple of other companies, notably News Corporation and the New York Times Company. They, too, gave us their capital in return for the right to have shares when we issued them. We could have gone to a bank, but I don't think any bank would have lent us money because we were losing too much money as it was. But because of the fascination with the stock market at that time, we hired a banker, Goldman Sachs, to tap the public's dollars. We knew people would buy shares in our enterprise for the reason they buy shares in many enterprises: They hoped we would one day either return a profit or be bought by another company for more than they paid for their shares. One of Goldman Sachs' main jobs was to raise money for us through an underwriting, or initial public offering (IPO). Everyone thinks he understands this underwriting process intuitively, but as one of the people who has worked on IPOs, from the entrepreneurial side to the sell side, I can tell you they are rather mystifying. Unless you are a serial entrepreneur, you probably will only go through the going-public process once, if you are unlucky enough to go through it at all.

I was hopelessly naïve. Here's the way it really works. Management of the company, which is typically clueless about Wall Street, has a meeting with the banker's corporate finance department, which draws up the documents for the offering and structures the deal, and the syndicate department, which prices the merchandise. The investment banking people tell you how many shares you are going to have outstanding and how many of those shares the company will float publicly. The syndicate person tells you what price those shares will

most likely be issued at. Our syndicate people told us that they looked at companies comparable to ours and said that given how much in sales we had—we had no profits—and how much money the New York Times and News Corp. had paid, the company should be worth $250 million dollars. The figure wasn't totally arbitrary—the New York Times and News Corp. had valued it similarly, although it sure was hard to figure out why it was worth anything given how much it was losing. Then the investment bank said, arbitrarily, that the company's ownership would be divided into 25 million shares. Of that, 19 million would be owned by the original investors and 6 million would be sold to the public. I give you these numbers because there is no magic to the number of shares a company has. Goldman could have said we were going to have 100 million shares and 24 million would have been issued to the public. It could have said we would have 200 million shares and 48 million were going to be issued. That's just how it works. The total share count matters tremendously only as a way to figure out how much earnings per share there are. Of course, TheStreet.com wasn't close to having any earnings per share, but you can still figure it out by taking the overall loss we were having in a year and dividing that by the number of shares to be issued, so you can compare TheStreet.com's earnings per share to those of other companies.

I initially owned 50 percent of the company with my cofounder Marty Peretz. When we invited the venture capitalists in, our 50 percent stake was diluted to about 30 percent each. With each new round of financing, we gave up more of our claim to the enterprise. By the time we contacted Goldman Sachs, my stake had been diluted to about 16 percent of the enterprise, since each new buyer was entitled to shares and the company issued shares to some of the people who worked there in addition to salaries. You may think that 16 percent is way too little versus where we started, but it is part of a much bigger pie than we started, so I was quite happy with the percentage.

Goldman Sachs then conducted what is known as a road show, where it flies management to a bunch of cities to stir up demand. We

already had a ton of demand for the shares before we started, so the roadshow was a complete waste of time and should have just been done over the Web. But theoretically you want to explain to people in person what the company does and what it plans to do. In actuality, the merchandise—the shares the company is issuing—was "hot" merchandise, meaning that everyone was clamoring for the darned stuff and we could have just as easily sold shares on eBay, but that's not how it works, unfortunately.

It is during this period that people at the company write the prospectus, or selling document, which tells you what the company does, how it is doing financially, what the backgrounds of the people involved are, and then gives you a huge list of reasons, or risks, that tell you why you would be nuts to buy the company. It's a funny way to do business, but, as I have said from the beginning, there's a lot of nutty, counterintuitive things about Wall Street that often are there just to confuse you and make you need someone who can help you—for a fee, of course. Most people throw the thing away immediately, but the prospectus can be an immense source of information about a company. You don't need to keep it—they are all online now, reachable with a keystroke.

After the company's top officers have been on a plane visiting a dozen cities, the merchandise gets repriced by the bankers to take into account the stirred-up demand as the deal gets closer. For me, this was another totally eye-opening process. While we started the trip thinking we would get $10 a share, the price got lifted seven times, the final bump to $19. It was only later that I found out that the plan was always to have it priced at $19 because that's the price Goldman thought would work best for everyone—the buyers and the company selling the shares. We insiders were restricted from selling for eighteen months, and then we were allowed only to dribble out stock slowly, so as not to crush the offering with too much supply. At this point we were only allowed to buy more on the deal, not sell any stock. If we had been allowed to sell stock, that would be considered "secondary" stock, not "primary" stock, which is just for the company.

Because the system for initial public offerings at the time couldn't really factor in all of the market orders, the company ended up selling 6,350,000 shares at $19. The stock opened, however, at $63, nowhere near the $19, as demand totally outstripped supply. Brokerages aren't allowed to issue more supply than they originally promised and so many uninformed folks in the public foolishly used market orders to buy. They ended up buying stock for 20, 30, and even 40 points more than they thought they would because they used the dreaded market order system. Never use it, as I will explain later, when you can use limit orders. Those who got the stock from Goldman Sachs at $19 on the actual offering mostly flipped the stock at those inflated prices and pocketed the $63 minus the $19 they paid. What a huge windfall for the customers and what a monster shortchange for the company! But there are no do-overs in this business. Even though, in retrospect, we could have sold many more shares at a much higher price, the company still had to pay Goldman Sachs 6 percent of the proceeds for this one-day sale.

Once the deal is done, the company has almost nothing to do with the shares again. The shares that come public, and then, in time, the shares of insiders such as the venture capitalists and the corporations and the founders like Marty and me, are free to be traded, although insiders can only peel them out slowly since there are tightly regulated rules for how much stock you can sell at one time—again, so as not to overwhelm the market. The price of the merchandise is reset every day through trading by the public, in this case on the NASDAQ, where companies can be listed that don't make money—you have to make money for a year before you can list on the New York Stock Exchange. While there are differences in how stocks trade on the two exchanges (the New York Stock Exchange uses what is known as a specialist system with humans manipulating the supply and demand, while the NASDAQ trades electronically from computer to computer with no human middle man), those differences are virtually irrelevant to all but those who trade in multiple thousands of shares, so we won't need to address the pros and cons here of the two systems. Suffice it to say

that once the deal goes public, the public sets the price from then on. For us at TheStreet.com, we had to watch the sickening slide from opening day at $63 to $1 a couple of years later, although it has since bounced back to more reasonable prices. You should remember those prices whenever you hear a silly academic say that the pricing system of stocks is "perfect," meaning that it prices in all data precisely. Within a period of two years the brilliant "market" valued TheStreet .com at both $1.2 billion and at $20 million. That's a lot of room for the savvy to make money and the naïve to get shafted.

3

HOW STOCKS ARE MEANT

to

BE TRADED

Now that you know the process that companies go through to become public, it's time to figure out how we—you and I—should value them. Determining a company's value tells you what's worth buying. Deciding what's right to buy and what's right to sell, and the best ways to do so, are the fundamentals of investing. Doing it correctly and intelligently can make you very rich. Doing it in an uninformed way, the way the vast majority of people do, can make you poor unless you get lucky. This book is about taking as much luck and hope out of the equation as possible.

People ask me every day what a stock they own is worth. They almost always say, "I bought TheStreet.com at ten dollars and it is now at four dollars. What should I do with it?" I tell them immediately, I don't care where a stock traded, I don't care about the past, I don't care where you bought the stock, the only thing I care about with a stock is what's going to happen next. I must say those words a dozen times a week on my radio show because most people don't grasp this simple

concept that determines just about everything you need in order to know whether a stock is going to go up or down: the future.

People are constantly trying to bring up the irrelevant when they talk stocks. Maybe you bought the stock well, maybe you bought it badly. It shouldn't influence your decision. They want to mention what went through their minds when they bought it and why they bought. I don't care about that either, because it obviously didn't turn out right or you wouldn't be referring to where you bought it and mentioning how you are down on it.

I'm driven so crazy by this web of meaningless alibis that the only time I take individual questions about individual stocks on my radio show is on Fridays when we play "The Lightning Round." I forbid callers to say anything but the name of the stock and I take it from there, telling them up or down, buy or sell, based strictly on what I think is going to happen in the future. That's because owning stock is a bet on the future, not the past. You must buy into that notion or you mustn't buy stocks yourself.

I didn't always feel this way. At one point, no doubt like you now, I was completely caught up in the notion of my "basis," the technical term, both on Wall Street and with the IRS, for the price I paid for a stock. If my basis for Maytag, say, was $34, and the stock was $28, I would let that unrealized loss get in the way of the decision-making process, because, I, like you, hate to take a loss. Of course, the situation is already in "loss mode" as I like to call it, a loss to anyone but you because you hold out hope that should play no role in the process.

In fact, I would let this basis factor so mar my judgment about the future of Maytag that I wouldn't be able to think clearly about whether I should give up on the position or buy more. I would say, "Maytag, I'm down six, maybe I have to buy more. Maybe I should be bigger, 'cause I'm down." Or, obviously, "Maybe if I buy more I can make it right even if I'm wrong now!" Lots of that kind of logic swarmed in my head when I was starting out.

This pigheadedness about my basis—in the face of obvious facts about how bright or poor the *future* of Maytag would be—made my

wife go ballistic. The Trading Goddess knew that the future was all that mattered, and she knew I was being blinded to it because I was down six bucks when I reviewed the piece of merchandise on which I was "long," or owned. In those grand old days of trading together at 56 Beaver Street in downtown Manhattan, a floor above the steak joint, Delmonico's, a downtown fixture, she would insist we get off the desk multiple times a day and go to a bare office located right above the kitchen of the restaurant. There, with steak fumes wafting in and threatening to embed themselves in our clothes and our nostrils, she would go over each position slowly and methodically, reciting each name from our position sheets. After each stock she would ask me what I thought and how I would rank it on a scale of one to five, a one being a stock I wanted to buy more of right now and a five being one I needed to sell pronto.

These sessions were extremely painful because there would be a dripping tone of sarcasm when a stock had obviously gone awry. She was always exacting in her methods; these weren't lovey-dovey klatches between husband and wife, believe me. They were discipline camps. I would try to think clearly about each position she would enunciate, but invariably I would be blinded by my basis. I just couldn't get past the decline from where I bought the darned thing. My judgment was stymied by the stigma of unrealized loss that each negative position carried.

Then one day, we got off the desk and went to the steak room, as I called it, and she handed out the sheets as always but the basis, the price I had paid, was whited out. That's right, she had grabbed a bottle of Wite-Out and painted over every price that I had originally paid for the stocks. "There," she said, "now you can think clearly."

Of course, when we got down to the Maytag position, I was able, at last, to measure Maytag for what mattered, the future, not what I was letting matter, the past, the 6 points I was down on the position. When not faced with the tether of history, I immediately admitted that Whirlpool and GE were kicking Maytag's butt and that we ought to just face the darned music and dump the stock.

From then on, she routinely whited out all the bases of every stock from our position sheets. And our performance increased dramatically. Lesson number one: When it comes to buying or selling a stock, don't tell me where you bought it, tell me where it's going. That's all that matters when it comes to buying or selling a stock.

Besides the past, people are way too hung up on price, the dollar amount you have to pay per share. Most beginners, but also many people who got in during the heyday, the bubble, when everything was working, don't even realize what "price" is, so let's explain that first before we explore whether we are paying too much or too little for a stock.

When you get a quote, or when you look at a stock's closing price in the morning papers, you are seeing the exact last price at which the merchandise—and this is just merchandise—changed hands. That doesn't mean it's where you can necessarily buy the stock. Stocks trade in bids and offers—you hit the bid, or sell it there, or you take the offer, or buy it there. The uninitiated use the terms "buy" and "sell," but we never do that on Wall Street; we say "take the stock" or "hit the bid." That's because we are intent on getting the job done. "Buy" and "sell" are amorphous terms, too amorphous for most professionals, but good enough for those who are just trying to buy small amounts, typically less than 100 shares. Any more than 100 shares and you are going to have to learn that "buy 200 shares of Nortel" is simply taking your life into your hands. Here's why. "Buy" and "sell" mean "buy at the market" and "sell at the market." Only amateurs and fools enter market orders. Our ridiculous system of buying and selling stocks is predicated upon your being ripped off by whoever gets that market order. And you will be. If you enter a generic market order, the order can be matched with another customer within the system or brokerage you are trading in, at a price perhaps at least surprising and at most entirely disadvantageous to you. Especially when the merchandise you are buying is illiquid or "trades by appointment," meaning that it is difficult to find multiple buyers and sellers. When I was just starting, trading stocks out of phone booths or sneaking out of law

school classes to place orders, I always used market orders and rarely did the order ever work to my satisfaction. I always felt I was getting ripped off. It was only much later, after I turned pro, that I realized that I *was* being systematically ripped off—by myself—because I foolishly believed that the system of buying and selling stocks at the market was set up to aid the little guy. Just the opposite. A market order is a license to abuse you, at the behest of a larger client or the brokerage itself trying to "find both sides of the trade" internally so it can get the full commission on both the selling and the buying instead of having to share it with another firm.

So what can you do?

Lesson number two in trading stocks: Always use limit orders when you buy or sell any stock, especially when you are buying in unseasoned situations, with new stocks or just-issued stocks, such as The Street.com on the day it came public. Decide what price you are willing to pay for a piece of merchandise, and then enter it. Never use a market order. You can determine yourself what you think is right, what you think is expensive, or what you think is cheap, and hold out for it. That's vital, that's what you have to do, and don't let yourself be abused by the system. This "limit" order is particularly important in so-called fast markets, when there is news impacting the stock you are trying to buy, making the merchandise a moving target. You determine the parameters. If I want to buy Nortel and the offered, or where I can buy it, is $3.50, but there is news out—a new contract gained from BellSouth, say, that will jack up the price—then I enter the order this way: "Take two thousand shares of Nortel at three fifty-five." That way I've set a limit on the price I will pay for the stock.

Similarly, if I want to sell Nortel and the bid, or where I can sell it, is $3.48, but Nortel has lost some important business to Cisco that I know will send the stock plummeting, then I say, "Sell two thousand shares of Nortel as low as three forty-five." I make up the price, I give the limit.

That way I buy it at the price I want, and if I buy it at the wrong price at least it's my fault, and not the fault of the system. Nobody tells

you not to use market orders because it is in nobody's interest except yours to do so. The broker wants you to do the trade so he gets the commission, but if you "limit" it, the trade might not happen, and then he doesn't get paid. (If the stock never reaches your target price, then the trade isn't executed.) The brokerage wants to cross your order with another order in house to get both of the commissions. A market order lets that happen, but at a price that you might not like. Never use market orders, ever! If this simple point is your only take-away from what I have learned the hard way, you are already well ahead of the game.

Now, how about that price, that last sale dollar amount. Do you know what that price means? If you go to Macy's and there are two cable-knit sweaters, one by Polo made of cashmere and one by Macy's house brand made of polyester and cotton, both selling for $100, you know that something's wrong with the price of at least one of these two items. The Polo cashmere should be $400. The poly-cotton Macy's deal should be $49. We can do stuff like that in our heads. We know bargains and we know rip-offs. We are sophisticated shoppers about things like sweaters at department stores. Alas, if only we were better at buying bigger ticket items like stocks at the malls I shop at every day, the NASDAQ or the New York Stock Exchange.

The reason why we can't spot bargains and rip-offs when it comes to stocks is that the prices we pay aren't "real"; they are simply ratios created by the companies through stock splits and share adjustments that often confuse even professionals but always confuse the little guys. When you buy a cashmere sweater for $400, you know it is worth more than the poly-cotton sweater at $49. But in the stock market—and only in the stock market—a $49 stock can be more expensive than a $400 stock!

We have to understand how these ratios are calculated so you can spot bargains and overvalued merchandise as easily as you can at Albertsons or Wal-Mart or Macy's. Don't freak out at the mention of the word "ratio." I was doing ratios with my fifth grader last night. They are simple division, something that our schools actually teach success-

fully to all but the socially promoted. You know I am going to get you through this with flying colors, so drop your objections and let's get to work.

To help us understand the real or underlying worth of merchandise versus the arbitrary price per share that we pay, let's stick with Maytag, the washer and dryer company everyone knows, and compare it to Whirlpool, its biggest competitor. Recently Maytag traded at $27 a share and Whirlpool traded at $67 a share. Are they roughly the same price? The beginner, of course, says no, one is $40 more than the other and is therefore much more expensive. Only on Wall Street, where so much is done to confuse the millions of people who shop at our store, is the answer "yes" to the question whether Maytag at $27 and Whirlpool at $67 are the same price. In fact, they are almost exactly the same price, as befits two competitors that duke it out pretty evenly. But you have to understand their price-to-earnings ratios to see through the $27 to $67 disparity. You have to understand the ratio to know that $67 isn't more expensive than $27.

You see, we don't care about the actual price that we pay per share. If Whirlpool, for example, were to announce a two-for-one stock split tomorrow, you would be paying $33 a share, and instead of saying that Whirlpool is selling for $40 more than Maytag, you would say it is selling for $6 more. Or, if Maytag were to do a two-for-one reverse split, so that it was selling at $54, you would think they are selling at similar prices. But share prices are just guideposts that a company can change at will. They don't help you figure out relative worth at all. (Never forget that while splits are exciting, they produce no more "pencil." That's my shorthand for taking a pencil and breaking it in half. You have two pencils, but you haven't created more lead. That's all a stock split is!)

What really matters isn't the price that you pay or that you see at the end of the long column of numbers next to a stock symbol or name in the newspaper stock tables each day. What matters is the price-to-earnings ratio of each stock. You have to take that last price on that line in the paper next to the stock's name, and you have to divide it—come on, take it and just put a line under it—by the

amount per share the company earned in the previous year. Maytag earned $2.18 last year. That's a number that can be found by simply inputting MYG, Maytag's symbol, into Quote.Yahoo.com. This will instantly tell you how much money, on a per share basis, Maytag made. (You can arrive at that number yourself, as you used to do before the Web's incredible explosion of free information, by dividing the amount the company earned for the year—that's back to the process of share issuance as we talked about with TheStreet.com—by the number of common stock shares there are.)

Now, you divide $27—the last price paid—by $2.18, and you get 12 (rounded to the nearest whole number). That's the magic number that you need to know, Maytag trades at 12 times earnings. You are paying 12 times Maytag's previous earnings per share for each share that you buy. That's the real price. The (M)ultiple, 12, times $2.18, the (E)arnings per share, equals the (P)rice per share. We express the price as an equation: $M \times E = P$.

You should always remember this equation as a way to understand how we arrive at prices. We take the earnings and we figure out what we are willing to pay for the earnings—the multiple—then we times them and we arrive at the price. This formula can also help us figure out future prices. If we know what the earnings estimates are going to be (E) and we can figure out what we might be willing to pay for those earnings (M) we can arrive at a future price or we can figure how much above or below a stock might be from where it might trade in the future. The multiple allows us to make apples-to-apples comparisons with the stocks of other companies in the cohort.

To put it another way, if we have the price, and we have the future earnings estimates, we can measure whether we are paying too much M or too little M for the stock right now versus its peers. Any change in the earnings estimates (faster growth, for example) or any change in the economic landscape (such as lower interest rates, as we shall see) can affect what M we will pay.

Congratulations, you have just mastered the art of figuring out what a stock is worth and what it might be worth in the future.

Professionals never say, "Maytag's a bargain because it trades at twenty-seven dollars." They say "Maytag's a bargain because it trades at twelve times earnings and yet it is a consistent grower that deserves to sell for a higher multiple." Or professionals might say, "Maytag's expensive at twelve times earnings given its spotty history." The subjectivity is in the comparisons to other equities of similar nature.

Whirlpool, on the other hand, earned about $6 last year and it trades for $67. What does it trade at times earnings? What's its magic number? Divide the $67 by the $6 and you get roughly 11 (again, we are rounding because the precise multiple isn't as important as the approximation). So Whirlpool trades at a multiple of 11 times earnings. Now we have something that allows us to compare the two companies; we have something that explains the *relative* worth of each company's shares. Maytag trades at 12 times earnings while Whirlpool trades at 11 times earnings.

Here's where it gets really interesting. While the Whirlpool at $67 seems almost $40 more expensive than Maytag at $27, when we make the comparison apples to apples, when we break it down by P/E (price-to-earnings) ratio, we see that Whirlpool trades at 11 times earnings and Maytag at 12 times earnings. That's right, Maytag at $27 is actually more expensive than Whirlpool at $67. Almost 10 percent more expensive, despite the prices quoted.

We say, using the vernacular of Wall Street, that Maytag is "one multiple point more expensive than Whirlpool." We are simply subtracting Whirlpool's 11 multiple from Maytag's 12 multiple to arrive at that one-point disparity. Do you know why a $27 stock can be more expensive than a $67 stock? There are many reasons. One is that a Maytag appliance might be slightly better than Whirlpool's. A second may be that Maytag's brand has a better reputation than Whirlpool. A third could be that Maytag's management might be better than Whirlpool's. All of those reasons do matter. But the real reason why one trades more expensively than the other is that one grows faster than the other. All reasons for changes in multiples pall compared to Wall Street's intense growth fixation. The main reason Maytag trades at

one-multiple-point premium to Whirlpool is that it grows faster than Whirlpool. On Wall Street we care about growth, growth, and then more growth of the future earnings stream of an enterprise. That's the major determinant of what we pay. The other reasons are quite secondary, despite what you have read or heard otherwise. Growth is the focus, the be-all, the end-all of investing, the mother's milk. Nothing trumps growth. If you understand that seeking growth, or more important, seeking *changes* in the growth rate that may be unexpected by others, is the most important factor to focus on as an investor, you will catch all the major spurts in stocks that can be had. That's because stocks move in relation to changes in growth of earnings at the underlying company. If you can predict or forecast changes in growth in the underlying company—either through management changes, or product development cycles, or changes in the competitive landscape, or through macroeconomic concerns like lower taxes or lower interest rates—you can predict big moves in a stock *before they happen*. That's what I have spent my whole life searching for, and I am living proof that these changes can be forecasted, found, and acted upon ahead of the crowd.

How is growth measured on Wall Street? To chart future growth, you have to start by looking at the pattern of earnings, particularly earnings per share, or EPS. If you pick up the annual reports, or download them online, you will discover that Maytag has been growing its earnings much faster than Whirlpool. In fact, if you do the arithmetic, or if you go to Yahoo! or TheStreet.com or any other Web site and ask for the "quote," you will also get the long-term growth of the enterprise. You will see, for example, that Maytag has been growing its earnings at 9 percent a year, while Whirlpool has been growing its earnings at 5 percent a year. Maytag has been growing its business much faster than Whirlpool. Again, Maytag trades at a higher multiple than Whirlpool, 12 to 11, because it grows its business faster. Wall Street pays a premium for high growth and awards a discount for slow growth. The multiple I have measured reflects past growth, but people on Wall Street presume that past growth can help indicate future

growth, and they judge companies accordingly unless the companies make acquisitions, change management, or discover something new and different that can make them grow faster. While not always an accurate predictor of future growth, past growth is a terrific starting point for projecting a company's future growth.

For many this growth fixation seems somewhat alien, if not counterintuitive. We tend not to rate any of the other goods we buy according to how fast they grow. It isn't an ordering principle in other walks of life. We don't buy cars, for example, for how fast they go, unless we are race car drivers. Houses don't go for growth, they go for looks and convenience. We don't choose mates or friends by growth. That's another reason why everything on Wall Street is so counterintuitive: Other than college basketball coaches trying to figure out which high school athletes to recruit, growth is a metric that matters only in the stock market.

We do, however, have a concept that all of us understand in the betting world that is analogous to the multiple we pay for growth. Despite its alien terminology, the multiple is actually nothing more than "the line" as expressed in Wall Street–speak. We take the line as second nature for every bet we have ever made. Anyone who has made even the friendliest of wagers, say, on the Super Bowl, knows that you can't bet on the favorite team without having to spot the other guys something. Teams are not traded even up. Their records matter and they get factored into the price of the bet. There's a favored team and a team that's the underdog. You often have to give or take points. The multiple is our own expression on Wall Street of the spread between the winners and the losers. You have to pay a higher price for growth on Wall Street just as you expect to have to give points to the lesser team in betting on a football game. In sports, the favorite could be favored because it is better coached, has better players, is bigger, or has a history of winning. In business, a company is favored because it has more consistent growth over time. That company is favored, and the cheaper company is the underdog. Just as in wagering, you have to pay up to place a bet on a superior company on Wall Street. The cheaper company, the un-

derdog, tends to stay cheap, just as the underdog tends to lose. Think of the lower multiple as the handicap, the discount factored into a lesser equity that makes it possibly compelling as something to wager on. But only when it gets so cheap as to make it seem that the line between the good team and the bad team is wrong does it pay to invest in the underdog.

Now, let's notch things up a bit and decide how to figure out if the line is right in stocks or whether the market's oddsmakers, all of those buyers and sellers, have created an opportunity because they might be wrong about a company's future. We know that all too often there are imperfections in the line when it comes to sports wagering. Are stocks any different? Let's figure out whether the cheaper of Maytag or Whirlpool is *too* cheap and might be worth buying. Remember, all we have done so far is figure out which one is trading for a higher multiple than the other. We have figured out which one is more expensive and determined that Maytag is one multiple point more expensive than Whirlpool because of its higher growth.

We are looking, in other words, for imperfection. Is there something about that pricing that could be wrong, either higher or lower than it should be? Unlike the supermarket, where there are scanning devices and checkers to be sure the store is selling the product for the right price, our store at Broad and Wall often misprices things. Just like in sports gambling, where we are trying to figure out where the line might be wrong, giving us too many or too few points, we have to exploit the mispricings. Again, Maytag's price-to-earnings ratio is 12 but we have calculated that it grows almost twice as fast as Whirlpool, which has an 11 multiple, or price-to-earnings ratio. I would argue that any company growing twice as fast as another in the same industry should sell at twice the price-to-earnings ratio of the other—not 9 percent higher as it is now—because growth is all that matters. So, in reality, Maytag at 12 times earnings is more of a bargain than Whirlpool at 11 times earnings, even though they are in the same business, because Maytag is doing better and growing faster. Maytag's the steal

at a 12 multiple, and Whirlpool's the more perfectly priced. Therefore Whirlpool will be less likely to produce a win. The line seems "wrong" enough to buy Maytag for an investment to bet it will go higher over time, at least as it trades against its competitor. That would be my initial take if people were to call in to my radio show, for example, and ask whether Maytag is a better buy than Whirlpool. Without having any other insight, I would go with Maytag.

The line can be wrong for a million reasons in well-known competitions like MYG versus WHR. But most investors don't look for the "games" where the line is most wrong—in younger, underresearched, and little-known companies. Instead, unaware of Andy Beyer's advice to seek out lesser tracks that don't attract the best handicappers, most investors traffic in only the big races, stocks like Microsoft or Intel or IBM. These are the Kentucky Derby and the Belmont Stakes of my business, the most known and written about, where the line is almost always perfect and very little money can be made. The imperfect line happens only when you stray away from the major players, go to the lesser tracks, in this case the companies worth $2 billion and less, and particularly the $100 million to $400 million companies. These stocks are considered more "speculative" by the cognoscenti, whether it be the talking heads you see on television or the authors of the dry books about finance. Nothing could be further from reality. The most terrible speculations, as defined by their risk-reward, are the big, well-known companies. You can't possibly get a homework edge on them; almost all the news on them is already "in," or discounted. That's why I preach that your homework should focus on the less well known situations, the markets with smaller, young growth companies. Although you must accept the risks that come with less knowledge, the rewards are far greater than with the perfect lines of the established players. Betting on the favorite to win at the Kentucky Derby might ensure a victory, but at a price that doesn't make the reward worth the risk. In other words, the logic behind Andy Beyer's *Picking Winners*—out-of-the-way tracks generate outsized earnings

because the line is often imperfect—is analogous to Wall Street, where the multiple is often set improperly for lesser-known, underfollowed companies.

Of course there are other details at work in evaluating companies' stocks besides the rate of growth of the corporation underneath the equity. For example, some of us might be yield-conscious. Given the fantastically low tax rate on dividends—15 percent goes to the government, you keep 85 percent—we might want to compare stocks on a yield basis. Whirlpool pays out 43¢ per share each quarter and Maytag pays out 18¢ per quarter. Again, we do our best to confuse the hell out of you on Wall Street because those two dividends are *equal!* You have to break out that fourth-grade division skill again and add in some multiplication. If you get dividends four times a year, you are getting 72¢ a share for Maytag (18¢ per share four times a year) and $1.72 for Whirlpool (4 times 43¢). You then divide that 72¢ by $27—last price—for Maytag and $1.72 by $67, Whirlpool's closing price, and you get 2.5 percent for both. Their dividends are exactly equal even though Whirlpool seems like it pays more. Again, that's because the dollar amount of the dividend isn't relevant; the yield, as expressed by the dividend divided by the price, is the apples-to-apples comparison.

So, on a dividend basis, these two stocks are equal and we can't differentiate them, although I would argue that a company growing its earnings twice as fast as another company might eventually boost its dividend at a faster pace, too.

Before investing in either company, we might examine their balance sheets. Again, when faced with a security laden with debt versus one with a clean balance sheet, I am going to favor the clean balance sheet, because when the economy turns down, too much debt can be a killer—to the equity holders. But if a fast-growing company with a great opportunity has to take down debt to finance a worthwhile investment, then the case can be made that the company's indebtedness should not be held against it in the competitive derby for your dollars. This brings us back to the price-to-earnings multiple versus that

growth rate again as a way to figure out whether Maytag is a better buy than Whirlpool. With dividends equal and balance sheets roughly equal, I will still want to buy the "more expensive" stock, Maytag, because it is only fractionally more expensive (1 multiple point: 12 P/E minus 11 P/E of Whirlpool) but it is growing almost twice as fast. That's simply more compelling than the stock of Whirlpool.

On Wall Street many of the professionals, the analysts on both the buy and sell side who compare companies with one another, simply stop when they calculate the P/E and the growth rate. They make their buy/sell decisions on those ratios. They take the growth rate of Maytag, and they match it against the growth rate of the average company in the Standard & Poor's 500, the ultimate benchmark betting line. They then compare the price-to-earnings multiple of Maytag to the price-to-earnings multiple of the S&P 500. They use the same process we used to calculate Maytag's price-to-earnings ratio. They figure out the "average" multiple that all of the stocks trade at. They average all of the P/Es together, and they use that as the benchmark. Recently, the average S&P 500 stock traded at 22 times earnings. So Maytag's price-to-earnings multiple is substantially lower than the S&P average. But Maytag also grows more slowly than the average company because the average company in the S&P 500 grows at about 9 percent a year. So while Maytag is cheaper than the average company in the S&P 500, as expressed by the P/E, or price-to-earnings multiple, it deserves to be cheaper. Most Wall Streeters declare that Maytag is "fairly valued" versus the S&P index because it doesn't grow fast enough to be attractive; it is therefore not much of a bargain even if it is a bargain versus its competitor Whirlpool. If it traded at a smaller multiple and grew much faster than the average company in the index, then it would be a huge bargain. If it traded at a large premium to the multiple of the average stock but grew much slower it would be much too expensive to buy. That's the kind of calculation that highly paid, I would say overpaid, people on Wall Street make every day.

You often hear some talking head on TV say, "Maytag's expensive." That calculus is almost solely based on the exercise we just went

through. If they didn't use shorthand, what these people would be saying is, "When you calculate the growth rate of Maytag, and the price-to-earnings ratio of Maytag, and you compare it with the average company as represented by the S&P 500's growth rate and multiple on earnings, you don't find Maytag particularly compelling." Or, to analogize back into sports and betting, the "line" on Maytag is accurate. There's no "steal" there, nothing that makes you feel Maytag's a great bet.

All of this makes sense in the world defined by Wall Street. But does it make sense in the real business world? Ahh, that's still another story. In the "real world" Maytag could be worth $40 a share if Electrolux decides it's worth that and adds Maytag to its business collection. In the real world Maytag could be worth $50 a share if General Electric decides it can't let Electrolux have the property. In the real world these aren't pieces of paper, they are companies that throw off cash and profits and can be used to augment the earnings of other companies. Businesses have a value to Wall Streeters and a value to Main Streeters. The Wall Streeters care about growth; the Main Streeters care about enterprise value and how much it would cost to buy the whole company. Wall Street loves to be bound by simple calculations like growth rates and prices of a company. All that gibberish about "overvalued" and "undervalued" or "fully valued" comes from comparing the price-to-earnings ratio and the growth rate of the average company to the price-to-earnings ratio and growth rate of the S&P 500 index.

Go back to the example of the two sweaters at Macy's. Wall Street is addicted to finding the mispriced anomaly, the cashmere sweater that is priced the same as the poly-cotton alternative. Unfortunately, the big cap part of the market, like the mall, doesn't allow for such obvious bargains, so most goods seem "fairly" valued to most participants because that cashmere item gets spotted by the millions of buyers out there and gets bought, even if it is buried in poly-cotton offerings.

Unfortunately, this kind of calculation, while intelligent and rational, won't make you rich. Too many people, smarter and more knowledgeable than you, can look up these kinds of data and make

these comparisons. So, while we want to understand how valuations work, we don't want to be trapped by them if we want to get rich. In fact, just the opposite: We must exploit the anomalies that this rigid arithmetical approach to investing creates every day. We don't want to invest to stay even with others; we want to invest to beat others at the contest of making money.

At one stage in my career I wanted to be an artist. I remember studying fine arts at Harvard, taking a course on modern art affectionately known as "Spots and Dots." In that class, the professor described how modern art didn't want to be bound by the four walls of the canvas, that artists like Braque and Picasso hated being bound by the canvas and actually attempted to make their art more like life itself, which is hardly two-dimensional. They placed things on the canvas to make them come alive.

I think that the analogy of modern art holds up well in the process of picking stocks, and it is one of the reasons why I regard myself as almost always able to pick out big winners among those stocks that are considered overvalued by Wall Street. While I accept the simple equation that $E \times M = P$, I refuse to be bounded by it. I want to think outside the walls of the earnings and multiple, outside the confines of simple earnings analysis to ascertain which companies are growing fast enough to own.

I run a public portfolio called ActionAlertsPLUS.com. Unlike every other commentator in the country, I don't mind showing what I am going to do beforehand so you can run ahead of me. And I love putting my money where my mouth is, which again distinguishes me from all of those talking-head reporter types who swear a vow of stock abstinence, which then makes them incapable of figuring out the process but certainly allows them to claim "honesty" in their ignorance. Frankly, I would rather be smarter and wiser and disclose my positions candidly up front than be divorced from the process. You can't be any good if you aren't a practitioner; you just don't get enough practice. You need to be in the hunt to find great stocks or you

shouldn't be commenting or telling people how to do it. I know it may look to some that I am corrupt because I praise stocks I own, even though I tell you that I own them. But think about the logic of it: I champion the stocks I own because I like them enough to put my money behind them. I champion stocks I own because I think they can make me money and you money, too. By similar logic I knock stocks I don't own because I think they are too rich and you could lose money if you buy them. I try to explain this all of the time on radio and TV. Nevertheless, people confuse my motives and believe that I am picking on bad guys and pumping stocks I own so I can make more money. If only life were that simple and if only I were that powerful! You spot bargains in the store the way I spot bargains on Wall Street, except that when I buy a bargain on Wall Street I am telling others and hoping they will take advantage of it, too. (I have established rules banning myself from taking advantage of any pop I might create by freezing my actions for five days if I mention a stock on radio or TV, and I won't sell a stock for at least a month after I buy it.) I regard myself as simply an oddsmaker trying to determine when the line is absurd and wrong.

Recently, for my ActionAlertsPLUS.com account, I had one of my biggest hits ever, AT&T Wireless, which you could have shared with me, and gotten better prices than me, if you had subscribed to that site. (You get better prices because I send out an e-mail about what I am about to buy to give you a head start before I buy it.) In a matter of weeks I had a double in AT&T Wireless that was accessible to all who read me. I am not bound by the two-dimensional thinking that hamstrings all of the high-paid analysts on Wall Street. I am not constrained by the growth mantra, as measured by the price-to-earnings multiple, even though Wall Street is. I see the piece of paper that I am trading and I remember that there is a business underneath it that the paper can lay claim to as long as the business is solvent. I recognize that stocks trade and, at times, companies trade, too. The stock trades on Wall Street, but the company trades on Main Street. Some companies are so huge that they trade only on Wall Street. Those are the

acquiring companies like Exxon or Microsoft or Intel or Pfizer or General Electric. They are too big in terms of their market capitalization to be taken over by anyone else. You can only trade their stock and their stock will be valued traditionally. You will always have to figure out whether the line on Pfizer or the line on GE is too expensive or too cheap to hold on to the stock. That's the best kind of analysis for stock in a company that is too big to be bought by another company. Obviously these better-known companies have more perfect pricing, and it takes a bountiful market to move them up faster than other stocks, given their size and their well-known-ness. How these stocks move up or down is discussed in a later chapter.

But when a company is even the second or third largest in an industry, then the whole shooting match, the control of the company, can trade. A takeover can occur that gives you an instantaneous win.

At the time that I issued an alert to buy AT&T Wireless, it was the third-biggest wireless company in the country. That was right before it was acquired by Cingular, a company put together by BellSouth and SBC Communications, two of the biggest landline companies out there. Before it was acquired the stock of AT&T Wireless had dropped from $32 to $6. I hated the stock in the $30s, when all of the analysts loved it because they thought the company had tremendous growth ahead of it. I thought the other companies in the wireless phone business would eat its lunch.

When the growth at AT&T Wireless faltered, in part because of poor management—something that the analysts who made the faulty estimates didn't take into account—the stock took a header. It went to the twenties, to the teens, and then to the single digits. When it got below $10, one analyst after another made the calculations we did earlier for Maytag—in other words, looked at the growth of AT&T Wireless's earnings and the price-to-earnings multiple—and decided that it was too expensive relative to the growth and the P/E of its peers and of the S&P 500. All seven of the major analysts were constrained by the growth mantra. They were considering AWE (its stock symbol) as a piece of paper, a stock, not as a company with an ongoing business.

Although I care about the apples-to-apples valuations of AWE versus the S&P 500 index and versus the other stocks of the players in the industry, just as I care about the P/Es of Maytag versus Whirlpool, I am not willing to be bound by such two-dimensional thinking when it comes to the actual enterprises the pieces of paper represent. I grew to love AT&T Wireless, the company, even as its stock was marked down by the market, because, unlike the counterintuitive thinkers on Wall Street, I actually believed the company was growing cheaper as it went down in price. No, I am not being cynical or sarcastic. As a stock price goes down, the business becomes cheaper as an enterprise, and we must never forget that ultimately these are enterprises we are trading. Wall Street loathes stocks as they come down because it thinks of them only as ratios versus the growth of earnings. I, on the other hand, love stocks as they come down, because I know the enterprise underneath may not be deteriorating as fast as the stock price. Just as in the mall, I am always trying to spot merchandise that is being marked down below its potential. Or, if we were talking about buying homes, I can see the value of a fixer-upper to someone with deep pockets even as others just think the home looks like an eyesore and has little worth. I am always on the hunt for damaged stocks where the merchandise underneath isn't that badly damaged—not damaged companies, but damaged stock prices. That's where the biggest anomalies among the established companies can be found. That's where the line is most wrong, among the visible but fallen stars.

How I came to buy AT&T Wireless, this fixer-upper of a stock, is somewhat typical of the kind of commonsense analysis that I do, that you can do, but that isn't done on Wall Street. My ten- and thirteen-year-old girls and I absolutely love the Fox show *American Idol*. We think it is tremendous that these talented youths duke it out in front of a panel of terrific judges, yet ultimately we decide who wins with our votes. Unfortunately, every time we call to vote on our faves, we get a busy signal. Every morning, I drive "the bus" to the middle school, taking my daughter and picking up kids along the way. It's the time

when I find out things I should know but never did during the days when I used to go to work at my hedge fund at 3:45 a.m. so I could trade in Europe. I got tired of hearing how everyone else in the car was voting and getting through and I wasn't, so I asked one of the girls how come she didn't get discouraged by the busy signals that I kept getting. Why, she explained, she text-messaged her vote. I told her that I wanted to text-message, too, and she told me you had to have an AT&T Wireless phone to text-message.

Ah-hah, now that's a gimmick. That day at work I pulled the file on AT&T Wireless and I saw that it had a huge installed base that happened to be growing by leaps and bounds in part because of this *Idol* promotion. The "file," just so you know, was simply the current quarterly report plus the most recent news clippings I found in Factiva and the most recent Wall Street reports that I found on FirstCall, all publicly available data that once was available in real time only to the richest and largest of mutual funds and hedge funds. I wanted to buy AT&T Wireless, but I could tell that these analysts didn't know why the numbers were so strong. Not one analyst alluded to the Fox promotion that was driving so much traffic to the company, traffic that I figured would certainly stop or diminish once America's most popular TV show finished for the season. I waited until the show ended and then watched as the numbers slid and the sign-ups, overinflated by the television show that probably none of these analysts watched, dropped precipitously. I noted the decline but still did nothing because I knew that come that November (2003) the FCC would force the carriers to adopt wireless portability, meaning we could easily switch carriers without losing our phone numbers in the process. Sure enough, when November and December rolled around, the complaints about AT&T Wireless were horrible. The other carriers did much, much better.

It didn't hurt that I went to a bunch of AT&T Wireless and Verizon Wireless stores to hear the complaints about the former and the praise of the latter. That kind of research, while anecdotal, steels your resolve

that you are operating in the right direction. I still do it; you can do it, too, if you have the time and inclination. It isn't must-do, but it does help to verify your thinking.

Of course, Wall Street listened too, and then began the sickening process of downgrading the stock from hold to sell, one analyst after another, as the weaker, non-*Idol*-inflated numbers collided with the poor service of AT&T Wireless sales centers during the portability switch.

But, I recognized that the brand name and the franchise weren't losing their cachet as fast as the stock was losing its valuation. It was only a matter of time before management would get fed up and realize it couldn't compete with the other players. These managements are made up of humans who make the calculation every day whether they should go it alone or cash out, succumb to others for a higher price than where their shares trade. They want to get rich, too, either short- or long-term, and if their stock isn't going up because the business isn't growing fast enough, they can elect to sell and take the money and run. As each analyst, seven in all, downgraded the stock to a sell and it fell from $9 to $6, I issued alerts saying that you should buy more. When the stock got to $6, I said double down, that this franchise wasn't nearly as damaged as the stock itself. Managements don't like looking stupid. They can and do recognize that their job is to make money for shareholders, although it takes an honest management to realize that it can make money for shareholders only by selling out. It does help, though, that management often has incentives to sell out, as was the case with the bountiful options package that was readily available for all to see in the AT&T Wireless proxy, the voting documents for the directors of the company. Remember Andy Beyer's rule number 3: Only invest in situations where you have total conviction.

What Wall Street didn't realize was that instead of being bound by the two dimensions of price-to-earnings and price-to-growth rate, there was a living, breathing entity, an actual business, that could be sold to the highest bidder. There has never been a case in history where a company that is not the first or second largest player in a five-

or six-company competition didn't succumb to a takeover by one of the other players that sought to become the premier largest player in order to take advantage of the tremendous economies of scale—for example, advertising and technology spending—that accrues to number one.

Sure enough, I had to wait only a few weeks before the initial inquiry came. And then another and another and then another again. Next thing you know, while every analyst had a sell on it, there were bidders willing to pay low double digits—all the other players out there.

Boom. Fifteen. That's right, I caught a $15 bid from $6, as the takeover war played out. The analysts caught nothing except scrambled egg on their faces.

It was all ours because we refused to be bound by the two dimensions of the canvas. How clueless was Wall Street? Even the best analyst on the stock, the Morgan Stanley fellow, who downgraded the stock at $7 on fears of wireless portability, upgraded it at $14 after the bid! How silly is that?

If you stay bound by the canvas of the stock, as the Morgan Stanley analyst did, you are always going to miss the bigger picture of the underlying entity. Wall Street cares about the growth of earnings, while businesspeople on Main Street care about the business underneath and how much it can add to their own earnings streams. That's why they will boost their own stock's worth by buying a fixer-upper.

There is no magic to pricing imperfections and finding bargains. You just have to know which streets to shop on and remember to compare the prices on Wall Street with Main Street before you buy.

4

SOME INVESTING BASICS

You now know how to buy stocks and how Wall Street and Main Street value merchandise. But what should you be buying and selling? What should you be owning? Should you own stocks at all? How many? For how much money? And for what purpose—for retirement, for fun, for college? How do you build your portfolio?

First, I hate one-size-fits-all answers to questions about you. We are all different, we all have different needs and different incomes, different worries and concerns. On radio, for example, I am always happy to answer questions on the relative worth of stocks, performing the exercise we just went through with the Maytag versus Whirlpool calculations. But those calculations don't help you if you don't have an investment strategy in the first place.

The most important reason why we invest, the most important reason why we will always invest, is that we don't make enough money in our day jobs to get us through the rest of life. We have to put money away, we have to save, because otherwise when we are done working and we don't have income coming in, we won't be able to afford life it-

self. But we also save because we know that if we can augment our incomes we can have more fun, or give more money away, or buy things that we otherwise couldn't afford. We can save to help buy a house or a car or any other large-ticket item. And we also save to give to others in our family, for our children, and for the cost of schooling.

I mention all of these obvious needs because the methods I advocate for each are different. When we are saving for retirement, that's Job One, so to speak, and we can't screw it up. The standards are higher and the risks we take are lower than for any other task because we must have money once we stop working. The other kinds of savings, because they simply augment current paychecks, don't require the conservative strategies that retirement money does.

We consider these two streams, the necessity stream (strictly for retirement) and the discretionary stream, as very different animals. Something that is right for the former could be extremely stupid for the latter. Complicating things further is the fact that we do different things and make different choices depending upon how old we are. When you are younger you can take far greater risks than when you are older because you have more time to make the money back from your paycheck. You also have more time to let the great cycle of stocks—in any twenty-year period high-quality stocks that pay dividends have outperformed all other asset classes—work for you.

Let's take the retirement stream first. It is vital that you start saving for retirement as early as possible. I had this drummed into my head, correctly, by my father, and to give you the true sense of how important it is, let me tell you a story.

Because of some reversals in my life, notably that someone—never caught—stalked me while I was a reporter living in Los Angeles two years out of college, I had the misfortune to live in my car for much of 1978 and 1979. Even though I had barely enough money to eat and pay the Allstate liability bill—I waived the collision!—I still managed to put away $1,500 toward retirement. That's how important it is to start saving early. I put the money with Fidelity and the compounding of that $1,500 would be enough for most people to live on for several

years of retirement. The logic of equities through thick and thin is that powerful.

I tell people that the younger you are the more important it is that you take even bigger speculative risks with that money because even if you get wiped out you have nearly your whole working life to make it back. That's why I favor the single most aggressive strategy available, accumulation of high-growth equities either through mutual funds or through your own selection—more on that later—until you are in your thirties, coupled with a percentage of assets devoted to speculation. When you get to the thirties, I like to throttle back the risk level to stocks that pay dividends or have the prospect of paying dividends within the near future and cut back the speculation. In your forties, I like to introduce bonds into the mix. Bonds don't allow much growth of income; they are more a preservative of capital, a place to hold money with a little bit of return to be sure you have it for later. Depending upon when you need the money, I alter the equation. If you want to retire at sixty, I would put more than half of your retirement money in fixed income in your forties. If you intend to work for years after sixty, I would put much less in those placeholders. Your fifties begins the big shift toward more and more fixed income. And finally, in your sixties, unless, again, you keep working, fixed income should dominate. Your opportunities to grow your money are now limited and the reward isn't worth the risk.

I mention the example of living in my car and saving for retirement because I am such a conservative when it comes to the later years. So many people call in to my radio show and say that they want to take more risks, that they want more aggressive investments because they didn't save early. Others in their sixties want my blessing to keep the vast majority of their assets in stocks. But I never bend on this. Here's why. I recognize the vulnerability of equities and the fallibility of my own judgment. Let's wind the tape back for a second to the spring of 2000. While I sensed that equities were overvalued, had I blessed a nontraditional, nonprudent course of action—staying in equities, particularly the kind of equities people were drawn to in that

era—I could have wiped out people if they overstayed their equity exposure. You never know when it is going to be the spring of 2000 again, and you can't allow your judgment to be swayed by the chance to make more money in stocks than they might allow. The desire to let it grow over time, to let the dividend and income streams come your way, is what should drive retirement investing. Only as you get closer to needing the money should your caution take hold so that you don't let a lifetime's worth of savings be wiped out by a swift downturn in the market right before you need the money.

What I tell people, though, is that for the second stream, the discretionary stream, the money not cordoned off for retirement, the money meant to augment the paycheck for other needs, the stakes are much lower. Consequently, you can take bigger chances with this portion of your assets. With discretionary investments, risks predominate and rewards can be outsized. With this stream you can and must speculate with at least a portion of your money, perhaps as much as 50 percent when younger, in your twenties, and then dropping back by 10 percent every decade, but never falling below 10 percent, if only because that's what you can afford to lose without damaging your necessity money. It is with this money that you can take chances. It is with this money that you can and should be trying to make yourself rich with some excellent outsized risks that could give you giant returns. There you can take as much chance as you would like and I will most likely bless it, as long as you follow the rules I lay out in subsequent chapters. You can put this money in the riskiest of ventures, provided you are willing to do the homework first. There I want you to seek out small-cap speculations, provided you follow my rules of good speculation. There I want the steak, the fat, the stuff you love but the traditional financial books say will be bad for your financial diet. They are dead wrong. They are as wrong as all of those doctors that pooh-poohed the Atkins diet over the years. I need you to become fascinated with the market with some of those assets of yours, the more so when you are younger. The younger you are the more speculative you can be!

That people don't routinely look at these two streams as entirely different kinds of money, so to speak, with radically different rules, drives me crazy. The mistaken conflation of the two streams leads people to be far more risky in their retirement and way too conservative in their discretionary pool choices. So, if you learn one takeaway lesson from this chapter, it is the need to think and act very differently with these two rivers of potential wealth. People who want to speculate in their retirement streams, particularly when they are older, will not get my blessing. People who *don't* speculate with their discretionary pool of capital are similarly making a huge mistake, provided they follow my rules on speculation. Mind you, this view is radical in its commonsense approach. Every other text I have read admonishes against speculation at all times. I think just the opposite. I want to build it in, provided you follow the rules of speculation, so that it is a tamed beast that can grow into something huge, then be stopped out before it can destroy your hard-earned capital.

Cramer's Law of Time and Inclination

Should you be running your 401(k)? Should you be managing your discretionary pool, or should you hand it off to others?

The federal government, in fits and starts, has made saving for retirement a priority. It has created various confusing programs such as the IRA and 401(k), allowed us to take control of the non–Social Security portion of our savings, in a tax-deferred way. The tax-deferred nature of the programs makes them imperative. If you don't have an IRA or a 401(k), by all means set one up this very minute to take advantage of the power of allowing your money to compound without your worrying how to pay the tax man. You must have a good menu of offerings to choose from and you shouldn't have to pay high fees to be in those investments.

It's terrific that we have been given control over some of our savings. But it is terrible that the government has given no instruction

about how we should control it, no rules to follow, and no training about how to do it. We have all been made our own personal portfolio managers by the IRA/401(k) revolution, but we haven't been given a dime's worth of education about how to be a portfolio manager. We teach kids in junior high and high school tons of things that are completely irrelevant, but we don't educate them one whit about how to take care of their own portfolios. It's flabbergasting to me to watch my kids read and learn about the Etruscans or about the hypotenuses and the order of the planets but nothing about stocks and bonds and portfolios! It drives me up a wall! Worse, the people whom the government wants us to rely on, the people in the financial services industries, have failed us mightily in instruction. In fact, I would argue that many of them have done their best to try to keep us in the dark, to make us less effective as clients or portfolio managers so we can be more reliant on them and they can make more money. I preach this every day when I say let me be your coach, let me show you how you can be your own portfolio manager, and if I can't do that, I know I can teach you to be a better client. You have to be one or the other, though, better client or better investor. There is no alternative. So let's see which one you are.

I like to build portfolios for both discretionary money and retirement money, with the former consisting of a diversified group of stocks as well as some speculation built in, and the latter being strictly common stocks when you are younger and then gradually moving to more fixed income as you go up in years.

What determines whether you are in shape to build a portfolio? When a caller asks me for help in managing or building a portfolio, I always tell her that I won't even help until she tells me if she has the time and inclination to manage money herself in a diversified fashion. I need to know both because not everyone can be a portfolio manager; some of us are always going to need the help of others who are professionals, either because we don't have the time to do the homework, or we lack the inclination to learn how to measure companies against one another to find the bargains that make for great investments. So

let's explore these two great variables—time and inclination—in the context of building a diversified portfolio to see where you fit in.

When I speak of time, I am speaking of the time to do homework on your portfolio. I will detail what the homework entails later, but suffice it to say that I think the rigors of the market demand one hour per week per stock to stay on top of it. (I have found that to keep up with all of the pieces of information publicly available for each stock, you need that much time. It is a shorthand measure, but I have clocked it over and over again and it almost always turns out to be right no matter how known or unknown the company might be.)

When I speak of inclination, I mean the desire to do the work. I believe the rudiments are so easy—you have already performed the most difficult task in calculating the multiple—that I have confidence that if you have gotten this far into this book you have the smarts to do it.

It's the inclination that trips people up. I always say that you need the same amount of time to keep up on your stocks as to keep up on your local sports teams. The problem isn't the time; it is the desire to do the work. If you don't have that natural inclination, you won't spend the hour per "team" that you need to follow. So, you have to ask yourself whether you like this stuff enough to stay on top of it. (If you don't have the time or inclination, then you need help. I explain how to get help in a later chapter, so don't get disgusted or discouraged. There are many ways to skin the investment cat.)

Now, you might have the time and the inclination to spend a couple of hours a week on your investments, which would be fine if you only had to own one or two stocks to get rich. But because of the third point, the need to diversify, you won't be able to spend just two hours a week on building your own portfolio. Diversification is the bedrock of portfolio management. Every Wednesday on *Jim Cramer's Real-Money* I play "Am I Diversified?" You dial 1-800-862-8686 and I ask you to give me your top five stocks. Then you ask, "Am I diversified?" I then play the "Hallelujah Chorus" or some funny jock jam if you are, or I give you the buzzer they use on *Jeopardy* if you aren't.

I play this simple game because diversification is the only free lunch in this whole gosh-darned business. Remember, owning stocks is a fallible process. You must never forget that these are pieces of paper. Pieces of paper can go down the drain as quickly as toilet paper if they are the wrong ones or we get into the wrong market.

That's why we have to diversify. When markets are going up, and when whole sectors are roaring, diversification seems like a huge drag. Why bother? When it is sunny, who the heck needs an umbrella or a raincoat? But when it is raining or stormy, or we get a hurricane like we had in the bear market of 2000–2003, diversification is your shelter, your virtual brick house that can't be brought down by the elements.

Diversification is also a weapon, a weapon against the malfeasance and the criminality that can engulf the investing process if we are not careful. You know how my game of "Am I Diversified?" came about? Do you know why I insist on playing it every Wednesday week in and week out? Remember the people who testified in front of Congress after the Enron debacle saying that their nest eggs were wiped out because they had kept all of their assets in Enron stock? They had all of their eggs in the Enron basket, in some cases millions of dollars in this one stock. The day that they testified, I happened to be talking on the radio about how badly I felt for these poor souls who had each lost hundreds of thousands and, in some cases, millions of dollars in Enron stock for their 401(k)s and their IRAs. My wife, the Trading Goddess, happened to be listening. She called in and let me have it. Just took me apart. She said how dare I feel bad for people who had millions of dollars and then gave it back in the market. How dare I feel bad for people who weren't smart enough to diversify and were so greedy as to not take the care to put their eggs in different baskets. I was just encouraging that kind of behavior for others when I could have been using their intellectual laziness and lack of knowledge about the value of diversification to drive home the point about how easily avoidable such heartbreak is. She was furious that I put the emphasis on the government's screwup in not catching Enron earlier. Diversification, she said, assumes that the government will screw up

and not protect us. It presumes that companies' execs will at least let us down if not loot their own enterprises. When she was through with me, I said, Holy cow, I better appease the Trading Goddess and find a way to make diversification come alive on the show, pronto. So we now play "Am I Diversified?" every Wednesday, and while it may seem hokey, it works.

Diversification is not only our greatest defense against chicanery, it is also our lone defense against the fizzling out of whole companies and whole sectors. We can't afford to put too much money in any one area because that whole area could wipe out our wealth.

I know, this too seems counterintuitive. How could we not want all of our money in the hottest sectors? Why would anyone want to put money in places that aren't hot, that aren't working?

History, however, tells us how wrong that kind of thinking is. When I got in this business, I used to review portfolios that were made up entirely of oil and gas holdings because, well, it was 1982 and wasn't oil going to $100 a barrel? Those portfolios would have been wiped out by the decline in oil to $10 that happened soon afterward had I not diversified these portfolios to less "hot" areas. Similarly, in the mid-1980s, the hottest stocks by far were food stocks. The great consolidation of the food stocks was occurring at the exact same time that the entities were going global. General Foods, Kraft, and Pillsbury were soaring. These stocks were insulated from the tremendous Japanese incursion that was occurring in manufacturing. Nobody wanted Mitsubishi ketchup; these food stocks were the lone safe spot as the Japanese wiped out much of our manufacturing base. I would see people whose portfolios looked like aisles two through seven in a Safeway or an Albertsons, for heaven's sake. That presumed that food was going to stay a growth business forever. Sure enough, by the 1990s, the food stocks had become stagnant. They have now underperformed for two decades, mooting the compounding process. They are barely investible because they have so little growth. You invest in them only for takeovers, and that's not a sound investment strategy. Those who have been betting on a Campbell or a Heinz takeover for the last de-

cade or two have suffered horribly while other enterprises have generated both large capital gains and bountiful dividends.

Of course, for the last decade all anyone wanted was technology, but we are now seeing the drawbacks of a portfolio made entirely of four or five of the great tech stalwarts of the 1990s. Owning those stocks now is like watching paint peel! Those who flee from all tech to all pharmaceuticals might have their portfolios wiped out by drug importation from Canada. Each sector at one time or another faces potential extinction. So we spread our stocks among many baskets.

While this seems counterintuitive given how much we want to be in the sectors that are in favor, we understand the hazards of concentration all too well. Would we really accept a diet, for example, that consisted only of Porterhouse, T-bone, chuck, and sirloin? Would we like a diet made up of bread, cake, pasta, and oranges? Of course not. We know how unhealthy those would be. It's the same with stocks; we need a balanced diet of stocks at all times.

For many people, though, this diversification concept slips right through their fingers. People call me and say, "Jim, I own Cisco, Dell, Intel, Microsoft, and EMC—am I diversified?" When I ask them if they are serious, they try to tell me that they think they are diversified because they own a networker, a personal computer maker, a semiconductor company, a software company, and a storage company. Heck, those stocks are as interrelated as a kneebone, shinbone, ankle bone, and footbone, for heaven's sake. These stocks all trade together.

I know that on a day when the NASDAQ, where a lot of tech lives, goes up 2 percent, you are going to feel like you are running with ankle weights if you own only one tech stock, but it is the two-ton weight on the downside we must fear, not the ankle weight when things are going well. And if you don't know the difference between these companies, if you don't know what they do for a living, then you don't have the time and inclination to do the homework necessary and you have to hand it off to a "professional." I put quotes around the word, though, because I can tell you that most "professionals" aren't much better about this stuff than you are. In fact, they amateurishly set up

and run funds that claim to be diversified but are no more diversified than the mock tech portfolio I just described to you. They claim the defensive power of diversification, when, in actuality, they are faux-diversified, owning a ton of stocks that will trade as closely as if you had Super Glued them together. They know this flaw, but if they can shoot the lights out for a quarter or two, and they usually can, their marketing departments can make hay out of your money while the sun shines, and the portfolio managers are paid by the dollars they take in, not by what they make for you.

How many stocks does it take to be diversified? I have found that you have to have a minimum of five to capture true diversification and protection from the undesirable elements. It would be terrific to be able to have as many as ten positions to really ensure diversification, but then you will be bumping up against the time and inclination requirements that I have already detailed. More important, more than fifteen stocks and you have simply become your own mutual fund, something I hear about often in the portfolios people talk to me about on radio or send to me via TheStreet.com. If that's the case, if you insist on fifteen or more stocks, you might as well hand off your money to one of those mutual fund fellows, although the costs, in fees, will be prohibitive unless you select a passive model, such as an index fund, which doesn't allow the manager to trade at his own discretion and charges you a higher fee, often for nothing special at all!

For retirement, I don't want to include speculative stocks, but for the discretionary stream, one of the five choices should be speculative, and perhaps as many as two or three of the five can be speculative when you are in your twenties or early thirties and you can make back the money in the event your investment fails.

How Much Do You Need to Get Started?

Given that you need at least five stocks in the portfolio to take advantage of the free lunch of diversification, how can you build a diversi-

fied portfolio of stocks for, say, less than $2,500? That leaves each position with no more than $500 per stock, making it so you simply can't own enough of any good stock north of $10. That's no good. You run the risk of owning five highly speculative stocks in small dollar amounts, and that's not acceptable. The only way to get enough of each stock with that little money is to be in an index fund, an exchange-traded fund like a Spyder (a stock that represents the S&P 500), or a mutual fund. If that's all you do have, you would do best to skip to chapter 7, where I evaluate those offerings for you. Of course, you can still own stocks if you have less than $2,500, but you cannot be diversified, and I care too much about diversification to approve a portfolio of fewer than four high-quality stocks and one speculative investment. (When you get to that $2,500 mark one day, then you can call your own porfolio's tune.)

But if you have more than $2,500, you can easily build a diversified portfolio that can allow you to make excellent money over time. I believe that $500—five positions each for a total of $2,500—of virtually any stock is enough to start out with, provided you add to the positions over time with new money.

How do you build that portfolio? You need to find stocks that will go up faster and more consistently than other stocks. I will show you how to do the homework to find them and then how to do the homework to maintain them—remember it's buy and homework, not buy and hold, that matters. And you need to buy them right, through methods that I will also detail when I talk about how to accumulate stocks correctly and sell them right when they go wrong. Staying on top of your portfolio, pruning it correctly, selecting new positions—these are the fundaments of the process and I love teaching them. I promise you will learn to do it just as I do and that you will enjoy it as I do. So don't despair because you think right now you don't have the time and inclination. My methods, I believe, are so much fun and so compelling that maybe you will be willing to give up that one sports event or TV show or movie to focus on getting rich beyond your salary. Believe me, it is worth it like nothing else in the world.

Lately some academic studies have shown that mutual funds can diversify too heavily. Two University of Michigan professors recently quoted in the *New York Times* studied funds that were more widespread in their holdings versus others and found that these managers underperformed those with concentrated holdings, thereby contradicting long-held notions of the virtue of diversification. Indeed, it is true, if you are an active manager of other people's money, you can indeed be "too" diversified. But that's not an important consideration when you are running your own money. We need to worry about having enough stocks to be diversified because it protects us from owning one stinker that takes down our whole portfolio. But we don't want to be so diversified that we are mutual funds ourselves. That's why I think that ten to twelve positions is the maximum for hobbyist investors, but being "overly" diversified is almost never a bad thing.

What Is the "Homework"?

When I say we no longer believe in buy and hold, that we have adopted a new regime of buy and homework, what does the homework mean? People ask me this question more than any other when I tell them you need an hour a week per position that you maintain. What am I looking for? What do you need to see? What can be seen? Is the "homework" even possible, and does it assure success?

First, understand that ever since the passage of Regulation FD, a rule set up to benefit you—and to hurt the full-time professionals like I was—everything that can be seen, everything that can be known about a company without being an insider, is available to all. And, candidly, it is all you need to make the right decisions. You will never have all the information you need, but this public data will suffice.

When I first got into this business I had to spend a tremendous amount of time just trying to find current information about companies. I used to have to go to the midtown Manhattan library to read old microfiches of quarterly reports two quarters after they were filed.

Research about companies was simply nonexistent unless you were rich enough to be a client of a major firm. Given that I wanted to get rich, it was a vicious Catch-22: Only the rich could learn which companies were worth buying!

But now everything's changed. Every quarterly report is instantly downloadable from the SEC's Web site for free. Almost every research firm makes its research readily available online, either on its own site or through Multex, which is owned by Reuters. So, the public documents and research are all right in front of you. No excuses.

I also used to have to get as many as twenty local papers a day to stay on top of the companies I owned. I would have to go through each business section every day to see if there was news about the companies. Now Google or Yahoo! or Factiva make all articles everywhere instantly available for free, or for a small fee. You can go to the Web site of any local paper in America and get data on a company that otherwise was totally unavailable unless you subscribed to the hard copy of the newspaper. And this data is perhaps the single most important stream of data because good investing is often local investing. Local investing, or at least simulated local investing, that is, looking up what is said about your company in its local paper, gives you one of the best information edges you can have.

When I broke into the business, working for wealthy families and small institutions, if you did enough commission business with me I might be able to get you to see a management presentation where you could get insights on companies nobody else would get. Those closed meetings are now illegal. Every meeting where anything of any materiality is discussed is webcast, again for free. You can't know something I don't know. It's not allowed.

Further, I used to be able to call management teams and speak to high-level executives about how their business was doing, something you could never do. Now I can still make those calls, but management can't answer them. They will be fined or prosecuted for talking to anyone without talking to everyone. There is no offline insight that some have that is denied to others.

Finally, when a company reported results, it used to hold a conference call for selected institutions and shareholders to brief people about how business was during the quarter and to give projections for the future. Now they still hold the calls, but everyone has to be allowed on them. There are no closed calls anymore.

That's the good news. The bad news? You have to read every report, from the quarterlies to the annuals, you have to read every important article, you have to listen to all of the conference calls, and you have to read the analysts' reports. That's the basic homework you have to do. The calls can be up to an hour and a half in length, but they provide the best information possible. Listen to them *before* you buy, although I have almost never heard of an individual investor who listened to two or three conference calls before he bought. I would never own a stock unless I had listened first. This information is too vital.

I know that seems excessive. But you would do much more research if you were going to buy a car or a home, and yet, a stock is every bit as big an investment. All of this work can be done on the Web, so there really are no excuses.

What are you looking for? What will you learn on a conference call that you wouldn't learn otherwise? You are looking to see how a company is doing, you are trying to take the company's temperature. When companies report, you are looking for clues about how fast the company is growing as measured by sales or revenues (they are the same) or how profitable the company might be—that's the earnings per share. If your company is a young company, you are looking for fast revenue growth. If your company is older, it should have been able to figure out how to monetize that growing revenue into earnings, and then into dividends. Old-line companies should be trying to maximize the cash they take in (the cash flow) to reward shareholders. Some buy back stock, others pay dividends. Given the low tax rate on dividends now, it could be especially important to you to find stocks that do pay or can pay good dividends.

How can we tell if a company is doing better or about to grow earnings faster than we would have expected? The rate of revenue growth

matters, but just as important is something called the "gross margin," or how much profitability each sale can generate. I know that this focus may seem a bit alien to you, but the simple way to look at it is to think about shopping at your supermarket. You know if you are buying a can of all-white albacore tuna for $1.40, and it cost the store $1.40 to buy the can it is selling, the store's taking a beating. If it is buying the can for $1.00 and selling it for $1.40, then it has a hefty profit margin. But if it then spends a lot of money on labor and plant and equipment and advertising to sell it to you, the business could still be a loser. And the store doesn't make it up in volume. A company has big margins when it can charge what it wants for what it makes. What determines that? Competition, cost of the items to make or procure, and the cost of doing business in general.

Some businesses are high-margin businesses because they have little competition. For example, Microsoft has little competition for Windows, save Apple Computer, so it makes a ton per Windows. In fact, it made so much that the government declared it a monopoly and tried to break it up. Intel makes a ton of money per microprocessor, almost 60 percent of the sale of each Pentium chip is profit. That's because, again, it has little competition. Utilities have no real competition, but not a lot of growth, either. Cable companies have natural monopolies, but those can be invaded by alternative methods of program delivery—satellite dishes—that can take down gross margins and destroy profitability. Some businesses, however, such as supermarkets, have tremendous competition and razor-thin margins. Other businesses, such as the basic materials businesses, can have hefty margins when their products are in short supply because there aren't enough plants making the products and then have terrible margins when the industries build too many factories. Still other businesses, such as drugs, have patent protection that gives them a hefty payout for seventeen years on new drugs but then, when the drugs go off patent, they are almost worthless to the companies. Some businesses have big profit margins only when the world's economies are booming. Those are "cyclical" concerns. Some businesses, such as

farming, or road building, or military spending, or aircraft building, have big profit margins when their own business cycles catch fire. Others have profit margins regardless of the world's economies. These are called "secular" growth stories, independent of the cyclicality of economies. People will use Dove soap or drink Coca-Cola regardless of how strong or weak the economy is. People don't skip taking medicine when they are sick unless they can't afford medicine, and most developed societies won't let that happen. This secular-versus-cyclical decision, as we shall see, is at the heart of a great deal of good investing and can generate tremendous outperformance if you catch the right moment to shift or rotate between secular growth and cyclical booms.

Each business has what is known as a metric or a series of metrics that measure how it is doing versus its peers. For the cable industry, for example, the enterprise value per subscriber; for hotels, it is the average revenue per room; for airlines, it is the average revenue per seat. In retail the measurement that gives you the best thermometer reading is the same-store sales, which compares how much business a store did last year versus this year. Restaurants are measured the same way. These metrics give a true measure of growth. Total revenues, on the other hand, could be augmented by new stores that are added to the mix. For technology, the metric is the gross margin per product sold. For financials, it is the net interest margin, or how much money was made on each dollar that the bank or insurance company or savings and loan had in assets.

If you are going to buy a stock in a business, you must find out what metric or metrics are important—always pretty self-evident from reading the research—so you know how your company measures up. If you don't understand the metric that an industry measures itself by, you haven't done enough homework to buy the stock. Go back and do the work until you do know. If you can't figure it out, you have not mastered the process enough to do it yourself, or you have chosen a stock from a group that is too hard to understand and you will not make the right move when the market goes against you, which it invariably will.

Let's go back to our Maytag-versus-Whirlpool example. If we are looking at revenues and revenue growth, that's simply the price of all the washers and dryers Maytag sells times the number of units sold. Pretty easy. Given that there is nothing magical about selling washers and dryers, one can suspect that unless Maytag invents some wholly new device, its product will be heavily dependent upon how well its consumers are doing. (And, by the way, I mean wholly new and spectacular. Maytag just began offering home soda and beer machines, vending machines, a terrific line extension from its normal vending machine brand, but it would have to do ten times the business it is doing ever to budge the multiple upwards.) Maytag is hostage to the economic cycles worldwide. If it wants to grow profits, it has to find a way to make each washer and dryer more cheaply. It can't just raise the price per unit because the competition in the appliance business is too fierce. Maytag is what is known as a cyclical business, because it does well when there is a cyclical upturn in the economy. Drug stocks, on the other hand, don't need cyclical upturns to grow. We call that kind of stock a "secular" growth stock, meaning it has its own growth levered to its products. The simple way to think about this is to view the companies as products you might or might not buy. You can't afford to skip taking medicine just because it is expensive, but you can withhold purchase of a new washer or dryer if you aren't doing well. That set of calculations happens to 300 million people in this country all of the time, which is why we are willing to pay a higher multiple-to-earnings for the growth of drug stocks than we are for the growth of washer and dryer companies. One can't be deferred; one can. One has protection from competition, the other is extremely competitive. You want to buy the latter only when the "line," or multiple to earnings is so out of whack with the growth prospects that you are compensated for the vicissitudes of the consumer and the economy.

Remember, when you do the homework, you are trying to measure how the company is doing—how the company is doing versus its peers and how the company is doing versus all of the companies out there as measured by the S&P 500. While there are many components

that can be measured, the main thing that your homework should identify is whether your company is growing faster than the average company. Once you can measure that—with information easily available in the management's discussion and analysis section in the public documents or even on Yahoo! Finance, TheStreet.com, or a host of other sites—you have to compare it to the average growth of the S&P 500. Then, you have to compare its P/E multiple to the P/E multiple of the average company. A bargain is a company that is growing sales and earnings faster than the average S&P 500 company but sells for a lower multiple than the average. An expensive stock is one that sells at a P/E premium to the averages but grows slower. I would almost always turn my back on a company that has the latter, but be intrigued by one that has the former.

If everyone is doing the same calculations, you might ask, how can there be any bargains? Aren't stocks perfect indicators of the future, as the academics insist? And, you might be wondering, how can you be better at this stuff at home than I can be as a professional?

First, remember the market cares more about future growth than it does about past growth, and to anticipate future growth you need insight that not everyone has. (Don't worry, I will give you my tips for how I have spotted future growth ahead of others for years.)

Second, the market's constantly throwing sales that allow you momentarily to find merchandise that is growing faster than the average company for less cost than the other company. In other words, if you are patient, and if you can keep the bat on your shoulder and let the pitch come to you, you will be able to buy stocks more cheaply than you should, which is the essence of good money management, whether it be done by pros or by you. Waiting for a company's stock to go from expensive to cheap because the market is throwing a sale may be the smartest thing you can do when you are building your portfolio. Similarly, when the market takes one of your stocks from cheap to expensive, paring back your holdings is essential so you can pick up some more of the stock when it inevitably becomes cheaper again.

Make Sure You Are Investing in Viable Companies Before You Measure Growth

Of course, it would be simple if the only thing we cared about is growth of earnings and sales. But we also have to be sure that the enterprise we are buying is financially sound. On my radio show I must refer to the balance sheet of the companies I talk about dozens of times per hour. I like companies with no debt and I don't like companies that have a lot of debt. When you have too much debt you can't pay the bills if your business runs into trouble. When you can't pay the bills, the creditors—the bond holders or the banks—take over the equity. It saddens me that so few people understand that if you just look at the "equity side"—the number of shares times the dollar price—you don't get the full enterprise picture. You must also consider the debt. A company like a Revlon or a Nortel or a Lucent looks incredibly cheap if you simply multiply the stock price times the shares. When you factor in the debt, though, it's not nearly as cheap as you think. That debt does matter. It can choke off the "healthy" business you think you are buying. Yet I must have gotten dozens of calls a week from people who owned the common stock of WorldCom or Kmart before they went bankrupt and thought they would be entitled to something. They didn't understand that they were holding a two of clubs against the bond holders' aces.

Don't be mystified by this stuff. It is easier than you think. If you are making $40,000 a year and you have payments of $40,000 a year in credit card debt and mortgages, you know you can't make it without having to file for bankruptcy. Same thing with companies. Companies present balance sheets every quarter that tell you whether they are taking in more than they are paying out in interest or not. When the companies do their conference calls, they also post their balance sheets on the Web or make them available to you so you can make judgments just as I am suggesting.

Of course, some businesses take down a lot of debt as part of their regular enterprise. Merchants take down debt in the fourth quarter so

they can have lots of goods to sell at Christmas. Airlines take down a lot of debt to buy planes. Cable companies borrow a lot of money to build out cable systems.

That's fine, as long as they are taking in enough money to pay back the debt. Given that I am an extremely conservative investor, I rarely own the stock of companies that borrow a lot of money. I like companies without a lot of debt. The reason is self-evident: It is much harder to lose your money when you invest in companies that don't borrow money or are not extremely leveraged. When companies borrow money, either in the form of bank debt or a bond sale, the collateral is, well, you! Your shares. Your ownership shares. The bond bullies strip you of your ownership rights and take over the companies when things go bad. That's why you must be vigilant about doing the homework. You must be sure that you aren't investing in something that could be taken away by the bullies because they have the legal right in bankruptcy to do so. I know this seems very basic, but when things turned bad in the economy, I listened to caller after caller on my radio show who had no idea that their shares could be crushed, literally made to disappear, as the ownership of the company switched from the common-stock holders to the bond holders and the banks.

We don't study corporate finance in high school or college. We don't understand the capital structure of companies. But we do understand mortgages and credit card debt. I am sure, if you are a bank officer, that there will be situations where a heavily indebted individual, one without a good income, is a good risk for a mortgage or a MasterCard. But the odds are against it, so you most likely pass up the opportunity. Same with stocks. I am sure that my method, which favors companies without a lot of debt, is going to steer you clear of some incredibly good situations, real home runs that you will regret not owning as they go over the fence. But unless you accept that an indebted company is purely speculative and it takes up your speculative spot in a diversified portfolio, I will always tell you to say no to the investment. As I say all of the time on *Jim Cramer's RealMoney*, it takes only one really bad investment, one totally belly-up situation, to ruin

your profits from all of the good stocks. And, believe me, as my old boss at Goldman Sachs, Richard Menschel, would remind me endlessly, there are no asterisks in this game. You can't say, "Well, I would have had a great year if it weren't for WorldCom," or "Without Enron, we would have made good money." Menschel drilled into my head the need to avoid the clunkers that can wreck all the good work of a diversified portfolio. Too much debt almost always crushes a company before it can make you enough money to merit the investment. Avoid the bad balance sheets, and most of the problems that befall investors will never visit you. Isn't that worth missing a one-in-ten shot that comes back from indebted hell?

In essence, the reasons you do homework are both offensive and defensive. The offensive portion is to identify companies that have the ability to grow earnings faster than the market thinks but are priced below what the market multiple is at the moment. You are trying to discover the unknown value of companies before others discover and exploit their value. You are also trying to identify whether everyone knows all that is good about your stocks and whether the company is more than fully valued versus others in the market. The defensive portion involves staying close enough to a company to see that it has fallen off the wagon and is beginning to take down more debt than it can afford. That, too, is readily obvious to those who do homework, but not to those who buy and hold. It is the latter situation that must be detected before it destroys all of the good elements of your portfolio. Remember, you have to play both defense and offense in order to turn small amounts of money into large amounts.

Before we leave the notion of homework, let me tell you what is not homework. Looking at the chart, the graphic demonstration of where a stock has gone, is not homework. It can tell you nothing. Some think it is the sole compilation of all investing thought and from it you can divine the next move. That's preposterous, and I have the tire tracks on my back to prove it, for I have been short, or have bet against, many a failed chart only to be hit by a huge takeover and a subsequent wipeout. In investing a picture is not worth a thousand

words; in fact, it is worth almost nothing. A chart is *never* enough to buy a stock from. Never. Don't be conned into believing that looking at a chart can suffice for homework; it simply can't.

Similarly, the commodity "tools" that brokerage houses try to portray as proprietary and therefore somehow generating an edge for you are meaningless in the real investing firmament. When you see a brokerage ad with people talking about how the "tools" are all there to pick stocks, you should run, not walk, to another broker. There are no "tools" that generate buys and sells, just hard work and research—which tools, if anything, will obscure. The reason why these brokerage houses advertise tools is that they don't provide any real research of any value but have to try to lure you in with some pretense of specialty.

Not to praise Wall Street research too much; as I have said many times, some of my biggest gains were made betting against Wall Street research. But the one thing that Wall Street does excellently is create primers about industries that allow you to help figure out the metrics. Before I ever buy a stock in a new industry I always do my best to locate the research primers from whatever houses have written them, whether it be nanotechnology or the clothing or restaurant industries. I need the benchmarks to make educated decisions. So do you. You can use Yahoo! Finance and TheStreet.com to find them.

Once you have decided to focus on a single stock for your portfolio—for either your retirement or discretionary account—you have to figure out mentally what's the risk-reward of that particular equity. You have to make a judgment about what the market will ultimately pay for a stock using the P/E parameters outlined earlier. Risk-reward analysis defines the short-term stock picking that professionals do, and I want you to understand the motivating forces behind it. Assessing the risk is a question of assessing the downside. Assessing the reward is a question of assessing the upside. The upside and the downside are created by two different buying and selling cohorts that you must understand in order to figure out the analysis correctly. The value guys create the bottom; the growth guys create the top. Fortu-

nately, because I am chameleonlike in nature and inherently unwilling to be anything but flexible, I understand both teams, the value team and the growth team, and I can tell you what constitutes wins and losses for each team. People are always calling my radio show and asking how I judge the risks and rewards of individual stocks. I tell them that I like to think about where the value guy will begin to buy a stock after the growth guy has given up on it, and when the growth guy will begin to sell the stock because the growth is slowing or no longer accelerating at an attractive enough level for the growth stock buyer.

I boil it down on my radio show to something quick and dirty: "Three up five down, or ten up, three down." That's because I like to know the upside and the downside before I buy so I know if I can handle the pain. But let's go through the exercise of how I judge the risk-reward in real life so you can do the same.

Recently a caller, Bob, asked me which I liked more, Rite Aid or Walgreens. He wanted my blessing to buy Rite Aid over Walgreens. I could tell that he would have vastly preferred me to recommend Rite Aid because, as is so often the case, it was simply more tempting because of its small dollar amount: Rite Aid was at $5.31 and Walgreens was roughly $30.

I told him I couldn't go there. I mentally calculated the upside and downside of both and concluded that Walgreens was the cheaper and less risky of the two and the better stock over the long term.

Here's how I did it. First, I took a look at the long-term growth rates of both companies, just as I taught you to look at Whirlpool versus Maytag. Walgreens is growing earnings at 15 percent, Rite Aid is growing earnings at 12.5 percent. WAG's growing faster than RAD. But when I calculated the price-to-earnings multiples of the two—remember that's how we figure out what's expensive and what's cheap, not by assessing the $5 that RAD trades at and the $30 that WAG trades at—I discovered that Rite Aid is trading at 40 times earnings while Walgreens is trading at 25 times earnings. Given that Walgreens earnings are growing 20 percent faster than Rite Aid's, it simply makes no sense to me—and will make no sense to the big money that con-

trols the marginal prices of stocks—that you should be paying a huge 15-point multiple premium for Rite Aid. The upside, set by the growth buyers, won't allow Rite Aid to trade much higher. The growth buyers will, indeed, be willing to pay more than 25 times earnings for Walgreens' consistent growth, because we have seen multiples of up to 40 times earnings for long-term consistent growth, especially at a time when other companies are having a hard time growing. (That's the upper limit of what disciplined growth buyers are willing to pay. There is always someone willing to pay any price, and later on I will talk about how to game those folks, but right now we are trying to do traditional risk-reward.) Given that Walgreens is slated to earn roughly $1.30, I could see the stock trading at an upper limit of 40 times earnings, or $52 a share. That's a sharp 70 percent gain from $30 a share where the stock was when Bob called me.

Now let's consider the upside of Rite Aid. It is already trading at the ceiling of what good, disciplined growth players will pay, 40 times earnings, so I think the reward for the stock is roughly where it is selling now. It is more than fully valued by the growth guys already. No gain.

Once we have quantified the upside, as defined by the growth buyers, we have to consider the downside, where value buyers would step in to stem the decline. As I have often described, most market players care about growth, but there is a smaller, yet still very disciplined cohort that actually likes to buy stocks as proxies for the businesses underneath. These are called value buyers, and they are the potential trampolines, or at least safety nets, that will get under a stock after it disappoints and create a bottom betting that something good—takeover or turnaround—will happen to the company the stock represents, and to you if you simply buy the stock cheaply enough.

These buyers look at abstractions such as the book, or replacement value, of an enterprise, or what other companies have been willing to pay for similar entities in the same industry. Given that Walgreens is the largest drugstore company in the United States, it is unlikely that it can be taken over. So what the value buyers in a WAG would look for

is a time when the stock is getting shelled, perhaps because of short-term considerations, like a missed monthly sales number or a weak Christmas, or a market sell-off in general, a time when they can get this fine grower for below its long-term growth rate. The way these folks think is, "Okay, Walgreens grows at 15 percent. If I can ever buy that stock at a P/E that is at a slight premium to that growth rate, instead of the excessive premium it sells for now, I could patiently wait until the growth-stock buyers realize what they are missing and they bid the stock up again."

Again, I expect Walgreens to earn $1.30 a share. Knowing that value guys start early and then buy as a stock goes down, I would expect the value buyers to show up at around 17 times earnings, or about $22 a share. That would put the downside of Walgreens at about $8 below the current price, which is a lot, but on a percentage basis, which is what matters, you are looking at around a 25 percent potential decline before the cushion sets in.

When will the value buyers settle in to stop a decline in Rite Aid? I expect Rite Aid to earn 26¢. Value guys would step in when the multiple is, again, at a small premium to its 12.5 percent growth rate. Using the same haircut I gave Walgreens, that would mean roughly 14 times earnings, or $3.64.

Now, let's recap the risk-reward so far: I see Walgreens as having 22 up and 8 down, a fantastic risk-reward. I see Rite Aid as having nothing up and around a buck and a half down. That's not an acceptable risk-reward ratio versus Walgreens.

Wait, it gets worse. We have only looked at the equity side of the balance sheet. I then did the balance-sheet analysis of Walgreens versus Rite Aid, which is incredibly important to let you be sure the bond bullies won't one day be in charge. The key to balance-sheet analysis, as always, is to figure out what kind of interest the company has to pay each year on its equivalent of a mortgage it might have taken out. Sure enough, Rite Aid has to pay $330 million in interest. But it only has $284 million in operating income. That's not a sustainable situation.

Walgreens, by contrast, has no debt. That means the risk-reward ratio I outlined on the equity is probably too kind to Rite Aid versus Walgreens because the value buyers might not be as tempted to start buying at $3.60 if there is a bond bully waiting in the wings to take the company away from them.

So far everything's pretty quantifiable. But I also like to factor in what I know about some other variables, variables involving the industry and the management of the two companies. These also assess future growth and help flesh out the "exact" nature of those earnings estimates that I was using to calculate multiples. They are necessary additions to the process because they inject real world concerns into an otherwise sterile arithmetic competition.

I know, for example, that the drugstore business is already "overstored," meaning that it is a mature industry. I know that because a quick search of the articles about the industry—a necessary part of anyone's homework—shows me that many of the players in the drugstore industry have nowhere to expand. Perhaps Walgreens can move into the food business or Rite Aid the dry-cleaning business, but that's not been in their skill set so far. I also know that JC Penney is selling Eckerd to CVS, which means that the competition is about to get even tougher because CVS is, like Walgreens, an excellent outfit. I can also see from the clips that Wal-Mart says it wants to enter the drugstore market, and we know that Wal-Mart laid waste to the supermarket business when it chose to go in, so who knows what havoc the big chain can cause drugstores.

That could mean that the highly indebted player, Rite Aid, might not even be able to make it. Walgreens, with its clean balance sheet, is also known as a well-run, stable enterprise when it comes to management. There's been very little turnover during its most recent past. A quick look at Rite Aid, though, shows pretty consistent turnover—including some because of criminal prosecutions—again a real negative.

All these subjective and balance-sheet tests tell me that if anything, the $8 down/$22 up analysis I have done for Walgreens is probably

conservative on the downside and the upside, whereas the downside of Rite Aid may be even greater than the buck and a half that I thought it might be, maybe as much as $2–3 more, given that no company will want to buy an indebted Rite Aid if it looks as though the company might have to declare bankruptcy because it can't pay its interest. Remember, in that situation the common stock gets wiped out, crushed. What you own will be gone.

So, it all gets translated like this: "Bob, the risk-reward of Walgreens versus Rite Aid is simply so much better that you can't afford to risk buying Rite Aid. You may have a very compelling reward with Walgreens."

Could I be wrong? Of course, there are multiple factors that are involved in the process that I haven't taken into account. Maybe Walgreens is having a better than expected quarter right now and it could be worth even more. Maybe Rite Aid could attract a takeover bid simply because lots of companies do stupid things. Maybe Wal-Mart buys Rite Aid, even though that seems unlikely because WMT is known as a disciplined buyer, and paying north of $5 for RAD is undisciplined, to say the least. There are always unknowable facts in the investment process, always, but we can't let them undermine judgment to the point that judgments can't be made. Because then we might as well put the money in the bank. For the purposes of Bob's query, I am confident that I have offered him the best judgment that can be made. Notice, Bob has made up his mind to own shares in a drugstore chain. It is not my job to talk him out of such an industry. It is simply my job to portray the risk-reward as best I can.

When I make these calculations, I am doing so only against other members of the drugstore cohort. In real life, nothing exists in a vacuum. But I would be doing the same calculus for Rite Aid versus, say, the S&P 500. I used the S&P 500 as a benchmark, not just to figure out what the whole market is doing, but also to figure out what I should pay versus individual stocks. If Rite Aid is cheaper than the S&P 500 but growing faster than the S&P 500, then indeed it is a bargain. But if

it is more expensive than the S&P 500 and is growing slower than the S&P 500, then it should be a sell, not a buy.

That's the basic daily decision-making process on Wall Street. These risk-reward parameters will work for any stock and are excellent for comparing one stock to another. But how do you find out when stocks are about to embark on their runs? How do you find out, for example, if Walgreens is about to journey to $50 instead of languishing at $30? How do you find the trigger, the catalyst for such a move? And, more important, how do you find stocks that can defy traditional risk-reward parameters, situations where there could be, say, 100 points up and 10 down, or even 300 points up and 20 down? How do you find the 10×ers, the super growers, without putting too much capital at risk in the process?

How can you spot gains of all varieties, from the small 3- to 5-point gains that can be fabulously winning on an average annual return basis, to the 20-, 30-, and 50-point gains that might disappear soon after or might continue on indefinitely? That's the subject of our next chapter.

5

SPOTTING STOCK MOVES BEFORE THEY HAPPEN

What makes stocks go up and down in price in the time we own them? How can we figure out which stock is going to go up *before* it goes up? How do we figure out which stocks are going to go up the fastest so we can capture those bursts? Aren't these more important questions than whether we like the "fundamentals" of a Computer Associates or the management of a Microsoft? Aren't these the real goals we're after, not just the reshuffling of the S&P 500 deck?

I asked all of those questions during the interviews when I was trying to get a job at Goldman Sachs out of law school. People would talk to me amorphously about how high-quality stocks went higher and low-quality stocks went lower. They would relate the management of the company and the prospects of the company to the stock price and hold up examples of how the decline or advance in fundamentals always seeped into the price of the stock, either immediately or eventually. I took it all in but still was confused about how a stock pushed from 10 to 11, or fell back from 11 to 10. The so-called obvious case of the fundamentals guiding the stock's movement just didn't seem self-

evident to me, and it may not seem self-evident to you. The moves, at least short-term, seem almost random, not based on the fundamentals.

Then one day, I annoyed a senior executive of the firm with my incessant questions about what causes a stock to go up a point. I just couldn't figure out how it all happened. He then called me over to his Quotron—that's what they were using then—and said, Okay, watch Stride Rite. He then hit up SRR and it showed the bid price (where the stock could be sold) and the offer price (where the stock could be bought), both of which were clustered around 7. He said to me, "You want to see a one-point gain; you want the anatomy of a one-point gain? Okay." He punched in a light on his keyboard and said, "Buy me fifty thousand Stride Rite at the market." Next thing I know the stock is tearing toward $8, careering toward it like a moth to a two-hundred-watt bulb on a hot summer evening. It was only after the exec said, "Okay, that's enough," after about 30,000 shares had been swept and the stock stopped at $7.50, that I recognized how easy it could be to move some stocks. It was the essence of supply and demand. The exec had created demand that could not be met by the sellers "on the books," so the specialist was letting the stock climb until it reached a level where sellers appeared.

Of course, most stocks aren't as illiquid, meaning there are many more sellers and buyers at all different levels, than Stride Rite had that day. But you get the idea. Demand and supply determine the minute-to-minute pricing of stocks, and if you blitz a stock with demand, unless it is one of the larger companies, unless it has more than $100 million in market capitalization, the level I think where you first get some real-time liquidity, you are going to produce your own anatomy of a one-point gain.

In the real world, the day-to-day world of stocks, there are many forces that can affect the pricing of an equity. The first and most basic is the sheer act of buying and selling a stock that doesn't have much volume. That's where we move stocks with our own buying. That won't happen very often to you as a smaller investor.

Even at the height of my firm, Cramer Berkowitz, I managed only about $450 million for a bunch of wealthy families, a pittance compared to the major mutual funds and some large hedge funds that control the marginal dollar that determines stock prices at the end of the day. I mention this to drill into your head the importance of considering supply and demand of the stock at all times. That's because way too many people get confused; they think we are trading the actual companies themselves, that the pieces of paper we are trading, investing, owning, are some sort of redemptive right, a coupon that will give you certain cents off, or an ownership right that will allow you to have a chunk of the brick and mortar if not the cash in the treasury of the joint. Untrue. These are, in the end, simply pieces of paper, to be bought, sold, or manipulated up and down by those with more capital than others. All other investment books stress the linkage between the stock and the company. Me? I stress the abject lack of short-term linkage and the opportunities that such an unconnectedness presents. While it is true that over the very, very long term—say your lifetime—stocks should indeed reflect the fundamentals, over the short term, the twelve- to eighteen-month time frame that is most applicable to most owners these days—like it or not that's how long most stocks are held—the fundamentals of the company play only a part in what moves a stock up or down. In fact, I believe the reason that so many professional managers and amateurs fail to beat the market or make big money is that they are way too hung up on the largely artificial linkage, short-term, between a company's health and the health of the stock. I think that deep down they like the linkage because it makes them feel that they aren't gambling with their money (or their clients' money). They think that if they stay focused on the fundamentals they have turned gambling into investing. I wish I could be so glib. I wish I could focus only on the company and not the stock, because it would be much easier. But it would also be much less lucrative.

Remember my litmus test: I am trying to get you to buy stocks that go up quickly, in a time frame that matters to you now, and get you to avoid stocks that go down rapidly, that could wipe you out. If I can do

that I can help you become wealthy. But if I choose to ignore that short-term direction of stock, I am leaving endless amounts of easy cash on the table for others to pick up, and that's just not going to allow me to outperform others and grow wealth in time for it to be used. If we lived for hundreds of years and didn't need the money for eighty to one hundred of those years and if we were incredibly rich to start, we could overlook these short-term bull markets quite easily. Yet, to me, it is just plain unrealistic and far too paternalistic to think and act otherwise, even though the vast majority of the practitioners out there ply this pristine but impractical advice.

More important, finding out when a stock is about to have what I call a Game Breaker move requires only some knowledge of the company and much knowledge about the way stocks work as they go about the process of growing. There will be lots of stocks that we will see move up by a billion dollars or more in capitalization—a totally catchable move—without any real, discernible change in or development at the underlying company. I have seen stocks tack on $500 million in market cap simply by saying that they are now nanotechnology stocks, not just technology stocks. I have seen fortunes made by adding a ".com" to a company and fortunes made by taking a ".com" off the name of the company. In each case these were fathomable moves. Remember the diet analogy: I don't care how we catch the moves, whether it is with carrots and melon and broccoli, or whether it is with steak and bacon. I just want us to catch the darned moves. Again, I know this is heresy. No investing text advocates trying to catch these moves. No market professional wants to be affiliated with these moves because they can be short-term in nature and they resemble gambling more than "investing." But so what? If we can catch Taser or Netflix or eBay or Yahoo! while not wholeheartedly believing in them long-term, if we clearly mark them as the speculative entry in our diversified portfolio, why should we not take the dozens of points that can be offered by these situations? Why can't we snare them? Why must we be bound by, for example, a bear market in most equities if

there is a bull market in some speculative enterprises that we can capture with buy-and-sell disciplines?

To me, the landscape looks like this. First, there are undiscovered companies with undervalued stocks—that's where most of the Game Breakers come from. Then there are discovered companies with undervalued stocks—that's the small-cap-to-mid-cap phenomenon, where some great gains can still be had regularly. Then there are discovered companies with fully valued stocks—that's where the vast majority of money managers play. We can make money in that cohort, but it's very difficult to make big money. I think of the gains from this segment as singles and doubles rather than home runs. Finally, there are undiscovered companies with fully valued stocks, the most dangerous sector of all for most undisciplined investors. That's where most of the speculation occurs and why most people lose money speculating. The typical uninformed speculators are buying stocks already exploited by the process of discovery. Once a stock is discovered, it is difficult for it to stay undervalued. And once a stock is fully valued, a whole new set of rules applies if you are going to make money investing.

All of these situations require disciplines: a buy discipline, which allows us to figure which quadrant we are in—for if we are in the discovered/fully valued quadrant we must be quite disciplined—and a sell discipline, which requires rigorous departures from stocks that we desire to keep.

How different are the quadrants? You need a market dislocation to buy in the discovered/fully valued segment, but you can act at will in what you will regard as a venture capitalist style in the undiscovered/undervalued segment. Each cohort is different, but none is more dangerous or risky than the other, provided you sell right in the early stages and buy right in the later.

We know that hoped-for future growth in earnings propels stocks. So, it is natural that we begin to believe that the catalyst for a big move requires a recognition that there is more growth to come than anyone knows.

What I have learned in my many years of trading and investing is that there are many different types of moves to be caught, and only some of them lend themselves to the traditional analysis that I outlined, say, in the Walgreens versus Rite Aid example. In fact, I think that the WAG vs. RAD is, in many ways, the most pedestrian, least exciting point gain to try to catch, even as it might be the easiest type to try to nab before it happens. Given my predilection for flexibility, I like to have metrics and doctrines and methodologies at hand to discover the secrets behind moves in all four groups—undiscovered/undervalued; discovered/undervalued; undiscovered/fully valued; and discovered/fully valued.

For some, these metrics might seem strange. Most stock pickers think of groups as small, medium, and large capitalization. But capitalizations can lie. Some stocks are large cap that shouldn't be. Some stocks are small cap, but not for long. If we want to make big money—the purpose of this book—the cohort that makes the most sense to look at is the undiscovered/undervalued, even as the graybeards would no doubt thumb their noses at these stocks, despite the likelihood of finding the next Starbucks or Home Depot or Comcast—all incredibly speculative at one time—among them.

Indeed, let's not kid ourselves. When you are buying the discovered stocks of discovered companies, you are simply doing handicapping and risk-reward work as we performed on Walgreens versus Rite Aid. But when you are trying to find the next Game Breaker move, you are strictly embracing speculation because, by nature, you are on unproven and subjective grounds. The earlier you move, the more your actions resemble gambling. However, as is so often the case, the earlier you pounce, the greater gain you can have. Once again, the investing that looks the least like gambling produces the most humbling returns, while the investing that seems much more like wagering produces the heftiest of returns. That's why this book not only doesn't frown on speculation, it insists that a part of your discretionary portfolio be dedicated to it.

The types of gains that can be had using this method are similar to

those of another form of investing: venture capital. You place a series of bets on a bunch of long shots—that's what VCs do—and you recognize that many, sometimes even most, will not work, but that the winners will more than make up for the losers. Amazingly, because of the asymmetric nature of losses—stocks stop at zero when they go bust—the losers can't possibly wipe out more than what the winners, with their infinite potential, can make. Further, when my trading rules for speculation are adhered to rigorously, you end up with a truly bountiful combination where your winners are allowed to run and your losers are stopped out *before* they get to zero. That's because the stocks that go from unknown and undervalued to unknown and overvalued exhibit similar characteristics that we can flag in order to exit before they flame out.

Let's take the different techniques and rules I use for each cohort and discuss how you can spot the big moves in each size of stock before it happens.

I am going to give you the traditional large cap analysis first, to walk you through the way that most managers do their thinking. Given that the vast majority of conventional stock picking involves choosing among higher quality blue-chip stocks that either pay dividends or can pay dividends, I want you to be grounded in the traditional methods and type of moves that can occur.

The reasons behind traditional moves of large cap stocks can be grouped into two logical catalysts:

1. Rotational catalysts: Decisions by portfolio managers to shift from group to group depending upon the macro backdrop: weak-to-strong economy or strong-to-weak economy, as dictated by the incredibly important actions of the Federal Reserve. These catalysts involve switching between secular growth *stories* and cyclical (smokestack) blastoffs that must be captured if you are to make money in all kinds of markets.

2. Estimate revision catalysts: Given the need all managers have to try to figure out where the biggest future earnings gains are going to

come from, we must be able to detect when companies' estimates are going to rise. We have to be able to spot product cycles or demand cycles before they occur so we can profit from surging estimates.

Once you have mastered these traditional stock-picking methodologies, I will show you how to spot undervalued stocks and undiscovered companies before others do so. That's where the biggest gains can be had. The disciplines involved in the undervalued and unknown stocks are completely different from those involving large capitalization entities. That's because most of the small caps *never* get to be big caps or even transition through to mid cap, yet they are still fertile places to look and explore and exploit.

Only after that discussion will I identify the rules you will need to trade and invest in all of these stocks correctly, as well as show you the mistakes that I have made in trying to exploit this methodology so you can learn from them.

The Secrets of Successful Large Cap Investing

As a successful hedge fund manager, running hundreds of millions of dollars of capital, I had to be sure that I could get in and out of stocks and be able to change my mind and direction without clipping huge percentages off my performance. The only stocks that allow that kind of flexibility are large capitalization stocks. As an individual, you are not so restricted. By the nature of the smaller size of your individual portfolio, you need not dwell in the house of the large cap. Nevertheless, that is where most people feel most comfortable selecting stocks, so we need to master the ways of making as much money as possible in this cohort.

Most discovered stocks do nothing but mimic the market. They trade largely on the underlying specific businesses and on the progress of their sectors in the overall domestic and worldwide economies. In fact, for discovered stocks, I find that sector analysis and specific stock

analysis each explain about 50 percent of the moves. In other words, knowing a business cold may not be as important as knowing how the sector is doing and how it performs in a given economic cycle. Whirlpool and Maytag are never going to trade like biotech companies no matter how great they are at washer and dryer making because the appliance sector only grows at about the same pace as the gross domestic product. There are a limited number of product modifications that Maytag or Whirlpool can add to spur growth before the sector overtakes and then stunts that growth. You don't have such an inhibiting course in biotech, where the drugs themselves define the limit. In other words, catching a Game Breaker move in Maytag or Whirlpool or most cyclical stories is difficult unless the world economy is growing at a huge pace, a cyclical theme such as a housing boom has ignited, or the company gets a takeover bid. But other industries, tech and biotech classically, are uniquely prone to these Game Breaker moves. I like to have a mixture of all of these kinds of situations with at least one entity, the speculative entity, where a Game Breaker move is more likely.

Sector thinking is so ingrained among the "big boys" at the mutual funds that they tend to determine the marginal prices not of businesses themselves—they don't take over anything, just the stocks—so that if you try to buy a good company in an out-of-favor sector you are most likely going to lose money until that sector comes back in favor, which will have little to do with the company's intrinsic fortunes. We call this the "best house in a bad neighborhood" thesis: No company, no matter how good, can truly transcend its sector.

I am not as concerned about sectors and companies right here, though. I am concerned about finding stocks that have catalysts, that are about to move, to put on huge point gains. All my life I've been fascinated by the ability to catch "the big move" in a stock, that spurt that makes you all the money there is to be made in a stock. Capturing that spurt was my specialty. (Remember that example of getting Gulf Oil before the takeover clearance? That is the outsized move we are trying to catch.) It is not enough to know Maytag versus Whirlpool on an

earnings basis. You have to know what makes Maytag or Whirlpool break out of the range that either will most likely be trading in most of the time. You need to figure out when Maytag is going to make that move, that multi-billion-dollar market capitalization move, that makes the stock worth so much more than it is now. Figuring out that inflection point, that catalyst, knowing when a stock goes from dormancy to action, from caterpillar to butterfly, is what you've got to be able to do if your stock picking is going to yield extraordinary results, results not bound by the S&P 500 or the Dow Jones or the NASDAQ 100. If you aren't soundly beating those indices, you might as well hand off your money to the mutual funds.

Remember $E \times M = P$? That simple equation is what drives the vast majority of stocks. The E is the earnings, or more accurately, the earnings estimates of a company. The M is the multiple, what multiple of those earnings estimates people will pay for a stock. P is the price of the stock. In other words, if you know what a company could earn and you know how much people value those earnings, you will be able to figure what price the stock is selling at. I know multiplication seems pretty easy. Solving for M is as simple as dividing the price by the earnings per share. Think back to the work we did on Maytag. If Maytag is going to earn $2 a share and it sells for $30 a share, the multiple the market will pay right now is 15. So, let's take that a step further. There are only two ways a stock should be able to obtain a higher price in the market: The earnings can go up *or* someone will pay a higher multiple for those earnings. So if Maytag is going to earn $3 per share instead of $2 and the multiple stays the same, the stock should trade to $45. If you knew or could build a thesis that Maytag might be earning $3 instead of $2 and the stock was at $30, you would know you are going to make money buying that stock because it will eventually go higher when the new earnings are reported.

Unfortunately, figuring out how Maytag is going to make $3 instead of $2 is not something that can be easily done by reading the documents and looking at the business model. Think about all of the

things that go into making those earnings per share. If you are going to predict that Maytag's estimates are a dollar too low, you have to know that Maytag's products are going to sell at a much better than expected level or that Maytag is going to make its products more cheaply than anyone thinks and sell them for more money than anyone thinks, or that Maytag's got some newfangled product that no one knows about that is going to make it a fortune. New product introduction, better sales, better margins—this is the stuff of higher earnings estimates, and if you can predict them, you are going to land a big win.

But what if instead of the earnings estimates changing radically, the M changes? What happens if you can figure out that the multiple is going to get bigger? Remember, if "E × M" equals the price of the stock, then we should be trying to predict when the M is going to get bigger even if the E is going to stay the same or go up just slightly. Let's say you know that Maytag's going to earn $2, etched in stone, but you believe that people should pay more for that $2 than the 15 times that they currently pay. Maybe you think Maytag should fetch 20 times earnings. That means you think the multiple is too low and should expand to a much higher level. If you are right, you could have a gigantic hit, as the stock would proceed to $40.

At Cramer Berkowitz, where I compounded at 24 percent year after year with no down years, I specialized in trying to determine whether the multiple was going to expand or contract on the same earnings. I spent most of my time trying to develop models and methods that would predict that the M would go up, often in conjunction with work that showed that the E was about to increase beyond what people expected.

I did this because it was obvious to me that if I could figure out which companies were going to beat expectations, I could get in front of large moves before they happened.

Fortunately, understanding why a multiple will expand or grow is something that anyone with common sense and a keen eye for what matters can learn to do. Unfortunately, the vast majority of people, in-

cluding professionals, have no idea about why a multiple will expand and don't even think it is possible to figure this out. These people are wrong. Given that I have repeatedly managed to predict multiple expansion, I know it is not only possible, but, given the directives I am about to describe, it is actually easy.

The first reason a multiple expands and contracts is the macro concerns that have nothing specifically to do with Maytag, Alcoa, International Paper, or any discovered company with a fully valued stock. Some in the business call this "top down" thinking, meaning that if you have a view of the nation's economy—and you always have to have a view if you are going to pick stocks with any consistency before they move—you can predict the direction of the multiple.

Let's stick with Maytag for a moment, because it is, in many ways, a perfect proxy for the macro elevation of the multiple. If the economy is heating up, or, more importantly, if you believe that the economy may heat up because the Federal Reserve is going to cut interest rates—something that always stimulates the economy—you should be betting that Maytag's multiple is going to expand. So, let's say the economy is growing at 2 percent and the Fed is not happy with that growth. And let's also say that Maytag is supposed to earn $2 a share. You can bet that that multiple is going to expand above 15 with an easier Fed. Will it go to 16 or 17? Perhaps, if the Fed steps on the gas. If the Fed cuts in small increments, I think you will see people "pay up" for Maytag, or pay a heightened multiple. If you think the economy is going to expand to 5 percent growth, I think you might be looking at a $40 stock, because with that level of growth there will be buyers willing to pay 20 times earnings, because you can see a similar multiple increase in past economic expansions. You can measure that multiple simply by looking at where a stock has traded in the past and what it has earned in the past. Some of that expansion is predictable—people will now pay 20 times because by the time we get to the next year, the stock might be earning $3 in an economic expansion. They pay it now

because they know that when we get to $3 the multiple will be 15 again, the average multiple of the stock, except the stock will now be substantially higher because of the E's gains. The way I look at this process is to say that the M anticipates the E, and if you can shift your portfolio toward stocks that should have a greater E when the economy is *about* to expand, you are going to find yourself riding a wave of multiple expansion to higher levels.

What if you think the economy is downshifting? Maytag's multiple will most likely collapse as it anticipates a decline from the $2 in earnings power that we thought it had. I could see the multiple go down to 10 times earnings or even 9 or 8 as it has in past slowdowns and recessions. Of course, when it gets there, when the economy slows, it might turn out that Maytag really earns only $1.25 and it is back at that same 15 times earnings. Maytag would be a "short" in such an instance. (I'll explain shorting techniques in the final chapter.) The M fluctuates in anticipation of the downshift or upshift in the broader economy.

The P/E multiple of all sectors responds to the giant macro picture, which is why it is so important to stay focused on where you think the economy is headed. Remember, I am not saying that you must have a view of the economy to own stocks, I am simply pointing out that if you don't have a view you won't be able to capture the spurts that are caused by multiple expansion or contraction. But I think the gains that can be had by this method are so significant that it is important to try to have the larger picture in the back of your mind when you are selecting stocks.

How important? I had a chart above my desk at my hedge fund at all times that showed what should be bought based on multiple expansion and what should be sold based on multiple contraction. That chart derived from the accelerations and decelerations of the economy. I call this chart, by the way, my mental "playbook" because, as in sports, it tells me which "players" to insert in the lineup, or the portfolio, when the economic circumstances demand changes. On my television show we spend a tremendous amount of time trying to divine

the next two to three percentage points of GDP (gross domestic product) precisely because of the point gains that can be had through multiple expansion or contraction based on that macro performance.

My chart, which looks like a wave, shows the ebb and flow of the economy and what works and what doesn't depending upon where the waves are going. Let me walk you through this. You need to know this if only because it explains what is known as "sector rotation," the driving force behind most days of trading in and out of groups of stocks that you see. Such trading drives the shorter-term performance of everything from Avon to Zimmer Holdings.

The chart starts at -2 percent with the economy expanding back toward flat-lining; zero to 7 percent growth. That's a classic recession condition. In a recession, the Federal Reserve can be counted on to cut interest rates on the short end, where it controls them, rather dramatically, as it has done in every recession since World War II. The longer-term rates, which are not set by the Federal Reserve, also drop as the demand for money declines.

At any given time, the market is churning toward the next possible outcome. When you get to a recession, the stocks that have maximum multiple expansion—the stocks with the highest multiples—are those of companies with recession-proof earnings: the drug companies, the food companies, the soap and toothpaste companies, and the beer and soda companies. At a slowdown's depth, but *before* the Fed takes any action, these companies' stocks are prized possessions because they still deliver the E in the $E \times M = P$ equation. (The cyclical companies are missing their estimates like mad at that point in the economy.) The M expands to what is known as a "peak" multiple right at this point in the recession. So, if Procter & Gamble, the quintessential "recession-proof" company, normally sells at 20 times earnings, it might sell at as much as 25 or even 30 times earnings, depending upon how desperate the market participants are for growth at any cost.

Now, let me tell you what confounds most market players. Just when you think that P&G can't go down, just when you think that the M is going to keep expanding past where it has ever gone, that's pre-

cisely when you have to switch horses and get on the most depressed horse, the cyclical horse. No matter how many times I explain this stuff in my columns and on my radio and TV shows, it always comes as a shock to people because it seems so counterintuitive. But when I walk you through it you will see not only why it makes the most sense, but why it is incredibly easy to predict and to catch the gobs of points that come with it.

Right when you think that only P&G can deliver earnings, the Federal Reserve floods the economy with low-priced money to head off a serious downturn. Remember, the Fed can control both the printing presses of dollars—through the reserve levels it allows banks to carry—and the price of those dollars, by setting low rates for how much it costs borrowers to take down that money.

For individuals, who live and die by mortgage rates that don't fluctuate that much or by credit cards that never fluctuate, the lower rates may mean nothing. But for companies that are constantly making decisions about deploying capital, the sudden decline in rates acts as a spur to investment and demand. I have found that stocks anticipate that money spigot by about six months. In other words, when you think the Fed is about to become accommodative, to start slashing interest rates, that's when you have to leave P&G and focus on the "smokestack" companies that are cyclical in nature, companies that actually make things that are discretionary, as opposed to the necessities from P&G. Again, it always helps to think of this process in terms of stocks. So, let's take P&G versus Maytag. As the economy slows down or shrinks, the market anticipates the Fed's actions. It anticipates that what currently may look bad for Maytag and look good for P&G is going to switch. So, in my wave chart, I would have "sell PG/buy MYG" because I was anticipating that while the E for PG is going to stay steady, the M would shrink, while the E for MYG is about to get better, and the M would therefore begin to grow. That's the opportunity to make the most money in Maytag; it's also the moment when you should anticipate losing money in P&G.

Remember, I always try to distinguish Wall Street from Main

Street. In real life, business at P&G remains constant. The company doesn't do any better or worse depending upon the Fed; we just "pay up" or expand the M because we trust the E so much versus all of those cyclically dependent companies.

At Maytag, however, the lowering of rates is a big event. The stock acts accordingly and anticipates that things are going to get better.

The reason why most people don't understand this process is that right at that very moment, the shift of, say, -2 percent going to 0 percent in the economy, Maytag seems incredibly expensive. Again, the process of the market seems remarkably counterintuitive. At the bottom of the economy, Maytag, which normally might earn $2, could make, say, only $1. As that downshift occurs, Maytag's stock gets crushed. If Maytag might have been at $30 when the economy was booming, I expect it to go down to $20 when the economy rolls over. That's the multiple contraction phase at work. (Why doesn't it pay even less than that? Because in the end, Maytag, the stock, can be bought by another company, one that wants Maytag's earnings for another cycle. The intrinsic worth buoys the stock of the company. That's the AT&T Wireless example in chapter 3. Market players are so fickle and care so much about future earnings that they often forget that these pieces of paper represent real companies and those companies are sought after by other real companies if the stocks of the potential targets trade through intrinsic value.)

Because stocks anticipate the fortunes of their companies, the collapse of Maytag the stock occurs *ahead* of the collapse of Maytag the company. Unfortunately, throughout this process of decline, the analysts who follow Maytag constantly reiterate their buys of the stock saying it seems so cheap based on the past earnings or on the earnings they are predicting. This moment is the most dangerous one for you as an investor. I have seen so many individual investors get burned at this juncture because a stock will seem so tempting as it comes down because it seems "cheap on the earnings." That's because they think both the E and the M are constant and that when multiplied they

should equal a higher price. The siren song goes like this: "Maytag, which will make $2, is now trading at only 12.5 times earnings; it should trade at 15 times earnings, so buy it." The analysts don't respect the power of the cycles enough.

Me, I step aside, or at my old hedge fund, I would be shorting—or betting against Maytag—furiously as I would recognize that the E would soon fall apart, making a mockery of those who are looking at the past. During this freefall period, the analysts are slashing their estimates, and with each estimate slash the stock goes still lower. The estimate slashing collectively drives even more money to the PGs and out of the MYGs as the market seeks safety of earnings and flees earnings at risk.

That keeps happening. PG keeps getting pumped up and MYG keeps getting punished until the estimates for Maytag finally reflect the reality of the company's true fortunes. Of course, that's when the analysts who have been recommending Maytag all the way down because it appears to be so "cheap" on the $2 they are expecting at last cut their estimates down to $1. Because the process of analysis as practiced on Wall Street is so flawed, the analysts downgrade the stocks. That's right, all the way down they kept reiterating their buys, saying how cheap the stock is, trapping you in Maytag for the horrible slide. But at the bottom, they cut their numbers and then they say the stock is no longer cheap—the E is cut in half, making the M look really big and expensive—and the analysts take the stock to a hold or a sell. If they don't do this, their investment policy committees will make them downgrade the stock because Maytag is now too expensive on next year's earnings versus other stocks the firm is recommending.

That's precisely the moment when I cover my short or begin to buy Maytag. At that price and after that decline, I can predict that the Fed will take action to stimulate the economy. I can also predict that the intrinsic worth of a Maytag will buoy it. I would also expect that the dividend of Maytag, which might have been not meaningful at $30, could support the stock at $20. It is true that in a really tough recession

Maytag might have to cut the dividend, but it can't cut its own intrinsic worth to another company that might want to own Maytag's business.

The reason why all of this processing seems so difficult is that with cyclical stocks, stocks hostage to the economic cycle, you must purchase them at precisely the moment when the M is highest. That's the opposite of what you do for noncyclical stocks. Noncyclical stocks must be *sold* when their M is highest.

Here's how the process plays out. As the economy downshifts, the stock of P&G goes up as market participants seek safety and pay more for P&G's earnings power. They sell Maytag because they recognize that Maytag's earnings power is too iffy. But once the economy shows significant deceleration, you have to have faith that the Fed will cut rates and start the expansion again, so you pay a super-high multiple for Maytag just when you must sell P&G at its super-high multiple. The process then works in reverse. As the economy improves, the analysts who deserted Maytag at the bottom and slashed estimates now have to take up their earnings estimates for MYG. Maytag begins to look cheaper and cheaper to them as the E is coming back in the $E \times M = P$ equation.

For me, as someone who anticipated the economy expanding, I now ride Maytag up, perhaps back to where it was, as the earnings estimates expand. During this period, one by one, the analysts come back to the stock and begin to recommend it. How do I know when to get off Maytag? I could, again, anticipate the slowdown that eventually occurs in all cyclical economies, but I have a much easier way. I sell it when all of the analysts love it again and start talking about how Maytag deserves an even higher multiple than 15 on that $2. I have captured the big move; I let others have the rest. In fact, that's when I tend to start embracing Procter & Gamble because at the top of the cycle nobody needs the safety of a PG, and its M shrinks.

So, you can see, as the wave progresses, from −2 percent to 0 percent to, say, 2 percent growth, I am riding MYG and shunning PG. As we get to where I expect the economy to peak out, 3–5 percent, I am

selling MYG and starting to shift to PG. When we get to that 5 percent, I expect the Fed to put the brakes on, slowing the economy, and the process of the crushing of Maytag and the expanding of PG begins anew as PG will make its estimates despite the Fed's forced slowdown.

I don't mean to limit the discussion to Maytag and Procter. Some stocks, known as secular growth stocks, can transcend almost all cycles because they grow so fast. Yahoo!, eBay, and Amazon, for example, face few of the pressures of the Maytags or the P&Gs because they have organic growth that isn't dependent on interest rates. These kinds of stocks—which are few and far between—don't get caught in the cyclical pull. I consider them "unsinkable" against any tide, even if their growth can't last forever.

But the vast majority of stocks at these various stages in economic growth are just like men on a chess board: They advance or decline in predictable patterns that can be gamed. When I anticipate that the economy is about to reverse waves because of the Fed and go from soft to strong, I buy Dow Chemical and DuPont and I sell Coke and Pepsi. When I see the economy acting too strong I begin to anticipate the process of M compression and I lighten up on my Phelps Dodges and my Alcoas as the Fed starts tightening. Again, it will seem counterintuitive to most outsiders because at the top of the economic cycle these big cyclical companies are making money hand over fist, but you must anticipate that such profits can't last and you must jump ship when the M is the smallest, just when all those analysts are telling you how cheap things are getting.

This sector rotation is perhaps the single most difficult part of the investing process because the notion of selling cheap and buying dear is totally antithetical to the beliefs of most investors. Yet it is a total article of faith with me to the point where it will seem that I am recklessly buying the most overvalued cyclical stocks and mindlessly selling the cheapest cyclical stocks.

I love sector rotations and have gamed them for years and years. Near the top of every economic cycle I reach into what I call my fridge and medicine chest stocks, all of which have been thrown away be-

cause no one wants dowdy old Procter or General Mills or Colgate when things are booming. And just when things look most terrible I banish all that stuff that you buy at the supermarket and the drugstore and I load up on the big uglies the market gives away. That's how you let the market work for you to catch the biggest sector rotation gains.

If this method strikes you as something you could do at home, you need not be limited to individual stocks to exercise it. While I have a predilection toward individual stocks, both the sector exchange traded funds and the Fidelity sector funds can be used to move in and out ahead of sector rotations.

Let's go through the typical scenarios of the wave of the economy so you too can anticipate the ebb and flow correctly when you are picking stocks. These scenarios are preciously important for those who are trading discretionary money for big profits, but less important for those playing the twenty-year investment cycle with retirement money. The classic texts all repeatedly deemphasize these cycles, but I have talked to thousands upon thousands of investors and they all have one thing in common: They don't like to lose money even if it means that they can make it back on the next cycle.

If the economic waves are coming in, meaning the economy is getting stronger, we have to monitor the Fed as soon as the GDP growth gets above 4 percent. That kind of growth rings bells at the Fed that it is time to cool things off, that it has to tighten—even if the Fed says otherwise. Am I calling the Federal Reserve governors or the chairman liars? Not really. But the Fed's job is not to figure out this stuff for you, it is to keep prices stabilized, and the governors send out multiple false signals. Just pay attention to the growth rate and don't listen to what they say, because you know what they will do. We can forecast what they will do based on what they have done in the past. When the economy heats up you will begin to see all things financial—real estate investment trusts, savings and loans, banks, insurers, brokers, mortgage companies, and homebuilders—trade down. It is ritualistic and can't be ignored by anyone trying to make bigger money than the market it-

CYCLICAL INVESTING AND TRADING

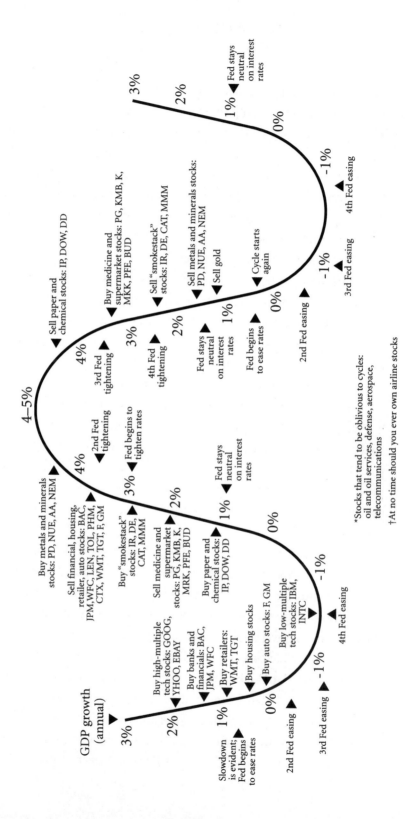

*Stocks that tend to be oblivious to cycles: oil and oil services, defense, aerospace, telecommunications

†At no time should you ever own your own airline stocks

self. That's because the big mutual fund elephants want out of these stocks before their earnings are impacted negatively—or the estimates get cut—because of rising interest rates. I know for many that's a big leap of faith. You might own companies that claim that they aren't rate sensitive. But if you are in the business of money you are by your very nature rate sensitive, regardless of what you say and tell investors. More important, remember that this book focuses on the stocks, not the companies, and whether the execs at the companies like it or not, financial stocks go down in this environment even if the businesses perform at better than expected levels.

At the same time, the techs and the cyclicals will react well during this period. The price of money, while important, isn't as important to them, and they are usually starting to fill up their order books nicely courtesy of the growth in the GDP. They "correlate" properly; this is why they are called cyclicals!

When the economy steamrolls even higher, to 5 percent, you have to start selling the stocks of the retailers and the autos because the higher interest rates that are coming are going to impact consumer spending. That drag will cause the earnings estimates to get cut and the M is going to shrink in advance of the E! You can still add to the positions of the deeper cyclical companies and tech companies, though, as their earnings momentum is slower to be broken by Fed tightenings.

By this point, at 6 percent, the Fed should have hiked once, maybe even twice or three or four times. If we are at 6 percent and the tide is coming in and the Fed is still tightening, we have to anticipate that the tide is about to go out—dramatically, as it did in 2000 and 2001 when the Fed sent us into recession by moving interest rates all the way up to 6.5 percent. We have to begin to sell the cyclical stocks and the techies that we accumulated when the economy was just accelerating and we have to anticipate that even as rates go higher, the Fed will soon become too vigilant. The moment after the third tightening is the most perilous moment in all investing. It is the time when I like to stay on the sidelines, build up maximum cash for all but the longest-dated of

my portfolios (my 401[k] and my IRA), and wait. Cash, not even bonds, is king at these junctures. In fact, because the Fed is raising rates regularly at this point, the price you get for your cash, for your money that is being kept in the bank, is beginning to look attractive, especially against the dividends that won't keep up with the Fed rate hikes. Cash is king. I like to presume that after the fifth or sixth tightening, the Fed's actions will have the desired effect. That's because, with short rates so elevated, it becomes prohibitive to build up inventory of just about everything, from stocks with margin loans to copper, plastic, wood, or any other kind of inventory. The business cycle shuts down at high rates because businesses can't afford to borrow to take down merchandise to sell. They also can't afford to bet that if they order a lot of stuff to sell they will do well, because the price of that stuff increases due to inflation. It is the inventory cycle that gets busted by high rates. It always happens. It happened in 1994 and in 2000, the first time with what was known as a "soft landing," meaning that the economy braked nicely, and the second time in a hard landing, where businesses quit taking down any inventory and sales just stopped.

It's at that moment when the economy still appears to be roaring that I switch to buying the most boring consumer staple stocks, the ones that do best without economic strength, the Procters and Kimberlys and Colgates. Then, when these stocks are all at their fifty-two-week highs for several months—it does last that long—when the m's are steepest on them, you sell them, sell them hard, and buy the homebuilders, the real estate investment trusts, the brokers and insurers and the mortgage companies and even those retailers that you threw out when things got too hot. Their time on the wave is now at hand as the tidal process begins again.

For the most part, the mental playbook that I have now put on paper for you rules. The playbook is so powerful that if the big market participants even think there could be rate hikes ahead, if they even *smell* rate hikes, they are going to sell whole groups because they anticipate the decline in the economy. It is incredibly important to have

a sense of where you are in the economic cycle if you are going to pick stocks even for the long term. Otherwise I predict you will get discouraged when you buy Coke and expect it to ramp up only to see Alcoa and International Paper taking off every day while Coke and other growth names languish.

These patterns are burnished into the thinking of all big-time portfolio managers; when these elephants move, they move stocks with them. To ignore their activities—especially when they are so easily predicted and anticipated—is a tremendous waste of money for all investors, short- or long-term. Given that you can set your clock to these patterns, why not take advantage of the big GDP cycles and make some good money at the expense of the elephants who simply can't help themselves. Except for takeovers, their movements are by and large the most important catalysts for large-scale moves in stocks.

The second and by far the most difficult way to predict a big move is to try to figure out possible changes in the E portion of the $E \times M = P$ equation for an individual stock away from the broader economic cycle. This is the method that the vast majority of people on Wall Street—sell side, buy side, hedge funds, mutual funds, strategists—try to live by and, predictably, it is the hardest and least rewarding. Put simply, every brilliant mind on the Street is playing in this field. It is, I am afraid, an almost Sisyphean task and not just because of the bruising competition.

For the longest time, I was able to chat with the chief financial officers of companies to see how their businesses were doing versus their competitors. With this information I was able to build models that showed me what companies might really earn versus what Wall Street thought they would earn. Sometimes I would divine that companies were going to report upside surprises, other times I could figure out when there would be shortfalls. It was never perfect because no CFO was allowed to talk to you during "quiet period" when they were within five weeks of the end of a quarter.

Still, when the companies reported their real earnings, Wall Street was surprised to the upside or the downside and I would sell my stock

into the upside surprises I predicted or cover my short into the downside. There were tremendous and quick profits to be had using this method.

But several years ago the SEC decided that these private conversations should no longer be allowed between private citizens and the CFOs or the CEOs. The SEC passed a rule that said there had to be fair disclosure of data to everyone simultaneously or that no one could get it. That meant that nobody could do homework working with the company to build a better model than anyone else, and the possibility of predicting surprises with help from the company ended for all, including the sell-side analysts who used to cozy up to and have special relationships with management.

That was a bummer for me as a professional, but it has proven a boon to me as an individual investor. Now I know that no one has an edge over anyone else at least as far as what the company might tell them legally. That doesn't mean, though, you can't predict the surprises. It is just either more cerebral or more time-consuming and requires a lot more research.

For example, when I was just starting at Goldman Sachs I was able to catch a big earnings upside in Reebok simply by noticing that Reeboks didn't stay on the shelves during the aerobics boom in the 1980s. Sure, I had to go to a dozen stores and chat up salesfolk to ask, but that's still legal. You can still build a model from the ground up. It just takes a tremendous amount of time and energy to do so, too much time and energy for anyone not doing the research full-time.

Similarly, I had the greatest short of my career by staking out a couple of Gantos, a now-defunct retailer, on several key Saturdays and noticing that no one was buying. My dad and I stationed ourselves right next to the register weekend after weekend for a month at selected Gantos and tallied how much—or in this case how little—was really being purchased. I was able to predict an astounding decline in earnings as the analysts took as gospel from management that the company was doing well. Those big store registers never lie. That's still fair game, too.

But that kind of difficult and time-consuming research is beyond the abilities of most, but not all, everyday investors. The more realistic approach to gaming the E is to try to anticipate *spending* cycles, particularly capital expenditure cycles, and ride the stocks from undervalued to overvalued as it dawns on other market participants that a big earnings cycle is at hand.

For example, the airline business is notoriously cyclical, with a seven fat year, seven lean year cycle almost etched in stone. Boeing, one of America's best companies, has been fairly good at predicting cycles through its own order book. When I detect that Boeing sees a cyclical upturn, I load up on the stocks of all of the companies that make parts for Boeing, all of which tend to be through the floor at the bottom of the cycle. I buy the stocks of companies that make fasteners or screws (Fairchild) or seats (BEA Aerospace) or cockpit instruments (Honeywell) and I wait until they see the orders and then the earnings that those orders provide and then, when everyone starts touting the stocks—usually at least a year into the run—I begin to scale back the holdings and sell into strength. It's tougher than it sounds; I start to sell when all of the analysts are furiously raising estimates and the stocks are expanding by leaps and bounds. But you must sell that strength gingerly, scaling out into the strength so as not to get caught at the top. The keys are to have lean enough inventory of the merchandise when the big Wall Street store is giving it away and have enough inventory so that you have enough to sell when your wares become ultrafashionable again.

There are many big economic cycles like the one in aerospace. Semiconductor equipment cycles, for example, are long and easily playable. When the semiconductor companies begin to do well, they raise money in the public markets to buy equipment. These companies can't resist doing so. You then have to buy the stocks of Applied Material and KLA-Tencor and Kulicke & Soffa and Novellus. However, once Wall Street starts raising too much money for these equipment companies, it is time to leave the table.

My favorite cycle to play is the telco equipment cycle. Here you

have an extremely competitive industry that has lean and fat years. When these big telephone companies are flush they always begin to buy equipment, and you can predict that the earnings estimates for the Nortels and the Lucents and the JDS Uniphases will soar. But when the companies start to get too competitive and the returns aren't there, or when they merge, they will cut back dramatically on equipment spending and the stocks get crushed. You can't judge these vendor companies by the managements; they almost never see it coming and have been known to blow analysts and investors out of the water regularly. You have to watch the customers themselves, the SBC Communications and the BellSouths and the Verizons and the Vodaphones and Nippon Telegraph & Telephones. When they are doing well, that's when you buy the telecom stocks. When they are doing poorly, regardless of what the vendors say, you must sell.

There are many cycles out there that are worth playing. Pharmaceutical companies are constantly introducing new drugs, some of which sell exceedingly well, boosting profits dramatically. And of course, the takeover cycle that I anticipated in the oil patch with Gulf Oil can make you a fortune if you are in a group that's about to consolidate because there are too many players. As I write in 2005 the oil cycle is very much "on," particularly for the under $1 billion equity names. You could have thrown darts at the participants in that cycle in 2004 and crush the S&P 500's return.

In these methods of predicting big moves, the multiple expansion-contraction process and the predictable sector spending cycle technique, it is the anticipation that matters. Once everyone realizes what you anticipated, it is time to take profits.

That makes investing, by the way, a much more lonely and difficult process than most people think. You have to love stocks when people hate them, you have to leave stocks when people love them. That's the most puzzling thing in the world to do because you will always feel alone and isolated. It is amazing, but those are the feelings I always have in my gut before I make the most money. Because I am so public with my ActionAlertsPLUS.com account, I am constantly sell-

ing what's hot and buying what's not, feeling the heat of the investing public telling me how wrong I am. I will know, though, that that's when the biggest gains are about to occur. The day I don't hear the cat-calls is the day I know that I have already missed the big chance for big money.

For many of you, this whole notion of catching cycles of any kind might just not be worth the effort. You simply want to own high-quality stocks all the time and you don't have the time or the inclination to make the switches or play the cycles. It is too labor intensive for you. Or you find it too difficult to fathom the changes and make the calls. That's okay, you can still do fine, maybe even as well as the market, *but you will never beat the market* and you will never catch the big moves that can make you rich in a shorter time than the long-term stock cycles will allow.

So let me tell you a story that might change your mind and get you to think more about these cycles. When I started my hedge fund in 1987, I was determined to buy the most consistent growth companies I could find. I was determined to avoid the rotations, to buy and hold good-quality companies and make money over time. I figured that those growth companies would continue to increase in value over time because the market loves growth so much. Isn't that what great investing was supposed to be about? Don't heed the short term, think long-term!

After two months of running my hedge fund I found myself down 9.9 percent. Unbelievable. I was being taken apart, just annihilated by my growth stocks, like Heinz and Merck and General Mills and Coke. My partnership had a "down 10 percent" clause—I go down below 10 percent and I have to give the money back. It's pretty frightening when you are about to lose your livelihood because of your poor performance; it concentrates the mind about the cycles like nothing else.

What was working? Why, Phelps Dodge and Dow Chemical and Alcoa. These stocks were killing my stocks. I thought it was incredibly unfair given that these big metal and chemical companies didn't have real growth over the long term, certainly not any growth in excess of

the rate at which the gross domestic product of the United States was growing. Their rallies seemed absurd. Didn't any of the buyers understand how they would eventually be led astray by PD and AA? Didn't people just want to buy and hold the great growth companies? Isn't that the best way to get rich?

At the time my girlfriend, Karen Backfisch, was on the trading desk of Steinhardt Partners, where every day she was taking down 500,000-share blocks of Alcoa and Phelps Dodge and Georgia Pacific and International Paper. She read me the riot act when I told her that I was sticking with my consistent growers. She explained to me that the market only likes "consistent" growth during an economic downturn or when the economy is doing nothing. Its first love affair is with "inconsistent growth" during one of its periodic explosions. She traced out a chart for me that I have been using ever since and that you can find on page 115. Put simply, when the economy is growing between 1 and 3 percent, you should own all of the Coke or Pepsi you can get. You should load up on the Pfizers and Mercks and Heinzes. When the economy is growing at a 3–6 percent clip, though, you have to own the cyclical stocks because they will have the best year-over-year comparisons. My future wife convinced me that most people who determine prices in the stock market have no real knowledge of history. They simply look at the number that is reported, and when they see PD .86 versus .38 (as in Phelps Dodge earned 86¢ this quarter versus last year when it earned 38¢), the market will go crazy for Phelps Dodge regardless of whether it will slip back to 38¢ or not by this time next year. While she was, of course, being a tad glib, to ignore these moves, to act as if you can sit out these moves, is the equivalent of saying, "You know what, I don't care if the elephants are about to trample me, I don't care if there is a stampede going on, I am just going to lie here and tough it out in these growth stocks and ignore the pain." How terrific it would be if I could tell you to do the same and you would do it.

Every single investment text I have ever read says you should ignore the thunder and just stay put in growth if not buy more. Every single one! But remember, I don't put much faith in investment con-

ventions. I know better. I know human behavior. I know what happens in real life when you ignore the playbook, when you stick with the so-called secular growth stocks while the elephants are dancing to the cyclical tune. What happens is that you panic. You sell at the worst time, the bottom. You bail. You say, I can't take the pain. I have seen this so many times that it bugs the heck out of me to hear the arid, bloodless graybeards say, "Oh, just ride it out," knowing full well that they aren't! Riding it out is for masochists, and I don't know a lot of masochists when it comes to money. I know that back in 1987, I switched then and there to the stocks that were working and I saved my company. I never again listened to those who advocated riding out the storm in so-called high-quality stocks. Oh, and for the record, my faves never came back; many are still priced at roughly where I sold them almost twenty years ago.

Let me give you another real-life example. A caller rang me up last year during one of my radio sessions where I play "Am I Diversified?" He owned a ton of bank stocks ahead of an imminent series of tightenings. He said he had heard me preach that he should step aside, avoid the pain, that the pain doesn't always produce gain. But he couldn't because he needed the yield that the financials offered, many of which were in excess of 3.5 percent at the time. I laughed. I said, The market works in strange and positive ways. For every major bank stock yielding 3.5 percent, I know an oil stock that yields 3.5 percent. The difference is that the banks are soon going to be yielding 4 percent because those stocks are going down (remember, the dividend stays constant, but you divide it into the stock price to get the yield, and the yield goes up when the denominator—the stock price—goes down) while the oils are going to be yielding 2 percent because they are going higher! My point was that the idea of staying in the financials for the dividends is pointless given the capital depreciation ahead, but if you insisted on yield I know I could find you a like group with a like yield that will go up, not down, ahead of rates.

The Importance of the Fed

We on TV are often accused of spending too much time trying to guess and anticipate the Federal Reserve. Lots of the criticism of the press is on the mark, but the "too-much-Fed-watching" rap sure isn't. Under all the methods I care about—the GDP method, the sector earnings cycle method—the Fed can play a role, either to screw it all up or make it work.

You need to know when the Fed is going to act and which way it is going to move not only because it directly affects what the big boys are going to do, but also because interest rates can be just as important as earnings streams in trying to predict the next big gob of points on a stock.

Interest rates matter intensely when you are trying to anticipate big moves in stocks. They also matter as competition to stocks. When interest rates are high, people prefer bonds to stocks. When the cash rate, or the amount that you get to keep your money in a bank account, skyrockets because the Federal Reserve is tightening rates severely, that can kill even the best stocks. Think about what happened in 2001, when cash gave you a 6.5 percent return. That interest rate helped cause the great turn-of-the-century bear market. Rates matter as a cost of buying stocks; the lower the rates, the more speculative people tend to be because you can borrow money cheaply to buy stocks. Margin buying, using cheap money, fueled the destructive 1999 rally that led to the bear market. I can't stress how important "easy money" from the Fed was in creating the bubble that has since been pricked by none other than much higher Fed rates.

Interest rates are also a major component of what we will pay for future earnings, for the "growth" of the enterprise we are investing in. Remember the process we use to find out what a stock *should* sell for in the future, as opposed to what it sells for now? First we figure out what a company can earn. That's the estimate portion of the price. Then we need to figure out what we will pay for those estimates—the price-to-earnings multiple. To calculate the multiple we take into ac-

count all sorts of considerations for the management, the earnings cycle, the macro economy, any political or economic risk. But what often tends to matter more than anything else is calculating the "discount" rate that we will pay for those earnings, something that is entirely dependent upon prevailing longer-term interest rates. I don't want to bore you with difficult nonarithmetic concerns here, but after we arrive at what we think the earnings will be in the future, and after we consider all the sector, macro, and micro issues that could affect those earnings, we then have to figure out what they are worth in the present to figure out what the price of the equity should be now. It is not enough to know what's in the future, we need to know how to relate that to a current value. We need to know what is called the "present value" of those earnings.

Present value analysis mystifies most people. They don't understand the discount mechanism of rates, and how rates help set the current value of assets. Yet we accept the discount premise intrinsically when it comes to our bank account. Let's use that example to drive home how interest rates help set the prices now for what we will pay in the future. If you are going to put $1 in the bank at a 2 percent rate per annum, you are going to get $1.02 a year later. That $1.02 a year later is worth only $1.00 now. That's another way of saying that the present value of $1.02 a year from now is $1.00. Same with earnings. Let's say we think Maytag could earn $5 in 2010. What's that worth now? How do we discount it back to the present? By using the same prevailing rate we would use for a bond. Stocks are considered "long-dated assets," meaning they are discounting the long-term earnings power of the companies underneath them. Just as we calculate how much $1.02 in the bank is worth today by using 2 percent per annum as a rate, we would look at comparable longer-term bond yields to assess what to pay now for those future earnings.

Normally, in a stable environment where there is low inflation, we would tend to want to pay a lot for those earnings. But at times when inflation is raging and bond prices are going down—yields going higher—we want to pay much less; we want to discount those future

earnings at a higher rate. Again, consider how much you would pay for Maytag this year if it were going to earn $5 a share next year, versus how much you would pay for Maytag this year if it weren't going to earn that $5 until 2010. This is the market's equivalent of a bird in the hand being worth two in the bush!

I don't want to get too technical. I don't want to slide into "Genuine Wall Street Gibberish," as I say on my radio show. For the purposes of trying to catch big moves off of changes in earnings estimates, what you need to know is that when interest rates are moving higher, the multiple you will pay for earnings shrinks. When rates are moving lower, the multiple you pay for earnings expands. Or expressed another way, when rates are going higher we will pay *less* for the future earnings and when rates are going lower we will pay *more* for future earnings. The economy ultimately determines the long-term interest rates, but the Fed controls the short rates *and* can help control inflation. When inflation runs unchecked, rates go higher, and we pay less for those earnings; we "discount" them more. When inflation runs lower, we pay more for the earnings because the discount rate will be lower.

So because of that present value factor we need to assess any signal that gives us the direction of future interest rates. How does this play out in the real market? When interest rates spiked dramatically in 2004, 1994, and 1990, the price-to-earnings multiple shrank for all stocks because that discount rate went up. When interest rates fell in 2003 we paid more for the earnings than we were willing to pay in 2004. We won't pay a lot for future earnings in a high-rate/high-inflation environment, no matter how good those near-term earnings are. In the beginning of 2004 the story was the incredible shrinking M, because the E didn't go down, but the prices did (M = P/E). People new to the game, people who didn't understand the relationship between stocks and interest rates, misinterpreted the price decline of stocks to mean that perhaps a recession was coming and that the E in the equation, the earnings estimates, wouldn't be made. That was nonsense. It was just the discounting mechanism bringing down

prices and chiseling away at the multiple. I call such a contraction in the multiple the silent stock killer because so many people can't see the cause of it—higher rates—until it is too late and stock prices are obliterated. The vast majority of individuals I speak to each week on my radio show pay no attention to rates; the homicidal effect rates can have on prices continually surprises neophytes and even relatively seasoned investors. You have to focus on interest rates if you are going to buy stocks. Or, to put it another way, rates are like the oil in a car. You don't want to bother with it, but if you don't, you know the engine goes bad. If you don't focus on interest rates as the lubricant to your portfolio, your portfolio will most surely go bad, too.

Remember, I am trying with every fiber and sinew to winnow out the stocks that have the greatest chances of losing a ton of points and focus on the stocks that have the greatest chances of gaining big. Knowing when and how aggressively the Fed will move can often be the key determinant, particularly with cyclical stocks, in assessing which equities will make you the most money in the shortest time (and keep you from losing the most money). I wish I could give you a series of indicators that would tell you when the Fed is going to move. The Fed assesses many things: the real interest rates that the market sets, the CPI (Consumer Price Index), the PPI (Producer Price Index), the price of gold, employment growth, wages. What matters if you are going to be picking stocks is that you recognize when inflation is picking up. I don't like to outthink this process, but when the CPI registers four straight upward moves, I think you should expect that the Fed will have to tighten. Remember, the essence of investing is anticipation. You can't wait until the Fed actually moves. You have to move ahead of the Fed if you are going to capture the maximum points. The reason is that the big mutual funds, which buy and sell stocks fairly emphatically if not recklessly, all know this stuff and own so much of each stock that they have to move well in advance of the actual deed. That's fine. We know it; we adjust accordingly.

Think of the Fed as some sort of bizarre schoolteacher who rewards the most stupid and uncooperative students and punishes

those who do the best, or, in the case of the economy, grow the fastest. Most of the time the economy, like students, is average, call it a B or a C. The Fed does nothing when things are average, virtually sits on its hands. When the economy is roaring, an A economy, the Fed gets all furious and starts using its only real instrument to slow things down, its ability to raise short rates. But the Fed rewards a D economy with joyous rate cuts, and if the economy's flunking, as ours was in 2002 after 9/11, the Fed takes rates as low as possible to get the economy moving again.

The effect on the companies is obvious. With cheaper credit companies can refinance, paying off high-interest debt, just as you might refinance your mortgage when rates decline. With cheaper debt companies can expand and hire and take down more inventory to sell at cheaper prices because it doesn't cost as much to borrow to hold inventory. That's how business gets going again. Of course, the companies are hurt when rates go higher as it may become too costly to build inventory or expand. So the Fed slows the economy when it's A rated and speeds it up when the economy's failing. But remember we aren't as interested in the specific impact of interest rates on individual companies as we are in the effect the Fed's moves have on the methods we use to predict outsized stock price moves. We care more about the perception of rising and falling of rates on future earnings than we care about what occurs to the companies, because the perception dictates the price movements.

I emphasize the Fed's actions here because if the economy were always strong, we would need to own only the stocks of the companies that were producing shoot-the-lights-out numbers. But because the Fed gets in the way all the time to slow down the economy or to speed it up when it is lagging, that shoot-the-lights-out method is a dangerous course of action. If you ignored the Fed, for example, you may have stayed fully invested well into 2001, which would have been a disaster for just about every kind of stock, but particularly for those caught in tech spending cycles, even if the textbooks said that you could still make good money in them.

If you want to minimize the Fed as a force—something you do at your own peril—you could lose unfathomable amounts of money in bad times or get blown out of the game entirely. That's why I emphasize both the Fed and these money-making cycles so much. Ignorance—and the buy-and-hold pattern it instills—is *not* bliss. It is why paying attention to your money makes it grow much faster than when you ignore it, and why you can, with some work, consistently beat the market over time.

A third method of divining big moves, an untraditional one I would like to think I have helped pioneer myself, comes from examining a different, unexploited cohort, which I call the undiscovered stocks of unknown companies. Most of the time individuals and institutions are simply trying to gauge and catch the moves of well-known companies with fully valued stocks—solving for M or solving for E, so to speak, trying to figure out the earnings or the multiple to those earnings that investors will pay—in order to gauge the ultimate objective, the price.

But what if there is no E? What if the companies are so new or so down on their luck that there are no earnings to be found, let alone earnings estimates? What if solving for E or M is impossible because E is too far away in the future? That's the case for many, many companies. Does that mean we have to give up and stay with the tried-and-true where the E and M are predictable and therefore the price somewhat logical if not perfect? Hardly. In fact, while these moves can be rewarding, as we have demonstrated above, they are dwarfed by the gains that can be had by newer companies without an E to game or an M to solve for. In fact, even after companies become discovered, their stocks can still be undervalued. We can make fabulous wine from these ignored and scorned vineyards, but we must also accept the fact that when we labor in the out-of-the-way fields we must be much more careful. We need both a buy and a sell price; we can't simply buy and forget about them. Many of these unseasoned stocks will poison our portfolios if they stay there too long.

Yet, if we don't toil in the unknown/undervalued company cohort, we are going to leave too much money on the table. Remember, they don't asterisk how fast you make the money—months, weeks, days, even hours—and they take it at the bank regardless of the velocity with which you minted it.

If my unknown company/undervalued stock terminology confuses you, it's because I don't like to use the term that Wall Street usually puts on these stocks: small capitalization stocks. I don't like to focus on small capitalization stocks; I like to focus on stocks that have a small capitalization that shouldn't be small because the companies underneath them have too much potential to be stuck with such an appellation.

My method puts a premium on identifying small capitalization stocks before they begin their journey to mid and large cap. As Willie Sutton said about robbing banks, that's where the money is.

It always amazes me that so many people accept the fact that investing in solid, well-known companies, even with the two ways we described before, produces the greatest return. It's simply counterintuitive. The well-known companies tend to be companies with billions of dollars in market capitalization, sometimes hundreds of billions. On a percentage basis, the shuffling back and forth of stocks that are already in the S&P 500 can certainly yield rewards. However, the biggest rewards come from identifying stocks of unknown companies at the beginning of their journey, when they might be worth no more than a hundred million dollars and are undiscovered, unknown, unloved, and, most important, *uncovered* by Wall Street. These situations have the least information, the most ignorance, and the greatest potential.

This method understands and anticipates that the real value of Wall Street is its ability to promote themes and companies that need money once they catch fire. This method tries to anticipate which of the themes and sectors will be the next Game Breakers. Wall Street is fabulous at taking the seemingly mundane and making it exciting and investible. It loves new concepts that need money to grow: teen fash-

ion, arts and crafts, big and tall, low-carb food, Mexican food, Asian food, down-home food, Indian gaming, nanotechnology, video on demand, homeland security devices, alternative energy ideas, you name it. All of these trends took many low-dollar, low-capitalization stocks on the journey from small to mid cap and, in some cases, large cap. Yet, for the most part investment professionals and amateurs alike shun this cohort as too dangerous and too speculative. Again, they consider it akin to wagering. They prefer to dwell in the vineyard of the perfect, the perfect companies with the perfect information and the perfect values. I like to dwell in the unexplored wilderness where much less is known about stocks and the information—and therefore the prices—can be wildly off the mark. They irrationally fear the losses that could come from the single-digit stocks that don't make it; they act as if stocks can go to minus something.

For the longest time, academics claimed that all stocks are priced perfectly, that there is no information edge available. You can't beat stocks, they say, so you might as well join them, perhaps through investing in an S&P 500 index fund. As you can tell, I have developed some ways to game the big moves from the discovered cohort, but I would be remiss if I told you that most investors can consistently beat the professionals within the vineyard of the known. But in the unknown cohort when the information is available, more money can be made here. Other forces, however, including crowd psychology—behavioral finance—rule this cohort. Given that we know that people inherently judge risk incorrectly, that they inherently buy at the top, that they can't restrain themselves from taking risks, particularly when they are losing, we can begin to predict patterns of behavior that can be anticipated to make you money. We know, for instance, that crowds get euphoric over certain concepts. We know that individuals are tragically overconfident when they should be underconfident, that they are swept away in ways that dwarf the efficient market and make it tremendously inefficient to the academic observer, but not to those who understand the patterns and see them over and over again. Put simply, the academics believe that the "market" will exert rational

pricing on all securities, but the "market" is rational only for the thousand or so largest stocks. After that, emotions and psychology play a large role, which you can profit from. When he was explaining why short sellers who bet against the irrationalities of the market often get blown up doing so, John Maynard Keynes wrote, "Markets can remain irrational longer than you can remain solvent." I stand that logic on its head and say that irrational markets can last long enough for you to get in and make hefty profits before you have to get out. Of course, my method will seem like gambling to those who think that all stocks are perfect and all behavior is rational. All I am recommending, though, is speculating prudently—meaning taking into account the behavioral tics of other investors and exploiting those tics to your own profit.

This third method of getting in and out before markets grow rational is perhaps the single best way to make huge sums in the shortest time possible. I am confident that the academics who research behavioral finance will one day exert themselves and trump the rational/efficient folks. When that happens my techniques will be the equivalent of "fundamental" investing. In the meantime, though, let's just make the money and forget about being blessed by the Ivory Tower.

I know that I never cared about such constraints at my hedge fund. I was willing at times to put up to 20 percent of my fund into these potentially gigantic rewarders despite their lack of long-term fundamentals. I had the freedom to do so because no one was watching over me saying, "You can't make that kind of money in a Viant or a Webvan"—to name two bankrupt dot-coms—"knowing that they will eventually burn out." No one was critiquing me or my buys of stocks that were unlikely to amount to anything in the long term, but that in the interim gave you a superb return as long as you didn't overstay your welcome.

At my hedge fund I called this the search for the "red hots," the stocks that were like red-hot potatoes: you could own them for a few days, weeks, or months, but you didn't want to get stuck holding the hot potato unless you had taken your existing capital and a profit out of the situation before letting it ride.

When I started out at my hedge fund, my goal was to try to game the promotional aspects of Wall Street brokerage firms, to try to get into the heads of the analysts who would recommend stocks because they wanted the banking business of the companies underneath them or because they were hoping to attract new companies to come public with their firms. I was excellent at spotting this kind of inherent corruption that existed at all the big firms and was able to game my fair share of upgrades before they happened, a perfectly legal psyching-out of the process. But Eliot Spitzer, the New York State attorney general, ended that game when he determined that the analysts were no more honest than movie critics who are employed by the movie companies themselves. Sure, occasionally they will like movies that are good, but far more often they will push movies that are bombs because that's what they are compensated for. Of course, in the case of a movie, you shell out ten bucks for something you don't like and you can leave, big deal. But when it is your investment money, and stocks are big money, you can shell out hundreds of thousands of dollars listening to corrupt research that was meant only to please the corporate finance client. With the research departments no longer allowed to shill nakedly for their clients, the predictive value of the Wall Street promotion machine is now nil. And believe me, the research game as I knew it has changed for good. You go to jail if you violate these rules. Wall Street analysts have calculated that no amount of bonus money from corporate finance is worth going to jail for.

But that doesn't mean we can't anticipate another kind of promotion that is just as powerful, in fact, more powerful, than the corrupt Wall Street promoters. We can anticipate what the crowd wants, the chattering classes, those people who can't control themselves because they think that every idea is the next Microsoft or Amgen. We can do it because we have enough empirical data about what they like and what sells for them, what piques their interest and gets them hyping things on the Internet, so that we can be ahead of the crowd and ride the wave that they create.

These kinds of stocks are another variety of "Game Breaker." They

are like supernovas, stars that shine bright for a short period of time before they explode from their own heat and gas. Game Breakers exist because the most compelling mantra of all investing is "Find the next Home Depot" or "Find the next Genentech" or Yahoo!, etc. Given the fantastic returns those famous stocks have produced, the search is logical even if in its suspension of skepticism it seems, at times, to be lacking in rigor. If we graft a buying discipline on what could look like the next big idea, the next Game Breaker, and tack on a selling discipline that cuts out the losers quickly and lets the winners run, we can make consistently good money simply piggybacking on others who are trying to find the next hot stock. We can limit our downside and, on the upside, take out our stake and then play with the house's money.

Since retiring from the hedge fund I have developed a keen sense of what could look like the next Game Breaker; I have honed the characteristics and systematized the otherwise haphazard process of culling the stocks to separate the potential diamonds from the dirt that surrounds them. This Game Breaker search tries to anticipate crowd psychology. To put it in the language of fashion, which is what this method attempts to exploit, we are trying to figure out which fads are going to sweep Wall Street and take companies' stocks up in wild excess of what would normally be expected. It is important to get into these stocks early, before they receive too much scrutiny from Wall Street, because that's when the best moves can be had.

For a new sector to get the attention necessary to be able to go from a small unknown idea to a mid cap idea with some real heft, the sector has to have what Andy Grove called "10× potential" in his excellent book *Only the Paranoid Survive.* In that book Grove postulates that there are some tremendous ideas out there, like Internet browsers, e-mail, the microprocessor—total game changers. "Technology changes all the time," Grove writes. "Most of this change is gradual: competitors deliver the next improvement, we respond, they respond in turn and so it goes. However, every once in a while, technology changes in a dramatic way. Something can be done that could not be done before, or something can be done 10× better, faster or

cheaper than it would have been done before." These "strategic inflection points" don't have to be limited to technology, Grove says. They can revolutionize everything from the movies (silent to talkies) to phone companies (the creation of competitive phone companies through government deregulation being a classic example). The trick for Grove was to recognize that these changes could come from left field and then learn how to anticipate them. The trick for us is to play in left field and see the ball better and earlier than others.

Of course, there are lots of ideas out there that aspire to be 10× ideas that never get there, but my method builds in those losses and accepts them. My method exploits the crowd's inability to distinguish a 10× idea from a lot of ideas that just fizzle and gets you in and out before the fizzling starts.

Let's take one of the more current fixations, nanotechnology, a science of manipulating small particles to make new compounds. Of course, the cynical trader in me says that this is simply the science of manipulating stocks so that more can be formed and bigger underwriting profits can be accrued. As is typical with the stocks of an unknown but exciting new sector, almost anything "nano" will get taken up. The trick is to figure out ahead of time what would have the most credibility if it were rewarded with a market capitalization that might be attractive to Wall Street, which typically doesn't want to touch anything smaller than a billion dollars in market cap.

In the initial stages, I examine which companies have a modicum of revenues, decent bloodlines when it comes to managements, and scientific prospects that sound somewhat legitimate. I do that by reading trade journals, newspaper and magazine articles, and academic studies on what might be working and what isn't. Typically there are a host of these kinds of stocks, many selling below $10. I like to place bets on "the field," meaning that I don't know which stocks will ultimately gain the most credence. To me this process resembles what venture capitalists do, except with odds slightly better for me because there is a ready public exit market whenever I need it for the losers, while the winners can more than make up for the losers. Venture cap-

italists ride the bad ones to zero; we can bail out whenever we realize they aren't going to fulfill the 10× potential.

If the venture capital analogy loses you, try this one: It's like fishing in a school of bluefish; it's impossible not to catch something when you are in the frenzied field. You've got to get that hook, line, and sinker in the water when a group like nanotechnology bites. You must seize it if you want to rack up big percentage gains in a remarkably short period of time, which is always what I am shooting for when I buy stocks.

Using the example of nanotechnology, to get the players for the field bet, I simply do a Google search for the companies involved, then find out which are public and examine their bona fides as described above. If I am early enough—judged by whether any major Wall Street firm yet covers the group—I pounce. If there is a lot of coverage of the group, particularly by the main firms based in New York, not just the regional firms from the hinterlands, I skip it. Major coverage means I am already too late to the party. The idea's been fully exploited.

Typically, if the science is sexy enough, or the demand strong enough, you can easily anticipate the group gaining steam. You see the trading volume of the stocks pick up, you see the chatter on the stock boards pick up, particularly the Yahoo! boards where my assistants trawl for comments, and you start seeing the more inventive Web sites, like TheStreet.com, writing up the ideas.

As soon as the companies in the cohort get some critical mass, the investment bankers at the regional brokers—not the ones in New York; that happens later—prowl the country and the world for companies that look like nanotechnology companies they can take public or write up with the hopes of getting some of their business down the road.

As stupid and as knee-jerk as this sounds, it is important at this moment to own as many nanotechnology stocks as you can because even the currently hobbled and uncorrupted Wall Street promotion machine can still be effective in moving stocks up when there are compelling technologies and big dollars on the line.

I continue to accumulate the stocks until the analysts at the major firms start their promotion and I stay long the group, that is, I hold these stocks, until the group is fished out, producing some of the best gains imaginable. How do you know when the group is fished out, that is, that the big gains have been made, when you can't trust the multiple process to yield any limits given that the group tends to have no E to put an M on? I let the Street's greed—almost as good a yardstick as its myopia in measuring stocks on earnings growth—tell me when to get out. During the expansion/frenzy process, the merchandise gets created at a fast and furious pace. Underwriting after underwriting occurs as the group goes higher and higher.

I can always tell when the frenzy's about to crash, though, by measuring supply and demand. Right near the absolute top—it's too difficult to call the exact top, and I have done that only once in my life, on March 15, 2000—the underwritings, all of which were fantastic to participate in, begin to fail. Merchandise that was considered "hot," meaning that it went to a premium almost immediately after it was launched, begins to sag. Deals open up and then slip to or below their deal prices. Secondaries—offerings of stocks already public—begin to pop up like mad as insiders, who can sell on those deals but couldn't sell previously because they were locked up on the initial public offerings—dump their shares. The secondaries don't stop despite the hammering they do to the stocks because the insiders know the pieces of paper are incredibly overvalued and want to get out.

At the exact top of the dot-com bubble, for example, every deal, every piece of merchandise, started failing or dropping below the level at which it was priced. None of the deals was working. That was the signal to get out. Supply had overwhelmed demand.

I have gotten into trouble with the intelligentsia and the pundits of the stock world because I tend to press the envelope of these stocks as aggressively as possible right to the very end of when you can still make money. I do that because that's when the gains are most mighty, as short sellers, who are always too eager to sell overvalued merchan-

dise, short and then cover the stocks higher because the pain of short-ing them is too great.

I take heat because it looks like I am recommending and buying the most overvalued stocks in the world relative to the companies un-derneath. But as I have stated over and over again, there is a world of difference between the companies and the pieces of paper that trade on behalf of them, and the biggest money is made exploiting those differences at crucial times. In fact, the rate of return of playing this promotion game, particularly if you can catch it *before* it starts, when you have undervalued stocks of unknown companies, is the single most lucrative game that can be played with the market. The purists hate this and hate to admit that the percentage gains from these levels dwarf any other in the investment process; heck, they think it is pure gambling! Again, I point out that if you are willing to speculate pru-dently, with rules, and obey the sell discipline, you should not care if the companies of the stock you buy ultimately ever amount to a hill of beans. They probably won't. Who cares? You will have made so much money exploiting potentially worthless pieces of paper that what hap-pens to the companies is irrelevant. You simply need to be able to see the world through the eyes of the optimists and recognize what they are willing to embrace without any skepticism. At the same time you must combine that rose-colored-glasses approach with the cunning and rigor that will allow you to anticipate when the jig is up, and many—but not all—of the companies are exposed as frauds or jokes. You can ride the 10× wave as long as you get out before it crashes, or before it is clear that only a handful of real companies is going to ben-efit. That's right—some companies actually do turn out to be the next Microsofts and Home Depots, and with my buy-sell discipline de-scribed later, you should still be able to hold on to some stock after taking profits off the table. You could end up with a portfolio of Yahoo!, eBay, and Amazon, as I did at my hedge fund, playing with the house's money while I shorted the junk mercilessly into the single digits.

It is at the moment when these kinds of stocks with no earnings look like they are going to infinity that the merchandise from all of the crummy and ersatz companies bulges from the woodwork and you have to scram as fast as you can. You have to be prepared to love the stocks at one moment and leave them unmercifully the next. You may have to flip on a dime; flexibility is everything when you trade these kinds of names.

How spectacular can the gains be if you initially suspend the skepticism and accept the possibilities out there? How fantastic can the gains be if you find the unknown and undervalued stocks ahead of others, simply because you are willing to accept that there might be a 10× idea out there? How much money can you make anticipating that something will be adopted by the masses as a potential 10×er? Remember, potential is all you need because with my sell discipline, I promise you will get out ahead of when the cataclysm strikes, or at least be playing with the house's money.

Consider the two charts on pages 141 and 142. The first one shows some spectacular moves I was able to anticipate at my hedge fund and in my writings over the course of the last decade, along with the duration of those moves and the gains that could have been had by the nimble in an amazingly short time. The second chart is the original list of companies I put together at the dawn of the dot-com period simply by reading the prospectuses at the time and trying to figure out who would be regarded as the providers of the picks and axes for the Internet gold rush. In that case, I and a partner, Matt Jacobs, who ran my research department at Cramer, actually created a rotisserie league—yep, like in baseball or football—where we had a mythical pool of money and had to draft players for the team. While we were drafting, the stocks were going up so fast that we quickly changed it to real dollars and were able to make a fantastic rate of return in an incredibly short period.

You can see how you would have done in like periods investing in the S&P 500, the perfect proxy for the stocks out there. The S&P doesn't come near these stocks. The gains on these speculative stocks

The Original Red Hots and the Gains They Made

Stock Symbol	8/30 1999	Share Price on Date 11/30 1999	2/29 2000	5/31 2000	Increase or Decrease in Share Price After 3 Months	6 Months	9 Months
ARBA	267.5	361.1248	1058	417	35%	296%	56%
BRCD	179.5	289.9376	578.2504	471.7504	62%	222%	163%
BRCM	125.3126	179.0626	394.75	260.125	43%	215%	108%
CMTN	3015.625	2085.9375	4346.875	4178.125	−31%	44%	39%
CNXT	371.9604	607.4418	1007.278	385.7364	63%	171%	4%
EXDSQ	19.0313	26.9531	71.1875	35.2813	42%	274%	85%
EXTR	65.625	66.375	111.25	48.875	1%	70%	−26%
JDSU	211.4376	457.5	1054.5	704	116%	399%	233%
JNPR	210.0624	277.125	822.9378	525.5628	32%	292%	150%
NTOP	72.625	58	57.875	29.5	−20%	−20%	−59%
OPWV	1072.125	2610	2513.25	1258.875	143%	134%	17%
PMCS	94.5	103.0626	386.125	306.5	9%	309%	224%
QCOM	183	362.3124	569.75	265.5	98%	211%	45%
QLGC	174	226.25	624	196.5	30%	259%	13%
RBAKQ	56.25	69.9688	149.25	83.875	24%	165%	49%
RHAT	75.5626	210	121.375	32.125	178%	61%	−57%
SPX	1324	1388	1366	1420	5%	3%	7%
VRSN	105.375	185.8126	506	270.75	76%	380%	157%
ZOOXQ	89.75	79	66.25	26.625	−12%	−26%	−70%

are so magnificent that you would have to be crazy not to want to try to get some and lock them in. You get in, you get out, and you sit in cash until the next wave appears. Mind you, this is not backdated stuff like so many huge gains that advisers brag to you that you *could* have had if you had used their service. These are gains that were had! I actually owned and recommended these stocks to others in the electronic pages of RealMoney.com. I simply got out in time, although at the moment I pulled the sell trigger, the move looked incredibly foolish if not actually traitorous to the cause. I took tremendous heat

The New Crop of Red Hots

Stock Symbol	Start Date	Start Price	Finish Date	Finish Price	% Gain	S&P Gain Same Period
BLTI	12/02	$5.00	1/04	$21.29	326%	31.58%
CHINA	10/02	$2.00	7/03	$14.46	623%	30.58%
CPHD	11/03	$5.00	1/04	$13.21	164%	7.42%
DNA	11/99	$160.00	3/00	$469.00	193%	−0.40%
EGHT	10/03	$2.50	11/03	$7.52	201%	4.24%
FARO	1/03	$2.00	1/04	$33.23	1562%	25.70%
FWHT	10/02	$3.50	9/03	$27.27	679%	30.69%
HLYW	4/01	$1.80	6/02	$20.68	1049%	−8.74%
ICOS	3/03	$15.00	6/03	$45.17	201%	24.69%
IOM	1/95	$6.00	5/96	$324.00	5300%	45.92%
MACE	4/04	$2.20	4/04	$10.15	361%	−1.79%
MAMA	2/04	$4.00	4/04	$15.90	298%	−0.25%
MICC	3/03	$1.25	4/04	$27.80	2124%	2.92%
SCHN	12/02	$15.00	1/04	$124.56	730%	24.79%
SINA	10/02	$3.00	9/03	$43.57	1352%	28.58%
SIRI	12/99	$26.00	3/00	$65.06	150%	−3.49%
SOHU	10/02	$2.00	7/03	$42.68	2034%	27.40%
SSTI	6/99	$1.75	6/00	$36.25	1971%	10.19%
SWIR	5/03	$4.00	4/04	$45.03	1026%	21.79%
TASR	7/03	$15.00	4/04	$356.10	2274%	17.20%
TBUS	3/04	$2.00	4/04	$14.27	614%	3.43%
UTSI	9/02	$12.50	8/03	$45.36	263%	15.15%
XMSR	11/02	$2.50	1/04	$30.96	1138%	23.12%

when I said in March 2000 that the jig is up, you have to sell; the heat from those last gains was just plain scorching. But if you understand my style and recognize that you are being a pig if you overstay those huge gains, you will recognize that the gains are so outsized as to be well worth the risk that some stocks won't appreciate at all.

As you can see, if you bought the red hots or the Game Breakers and then sold them and invested in T-bills after each one until the next one bubbled up, you absolutely clobbered the averages. Empirically, the outsized returns simply can't be denied. So then why don't more people seek out these stocks? Why is the investing intelligentsia so unwilling to embrace a Game Breaker strategy? I think it's because such a strategy requires two decisions, a buy and a sell. The traditional buy-and-hold approach to investing, which I scorn, simply doesn't consider any purchase of a stock that requires a later sell as part of the investment process. That's considered wagering and therefore beneath the strictures and gospel of traditional investing *even though it slaughters traditional investing when it comes to returns*, which is and will always be the *only* way to measure performance.

To those who still insist that it is impossible to identify and isolate the Game Breakers before they happen, consider the stories we highlight on my CNBC show. Anyone who watches knows we frequently vet these small caps before they take off on their trajectory. Take the stock of Taser, which I discovered on national TV when it was less than a $100 million company after I had the company's management on my CNBC show.

After studying the company's fundamentals and its technicals—including the small number of shares outstanding—I said it could easily go to $1 billion in a short time. It was not hard to see that Taser could put on a lot of capitalization. It had a unique product, a good buzz—remember we are anticipating fashion—and, best of all, an extremely limited float (number of shares outstanding), so if some institutions tried to buy it they would have to take the stock up beyond what most thought was possible. Six weeks later the stock became a $1 billion market capitalization stock as the frenzy took over. When it got to $1 billion, I said enough was enough and suggested people take profits, that the frenzy had grown out of control. It peaked shortly thereafter and declined precipitously, as these stocks often do when

they reach the $1 billion level and the volume expands, signaling that there is, at last, too much float and the stock has finished its upward trajectory.

Getting in and getting out in time is possible and doable if you follow my buy and sell disciplines.

For two years people have been buying Sun Microsystems because it is a nice low-dollar stock. For two years it has been among the most active stocks on the NASDAQ. And for two years it has done nothing. That's because we are late to the game of Sun. It's an old stock, one that has already had its day. Same with Gateway. Or EMC. I am looking for stocks with velocity, stocks that can move, and move quickly, not quagmire stocks that sit and move in small increments. Low price alone does not make a stock a good investment.

What are the ingredients for the recipe of a mass-psychology-driven move upward? What should you be looking for in order to spot these huge gainers ahead of the monster leaps? I break it down like this:

40 percent management. This includes speaking with the company and evaluating management ownership and recent changes in ownership, ability to sell the story, and accessibility of information on the company. The salability of the story and the credibility of management are subjectives that can't truly be measured. They provide the springboard for all other work on the topic. I talk to the management of almost every company I can get on the phone; firsthand knowledge is important when you are riding these rockets.

30 percent fundamentals. That means cash-flow growth, earnings growth/potential, balance sheet, liquidity. The stocks that could turn into Game Breakers tend to have real financials; they are not shell companies. At times they have real profits; they always have revenues and rapid revenue growth. They are not just penny stocks thrust upon the market by the fraudsters in the boiler room.

15 percent technical analysis. This includes stock momentum, support levels, simple chart reading. I am not a chartist, but I am looking

for stocks that have been basing for a long time. I want to see stocks that could break out or are about to soar if the crowd lights a match under them. Consider the chart work the search for a bag of Kingsford Match Light charcoal before the match gets struck.

15 percent what I call "TheStreet.com alpha factor." That's a proprietary measure I have created based on the stock's float, low volume relative to the float, how the stock has reacted to strong news in the past, and the short interest ratio. It is a measurement of the potential "short" pressure on the name, meaning whether there is enough stock out there, physically enough stock, to absorb the buyers' demands without it flying through the roof. This factor is a precursor to a stock's velocity, a tell that allows you to approximate how fast a stock can go from zero to sixty, if you will, without gravity or stock supply interrupting. These stocks work only when the size of the stock is "too small" for the concept and has to be supersized quickly by the crowd. That's one of the reasons I like to work off a screen that yields stocks that have a minimum of 100,000 shares, $100 million in market cap, and a price between $1 and $15. That's where most of these stocks live. Supply—merchandise for sale—has to be hard to come by, and when it isn't hard to come by, the move is probably already over. Supply must be so tight that when a buyer of 5,000 shares comes in, the stock is tough to find without moving it up to where sellers are. That's the Match Light scenario in action.

Consider the gauntlet we put Taser through. First, the company had seasoned management that had been in the business of developing stun guns for years but had not been able to crack any major police market. The balance sheet and the cash flow were superb. The stock had been basing for ages and most of it was held by just a few people, including insiders. Given the incredible news backdrop—that police departments all over the country were suddenly united in adopting Tasers because the number of fatal police shootings is a politically charged issue that hurts the overall functioning of the police and the elected officials—once one or two major police departments went to

Taser, it wasn't much of a leap of faith to think that there would be many others behind them. The Miami force, known as both progressive and reformist, gave the signal when it picked Taser over the standard handgun for its manslaughter-plagued officers. Given the "tight" float (there were barely 1.5 million shares outstanding) and the demands on that float, it was, in essence, a predictable short squeeze that created instant wealth as the stock galloped from $100 million to $1 billion. It ramped and kept ramping until the market was overwhelmed with supply and the move was over, even though the news background stayed positive. How could we measure when the supply had caught up with demand? The explosion in volume told us that the stock had at last found a level where more wanted out than before; that changed the balance and left the stock hanging too limply. If we had waited until the fundamentals turned (the company would soon begin to lose business because of fears that Taser might be thought of as an instrument of torture and because the stock's capitalization gave it no room to lose any contract in any major metro area) we would have given back much of the easy gain.

What's working right now at this very minute, you ask? Tough question, because this is a moment-to-moment cohort with no room for buying and holding. That doesn't mean, though, that I can't be toiling in this vineyard for you anyway. For those of you who are Web savvy, because you have bought this book I will give you this URL: www.thestreet.com/stocksunderten. It allows you to participate for free in a service that isolates the potential next 10×ers before they occur and while they are still under $10. It is called the "StocksUnder$10" electronic newsletter, and while I would love to give you a list right here of what fits, the short time frame for selecting such winners makes it impossible to do anything other than send you to the site with my compliments. What's working is too fluid, changes too often. Try it out. You will see that this type of investing—gambling, if you like—is actually far more predictable and gameable than the Wall Street experts think. The next Game Breakers are out there. Like a good venture capitalist, you can own a bunch of them with this ser-

vice, and you can get out of the losers before they crash and stay with the winners as they produce ever bigger gains.

As is so often the case, the process seems counterintuitive to many investors, who are often caught at the top when playing these stocks without strict rules regarding losses and without regard to the fundamentals, which, as always, do matter. That's why I have taken to using the metaphor of the Holland Tunnel Diner to explain this kind of investing to the public. After a brutal night in the city where we'd drunk too much, my wife and I used to like to stop at the Holland Tunnel Diner, a grungy place with a red-hot griddle, for a couple of egg sandwiches to sop up the inebriation. I used to marvel at that griddle man because that griddle was so hot it could fry an egg to perfection in what I measured to be nine seconds. But if the egg was left on for a tenth second, the griddle man would burn the bejesus out of it.

When you are playing the crowd promotion game, when you are solving for M without an E, you've got to be that griddle man at the Holland Tunnel Diner. You have to play it until the heat gets so hot that it makes a perfect egg sandwich, but you must bolt from the griddle before you overstay for even one second. Otherwise you could wreck your whole portfolio.

Fortunately, unlike the Holland Tunnel Diner, our griddle emits warnings. For individual Game Breaker stocks we see the volume expand; we see the secondaries get filed; we notice the insiders bailing. For the group moves, we see new underwritings and we see those fail as the IPOs go to a discount to price almost immediately. These pitfalls are obvious to anyone paying attention not to the companies themselves, but to the supply and demand in the marketplace. When the secondaries break down at inception and the primaries, or IPOs, retreat to a discount immediately, those are signs that things have overheated and you have to go elsewhere pronto. Don't worry, it is incredibly easy to spot these warning signs. With sector moves it's the moment when underwritings are coming through the chute like torrential rain only to sink in the muddy discount almost immediately. Every single group move of consequence has experienced this pattern,

where you still have time to get out before dreadful financial consequences occur. It is usually at this moment that the press discovers the trend and there are dozens of articles everywhere about the "craze" that is no longer a craze but is a solid idea that is going to produce the next Home Depot or Genentech or Microsoft. That's the moment when the skeptics seem silly and the "new era" folks seem most wise. That's the moment when it looks like money grows on low-hanging branches and you don't need a ladder to pick it off.

When you hear that kind of talk, when you read that kind of gibberish, be prepared to get the hell out of the diner or pay the price for the burned egg sandwich.

6

STOCK-PICKING RULES

to

LIVE BY

You now know all the strategies I know about finding the biggest gains in stocks. Now, what tactics do you use to keep those gains and to sell before your gains turn to losses.

When I started writing for TheStreet.com eight years ago, I entitled my column "Wrong" because I believed fervently that if you lost money, even if only for a day, it would be "wrong." As a hedge fund manager I thought there was no excuse to lose money on trading. None. Although of course it happened all the time. That didn't make it forgivable, though.

As a hedge fund manager, managing impatient wealthy money (and, by the way, all wealthy money is impatient), I had little tolerance for losses. I could say only so many times, "Look, I really believe if we wait long enough we can have a home run here." At times the speed of the gains was more important than the size of the gains. The preoccupation with near-term performance was amazing to me and gripped me as soon as I started my fund in 1987. What rich people cared about was being with the "hot hand," with who was making money now,

hand over fist, who was beating everyone else *now*. It was so NFL-like, you were either the champion or "they," the investors, went home with someone else.

When I started running other people's money I thought I could report yearly. But no one would give me money unless I agreed to report quarterly. Heck, it was their money, so naturally I agreed. A couple of years into the process and the next thing I know, they want reports monthly. A few years later and they want weekly. In my last few years many of the partners wanted daily performance. They didn't want to wake up one day and find they had lost money, so they grilled me endlessly about how we were doing. As someone who could go long or short, I knew that meant that when the market was up they expected me to make money and when the market was down they expected me to make money. If I could short and the market dropped 2 percent, they expected me to make 2 or 3 percent. If the market rallied 2 or 3 percent they expected to hear that they made 4 percent.

I used to complain to my wife that I had become a dancing bear *and* a dancing bull, a circus animal. I had to deliver results constantly. With that kind of partner-fueled obsession you are driven to trade. You can't let positions run against you, even for a minute, or you risk remonstration at the close of the market (I wouldn't let the partners speak to me when the market was open). You have to stop out all losses before they become consequential, even if it is for positions that you believe in. You can't sit in a good position, an AT&T Wireless, for example, while it goes down and you build it up, because the partner critics won't tolerate the short-term unrealized loss. They think that any loss on the way to riches is "wrong." You have to book every gain as quickly as it can be taken, lest it be taken away. I had to expand my trading day to between 4:00 a.m. and 11:00 p.m., trading in any market that was open—Finland, Japan, Hong Kong—just to be able to rack up enough short-term gains to please the partners.

There is no doubt that the model I adopted, quick trading gains whenever possible, is a good one that led to immense riches. But it isn't at all replicable for you, unless you want to give up every aspect of

your life—including your family, as I did—to succeed. The price is just too high for a model of extreme short-term performance, even if it delivers above-average returns. When I quit my hedge fund at the end of 2000, I vowed that I would never again put myself in that position. I knew that such a short-term trading style was not sustainable and would not even necessarily beat a longer-term, more tax-advantaged style of investing. I had an opportunity, not long after I retired from the hedge fund, to manage money in a slower fashion, at a mutual fund. There I wouldn't be taking 20 percent of the gains, both realized and unrealized, as I was at my hedge fund. I would be taking only 1 percent of the entire asset base as a fee. That intrigued me, until I recognized two terrible aspects of the mutual fund business: One, I would have to be selling my fund constantly, and two, I would have to be accepting money all of the time, regardless of whether I needed it or could use it.

As difficult as it was as a hedge fund manager with daily demands on performance, I could see where these two demands, the selling demand and the imperative to take in more money all of the time, could be disastrous to performance. I rarely, if ever, opened my hedge fund to new money. I insisted that you be nominated by a partner in the fund already, as a way to be able to keep the asset base from growing too quickly. Nothing's worse than taking in too much money when you can't handle it. Almost all my temporary bouts with underperformance came when I took in new chunks of money and couldn't adjust to the new position size. My goal as a hedge fund manager was to make 24 percent after all fees, year after year. That was what I had done initially and I thought it was a great goal to maintain. But making 24 percent when you are running $10 million or $100 million is quite different from when you are running $250 million or $500 million, let alone the billions that all of the successful mutual funds have under management. At my hedge fund initially I could make $20,000 a day and hit my benchmark. By the time I quit I needed to make $423,000 every day to make my "quota." I did it, but it was incredibly hard.

Given the incentive of the mutual fund model, though, which pays

you for asset growth through sales more than for performance, you are setting yourself up to underperform the averages. If I kept growing I would have had to be making a million dollars a day just to stay even with my record. The biggest enemy of great returns is the law of large numbers; it's simply too hard for most mortals to beat the market when they are running gigantic sums, particularly when those sums are coming in over the transom every day. Especially when you are out there glad-handing to raise more money when you should be inside analyzing companies.

So, I decided to heck with it. I'm not running other people's money in a hedge fund manner; too stressful. And I am not going to run other people's money in a mutual fund manner; too prone to underperformance. What's the point of playing the game if you aren't going to make big money, bigger than the next guy?

Instead, what I decided to do was free myself of the constraints of both business models. I would run money myself, my money, and I would do all of the things that I couldn't do that constrained my performance at the hedge fund. I would build big positions in companies I loved and own them over time regardless of the short-term vicissitudes. I would stop worrying about the day-to-day performance and concentrate on long-term performance. I would no longer blast as "wrong" short-term glitches on the road to long-term wins. I would have a trading discipline and an investing discipline commensurate with this new, commonsensical view, and I would make money both short- and long-term when I thought it was right, not when they, the investors, thought it was right.

In short, I became, in a word, *you*. And you know what I discovered? Being a private investor like you beats both models. You can easily outperform the short-term-obsessed hedge fund manager who is always looking over his shoulder trying to please the partners. And you can totally trump the mutual fund model with its endless obsession with growing assets under management and salesmanship.

Strangely, many of you have no idea how good you have it. I take calls from people on my radio show who complain that such and such

a stock is going against them or that it is dropping when it should be rallying. I will say, "Don't you believe, don't you have conviction?" If they say no, I say, "Well, by all means sell it." But if you are on your own, and you like the company underneath, and the stock is being marked down because of the occasional craziness of the market, that's an opportunity, a blessing, a gift! Most people just can't run their own money well, though. They just don't have the qualities or the rules they need—the discipline to see it through and to beat all of the others out there, including the high-priced managers that they are willing to throw their money at for no reason at all.

The following sections of this book are about the discipline you need to trade and invest like a pro without the inherent bias against performance that pros in the hedge fund and mutual fund camps have. This chapter will help you to get all the advantages the pros have in handling money with none of the disadvantages. You already have all the basics: the skills to analyze price-to-earnings multiples, the ability to understand the cycles that drive stocks, the knowledge of the best places to look for big gains. Now you need the tools—the real tools, not the silly stuff that passes for tools advertised by brokers desperate for your business—to trade and invest your portfolio to riches.

The Ten Commandments of Trading

1. **Never turn a trade into an investment.** If there is one concept you must take away from this book, it's that you must never, ever turn a trade into an investment. First, let's talk about the process of buying a stock. When I decide I am going to buy Kmart, the reconstituted real estate and retail play, I have to declare right up front whether I am buying it for a trade or an investment. A trade means that I am buying it because of a specific catalyst, a reason that will drive it higher. That catalyst is a data point, a recommendation, a belief that things are better than expected when the earnings come out, some news about a restructuring, or something material that could occur. There is a mo-

ment to buy and a moment to sell. But you must declare first before you buy. Here's why. The vast majority of you will buy a stock for a reason and then either the reason occurs and nothing happens, so you then decide, darn, I'll just call it an investment and I will buy more as it goes down, or else the reason doesn't occur—the reason may never occur—and you decide to hold on to it because, well, what's the worst thing that can happen? The answer of course is plenty, and almost all of it bad. The answer is that you would never have bought it in the first place if you didn't think the reason was going to occur, so there is no reason for you to own it now. I have seen myriad investors turn trades into investments, developing a rationale or an alibi to fool themselves that they are doing the right thing. That's because they don't make the distinction between a trade and an investment. When I want to "invest" in a company I buy a small amount of it to start and then hope the market will knock the stock down so I can buy more. When I want to trade, I put the maximum on at the beginning because I believe the data point is about to occur. I never buy anything for a trade without that catalyst. I never buy anything for a trade just hoping it will go higher; there can be no hope in the equation. I buy down when I am investing. I cut my losses immediately when I am trading if the reason I am trading the stock doesn't pan out.

2. Your first loss is your best loss. People know when trades have gone awry. They know the stock doesn't act well. On my radio show I talk about how stocks talk to me; they tell me things. Actually, of course, they tell everybody everything, but most people don't know how to listen. If you buy a stock for a trade and it starts going against you in a meaningful way, perhaps a decline of 50¢ or more, you may have a real problem on your hands. I am not kidding. When it comes to trading I am an extremely disciplined person. I like to cut my losses quickly and get over them quickly. That's why I say that my first loss is my best loss. All other losses tend to be from lower levels and at bigger cost to me. Again, people instinctively can feel the trade going awry

but because of ego or pigheadedness, they don't want to heed the thunder and they stay in only to have to panic out at lower levels.

3. It's okay to take a loss when you already have one. One of the silliest things individual investors do is to pretend that they aren't losing money simply because they haven't realized the loss. I talk to investors all the time who rationalize that they are in the money until they take it off the table—regardless of whether they are profitable or not. Nonsense. A loss is a loss, realized or unrealized, and most of the time it is better just to take it than to act as though you don't have one. My goal is to get you to realize the loss before it does so much damage that it cuts into your gains. No one can come back from the chronic loss position; no one is good enough or has enough ammo to stay in the game. Cut your losses now; let your winners do the running.

4. Never turn a trading gain into an investment loss. You've just made a terrific trade, you bought Philip Morris (now Altria) before a great quarter and watched it go up 4 points on the good earnings news. Do you take the trade? Or do you begin to wonder, "Hmm, this MO is better than I think; I should hold on to this." I did that once, that exact trade. I bragged to the Trading Goddess as I was driving her to the airport for a flight to Paris. I told her I had a big gain on a couple of hundred thousand shares. She reminded me immediately never to use the word "gain" unless it was taken, because as far as she was concerned, there was nothing booked so nothing had been done. A week later I picked her up at the airport, back from France and gay as I have ever seen her. She could see through my sullen look immediately. "What did you screw up on?" she asked, knowing full well that the only thing that could have made me unhappy at that juncture was a big loss in the market. I then had to describe to her that a day after she left a court had ordered Morris to pay billions in tobacco medical damages to everyone who had ever smoked a cigarette, or something like that. The stock had dropped 15 points. She reminded me of the cardinal rule, that a trade is just a trade, and when you turn it into an investment

you have overstayed your welcome. I had turned my solid six-figure gain into a multi-million-dollar loss. Let my loss be the lesson to you, so you don't have to learn it yourself.

5. Tips are for waiters. At one point in both our lives, my wife and I were waiters. To be more accurate, I was a busboy, because you had to be twenty-one to serve alcohol in the state of Pennsylvania. She was a waitress. Later, when we worked together, my wife would handle all the incoming calls from brokers. That meant that at least four times a week I had to hear her lecture someone about the tip they were giving us, telling the poor shmoe on the other end of the line that we were both waiters once and that they should save the tips for those in that profession and not hit us with them. Why was she so adamant? Because the logic of a tip, or really, the illogic, is so palpable. If you really "know something," then you are per se an insider and aren't supposed to tell anyone without running afoul of the securities laws. And if you don't know something, you should shut the hell up because you don't know what you are talking about. So, any tip is, per se, a bum steer— unless it is left at a restaurant. This no-tip rule is a very hard lesson, because invariably the people offering tips are experts at making them sound like genuine insight. But believe me, the only reason someone really gives a tip is so he can get out of what would otherwise be a terrible position that he's stuck in and will definitely lose money on if he doesn't get you to take him out of it.

6. You don't have a profit until you sell. This commandment is a variation of the rule of not turning a trade into an investment. People constantly confuse booked gains, real gains that you can take to the bank, with phony paper gains that are meaningless because they can be taken away. Most people are also reluctant ever to take a profit because they don't want to pay taxes. I always tell people that if we could just rewind the videotape to January 2000, when people were sitting on trillions of dollars of unrealized gains, we would be able to drill this point home well enough that people would respect it. Gains not taken can be losses. Gains taken can never be losses. It's that simple. I stress

this point because we have all been brainwashed not to sell; we think it is sinful. It is commonsensical. It is logical. And it is the only way to be sure you get rich in this business.

7. Control losses; winners take care of themselves. One of the amazing things about this business is how often I hear people say, "If it weren't for that Nortel position, I would have been up big," or, "I would be making a huge amount of money in the market if only I hadn't let Lucent run against me." It takes only one or two losers to wreck a portfolio. I try to devote far more of my time toward my losing stocks than my winners, and not because of some sort of masochistic streak. Rather, I recognize that stocks often telegraph declines. I recently bumped into a policeman in town who owned a couple hundred shares of Enron. He was thanking me profusely because I told him at $20 he had to bail. Of course he was reluctant to do so; the stock had been at $80 not long before. I told him that loss control is the paramount concern for all of those in the market, because the winners, the good stocks, tend to take care of themselves. He sold the Enron. He told me that if he hadn't he would have wiped out all of the gains he had had in all the other stocks in his portfolio. I tell the story because it is typical; one bad apple in this business truly does destroy the whole barrel. Take the loss before it gets hideous. Don't buy into the notion that you can't sell until it comes back and then you promise not to do it again. That's how losers think. You need to think like a winner.

8. Don't fear missing anything. I can't tell you how many times I have had my heart in my throat, pounding, pounding, because I didn't have enough in the market. I can't tell you how often I felt that I had to "play," I had to be in because the market was going higher and higher and higher without me. Do you know that almost every time I had that feeling, almost every time I had that "I can't miss this action" drama playing around in my head, I lost money? Discipline is the most important rule in winning investing, and sometimes that discipline means admitting that you missed the opportunity and it is too

late. I almost always feel like I have missed something right near the top of the move. When I was in the Bigs, I used to turn that sentiment into a profit in my final years by actually betting against the market when I thought I was missing something, because that heart-stuck-in-throat feeling correlates with the tops of moves, not the bottoms. Always remember that the best time to buy is when it feels most awful, not when it would relieve the incessant pain of fearing the next big rally, especially given that that rally invariably has already occurred.

9. Don't trade headlines. The press is almost always wrong in its quick takeaways of what business news is about. Some of it is the rush; Reuters wants to beat Dow; Dow wants to beat Bloomberg. Some of it is the lack of grounding of most journalists in business news. And some of it is complexity: The headline can't capture the reality because the reality is a jumble. Headlines that present stories about such and such a number being "better than expected" are the types of headlines that punish traders constantly. They can't understand how they could be wrong because the "tape" just said that the quarter was better. Typically, the reality is that there is something else, some other metric that might be important, or that the quarter is finagled with one-time gains. I think that you have to wait to read the whole story and you can never be sure of what that story is going to be from the headline. This point is very important because with electronic trading you can move too fast, and often many of you do. Learn the whole story. If this really is a great opportunity, you will not miss it by taking time to iniform yourself.

10. Don't trade flow. You are watching CNBC, you see multiple "takes" or trades to the upside in IPIX or MACE or some other four-lettered hot stock. Do you want to go buy it? That's called trading flow. People always want to trade flow. I used to get calls from dozens of brokers saying that they had big buyers of Microsoft or big sellers of EMC, and my instincts were to go along with the trades, to buy because they were buying. Wrong! When you have no idea why people are buying, when you are just operating on the buys and sells of oth-

ers, you are trading on ignorance. Ignorant traders never ever win. I promise you that by trading flow you will lose far more often than you will make money, even though it seems so easy. Why would they buy if they weren't right? The answer, of course, is that many investments made by others are ill-considered and attempting to piggyback off them is nonsensical even if it feels great. No matter how many times I stress this point, people still see large buyers on the bottom of the TV screen and they go nuts imitating them. That's just plain stupid. Do you think they will tell you when to sell, too?

Twenty-Five Investment Rules to Live By

1. Bulls and bears make money; pigs get slaughtered. My favorite expression of all when it comes to the market is that bulls make money, bears make money, and pigs get slaughtered. In fact I have a tape of pigs snorting that I play on *Jim Cramer's RealMoney* when I think that someone's been too greedy. I am all about common sense, which, unfortunately, seems rarely to be interjected into the investing dialogue. It makes sense that a bull can make money when the market moves up, and it makes sense that a bear can make money when the market moves down; both going long and shorting are noble endeavors. It's when you act piggish, when you refuse to take anything off the table after a huge run, that you get hurt. My style of investing is to buy down, simply because I believe, when I am *investing*, that I am buying shares in an enterprise, and unless that enterprise has faltered in the interim between my decision to buy and my buying, I stick with it. I use the market's irrationality and randomness in my favor to accumulate more stock, to the point where I am perfectly willing to have up to 25 percent of my portfolio in one name if I think it is absurdly valued. Just as a market can take a stock down irrationally, it can also take a stock up irrationally, although far too few individual investors think this way. The difference is that when a stock goes down irrationally it is getting cheaper and cheaper, but when a stock goes up irrationally it

is getting more and more expensive. In any walk of life other than investing in stocks there comes a price that we are not willing to pay and a price where we would be a seller of goods. Only in stocks do we feel we should hang on regardless. That's just plain against common sense. When you are a pig, therefore, I expect you will be slaughtered. Many people have asked me how in March 2000, within ten days of the top of the market, I knew to take money off the table and begin to short (arguably my best call since the cash for the crash call in 1987 that my wife steered me to). The answer, in a rather unrigorous and noneloquent moment, is that I was not willing to be a pig. I had made a ton of money virtually in a straight line and had watched many of my stocks go to absurd valuations. Of course, at the time, people had plenty of justifications, intelligent, rational-sounding justifications for staying in the market. But my "bulls make money, bears make money, pigs get slaughtered" philosophy got me out right on time.

2. It's okay to pay the taxes. At the time when I said to take money off the table in March 2000, I received close to a thousand e-mails from people saying that if they took the profits that I was advising them to do, they would have to pay a tremendous amount of tax, much of it short-term, which, of course, carries with it much higher rates than long-term gains. I wrote back to each person individually saying that if you don't take profits, you won't have profits, that the least of your worries is the tax man. Not one agreed with me. The abhorrence of taxes transcended good judgment. Years later, I am still getting e-mails of apology from people bemoaning the fact that they cared more about paying taxes than taking profits and that their portfolios subsequently shifted from being well into the black to dripping with red. *Never* consider taxes as a reason to hold a stock if the stock has gone up too far too fast and can head back down hard. *Never* hold on to something not worth holding on to or something that has gotten dangerously overvalued simply so you can wait until the gain goes long-term. This is the single biggest investment mistake people have made in our generation, and despite the trillions lost in the bear mar-

ket of the turn of this century, I still see people making this error. Shameful, just shameful. Taxes do not trump fundamentals; dangerous stocks are dangerous whether they are owned long- or short-term. You can't base investment decisions on the tax man.

3. Don't buy all at once; arrogance is a sin. I consider myself one of the greatest market timers of my era. I was able to accumulate wealth as quickly as I did because I timed lots of big moves, getting in right and exiting right. Yet, when it comes to buying stocks, to the way of buying stocks, I never buy all at once. I buy increments on the way down, spaced out gingerly to avoid emotion. Similarly, I never commit a lot of capital at one level, and I space out my capital commitments. Let me give you some examples. For my retirement account, my 401(k), I like to put aside a twelfth of my commitment every month. But if I catch a market break, a substantial market break of 10 percent, I speed up the next month's contribution. If I catch a break in excess of 15 percent I put in the next quarter's contribution. And twice in the last ten years, when there was a 20 percent decline, I invested all that I had left to contribute. That way I was able to take advantage of the declines and average in at great prices. I did it this way because I know I am fallible. I also know behavior and common sense. I know that if I commit all my money at one level and then the market takes a huge tumble, I will be so angry and sullen that I'll believe that the market itself is rigged or that it can't be tamed or that it is just too hard. I hear those sentiments from callers every day on my radio show, and I know that they can only be combatted by humility and a recognition that the market can be an unpredictable morass at times, but over the long term it makes plenty of sense.

Similarly, when I wanted to build a position, a sizable position in a stock, I never bought it all at once. I recognized that there was inherent fallibility in my moment of buying. Perhaps the market was about to take a huge tumble. Perhaps some negative event would occur that would make the buy seem ludicrous a few minutes later. So space them out. That's always been the way with me, even though it often

drove my brokers up the wall. They hated the fact that instead of going in and buying 50,000 shares of Caterpillar in one fell swoop, I bought 5,000 every hour, or 5,000 at one level and then waited for a 25¢ drop to buy the next 5,000. They wanted to get my order done; I wanted to get my order done right. You are the client; you are in command of your money. Don't let anyone rush you or make you put it all to work at one level. How do you know that tomorrow the market won't crash? How do you know that tomorrow there might not be an unbelievable opportunity to buy one of your favorite stocks at a much better level, but you have just committed all the money you had? Accept the fallibility of man's judgment and use it to your advantage. The worst that happens with my method? Simple: You don't get enough stock on before a very big move. You don't have as big a profit as you would like. Now that's what I call a high-quality problem!

4. Look for broken stocks, not broken companies. Most people so closely affiliate the stock with the company in their minds that they can't tell the difference between the two. That's nonsense. There are lots of very bad companies with very bad stocks. But there are also lots of good companies with very bad stocks. Your job is to know the difference, because the former is no bargain and the latter defines a bargain. After every sell-off of any magnitude, and we will surely get a dozen of them every year, there will be stocks that have been crushed unfairly. Most people gravitate toward the broken stocks of broken companies, the Suns, the Gateways, the CMGIs. Instead, they should focus on the companies that have been unfairly beaten up. On my radio show, I say, Don't buy damaged goods, buy damaged stocks of companies that are on the mend or improving. How can you spot the disparity? Simple homework. I can't tell you how many conference calls I go on with companies where they say, in plain English, even though our stock is down, our business is particularly strong. A year ago, Yellow Roadway, the best trucking company on earth, reported a shortfall because of some execution problems involving the merger. The CEO, Bill Zollars, came on my CNBC show and said the model

wasn't broken; the business suffered a hiccup, but the stock was refusing to recognize what the business knows: the hiccup's over. Sure enough, the stock subsequently moved up 50 percent when the company reported its next quarter. It was the classic example of the broken stock masking the healthy company.

During sell-offs I always tell people to build a shopping list of what they want to buy while it is happening and stay current about those companies so they can buy them at markdown prices. Remember, in the end, the stock market is just a big store where inventory at times has to be moved. Sometimes the marked-down merchandise at a department store or a supermarket is broken. Don't waste your time speculating on broken companies—those are the spoiled fruit on sale at the supermarket. There are enough healthy companies out there whose stocks have been knocked down for unfair reasons that you don't need to buy spoiled rotted companies that are crummy at any price. Chances are that most companies deserve those low prices and won't go up unless you get real lucky. You don't want luck, or hope, to be part of the equation.

5. Diversification is the only free lunch. Nonetheless, nobody wants to be diversified in real life. They want 100 percent of the next Microsoft; they want to put it all in a couple of stocks that could rally off the next big tech thing. But life's not like that. You have to be diversified to spread the risk. I always explain this in the commonsense way that takes you back to the supermarket: Would you put all of your eggs in one basket? Would you be willing to let all your chips ride on one number at roulette? Of course not. Then how can you have all of your money on tech or health care? How can you make such a big bet on one sector? It's just plain foolhardy.

Why don't people realize it? Because most people process the downside ineffectively. They don't understand that you can lose everything if you are concentrated. You know, though, that the same people who would buy nothing but tech would quickly realize that a dinner made up of four beef dishes is just plain unhealthy. These same

people who would put all of their money in Enron would recognize that betting the farm on a lottery ticket is the height of folly. These are pieces of paper, for heaven's sake. Some of the pieces of paper are going to turn out to be worthless, even ones you think are worth a lot. Some are going to zero. The only way to ensure that you are not destroying your nest eggs is to diversify the cartons you place them in.

The toughest thing about diversification is that it is a real party spoiler. When I started my radio show the NASDAQ was much higher than it would be a year later. I wanted people to sell some tech and buy some dividend-producing stocks. I got so despondent about how unwilling they were to do so that I started the game "Am I Diversified?" I believe I have personally helped tens of thousands of people fight off the unmitigated assault on their wealth that was the bear market of 2000. But there's plenty more work to be done. Not one year after the bottom, I started getting those "I own EMC, Oracle, Microsoft, Hewlett-Packard, and Intel" calls all over again. I had to painstakingly remind them how all of these stocks trade together, and if you catch a squall in the market, you are liable to drown in tech stocks. If the goal is to stay in the game, there is no worse way to try to accomplish that goal than to stay in one sector. You will hate me when the market is straight up, but you will love me when the market goes down and the sector you would have otherwise owned is swamped by sellers.

6. Buy and homework, not buy and hold. When I started *Jim Cramer's RealMoney* I had a ton of people who didn't want to part with their failing tech or biotech stocks. I always told them, fine, they could continue to own them if they could just answer a few simple questions in English: What does the company do, what price-to-earnings multiple does it sell for, and whom does it compete against? No one could tell me. They just said that they were taught to buy and hold and that anything else was just speculation. I thought long and hard about this misapprehension and decided that the key issue was that they were buying and holding when they should be buying and doing homework about what they bought. Homework is analyzing the Web page,

conference call, articles, research, and the like that I discussed earlier. If an investor didn't do those things after he bought, one hour per week per position, I thought he was being reckless, and I said it out loud. I told people that they had no business being their own portfolio managers. They either had to give it up to an index fund, if they had no time, or they should just put it with a couple of funds or managers and review them regularly. But the idea of buy and hold after the tragedy we went through in 2000–2003, one that is on bad days still very much with us, is just preposterous.

If there were truly an arbiter, if there were really an organization or an entity that regulated who had a right to come public, with some standards about how much money they are making and how good their balance sheets are, then you could buy and hold. But the one thing we have learned in the last five years is that anybody can bring anything public and we can't let the low barriers to entry into the stock market hurt us. So the mantra is buy and homework, not buy and hold. Always remember that no asset class over the long term—defined as twenty years—has ever beaten high-quality stocks that pay dividends. But unless you keep up and do the homework, how do you know if your stocks are high quality enough to pay a dividend one day? Without the homework you shouldn't own individual stocks. It is too likely that you will stumble and too likely that the long-term payoff of stocks will elude you. I can't tell you how many times I have bought the stocks of good companies that subsequently went bad. That's what the homework should tell you. It is a check on when to bail because a company's not coming back. It is not designed to find a hot stock so much as it ensures that you don't have your portfolio wrecked by an ice-cold one.

7. No one ever made a dime by panicking. No matter how many times I tell people that panic is not an investment strategy, I see people cut and run at the very worst time. When you sell into the maw, when you join the rout, you *never* get a good price. You feel good momentarily, you feel relieved that the pain is "gone," but it's always wrong.

When I ran my hedge fund I made millions of trades. I dutifully saved all the trading records in giant boxes and then at year end went over every single trade to look for the biggest panicked losses—you know which ones you panicked on—and then I would look at a chart of the stocks the day before I sold them, the day after I sold them, and a week after I sold them. Do you know in almost every single case—and I am talking millions of trades—the stocks were up the next day and up appreciably a week later. That doesn't mean they weren't substantially lower a month, a quarter, or even a year later. It does mean that it was the wrong time to execute the sell strategy. A patient, less panicked style always generates a higher return. Always. That's a certainty in a world where there is very little certainty.

In the mid-1990s I let a film crew into my office as part of a *Frontline* documentary on the markets. It happened to be a day where I panicked and sold half of my portfolio to Goldman Sachs at a price about 5 percent lower than the previous day because I thought the market was going to be down 10 to 15 percent. I kept a copy of the tape and I watched it every time I felt a panic attack coming on, because on that day, the very day where I felt that things were coming unglued, the market actually rallied. I wish I could say that it was just irony, but it was rationality. Typically the panic comes at the *end* of the sell-off, not the beginning or even the middle. The panic marks the capitulation of all of those who tried to stay the course. That's why the panic tends to be the bottom. In October 1998 I forgot about *Frontline* and panicked into a gawdawful tape, the second time in three years that I went against my discipline. Then, too, the market looked like it was going to crash. Instead it rallied steadily after I made my sales.

If you are one of those people who simply refuse to believe me and my empirical work on this, do me a favor. Next time you feel a panic attack coming on that tricks you into wanting to sell, adopt the approach of the Trading Goddess and "throw a maiden into a volcano." That's where you take one stock and sacrifice it in order to forestall taking a more drastic action. Remember my goal: to keep you in the game. Nothing drives people out of the game faster than waiting and

holding and then selling at the panic bottom. Don't let it happen to you.

8. Own the best of breed; it is worth it. Here's a principle that is followed strictly among professionals, yet is studiously ignored among the hobbyists and amateurs. So many people are suckers for cheap. So many people look at the $E \times M = P$ and say, "Wait a second, that's too high a multiple to pay; Intel's not that much better than AMD." Or, "There's no way that I will pay that much of a premium for Procter over Colgate." Shame on you. The biggest bargains tend to be the best of breed. The amateur loves a "cheaper" alternative, whether it is cheaper in stock price or cheaper in multiple. The professional says the reason why Walgreens has a more expensive multiple than Rite Aid is that it is much better, and when things get difficult, management is more likely to figure out their problems than to get buried by them. When the choice is among two or three companies in an industry, always go for the one that's the best of breed regardless of the price. Far too often the market simply misprices the weaker of the two, giving it too much credit. The underdog hardly ever wins in this game.

9. He who defends everything defends nothing, or why discipline trumps conviction. One question I am asked repeatedly in my business is, "Don't you worry about your stocks?" The answer is that I am always worried about my stocks, always, but I am particularly worried when they go *down!* I am doubly worried when they go down when the market as a whole is going up. That's a sign to me that something's wrong, that someone knows something I don't know and that I'd better find out or I won't be able to take advantage of the weakness to buy more—I will have to sell instead. That's why I demand that if you are going to have your own portfolio you have the time and inclination to make the calls, or read the homework or listen to the conference calls or check the Web sites and articles that will determine whether it is a buying opportunity or a selling opportunity. Of course, there are plenty of times when stocks go down and the homework shows you nothing. There are plenty of times when there is chicanery in the

numbers, or there is puffing by the management, and we don't really know the truth. Or, worse, someone does know the truth, and it was found out at the seventeenth hole at Baltusrol and is known only to a select—and illegal—bunch of insiders. There are also tons of times where you simply have too much stock in the market versus what the market's going to do; you are too "long," as we say in the vernacular. So, what do you do? How do you manage a portfolio under conditions where things go wrong with the stocks you own and things go wrong in the market? There are no magic bullets, but I believe that when in doubt, discipline trumps conviction. You have to have a discipline, a discipline that ranks all of your stocks so that you know which ones you are willing to buy right now and which ones you are willing to sell if you need the capital to sell. You need to rank stocks because not all stocks are created equal and when things go awry you have to be willing to "circle the wagons" around a few good stocks and buy them down so you get a better basis.

I can't tell you how many times, either because of overconfidence or because of an excessively benign period of market rallying, I was lulled into being too long. That's why I developed a four-step system of ranking every stock I own: 1 is a stock I want to buy more of right now, 2 is a stock I want to buy more of if it goes lower, 3 is a stock I want to sell if it goes higher, and 4 is a stock I want to sell now. I actually used to get off the trading desk at my hedge fund every two hours and rank the stocks I owned, forcing my portfolio managers to have only one or two 1s and making them choose what they really liked. The rankings force discipline and make discipline trump conviction. A wise soldier once said, "He who defends everything defends nothing." In war that means don't defend every beachhead and valley. In investing, that means trying to buy all of the stocks that you "like," because no one, not even Bill Gates, has that kind of money. That's how I run my money. I know that I can't protect every stock, so I choose the ones I believe in the most and I buy them down, I "defend" them and let the others go. In a serious sell-off, the 1s become the only stocks I will own, and I will sell off all the others. This method keeps you from

being a kid in a candy store at the worst possible time—when you are about to get your fingers cut off. It requires you to examine every decline as a potential point of action. It also is proactive. *You* are determining what you are selling, not the market. Most people sell because they can't take the pain; this method builds in the pain and turns a decline into an asset. Almost all my great investments since I started ranking stocks ten years ago came from buying my 1s at the time when everyone else was selling them.

10. The fundamentals must be good in takeovers. You want to speculate in takeovers; who can blame you? You want to catch the next Mandalay Bay or the next Nextel Communications. You think that you can wait it out because the payoff will be big. Let me tell you what I think of that: You are a fool if you speculate on takeovers. What you must do is buy undervalued good companies that are doing well. If you go and buy stocks with poor fundamentals betting that someone will take you out with a high bid, you are going to be wrong far more often than you will be right. In my last year at my hedge fund I decided that after Best Foods got a takeover bid it was inconceivable that Campbell would stay independent. Just inconceivable. Too good a brand, too easily acquired. I knew that the family behind the brand was getting restless, and in the meantime the stock had a 4 percent yield. My associate Matt Jacobs, who later became my research director, asked me how the fundamentals were. I told him that the takeover story was "too good to check out," and that if I really drilled down on the fundamentals I would probably not buy it. A year later, after a slash in the dividend and several shortfalls of a gigantic magnitude, I had lost more than 10 points on Campbell. Funny thing about the fundamentals: If the market doesn't like them, the potential acquirers won't, either. When you buy crummy companies and they go down, you can try to console yourself by saying that "maybe I will get a bid." It is far more likely, though, that you will have a Campbell on your hands. Remember the premise of this book: Let me be your lab; I have made every mistake in the book. You can't speculate on bad companies bet-

ting that they will get bids. They don't. Nobody wants them, least of all other companies.

11. Don't own too many stocks. You can overdo the virtues of diversification and become your own mutual fund. Given my constraints about time and inclination—you need one hour per week per stock to stay on top of the fundamentals—it is impossible to own more than twenty stocks unless you are a full-time stock junkie. The right-sized diversified portfolio where you can do it yourself is a five-stock portfolio. Too few and you lack diversification; too many, and you can't stay on top of them. Try to come up with a "just right" formula that allows you the comfort of staying on top of every position.

12. Cash and sitting on the sidelines are fine alternatives. Lots of people believe in being fully invested at all times. Lots of managers think they are supposed to be fully invested at all times. This is total nonsense. Lots of times the market just stinks and you want to have cash. Lots of times there is nothing to do except sit in cash. One of the reasons why I outperformed every manager in the business in my fourteen years at my hedge fund is that there were substantial blocks of time when I was largely in cash, including the 1987 crash. Cash is a great investment at times. It is a perfect hedge, as opposed to shorting the market, because if the market keeps going higher as it did, say in 1999, far longer than anyone thought, you could face devastating losses. I think that cash is the most underrated of investments because nothing feels as good as cash when that market comes down. It is one of the reasons why if you follow my method of how to trade around a stock, you will know that as the market spikes I take stock off, raise cash, and reposition myself for the next decline. Some people confuse this with buying on dips. I don't buy on dips; I sell strength and buy weakness in the stocks of the companies I love. When the time is right I almost always have the cash to put to work because I believe so strongly in cash as an option.

13. No woulda shoulda coulda. One of the most despicable traits of amateurs, and even some professionals, is second-guessing. You make

a call, you go to buy Newell Rubbermaid, and then it has a short-fall. You sit there and stew about what should have happened. Or you sell Cyberonics the day before it doubles and you ruminate all the next day about what might have been. That's all nonsense. The market requires you to have the right head on at all times. You have to be ready to see the ball right for the next pitch. There is no time to re-monstrate. You clear your head and go right back out there. If you want to be introspective and constructive, bracket some time at the end of each month, or maybe the end of each quarter, to assess your strategy. But to second-guess decisions is to put yourself in a loser mind-set. Mind you, I want the pain felt. When I thought one of the younger people in my office made a mistake that was costly, I made them wear the symbol of the stock that they screwed up on as a Post-it on their forehead for the day. But I insist that any time spent saying, "If only I . . ." is time that keeps you from getting the next big stock. My wife, by the way, believes that women are such good traders because they lack the second-guessing instinct that men have. Whatever, but she taught me to steel myself and to come in the next day without the mental baggage of a screw-up so I could be ready to swing at the next fat pitch.

14. Expect corrections; don't be afraid of them. When a correction happens, investors sometimes decide that they want nothing to do with the market, that the correction signifies that something is wrong and the market can't be touched. That's another very big mistake. Corrections happen all the time after big runs and they are to be ex-pected, but you can't write off the market when they happen. I always tell the story of Joe DiMaggio after his fifty-six-game hitting streak— still the most amazing baseball feat of all time. When he failed to hit in game fifty-seven, should you have traded DiMaggio? Was he finished? Is that smart thinking? Same with the market. Corrections are to be expected; when they happen they are not a reason to panic. They can be great opportunities even as people insist that they've wrecked the charts, taken out the two-hundred-day moving average, or made the

market unpalatable, claptrap that I hear every time the market snaps a winning streak with a couple of big losses.

15. Don't forget bonds. We always look at the stock market as a hermetically sealed operation. We don't think of it in the broader context of all markets. Big, big mistake. You have to be aware at all times that there is an intense competition going on among assets. The most important rivalry is stocks versus bonds. When interest rates are high, particularly for risk-free investments like U.S. treasuries, that's formidable competition for stocks, where there is a ton of risk. The tug of war between the two goes on at all times. When interest rates go higher there will *always* be someone who says "I like these more than stocks" and stocks get sold off. That always happens. But many of the people who got in the market in the last decade don't even think of bonds. That's financial suicide. It was no coincidence that the Fed had the overnight cash rates as high as 6.5 percent at about the time that the bear market of 2000–2003 began. The ratcheting of rates that the Fed did in 1999–2000 and back in 1994 crushed the market, just crushed it. And that will always be the case. Pay attention to interest rates and bonds; ignore them at your own peril.

16. Never subsidize losers with winners. So many bad portfolio managers and so many terrible individual investors always sell their best stocks so they can hold on to their worst stocks. You can always tell when you see this pattern. You will be reviewing someone's portfolio and it will be the biggest pile of junk, and you will say, "What happened to your blue chips?" They will say, "I had to sell them to buy more of these stocks because these stocks kept going down." Everyone has this problem. I have counseled enough hedge funds that were in trouble to know that the first thing that gets sold are the best ones because "they can be sold." There's always a bid for the good stocks. But when you have a handful of good and awful stocks, you don't sell the awful ones because "they are down too much," or because you "will knock them down" if they are small stocks and you have a lot of them. I understand that problem for institutional readers, but individuals,

please, do not subsidize losers with winners. If you own companies with deteriorating fundamentals—as opposed to good companies with deteriorating stock prices—please sell the bad ones, take the loss, reapply the proceeds to the good ones, and move on.

17. Hope is not a part of the equation. Emotions have to be checked at the door in this business. I often hear people say "I hope" that a stock goes up. This is not a sporting event; this is money. We have no room for rooting or hoping. We are buying stocks that we believe should go higher because of the fundamentals and avoiding stocks where the underlying business is bad and getting worse. Where should hope fit in? Nowhere. People treat this business at times like a religion. They believe that if they pray that things will work out, maybe they will. Or they fall in love with these miserable pieces of paper with the idea that the love will be requited. Be realistic. Hope, pray, love, rooting—these are all the enemies of good stock picking. Hard work, research, being realistic about the prospects is the stuff of good stock picking. I can still recall the ringing in my ears when I would get off the trading desk with my wife and she would say, "What's the deal with this Memorex," and I would say, "I am hoping it gets a big contract." She would scream, "Hope? *Hope?* We need *hope* to make this work? Sell it and get me something where we have more in our favor than just hope." Many times she didn't even ask, she just sold it after I used the word "hope" to see if I would buy it back. Invariably I didn't buy back the stocks I was hoping something good would happen to.

18. Be flexible. Readers of TheStreet.com hated me in the spring of 2000 when I turned bearish. They despised the fact that I could turn on a dime, hate the very stocks that I had liked, suddenly shorting what I was going long just a month before. They thought I was lacking in rigor, a joker even. I even got plenty of death threats and was worried about my personal safety because the change I made was so stark. But you know who agreed with me? The insiders. All of my views that changed had to do with hearing the companies at conferences—all available on the Web—saying "something's not as

good as it was before." This was granular stuff, like being at the Nortel meeting when former CEO John Roth said, "Business has gotten softer in the last few weeks," or being with Cisco when the company said, "The quarter is not yet in the bag," when the quarter was always in the bag by this time in previous years. You see the situations change, the business conditions change. Something that might be good one month can turn bad.

Maybe you don't care and you are only in it for the long term, but if you are playing fireflies, Game Breaker stocks, and their business hits a wall, their stocks will soon hit a wall, too. I never took action on a stock, going from buy to short sell, unless I heard from the company first that things had gotten less predictable or that business had softened. That's why the homework and the conference calls and the writings are so important, because if a business is saying that things have gotten soft, it must do so in a public forum, and you have to be listening to that public forum as or soon after it is happening. If you are devoting only fifteen minutes a week to each position you have, you aren't doing enough homework to be there at the inflection point of good to bad and you will be caught, as so many were caught in the great bear market of 2000.

19. When high-level people quit a company, something is wrong. I don't believe in shooting first and asking questions later. I think that there is almost always time to do homework to see what's up with a stock—except when a major executive leaves unexpectedly. One of my cardinal rules—and these are all cardinal rules here—is that I will not own a stock when a CEO or a CFO leaves suddenly. I just sell it. I might buy it back later, even if it is higher, but I don't like to own stocks where either of these two heads suddenly departs. Sometimes I am going to lose money because I will have acted rashly. But then again, for every one of those situations there are ten like that of Enron, where CEO Jeffrey Skilling quit abruptly for the usual "family reasons" in the summer of 2002 when the stock was at $47. The stock went to zero soon after. People don't quit for family reasons when they are needed

at companies. They just don't. You can't be sure what the real reason is, but when someone leaves like that, someone is making a statement. You have to make a statement, too. You have to sell.

20. Patience is a virtue—giving up on value is a sin. Sometimes stocks you like do nothing. They can do nothing for ages. If you are a professional investor at a hedge fund, this waiting can be unnerving. You have people calling you daily and asking you how you are doing with their money. If you have lots of stocks that are doing nothing, they will take the money away and you will have to sell those stocks anyway. But individuals have no such pain. Individuals can sit on stocks as long as they want. Unfortunately, when I counsel patience individuals get antsy. "If it were any good it would be going up now, no?" Do you know how patient I was in owning Intel? For eighteen months I watched Intel do nothing in the late 1980s. But I believed. I held on to it because at that time I had only a few partners, and none of them needed to know every minute how much they were worth. Later in my career I could never have held on to an Intel that long. Lots of stories take a long time to develop. Lots of turnarounds take eighteen months to two years. When you buy a stock and you recognize that it could take a long time to turn, mark it as such in your mind so you don't get tired of it and just sell it. Stocks that are stuck in the mud a long time tend to romp like thoroughbreds when they are freed from the gate. Do you have the patience? If you don't, let someone else run your money.

21. Just because someone says it on TV doesn't make it so. This is one of my favorite tenets. So many jokers come on TV. So many clowns, people who know nothing. Sometimes people get on because they are telegenic. Sometimes they get on because they look good. Sometimes they get on because they have great PR people. Sometimes they get on because they are friends or because we owe them a favor. Oh yes, and sometimes they get on because they are good. The last is the exception. I can't tell you how unimportant performance is to the media. They are embarrassed to ask about it. They don't want to be in

the business of grading content or making decisions about whether someone is any good or not. That could leave them with no one to come on the show! That's right, they need to book these shows; that's the primary motivation, *not* bringing you people who know the most about stocks. Not all programs are like this, of course, but far more than you would like to believe. Yet I constantly see people who say, "I bought Covad because I heard this really smart guy say he liked it on TV." Well, let me ask you something. Was he selling it to you when he did? Do you know? Here's an odd fact: I am the only person who comes on TV who has to disclose his positions publicly. I volunteered to do this to protect everyone—my listeners and myself—from charges of pumping and dumping. Nobody else has that restriction, even though it is illegal to pump and dump. But if we asked managers to swear that they don't use the networks to sell their stocks, would they come on our programs? Don't they have an obligation to do the right things for their shareholders? If someone recommends a Covad and it goes up 15 percent when they do, do you really think they keep it? If so, think again. Don't trust anything you hear; go do the homework. If you like it, then buy it. But remember you are *never* going to get the sell call from the TV. Ever.

22. Always wait thirty days after an earnings preannouncement before you buy. Nothing seems more tempting than to buy a stock after it's been completely poleaxed by an earnings shortfall preannouncement. Nothing, however, could be more foolhardy. Here's why: A company preannounces a soft quarter not because it is having a soft quarter—that goes without saying—but because there is no way out and things are getting worse, not better. That means you are buying into a situation where things are deteriorating as you are buying. My advice: Wait at least thirty days from the preannouncement if you insist on buying. By that time the bad news, the ongoing bad news, should be factored into the stock price and you can begin to anticipate positives going down the line. Never buy a stock just because it's down on a preannouncement. That never works. You will lose money. I promise you.

23. Never underestimate the Wall Street promotion machine. When Wall Street gets behind a stock, that stock can go much farther than if the fundamentals were doing the driving. There was a time when Wall Street firms would compete with one another to sponsor companies so that when the stocks of the companies got high enough, the managers would hire the brokers to do deals. That stuff still goes on, but it is no longer linked so closely because the analysts who do the shilling can't be paid by the investment bankers, courtesy of the investigatory work of New York attorney general Eliot Spitzer. Still, when a company's stock gets picked up with a buy from a major firm, that stock is going to go higher than it should. That kind of sponsorship is what I like to sell into. Remember, I believe that that stocks are inherently poor, short term, at tracking the fundamentals of the companies. Longer term they are great; shorter term, though, when they ratchet up because of sponsorship, that's the time to bail, not buy. That's one of the reasons why I advocate buying weakness and selling strength at all times. When you get the artificial strength of a buy recommendation—there are very few sell recommendations, so I don't care about those—use it to do the unnatural, counterintuitive thing, and sell.

24. Be able to explain your stock picks to someone else. One of the worst things that ever happened to stock picking was the Internet, because it took away one of the most important brakes on the process: talking to someone about a buy. Buying stocks is a solitary event, too solitary. As I love to say, we are all prone to make mistakes, sometimes big ones. One way to cut down on those mistakes is to force yourself to articulate why you would like to buy something. When I was at my hedge fund I always made every portfolio manager sell me the stock, literally sell it to me like a salesperson, before I would buy it. If you are in a position where you are picking stocks by yourself, get someone to listen to you, let you articulate the reasoning, the philosophy behind the buy, why you like it. The simple selling of the idea, the notion of fleshing it out in a coherent way, often reveals one or more flaws.

When my wife played this role she always asked me questions like a journalist. Here are some samples of questions that she asked me over and over again, some of which often stopped buys in their tracks:

1. What's going to make this stock go up?
2. Why is it going to go up when you think it is?
3. Is this really the best time to buy it?
4. Haven't we already missed a lot of the move?
5. Shouldn't we wait until it comes down a little more?
6. What do you know about this stock that others don't?
7. What's your edge?
8. Do you like this stock any more than any of the others you own and why?

The last question was particularly crucial because my wife never liked to add a stock without subtracting one, in part because she believed it was impossible to have dozens of good ideas at once that you could have an edge on. That's valuable advice. Without a sounding board, you simply aren't being rigorous enough. If you are in a jam, heck, call me on my radio show on Friday and articulate it, and I will give you the straight up or down in the "Lightning Round," the ultimate test of your conviction. Buying a stock should be like buying a car; there's a lot that goes into it. Don't short-circuit the process. Or as my wife would say, "Look for reasons not to do it," because they will certainly surface soon after you buy the stock.

25. There is always a bull market somewhere. At the end of every radio show I sign off with, "This is Jim Cramer reminding you that there is always a bull market somewhere." I say that because I can't stand the bellyaching I hear from professionals and amateurs that there are no good stocks out there. There are always markets and sectors and exchanges that are in bull mode. Even at the height of the just-completed bear market in 2000–2003, you had tremendous out-

performance first in the food and beer stocks and then in the silver and gold stocks. These weren't proverbial flash in the pan moves, either. These were real, sustained, and totally catchable. There's a terrible desire among professionals and amateurs not to try something new, not to look at new markets or new stocks. The aversion comes from the amount of work that is required to learn new groups and from the belief that you can't stretch your knowledge. That's nonsense, as I showed you in the metrics section. In every situation, $E \times M = P$, and it can be solved for. More important, the obvious nature of the bull sectors should be self-evident to you by looking at the tables of exchange-traded funds that are readily available online in dozens of places. If you want to read about where the best bull markets are in what sectors, there's a terrific free publication put out twice a year by Fidelity for its investors, *The Fidelity Sector Fund Report*, which is the single best text about which sectors are doing what and why. I devour it as soon as it comes out, as I have for ten years. It's a brilliant document, and it will be obvious to you, as it is obvious to me, that there is always a bull market occurring at any given time somewhere on the planet, and is totally worth nailing, instead of bellyaching about how Cisco and Intel and Microsoft don't move anymore.

7

CREATING YOUR DISCRETIONARY PORTFOLIO

You're a baby boomer who just inherited $50,000. You are a young executive who finally has saved $10,000 from his paycheck. You just got married and you want to make some money in the market, not just watch your retirement index fund grow. You want to build a portfolio of stocks. You want to manage it yourself. How do you begin? Do you just grab a couple of stocks that are top rated from some broker or that score well on some quantitative tracker and let 'er rip? Or is there more to it?

If you are like most people, jammed to the gills with work, not a spare hour of time to be had in a week, let alone a day, and you still want to pick individual stocks, I've got some bad news for you. I won't play. I won't endorse your owning stocks or building a portfolio. You can't do the homework necessary to do it yourself. You don't have the time or inclination. Period. You will lose too much money. Hand over your money to the mutual fund manager.

I have spent the better part of the last five years doing repair work for individuals in your shoes who built their own portfolios during

the heyday only to see all their hard-earned work immolated in a pyre of Commerce One, Internet Capital, and Lycos. Money just shredded into cold coals and burned out sparks. Fizzled to nothing, because people didn't know the basics, they didn't do the homework, and they ignored the cardinal rule to diversify to minimize the risks of single-sector annihilation.

I know the pushback. I can read your mind right now: The professionals didn't do it any better, either, most of them lost big, too. So I can do it better and it will cost me less. Here's the problem: Managing money is difficult, time-consuming, draining, and a totally alien experience for almost everyone who has come out of the educational system of the United States, where, if you are lucky, you may have learned the difference between a stock and a bond. You most likely figured out how to balance a checkbook on your own, but beyond that, handling money is tough for you. And now you want me to endorse your setting up a portfolio? Dream on. You'll be like all the other callers I talk to every day on my radio show who have crushed their own nest egg with reckless purchases based on bogus investment tools and advice that made them feel more confident about buying than they should have been.

But you've paid for the book, you've gotten this far through my basic training, you've digested my Miranda warnings against doing it yourself, and you won't take no for an answer. You insist that you can take control of your finances, that you are not going to let some broker churn you or some mutual fund rip you off. Your confidence that you can do better is unshaken. I will help you, but only on the following conditions:

1. You will do the time-consuming, sometimes tedious homework that I described earlier in the book. No shortcuts. You have to do it all. Remember, in my world it's buy and homework, not buy and hold. Take it from me, I speak to dozens of people who bought and held crummy stocks that they never should have purchased, let alone held. You have to listen to the conference calls—they are very time-

consuming and dense—read the articles, get the annual and quarterly statements and reports and understand them. If you don't, I will mentally buzzer you as I had to do to Dorothy from Queens, New York, who called me on my radio show last year claiming she had done all the homework that was necessary to buy International Game Technology and was "ready to pull the trigger." Just one thing, though, she said; she wanted to know why the stock was down 3 points, given that everything was so hunky-dory. I asked her, "Did you listen to the conference call on the quarter?" She said no way. I said had she listened she would have heard management say that contrary to the last few years of great consistent earnings, this year was going to be "lumpy." You pay up for companies with consistent growth, as I have demonstrated. You slaughter consistent growers that suddenly turn lumpy in their earnings generation. Now the stock will have to go from growth to value hands, and that takes many quarters and takes off many points. Dorothy was all set to be fleeced by the process because she thought she had done the homework after reading some articles about the potential of Indian gaming. Turns out she hadn't done anything substantive to merit her opinion. Thank heavens she called; the stock got obliterated shortly thereafter. Most of my callers, when asked if they did even the most basic level of homework, admit that they haven't when I define the homework substantively. Don't be a casualty; do the kind of studying that you would have done for a social studies test in seventh grade. You would do the work if you set out to buy a new car; stocks are even more expensive and don't come with warranty protection. No money-back guarantees here! Caveat emptor still lives in the stock market, despite the attempts by the tort lawyers to change it.

2. Which brings me to the second caveat that you must agree to before you get my blessing to run your own money instead of turning it over to others. You must promise to spend a minimum of one hour per position per week doing the research. I know this commitment sounds onerous. It isn't; it is commonsensical. There's a lot to do to

maintain a portfolio, and I find myself routinely spending at least an hour a week staying on top of each of my positions. That's why I arbitrarily cap my positions at twenty-five; I have only about twenty-five hours each week free to do research because of my various commitments. When I have more positions than that, I fall down on the job and can't stay on top of things. And I am a very fast researcher and fact-gatherer about my companies. The difficult thing about this rule is that you can't be diversified to my liking unless you have five stocks in your portfolio, which means that you need to have five hours free a week to run your own money. Don't freak out; it takes five hours to watch an afternoon of football. It takes about five hours to go to a baseball game. You go to the movies, it's about a four-hour experience. Are those activities more important than your money? I didn't think so. If you don't have the time, skip to page 198, because you are not going to be a good enough portfolio manager. You just don't have the time. If you have only four hours, give the money to one of the fund managers I recommend. You can be a great client in four hours.

3. You must be interested in business, in what makes a business tick, to do it yourself. You must be curious about how a business makes its money, what its metric is that has to be beaten—gross margins, revenues, seat miles, average selling price per unit, etc.—and how much growth you think a company may have. If you don't have that inclination to find out these things, you won't know whether a decline in a stock is a buying opportunity or a time to puke up the stock—and if you don't know that, I guarantee you will lose money. If you can't explain to me in thirty seconds what a company does and what you are expecting out of that company, go be a great client; you won't be a great investor. I am not asking you to be a stock junkie, like me; I am asking you to have some authority and curiosity about companies before you buy them.

4. You must have someone, not necessarily a broker, you can bounce an idea off of, someone whom you trust, so you can get a second opinion on the stock before you buy it. I didn't use to believe this,

but Byron Wien, the great strategist at Morgan Stanley, put this idea into my head during the beginning of the dot-com period. I was telling him my idea for TheStreet.com. I said that lots of people were going to go "self-directed," industry parlance for doing it yourself. He laughed and said it will never happen because people, in the end, are so fallible, they are going to want to interact with another human being first, as a sounding board, if not talk directly to a human broker, just to get some sense of whether the idea is so stupid and reckless that it shouldn't be done. I told him that millions of people were flocking to online trading. He told me that it was just a matter of time before they lost everything, in part because the idea of having to explain a buy to someone, explaining why you own something and why it is worth owning, requires the scrutiny of another person. The sounding board is worth the commission, he said. Of course, I was right and he was right. Millions went online and bought, and then those millions lost billions in part because they never bounced the zany, wacky ideas off anyone else. They never articulated why they liked something. You remove that embarrassing interchange and you will embarrass yourself a heck of a lot more on the back end. Get a sounding board before you buy. Don't have one? Call me Fridays on the "Lightning Round" at 1-800-862-8686 or during one of my second-opinion shows, where I can help you. Otherwise, again, have someone else run your money.

5. Finally, I can't have you get discouraged and quit. The whole process is a game of endurance. Think long-distance running. There are periods where you want all your discretionary money in cash, and there are periods where you want every dollar on the board wagering for you. Remember, I'm not talking about the retirement account. That's too sacrosanct to play with; you need to keep that with others unless you know already that you can beat the market. As I have said elsewhere, I am a rank conservative when it comes to retirement: I want the money as diversified as possible into high-quality equities as defined by an index fund or a mutual fund that acts as an index fund with a brain. We aren't fooling around here. As you get older, you need

to have fewer stocks and more bonds. But that's not the kind of investing we are talking about here. What I am talking about here is the notion of setting up the portfolio and then having the discipline to stay with it, to review it, and to cull it and revise it. I will give you very specific advice later in the chapter how to rank things like a pro. We know that no asset class has beaten high-quality stocks that pay dividends over a twenty-year period. But we also know that many people get fed up during the tough times and blow their stocks out either because they can't take the pain or their stocks aren't of high enough quality to meet the test. Sign on for the long term, not a couple-of-years hitch. That will solve a lot of your problems.

Okay, now you have gone through the warnings and you have checked off on all five preconditions. You are now ready to build a portfolio to augment your paycheck. I am going to assume that you can build up to ten stocks, that you are willing to give it ten hours a week. If you can't do ten, cut it back to five and just take my top five from the Chinese menu I have prepared.

    I am not intentionally trying to steer you to any one company. I have come up with a menu that makes it so you can get involved with a portfolio and stay involved, and use your expertise (which you may not even realize you have) to pick stocks. I want you to feel free to deviate from the list, but if you pick from it, I know you will be diversified in areas and types of stocks, and that will keep your risk to a minimum and your rewards to levels you are not used to achieving. I present it in menu form by sector or by risk-reward. You have to choose the stocks because, after all, it is *your* portfolio. This way, with this menu, I know you won't just own five tech stocks. I know you will be diversified and not get clobbered on the down days. I know you will stay involved because you are doing the picking, not me. I can't be your guru; who knows when I won't be there to hold your hand. You need to be your own guru, but I can give you the parameters, the guard rails so to speak, to be sure you don't plunge off the bridge into the sea of red ink that awaits so many who try to do it themselves.

1. Your first pick should be a stock of a company from your neighborhood, something that you know or can relate to, a company that employs people close to you or you can ask around about. Let me give you some examples. My first stock was an aircraft parts manufacturer in my hometown that was desperately searching for employees soon after I got out of college. I knew that in my lifetime the company had periodically been hiring and periodically laying off people, but I had never seen it recruit as aggressively as in 1979. I looked at the financials. It didn't have a lot of debt. I read what was available publicly—not much then, a lot more now. I bought the stock. It doubled in about seven months' time. The next stock I picked was out of a business magazine, a company in a business I knew nothing about, women's clothing, and I lost about 70 percent of my money in about seven weeks' time. That doesn't mean you are immune when you buy locally; it does mean, however, that if the stock goes down at first or if it gets hammered, you can more easily check around with friends and neighbors than if you are buying the stock of something with which you are not familiar. After that, I stuck close to home, or at least to something I would have some firsthand call on.

Please be careful when you work this hometown advantage. I bought the stock of a company once that had a factory that made precision instruments for aircraft dashboards. The local paper kept talking about how the division was hiring like crazy and getting big orders, but it was part of a larger company that at the same time was imploding under a mountain of debt. My method doesn't absolve you of homework; it is just a way to be able to get a feel beyond what you might get by just buying shares in some tech company that you know nothing about that could be slaughtered as you continue to buy down for no good reason.

There used to be a toy and novelty store down the block from where I lived in Brooklyn. I went by it every day to pick up a little trinket for my kids, something my dad used to do for me when I was growing up. Each day I heard the "boys" who ran it talking about what was hot and what wasn't. From them I had a very nice hit in Mattel, a

comeback story. But one day I heard them cursing about the stock market. They had no idea who I was. One had bought Seagate, the other Daisy Systems. I told them at the register that I was always interested in stocks and that I was intrigued by what they knew about Seagate and Daisy, both of which I happened to have been shorting for my fund. They freely admitted they knew nothing; they had just heard these were hot stocks from someone on TV. I laughed and told them to get out now. Seagate was cut in half soon after; Daisy filed for bankruptcy. Classic—they were making me money with their inventory and they were buying stocks they knew nothing about.

Having trouble finding a local company or local news about one, like Mattel? Check the business pages of your local paper. They usually have a good read on the companies in and around town. Of course, you need to be able to stay current beyond reading that paper. All of the rules of homework apply, but that is a nice way to start. Many papers have beefed up their business coverage these last few years, and I always found them—still do—to be of tremendous value in finding new ideas. The best papers are the real local papers, the weekly local paper that covers just your area, your suburb, your neck of the woods. That's where the really great ideas come from.

2. Your next pick should be an oil stock. I almost never see a portfolio with an oil stock in it and it drives me crazy. These are some of the most consistent performers, with high-dividend yields, great cash flows, and businesses that do well in times of tension. I am a huge believer that we are going to see continual increases in demand for oil worldwide, and until a better fuel is found you should own shares in one of these companies. Exxon, British Petroleum, ChevronTexaco, ConocoPhillips, and Kerr-McGee all could be great for many, many years. They will be boosting their buybacks and raising their dividends as their cash flows have increased faster than any other sector. Oil is in what we call a "secular bull market," meaning that it has characteristics of longevity that counteract the traditional cyclical nature of so many businesses. Strong or weak economy, it seems, oil's staying

up there as a valued commodity. Can't come up with a stock? What brand of gas do you buy? That will probably be fine. Yeah, it is that simple.

Oil used to be 20 percent of the S&P 500 when I got into the business of stocks. It subsequently went all the way down to 5 percent two years ago. As I write it is only at 7 percent. I think that it belongs at 10 percent. When you see it there, you are free to take a profit if you want to. Not until then, though. These stocks have fallen well behind the price of crude; that will change over time and you will be the beneficiary.

3. You need a brand-name blue chip that currently sells at a 2.5 percent yield or greater. At any given time the market's putting on a sale of one of these and you just need to find which one is right. Why 2.5 percent yield? That's above average for the S&P and it affords you protection if the stock gets hit. I don't find a lot of 2.5 percent yielders getting crushed because they have a floor. The floor will be lower when the Fed finishes raising rates, but I think that it is nice to know that the worst thing that happens is you are getting an even bigger yield as the stock goes down. Consider one of the major chemical companies or conglomerates if you are having a hard time choosing. Try to get one with a history of raising dividends when possible. Please, please, don't buy the stock of a company that is borrowing to fund the dividend. I know I can count on you to spot that, because you agreed to my Miranda warnings earlier in this chapter. Remember to use the weakness in the market to buy a high-quality dividender on your terms.

4. You need to own shares in a financial, one of the largest portions of the S&P 500. I like to own local. I have had phenomenal success over a twenty-year period owning a local bank or a savings and loan. One of my biggest hits came from Commerce Bancorp. When it opened near me I was attracted to its seven-day-a-week service, and we decided to bank there. About three months after we put our money in CBH, I told my wife that I was going to be attending a conference

where the CEO of CBH was going to be speaking. She told me that I should give him a piece of her mind because the sun glare in the afternoon made it impossible for her to read the screen at the automated teller. Sure enough, I got a moment with Vernon Hill and I told him that we were Commerce Bancorp users but that my wife didn't like the glare at her branch. He asked which branch, I gave him the location. It was a Saturday. On Monday my wife went to the branch and a glare shield had been added. That's my kind of service. And that's my kind of stock. I had a similarly positive experience with a Third Federal Savings when I used to live in Doylestown, Pennsylvania. I needed a mortgage; they came to my house, at night. Didn't even have to ask them to. I checked out their branch, looked at their financials, and ended up taking down a big chunk and getting a nice payback within a couple of years, with a good dividend, too. Every town has some publicly traded banks. If you have a good experience, go buy shares in it, provided that it has a good history of earnings and dividends, something that you know how to find out because you have agreed to do the homework in advance. Your visits to your bank are your gut checks that are so necessary to know whether you should buy more or not when the stock gets hit. And the stock will get hit and hit hard at some point while it is in your custody, as Commerce Bancorp did. I don't care whether you buy a savings and loan or a bank; I do care that there be insider buying in the institution—just some because I need to see conviction—and it sure helps if there is a nice-sized dividend relative to the rest of the market. I especially like situations where you can get in on shares in an IPO of a new savings and loan because you are a depositor. That's been the single biggest source of wins for thousands of investors who pay attention to where they bank.

5. No other financial writer in America is going to tell you what I am about to tell you next and frankly, I could not care less. I know you crave speculation and I know that some speculative investments can be rewarding. I am not willing, like so many others who write and talk about the market, to deny you that feeling. It is too ascetic and unnat-

ural. I know you will speculate anyway. It's human nature, in the same way that gambling and lottery tickets attract so many takers, no matter how many times you tell people it is a sucker's game. That's why to round out your top five investments I am blessing an investment in some risky, on the come, next Microsoft, Home Depot situation. You can choose something that is being recommended by the *Stocks Under $10* newsletter, perhaps, which I have a hand in. Or you can choose a tech or a biotech company that has some potential to be a huge company. I am blessing this because I have found that investing is a lot like parenting; if you don't give your kids a little room to do something daring, to break a few rules, then they will break all of the rules and cause tremendous heartache. I am telling you, go, with 20 percent of your money, and buy something that you think could be a terrific investment, a hunch, a potential home run. But if you do, please, I don't want you to put one penny more into speculation than that. You are taking a pledge. You must swear to me you won't put more into the speculative portion of your portfolio even if it is crushed and you want to average down. This is the portion of the portfolio where you can expect to lose your investment, and you should accept that. I don't want you losing more than your 20 percent, though, because you can't make it back with the consistent growers you own elsewhere in your portfolio. The math's just too brutal.

Mind you, if you have the time and the inclination, you might use this slot, again keeping in mind it is only 20 percent of your investment, in a pooled fashion. Some of the best investments I have ever made are in baskets of down-and-out stocks that can either go to zero or make you a fortune. In October 2002, for example, I recommended a basket of telecommunications stocks, all of which sold under $2: Lucent, Nortel, JDSU, Corning, and Qwest. With the downside factored in—thank heavens stocks can't go to negative 4—I watched as some of these stocks doubled and doubled again. Each time I took some of the investment off the table but let the rest run. I did a similar field bet in 2003 with the merchant energy companies like Dynegy and El Paso that were down on their luck and trading under $7. These kinds of

field bets can serve as the speculative portion of your portfolio just as well as if you are trying to hunt for the next Amgen. Typically, in a field bet, one of the five will go to zero, another one or two will do nothing, but the others will create profit enough to make the whole thing worthwhile. I make these bets whenever a sector falls so out of favor that even if the stocks fall from where they are, the loss will not be of great magnitude. Again, you can't let the speculative portion of your portfolio exceed 20 percent of your invested capital or you are taking on too much risk. By the way, I am always making field bets in distressed areas, so stay close to what I'm up to for ActionAlerts PLUS.com, my private account where I send out e-mails to you telling you what I am going to do before I do it. I play with an open hand. For a trial simply log in at www.thestreet.com/actionalertsplus, another special URL for readers of the book only.

You have now selected five stocks from a list of diversified sectors. You can stop there or, if you have the time and inclination, you can diversify further, adding something from each of the next five items as you get more capital.

6. Rotations of the type I have described—where market players flee safety for aggressive cyclicals because the Fed is about to ease rates aggressively—often create tremendous buying opportunities in the staid and true, the Procter & Gambles, Kelloggs, the Colgates, BUDs, General Millses and Gillettes, the so-called medicine chest and fridge stocks. As you have already selected your diversified five stocks, why not wait to add the sixth, a soft-goods secular growth stock, until the market deems it out of fashion. You have a long-term time horizon; be smart and pick the stock up when nobody likes it. Use the rotation to pick it up much cheaper than you would otherwise. Use the decline to win, not lose, for once, with your portfolio. Lots of times these stocks go down hard after a particular quarter because some fund or funds get disappointed. But it is a tribute to the high quality of these branded companies that they almost always snap back. So don't be

afraid to buy the most dislocated of the companies that have big shelf space in the supermarket. That's how I gauge it—with my eyes.

7. Now, to augment that soft-goods play, I want you to buy one high-quality cyclical stock when it is clear that the economy is going to go bust and the smokestack stocks are being trashed repeatedly. My favorites: Dow, Deere, DuPont, Caterpillar, Boeing, Ingersoll-Rand, United Technologies, and 3M. These stocks, like those of the category above, *always* get slammed if you wait long enough, and the slamming will produce value for a long period of time. Again, you have to regard the rotation as your chance to pounce on the proverbial straw hat in winter or snowshoes in July. You are not affected by the "inventory" concerns that plague so many professional money managers. No one is looking over your shoulder, no one is reviewing your portfolio daily, so use that advantage to snap up the stocks that the lemmings have to get rid of to show they were "in the know." These are great American companies that, several times a year, get thrown into the discount bin or are marked down by market hysteria. You have to be ready when it happens.

8. Technology companies are risky; but not to have a technology company has proven to be a terrible risk for all but three of the last twenty years. That's why I think you have room for one after you have selected the other seven stocks. Me, I am so conservative, I like tech companies with yield. That means they are mature enough to be steady growers and you haven't necessarily sacrificed double-digit growth. If you think that I am being too stodgy, you have an easy choice: Make your tech stock your speculative stock. I have seen so many portfolios with the same old poorly performing bunch of techs that I can't bear to see you load up with too many of them. I would hate to have to buzzer you if you called me on a Wednesday when I am playing "Am I Diversified?" I know that tech can be considered the lifeblood of the economy, but so many have put tech at the first, second, and third portions of their portfolios, much to their own ruina-

tion, that I need you to deemphasize the sector. It is too dangerous to overweight until all the others have capitulated. And remember, that comes from me, an Intelaholic.

9. Add one young retailer that hasn't yet expanded to the majority of the country, and has preferably saturated only one region of the nation on a march to national status. People are always saying that the retailers are great investments, but they don't understand that it is not "the retailers" in general, but the retailers that are still expanding geographically around the nation. In fact, once the companies are everywhere they tend to be pretty poor investments, as anyone who has owned May or Federated or even Wal-Mart can attest. I like to buy retailers when they are just getting started and they have a concept that, if it works in one place, can work all over the country. That's how I discovered and owned so many great retailers, including great one-time growth stocks like the Limited, Gap, Wal-Mart, Kohl's, and even Lowes and Home Depot. Once they were everywhere, though, I sold them and never looked back. Currently I like Cabela's because it is a high-end camping and hunting store that could go for years before it saturates the landscape. Be careful, though, you must check them out firsthand.

10. Finally, buy a "hope for the future" nontech stock, perhaps a biotech company or another kind of company from the S&P 600, which is the mid cap index. Many of these companies will turn out to be the Amgens and Starbucks of tomorrow. You have to be a legit company to get into the S&P 600, and it is the proving ground for the S&P 500. It's a natural place to hunt for some good names. That's a great list to choose from; if you can't come up with something, pick a holding from the New America index of *Investor's Business Daily*. They have a phenomenal track record for selecting these kinds of medium-stage companies. Again, do your homework. *IBD* is no substitute, just another terrific starting point for ideas that you can use to find the next big stock.

Now that you have picked your stocks, you have to learn how to buy and sell for your portfolio.

I am a huge believer, as you know, in my own fallibility. I also like to make the market work for me. It puts on sales all the time. I like to use those sales to buy my stocks cheaply. That's why I have urged you to set up your portfolio to take advantage of the sales. Rotation sales are like post-Christmas sales. You know they are going to come. Unlike Christmas, you don't purchase a stock for someone else; this is for you. So wait for the sale and take advantage of it.

I also don't believe in putting too much money to work at one level. I know that the market tends to fool the most people it can. So why be faked out? Why not accept that your first buy may not be your last buy and build in the weakness? That way you are never top-ticking, something that's incredibly important if you are going to stay in the game. I know most people think that the market is rigged against them. That's because they buy a stock and it immediately goes down. Heck, if so many people complain about this—and they do on my radio show all of the time—let's do something about it.

So, let's say I want to own 200 shares of Cabela's as part of a retail bet because this retailer is only in a small part of the country and it can grow forever. It will take a decade before Cabela's has saturated anything. That means anytime it dips it could be a terrific buy.

What I like to do is buy my first 100 shares and then wait. If the stock goes down a buck or two, I will buy it; if it goes up, oh well, the worst that happens is I have made a little less money than I would like. That's how I buy everything. I like to buy weakness. Similarly, I like to sell strength. When I have decided to take something off the table I wait until a day when my stocks are running and I offer them out. I never like to exit all at once; I pare back. That's the best way; don't let your broker press you into being the big man and selling all at once.

At any given time I maintain a wish list of stocks to buy and to sell as part of my portfolio. I don't know when the sell-off is going to take place; I just presume it will happen and then I pounce. I am so reli-

gious about not buying stock all at one level that I actually sketch out the levels I will pull the trigger at, and I will widen or narrow the scale of the bids depending on how well or badly the market might be doing at the time. If I believe, for example, as I did in 2000–2002, that the market itself would serve to hinder my buys, I use a wide scale. If the market was poised to make a move because, as a whole, it seemed cheap and was ready to roll higher, I would use tighter scales. I let the market throw its sales to get my merchandise at better prices.

Of course, there will always be situations where you have been too aggressive and the market becomes brutal. There will always be situations where you simply misjudge the market. I don't care about misjudging it too conservatively: The worst that happens is you make less money. I care about being too aggressive when the timing is bad and getting your head handed to you. Again, those kinds of misjudgments come with the risky assets we are accumulating. My insurance against my own fallibility, besides the use of scales to buy on the way down, is to rank my stocks, perform a sort of battlefield triage for the moments when it seems as if the world's coming to an end and all of my stocks are getting killed. That's why I rank my stocks every Friday on a scale of 1 to 4. It helps me make judgments in a cool moment that can then hold up during the hurly-burly of the trading day. (I don't like to make these rankings during the trading day because that influences my fears more than it should. Fear is too powerful when the market's open.) My four-part scale makes the process much easier. You can easily employ the same strategy with your portfolio. A 1 is a stock that if I have capital handy—some sidelined cash or new money—I want to apply it right now, that's how good it is. A 2 is a stock that if it pulled back 5–7 percent, or a couple of points, I would buy more. A 3 is a stock that if it were to go up 5–7 percent, or a few points, I would begin to sell it. And a 4 is the mirror image of a 1, it is a stock I want to get rid of ASAP, either because it has gone up enough or because I think it could be a real bone-crusher in an ugly tape. Because I have ranked my stocks, when things get nasty I circle the wagons around my 1s and 2s and I let go of my 3s and 4s. I would be willing on the fly to whittle my

positions down to my top five from ten if I felt that I was in danger of getting crushed by the market. I also know that if there are stocks that I wouldn't buy right now, then I don't have the conviction I need, I am too heavily invested, and I will panic out of my holdings when the tape turns really ugly. (If this is all foreign to you, take a trial of my ActionAlertsPLUS.com where I run my own money publicly. Lots of good ideas there, and I use this identical ranking system to make all my buy and sell decisions.)

Ranking stocks is a tremendous way to test your discipline and your conviction. If you don't want to buy more of a stock right now, right here, that says something. That says when things get tough you will jettison it in a heartbeat. What we are looking for, what ranking does, is make it so that weakness is *welcomed*. It stands the psychology on its head and turns fear into a method of buying your stocks on terms you want, instead of selling them on terms the markets dictate.

I love the flexibility, by the way, of selling a quarter or even half of my shares as a stock goes up. Selling strength is another of my trademarks. If you want to buy on a sale at a store, wouldn't you like to return some of the merchandise at a higher price if possible? When I put it like that, I'm sure you understand my "scaling out" on the way up. If the stock falls back, I can always repurchase it. If it keeps rallying, I just make a little less money than I would like. By selling partially into strength, I don't violate my bulls, bears, and pigs adage. But I also let my winners run, which is vital, particularly because I often see people sell really good stocks that are going higher where they have done a giant amount of homework, only to reinvest the money in a loser.

Ranking stocks, making sure not to defend everything because then you really are defending nothing, and waiting for broad market sell-offs that have nothing to do with the companies you are buying but are knocking down the stocks you like anyway are the disciplines necessary to maintain your portfolio in tip-top shape. They are the key to implementing a disciplined approach that allows conviction to make you money but limits the losses during the inevitable vicious markets that we have all become so fearful of. You must feel embold-

ened by sell-offs, not paralyzed by them. You must recognize that a sale in the market is no more frightening than a sale at Macy's. If you do that, you will prosper when others are beside themselves with pain or throwing up their hands with resignation.

You don't have the time or the inclination to build and maintain a portfolio with your discretionary savings. What can you do instead? I've got a couple of options, none of them optimal, but all of them acceptable. First, you can get your diversity and beat almost every single mutual fund manager simply by buying shares in stock index fund. Almost every major firm has them; the key is to find the lowest fees possible as these are commodities. Vanguard pioneered the S&P 500 index fund and is the cheapest and best one I can find.

Why do most managers fail to beat index funds? Because it's a lot harder to manage a lot of money than it looks. If you manage a traditional mutual fund and you do well, you will soon be inundated with money, which will cause you to change your style and, over time, unless you are incredibly good, you will begin to mirror an index fund, except you will be charging your investors higher fees.

John Bogle, the most honest money manager in the business, and the creator of the index fund, once appeared on one of my TV shows after I had run money professionally for about ten years. He said that no successful manager, over the long run, can beat an index fund. I told him that was just untrue, that I was a living, breathing example of someone who consistently beat index funds. He then asked me, "Do you limit the amount of money you take in?" I told him that not only did I limit the amount of money that I took in but that I was almost always closed to new investors.

He then asked me how much I ran. At the time I had about $200 million under management. He said that as long as I stayed under $500 million and was closed to new investors—relying only on capital appreciation for more money under management—I would be able, if I continued to be really good, to beat the market. But once I got above those levels and changed my exclusionary policy I would eventually

become a glorified index fund with high fees. I never forgot that and I never went bigger than $500 million. I also never got beat. That's why.

Most mutual funds, which have a different incentive structure from a hedge fund, can't be so exclusionary. Hedge funds take a percentage of the gains—realized and unrealized. I took 20 percent. Mutual funds take a percentage of the money under management, usually about 1 percent. Given that everyone on Wall Street wants growth, the way to grow your fees is to take in more money. So the natural tendency is to get big fast, particularly after you have a hot hand. That's just the recipe for underperformance that Bogle sketched out. Nevertheless, there are some managers, individual managers, who are so good that they have been able to overcome the Bogle problem. Unfortunately, they are few and far between. Consider the game like the NBA; 99.9 percent of the basketball players aren't good enough to get in the NBA, and even when you get there, only a handful are bona fide superstars.

Before I give you the names of the great managers, let me just add that I hate giving mutual fund recommendations. As an experiment five years ago I put $2,500 into each of fifty mutual funds to see if I could keep up with who was good and discover some stars, some people worth writing about. Only three of the funds made me money, and none made enough money to get mentioned here. Bogle's right.

Still, there are some managers I recommend because they are truly world-class stock pickers. Notice, I am giving you the name of the manager, as well as the fund. *If* the managers were to leave or retire—and the industry is notorious about not telling you if they do, so you have to stay on top of it—you will have to pull your money out pronto because you only buy a manager in this business, not a fund.

The first is Will Danoff of Fidelity Contrafund. Danoff worked with my wife in the 1980s, and it always burned me up that she said he was as smart as I was. I always figured that if she weren't married to me she would be telling people that he was smarter than I am. I am a jealous guy. The only way to get even is to give the guy you think might be better than you some money, which is why I have a lot of my personal

retirement money with Contra. Danoff's the real deal. He's had the fund since 1990. While his five-year performance is not a knockout at 1.69 percent, he's your index fund with a brain, as the S&P returned −2.30 percent during the same period. I like to use Danoff's Contra as a substitute index fund because it always does a little better with less risk. You can't ask for more than that from big money.

My second pick is Richie Freeman of the Smith Barney Aggressive Growth Fund. Freeman's fantastic; a stock picker *par excellence,* someone who lives and breathes stocks the way I do. He's incredibly focused and driven to beat the averages. You want him in your corner. Freeman's always good, but I particularly like to give him money after he's had a rough patch; he's so competitive that that's when he is most bankable. Richie's been in the game since 1983. In the last five years he's averaged 5.83 percent, with terrific recovery from a very tough 2002.

My third pick is the John Hancock Classic Value Fund, run by Rich Pzena. Rich got in the business about the same time I did and has always been a fantastic value guy. I'd entrust him with any amount of money because he picks stocks with the lowest risk and highest reward of anyone I know. Always has. Rich has chalked up a 13 percent annual return over the last five years. Wow!

Lawrence Auriana's been a guest numerous times on my CNBC show. He and his partner Hans Utsch have been running the Federated Kaufmann Fund for almost two decades. They are driven to find new names, great health-care and tech companies. They are wild-card players, but they play those cards more consistently than any managers I know. These two have shot the lights out over a long period of time, notching 12.5 percent annually in the last five years.

Finally, the only manager I don't know personally whom I will recommend is Clyde McGregor, who runs the Oakmark Equity and Income Fund. Unlike all of the other funds, this one has a heavy bond exposure, so consider it the most conservative of the lot. Given this fund's risk aversion, the 11.76 percent return is just plain stellar.

Remember that mutual funds are already diversified, so you don't

need to own a whole bunch of them. I am always getting phone calls and e-mails from people who own ten or twenty mutual funds, which is absurd. Who can keep up with that? I would invest in the Oakmark Equity and Income Fund if you are conservative, Federated Kaufmann or Smith Barney Aggressive Growth if you want to have some risk with big reward, and the Contrafund if you are somewhere in the middle like the vast majority of folks out there. If you just had to own one fund, I would make it Contra. I don't want to overthink this process. I bet all of these managers are going to beat the index funds simply because they are better than 99 percent of the managers.

What happens if you say, Hold it, I want to be in a hedge fund, not a mutual fund. I want some of the service that Cramer gave to his partners at his firm, where he talked to his clients whenever they wanted and told them what they owned and consistently outperformed. (Mutual funds tell you nothing about what they own in real time, so you just have to trust the manager.) I have bad news for you. I have no recommendations for you. First of all, hedge funds can take only "qualified" investors, meaning rich people. Second, I don't know anyone I would like to recommend to you. I can tell you, though, that you need to interview the manager personally and be sure that he has done well in good *and* bad times. It is incredibly important that the manager give you two references whom you can call. If he can't do that, don't bother. He also has to have an outside accountant who works just for the partners. That accountant works for you, gets all of the confirmations and documents, and can tell you where you stand. Without such an arrangement, I would be scared to have my money with that fund, because hedge funds aren't regulated by the SEC in the same way that mutual funds are.

Should you be worried about shenanigans at the mutual funds, after the terrible disclosures that some made about selling the net asset value of the individuals to the hedge funds to take advantage of pricing discrepancies? Not any more. The regulators have cracked down. But far worse than the chicanery, frankly, is the poor management and the return after the fees are taken. The managers I recommend above

all charge fees, but the net return of their funds after fees is still much better than the averages, and only the net matters.

If instead of giving your money to a hedge fund or a mutual fund you want to give it to an individual broker, all I can say is good luck. My experience is that no really good broker, who has made money consistently for his clients, can service you if you have less than $250,000. Of course, there will be thousands who disagree, so here's what I suggest. Find someone with your size nest egg who can recommend a broker. It is a total word-of-mouth business. The firm itself means nothing to me, only the broker, because at any firm there are hundreds of ideas and ways to make money. You need someone who can harness the best and cull the worst. Only a word-of-mouth recommendation is going to cut it for me, because, again, I have no recommendations. I don't mean that meanly, I am just saying that it is a one-to-one business, like health care, and you have to find the broker you would be most comfortable with.

If you have less than $250,000 and you want a broker, I don't think I can protect you from being treated poorly. So you either have to learn to do it yourself or you split up the money among the managers I have highlighted here.

I know I sound cynical, but just call me skeptical. Having worked as a commission broker, an investment adviser, and a hedge fund manager, and having taken and answered literally tens of thousands of calls and e-mails from investors, I know the business's limitations. I am not going to sugarcoat them. If you care about your money and you want to see it grow and you don't want it screwed up, you must take the time and develop the inclination to do the things I say here. Together we can do it; otherwise everything else is just, well, settling for less than you deserve.

Oh, one other thing: please be wary of hot funds. One time, while I was working with my wife, a decade before I talked with Bogle, I opened my fund after a fantastic quarter. I took in almost the same amount of money that I was running. What happened? Well, when I was a kid there was a game show called *Supermarket Sweep*. In the

show contestants would have a couple of minutes to run through a supermarket with a cart, gathering as many expensive goods as they could. Whoever grabbed the highest-priced merchandise won the game—"Look, he's going for the hams!"

That was me. I had to put that money to work. Fast as possible. They didn't give me the money to sit on the sidelines, I rationalized. I went for the hams! Sure enough I got the market's equivalent of trichinosis. As soon as I spent the money I knew I had done the wrong thing. Within two weeks the fund had dropped 10 percent. I spent the rest of the year making up for the decline.

Why does this happen? Couple of reasons. One is that you feel the responsibility of the new money. You feel that you have to justify why you took it in. The only way to justify it is to invest it.

Second, the size that you use to buy, your deployment tactics, change when you run twice as much money. You don't know how much you should put to work at one level. You don't how you should buy things. If I used to buy 5,000 shares at a time should I now buy 25,000? I blew my head off because my usual method, 5,000 shares at a time, seemed too slow to me. I started committing capital too aggressively.

Third, what works for $20 million may not work for $50 million or $500 million or $5 billion. Maybe the secret of your first-quarter success was finding precisely the right small cap stocks. Now that you took in all of this money you feel like you have to invest, but you can't find the right small caps to meet your rigorous criteria. So you force things. That's how you make even bigger mistakes.

Eventually the stress of the money cascading through the door becomes too much for any mortal to take. The job becomes managing the input, not picking stocks, and the great stock pickers get sacrificed. The fund managers I recommend have dealt with this issue, confronted it, and have the tenure and power to tell the marketing department, "Look, I can't handle the money right now. That's why I feel so confident about them and so nervous about the new ones I don't know."

8

SPOTTING BOTTOMS
in
STOCKS

If someone asked me what I do for a living, what's my modus operandi, I would have to tell them that I spot bottoms in stocks. That's my specialty. That's what I am best at. I'm good at buying a stock when it is down and nobody much cares for it. Most investors are momentum driven. They want to try to catch a stock while it is having a huge move. They like to buy up, pay up, find a stock that's moving like Secretariat and catch the last five furlongs. That's not for me. Not enough reward, too much risk, especially given what I know about how a company's stock can diverge substantially from the worth of the underlying company. That's why I am not a chaser; I'm a classic bottom fisher. I try to buy situations where stocks have gone down to some level that to me is just plain wrong, that is totally and unequivocally out of synch with the underlying company the stock represents. I try to buy stocks with such a limited downside that I feel they are gifts if they go any lower, not accidents waiting to happen. Given that we accept that the fundamentals and the stocks that are supposed to track these fundamentals don't act in synch, obviously

the most lucrative time to buy the divergence is when the company's otherwise sound fundamentals are temporarily impaired and the stock takes a header well beyond what is warranted. That's when the company's long-term virtues are totally out of whack with the equity.

It stands to reason then that the same goes for the market as a whole. There are moments of sheer lunacy involving the S&P 500, the benchmark index that we all follow, or in the NASDAQ or even the Dow Jones averages, where these gold standards of investing go awry because of panicky sellers. They can be completely and totally wrong versus how the underlying companies or the economy is really doing. That happens at bottoms. The positive realities separate themselves from the panicked fantasies of bizarre, uneconomical, and irrational closing prices, and you have to pounce when they do.

Understand that bottom fishing is not a "technique" per se, as in "buy a stock down 10 percent from its fifty-two-week high" or "buy the market on a big dip." That's way too ephemeral for me. Nor is it a formula, as in "wait until a stock trades through its growth rate" or "don't pull the trigger until a stock trades at a 25 percent discount to the market, or at 10 times earnings." That's too hard and fast for reality. Lots of really crummy stocks of really crummy companies are going to trade down 25 percent and then go down another 75 percent. That's a fishing net that catches some salmon as well as a lot of killer orcas, murderers of your financial well-being. My bottom fishing is a collection of perceived working patterns that have held up over a substantial period of time for both individual stocks and the market as a whole. Just like the sport that I compare it to, bottom fishing requires incredible patience and a sense that just when you are about to give up is the moment that greatness strikes. You can't rush bottoms. It is no more scientific than fishing—there's a definite feel to it. The biggest mistake people make in finding bottoms is that they find too many of them and find them too often. The bottoms I am talking about are rare, rare and dramatic. True long-lasting bottoms just don't occur every day, or every month, or even every quarter. They occur just often enough to make the patient rich and to reward the out-of-favor buyer.

When selecting individual stocks, most people try to catch bottoms by looking at a chart, one of those with candles on it, or with squiggly lines that mark a two-hundred-day average of how the stock has traded. They see that a stock has gone down for a long time; perhaps it has retreated to something like its norm, as represented by the fifty-two-week moving average, and lately the stock has stopped bleeding. That's enough for many of these chartists, regardless of whether the patient has stopped bleeding because he is dead or because he's healed. To me, bottom fishing by chart is reckless. It often sends a false signal and puts you in a stock or the market way too early and without any grounding if the stock breaks down again from that level. To me a "chart bottom" doesn't make you any money and gives you an artificial and unwarranted sense of confidence. You will never spot a real stock market bottom simply by looking at a chart. Even Mrs. Cramer, who regarded herself as the quintessential chart bottom caller, was off by as much as 50 percent from the start of some of her small stock bottoms that she picked from the chart alone. That's too dangerous for me.

Nor are there successful software packages or Web sites that produce lists of surefire bottoms, even though many people pitch these products in that vernacular. Don't be taken by shameless charlatans; things aren't that easy out there. Avoid those packages that show you well-defined channels or successful entry points. They are all bogus and will cause you to double down or sell at the worst possible moments. My kind of bottom calling is also different from the unoriginal and often corrupted world of Wall Street research, where hedge funds or mutual funds lean on analysts at sell-side firms, telling them to call bottoms in some of their flagging stocks or else they will take their commission dollars elsewhere. Don't think this stuff has happened? Then you were never on the other end of the line when I berated analysts to climb out of their foxholes and make a stand to defend a Cisco or an Intel when I owned them. I used to do it all of the time; thank heavens I am out of that contest. Nor do I spot bottoms by watching and listening to the much hyped "earnings" reports during earnings

season. Despite all of those "upside" and "downside" surprises, none of the bottoms I have studied were ever caused by those reports. These are almost all artificial anyway, a product of the companies' whispering to analysts what numbers to use so they can beat those lowball projections by a penny or two and take in unsuspecting new shareholders, or buyers. That was supposed to have stopped with the corporate reform—the Sarbanes-Oxley Act—but it still goes on. So you can forget about that mumbo jumbo for finding bottoms after a long slide; it doesn't compute.

Nor am I talking about capturing momentary trading bottoms, either. I am not trying to persuade you to try to scalp flow off institutional buy and sell orders, as I did at my hedge fund. You need to generate monster commissions before you will get "the call" that a seller who has mercilessly knocked a stock down while exiting has at last finished his nefarious work and the temporarily depressed stock is ready to bounce. That kind of ephemeral bottom doesn't make you big money and is completely inaccessible to you anyway. It just generates a lot of short-term profits for the hedge fund operators and a new set of commissions for the brokerage houses on top of the ones gained from working the stock down.

Not one big bottom that I have found was ever called by a Wall Street analyst with a buy recommendation, either. The "hold to buy" parlance never coincided or was predictive of the bottoms I am trying to catch. These people make you money, for the most part, by luck. Almost all of the major analysts at the large firms got hired for banking prowess—bringing in the next underwriting deals—not for stock picking. If you have to use one, be sure he doesn't do banking first, so you at least know that *you* are the client and not the investment banker down the hall. In a study of literally thousands of big bottoms in the stock market or in individual stocks I couldn't find a single big bottom that was snared by these folks. In fact, it is the opposite. I found their downgrades to be more predictive of important bottoms than their upgrades because of their inability to see the bottoms coming. So there's nothing in this chapter that relies upon my hedge fund spe-

cialty, my good calls from brokers for all the business I did, nor my close contacts with dozens of analysts from around the country. In fact, sadly, the closer you get to the vortex of information that I swirled in at my old office, the more likely that a bottom will be drowned out by the accompanying noise that often causes it.

My bottoms are what I call "megabottoms." These are the kinds of bottoms that you brag about getting for years, the kind that occur after vicious and often wildly exaggerated declines. The kind that happen when a stock seems permanently damaged even as the company underneath is suffering no more than a scant hiccup. My work on the topic is the result of examining and studying thousands of true bottoms that I have called—and some that I have missed—in both the stock market and in individual stocks. When you invest in these kinds of bottoms, you don't have to be nearly as worried about all of the other things that I caution and counsel about in this book. You can stay a bull for a while, you have a longer time to wait until you become a pig. You don't have to fear imminent overvaluation because you have caught a stock at its most severe undervaluation and the pendulum just doesn't swing that fast in this game. Your reward so outweighs your risk that you can come as close to relaxing and living off a stock as you ever will in this business. You have gigantic leeway to let your gain run. That's the best kind of gain and one that can make up for a lot of losers.

I divide the patterns into two kinds of bottoms, investment bottoms and trading bottoms. Trading bottoms don't last but are so juicy, and, in these days of low commissions and instant trading, so obtainable, that I don't want you to miss them. Investment bottoms, however, are long lasting and you can get in some fantastic prices for discretionary savings or retirement. Some coincide with overall bottoms of the stock market itself.

I love to talk about individual stocks more than anything else in the world. I would like to think I can spot a stock that is finished going down better than anyone. But with that talent comes a recognition that no matter how good you are at divining the moves of individual

stocks, the vast majority of bottoms occur simultaneously with market bottoms. That's because there is so much money "indexed," or bet on the S&P 500, that if you can pick a bottom in that index, you can pick a bottom in most stocks. There are always exceptions. The gold stocks don't trade with the index; they represent an industry that tends to do well when the index does badly. Same with the oil stocks; they are a counterindex. If you can nail the index at its bottom, though, suffice it to say that you have a lot of bases covered. That's why we will review market bottoms first. At market bottoms you could have five hundred to six hundred new lows to choose from, and even the worst ones bounce if you catch the move right.

In the past twenty years we have seen four market bottoms of consequence: the 1987 crash bottom, the 1990 Iraq-Kuwait bottom, the 1998 Long-Term Capital bottom, and the 2002–2003 post-dot-com, pre-second-Iraq-war bottom. All four of those bottoms were exquisite moments to buy because if you nailed them, if you kept some cash on the sidelines for them and applied it correctly, or if you went all into equities at these moments, you beat the vast majority of managers and made fortunes for yourself or your investors. There were many other false bottoms during this study period, but none of them measured up in terms of opportunities worth committing that excess capital aggressively into the market. What mattered, in each case, was that indicators reached extremes that told you it was safe to land your capital. I chose that analogy because I like to look at the market the way a pilot examines an instrument panel when there is so much fog that he can't land on visibility alone. I like to consider the indicators as a checklist that, when enough criteria are met, signals that it is okay to bring down the airplane, or to commit capital to the market. That's why I present them in checklist form so you can use them during the periods when most market gurus and mavens are saying it is safe. You can know better.

I have studied these bottoms intensively, both as a participant and

as a historian. They each had one-of-a-kind characteristics, but not enough to make the study of them useless and nonpredictive. They had so many readily observable commonalities that these bottoms are, in retrospect, discernable and investable, and, most important, worth waiting for.

Every bottom is caused by different events. In the 1987 bottom, which occurred the day after the crash of 1987, a series of mergers and acquisitions took place as corporate America recognized that the monstrous 22 percent sell-off didn't foreshadow any economic downturn and was more a matter of computerized program trading run amuck. (We haven't had a decline like that since then because of sensible moves put in by the New York Stock Exchange to control the velocity of declines.) The 1990 bottom occurred after Iraq's invasion of Kuwait, which led to a dramatic decline in the price of oil after an initial spike. The 1998 decline got staunched, ostensibly because of a cut in interest rates by the Fed. The 2002–2003 double bottom (October 2002 and February 2003) occurred with the run-up to and start of the Iraqi war.

It's because of the disparity of events and their unusual nature— the next bottom will most likely not be triggered by another Iraq war—that most people tend to think that market bottoms are too aberrational to call. That lack of history repeating itself has led to an investment philosophy that says, basically, "We don't know when a bottom is going to be reached, so you should just stay long all of the time and not worry about it." There is a certain logic to this notion: The academic work of Jeremy Siegel, the nation's foremost stock historian, shows that high-quality equities have outperformed every other asset class over a twenty-year period, so you could say, what does it matter if you spot a bottom when you already own stocks for a much larger cycle? Indeed, for retirement investment, I am in the camp that says bottom calling is not an important exercise. I routinely invest one-twelfth of my allowable retirement funds each month, accelerating that process only if we have a significant decline, one that I define

as 20 percent, in the market. That staged investment, coupled with the occasional plunge during a big decline, however, has produced far above average results.

More important, though, discretionary money, money meant to augment your paycheck, should always be at hand so you can take advantage of bottoms. I almost always keep a minimum of 10 percent up to a maximum of 25 percent of my discretionary money in cash, to profit from when I see the signs of a bottom developing.

With that, let's examine what all four of these market bottoms had in common, what had to happen in each case before the stock market could stop going down. All of this information is readily accessible, by the way, through reading a combination of *USA Today,* the *New York Times, Investor's Business Daily,* and the *Wall Street Journal.* If that's too time-consuming, I constantly update this stuff during the trying periods in TheStreet.com.

1. **Market sentiment.** The first dashboard instrument we have to check to determine whether we have a bottom at hand is market sentiment. Sentiment's a tough thing to gauge. There are tons of anecdotal indicators and services that produce "bottom calls," but I find them dubious because they tend to be without long-term significance. We are, in the end, measuring pain, and when the pain gets to the maximum, we are going to get a bottom, which was the case in all four of our megabottoms of the last twenty years.

That said, here's my sentiment/psychology checklist of what must occur before we can be sure that a bottom might be at hand. Until you see *every* one of these indicators, you would be nuts to commit any excess capital to the market. It would be akin to running outside of a bomb shelter during the London Blitz without waiting for the sirens.

First: The pain makes the front page of the *New York Times.* This indicator, one of the absolute favorites of Mrs. Cramer, has literally never been wrong. Such a simple thing, but is worth considering why it works so well. First, the supposition here is that during the periods of incredible pain there are always people who show up in the business

sections of your newspaper, in the business magazine press, and, of course, on business TV, saying that a bottom is at hand. For the most part, those who say these things are pushing an agenda. They typically have liked the market for some time and didn't get out, or they are always liking the market because it is good, at least short-term, for their business, whatever that business might be. Maybe they run a mutual fund and that fund can't short. It's therefore "always" a good time to invest in that firm. Maybe they run a brokerage business that makes its money in commissions and the worst thing that can happen is to say, "I wouldn't buy now." Given that most of the profits from equities come from writing buy tickets, chiefly of underwritings, where the sales fee is much bigger than anything that could be gotten on the sell side, the notion of trusting any of these people is simply preposterous.

Nor does it help to read in the business section of the *New York Times* or the green "Money" section of *USA Today,* the two most important papers when it comes to calling a bottom, that there is a lot of blood on the streets or that the pain is getting too great. Those are classic canards, too. In my research on bottoms I found dozens of articles about pain and losses in these sections that were written *before* some of the biggest parts of declines occurred. But all bearish bets are off when the *New York Times* or *USA Today* puts the market's pain in a prominent place on the *front* page of their papers. Amazingly, at every bottom, stories about how horrid the market is have become a staple. If the market-woes stories aren't on the front page, then simply wait; the bottom hasn't been reached yet. There hasn't been enough pain outside the little financial world to create a bottom. It is simply incredible how right this indicator always is. It's so right that every time I have come up against a terrible bear market phase, and there have been a ton of them in the last twenty-five years, I find myself arguing with my wife about the possibility of a bottom, and she will casually ask me whether the *Times* has put the markets' woes on page one. When the answer is no, stay on hold; you aren't there yet. You will miss some transient bottoms for sure, but all megabottoms meet this characteristic before rallying sharply and, largely, for good.

A **second** gauge of sentiment that has never been wrong and has snared all four of these megabottoms is the Investors Intelligence survey of money managers. Again, like the *New York Times* indicator, it is a contraindicator, a counterintuitive sign that will make sense only after you understand the dynamics of the poll.

For twenty years, Investors Intelligence, a nationwide service, has questioned newsletter writers about whether they are bullish or bearish. While you might expect that a good time to invest is when the managers are bullish, that's actually the worst time to invest. Anyone who answers the poll by saying he is bullish is admitting that he likes the market. If he likes the market, he is by definition already in and invested. It therefore stands to reason that if everybody's bullish, then everyone's spent his cash and bought his stock. Which is why the single most important sentiment indicator I follow after the front-page *New York Times* indicator is when a majority of money managers polled dislike the market. When the bull-bear ratio shows a definitive majority of bears or even a plurality of bears with less than 40 percent bulls, you are in the safety sentiment zone. Mind you, a reading alone of less than 40 percent bulls doesn't per se mean a bottom. But remember this is a checklist, and this is one of the most important indicators to hold out for to be sure you are not getting a false reading. If you jump the gun and commit your reserves because you think the market's bottomed and you aren't there yet on this ratio, you will always be wrong. That level of certainty is rarely available in any other kind of gauge. For those unfamiliar with this indicator, it can be found among all of the indicators in the *Investor's Business Daily* and is available every Thursday morning in the paper. Never buck it; doing so has cost me tens of millions of dollars. Why should you lose money after I have proven that the losses always occur when you anticipate the bull-bear percentages too soon.

It is somewhat unfortunate that so many of my sentiment indicators take advantage of the wrong-way nature of so many market participants, but remember, when you are calling bottoms you have to believe that all hope is extinguished, and so therefore everyone who

has to sell has already sold. That's why I regard the **third** and one of the "meanest" indicators to be one of the best: mutual fund withdrawals. No important bottom is without these. No bottom is sustainable without mutual fund flows occurring steadily for at least two months. There can always be periods of one or two or even three weeks where you might get outflows related either to tax concerns or to unusual events that scare people. But consistent, repeated outflows of several months in duration accompany all the big bottoms. These numbers, available on Fridays through an organization call AMG, are almost always in the papers Saturday or Monday, so, again, we are not talking about esoteric hard-to-find data. If you haven't seen big outflows, again, you aren't there yet.

Perhaps the most esoteric of my sentiment indicators, and the only one that isn't readily accessible in your local paper, is the **fourth** indicator: the VIX. The VIX, or volatility index, is a measure of stress in the system. It is a compilation of worry as defined by various ratios of puts and calls (I'll explain these terms in the final chapter) that gauge either complacency or panic. Panic signals the freak-out selling that always accompanies market bottoms. A reading above 40 in the VIX— a measure of pure panic in the marketplace—indicates a market bottom. In fact, anything above 35 can trigger a possible bottom, but +40 is a requirement that all four of our significant bottoms have met. Any reading below 30 indicates that the bottom can't be trusted. One note of caution: The first reading above 35 isn't going to be the last. If you have the luxury, my work says the third week of +40 readings is the safest time to buy.

When I first heard the word "oscillator," I said to myself, Now here's some Genuine Wall Street Gibberish, some indicator that tells you whether stocks are "oversold" or not. How can some indicator that tabulates how eager people are to unload stocks by measuring how many sales occur on downticks and at distressed levels really help you identify a bottom? But as someone who daily measures the overbought-oversold condition through the columns of TheStreet.com's Helene Meisler, someone who I believe is the world's number one

technician, I have come to respect this instrument to the point that I never buck it, ever, when calling a bottom. It is my **fifth** bottom indicator.

Most of the time markets are in equilibrium. Buyers buy at reasonable levels relative to the last sale and sellers sell at reasonable levels relative to the last sale. But at times market players en masse are so exuberant that they push up prices constantly with their buying. They don't wait for supply and demand to be in balance and they chase stocks up, causing higher prices.

Similarly, there are moments when sellers want out so badly that they will not wait for buyers to step up to the plate. They seek out the buyers wherever they can find them, chiefly well below prevailing levels. Oscillators measure these pressures. (There are a number of different oscillator gauges. The Standard & Poor's company updates one every night that is available for $1,000, but I prefer the one that Helene Meisler calculates herself that can be found on Realmoney.com.)

Equilibrium buying occurs when an oscillator registers in the middle, which is defined by 0 ± 2. A $+2$ reading or a -2 reading signifies nothing. Only extremes matter. At every negative extreme, defined as -5 or lower, we have gotten a terrific opportunity to buy stocks. All four of the bottoms I have researched gave us extreme readings of -7 before they bottomed. The oscillator indicator, unlike the VIX, is something that produces almost instant results. The bottom is "in" when you get that reading along with all of the others that I have described here.

If you get all of these—a -7 reading on the oscillator, a $+35$ reading or more on the VIX for three weeks, sustained mutual fund withdrawals, a reading of 40 bulls or fewer in the Investors Intelligence survey, and a front-page story in the *New York Times* or *USA Today* detailing the pain the market is causing the man in the street—you will have satisfied the sentiment indicator for a megabottom.

It sounds so simple, but in reality, using these indicators is an exercise in extreme patience. I can't tell you how many times people have called me during the last four years and said, "It's so painful, we must

be near a bottom." And I have to go over the checklist and disabuse them about when we really are. Usually they say, "That's okay, I can hold out," but I will let you in on a secret—nobody, not even the Trading Goddess, can take the amount of pain that has to occur in a swing from euphoria to a swing of despair. That's why if you are feeling the tightening around your throat or the knots in your stomach and we are nowhere near negative on the oscillator or near superbearish on the Investors Intelligence, I recommend that you trim your holdings back, perhaps dramatically. That's what I usually advise people who call in to my radio program.

2. Capitulation. The next set of indicators that we must see before we can call an investible bottom gauge capitulation. In every one of the megabottoms, we had what I describe as a "crescendo sell-off" before we had an "exquisite moment." In a crescendo sell-off we have massive capitulation. Players who had been hoping to stay with the market finally give up and can't take the pain anymore.

Spotting a crescendo bottom isn't as easy as it sounds. But there are some overt signs that can be seen in the daily paper. A crescendo bottom is a bottom where a great many sellers converge at once to take stocks down to unusual levels versus the fundamentals. The accompanying detail that has marked all crescendo sell-offs is a dramatic imbalance in the amount of new highs to new lows. At all of the bottoms that I have found to be investible, you have between four hundred and seven hundred new lows and only a handful of new highs. That kind of capitulation is a must-have before you can be sure that the majority of selling is over. When you have only a couple of hundred new lows, not enough damage has been done to reach a buyable crescendo.

A second characteristic of a crescendo bottom comes from the bizarre forced-selling method that the brokers apply at all major brokerage houses. Throughout all sell-offs, marginal players and speculators attempt to call bottoms on a repeated basis. Their meager efforts are often a sign that we are not anywhere near the bottom. That is why

we have to monitor their selling closely to see when it comes to an end and they are washed out of the picture. Fortunately, their telltale selling comes almost entirely between 1:30 and 2:30 in the afternoon. That's because brokers everywhere are on the hook for trades done by their clients in violation of margin rules. The rules state that unless the customer borrowing from the firm puts up more equity when positions go against him to the point where his collateral no longer meets the requirements, the positions must be cashed out. The brokers badger these customers all morning, but the brokerage house finally stops fooling around and after the Federal Wire system closes at 1:00 p.m. the margin clerks swing into action and brutally sell out the common stock of overly margined players. The selling lasts until about 2:30. You will see during prolonged downturns that the selling during this margin-clerk hour is by far the most brutal of the day. If you have to buy a stock during a downturn, you would always be wisest to wait until the forced-selling period is over.

But for spotting bottoms, it is more important to recognize when the hour of trading doesn't bring further pressure on the market. If there is no strong sell-off by 2:30, then that's a sign that margin debt has shrunk to acceptable levels and speculation has been wrenched from the system. You never get a bottom before that speculation has been flushed out. You can always wait until the SEC releases the monthly margin debt numbers, but I have found that before every radical decline in margin buying has occurred, you can spot that decline simply by focusing on the 1:30 to 2:30 p.m. margin-clerk selling. Mind you, this indicator only works on down days. You need to see no selling to speak of during that hour after a series of declines, or even weeks of decline, before you know that the market has bottomed out.

Until about a decade ago, we had no one pool of capital large enough and reckless enough that its own busting could be a form of capitulation. But that changed with the 1998 bottom, when Long-Term Capital, a gigantic hedge fund, made a series of monster bets that went wrong, resulting in that company going belly-up. Its forced liquidation, which took place over the final days of September and

early October, produced the only tradeable bottom that wasn't caused by widespread capitulation on the part of a multitude of speculators. I point this out only because the 1998 bottom did not produce a wave of margin selling at the retail level, just at the hedge-fund level. Fortunately, that hedge fund's decline was well chronicled and therefore could be gauged even easier than the margin selling that helped create all of the other bottoms I have studied. During big declines you will find me hard at work between 1:30 and 2:30 checking the levels of forced selling and looking for imbalances that indicate the margined folk are being led to the slaughterhouse. Once they are out of the picture for good, bottoms can be found much more easily. In 2000 there was so much margin debt that we didn't clear things up until October 2002, when the forced margin selling was so palpable that it amazed you. And then it ended. Within a few weeks, you got your bottom.

A third characteristic of a crescendo bottom is a dramatic spike in volume on the exchanges. There can be day after day of lethargic selling that produce no bottoms. You get a crescendo only when the volume is loud enough to indicate that many sellers are cleaned up.

This method of spotting a crescendo always eluded me until I became a part of one during a mini sell-off in the mid-90s. That was when *Frontline* chose to do a special about speculation and I agreed to let a film crew come in and film me at my hedge fund. Because the market had been quite terrible for almost two months and we had been buying in anticipation of a crescendo bottom, we had reached our maximum allowable buying power. During the morning when the film crew came in, the market looked colossally ugly, and we sensed still one more day of pain. Because of that we went to Goldman Sachs, one of our best brokers, and said we wanted to unload one-tenth of our merchandise, or $30 million in stock, before the market opened. We wanted the security of some cash; we were selling scared. The firm sized up our offerings and bid us down a point for each stock. We were quite relieved, and we sold them the stock. Within a half hour after the opening, Goldman came back and bid about a quarter point higher for more of the same merchandise. Volume ex-

ploded all over the Street by ten o'clock, with much higher levels of trading than we had experienced in months. We took that to mean that our own panic sale had been joined by many others. Suddenly buyers came out of the woodwork because an acceptable level had been found. The hourly volume spike made it evident that at last buyers were alive and sellers had been able to unload substantial chunks rather than dribs and drabs all the way down. Again, that cleared the decks of institutional sellers in the same way that the margin clerks clear the decks of the individual sellers. Of course, we have our bottom selling memorialized in a documentary; let it serve as a reminder to you not to sell into the big volume after a long decline. That's the time to buy, not sell. A minicrescendo had occurred, and we were part of it.

Another telltale sign of capitulation involves the flow of underwritings. Brokerage houses live by the selling of merchandise through underwritings. It is second in profitability to merger and acquisition work and the lifeblood of many of the larger sales houses. Because it is so important, firms will push these deals through the door no matter what, until there are simply no more buyers left. At that point, at last, they stop, because if they can't sell the deals, they get stuck with the merchandise. They won't bring a new set of deals until they have worked off the old merchandise. You don't commit capital until the most recent underwritings have worked. That means the excess inventory has at last been worked off in the system and the all-clear has been sounded; there's too much cash idle again at last. That's why underwritings are such perfect tests of when a bottom might be coming.

Remember the order of the stock market's underwriting cycle because it always anticipates the stock market's cycle as a whole. When you get an overheated underwriting market with wild openings (where stocks go up and up on the day they first come to market) and tons of offerings each week, that's a sign of a developing top (more on that later). So get ready to sell a lot of stock. Soon you get deals opening up unchanged, with little or no premium; that's a sign the market's getting sated and you should be in a minimum of equities. When deals just fail from the moment they come out, that's a sign of a weak

market, one the underwriters will still pummel with greed. Don't be tempted to buy yet; many will be. That's a false bottom. It's only after deal after deal breaks down that the pipeline of new equity at last dries up. That's when the speculative juices are being wrung out of the market and liquidity is building up. During the period when no equity is being issued you will see a radical change in the supply and demand of equities. Well into a downturn companies will continue to buy back equity as a matter of course, but issuance dries up when the brokers get totally stung by deals. So supply and demand get way out of whack as money naturally comes into the market, through 401(k)s and other retirement accounts, and there's a continuing and natural decline in the overall numbers of shares available to buy.

You can't catch a bottom as soon as the underwriting dries up because there are still so many excess shares kicking around in marginal accounts that don't want to hold them. But one or two months after the flood of new deals ceases—never longer—you begin to see a few terrific IPOs that come public and the stocks don't go down. That's the sign that you are now past the crescendo and should be in there buying stocks. You must wait until the whole cycle plays out, though. Moving in before the new set of deals goes to a premium is suicidal. These brokers know what they are doing. They aren't taking chances at that stage; they know that the market is at last fine to operate on from the long side.

A final indicator that you might be in a crescendo bottom comes from something so odd that it is *only* seen at market bottoms. That's the "stop trading, order imbalance" sign. This signal is tricky because you need to be at a machine to see it happen. It is, in fact, the only indicator of a crescendo that cannot be spotted simply by reading the papers. It is rare, although all four megabottoms had multiple days— but not weeks—of this behavior while the capitulation was occurring.

We often get order imbalances on individual equities when we have bad news on individual companies, such as some sort of executive resignation or earnings blowup or chicanery that causes a stock to open at a deep discount to its former price. But there are moments

when we get "stop trading, order imbalance" across the whole stock market, with lots of stocks opening down huge simultaneously on no news. We had precisely this kind of behavior on the day after the 1987 stock market crash—the single best buying day in the recent history of the market—and we had it again in 1990 and in September and October of 1998 and again in October of 2002. Repeated order imbalances sans news are sure signs that the capitulation has reached absurd levels and you have to make your move to buy.

I love order imbalances after big declines in stocks; they clear out all of the panicky sellers—just the people you don't want in your foxhole—all at once. That's perfect; the safest time to buy.

3. Catalyst. The ultimate goal when you spot crescendo selling and you match it with the sentiment indicators is to consider what event could occur that would trigger what I call an "exquisite moment" where you have to buy because the opportunity is so great. In 1991, at the end of a seven-month bear market, and in 2003, at the end of a three-year bear market, we got the same exact catalyst: the start of a war with Iraq. In both cases we had a pretty high degree of confidence about when the event would occur. In both cases, as is often the case with what I call the "Big Bad Event Syndrome," where a news event that so dwarfs others is about to occur, the stock market factored in all of the negatives and none of the positives.

In 1998, the catalyst that triggered the upsurge was a "surprise" federal funds cut. I write "surprise" because the Federal Reserve let some of its buddies that talk to the press have a head's-up that the rate cut was going to occur. That was the signal to jolt stocks upward.

In 1987, the catalyst was again the Fed, which when it saw all of the delayed openings in stocks, said that it would provide all the liquidity needed to make sure the markets were orderly.

Again, after each sell-off a different trigger will cause the averages to reverse. The trick is to recognize ahead of time whether enough of the precursors are in place so that you are prepared when the catalyst comes to change the direction. The trick is *not* to know or try to pre-

dict the catalyst itself; that's rarely known. But the setup for the exqui-site moment can be predicted much more easily than the actual trig-ger that pushes the market higher. The catalysts are always different, but in each case we had priced in all the negatives and none of the pos-itives. That's why the setups are the key and are reproducible repeat-edly even though the catalyst remains something mysterious. Think of it ultimately as a forest fire waiting to happen. The sellers' inventory, the liquid that keeps the forest damp, has run dry. Then you know that the tinder is ready, and the exquisite moment is about to strike. You don't need to know when or where the spark will come from to know things are ready to ignite.

I called the exquisite moment on TV for the 2003 rally, right at the exact bottom, give or take 100 Dow points. People thought I was a genius—this was right before the war began—when in actuality all my indicators were flashing the brightest green. I am not saying it was easy; I am just saying the signs were consistent and you, too, could have spotted them if you knew what to look for. There's no magic or alchemy, just patterns readily available to all who have studied the market these last three decades.

For some people—I call them the "permabears"—these certain in-dicators and the exquisite moments they have begotten are still not enough to commit capital. I would point out to these permabears that the conditions are never perfect enough for us to know the exact bot-tom. But if we correctly identify these situations, even if we are wrong and we don't get an exquisite moment to buy, we are still not injured for trying. In every case where all these conditions occurred and we didn't get a bottom within four weeks, we still experienced no decline in capital. That's all you can ask for.

How do you know if you have missed the bottom or are too late to take advantage of it? There are dozens of subindices out there that bottom after the market as a whole has bottomed, but only one index has been coincident with or has led the market bottom in every case: the BKX, the Bank Index. If you see a 10 percent move up in the Bank

Index you are already well into the upswing, and it might pay to wait for a couple of profit-taking days to transpire before you commit capital. I always keep the BKX at the upper left hand top of my columns, right under the S&P, because of its canary-in-the-coalmine ability to detect that a big move is about to get under way. Unfortunately, a rally in the BKX has also produced several false tells, so be sure all the other indicators are working for you before you bite. The BKX predicts a lot of declines, too many to be useful, but it has always been right at confirming real bottoms as they have happened or right before them.

One other consideration: Sometimes the bottoms are so vicious and elusive that you need to test the waters first so you don't get too exposed to the market before it really bottoms and collapses again. For that, may I suggest something that has kept losses to a minimum when I am market bottom fishing? Start your buys on the morning of the bottom not with your favorites, but with some stocks that might have additional support from day traders and institutions. Buy the stocks that have been upgraded that morning. If the market does falter, the artificial buying that comes with every upgrade will at least cushion the downside for the stocks you are using to test. Don't leave it to chance or buy a stock that has no institutional support that day. You may end up in an equity that gets slammed if the market reverses down sharply, and you will be too shell-shocked to attempt the next bottom—and bottoms, real bottoms, are too precious not to try for. You can use that method to test every single bottom and never have to pay so much as a ticket for admission. It's a terrific way to feel for a bottom with minimum pain.

Believe it or not, bottoms on individual stocks are a lot harder to call than market bottoms. That's because divining the behavior of a single entity is much more difficult than trying to fathom thousands of equities that, in many ways, do trade together.

How hard is it? About fifteen years ago I was building a massive position in Control Data, now Ceridian, in an attempt to call a multiyear bottom. The stock had declined from about $150 to $15, and I

thought we were nearing a bottom. So I began to build a position using what I call a "wide scale." That means that down every point I would buy another tranche of equity, and when I thought it reached absurd levels, I would make my buys even larger, pyramid style. During this period I was trading with my wife, and she used "strict" scales, meaning that she refused to deviate and try to call a bottom at a particular level in part because a bottom had eluded Control Data for more than a decade. When the stock got to 10 we had about 200,000 shares, bidding for 50,000 every point down. It then quickly dropped to 9. I got on a plane to go see the company in Minneapolis. I spent a day with management and I came back confident because the CEO at the time was truly bullish on the outlook. When I got back I wanted to double down at 8, that's how positive management had been, but Karen was convinced that we hadn't reached max pain level. Karen said we were sticking by our scale of 50,000 every point. Sure enough, the stock traded through 8, where we bought 50,000, and then through 7, where we bought another 50,000. Amazingly, the stock kept dropping. I kept calling management, they kept telling me, Chin up, not to worry; it was all going to be okay. Those were the days where we were trading out of our garden shed in Bucks County, and my wife would constantly tell me to call the company and go through the drill again and again to be sure I was right.

Then one Friday, when the market was particularly ugly and Control Data was trading at slightly above $6 and we were bidding for our usual 50,000 shares, Karen said that she saw signs of capitulation. The sellers were coming in faster and harder now and were asking for bids from the different brokerage firms. She said she was on the verge of the double down.

To me, she seemed nuts. We hadn't known each other long enough for me to acquire those German nerves of steel of hers yet. I was shaking, shaking so hard we just stood there while the sellers were out whacking everything. Shouldn't we step aside, I asked? Shouldn't we break our scale, or walk away? That's how hard the selling was.

She looked at me as though I had no idea what I was doing and

then picked up the phone to our trading wire to be sure that the $6 bid was in and nobody pulled it while the sellers were busy panicking.

A few minutes later, the phone rang. Karen got it and said, "Jim, it's for you, some guy named Larry." I gulped. Could it be Larry Perlman, the CEO of Control Data, calling little old me in Bucks County, the guy who had 350,000 shares of his stock, which represented more than a quarter of my fund?

Sure enough, it was. Larry wanted to know what the heck was wrong with his stock. All was going so well, so exceptionally well, that he couldn't figure out what was causing the selling. He was at wits' end. I told him I wish I knew, that it was one tough row to hoe, and I hung up, totally rattled.

Karen asked me why I had turned so white. I said that I just got a call from a shaky CEO who wanted to know who the heck was selling his stock down and why, given how good things were. What was out there destroying the stock? I told her if he's worried, maybe I'm nuts to be so confident. I thought we should join the sellers.

Nonsense, she said, just the opposite. Only in the comic strips do lightbulbs go off over people's heads, but I swear I saw some light go on somewhere near her cranium. She picked up the phone to Jimmy, our position trader on the account, and said, "Bid six and a quarter outloud for one hundred thousand shares and keep reloading at the same price until you are filled three hundred and fifty thousand times."

She was doubling down, right then, right there.

I told her she had to be a whack job, that's how out of her mind she was. We just got a call from the CEO, I said, who has no idea what the heck's going wrong and your instinct is to double down?

Of course, she said. The definition of the bottom is when the two biggest bulls, her husband and the CEO, panic at the same time, when only the CEO knows more about the company than her husband. That's when you stand there, she said.

It got more painful initially. After we got filled on 350,000 shares at 6.25, she went "up," not down, and said bid 6.5 for another 100,000.

Filled again. Darned seller reloading. Bid again, she said. Now we had about half of our fund in Control Data.

Sure enough, we weren't filled the second time. The seller had dried up. The buyers came in. Take a look at a multiyear chart of that security. It never looked back from that moment, and we feasted off our Control Data position for many years to come.

Yes, bottoms can be called on individual stocks, but usually because the people who love the stock finally throw their hands up and the cooler heads step in and profit from the capitulation. At the bottom even the CEOs are confused. Accept the chaos!

Stock bottoms may be elusive, but like market bottoms, there are some telltale signs you can use to spot them. You just have to remember what you are looking for: the pricing in of the negatives without any of the positives being included.

One of the reasons spotting bottoms in equities is so elusive versus the averages is that the averages rarely go to zero—I can't recall even any sector indices that went to zero, and that includes the DOT, TheStreet.com's Internet index, during the worst of the dot-com bust. Given that debt causes the stocks of good businesses to go to zero, I would heavily recommend that you not try to spot many bottoms among the more heavily indebted companies out there. That said, let me give you my checklist of what to look for to detect a bottom in an individual stock.

First, a stock needs to lose most if not all of its sponsorship to form a true bottom. Even in the tough market of 2004, with just a handful of winners, it is amazing to see that in each winner's case, it didn't bottom and then begin to move up until it lost most if not all of its sponsorship. Amazon, Yahoo!, and eBay, together among the best-acting stocks in the market, each received multiple downgrades and were even the recipients of sell recommendations at the bottom. That's a classic tell, when a stock loses whatever support it has left on Wall Street. It's predictable and bankable because of the method analysts use to pick stocks. Typically they build a model of earnings, and when they can find stocks that they think are cheap on earnings rela-

tive to the growth rate, they want to pull the trigger and buy. Unfortunately, business is rarely as predictable as these analysts might have you think. When a company makes the estimates, the analysts reiterate their buys. When a company exceeds the estimates they go from hold to buy. But when a company, no matter how temporarily, misses the numbers, they by nature have to downgrade the stock. Since all of the analysts use these earnings models instead of trying to value companies for their intrinsic worth, they all tend to downgrade at the same time for the same reasons. You get a bottom when even the most patient or brain dead of those using these methods downgrades the stocks, typically because management is embarrassed that such bad stocks remain on the recommended list. After the investigations Eliot Spitzer has made, this process has become even easier because in the old days the stocks went from buys to holds. Now the analysts take them to sells because they didn't have enough sells on during the crash to please the authorities; in fact, they had almost none! At the bottom in 2002–2003, almost every great stock that had been hit by the temporary slowdown of the economy had sells on it. Broadcom, shortly before it doubled, had four sells on it! What a terrific indicator! Same with Lucent and Nortel and Corning before their giant moves.

The bad news about spotting the sells is that it might take several quarters for the turn to occur, because these analysts won't get back on the horse until it has a couple of good quarters. They've been too burned to be anything but twice shy. The good news is that when everyone has downgraded a stock, and it has a decent balance sheet, your downside is extremely limited. The most dangerous thing that can occur is that you might end up sitting out of whatever rally you might be trying to play. They can't "hurt" you with any more downgrades; they've already occurred!

A second "tell" of a bottom occurs when bad news hits and the stock ceases to go down. This indicator is a simple one, and it is common in every single bottom. That's because bottoms get formed only when all of the sellers have finished, so there is no one left who cares about the new negatives to want to dump the stocks. Again, remem-

ber, this works only with a good balance sheet, because with a bad one, the bad news could lead to some sort of impairment that removes the equity from your hands and puts it in the hands of the bond or note holders. I love situations like one that occurred in EMC in 2003 when it reported a so-so quarter, guided estimates lower, and said business is just okay. The stock went up on the news. No one was left to be shaken out. That's a classic bottom, one definitely worth waiting for. EMC had fallen 40 percent before it found its sea legs.

A third indicator is consistent, large insider buying. Insiders sell for a myriad of reasons: taxes, estate planning, divorce, prudence. They buy for only one reason: to make money. Beware here, though. The managements know that they can draw attention to their companies with token buying or with widespread but small buying by all board members. This kind of forced buying shouldn't fool you. Don't bite when you see small dollar amounts of buying by individuals at the top. They could be "painting the tape" with their buys. You need to see buys in the millions of dollars to be sure that someone isn't trying to trick you into the stock, or con some reporter. Buy only when you see multiple buys, too. There's always one board member with a lot of cash around. But multiple and repeat buyers of significant amounts shows you the insiders mean business. It's a great tell and often signals the absolute bottom in an enterprise's stock.

A fourth indicator of a bottom occurs when a stock is rumored upon negatively and nothing happens. At all times there are plenty of hedge funds that need merchandise to go lower so they can bring in their shorts, either successfully or unsuccessfully. At all times there are also unscrupulous people who are willing to say anything about a company to anybody—particularly the press—to knock the price down, knowing that it will be repeated by willing brokers who want the short sellers' business. For most of you this process seems completely insidious. You think it is outrageous that short sellers plant rumors and tell tall tales to knock stock prices down. Not for me. I am always looking for all-clear signs to beat the system. I regard it as the ultimate tell of a stock going from weak to strong hands when I

hear a negative rumor about the company—broadcast widely either through a network or a national newspaper, a Web site or magazine—and the stock, which most likely would have been totaled by the rumor at a higher price, does nothing. I especially like it when a hefty dollop of puts has been purchased beforehand. That's a terrific fire to the upside just waiting to happen. There's nothing like trapping a short seller with his own lying story and getting him to feel the pain himself of a stock that won't come down so he has to come in and sell the puts, which will automatically move the stock up. Particularly because the broker who bought the puts probably told others to expect something negative, and when the negative occurs and the stock doesn't go down, these tagalongs panic and cover the target company's stock.

So, I like to keep up on the negatives of stocks that have been breaking down to figure out when all the negative news is in. That usually means some positive news is about to come down the pike or the major damage is done and you are safe to speculate on a bottom.

The final kind of bottoms I look for are bottoms based on macro considerations. These are sector-rotation bottoms, and they are the key to making unusually large profits. Let's spend some time on them, especially because these are some of the most counterintuitive bottoms out there, yet they are begging to be had if you simply stand conventional wisdom on its head. These bottoms involve decisions by big money to make moves to get out of some stocks that have been very hot and into others that have been very cold, almost entirely because of macro decisions, like Fed tightening or loosening policies. Let's stick with them because they are consistent in each cycle.

Sector bottoms, picking individual stocks as part of a big sector bet, means going back to the model of earnings and Fed tightenings and loosenings that I described earlier. There is a simple theme to these rotations. When you believe that the tightenings are beginning to have an effect, you will see a sudden rush of money over a four- or five-day period into the Kelloggs, Gillettes, Avons, Procters, and Kimberlys, the stuff that is in your kitchen and your medicine chest. I used

to like to place these bets close to the midway point in the tightening portion of the cycle, but these days so many people anticipate the Fed's moves that I think you would be best to start buying right at the time of the first tightening. Usually you get the tightening after a prolonged period of inflation, which erodes the value of these key franchises. But when the Fed tightens, you get a freeze in the economy and the erosion stops. Also, when the Fed tightens, you get a fear that the cyclical companies will not make their numbers the following year, or that the future will be clouded for the companies that are heavily dependent upon the economy. That's why you have to jump into these situations in advance. One of the reasons why I was able to successfully navigate the severe downturn in tech stocks in 2000 was that I used this method to switch into a portfolio of food, soap, drug, and cosmetic companies, the type that don't slow down when the Fed ratchets rates up.

Of course, the opposite happens when the Fed does its first loosening. Traditionally you need to switch into a sector that does well with the economy, typically companies like the autos and the retailers. You rotate into the heavier cyclicals as the easings go on, until in the end you are stuck with the dirtiest of stocks out there, such as, steel, copper, and aluminum.

I point all of this out not to belabor something discussed earlier, but to point out that throughout these periods, brokers and TV pundits and mutual fund folk will be recommending the "cheap" food and drug stocks betting on a comeback, right in the middle of an economic expansion or when they have just started selling off. Think to yourself, false bottom! Same with the cyclicals. You like the cyclicals when they are most expensive, when their earnings have cratered, when they traditionally seem outrageously overvalued. But when their multiples are cheap, when you hear that Phelps Dodge trades at 6 times next year's earnings, run for the hills. It will never make that number. It might not even make half of that. That's the slowdown coming. Never be lulled into cyclical stocks when they are cheap; sell the safety stocks when they are ultra expensive. Their bottoms are

both counterintuitively reached and formed by the Fed cycle, not by their intrinsic earnings power.

There are a couple of other kinds of bottoms to be aware of. Some bottoms occur when companies get so cheap as to be taken over by others, but again, I don't speculate on takeovers with bad fundamentals, unless all the risk is taken out of them and nobody likes them apropos of the bottoming process described above.

One other type of bottom is worth commenting on: the tax-loss bottom. Every year at the end of October, when most mutual funds end their fiscal year, the funds like to take their losses. There is a perception that you should wait until December to buy tax-loss names, but that's a canard because it is institutional selling that drives most stocks down, not individuals. The third and fourth weeks of October—hah, now you know why there are so many crashes during that period—represents the height of this kind of selling.

My experience is that if you are picking stocks off tax-loss selling, you should begin most of your buying in the last week of October, but leave some money for the occasional "legit" sell-off to demonstrate itself. Spend that money in the last week of November. I don't like buying stocks just because tax-loss selling is over. There are a million reasons why stocks go down, but I know enough to take advantage of the seasonal pattern that constantly manifests itself.

9

SPOTTING TOPS

Two great investment themes create the day-to-day tension in the stock market: capital appreciation and capital preservation. We have historically—and I think inaccurately—called capital appreciation by a different name: "buy and hold." I have shown that buy and hold has no place in the logical investing lexicon and that buy and homework must be the modus operandi. Buy and hold presumes, preposterously, that tops—permanent impairment of stocks after a certain attained height—don't exist. Yet dozens of tops are formed every week that could wipe out whatever capital appreciation you may have gained by buying and holding. Tops are the bane of all investing. At a top buy and hold is the enemy and capital preservation becomes king.

Yet the amount of attention paid to spotting and avoiding holding after a top in the investment canon is paltry when you consider the damage and the havoc that tops can wreak on your portfolio. If there were genuine scrutiny and rigor to how stocks originate in the first place, if there were somehow some strictures about what kind of stocks are "suitable" for investment, we wouldn't have to worry

about tops. All stocks would generate solid returns, save a handful that fail. Those would be chalked up as occasional accidents that happen, nothing more than that. We would factor them in; a diversified portfolio would cushion whatever damage an occasional top might generate.

Unfortunately, we are never at a loss for bad stocks in the market. Virtually any company can issue stock without much scrutiny from the feds beyond the securities equivalent of a name, rank, and serial number. Recently, the SEC revealed the names of some thirty stocks that traded with multiple billions in capitalization that had no companies underneath them. That's right, they were made-up companies—shells—that had no earnings, revenues, or even, in some cases, headquarters or employees. These nonexistent companies traded freely for years in the hundreds of millions of shares without being flagged by any authority. The government didn't blow the whistle on the stocks until most of them had been reduced to zero, of course, not before robbing unsuspecting "investors"—if you can call this process investing—of billions of dollars in wealth. Before the government halted trading in these empty, worthless vehicles, they had been blessed, de facto, as if they were operating companies with real financials. No government entity ever came out and said, "Be careful, these aren't real companies." You can't expect the SEC or the exchanges to protect us from the fraudsters, though. And there's too much corruption out there for the SEC to be a cop on the valuation beat; it's not the government's job to examine whether a stock is worth something or nothing at all.

You can't rely on the market to sort them out correctly, either. It fails so often to do that job that you should have lost whatever faith you might have had in the screening and valuation processes of the collective wisdom of the market by now. But many of you still haven't been disabused of the market's illogic because of the buy-and-hold brainwashing that Wall Street relies upon to keep you from taking back *your* assets under *its* management. If you knew what the Street knows, you would rather be in control of the money yourself. That

way your guard would be up and you could be more vigilant than Wall Streeters want to be, or, given the conflicts of interests they live under, can afford to be.

Although we are a nation that has produced stocks with phenomenal long-term returns from both dividends and stock appreciation, we are also a nation that has produced more investment fads, more short-term gimmickry, and more white-collar corruption leading to multi-billion-dollar losses than any nation other than Japan during that country's phenomenal bubble (which is still bursting). There are tons of stocks that don't deserve even to trade and a myriad of others that are topping right now and could be incredibly dangerous to your financial health.

For me, spotting a top is the equivalent of embarking on a long and winding train ride and trying to figure out if the engine's about to jump the tracks any time soon. We know nearly all trains get to their destinations, yet we accept the fact that occasional derailments do happen. This chapter's about trying to get as much mileage out of stock as possible, but not so much that you hang on while the stock jumps the track or plummets through a broken trestle. Sometimes, you've got to jump off the train to survive. It's no sin to do so and, of course, it would be pretty stupid if you knew a crash was coming and you stuck around for it. Yet, despite the common sense of it, my view is *not* the prevailing wisdom on Wall Street.

On Wall Street "sell" is a dirty word and tops don't exist; they are only temporary breakdowns that will eventually be surmounted. When I first got to Goldman Sachs I remember asking people, "When do I tell clients to sell? What's the exit plan?" The greybeards would say, "When the stock gets downgraded; that's when you sell." But downgrades, when they happen, most often come after the train has abandoned the track. The selling process is pretty alien, especially when another portion of a firm might be vying for business of the company that might be downgraded, and that business is a much larger business than whatever trading profits can be made in the stock. Even though Eliot Spitzer, the New York State attorney general, has

performed yeoman's work vetting this process, it still happens as long as investment banking and research are under the same roof. You just don't get a lot of correct sell recommendations on Wall Street, and when you do, it is usually too late to sell. Indeed, there are hundreds of texts and analysts that can tell you when to buy. But selling is considered to be a sporadic, haphazard art. I contend that selling and knowing when to sell are more important than knowing when to buy. That's been the lesson during the last seven years where the S&P 500 compounded at 5 percent and many stocks lost you tons of money during that period. I have spent much of my life poring over chartbooks looking for patterns, looking for repetitive warning signs that would get you out before the top. I wanted to find a commonality, or a set of commonalities, that could be warning bells for stocks that otherwise would be too dangerous to touch, the stocks that produce short-term gains in almost parabolic style, the stocks that go up fast but fall even faster. The idea behind such reasoning is that you shouldn't deny yourself an iVillage or a Commerce One or an eBay on the way up, provided you know when to get out. You can own the sizzling stocks, take the huge gains that they provide, and then exit before the steak gets burned.

Spotting tops allows you to embrace lots more equities, including riskier ones that can be very rewarding, much more rewarding than most people think possible. If you hone your selling skills, you can take advantage of the four- and five-fold rallies that can occur in unseasoned merchandise, even if, in the end, the merchandise craters to zero—as long as it does so without you on board. This flexibility has made me fortunes even as it has created a legion of Cramer-haters who think that I have no right to hop off the griddle. This top stuff truly is like cooking. You can cook something to perfection. If you take it off before you get it there, nobody's happy, but you can always throw it back on. But once it is burned, it's finished, done, destroyed. Why stay on the griddle for that punishment when you can learn to spot the moment something's about to get fried into oblivion? This bit of

cooking advice is better than anything you will ever get from most investment books. I can't tell you how many times recognizing that things have gotten too hot after a big run has allowed me to take terrific gains even as others say, "Hold it, I thought you said you liked this stock, you can't sell it now." My view? You bet I can. I am not sticking around for my meal to burn to a crisp even if I liked it a moment before. That's foolish. These are stocks; just like food, they can vaporize in an instant. They can and do go bad, all the time.

The more we are wedded to stocks, the more we ignore the changes that might be occurring in the ever-fluctuating landscape, changes that might knock our companies out if we aren't careful. Ideology's an unsteady crutch in this game; the more we have of it, the more money we will lose. This is a business of flexibility; you may have to like a stock one minute and hate it the next because the fundamentals underneath change that fast. If you think this is a business of firm, resolute stands no matter what the facts say, you are going to end up poor as a church mouse. That's no way to run money, your own or others'.

Let me give you a couple of other caveats to the top process. First, this is not a chapter on spotting *market* tops. I am focusing on when to sell individual stocks, although I reach a conclusion about the entire market and when it should be sold, more as a recognition that there have been and will be "tops" in the S&P 500 that will last long enough that they should be solidified. However, I always believe the casino will be open, and if you take it case by case, game by game, that's a lot better than saying, "That's it, I want everything out." That's worked only once, in the third week of March 2000. I don't suspect we will see such a renegade market bubble in our lifetime. If anything, I am far more concerned with some sort of biblical seven lean years after seven fat years. I don't mind mixing biblical metaphors with Vegas-style reasoning. By now you know that I think that any analogies to casinos are far-fetched; the table games have much more rigorous rules and regulations. Letting you bet on a bogus entity—something that happens with stocks all of the time—would be ruinous to the house, and the

casino business just wouldn't allow it to happen. Same with illegal NFL gambling, which I regard as much more honest and less rigged than much of what passes for fair in the stock market.

Second, I am not a technician, and this is not a collection of chart patterns that lead up to tops. Chart people spot many tops; in fact, they spot many more tops than there are. That's just not valuable to me. In fact, one of the biggest mistakes I ever had in my career was to be short Genentech based on a classic top formation, which, a prominent technician told me, ninety-nine times out of hundred produced a significant decline. I got my face handed to me when, the next week, Genentech got a humongous takeover bid! I had to buy the stock back up about 70 percent. Nasty, embarrassing, and astonishingly costly. As I hung up on the technician after cussing him out for the hot tip, he was squealing, "But the chart says it should go down!" To heck with the chart! To heck with the chartists! Except Mrs. Cramer, who still manages to integrate the fundies and accepts that the chart can *never* be the final judgment, but *can* be consulted to generate ideas.

Nor am I talking about temporary fluctuations in stocks, avoiding short-term drops. If you follow my rules on portfolio management—my bulls-bears-and-pigs mantra that involves taking a little something off the table as a stock goes up—these short-term tops, false tops so to speak, take care of themselves. You quickly put the money back to work in the same equity at a lower, cooler level. Low taxes and low transaction costs now allow such moves. This kind of approach not only is important, it is prudent in a world gone buy-and-hold haywire.

The real danger of false tops is that you might be spooked out of a high-quality stock; they are hard to find and you should treasure them for as long as they last, not jettison them quickly for some lesser merchandise. Sometimes it takes months to develop really good ideas. You should depart from them only when you have serious reservations such as the kind I am about to explain to you.

No, I am addressing here the basic reasons why, unfortunately, at times, you should abandon stocks you know and love. They are rea-

sons why you should take the money off the table and look elsewhere for opportunity because something has changed, something in the landscape either for the equity or the company itself has gone sour or is about to go sour and very few people know it. Here are the main antagonists to buy and hold, the place where tops are in sight and you can assume that the train will derail if you stay along for the ride.

1. **Competition**. The most common form of top explains why you must stay involved with the day-to-day operations of your companies, why you can't do "buy and hold" but have to do homework instead: the competitive top, when someone else comes in and destroys your company's business. You can tell when the competition is heating up only if you stay vigilant and monitor not just your company but the whole industry, one of the main reasons why I say you need to give your portfolio one hour a week per position if you are going to get it right. Seventy percent of the tops I have studied have this dominant competitive characteristic at their roots. Typically, the company itself doesn't see it coming. You may own a company with fairly decent margins on sales that is forecasting great multiyear visibility because it has terrific market share and has vanquished its competitors. Suddenly a new entrant comes in, one who can make the same product or do the same service or sell the same goods as your company, but with lower margins. The new competitor, if it means business, and they often do, will destroy your company even as your company pretends that such a thing can't happen, or doesn't even know that a competitor is lurking because it is watching only the existing players, not anyone off the radar screen.

Let's examine the greatest top I have ever seen in my life, the top involving United States Surgical. Everyone who was anybody in the market owned U.S. Surgical during the 1990s. It was a universal principle that you had to have stock in this dominator of the surgical staples, because it had sky's-the-limit growth with no competition and unlimited market potential. USS had a revolutionary proprietary technology of staples that could be used instead of stitches. USS's

business was big, bigger than big. It was the only stock you just *had* to own.

In the 1990s I worked as a trustee to a fund that owned 8 percent of the stock. The position kept going up and it became a bigger and bigger portion of the fund simply because of the mammoth capital appreciation. I grew worried that we were too levered to the stock and demanded that we sell some because I thought we were being pigs. I must have asked them to take some profits for almost two years because I thought it was so rich, but no top ever developed and the stock just kept increasing in price. I ended up being kicked off the board in part because I was so negative about this wonderful stock that I felt just couldn't continue forever. It apparently could.

Just when everybody loved this stock and it was among the most widely held equities in the country, with the highest gross margins of any mass-produced product I had ever seen, Johnson & Johnson, which made Band-Aids and a lot of hospital and surgical products, decided that it had had enough of United States Surgical's domination in the operating room. Management at JNJ made up its mind that it was going to challenge USS. Management made this judgment even though everyone on Wall Street thought that USS couldn't be removed from its hammerlock on America's operating rooms. Critics of JNJ and supporters of USS thought it was reckless for JNJ even to think about taking on USS. There was one key difference between JNJ and USS. USS had high margins on its staples, JNJ had low margins on its Band-Aids and its other hospital-based commodity products. JNJ made very little money on Band-Aids; USS made huge money on its staples. If JNJ had any success at all, the company would be able to raise its margins because a new higher-margined product, staples, would be a part of its mix.

At the time JNJ announced it was moving into USS's business, USS was at $120. Every one of the USS analysts ignored the JNJ threat; most USS analysts didn't even follow the stock of JNJ. Others felt that stodgy JNJ couldn't possibly beat fleet-footed USS. I knew it didn't matter. Given that JNJ's margins would increase even if it sold its sta-

ples for half the price of USS's it was only a matter of time before USS's margins were cut to ribbons and the stock slid. I looked at the margins of the two companies and decided that USS was finished, kaput, done for. I shorted every share I could get.

As JNJ moved in with its lower-priced alternative, USS slid from $120 to $80. At that level those USS adherents who were in denial about JNJ started talking about price competition in the operating room. Heck, USS had never done anything but raise prices. Now it was cutting them?

The stock went to $30 overnight on that kind of talk as USS's margins tumbled in a price war. None of the USS acolytes even saw the JNJ train coming. If you were following only USS, you were totally blindsided. I covered the stock in the mid 20s, but I could have waited because it went still lower before ultimately, spent and confused, the company succumbed to a takeover bid.

Rule number one when you are riding a great long: Always assume that there is someone out there who could come in and make your company's product for less with lower margins. A committed competitor moving into your company's area with overall gross margins that are lower than the margins your company has signals the time to run, not hide. This kind of pattern happens over and over again in everything from tech to tampons. No one-product or two-product company with high margins can withstand a well-capitalized lower-margined competitor. Given that the competitor tends to be of the Merck or IBM or Intel or Oracle, Procter & Gamble or JNJ variety—a global behemoth with lower margins than any specialty players—you have to be totally on top of what could be a terrific momentum situation one day and a stupendously overvalued stock the next. In fact, much of the big top of the year 2000 was directly related to established, well-known, but lower-margined tech companies barging in on lots of little specialty dot-com companies that had one product and high margins. The market was littered with stocks that went from $100 or even $200 to zero almost overnight, and you would never have known to get off if you were just talking to the target companies

themselves. Viant and Scient, billion-dollar consulting companies one minute, were bankrupt consulting companies the next when IBM and EDS moved in. Tampax, a fantastic single-brand company, got sideswiped when Procter and JNJ moved in with products that crushed Tampax's margins but elevated their own. None of these little companies and their acolytes on Wall Street saw the locomotive was out of control and about to jump the track. These were horrid accidents just waiting to happen. Simply put, when you hear about new competition, you must worry, whether you would like to or not. Not unimportantly, the periods of profound underperformance for Intel have come when AMD geared up with a competitive offering. Similarly, much of the underperformance for Microsoft in the 2003–2004 period before the big dividend change was related to competition from Linux provider Red Hat. Did these cause tops? We still don't know. Your takeaway should be that you must *never* underestimate the power of the competition to hurt your stock, even if it doesn't immediately hurt the company.

2. **Vagueness.** Whenever a management is vague about specifics, whenever a management tells you it isn't worried about the numbers, or that it doesn't want to be constrained by the projections or by the forecasts because it is talking and thinking about bigger things, sell the stock. There are no bigger things than the numbers. This is not a game of trying to make people feel better or making them more broadminded. This is not a liberal arts bull session. It's a business of hitting the numbers. When management goes vague in an interview—any interview—run for the hills. You've got a real top on your hands. Spotting this type of top can be done only if you do the homework and read about the companies that you own. You have to search for the interviews and watch them when they come on television just to see whether they are shucking and jiving or they are sticking by the hard facts.

This method, analyzing the vagueness, is how I discovered the top

at Sunbeam, another one of those classic falls from grace that took a tremendous number of value and growth managers with it.

Al Dunlap, the now disgraced former CEO of Sunbeam, came into my office when the stock was riding high, in the mid 40s. He used to come on TV, notably *Squawk Box,* and be very adamant about the projections, the numbers. Adamant and positive. One time, after a TV appearance, he decided to swing by my office. Comes in with the sunglasses. Oh yeah, always distrust guys with sunglasses in a room without a lot of light like my trading room, where I hated the glare from the lights on my machines. He wanted to talk to me and my partner at the time, Jeff Berkowitz, about new products, notably some heart monitor gizmo for dogs. I kid you not. The pet market's huge, he's telling us. Berkowitz says that's super, great to hear, but how's the quarter? Dunlap looks at him with contempt and drones on about the dog heart monitor. So Jeff asks again. Dunlap ignores him and starts talking about a new gas grill that's in four parts, down from thirty. Much easier to put together, he says. I start talking about how much time it took me to put together the grill I had bought at Fortunoff a few weeks before, parts all over the place, and it still didn't work when I finished it. Berkowitz? He's listening and nodding, and then he says to Dunlap, "How's sales from grills?" Dunlap fires back that Wal-Mart and Kmart can't get enough Sunbeam products. Jeff persists, wanting to know real sales data, something that Dunlap had always provided before when asked. "Are sales good right now?" Jeff asks. That's it, Dunlap blows his top. He turns to me and asks how much more of this crap does he have to take? I wink at Jeff. Jeff steps out and sells every share.

When someone who talks up his business at every turn, who is incessantly upbeat, suddenly won't talk about the numbers and won't brag about the business, and instead wants to talk about a heart monitor for dogs, you've got a classic tell that the business has gone sour. A year later Sunbeam was bankrupt.

How else can vagueness manifest itself? A company that formerly

wanted to tell you everything about its future no longer wants to give guidance, or says it can't forecast its business. That's a top because the buyers and owners of that stock most definitely owned it because they liked the predictability that the company no longer has. Another form of vagueness can be a company that won't give you breakdowns of sales when it used to, especially when it is saying it can't do this for competitive reasons. General Electric is the single most competitive company I know and it gives you all the data. Shame on those who won't.

Vagueness can also be bravado. Scott Butera, the Trump executive in charge of casinos, told us not to worry about the numbers because bankruptcy would be averted, making the $2 DJT, Trump casino stock, look like a buy. When the stock got cut to 37¢ immediately after the bankruptcy, you shouldn't have had to worry, because bravado without numbers spells a top, and you should have already sold.

Vagueness, like competition, is something that you can find out about only if you are paying attention and are benchmarking the company. If you don't listen to the conference calls and don't read the interviews or articles, how will you know about new competition and how will you know when management's gone vague? The chart sure as heck won't tell you! Only vigilance will get you out before the top strikes when management has gone opaque.

3. Overexpansion. Nothing defeats a company's dreams like over-expansion. I have written throughout this book that growth is all that matters. In the end, if you can't create growth organically you either have to buy growth or you have to use steroids to grow. Knowing when a company is overexpanding and expanding too quickly, the functional equivalent of steroids, is integral to spotting a top ahead of a train wreck.

Unfortunately, overexpansion is inherently difficult to analyze. It is tough to spot because Wall Street doesn't want you to spot it. Wall Street masks the problems of too much growth. That's because Wall Street loves acquisitions and rapid expansion, the primary ways

to make quick growth happen. Acquisitions can make for instant growth, but they can also make for instant problems. Frenetic store openings or office expansions strain a young management's attention and dollars. Both are catastrophic to the core enterprise unless checked by some degree of common sense as well as the wisdom to stand up to the growth jihadists who populate mutual and hedge funds.

Often companies do acquisitions to please analysts who are working hand in glove with another department at their firm that does M&A work. An investment house makes more money doing M&A than any other activity, but the babe-in-the-woods managements that come to Wall Street don't know that. They want to please the analysts, the analysts want payback from bonuses that are controlled by the hierarchy, and the hierarchy knows nothing generates fees like M&A. The investment bankers want to do the deal, any deal, all deals! If a company cannot grow numbers fast enough on Wall Street, it has to go buy the numbers or succumb to downgrades, and those are often too much for unseasoned managements to recover from.

The integration of the takeovers, though, is something so difficult, so taxing, that even the pros screw it up. Time and time again after a company makes an acquisition, the analysts dutifully raise numbers and the stocks initially go higher. I almost always sell into that hoopla because the acquisitions don't go smoothly in most cases and the numbers come down when they don't.

What's the sell signal here if you can't pull the trigger when the numbers go higher? I will give you the code. Whenever you hear management talk about "integration problems" as in "integration problems are slowing our ability to merge these two entities," run, don't walk, to the exit. All deals have integration problems; they are a given. If they are affecting the numbers to the point that management has to acknowledge them, believe me, that's fatal.

Some companies are so desperate for growth that they do acquisitions at any cost. That's what destroyed the once-great AT&T. Michael Armstrong, the former CEO, felt his company was too stodgy and

simply wasn't growing fast enough to please the Wall Street analysts who were measuring the company's growth against what we now know to have been the bogus and inflated numbers of competitor MCI-WorldCom. So Armstrong let a bunch of bankers and glad-handing analysts talk him into spending money to make acquisitions so he could grow numbers. Of course, the integration couldn't be done easily, the debt costs were unbearable, and eventually the company virtually collapsed under its own weight in borrowings. The tip-off for that collapse, the top-spotter so to speak, was the unbelievably aggressive acquisition strategy, one that happened at a pace that no management could possibly accommodate. Enron did the same; it made a flood of acquisitions and transactions designed strictly to mask the real lack of growth and the inability of management to create products or business lines itself to put points on the board. Not all companies are meant to be fast growers. Revolutionizing a slow grower into a fast grower is almost impossible; don't fall for it.

If you don't believe me, just remind yourself of what happened with AOL Time Warner. AOL made that acquisition, we now know, because business had slowed dramatically. The only way to mask that incredible slowdown was to buy another company and throw everybody, every doubter, off the scent. It was a brilliant plan. If you had sold AOL when it made that deal you'd have locked in a huge gain at a time when everyone talked about one plus one equals three. Of course a half plus one doesn't even equal one if you pay many times the worth of that half. Everyone who held still has losses and will, I believe, for many years to come. It was just that bad and desperate a combination.

Of course there will be companies that make intelligent acquisitions that don't signal the end of their growth. Procter & Gamble has made several acquisitions that have boosted its bottom line successfully; so has General Electric. But they were measured and considered and *incremental* to their core businesses, not roll-the-dice mergers done one after another to throw you off the scent. GE and P&G are established companies where mergers and acquisitions are part of the business structure. They are not anemic growers desperate to please

by trying to integrate new businesses into existing product lines. P&G and GE, by the way, have never had integration problems in all the years I have been following those two great companies.

Overexpansion doesn't happen just through acquisitions. Retailers, which are under tremendous pressure to grow to please Wall Street, have often opened too many stores at once just to meet the demands of analysts who like their stocks. When you see companies put up a phenomenal number of stores all at once relative to their base, I think you have to shoot first and ask questions later. It just isn't possible for a management to maintain the quality control through that kind of expansion. It is a sign of weakness, not strength. It is also why, when a company is in extreme growth mode, I look at same-store sales, not total sales, to detect a fiasco. When retailers are growing by leaps and bounds you can't gauge a business from total sales: Adding stores overnight grows bigger numbers. So look at same-store sales, "comp store sales" as they are known, to judge how much the existing business is being hurt by the expansion.

By the way, that's one of the reasons that I would urge you, if you decide to own the stock of a retailer, to visit the stores regularly. I was able to spot a top in Restoration Hardware by a combination of visiting stores and monitoring that company's breakneck expansion to please Wall Street. When I got yelled at in the local store at the Short Hills mall, even though I had to be one of the biggest patrons of the chain, that set me to work on what ultimately turned out to be a magnificent short sale.

These companies, by the way, almost never recover when they expand at that pace, which is why I am so adamant that when you see this kind of nonmeasured expansion you have to hit the ejection button. The ultimate top is formed when a company stumbles after breakneck expansion, any company. Don't even attempt to bottom-fish; there tends to be no there, there. Particularly when the expansion is of the "roll-up" variety, where the home office keeps issuing stock to buy mom-and-pop companies. Once the earnings cool and the stock flops, there's no way to get the momentum back. No mom and pop

will sacrifice its hard-earned businesses for that devalued currency. The Street is littered with bankrupt companies that didn't understand that ironclad law.

4. Government blindside. The front page of the *New York Times* spots more tops than the business page. That's because governments, both federal and state, can do more to hurt companies or permanently debilitate their earnings than any competitor. Oddly, though, the Wall Street analysts who are supposed to flag the real problems for companies to us mortals who await their verdicts don't pay much attention to government edicts. The large institutions that control the marginal shares of companies are so focused on earnings growth from internal sources that they, too, miss the big negatives that can come from any administration.

In the late 1990s, for example, the greatest stocks, the most recession-proof stocks, were the nursing home stocks. These had momentum and a thesis, the graying of America. All of the major investment houses embraced the aging theme, and everyone presumed that the government would just keep paying major portions of the nursing home bills for the elderly. Wasn't that the politically popular position? Didn't the elderly control lots of key states and vote their pocketbooks? That was the logic, certainly, of the lofty multiples these stocks sold at in the late 1990s.

Perhaps the most popular stock of the era, Genesis Health Ventures, a gigantic East Coast nursing home chain that kept issuing stock to roll up mom-and-pop nursing homes, just kept roaring and roaring higher as this thesis ascended. But President Clinton, right before the turn of the century, decided he had to rein in some health-care costs lest the country slip back into deficit spending. The feds decided, virtually out of nowhere, to change the reimbursement rate to operators of nursing homes. The companies didn't see it coming. The analysts didn't see it coming. Yet, when it happened, it was devastating news delivered from the front page of the *New York Times*. I recently looked up the First Call notes—the analysts' contemporaneous comments—and

not one flagged the articles that were hidden in plain sight on the front page of the paper of record. They all missed it. This reimbursement change was the single most devastating piece of news ever, but the stocks just hung there as the owners and their analyst buddies ignored the guillotine that slammed down on the news pages. Once the reimbursement rates changed, every one of these companies went from great longs to great shorts, overnight. Genesis Health, the bellwether of the industry, the gold standard, would be in bankruptcy within a year. It went bankrupt while many of the buy recommendations were still intact.

How do you spot this kind of top? You have to start by reading the front pages, not just the business sections, of the *New York Times,* the *Wall Street Journal, USA Today,* and the *Washington Post.* I start my day with them, electronically, inserting my stocks' names in their indices to see where the articles come up. I never constrain myself to the business sections; that's just foolish.

During the downfall of Genesis, I spoke to a relative who had sold a company to Genesis Health. The stock had just fallen 10 points from its top and every analyst was telling me to buy it. I asked him what I should do. He had a simple answer: "Don't you read the papers? The businesses are finished." I told him that couldn't be because the companies were all saying not to worry. He said they were saying that to the analysts, urging them to keep a stiff upper lip, but in truth they were petrified. The great nursing home buy-and-hold craze was a huge top the moment that the reimbursement rates changed. It never came back.

Similarly, DoubleClick, among the most successful of the dotcoms and among the quickest to reach a multi-billion-dollar valuation, decided at what amounted to its peak that it was going to enter the business of knowing everything about its customers. It paid a couple of billion dollars for Abacus, a marketing company with a huge database of users. No sooner had the deal been completed than the government questioned whether these kinds of services invaded consumers' privacy. DoubleClick ultimately had to write off billions of

dollars as it misjudged the political tremors that were evident for all to feel. As is typical, the analysts took their cue from the smug DoubleClick folks, who never knew what had hit them. Still don't for that matter.

I got hit by one of these governmental blindsides just last year when I rode Forest Labs, a drug company, all the way down from what now appears to have been a certain top. My mistake? I didn't take seriously the notion that the FDA and Congress would begin to focus on the suicide rates of young children on antidepressants, the core of the growth for Forest Lab's most important drug, Lexapro. The analysts didn't believe it, either. But it was right on the front page when the stock was in the 70s. Thirty points later, when the analysts finally started addressing the problem, it was too late for me. One of my largest losses since I left my hedge fund.

5. Top in retail. Retail tops are easy to spot. Some think you can spot them by measuring same-store sales, sales that are compared on an apples-to-apples basis. If sales in one store were $1 million in year one and $900,000 in year two, that's a same-store sales decline of 10 percent for that store. I like that as a measure of rapid-growing retailers, but for mature retailers, I use a different litmus test. Companies have good months and bad, and while the same-store sales are important, they inconsistently call more tops than they should. False tops are the bane of investors who own retailers, so you have to be very careful not to exit just because a company, particularly an apparel company, had a bad month.

No, the real top in retail comes when a retailer has stores in every state, when there are no new areas in which to expand. Every retailer, whether it be Gap or Wal-Mart or Kohl's or Home Depot or the Limited or Toys R Us, hits a wall when that happens. I love to own retailers early in their growth cycle when they are regional going national: lots of states ahead, and if the concept is a good one you can use every single same-store sales decline to buy more. But, and it is a huge but, once

all of the locations are used up, as represented by a truly national presence, I have no desire ever to own that retailer again. It's been a terrific way to own these stocks, and I have managed to get the maximum out of every one of the majors and then leave them, never to own them again when they cracked into the last corners and crannies of American malls. Be careful. Analysts hate to get off retail horses while they are running; they will deny that this nationwide test matters. I know better; it works *every time.*

6. Fad stock tops. I can't blame anyone for playing any fad. The runs we have had in everything from Reebok to Palm to Research in Motion have been fantastic. There's always a product out there that is in short supply because it has caught the fancy of the American consumer. You can make fortunes as the stocks go higher. But as soon as the supply catches up to demand, whether it be iPods built by Apple Computer or aerobic sneakers made by Reebok, you must sell it and never look back.

How do you spot a fad top? You have to monitor the stores that sell the product. You have to listen to the conference calls. I was able to sell fads at the top in everything from Palms to Filas to Guess jeans to Keds simply by listening to the conference calls of places that sell these goods, not by the managements of the companies themselves, who never saw the tops coming. As long as the merchants said they couldn't get enough of the product, I knew I was fine and the stock would go higher. Once they said that they had enough product to be able to meet the demand, there was no price at which I wouldn't sell the supplying company's stock. It's just that simple. But if you are going to play a fad, and you don't have the time to listen to conference calls where the fad product is sold, a Best Buy or a Radio Shack for electronics, a JC Penney or Federated for a clothing line, you are going to be crushed like a bug on a windshield. Doing that extra homework, checking outside what management of your company has to say, will save you from holding the stock after a top and losing a fortune, espe-

cially because as is typical with fads, the fortune is huge but ephemeral to all but those who pay attention to the outlets where the product is sold.

7. In-the-hole secondary. One of the incredibly easy tops to spy is when a company does a "deep in the hole" secondary after a huge run. Talk about sure tops. When a company sells stock that is at a huge discount to the last sale of its equity, that's a gigantic red flag that will soon turn into the Jolly Roger to steal your gains.

At one time in the 1990s, Iomega developed a cult following. It had a Zip drive that people thought was proprietary and was always going to be in short supply. The Iomegans worshiped the stock. Me? I don't worship any stock. But I recognize that a cult following can be milked for all it's worth. Investors and friends would chastise me, saying that it was simply a piece of junk that was overly loved. I said, So what? The stock is in tight supply; the short sellers are killing themselves over it; and I am riding it until I see a secondary that is priced in the hole for it, meaning a piece of merchandise from insiders at the company that is sold by underwriters at a substantial discount to the last sale. When that happens, you sell, period, and you never look back. That's because the insiders know the jig is up. The real institutional buyers, the smart guys, have no appetite for the merchandise. Voilà, immediately after the short squeeze is alleviated, the chart goes bad, the institutions puke it up, and the stock just dies. That's exactly what happened in Iomega. The stock went from $1 to $50 and then came down to $40, where Iomega priced a secondary at $35. Okay, I didn't get out at $50, but I was able to hit that $35 bid provided by the underwriters who, foolishly, tried to support the stock. What a home run. Another few months and it would have been a strikeout.

I can't tell you how many in-the-hole secondaries were done between October 1999 and October 2000, the ultimate topping-out period for the market. Every one of the major dot-coms did these in-the-hole secondaries. It got to be like shooting fish in a barrel; you

could own them until the deal came, and then you had to blow them to kingdom come. One reason why I had such a big year in 2000 was that after every one of these in-the-hole secondaries I went short the stocks that did them. You can't get a clearer top tell.

In case you still need help in understanding this one and remembering how vital it is that you sell when you see one of these secondaries that is sold deep and still doesn't hold, let me tell you the story of DIGI.

If there was a stock that embodied the more manic years of my hedge fund, it was DSC Communications, stock symbol DIGI. We owned it from $25 to $75, and it was the type of ramp that used to make our day, every day. Oh we loved DIGI. Jeff Berkowitz had just joined our firm out of the Goldman Sachs research department, where he covered tech. My wife headed the trading desk then. When we had a great stock going, my wife used to lead us in chants about it. They always chanted and played music with bongos and drums at her old shop to alleviate the pressure, and she had brought that style to our desk. Her chanting sounded like a mixture of "King of the Congo" by Kipling and a Gregorian version of the Florida State Seminole cheerleaders at the big game against the hated Gators. Every time the hope-filled stock would rise more than a dollar she would start in with "Didg-ee, Didg-ee, Didg-ee" until the stock would be up a couple of smackers. She would directly attribute the stock's levitation to the mystical powers of her chanting. Of course, it was DIGI's growth that drove it, but the stock business does have a strange karma to it at times.

In the meantime, the beat of the whole market was being set by DIGI's earnings-estimate increases, the real tonic that moved the stock higher. When estimates weren't being upped, DIGI was busy announcing contract after contract from Baby Bells and foreign companies that would eventually lead to higher earnings.

A day never seemed to go by without hot news for DIGI. This stock was telephony's gift to the Street. It had everything: fiber to the loop,

home video, pay TV, you name it. It was the equivalent of Lucent, Cisco, and Nortel all rolled up into one when those stocks were revered on Wall Street.

The stock, like any hot stock of consequence, also attracted the attention of the shorts, who, every day, would die a thousand deaths as the stock would be taken and taken and taken. We would all be glued to our screens watching this marvelous animal leap through whole new handles (each new $10 level is a handle: $10, $20, $30). As the offerings lifted we would wonder aloud what short fund would be cremated today by DIGI. Short squeezes, possible takeover, earnings-estimate increases, contracts—we lapped it all up and hoped it could go on forever. We were, for all intents and purposes, the DIGI Fund.

And then one day Goldman Sachs filed a secondary for a boatload of insiders at DIGI who hadn't done any selling of late. Sometimes these big holdings get bunched and sold all at once, and that's what Goldman did with the stock of the DIGI insiders. The offering was gigantic, big enough to sate everyone's interest who wanted it. It overwhelmed the market, as these secondaries often do. The deal was big enough to allow as many short sellers who wanted to cover in on the stock that had been tight as a drum and unavailable to borrow. (Funds had sold the stock short, hoping it would go down, and then couldn't physically deliver the stock because, of course, they didn't own it, and they couldn't find any stock to borrow.) The secondary was big enough to alleviate the squeeze that had helped propel this stock so far.

Suddenly, DIGI the rock of Gibraltar became DIGI the house of cards. The day the big slug of merchandise was priced, the stock was abnormally soft. The offering got priced right through the bid, deep in the hole. It still seemed shaky, even though it was much lower than where the stock sold the day before.

The moment it was priced my wife turned to me and said, "DIGI is done-ee." I told her not to be ridiculous, that this stock had all the right moves, big orders coming, some I even knew about, and that we had to go right back in and play the DIGI game. She nodded to me, smiled,

and sold every share we owned. Hundreds of thousands of shares. She just drilled the bid, the big juicy syndicate bid, and just like that DIGI was out of our lives. I was furious. I knew good things were about to occur. She just laughed.

The stock didn't hold that price. Others puked it, too. Others who knew what Karen knew, which is that deep-in-the-hole secondaries are like fire in your portfolio. The stock soon broke down and wilted. By midmorning. I felt like I had lost a limb. I didn't understand Karen's rules yet. I thought we should just buy it again. Where would I ever find as good a story as this? I demanded to get back in. She said absolutely not, that we were going to wait until the guillotine stopped falling.

The stock rolled down again the next day and the next. Then, a week later, DIGI lost a contract that I thought it should surely have won, to the manufacturing arm (later Lucent) of what was then AT&T. This was the first big order Lucent had won of the type and it virtually gave the darned thing away to get the business. (See low-margin enterprises versus high-margin enterprises and tops, above.)

DIGI's stock never recovered from that loss. The very next quarter it missed numbers. And then it blew about a half-dozen quarters until it finally got so low that Alcatel snapped it up for below where the whole move started.

If you had paid attention only to the analysts—almost all of whom loved DIGI and didn't downgrade it until shortly before the Alcatel bid—or if you had just focused on the company, or if you had fallen in love and decided that buy and hold was all that mattered, you would have given it all back and then some.

But if you followed the simple rule, Sell the deep-in-the-hole secondary, because it's being done for mystical reasons you don't know but will most certainly soon find out, you will get out with your gains intact and a smile perpetually on your face.

8. Accounting mayhem. The final top that manifests itself with frequency is the accounting shenanigans top. The main reason a com-

pany jiggers the numbers is that it can't make them. When a company can't make its estimates and resorts to these kinds of games, whether the company is Tyco or Cardinal Health or Bristol-Myers or Enron or Schering-Plough, you simply *must* sell it. There is no excuse, no justification to hold on to it. I have a sign that says "Accounting irregularities equals sell" on my quote machine. Mistakenly, in the post–Sarbanes-Oxley period, when I thought that the courts had gotten so tough that you had to be out of your mind to pull off this kind of legerdemain, I took the sign down. A week later Nortel, at $7, announced that it had found some irregularities. I was off my guard. I held instead of selling. The stock promptly went to $3. I couldn't ever recover the money invested.

Never hold on when these come up. Never. Cendant is still not back to where it was when it first served notice that its accounting was shaky. It's simply the kiss of death when these tricks surface. You must shoot first and not even bother to ask questions later. Will you end up selling some stocks too soon because of this? No doubt. But would you end up selling all of the accounting disasters higher than where they ended up? Yes, 100 percent of the time.

9. Holland Tunnel Diner top. We have whole markets that are like the griddle in that diner I described earlier (see page 147), where the market is just so darned red hot that you have to take something off the heat or get burned. Sometimes that will cause you to lose some of a good stock that keeps going higher; other times it will allow you to avoid a top or lessen exposure to a stock that has topped. Unlike the other tops, of course, it is more of a look and feel than a set measure. But when a red-hot market is coupled with an S&P oscillator reading of +5 or more and there are more than 50 percent bulls, you better believe the merchandise is going to fry. (Through its own proprietary oscillator, which I pay to consult, the McGraw-Hill Company's S&P Division keeps track of overbought and oversold markets.) Holland Tunnel Diner tops are often followed by 7–10 percent declines that the market eventually recovers from. But you would be amazed at how

many stocks top for good during those viciously heated moments. Don't let your portfolio be cooked with them.

When I got out of the market in March 2000, I was heavily criticized because I had been so bullish just a few weeks before. But tops are like that. Right before you reach the summit, things are cooking to perfection and you want to be in. You have to be in to get those great gains. But one moment past and you have lethally overstayed your welcome. Don't be afraid to change your mind. This is one place where when the heat is too hot, you *must* get out of the kitchen.

10

ADVANCED STRATEGIES *for* SPECULATORS

Most of my financial life I have worn two hats: I'm a practitioner and a real-time explainer of what I am doing to those trying to learn. I try to put the process in English, so that you aren't confused by the mathematics or the science of it. I try to make it simple because so many people in my business try to make it hard. They use Genuine Wall Street Gibberish, a form of mumbo jumbo; wittingly or unwittingly, they seem to do their best to confuse. I know when I was a salesperson, I could take advantage of those who were ignorant of the way we on Wall Street work if I wanted to be short-term greedy. Those who knew the most and had the best facility with money, though, did get the best treatment and benefited considerably versus those who just couldn't figure it out.

Most of what I had to explain would make sense to anyone who has more than a fifth-grade education: Stocks are arithmetic; the logic behind them is psychology, not quantum physics. Buying and selling a stock is no different from buying and selling a house. You are making money if it goes up after you bought it; you are losing money if it goes

down. But there are two parts of what I did with securities as a practitioner that are particularly difficult to fathom and execute: options and shorting. For these there are no easy explanations, no fifth-grade analogs that make them more understandable. But they should be learned nonetheless. Why should you not be able to take advantage of all of the instruments and methods that the most advanced players use simply because they are complex and arcane? They can be incredibly valuable even to novices if used correctly. They might help you as you get started in building a winning portfolio, regardless of the environment.

Shorting is difficult to understand and potentially dangerous. It's difficult to understand because shorting involves selling something that you don't own. You can't do that in any other line of business. You can't sell a glass of lemonade you don't own, you can't sell a home you don't own, and you can't sell a car you don't own, so it's incomprehensible to many how you can sell stock you don't own. How do you deliver to the buyer shares you don't own? Where do you find someone willing to give it to you so you can sell it without owning it? How about if you first borrow it from your broker before you sell it short?

Let's go through the hypothetical. Let's say you think Intel's too high and you want to profit from the decline you expect to happen. When you sell a stock short, you say to your broker, "I want to sell one thousand shares of Intel short." The broker borrows the stock for you first, places it in your account, and then sells it for you from your account. You even get the proceeds from the sale of 1,000 Intel right into your account. If the stock goes down after you sell it, you make money, the mirror image of what happens when you buy a stock and it goes up. Of course, the opposite is true, too: If you short Intel and it goes higher, you are losing money.

When you buy the stock back that you shorted you are "covering" the short, and you should say that in the order so the broker knows exactly what you are intending. Let's say you sold 1,000 shares of Intel short at $20 and it drops to $16. You tell your broker, "I want to cover

the Intel short, I want to buy back one thousand shares of Intel." If you buy back the stock at this price you make $4,000. Ah, but what if Intel went up? Then you could cover for a loss, as in, "I am covering the one thousand Intel I sold short at twenty dollars at twenty-four dollars," where you would lose $4,000. You could always continue to battle the Intel and sell more, or you could just let it run; that's up to you. But be careful, you can lose lots of money if the stock keeps going higher. The loss or the gain isn't booked until you cover the trade.

Shorting is dangerous because stocks can only go down to zero but in theory at least they can go up to infinity. That's a terribly asymmetrical risk-reward, one that could allow you to lose millions of dollars as a stock goes up and up, but make only a finite amount as the stock of even a bankrupt company stops at zero—although some stinkers I owned felt like they could go even lower.

It's tough enough when you own a stock and it goes down, but it's excruciating when you are short a stock and it goes up. It's financial suicide when you short a stock that so many other folks are short, and the brokerages can't find the stock in the vault to lend out because all shares are out already. The seller can never fail to deliver. So the brokers have to go into the open market to find stock to deliver to the buyers. Their frantic buying creates a squeeze that can produce wild gains for the longs and stupendous losses for the short sellers. That's why such moves are called short squeezes. Stocks can zoom when a large percentage of the "float," or shares that can trade freely, are sold short and new short sellers come in and fail to locate borrowed shares before they sell. That's illegal—you always have to locate stock first—but lots of bad brokers let it happen because they want the commission, and lots of stupid customers don't tell the broker up front that the sale is a short one. When the unscrupulous meet the uninformed, and execute short sales of stocks that shouldn't be shorted, it's a combustible combination. Often these squeezes happen to the phoniest of stocks, so that you could be right on the fundamentals but be betrayed by the mechanics of shorting. The shorting process entails too high a degree

of difficulty and risk for the vast majority of investors because you can lose more than you have in your account if the shorted stock skyrockets. It's particularly awful to short a company many know is phony, because the real bad ones are so often targeted by multiple short sellers. That's why occasionally you see these counterintuitive 10- and 15- and 20-point jumps for stocks of companies that barely exist or are simply hype. So be very careful before you sell short. If you want to save yourself some stress and put a cap on your losses up front, you should first try to bet against the stock using put options.

Options are hard to explain. I have never met anyone who could explain these complex instruments in a simple way. So I will tell you that their degree of difficulty is beyond the average investor's ken. Options have their own language—"calls" give you the right but not the obligation to buy common stock, while "puts" give you the right but not the obligation to *sell* common stock. They also have their own rules—you need to decide to exercise or sell them when they are "in the money" at expiration. If they are misused they are extremely dangerous.

So why go into options at all? Lots of reasons. First, you are almost ready to go out on your own and nab some higher returns using the tricks of the trade I have taught you. But I don't want you going out there without knowing all of the weapons that can be in your arsenal. The main reason you bought this book is so that you could learn how to be better at handling your money, better at being a good investor or a good client. No one is going to care about your money as much as you do. Part of being a wise investor is being familiar enough with all the conventional and unconventional strategies so you can be sufficiently knowledgeable to evaluate your broker, decide if he or she is right for you. You need to retain control and not lose it to someone who might do wrong things to or for you. I have learned the hard way that bad brokers and bad managers use fear and ignorance to milk naïve clients. If you don't understand options I believe you will get ripped off by someone who recognizes your ignorance and tries to

take advantage of it. Further, options are part of sophisticated but sound stock analysis. Investors need to know—at least in general terms—how everyone is betting on a stock before they buy shares in it.

I understand that options can be intimidating. I have met seasoned common stock traders, people who have traded common stock for decades, who don't understand what puts and calls are and why anyone would use them. These are complex pieces of paper (also known as "derivatives") that allow you to use a little capital to go a long way. You buy calls when you want to make a bet that a stock—or an index—is going to go higher in a short period of time. You buy puts when you think a stock or an index is about to sink quickly. You buy them like this: "I want to buy calls on Intel" or "I want to buy puts on Intel." Then the broker offers you a menu of options struck at various prices at various months out in the future. He asks you how many you want, with every option equal to 100 shares of common stock. (Don't worry, I will walk you through examples.) The puts or calls are entered into your statement in the same way that common stock is. They don't obligate you to do anything, though, and the vast majority of all puts and calls expire worthless, meaning that the owners and holders lose money on the bets. You never *have* to use either puts or calls. You can always buy common stock or a basket of common stocks if you want to profit from the upside. You can always sell a common stock or even sell all your stocks when you think that the market's going lower. My wife, for example, never understood options. She used to rail that if I really hated the market, what the heck was I doing buying insurance against my stocks in the form of puts, or contracts, that give me the right to sell the stock at the current price ("in-the-money" put) or at a lower price than it currently sold at ("out-of-the-money" put). She would tell me that stocks aren't houses; you don't have to live in them. Why insure something you don't have to live in? Just sell it. That's not bad advice.

These days, because I am limited by various media obligations, I

can't use puts or calls. If I think a stock is going to go down, I just sell it; I don't buy puts on it to protect it. But I used both puts and calls to tremendous effect when I first started out as a little investor and ultimately at my multi-million-dollar hedge fund. Over the years I found that options were a fantastic way to make a little money into a lot of money. As I am a constant risk-reward hunter, I loved the idea that I could risk some money on calls to make much bigger money than I could make buying common stock. I also loved the idea that I could bet against a stock using puts without worrying about a short squeeze, where a stock rallied hard because so many others were making the same bet that brokerage houses couldn't find any more stock to borrow.

I have wrestled with this chapter more than the others because I know that the stuff I did with options in my later career may simply be too difficult and time-consuming for all but the most hard-bitten professionals. Yet I know I have to expose you to them, just so you can understand what's out there, so you can understand what to do if you ever have a hunch so good that it is worth speculating on. I've had a ton of these and I am always grateful that someone came up with options so I could take advantage of their bang for the buck. Let me walk you through how options work and how they differ from purchasing or selling common stock so you can understand their magic. Then I can present you with some advanced strategies about how to use options in a conservative way to leverage your cash and your best hunches.

As mentioned, there are two kinds of options, calls and puts. Call options are the right but not the obligation to purchase an agreed-upon amount of stock at a particular price in the future. Put options are the right but not the obligation to sell a stock at a particular price in the future. We buy calls when we have a hunch that something big is going to happen that's terrific for a stock or for the market. We buy puts when we think that a stock's going to implode and we want to be there, gaining from the collapse, rather than just being blasted out of our wealth. We can buy puts or calls on stocks or indices. Don't like the

NASDAQ? Buy a put on the QQQ, the Nasdaq 100. Like the Dow? Buy Dow Jones calls. Think the overall S&P 500 is going higher in the near term? Buy a call on it. Worried that the market's about to dive? Buy puts on the S&P 500.

You can buy a call or a put like a regular stock. The difference is that when you buy a put or a call you are buying a bet on the direction of the stock; you are not buying the stock itself. You have to be able to isolate the time frame that you want to bet on that appreciation or depreciation *before* you buy one. You can't say, "I want a put that will last forever" or "I want a call that will never end" because these are contracts with a delivery date. And you have to predict where the stock will appreciate or depreciate to, an actual level that you think it will go to. In other words, you can't just say, "I want an Intel call." You have to say, "I want a call on Intel that will allow me to capture the appreciation of the next ten points over a period of, say, eight months." If it is February and Intel is at 20, your broker or your electronic screen will give you a list of calls that would reflect that time period. He might suggest that you buy the "October 20 calls," phrased that way because it would mean that you would have until October of that year to capture the appreciation. The "20" is the "strike," the price level you are paying for all of the points Intel might make above 20 by the third week in October (all options expire on the third week of the month). Let's go through the hypothetical.

It's February and Intel's at $20. Let's buy some Intel October 20 calls. You pick up the phone and you say to your broker, "I want to buy some October 20 calls on Intel." The broker would then look up on his options monitor—they all have them and you could have one too, if you wanted to—and the broker might see that the calls are at $1.75 bid $2.00 ask, meaning that you can sell or buy an October 20 call at those prices respectively. Let's say you want 10 of them. That will cost you $2 per option. Each option allows you to buy 100 shares of common stock at $20. The arithmetic is a tad difficult to remember, because you have to multiply that $2 by 100 first. Then you have to multiply the sum of $2 times 100 by the number of calls you are buying. So, 10 calls

costs \$2,000 (\$2 $\times$ 100 $\times$ 10 = \$2,000). There are no shortcuts for understanding this process. You must know that the \$2 price is the starting point to calculate the amount you are spending. If you can't follow it, work with your broker to figure it out.

Let's say Intel goes to \$25 in October. Your Intel October 20 call, which you bought at \$2, is now worth \$5. How? You simply subtract the strike from the price of the stock to figure out what the call is worth when it expires. Congratulations, you have paid \$2,000 and you have something now worth \$5,000. You made \$3,000 betting that Intel would go up.

But let's say you feel Intel is going down, not up, during that same period. You might want to buy the Intel October 20 puts, which would allow you to capture all of the depreciation below \$20. Again, with the stock at \$20 in February, the October 20 put may cost \$2. You buy 10—each put allows you to sell 100 shares of Intel stock—for \$2,000. If the stock drops to \$15 by October, you subtract the closing price from the strike to figure out how much you have. Twenty minus fifteen is five. The \$2 puts you bought for \$2,000 are now worth \$5,000. Congratulations. You made \$3,000 betting against Intel.

Who determines the price of the puts and calls? The thousands of buyers and sellers of these instruments. Institutions sell calls and puts to bring in additional income. Individuals and hedge funds, the type of fund I used to run, for example, buy them to magnify bets, to put a little capital to work to make a lot. They determine prices for puts and calls much like stocks through the marketplace, as a function of supply and demand. You can get posted prices for small increments of puts and calls from your computer screen. Consult your broker if you want to buy more than a 10 lot, though, because the screen market may not be big enough for more than that.

Options are quite handy, and most of us have used them; we just haven't used them to buy or sell stock. When we speculate in real estate, we often ask for an option to buy something. We pay for that option even if we end up not buying the land underneath it. When we buy insurance, we are buying a put. We are putting out a little money

to protect a lot. We don't want the insurance put to pay off, but if it does, we consider ourselves lucky to have had it. The insurance put and the real estate call are just like stock options in their most basic form.

Let's flesh out the real estate call so we are more comfortable with examples that look and feel a lot like options that you are familiar with. Let's say you live in a town near a heavily traveled interstate highway. You have a hunch that sometime in the next year or two, the federal government might build an off-ramp not far from where you live. You recognize that when off-ramps get built, retailers flock to these sites as natural places to erect new stores. You, yourself, are not a developer and have no desire to develop the land. You may not even be able to afford the land—far from it, in fact. But you don't want to miss this chance. It would be natural for you to call a Realtor and say that you would like an option to buy the land for the next two years, if one were available. That way, if the off-ramp is proposed, you know that you can exercise the option and sell the land, perhaps to a Target or a Wal-Mart, for a heck of a lot more than anyone thought possible. Let's put some numbers on it. Let's say the parcel of land was for sale for $300,000. You didn't have that money on hand. It is possible that you might be able to propose that for some percentage of that $300,000, whatever you think negotiable, perhaps $10,000 a year, you reserve the right to buy that property for $300,000. If you could get that option contract and the off-ramp is approved, you might be able to exercise that option and, without ever putting down the $300,000, sell it, say to Wal-Mart for $3 million. You just made an astronomical profit by exercising the option and selling it.

That's how I got started using call options. I wouldn't have the money that I needed to buy a lot of common stock, but I could put a much smaller amount of money down in order to buy the common stock some time in the future at a fixed price, and then sell the option, or exercise the option and sell the common stock afterward. Let's walk through an actual trade so you can see how I was able to use call options to make a ton of money in a legal way.

When I was a young investor at Goldman Sachs, I was always trying to figure out whether a drug company had a major new drug find that could impact the bottom line enough to make the stock worth owning. In the fall of 1986, Merck had been working on a novel cholesterol-lowering drug. The company's scientists had determined that if they could lower cholesterol through medication, they could save millions of people from having heart attacks. Today, of course, these drugs are among the most popular pills sold on earth. At the time, though, most of the analysts who covered the drug companies didn't think much of the concept of cholesterol-lowering drugs. They thought the category would be small. One of my investors, though, a cardiologist, was very excited by the results he saw in those who took the cholesterol-lowering pills. It was his hunch that these drugs could be a billion-dollar seller rather quickly for Merck. I canvassed Wall Street seeing what numbers people were using for the new medication, and no analyst thought it would amount to more than $200 million in annual sales. Once I knew that such a figure seemed absurdly low to my doctor friend, I recognized that I might have stumbled onto something that could propel Merck, a good drug company, to incredibly high levels.

At the time I was doing my canvassing, Merck traded at $80 a share. If I wanted to buy 100 shares of Merck, I would have had to pay $8,000. That's a lot of money to put to work for a limited amount of shares, especially because—as in that case of the real estate by the off-ramp—I didn't care to own the actual stock; I just wanted to own the appreciation of the stock. I just wanted the upside from $80.

How about if I could buy a right to the appreciation of Merck, *just* the appreciation of Merck, not the stock itself? What if I could get someone to give me an option on the appreciation of Merck above $80, given that I thought Merck would jump in the same way that the undeveloped parcel of land might jump? That would be a better way, especially given that I knew when the drug was going to go to market and that it would immediately impact the sales estimates, which, theoretically, would drive the company's stock higher.

That's the best example of what calls are about.

So, naturally, I asked my broker for a call on everything above $80. Here's where the fun begins. He would say, "I can offer you a contract that will allow you to get all of the appreciation above seventy-five dollars, or above eighty or above eighty-five or above ninety or even above one hundred? Which one do you want?"

You want to know how much each option costs and how much you can buy above each one. You want to figure out which has the most value, the most bang for the buck and the least likelihood that you will lose it all. Let's play it out conversationally, the way I have had to explain it to hundreds of customers.

"I would like the call that begins at eighty dollars," the first-time options customer says.

"And when do you want your contract to last to?" I, the broker, would ask.

Given the time frame of the new drug's launch, the customer says, "I need to have the option last until at least February."

I would then scroll through the menu of Merck calls that are currently being made on one of the big options exchanges and suggest as a start, "We should look at the Merck calls that last until the third week of February." Let's consider the Merck February 80s, shorthand for Merck calls struck at $80, meaning that you get all of the appreciation above $80 until the third Friday of February.

"How much will those cost?" the customer asks.

I would then tell the customer, before I mentioned the price, that each call is the right but not the obligation to buy 100 shares of stock above $80, so I would be quoting a dollar amount that would be multiplied by 100. Confusing, I know, but a call doesn't equal 1 share of stock, it equals 100 shares. So I would say, "Each call is priced at five dollars, so you would have to spend five hundred dollars per call."

Now, the customer thinks, Hold it, the call costs me $5, that's a lot of money. "If I buy this call, if I buy one call, and Merck goes to eighty-five by the third week of February, how will I have done?"

Not too well, I say. You are spending $500 for the right to buy 100

shares of Merck above $80, but that right will make it so you make no money until Merck goes above $85—the $5 you paid for the call plus $80 equals $85. You will be wagering $5 to make $5 unless it goes higher than $85.

How about the calls that allow me to get everything above $85? the customer would then ask.

"Those," I would say, "are three dollars per contract, meaning that you would get the appreciation for one hundred shares above eighty-five dollars but that would cost you three hundred dollars. Now the stock has to go to eighty-eight before you start making money." (I am approximating what the prices would be, but you get the picture.)

Most of the time you might just say at that point, Wait a second, this is too expensive. I am not going to risk all of that cash and then watch Merck go up 5 or 8 points and make nothing. I would rather take that $500 or $300 and buy the common stock. Of course, you can see the problem with that. You don't get a lot of Merck stock for $300 or even $500. You buy three shares of $80 Merck stock for $300 and it goes up 5 points, you've made $15. That's not much at all. You buy six shares for $500 and make $30.

But let's say the customer is adamant that this new drug is going to shoot the lights out, as I was. I believed that Merck could go to $100 by February. So the customer comes back and says, "I have eight thousand dollars to invest in Merck calls. You tell me what to do. I think the stock will be way above a hundred come February."

I would test the customer's confidence. If he sticks to his guns, then I would say, "Okay, you have great conviction. Let's look at the Merck calls struck at ninety dollars. They are one dollar per contract, meaning you can buy, for one hundred dollars, all the appreciation above ninety dollars for one hundred shares. You can either buy one hundred shares of Merck stock for that eight thousand dollars or you can buy up to eighty of the Merck nineties for that eight thousand dollars." (Remember, each call must be multiplied by 100 because each call represents 100 shares. So a dollar call costs $100 and with $8,000 you can buy 80 calls.) If you buy 80 of those calls, you will control the appreci-

ation above $90 of 8,000 shares. Each call is the right to 100 shares worth of Merck.

So now let's contrast the two choices, the common stock guy who buys 100 shares of Merck for $8,000 and the options guy who buys 80 of the February 90 calls for $8,000.

If Merck does nothing, stays at $80 for the next four months, what will happen? The common stock guy's doing fine. He has his $8,000 and has probably picked up a Merck dividend along the way—the dividends go only to common stock holders, not call holders. The option holder? He's out all $8,000. Horrible trade. Just horrible. That Merck 90 call went out worthless.

How about if Merck goes to $85? The common stock guy just made $500 on his $8,000 investment. Not bad, not bad at all. Good rate of return. The options guy? He's the big loser again, out all $8,000.

How about if Merck goes to $90? The common stock buyer is now in clover for 10 points, he's up $800, he's made 10 percent on his money. Better than a sharp stick in the eye. The call holder? Still wiped out. All $8,000. How much is the right to buy a stock at $90 worth when the stock is at $90? Nothing!

So far, under every scenario, the options guy is a chump, a moron, a total loser. The common stock guy is the winner, big time.

But how about if Merck goes to $100. Then what happens?

Paydirt for the call holder.

You own the rights to all of the appreciation above $90. You just made 10 points. You have 80 calls, controlling 8,000 shares! You just made 10 points on 8,000 shares. That's $80,000! Of course you don't have to buy the common stock, you just have to exercise the call when it gets there and sell the common stock.

It goes like this. You tell me, your broker, to exercise the 80 calls in Merck. You simultaneously tell me to sell 8,000 shares of Merck, because when you exercise the calls my brokerage will deposit 8,000 shares of common stock into your account, and you don't have the $800,000 you need to own 8,000 shares of a $100 stock.

In real estate that's the same as selling the land to Wal-Mart with-

out having to take delivery of the land. You couldn't afford to buy it, but it doesn't matter because you exercise the sale at the exact same time that you exercise your option.

You bought all of the appreciation rights for 8,000 shares of Merck between $90 and $100. That's 10 points of appreciation. Your $8,000 call turned out to be worth $80,000 (10 points times 8,000 shares because each of the 80 calls controls the appreciation of 100 shares, and 80 times 100 is 8,000).

How did the common stock shareholder do? He bought 100 shares at $80. The stock went to $100. He made 20 points; 20 times 100 is $2,000. He made $2,000 on his $8,000 investment. You plunked down $8,000 and saw it go to $80,000. You just made $72,000 on that same $8,000.

Now I've got you interested.

Let me tell you what happened to me in that example. I put about $80,000 on those calls. They went up ten times. And I had enough money to quit my job to go run a hedge fund. I know I could have been out all $80,000, but I thought the reward justified the risk.

I know I have made it sound simple, and it *is* simple when the stock explodes up. Most stocks don't. Most people get wiped out by what is known as "out of the money" calls. But if you are intrigued, I urge you to consider calls when you know something so special that it might merit such a wager.

Now, let's play the downside.

Let's say Merck's stock has gone to $100 and you get a sense that the U.S. government is going to allow people to buy Merck's Mevacor in Canada for one-quarter the price of what it sells for in the United States. That would be a disaster for Merck. You think Merck will go down 20 points when it happens. If you own the common stock, of course you would sell it. But you might be tempted to short Merck, or bet against the stock. You would call up your broker and say, "I want to bet against Merck because of a change I see coming, what do you advise me?"

I would say, "You can sell some Merck you don't own and profit from it. Let me see if I can borrow a thousand shares from someone here that you can sell short. Let's say you sold a thousand shares of Merck *short* at a hundred dollars and it went down twenty points. We could then buy back those shares you don't down twenty and make twenty thousand dollars. That's a nice trade. That's how the short side works."

But, I would quickly add, if you are wrong, you could lose your money. Worse yet, if Merck goes up, you could be out infinite amounts of money. Let's say Merck goes up 10 points. You would owe that 10 points to the guy from whom you borrowed the stock. You'd be out $10,000. And if it went to up 20, you could be out $20,000!

No customer wants that risk. So you might ask for a menu of puts, which give you the right but not the obligation to sell the stock at various prices. I would call up the menu and say that I could sell you a put that allows you to gain everything under $100, under $95, under $90, and so on, as low as you want to go.

The $100 put costs $5. The $95 put costs $3, and the $90 put costs $1. Again, we walk through the mirror image of the call arithmetic. If you buy the Merck $100 put and the stock goes down 5 points, you make nothing. The cost of the put equaled the loss in price of the stock. If you buy the $95 put and the stock goes to $90, you make a little bit of money. But if you buy the $90 put and the stock goes to $80, you could make $10 per put.

So, let's do it, let's buy the $90 put. Here's what happens. Let's keep the investment amount the same, $8,000. You buy 80 puts struck at $90 for that $8,000. Those puts give you the right to all the decline below $90 for 8,000 shares—80 puts times 100 equals 8,000 shares. If the stock goes down only to $90, you make nothing. But if it plummets to $80, you have sold the equivalent of 8,000 shares at $90 and it went to $80. You made ten points times 8,000 shares or $80,000.

Now let's compare the short seller who sells 1,000 shares of common stock at $100. He makes 20 points per share if Merck drops to $80. That's $20,000. Not bad. But he also *risks* getting crushed if the

stock goes higher than $100. Twenty-thousand-dollar gain versus an infinite loss if Merck runs. Not a good risk-reward.

The put holder, though, limits his risk to his investment. He can't lose more than $8,000, and if the stock declines to $80, he makes the equivalent of 10 points on his 800 shares that he controls through the puts. He's up $80,000 versus a loss of $8,000. That's a fabulous risk-reward.

Both of these examples, the put and the call, show the true power of options when they work right. They also show that you could be out a lot of dough when you are wrong. When you know that you have something big, either way, the best way to play it is in puts or calls. But if it isn't big—and about 99 percent of the situations I hear daily aren't big—it is better to use the common stock. It's that last caveat—that 99 percent of what I see and hear should be played in common stock—that keeps me from spending more time telling you about the more tricky and dangerous ways to use calls and puts. We'll have to save that for another time.

Which stocks should be shorted? Anything you think should be going down rather than going up. I don't mean that facetiously. I like to be able to look at or argue every stock from the point of view of a long or short. When associates of mine would come to me at my hedge fund with a long, I would view it as a short seller would, and vice versa. I think it is important to be able to examine both sides and not to be dogmatic about which side to take. Given that predilection, I think what you need more than a list of which stocks should be shorted is a set of rules that exclude certain stocks from being shorted. My wife developed just such a list of basic tenets and I will share it with you. Remember it, write it down next to your monitor, whatever it takes, but don't violate it. I believe that statistically you will be doomed to lose money on a short if you do. These rules have saved me tens of millions of dollars. And as Karen is incredibly plain speaking, you won't have any trouble understanding them.

First, the *BusinessWeek* cover rule. Karen would always ask me, Do

you think the company could be on the cover of *BusinessWeek* this Friday as the world's greatest company? Simple rule. Life saver. Don't go after good companies that you think are screwing up short-term. There's nothing worse, for example, than being short Merck, as I once was, and then reading a loving *BusinessWeek* cover story on Merck three days later. If your short involves a company great enough to be on the cover of *BusinessWeek,* forget it. Even if you have insight, just forget it. Great companies shouldn't be shorted.

Second, can the company be taken over? If yes, Karen would say to me, "You are on your own, just do it in puts." In my career, I've been short three companies that received takeover bids, all at a huge premium: NCR, Systemix, and Genentech. With each one I had what I thought was a great reason to be short. The first two had disastrous fundamentals, as the acquiring companies later found out. The third had traced out a perfect head-and-shoulders pattern (technical jargon for a stock that's supposed to roll over imminently), something I guess Hoffmann–La Roche didn't care about when it made its partial tender at a gigantic price above where I shorted the stock. In all three cases, I must admit, I could have guessed that a takeover could have occurred, as all three companies were in industries experiencing consolidation. I should never have shorted them. This point alone is worth millions of dollars. A possible takeover should transform a short into a put special, or you should just not play at all.

Third, never short because of valuation. Never short because you think the stock's too expensive. Expensive stocks have a way of getting more expensive. I don't care what P/E Qualcomm sells for, I don't care whether you think Yahoo! or Google is absurdly valued. It is irrelevant that some stock that trades at $50 has no earnings. You must never, ever try to call an irrational top based solely on multiples of sales earnings. There will *always* be some mutual fund out there that will keep the ball in the air and crush you with its buying. Michael Steinhardt, my wife's guru, taught this basic point to her, but repeatedly violated it himself. He lost oodles of money shorting overvalued stocks.

Is there a rational for why this method of shorting doesn't work?

Indeed, often companies that seem overvalued now turn out to be incredibly cheap when you look back at them. For instance, eBay and Yahoo! both sold at astonishingly low prices to what turned out to be the future earnings when they were in their 40s and 10s respectively. The long-side players simply ignored the near-term P/E consideration and focused on the out years. They recognized that these stocks were going to grow into their multiples eventually. Or, as Karen would say, they were smarter than those who took the other side.

Of course, there are plenty of times when the out years don't materialize, but that's not the point. You have to consider the fact that other investors might believe that they might materialize. You need a better, more rigorous answer about why a stock will come down than "it is too expensive." That doesn't cut it. You need a catalyst that you believe will turn that high-flying stock into a stock too expensive for even the hardiest of believers. You need some number, some report, some competitor that could come in and wreck the margins. Without a specific, objective reason to turn the buyers' heads around, you must remember that stocks that go up gain adherents—chartists. They will ride these winners until something fundamental happens to break the overvaluation. If you don't know what that is, don't short. You may not live long enough to collect the gains.

Fourth, please use puts when you can instead of borrowing and selling short stock. Puts don't subject you to the buy-in; they allow you to limit your losses to the value of the put, not to the potentially parabolic run of a stock. Lots of great short sellers went out of business in the 1990s because they shorted common stock, and they discovered that stocks do go to infinity, or close to it, as many of the dot-coms did before collapsing. If you are sure something is going to go down but don't know when, use deep puts going out many, many months. You will never regret paying the extra money. That way you can't be wiped out by an Energizer Bunny like a Research in Motion or eBay or Qualcomm, stocks that hung on longer than anyone thought they would. I can't tell you how many times people got caught in squeezes

because they refused to pay the premium for the puts that would have at least limited their losses. You never want a short to put you out of business, but I have seen it happen dozens of times among my own friends. Don't let this be your undoing.

Fifth, never be part of what I call a gang tackle short. If you ever hear of a bunch of people shorting the same names that you are shorting, I can tell you that you are a dead man. Karen would always ask me, "Does anyone else have this call?" If the answer was yes, her answer was always no. She always wanted the information to be homegrown, not borrowed from someone else; created by my own research, not by the research of others. That's because there could be people much bigger than me shorting the stock and then covering to wreck the short when they grew impatient. Too many short sellers means too little stock to borrow means too much of an opportunity for a buy-in to occur.

Sixth, and most important: It is not cool to be short. It is not something to get a kick out of or earn your bones on. Karen sold short for a living. It is gut-wrenching, harrowing, and extremely rewarding when you are right and mind-numbingly painful when you are wrong. There's nothing gallant or suave about shorting. Hedge fund managers always like to brag about their shorts. They think that it distinguishes them as truly intense, sharp thinkers. Nah, my wife would always say. "It's the same as going long, except you can't quantify the loss."

Just in case you don't respect the power of the short squeeze, in case you don't understand how painful these can be, let me leave you with a story that happened to me early in my career and taught me to have a better case and not target takeover stocks as part of my short-selling methodology.

Before I got into the business, I remember being completely mystified by the newspaper phrase "short-covering rally." All buying seemed like "real" buying to me, so what difference did it make whether it was buying to cover a short or not? I couldn't believe that

any big stock could be bid up as part of a short squeeze or, more important, a short-term imbalance that an aggressive short seller could create.

One day, after I had been trading alone for a while, I met an analyst who told me he felt that Noxell, now a subsidiary of P&G, but at the time an independent company, could be in for a disappointing quarter. As a young hedge fund operator I jumped at the chance to show my shorting colors. Weren't we supposed to be taking bold, contrary stands against companies? Noxell, an expensive NASDAQ stock, seemed ripe for a whacking. After doing my homework I started shorting Noxell gingerly, the same way I would buy a long, shorting a little at first, hoping higher prices would come so I could put out (short) more at better, more ridiculously priced levels. I sold short 10,000 shares at $50 and then said I would short my next tranche of 10,000 every half a point up. The market quickly obliged, and two days later the stock was at $54 and I was short more than 80,000 shares.

When positions would go against me like this, I would frequently go back to the analyst who turned me on to the short and grill him. In this case, the analyst was more convinced than ever that the quarter was weak. I called other analysts around the Street, including those who had a buy on Noxell, and they, too, seemed a bit concerned about how sales and margins were coming through for the cosmetics company. So I put out more stock. I kept to my scale and the stock kept climbing. At $58, now up 8 straight points from where the stock was trading when I started the process, I was short 150,000 shares. When you are running less than $100 million, which I was at that point, you begin to get pretty concerned. I became the Short Noxell Fund.

Over that weekend, of course, I stopped shaving with Noxema Medicated Comfort shaving cream. I had the familiar flush of perspiration of when I had done something wrong every time I looked at the balance sheets and saw that mammoth position. I was panicked, but I stuck with my discipline and shorted more as it kept climbing, even increasing my levels to 20,000 shares every half point because I needed

to bring up my basis (the point at which I'd begin to make money). I had to believe that there was no way that profit-takers wouldn't come in to bring the stock down, allowing me to cover some of the shares that I had shorted. I trade around shorts the way I trade around longs, buying some back when a stock gets hit so I can short it again when it rebounds. That way I always feel like I have room to take advantage of the ensuing spikes. But this stock never came down, not a half point even, the whole time I was shorting it.

On Tuesday after the Noxema-free weekend, the stock jumped to $60—up 10 points from my opening short. To heck with the analysts, I said to myself, I started calling anyone, everyone in the business to ask if they had heard anything positive about what the heck was propelling Noxell. "Look, I am short the &%*%^% thing," I would say, "and I just need an explanation for what's wrong." Nobody had one. Everyone was encouraging me to put out more because it was obviously going up for no good reason.

The very next day the stock traded through $63. Now I was asking traders at the big stock houses what was happening, calling all of the honchos who made markets in Noxell asking them what they were hearing. As I was making these desperate calls I saw the stock shoot through $64 to hit $65.

Finally, I broke down and called Karen Backfisch, who would become Karen Cramer, but this was way before I thought that possible. I asked her to find out what the heck was going on with Noxell. I was too embarrassed to tell her that her boyfriend was short the darned thing. But I knew I couldn't figure it out without her. Karen tapped into her network of short sellers who do nothing but talk all the time about who is shorting what and what might be ripe for the taking. These guys knew where every short was buried; they probably even did some of the killing. The news I got chills me to this day and reminds me always how tough being short can be. She said, and I will never forget these words: "Some little joker hedge fund's been shorting the *&&^%^& out of it and now the traders are all spreading the word to

anybody who will listen that Procter and Gamble is going to bid ninety dollars for the thing. He's got to capitulate and buy it back. They're going to put the little guy out of business, or force him to cover. Get on board!"

Of course little joker hedge fund guy was me.

Oh no, I thought, I am going to be put out of business. I couldn't stand the pain any longer. Not one second. I frantically called a major trading desk and told them I had 250,000 Noxell to buy. With the stock at $64, I would be willing to pay up to $69 for it all. Anything to take away the pain.

One hour later, battling a collective short squeeze of my own making, I took the biggest loss of my career. Noxell 69; Cramer zero. That's right, I paid $69 to bring the whole short position in. I was relieved, I could breathe—heck, I could shave—but the loss was simply unfathomable.

Crushed. Just crushed.

Not long after I covered, Noxell reported extremely disappointing earnings, much worse than I had expected when I put out the short. The stock plummeted to levels well below where it would be considered a terrific trade, right back to the low 50s. I had been completely and utterly had by a group of traders who fomented what amounted to a nonbuying short squeeze that snared me and only me. Such is the lot of the shorts, though, that this type of incident is all too common. I can't tell you how many times after this that I got the call about some moronic hedge fund that was short a stock that I liked and I was encouraged to walk it up in his face by a trader. Just the way I got hosed in Noxell. And I admit to doing it. The money's just that easy.

Noxell was later acquired by P&G—the rumor had gravitas, but the bid came at a price not much higher than I covered. I simply got beaten by the artificial squeeze.

You would think that the market wouldn't care about one little hedge fund that was correctly shorting a stock. You would think that somehow there would be justice or there would be more of a motivation for a stock to go higher than that a few funds were ganging up on

another fund that was short. But that's not how it works. Everyone on Wall Street is out to make a buck any way possible, and if it means trying to put a short seller out of business, then so be it. The dark forces coalesce on both sides of the trade and can force victories and losses regardless of fundamental reality.

What should I have done? Simple. I should have bought deep in the money puts from a far out month that would have allowed me to preserve the trade until the time the company reported earnings. And that's just what I did whenever I shorted after the Noxell annihilation.

EPILOGUE

We've experienced a remarkable swing of the financial pendulum in the last five years. We've gone from embracing the stock market, cheering the relentlessly higher levels of the averages, to spurning equities and accepting that they are difficult to fathom, manage, or profit from. We lusted for shareholder democracy, where each person built his own portfolio and monitored and maintained stock positions, eager to take advantage of the hottest trends. Now many people believe that stocks are a crooked affair, one that only the richest and most well-connected people can possibly afford. Stocks, which regularly trumped homes in rising values for all of the 1990s, have now stayed flat while we've gotten used to 20 percent appreciation year after year for the properties we live in. We've gone from checking our portfolios daily, even hourly, to selling all our stocks and not even bothering to open the statement from our mutual funds. Firms we trusted to be fiduciaries sold our net asset values from underneath us. Research that we thought was honest turned out to be corrupt, paid for by the very companies that were being reviewed. We put faith in managements that soon will be occupying whole wings of federal prisons. We stopped funding our 401(k)s; we gave up trying to fathom which stocks went up and which ones went to zero.

My chief motivation for writing this book was to get you to under-

stand that there are always opportunities to make money, always
bull markets to find, always stocks that will go higher, even in the
crummiest of markets. I think the pendulum has swung too far now,
that as silly as it might have been to check our net worth by the minute
on the Web, it might even be sillier—and more dangerous—to do
nothing with your money today. Retirement's always around the corner. Your paycheck isn't big enough and it won't last forever. You can't
sell your house without buying something else to live in, and that
makes the wealth of your house impossible to tap without a dramatic
change in circumstance.

That's why I know it's time for you to get back in. This time
though, because you will use the principles and common sense of this
book, it won't end the way it did at the turn of the last century. In fact,
it won't end at all.

But let's say I am wrong about the market swinging too negatively.
Let's say that the awful roller-coaster market—up and down and up
and down and then finish the exact same place but with a sick-to-our-
stomach feeling that makes us dread the process—continues; seven fat
years, seven lean years so to speak. I think I have shown in this book
that there are always needles in the haystack, groups that work, always
bull markets out there somewhere. You just need these tools to know
where to look for them.

By no means am I saying it is easy. I insist on buys only with homework, I insist on staying on top of your portfolio. I demand that if you
are going to buy individual stocks you get involved and stay involved,
and that if you don't have the time or the inclination you must hand it
off to others. I know, though, without a doubt, that you have to learn
to be either a better investor or a better client; there is no other choice.

Home Depot has a terrific saying: "You can do it; we can help." I
think that most professionals, including those you see on television or
read in print, have come to a different conclusion: "You can't do it and
we can't help." As someone who has traded and made money in all
sorts of terrible markets since 1979, I know you can do it, and I know

I most certainly can help. My methods, which involve hard, time-consuming work and lots of common sense, constantly generate winning ideas and cull out losers that could wipe out whatever good you might be doing. I know what you did wrong the last time around, and I know that I have offered cures, not panaceas, to that behavior.

I know I will never be willing to concede what so many folks do now, which is that you can't beat the averages, so you might as well join them. In sports, that would be the equivalent of saying that no college player can ever rise to the NBA or the NFL level so why bother to aspire. We know that some do make it, we know that in this game we don't need the God-given talents that those players have to have. We just need hard work, some rules and some discipline, and we will beat the averages.

My styles and methods aren't in the textbooks. Nobody I know divides the universe into the retirement stream and the discretionary stream and allows you to be as aggressive in the discretionary stream as you should be conservative in the retirement stream. No one I know embraces speculation, embraces the finding of lowly stocks, trying to catch the unexploited before the pack, even if the unexploited never, ultimately, amounts to anything. As long as you restrain yourself to no more than 20 percent of your discretionary funds in speculative holdings, you are not violating any rule that will come back to haunt you. And if you are still rolling the dice with 100 percent equities for retirement a few years before you need that money, you just wasted your time and money reading this book.

Will we ever return to the days when fortunes were made overnight in the market, when the closing prices flashed on billboards around baseball stadiums and every bar and health club had CNBC on round-the-clock? I don't think so. I don't want it, either, because then it is too easy, and when it is too easy, we lose the rigor, and ultimately, we lose the money that we have invested. I like it hard; I like it difficult to fathom. That makes it so there are fewer people out there to grab the great ideas. The great stocks don't get bid up so fast that we have to sell

them as soon as we buy them. And sell them we must if we are going to hold on to the gains, because selling's part of the discipline of stocks that we have all forgotten.

So, go build that portfolio. Remember, even someone like me, swinging around hundreds of millions of dollars at one point, never did anything rash, never did anything all at once, never felt he had to be "big" at one level, only to see the market get cracked right after I spent all my hard-earned money. Take your time this time. Do it right, do it with caution, approach it with the same thought you would give any large dollar purchase. Live by the rules here, recognize that your rules and your discipline are your only friends in a world where the government can't protect you from the rapacious folks who we now know dominated the boardrooms of both Main Street and Wall Street.

You will make mistakes. You will lose some money. You might not become a millionaire overnight, as so many charlatans in my business claim at seminars and in books. But you will be doing it the way the real pros do, the ones who beat the markets, all markets, the ones who know that you don't have to have a bull market in all stocks to make money. I can't ask you to love stocks as much as I do, but I can ask you to take care of yourself financially, because, alas, no one will ever care as much about your money as you. Get started toward saving. Today. Unlike so many things in life, you will never regret it. And one day, I hope, you will look back and think, Holy cow, I can't believe how much money I was able to make, just when everyone else thought that stocks would never ever work again.

INDEX

Al: Okay, let's move off of how fat you are. Because there's something pretty serious I want to ask you about. Recently on one of your radio—

Rush: Have you ever noticed how all newspaper composite pictures of wanted criminals resemble Jesse Jackson? (*Newsday*, 10/8/90)

Al: My Lord, that is racist. And please don't interrupt me.

Rush: Let's go to the issue of condoms. (Heritage Foundation, *Policy Review*, Fall 1994, p. 8)

Al: No, this is my interview. I want to get into something serious here, which is a startling revelation you made on the radio recently. You broke down and admitted to your listeners that you actually collected unemployment insurance, am I right?

Rush: Well, I was without income once when I was married and my wife made me go and file for unemployment, and it was the most gut-wrenching thing I've ever done. (Radio show, 5/10/95)

Al: Wow! That is astounding! So Rush Limbaugh was actually on the dole? How could you of all people accept money from the government?

Rush: I had a bunch of expenses I couldn't meet. I had one credit card—I couldn't pay my MasterCard bill because it came at a time of the month when the rent came. (Radio, 5/10/95)

Al: My God! You are perhaps the world's biggest hypocrite. I mean in *The Way Things Ought to Be* you say, "The poor in this country are the biggest piglets at the mother pig and her nipples." And yet it turns out that you, yourself, suckled at the federal teat, and are, in fact, a loathsome piglet. I mean pig, because you're so fat.

Rush: I had a cash flow problem . . . grocery stores then didn't take credit cards—I literally, for a couple of years, was going to snack-food kinds of places, that did take credit cards, and buying junk, potato chips and so forth. (Radio show, 5/10/95)

Al: Hence your enormous weight. Lord in heaven, you are a sad person. Can you give us more of your pathetic sob story?

Rush: I was able to afford shelter, but that was it. I wasn't able to afford the upkeep on the shelter. If it weren't for the fact that I had a friend whose boys would mow my yard, then I would have had weeds instead of a yard. (Radio show, 5/10/95)

Al: I think I get the picture. You were unemployed, eating potato chips, and too lazy to mow your own lawn. Could this story get any more pitiful?

Rush: The air conditioner broke down—couldn't get it fixed. Roof, paint, all that. And I eventually had to sell it and lost money in the process, because, of course, the place had turned into a ramshackle old shack. (Radio show, 5/10/95)

Al: Of course. You know, Rush, I still don't understand why you collected unemployment instead of working. There *must* have been some work available in Kansas City for an able-

bodied man with three hundred pounds on the hoof. Perhaps as ballast on a barge traveling down the Missouri.

Rush: My wife made me go and file for unemployment. (Radio show, 5/10/95)

Al: That's right, you already said that. I swear, you must be the biggest pussy on God's green Earth.

Rush: [Y]es. (*The Way Things Ought To Be*, p. 315)

Al: My God, you are a sad, sad creature, aren't you? Sort of a she-male?

Rush: [Y]es. (*The Way Things Ought to Be*, p. 315)

Al: Well, that's about it. Before we go, is there anything you'd like to say to my readers about the state of America?

Rush: We're in bad shape in this country when you can't look at a couple of huge knockers and notice it. (TV show, 2/2/94)

RUSH LIMBAUGH—SUCCESS STORY

That was fun, wasn't it? But it's occurred to me that maybe I'm being so rough on Rush because I'm a little jealous. After all, Rush is more successful than I am, at least if you leave out the failed marriages and sad physical condition. He is, after all, the undisputed master of the format radio consultants have dubbed "non-guested confrontation." He does make $25 million a year, maybe more now with the No Boundaries tie collection.

RUSH AT A GLANCE

1951. RUSH HUDSON LIMBAUGH III BORN IN CAPE GIRARDEAU, MISSOURI.

AGE 16. FIRST JOB AS RADIO DJ RUSTY SHARPE AT STATION OWNED BY 300-POUND RUSH SENIOR.

"HE DID HAVE A WEIGHT PROBLEM GROWING UP." —DAVID LIMBAUGH

1969. ENROLLS AT S.E. MISSOURI STATE. 1970. DROPS OUT. CLASSIFIED 1-Y BY DRAFT BOARD.

DURING SPIN-THE-BOTTLE GAME, CHEERLEADER REFUSES TO KISS "RUSTY."

1951   1965   1967   1969-1970

And he's used his platform to become national precinct chairman for the Republican party. As much as anyone, including Newt Gingrich, he is responsible for the current Republican majority in Congress. Just ask the seventy-three freshman Republicans who made Rush an honorary member of the Class of '94. So, yes, Rush deserves more respect. And that's why I've prepared this time line to give you some idea of how and where American conservatism found its voice.

DIVORCED BY ROXY M. BALLOONS TO 260 LBS.

HIRED BY KMBZ IN K.C., WHERE "I FOUND OUT I WAS REALLY GOOD AT INSULTING PEOPLE."

FALL '84. HIRED BY KFPK, SACRAMENTO.

MARRIES MICHELLE SIXTA. LOSES SIX TO EIGHT LBS.

FIRED BY KMBZ. PUTS BACK WEIGHT AND THEN SOME.

"UNGUESTED CONFRONTATION" FORMAT CATCHING ON. LOSES 60 LBS AS SACRAMENTO SPOKESMAN FOR NUTRI/SYSTEM. WEIGHS LESS THAN OPRAH.

1980   1983   1984   1986

NUMBER OF SYNDICATED STATIONS EXCEEDS RUSH'S WEIGHT IN POUNDS FOR FIRST TIME—REACHING 350.

TV SHOW BEGINS. THE WAY THINGS OUGHT TO BE TOPS BESTSELLER LIST. IN IT, RUSH RAILS AGAINST UGLO-AMERICANS, ANTI-MALES, SUBSIDY HOGS, ENVIRO-RELIGIOUS FANATICS, ANTICAPITALISTS, AND LIBERALS.

SEE, I TOLD YOU SO HITS BESTSELLER LIST. IN IT, RUSH ANNOUNCES THAT "I, FOR ONE, AM TIRED OF ALL THE NEGATIVITY."

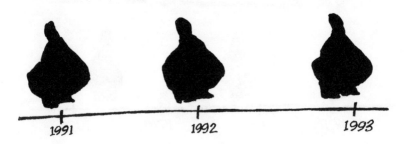

1991   1992   1993

AFTER A COLUMNIST EXPOSES THAT HE'S NEVER VOTED, RUSH REGISTERS FOR THE FIRST TIME IN HIS LIFE.

HIRED BY WABC. MOVES TO NYC, HOME OF OVER 100,000 RESTAURANTS

OPRAH LOSES 90 LBS. RUSH GAINS 80, PUSHING 300.

SYNDICATED SHOW HITS 200 STATIONS. DIVORCED BY MICHELLE SIXTA. EXPANDS TO 320 LBS.

1986   1987   1988   1989

MARRIES THIRD WIFE, MARTA FITZGERALD.

REPUBLICANS TAKE CONTROL OF CONGRESS. INCOMING G.O.P. FRESHMEN DUB LIMBAUGH AS "MAJORITY MAKER." RUSH STARTS HAWKING SANDALS ON RADIO SHOW.

TV SHOW LOSES 9 MARKETS. NO COMPARABLE LOSS IN WEIGHT. BEGINNING OF END?

ON RADIO, LIMBAUGH SPREADS RUMOR THAT "VINCE FOSTER WAS MURDERED IN AN APARTMENT OWNED BY HILLARY CLINTON AND THE BODY TAKEN TO FORT MARCY PARK."

LIMBAUGH, GINGRICH, AND BILL BENNETT SPEND MEMORIAL DAY TOGETHER. PLOT STRATEGY FOR '96.

1994   1995   1996

3

ONE GIANT LEAP TOWARD SOLVING THE BUDGET CRISIS

The big movie last summer was the inspiring rescue story of *Apollo 13*. Yet despite the boost to NASA's public image, the agency is still under the budget knife. That's because the big political story these days is balancing the budget.

How can we cut all these programs, retain civilization as we know it, and become a better and more compassionate country, as the Republicans are suggesting? I've looked at the budget and it can be done, but we need creative thinking to make it work. In the spirit of Gingrich and Kasich, I have an idea.

The new budget includes big cuts for both Medicare and NASA. Now here are two seemingly unrelated facts.

> *Fact one:* 30 percent of Medicare expenditures are incurred by people in the last year of their lives.

> *Fact two:* NASA spends billions per year on astronaut safety.

Maybe you see where I'm going. Recent poll data show that our senior citizens are willing to make sacrifices, if they will

help lower the staggering debt on future generations. Most think these sacrifices would take the form of lower social security benefits. My idea is more radical.

Why not shoot the elderly into space? Stay with me. Because I'm not just thinking about the budget here. I'm talking about science. Just think how many more manned space operations NASA could undertake if they didn't have to worry about getting the astronauts back.

Now, I'm not saying we don't try to get them back. We just don't make such a big deal about it. That way we don't have to use the shuttle every time, which is very expensive. Put an old Mercury capsule on top of a Saturn rocket, fire it up, and see what happens. And if the "Houston, we've got a problem" call comes, Mission Control can simply reply, "Best of luck. We're rooting for you."

We could learn so much. What is the effect of weightlessness on arthritis? Let's make it our goal to perform the first hip replacement in space before the millenium!

Would aluminum foil make a good space suit for a space walk? Or would you bake like a potato? That would be fun to know. Would a '72 Buick Le Sabre make a good space capsule? This whole thing could be a tremendous boon to what is called "raw science." That is, knowledge for which there is no real immediate use, but which could have great long-term benefits. For example, how close to the sun can a person get before he bursts into flame? Would it make any difference if he's fat?

If my idea works, we could expand the program to include the terminally ill. Who doesn't want to go out making a contribution?

Here's a related idea. Stunts. How much did Evel Knievel get for jumping the Snake River Canyon? Millions, right? OK. Every Sunday we put an elderly (or terminally ill) person

in a rocket, fire it over the Snake River, and put it on pay-per-view. The revenues go straight to reducing the debt.

Here's another idea. I am not a military expert, so I'm not sure that this is feasible. But here it is. From what I've read I understand there is nothing more terrifying in battle than seeing enemy hordes charging at you with no regard for their own lives. Why have we always insisted on asking our young men, and now young women, in the flower of their lives, to risk themselves in combat? Why not, in the right situation, use a human wave of our elderly to scare the enemy?

Think about it. You're an Iraqi or a North Korean or a Serbian soldier. Suddenly, over the horizon, you see a battalion of Americans. They won't attack, you think. America wouldn't risk the blood of its precious youth when it could simply employ their sophisticated, expensive weapons. Then you look through your binoculars, and a chill goes down your spine. Retirees! Thousands and thousands of them! Each one older than the next. Each with a life expectancy of three or four years at most. You think to yourself, "What do these people really have to lose? The four worst years of their lives?" You're terrified. Then they charge. A slow charge, yes, but that makes it even more frightening.

Admittedly, there're some kinks to work out. Mobilization would be tough. Have you ever organized a group of seniors for a theater trip? I don't think training would be that much of a problem. It'd be kind of like, "Go out there and run." And this would give our World War II–era Americans a chance to contribute yet again to our country. Just when they thought they were forgotten.

I guess what I'm saying is let's not just talk about our problems. Let's talk about *solutions*.

4
ADVENTURES IN POLITICS
1951-1975

I've always been fascinated with politics. When I was growing up in Minnesota, my family would discuss current events at the dinner table. My father was a lifelong Republican even though he never made more than eight thousand dollars in a year. I like to say we were lower middle class but didn't know it. Dad was born in New York in 1908, and we didn't move to Minnesota until 1955, when I was four. For those of you in the Michigan Militia, that means I was born in 1951.

We moved to this small town in southern Minnesota, where Dad opened a factory that manufactured quilting. Quilting is the, well, quilted fabric that lines winter coats. My mother's dad, Simon, a Russian immigrant who arrived in this country when he was sixteen speaking no English, built a fabric business and passed up a golden opportunity to become rich during World War II, when he refused to cheat on wartime regulations, which a lot of manufacturers did. At least, this was family lore, but the point is my mom was proud of it, and it was an ethics lesson in our house. So in 1955 Grandpa opened this factory in Albert Lea, Minnesota, and sent my dad, who at 47 had never been west of the Alleghenies, to

manage it. I asked Dad a few years ago, why Albert Lea? and Dad said it was because the railroad ran through Albert Lea, but when we got there we found out the railroad wouldn't *stop* in Albert Lea. At least not to pick up our goods. Dad was not a good businessman. Even though he worked fourteen-hour days, the factory failed.

So when I was six, we moved up to Minneapolis. Actually a suburb, St. Louis Park, called "St. Jewish Park" by most of the Twin Cities, because it was the Jewish suburb of Minneapolis, that is to say it was about 20 percent Jewish. Not exactly a *shtetl* (for those of you in the Christian Coalition, a small city of Jews), but by Minnesota standards, a *lot* of Jews. Minneapolis had something of a reputation for anti-Semitism, fueled in part by the pernicious presence of a Jewish organized crime syndicate that Hubert Humphrey chased out in the late 40s when he was mayor.

Dad got work as a printing salesman, and since my brother and I were both in school, Mom got her real estate license. At the dinner table my parents would talk about their day. Dad's highlight was always lunch and one of his buddies' bad jokes. Mom would tell us stories about the practice that didn't have a name at the time but would later become known as redlining. Basically, developers, bankers, and real estate agents had a spoken or unspoken agreement to restrict blacks or Jews from buying homes in certain areas. I assume the term "redline" came from a line, I guess a red one, drawn down streets like Texas Avenue in St. Louis Park. So on one side of Texas you'd have a development with tiny houses owned by people with names like Anderson, Carlson, Lundahl, and Anderson again, and right across the street, living in the exact same houses with the exact same floor plan, families named Goldberg, Shapiro, and Grossman.

Mom wouldn't tell her clients she was Jewish. So every once in a while she'd be driving a couple around, and the

woman would say something like, "I don't want to buy a house from a Jew. I hear Jewish women are terrible house-keepers." And my mom would smile and kind of bat her eyes involuntarily, which she'd do when she hated someone, and say something like, "In my experience there are good Jewish housekeepers and a few who aren't so good, just like Christian housekeepers." And leave it at that.

Mom was a Democrat, and I remember the 1960 presidential election as a source of some friction in our home. I was for Nixon, because I liked my dad better than my mom. My older brother, Owen, was for Kennedy. I think it had something to do with a visceral aversion to Nixon. Anyway, in 1964 Dad switched parties. A card-carrying member of the NAACP, he was disgusted with Goldwater's opposition to the 1964 Civil Rights Act. We'd sit in front of the TV and watch them turn police dogs and fire hoses on Negro demonstrators, and Mom and Dad would compare it to the Holocaust and tell us it was our duty as Jews to support civil rights. Dad just couldn't understand how Goldwater or anyone could oppose equal access to public accommodations. But the Republican party, people like Strom Thurmond, and George Bush, and Robert Bork, did reject a law that made it a crime to refuse to serve a person because of the color of his skin.

So Dad left the Republican party and never went back. A man who had voted for Herbert Hoover, Alf Landon, Wendell Willkie, and Thomas Dewey (twice!) turned around and voted for Lyndon Johnson, Hubert Humphrey, George McGovern, Jimmy Carter, Walter Mondale, Michael Dukakis, and finally, at age 84, for Bill Clinton. During Vietnam, Dad didn't want his sons to go to war. Just like Dan Quayle's father. The only difference was Dad didn't want anyone else's son to go to Vietnam. So he demonstrated against it.

So I've always been interested in politics. And I thank my parents for that. As you can see, there was a strong element of

moral indignation behind this interest, and indignation is well and good in doses, but I noticed fairly early in life that some people *live* to find stuff to be indignant about. And it's pretty unattractive. That's why I decided to become a wiseass.

1971–1975. I Get My Brother Out of the Draft and Give Mo Udall a Cruel Measure of False Hope

Late fall 1975. For those of you in the Montana Militia, I was now twenty-four years old. I had my first steady job, writing for a new show on NBC called *Saturday Night Live*. It was an exciting time, and my only regret was that my dad wasn't alive to see it. No, wait. What am I saying? He didn't die until 1993.

After our first few shows in October, we had a one-week break. My brother Owen, who also had become a wiseass, though not professionally, was now a photographer, and he suggested I ride the press bus with him in New Hampshire and follow Ronald Reagan around. Reagan was one of those guys who in 1964 opposed the Civil Rights Act. Can't legislate morality was the rationale.

Our first stop was Cambridge, Massachusetts. Mo Udall was speaking at M.I.T., Owen's alma mater. My brother, the first member of our family to go to college (Dad never graduated high school), holds a degree in physics from M.I.T. But he was there during the height of the war and saw that most of the applications of physics at the time involved finding better ways to kill people. So after graduating, he became a photojournalist.

We arrived late at Kresge Auditorium, which was packed with bespectacled young Jewish and Asian American men with slide rules stuffed in the breast pockets of their white shirts. I tried to keep up with Owen as he snaked his way

through the crowd to the front, a talent he had developed in his years covering these kinds of events. Also he was very skinny, which was an advantage. In 1971 Owen got out of the draft by being underweight. He's five-ten, and at his draft physical he weighed in at 109. Pounds.

In fact, I was his trainer. I wrestled in high school and knew how to lose weight. (Attention, Rush: It involves diet and exercise.) Owen had graduated and gotten his draft notice. I was a sophomore at Harvard (I tested well in high school), so Owen moved into my dorm room, and I supervised his weight-loss program. We didn't have that far to go; he weighed 125 and we had to get him down below 115–110 to be safe. On the other hand, try getting fifteen pounds off a guy who's built like a whippet.

Basically, I fed him two things. Steamed spinach and raw oysters. The latter on the hope that he'd get some nasty gastrointestinal disorder. And I'd play squash with him for hours at a time. My dorm had squash courts in the basement and you could play twenty-four hours a day. The week of the physical I had Owen down there in the middle of the night in his sweats and he'd literally collapse during volleys. And I'd yell at him, "Get up! Charlie's coming! Charlie's gonna get ya!" Meaning, of course, the Vietcong. Owen would jump right up and play till he collapsed again, and we got him down to 109. He thinks less, because he swears they added some weight to the scale when they saw him coming.

But in Kresge Auditorium Owen was at his fighting weight, now probably 127 pounds, working his way through this mass of wonks, geeks, and techies while hauling three Nikons and a camera bag with all kinds of shit in it. Fortunately, we hadn't missed anything, because Udall was late too.

Very late, it would turn out, and as the crowd grew restless, a young man from the M.I.T. forum committee got up and praised the turnout and went on for about fifteen minutes

about participatory democracy and started pissing everybody off. Only he didn't announce that he was from M.I.T. and the crowd thought he was from the Udall campaign. By now, Owen and I were actually on the stage, and I turned to a Udall staffer and said, "Somebody from your campaign really should say something." But the staffer just stared at me.

This guy has no sense of show business, I thought. I who had been in show business for about a month. As the guy from the forum committee wrapped up, there was a smattering of boos, and I looked around for someone with a Udall button to address the situation. The jeers started to build and I just couldn't help myself.

By the time I got to the podium, the boos were pretty deafening. But when I tapped the microphone, they started quieting down. Owen looked at me kinda puzzled, but then started snapping pictures. His little brother was speaking. "The Udall campaign would just like to announce that the tedious gentlemen who just spoke was from your institution and not, I repeat, *not* a member of the Udall campaign!"

First came a really big laugh. Then cheers. More than anything it was about the hour and fifteen minutes of mind-numbing boredom that preceded my announcement. And just as the cheer was coming to a crescendo, my gaze went to the back, where Morris Udall was just entering the hall, looking tired and a little distracted. Even his non-glass eye was a little glassy. He was, after all, an hour behind. That's when I got really close to the mike, so everyone could hear my voice booming over the cheers, "Ladies and gentlemen, the next president of the United States, Mo Udall!" A tumultuous roar! The place went nuts! As Udall worked his way through the frenzied crowd, I could see that for probably the first time, and maybe the last, Mo Udall was convinced he could win this thing.

Owen told me not to do that again.

NEW HAMPSHIRE, 1975. I SOW THE SEEDS OF GERALD FORD'S DEMISE

The day after Udall's M.I.T. speech we headed up to New Hampshire. First we went to a Ford event. It was *really* boring. I don't think I even saw him. The press corps and I sat in a high school gymnasium where they piped in a speech Ford was giving to the students in a nearby auditorium. So I just wandered around, talking with press people who were even more bored than me.

I was excited to see Ron Nessen. Now, there's a sentence you don't read every day. Ron Nessen was press secretary to the president, so I was excited to see him, and I struck up a conversation. It came out that I worked for *Saturday Night Live*, which I was surprised to learn he had seen and enjoyed. He even said he liked Chevy Chase's Ford sketches, which depicted the president as a fatuous stumblebum. I said, "You should be on the show." And he said, "I'd love to."

When I went back to work the next week, Lorne Michaels made it clear that, since he, not I, was the producer of *Saturday Night Live*, it was inappropriate for me, an apprentice writer, to invite people to appear on the show. Nevertheless, Nessen did host a few months later, and it was pretty much a total disaster for the president. It was never our intention to "take the President and shove his press secretary up his ass," as Lorne would later put it. It just kind of worked out that way.

Nessen appeared in an Oval Office sketch I helped write in which Chevy as Ford kicked a wastebasket around the room, stapled his ear, and shouted, "Heel, Liberty!" to a stuffed dog. Worse for the White House were sketches Nessen didn't appear in: A couple (Chevy and Jane Curtin) writhing under sheets in their bedroom as robed Supreme Court Justices make sure they don't do anything too kinky; an Emily Litella

(Gilda Radner) "Weekend Update" editorial on "presidential erections"; and a hilarious parody of the "with a name like Smuckers, it has to be good" commercial written by Michael O'Donoghue featuring names for jams such as Nose Hair, Death Camp, Mangled Baby Ducks, Dog Vomit, Monkey Pus, and Painful Rectal Itch.

Oh yeah. And Nessen had talked the president into pre-recording an opening for our show. A very, very stilted Gerald Ford saying, "Live from New York, it's *Saturday Night!*" You know, kind of a presidential endorsement. And I forgot the Autumn Fizz parody. Gilda pitching a carbonated douche.

According to wire service reports, White House staffers said the president was "not pleased." When Nessen returned to Washington, he received a handwritten note from the president's son, Jack. "I thought as Press Sec. you're supposed to make professional decisions that get the Pres. good press! If you get a min. I'd be happy to explain to you that your job is to further the Pres. interest, not yours or your family's!" Evidently he agreed with White House aides who found the show "vulgar" and thought it made the president "look stupid."

Fortunately, the White House had a plan to restore the President's stature. The WIN! buttons. Whip Inflation Now!

SAME TRIP. LYN NOFZIGER THROWS ME OFF THE PRESS BUS FOR ASKING RONALD REAGAN A SNIDE QUESTION

I seemed to be cutting quite a swath through New England. Now Owen and I found ourselves in Hanover, New Hampshire, following Ronald Reagan. We stayed overnight with the rest of the press corps at a quaint hotel on the campus of Dartmouth College, and the bus left very early in the morning for Reagan's first campaign event of the day, an appear-

ance at the most adorable little country store you've ever fucking seen.

I was kind of sleepy, but this was fun! I, like the rest of the press corps (well, I wasn't really part of the press corps, but I was getting confused), was standing about fifteen feet from Reagan inside this set for a Pepperidge Farm commercial as he answered questions from guys named Caleb and Ichabod.

It would be pretty much impossible to overestimate the extent to which I underestimated Ronald Reagan at this point in time. Yes, he was a former two-term governor of California, but I thought of him mainly as the host of *Death Valley Days* and spokesman for Boraxo.

This is probably something you should know about me as you read this book. I do not have the best track record as a prognosticator. Remember back to about 1984 when both Madonna and Cyndi Lauper were emerging? I would have put all my money on Cyndi Lauper. Great voice, really cute and fresh-faced in a saucy kind of way, with a Gracie Allen comic thing happening. Yeah, Cyndi Lauper over Madonna. Of course, in fairness to me, I had no way of knowing at that time the extent to which Madonna would be willing to degrade herself to win such a huge following.

So some guy asks Reagan about mandatory motorcycle helmets, which was a big issue in California. A couple years before, a few thousand Hell's Angels had bombed into Sacramento to protest a proposed law which would have made it mandatory to wear a brain bucket when riding a motorcycle. Now I guess it had become an issue in New Hampshire, and Reagan was on the side of the Angels. "It's a limit to personal freedom," he told the man.

On to the next event, and the next. On and off the bus, then back on. And it's kinda cool; I'm one of the boys on the bus. Back off and we're at a junior high assembly where a kid

asks if Reagan favors decriminalizing marijuana. Reagan says no, "because medical evidence shows that marijuana causes brain damage."

The last event is back at the Dartmouth hockey arena. It's evening, and there are several thousand people, all Reagan supporters, except for those of us in the press who are neutral, sitting in a neutral roped-off area. Reagan gives his speech and then it's time for questions. It's a big arena, so there are microphones in the aisles. So I climb over the rope and get in line to ask my question.

"Yeah. I've been following you on the press bus all day, and this morning in Derby Falls you said you were against mandatory motorcycle helmets because it's a limit to personal freedom. . . ."

People had already started booing.

". . . And then later this afternoon in Cornish Flat you said you were against decriminalizing marijuana because it causes brain damage. . . ."

BOOO!!

"What's your question?" says the candidate.

"Well . . . can't not wearing a motorcycle helmet cause brain damage a lot quicker than marijuana by, for example, the head splitting open so that actual material from the road enters the brain?"

BOOOOOO!!!!!!!

Reagan let the crowd go on for quite some time while he seemed to grope for an answer to my question. Finally, they quieted and he bobbed his head the way he would and said, "Well. If I was on an airplane, and the pilot was drunk, I'd be able to tell. But if he was high on marijuana, I wouldn't. Be able to tell."

Lots of applause.

When I got back to the press bus, Lyn Nofziger was waiting for me. Nofziger was a bulldog of a guy with the kind of a goatee that if he was Jewish and in a little worse shape, you might think he was a pornographer. I think he was Reagan's press secretary at the time. Anyway, he ran the bus. He actually let me on so everyone could hear him say, "Either you're a member of the press or a member of the public!" And, of course, he was right. Then he kicked me off, and I had to walk back to the hotel, which was about three blocks away, and since there was so much traffic from the event, I easily beat the bus back to the hotel and made sure to greet it with a big grin on my face.

When Owen got off the bus, he acted like he didn't know me. Later he suggested that we kind of put a moratorium on these little fraternal campaign junkets.

5

THE NEWT CANCER SURGERY STORY

WHAT THE LIBERAL MEDIA MIGHT NOT BE TELLING YOU

You've probably heard the famous story about Newt Gingrich and his first wife, Jackie. The one in which he visited her in the hospital when she was recovering from cancer surgery. As the story goes, Gingrich brought along their two daughters *and* a yellow legal pad with his terms for a divorce, which he read to her while she was still groggy.

One thing you should know about the story is this: It's true. Gingrich has acknowledged all but the groggy part, telling *Time* magazine that the story was "a caricature." And to be fair, there is no way to know what goes on between two people. Anyone who's been married knows that.

In fact, I think the liberal media's portrayal of this whole ugly episode has been a little unfair to Newt. Maybe if we knew the real story, Newt wouldn't come out looking like such a pig.

Maybe it went like this:

Jackie calls Newt at home just before she goes into surgery. "Newt, I'm more certain than ever that I want a divorce."

"But, honey, you're about to undergo cancer surgery! You don't know what you're saying!"

"Newt, please. When you bring the girls today, I also want you to bring a legal pad with terms for a divorce."

"For godsakes! You're having cancer surgery!"

"Would you stop it?! This is what I want. What I *don't* want is for you to blame yourself. You're too good a person for that."

It could have been like that. And to assume otherwise would be unfair.

Of course, what we do know is that after the divorce, he was late with his alimony payments, and she had to take him to court twice to provide adequate support for her and the girls and that her church took up a collection to help them get by. That we do know.

6

GINGRICH: SEX, GIRAFFES, AND WEIGHTLESSNESS

So Newt Gingrich is a deadbeat dad who presented his first wife with terms for divorce while she was in the hospital recovering from cancer surgery. That's not the point of this piece. But it's fun to repeat.

Newt is nothing if not a man of ideas: We should give poor kids laptops. We should put poor kids in orphanages. We should appoint militia-loving Idaho representative Helen Chenoweth to a gun control task force.

Some of Newt's ideas have not been popular among feminazis. Last January, while teaching his "Renewing American Civilization" course, Newt discussed some of the innate differences between the male of the species and the female:

> If combat means living in a ditch, females have biological problems staying in a ditch for 30 days because they get infections. . . . On the other hand, if combat means being on an aegis class cruiser managing the computer controls for twelve ships, a female may be again dramatically better than a male, who gets

very, very frustrated sitting in a chair all the time because males are biologically driven to go out and hunt
giraffes.

Two images come to mind. The first is of the grasslands of
Africa. During the Neolithic Period. Rush, Newt, and Bill
Bennett, all 825 pounds of them, are trying to run down a
giraffe. The giraffe is thinking, "No problem here."

The second image is of Newt, about fifteen years ago, explaining to his thirteen-year-old daughter that she just got her
first "infection."

The question is: Where does Newt get all of his ideas?
Well, I turned to his bestseller *To Renew America* for clues.

If you want a sense of the personal values we should
be communicating to children, get the Boy Scout or
Girl Scout handbook. Or go and look at *Reader's Digest* and *The Saturday Evening Post* from around 1955.

So I sent my assistant, Geoff, to the New York public library (government program) to do a little research. And
wouldn't you know it? He found what appears to be the primary source of Newt's gender theories. From the November
1955 *Reader's Digest* comes "Why Women Act That Way."

The article answers such thorny, politically charged questions as: "Why are women so clumsy at pitching a ball and
running?" (bone structure); "Why do women go on periodic
frenzies of housecleaning and furniture moving?" (thyroid
gland); "Why are women forever smelling something burning
or hearing burglars?" (keener senses); and "Why are women
such glib fibbers?" (to compensate for lesser strength).

But the core of Newt's beliefs seems to be derived from the
section entitled, "Why do women go in for concerts and 'culture' so much more than men?"

There's a biological basis. Such things call for sitting still, and it's hard for a man to sit still. Woman's greatest avoirdupois is around her hips. This anchors her down in chairs and makes her more comfortable. A man is top-heavy, with his maximum weight around his chest and shoulders. He's built for action, not sitting.

See? Just add the words "aegis class cruiser" and "giraffe."

There is one area of male-female relations, however, in which the Speaker's views seem to diverge sharply from those of our nation's literary condenser of record. To wit: the honeymoon.

For more than a decade, Newt has contended that in the not-so-distant future, couples will be celebrating their nuptials in space. He first suggested this in his 1984 book *Window of Opportunity*, and it's back again in *To Renew America*.

I believe space tourism will be a common fact of life during the adulthood of children born this year, that honeymoons in space will be the vogue by 2020. Imagine weightlessness and its effects and you will understand some of the attractions.

You don't have to be Hugh Hefner to know that Newt is talking about sex. Well, from what I know about sex, Newt couldn't be more wrong. Gravity is an important, maybe even necessary, element in the physics of marital union. This is especially true for the uninitiated, for whom the wedding night is a source of extreme anxiety and apprehension. I refer you to the September 1955 edition of *Reader's Digest** and the article "Before Young People Marry."

---

* The same issue also features an article entitled "The Negroes Among Us."

People harbor many needless anxieties about sex. Men may be afraid they may be anatomically inadequate; girls may be apprehensive about the first sex experiences. Most of these fears are baseless. Anatomical disproportion is very rare, and the dilation of the hymen is seldom accompanied by much discomfort. . . . Honeymoon experiences are no criterion by which to judge sexual compatibility. Tired from weeks of wedding preparations, both bride and groom may be too exhausted, by the time they are alone, to function normally or to react adequately.

My God! The *last* thing these kids need is to be weightless! What is Gingrich thinking?

Imagine for a moment that you are a bashful young groom, exhausted not just from weeks of preparation and the wedding itself, but from the stress of the massive G-forces exerted on your body during liftoff. It's been a long day.

Now, finally alone in the honeymoon suite of the space station, you and your bride prepare to consummate your marriage. As you offer her a tube of complimentary space champagne, she floats away. As you try to unzip her space suit, she floats away. As you attempt to find the switch for the artificial fireplace, once again, she floats away. What is already a very awkward situation for the both of you becomes a horrifying, potentially scarring, test of acrobatic agility.

If this is any indication of how impractical Gingrich's ideas are, imagine what a mess welfare reform is going to be.

RUSH LIMBAUGH'S
FACT CHECKER

W hat's the easiest job in America? Washington, D.C., Shadow Senator? That's pretty easy. How about "undeclared candidate for president"? That's easy *and* lucrative. Ask Colin Powell's publisher. But if you ask me, the man who has the easiest job in America is Rush Limbaugh's fact checker. I asked my own fact checker, Geoff, to track him down. He called us back and we got it all on tape.

Telephone ring

Geoff: Hello! Rush Limbaugh Is a Big Fat Idiot. How may I direct your call?

Waylon: Excuse me. I thought I was calling Empower USA.

Geoff: Oh. Um . . . I'm sorry, you must have the wrong number.

Waylon: Is this 212-555-0238?

Geoff: Ooooh, no. I guess you misdialed.

Waylon: Sorry.

Geoff: S'okay.

Moments later . . .

Geoff: Hello! Empower USA. How may I direct your call?

Waylon: Oh good. Is this Geoff?

Geoff: Hi, Waylon! Let me put my boss on.

Al: Hi, Waylon! Megadittoes!

Waylon: What?

Al: Megadittoes. You know . . . megadittoes.

Waylon: Oh!! Yeah, right. Megadittoes.

Al: Waylon, thanks for calling. As I think Geoff told you, we here at Empower USA are a brand-new right-wing think tank, and we're just gearing up. Now, I understand you've been Rush Limbaugh's fact checker from the get go.

Waylon: Yeah, I've been with him for eight, ten years. Something like that.

Al: I guess he must be very happy with you.

Waylon: Well, if it ain't broke.

Al: Waylon, we're trying to get our fact-checking unit up and running, and we thought we'd come to the best. So I wanted to ask you about a few of these . . . facts. First of all, in April of 1994, Rush said on the radio that "there is no conclusive proof that nicotine's addictive. . . . And the same thing with cigarettes causing emphysema, lung cancer, heart disease."

Waylon: Yes. That's a bona fide, one hundred percent correct.

Al: I see. And where did you get that information?

Waylon: Ummm . . . jeez, you know, I got that around here somewhere. The place is kind of a mess. I never throw anything out. 'Cause, you know, fact checker.

Al: Right. Well, here's another one. It seems that on June 9th, 1994, Rush claimed on his TV show that there's a federal regulation which says if you have a Bible at your desk at work, then you're guilty of religious harassment.

Waylon: Okay. Turns out that's wrong. But it wasn't my fault. See, I took June off that year. And July.

Al: You get a lot of vacation?

Waylon: Yeah. Rush is great that way. Makes up for the very low salary.

Al: All right. How 'bout this one? In his second book, *See, I Told You So*, Rush writes, "There are more American Indians alive today than there were when Columbus arrived."

Waylon: There are? That doesn't sound right.

Al: Well, actually, it's not. According to the Bureau of Indian Affairs, in 1492 there were between five and fifteen million Native Americans in what later became the United States. Today, there are fewer than two million Americans who claim Indian ancestry.

Waylon: Wow! How would you find out something like that?

Al: We did a Nexis search. It's a computer database.

Waylon: Hmmm. Is that anything like that E-mail stuff I've been hearing about?

Al: Yeah. Sort of. Well, Waylon, I want to thank you. You've been very—

Waylon: Hey! Guess what! I found that source for that nicotine, lung cancer thingy.

Al: Let me guess. Tobacco Institute.

Waylon: Bingo!

Al: Well, this has been very helpful, Waylon. Thanks.

Waylon: My pleasure. Listen, any time you guys need any information . . . I got great stuff on the poor.

Al: Can't wait.

Waylon: Megadittoes!

Al: Megadittoes!

8

OPERATION CHICKENHAWK

I f you've spent any time listening to Limbaugh, you've probably heard him call Bill Clinton a draft dodger. But what about Rush's military service record? Surely a man of his age and political conviction would have volunteered for duty in Vietnam. After all, he supported the war.

So you might wonder where exactly in 'Nam Limbaugh served. The steaming rice paddies of the Delta? Or was he a Marine, dug in at Khe Sanh? Special Forces, perhaps, crossing the DMZ on a Search and Destroy with "Born to Kill" tattooed on his biceps? Or maybe he stayed in Saigon and used that talent on loan from God to entertain the boys in the field. That's it! Of course! Robin Williams's *Good Morning, Vietnam* character must have been based on Rush!

Not quite. When questioned about his draft history in 1992, Limbaugh responded, "I had student deferments in college, and upon taking a physical, was discovered to have a physical—uh, by virtue of what the military says, I didn't even know it existed—a physical deferment and then the lottery

system, when they chose your lot by your birth date and mine was high."

Sounds like they discovered some debilitating injury at the draft physical, doesn't it? Nope. Limbaugh, who has said about the draft, "I made no effort to evade or avoid it," never took a draft physical. Instead, records show that Limbaugh pre-empted a physical by providing his draft board with information of some disqualifying condition. Limbaugh's story has changed several times. According to Limbaugh, the physical deferment was for either a "football knee from high school" or a "pilonidal cyst." A pilonidal cyst is a congenital incomplete closure of the neural groove at the base of the spinal cord in which excess tissue and hair may collect, causing discomfort and discharge. As disgusting as this sounds, there is no evidence that Limbaugh's cyst contributed to the breakup of his two marriages. There is, however, also no evidence of a football injury.

It's funny how many hawkish Republicans didn't go. Phil Gramm had student and teaching deferments; George Will had student deferments; Clarence Thomas was 4-F.

So was Pat Buchanan, who had a bad knee. He spent the war writing speeches for Nixon. Interestingly, he is now an avid jogger. Jogs regularly, I understand.

After his *Murphy Brown* speech, Dan Quayle took a lot of unfair hits, especially from Hollywood. Quayle wasn't attacking single parents; he was talking about the importance of fathers. For example, Quayle's father found his son a slot in the Indiana National Guard, and the boy didn't have to go to 'Nam.

Newt Gingrich didn't go. But sometimes he regrets it. He's said that by avoiding Vietnam, he "missed something . . . a large part of me thinks I should have gone over." I wonder if Bob Kerrey ever thinks: "I'm missing something . . . a large part of me." Just wondering.

Central Highlands, South Vietnam
August 1969

"Shit," murmured Gingrich, wiping the sweat from his brow.

"Are we in trouble?" Quayle whispered. Quayle was "new meat." This was his first night ambush and he was shaking.

"You wanted to know what that smell was," Gingrich said with disgust, as they trudged down the jungle trail. "It's shit. Limbaugh shits his pants whenever he's scared. That's why no one wants to be in a hole with Limbaugh."

"It's my pilonidal cyst!" came the voice from the rear. "It's a congenital incomplete closure of the neural groove at the base of my spinal cord in which excess tissue and hair may collect, causing discomfort and discharge. I shouldn't be here."

"Bullshit!" shouted Buchanan. "You've dropped a load in your shorts, and it stinks!"

"It's my pilonidal cyst!" huffed Limbaugh as he struggled to keep up.

"Fuck your pilonidal cyst! Ah'm sick of hearing about it!" came the thick southern drawl.

"Fuck you, Gramm," the corpulent radio operator shot back.

"Eat me, fatso!"

Now they were all yelling at Limbaugh. Gingrich, Gramm, Thomas, Buchanan. All but Quayle, who was too new and too scared to take sides, and Will, who was too high on acid. That's why Will was the one they called "Stoner."

"Shut up, you meatheads!" Lieutenant North was pissed. "You're gonna get us killed!" North couldn't believe he was out with this bunch of sorry-ass losers. He was platoon leader, and normally a buck sergeant would be taking a squad out on ambush. But this squad was giving his whole platoon a bad rep. Word had spread up and down III Corps: North had a

squad of chickenshits who wouldn't fight. Well, tonight, that would change.

North knew that sound carries at night. Fortunately, they were only a few hundred meters from base camp. A reconaissance team had reported "beaucoup NVA movement" a few klicks north, and the chickenshit squad was headed out to surprise a few dinks.

North was still sizing them up. Knowing who you could rely on could save your life. Not knowing could get you killed. "Will, you take point."

"Go ask Alice." The private grinned.

"What?!" North hoped he had heard the man wrong.

"When she's ten feet tall."

He hadn't. "What are you talking about, soldier?!"

"One pill makes you larger, and one pill makes you small," Will explained.

"Gingrich, what's wrong with Will?"

"First day in 'Nam, Stoner saw a buddy get greased. Guy named Bill Bennett. Got it right in the eye. Stoner tried to plug the hole, came up holding a handful of goop that used to be Bennett's brain. It was pretty grotesque. Bizarre and grotesque, to be honest. Stoner hasn't been the same since."

"And the ones that Mother gives you don't do anything at all." Will giggled.

North just shook his head. Too late to send Will back. "Limbaugh, take Will. From now on you two are buddies." Limbaugh nodded. He didn't mind. Will was the only one who didn't complain when he dropped a load. North turned to Thomas. "Clarence, you take point."

"Why?" Thomas shot back indignantly. " 'Cause I'm black?!"

North knew he couldn't tolerate insubordination. But racial tensions had been high within the platoon. "Okay, Buchanan, you got point."

"But my knee." Buchanan winced to make his point.

"Sometimes it goes out, and I scream. You don't want the point man giving away our position." Gramm rolled his eyes. How many times had they heard about Buchanan's knee?

"Buchanan. My momma told me there's two kinds of people." Gramm scrunched his face like a bulldog. "The kind that pulls the wagon, and the kind that rides in the wagon. It's time you got out of the wagon."

"Then *you* take point," the Irishman shot back.

"Ah took it last tahm," drawled the Texan.

"Bullshit!" "*I* took it last time!" "No, *Ah* did!" Gingrich, Limbaugh, and Gramm were at each other now.

North just wanted it to stop. "All right! *I'll* take point. Now, let's move." North started forward, taking the point

position about twenty meters in front of his men. As he worked his way down the moonlit trail, North began to get a bad feeling. He had led a lot of men into battle. He had seen fear before. But not like this. And North knew one thing. Fear at night is a killer.

The trail led to a steep embankment. North clutched the M16 close to his chest and slid down feet first on his butt. It was a bumpy ride, but North didn't mind. In fact, he kind of liked it. He just wondered if his men could navigate it. Especially Limbaugh. He's so fat and smelly, thought North. He turned and waited. And waited. Where are they?

———————

By the time North caught up with the squad, they were just fifty meters from the base camp perimeter. "We got lost," shrugged Limbaugh.

"The only rational thing to do was turn back," Gingrich explained.

Gramm nodded. "Gettin' late, sir. Maybe we should pack it in, chalk this one up to bad luck." The others agreed. Will was the last to speak:

"Excuse me, while I kiss the sky."

———————

North planted a pair of claymores in the high grass. That made ten in the kill zone. He ran back to the trees where his men were waiting—cowering, really. They had put in their ambush along a stream about three klicks west of the base. North gave two clackers to Quayle, and pointing to the arm on the firing device, whispered, "You push this down, it sends a current to the blasting cap and detonates the mine."

"Huh?" North couldn't tell if the boy was stupid or just scared stupid. He did know this. Quayle had the look of a deer caught in the headlights.

"Never mind." North gave the clackers to Gingrich and

hoped for the best. "It's going to be a long night, men. You wanna catch some z's, work it out with your buddy."

Limbaugh smiled through his fear. He knew Will was too wired to sleep. The rotund radio operator had just polished off both their C rations and was getting drowsy, so he leaned against the radio set and drifted off.

In the dark and silence now, each man sat alone with his thoughts. And his dread. "My God," thought Quayle, "I'm so scared! I should have listened to Dad and taken that place in the National Guard. But no, I was too worried about my political future. I didn't want to look like some rich coward in the year 2004, when I'd be mature enough to run for national political office. God, I'm a fool!"

Thomas used the moonlight to write his girl: "Dear Honeybunch, Sometimes this war frightens me to depth of very my

THE NEXT FORTY MINUTES WERE THE LONGEST OF HIS ADULT LIFE...

soul. But I promise you I'll make it out of here alive, sugar, so I can come home into your embrace and gaze into your loving eyes. Love, Clarence. P.S. Send more pornography."

Ten meters away, Gramm gazed up at the stars. He'd never believed he could kill a man. And so far he hadn't. But women and children were another story. He thought back to the village and how he'd lost control. Funny what fear will do.

Gingrich cursed North under his breath. Four more days and his tour would be over. Then he'd be out of this nightmare. Three hundred and sixty-one days he'd lived with this unbearable, unrelenting, gut-wrenching fear. Fear that had lifted only once. He thought back to the Saigon bar.

"You number one G.I. I fuck you till tomorrow. I suck you all night long," sighed the pouty sex kitten.

"Could you sit athwart my chest," Gingrich asked excitedly, "and make me do terrible things?"

"You number ten G.I. You disgust me." She spit in his face and walked away.

Gingrich smiled at the memory. He hadn't found the release he had sought, but at least the humiliation had taken his mind off the fear.

For the moment anyway, sleep had erased the fear from PFC Quayle's young mind. His dream took him back to the sun-dappled hills of Indiana and a raven-haired beauty named Marilyn. His head cradled in her tender arms, they watched the wind ripple through the rows of Hoosier corn. Caressing him lovingly, she nibbled at his ear, then whispered softly . . .

"We're never going to get out of this jungle." Quayle woke with a start. Someone was still nibbling at his ear.

"I'm so frightened, Quayle. Hold me. Hold me tight." Buchanan's strong arms clutched the new man firmly. Quayle froze in terror. The next forty minutes were the longest of his adult life.

North's catlike eyes pierced the dark. He lifted his nose to

the air. On a good night he could smell Charlie from half a klick away. Not tonight. Not with Limbaugh fouling the air.

Then he heard it. A twig snapping in the distance. North ID'd it immediately. Bamboo, seventy-five yards. They were going to have company.

North saw the scout first. NVA regulars, heading right for the kill zone. North's mouth split into a grin. He signaled silently to Gingrich, whose hand tightened on the clacker. In a moment, these dinks would be in for the surprise of their lives.

Suddenly, the still night silence was shattered. THE MAGICAL MYSTERY TOUR IS COMING TO TAKE YOU AWAY! Fucking Will! North yelled at Stoner to turn off the boom box, but a burst of AK-47 fire did it for him. The boom

STONER HAD TOKED HIS LAST DOOBIE...

box had played its last tune. And Stoner had toked his last doobie.

The jungle erupted in a maelstrom of hot, flying lead. North squeezed his M16, cutting down the scout with a bullet through the head as red tracers from a spewing NVA M-60 lit up the night.

North turned to see Quayle catch one in the throat, leaving a gaping wound that spurted blood onto the terrified Buchanan. Buchanan had just one thought. Play dead.

When North stopped to reload, he noticed that all the fire was coming from one direction. His squad had not shot one round! The lieutenant caught a glimpse of a panicked Thomas, trying to squeeze the trigger. "Click off the safety!" North cried as he slapped in a magazine while dodging a hail of AK-47 bullets. Too late. Thomas jerked backward, the bullet that took his life ripping through his chest.

As North watched thirty NVA regulars charge toward them, he called to Gingrich. "The clacker! Now!" But Gingrich's eyes were wide and his hands frozen with terror. "Now, dammit! They're in the kill zone!" Again nothing. North made a mad dash toward Gingrich, AK rounds whizzing by his head and thudding at his feet. A final dive and roll, his hand pushed the handle down. BLAM!!! The ground shook from the explosion, and thirty dinks went to their gory deaths.

Still they kept coming. My God, North thought, it's a whole company! "Limbaugh! Call in the artillery!!" No response. When North turned to find his radio operator, he couldn't believe his eyes. Limbaugh had pulled Will's corpse over himself, and Stoner's lifeless body heaved in rhythm to the fat man's terror-stricken sobs.

For the first time in my life, thought North, I feel ashamed to be an American.

At first, Gramm had panicked too. But now he knew what to do. "Ah'm not going home in no body bag," he thought.

WITH QUAYLE'S VIRGIN M-16 IN ONE HAND, AND THOMAS'S IN THE OTHER, HE LEAPT UP AND CHARGED.

"Phil Gramm's momma didn't raise no fool." He clicked off the safety on his M16, lined up his target, and squeezed the trigger. BLAM! He stared at the smoking hole in his boot, then passed out.

North looked around at his unit. He realized it was just him and the enemy. Thirty yards ahead two NVA's had set up a machine gun and were spitting out .50 caliber rounds at will. North took one in the leg. His face hardened. He plucked a grenade from his vest, pulled the pin with his teeth, and sent it hurtling through the night air. When the smoke cleared, all that was left was a grisly tangle of flesh and metal.

North emptied the clip in his machine gun, mowing down a couple dozen dinks in the process. Tossing the spent weapon aside, he decided to take the fight to the enemy. He pulled a knife from his belt, placing it between his teeth. Then with Quayle's virgin M16 in one hand and Thomas's in the other, he leapt up and charged. Running, dodging, jumping, shoot-

ing, knifing, clubbing, and strangling where necessary, he cut a swath of destruction through the astonished ranks of the enemy.

Meanwhile, Gingrich had snapped out of his stupor. He grabbed the radio. "Limbaugh, tell me how to work this thing!" No answer. Just the feeble whimper of a man sitting in his own excrement.

Gingrich slapped him across the face. "Snap out of it!" But Limbaugh couldn't stop crying. "Fuck it, I'll do it myself! Where do you keep the manual?"

Limbaugh had the hiccups. "In, in, in, in . . . in my back pocket."

"Oh, Christ!" This was going to be unpleasant.

First light was appearing on the horizon as North slit the throat of an NVA corporal and tossed his body on the pile. Suddenly, his ears pricked up. The sound was unmistakable. The distant thwop-thwop-thwop of a Huey slick. North turned to see the remains of his unit hobbling toward a clearing in the distance.

The chopper was almost overhead when North caught up with them. "Why the hell you calling in a medevac?! This fire zone is still hot!!"

"But, sir, we've got wounded," shouted Gingrich over the roar of the helicopter. Gramm shook his foot demonstratively, unable to hide his smile.

"There's still a third of a company of NVA back there, dammit! Now you turn and fight or I'll court-martial every damn one of you!!" North spun around on his good leg and started back to engage the enemy.

Gramm turned to Gingrich. "You thinking what I'm thinking?" Gingrich nodded grimly. Limbaugh choked out a feeble, "Uh-huh." Buchanan gave a hearty thumbs up.

Crack! North fell to the earth, facedown. Blood gushed from the hole that had just opened in his back. He rose to his

knees, only to fall again as another slug caught him between the shoulder blades.

"Sonofabitch," thought Gramm. "Ah *am* capable of killing a man."

He turned to the others. "Nobody saw nothing, right?"

"Nope."

"Not me."

"Unh, unh, unh . . . unh-unh."

The sun was rising over the battlefield as the Huey lifted the four grunts to safety. Gramm surveyed his wounded foot

"LIMBAUGH! TELL ME HOW TO WORK THIS THING!"

"SONOFABITCH! AH AM CAPABLE OF KILLING A MAN!"

with a smile. "Purple Heart's gonna look mighty fahn some first Tuesday after the first Monday in November." Gingrich and Buchanan exchanged a look. Solemnly, each man drew his knife and plunged it into the other's thigh.

The pilot turned back to look at them, his nose wrinkling in disgust. Uh-oh, thought Gingrich, he's onto us.

"Hey! Did one of you grunts shit your pants?!"

(Mr. Franken is a regular contributor to Soldier of Fortune *magazine.)*

9

BOB DOLE'S NIGHTMARE OF DEPRAVITY

Last May, Bob Dole made his famous attack on the Hollywood filth factory, or what around my house is called "Daddy's meal ticket." In the speech he divided motion pictures into two categories. Movies, according to Dole, are either "Friendly to Families" or "Nightmares of Depravity."

Forrest Gump, *The Lion King*, and *True Lies*, said Dole, are Friendly to Families, while *Natural Born Killers* and *True Romance* are Nightmares of Depravity. And he felt *very* strongly about this. Even though he hadn't actually seen any of the movies.

But the movies he mentioned have come and gone. How is a parent to know which category a film falls into when it's released? The last thing you want to do on a weekend is take your kids to what you think is a nice family film and have the whole experience turn into a nightmare of depravity. And believe me, it's happened to us. More than once. Pauly Shore's *Jury Duty*, for example.

Extrapolating from Dole's list, I've come up with a very brief . . .

Bob Dole Guide to Moviegoing

1. If there are multiple murders involving weapons on which the Republican party wants to repeal the ban, the movie is a Nightmare of Depravity.

2. Unless the movie stars Arnold Schwarzenegger.

3. Or anybody on the Republican donor list. Bruce Willis or Sylvester Stallone, for example.

4. If the plot of the movie involves an evil one-armed killer, as in *The Fugitive*, the movie qualifies as a Bob Dole Nightmare of Depravity. And the one-armed man doesn't have to be a killer; he need only be portrayed as "mean-spirited."

I apologize for that. It was wrong. Dole, of course, lost the use of his arm while defending my right to make a cheap, offensive, and not all that clever joke.

In his terrific book on the '88 presidential campaign, *What It Takes*, Richard Ben Cramer writes very admiringly of Dole's courage recovering from the nearly fatal wound he suffered in Italy. In one particularly jarring passage, Dole is sent home by train in a full body cast and met by his mother, Bina.

Bina was there when he got to Winter General on June 12, 1945. Bob had the nurses take his arm out and lay it on his cast, so his mother could see it. She'd steeled herself, but the minute she came into the room, Bina broke down in tears. When she saw the

way he looked at her, she told herself that was the last time she'd cry in front of Bob. And she sat down next to him and touched his face.

She had to pick eight cigarette butts out of his plaster cast. She told her sisters: they'd used her boy for an ashtray on the train.

When I read that, I gasped. My wife was reading in bed next to me, and said, "What?" I handed her the book, and she read the passage. "My God," she said. "You'd think going through something like that would make a person very compassionate."

"Yeah," I said. "Or really angry."

I liked the Bob Dole I read about in Cramer's book, even though the ambition that made him an absentee husband and dad caused his first marriage to end in divorce. Frankly, I'm getting a little sick of cranky Republicans who can't keep their own families together telling everybody else about family values. Quick. What do Newt Gingrich, Bob Dole, Phil Gramm, and George Will have in common? Answer. They've all been married only one less time than Rush Limbaugh.

I spend time with my kids. And lots of it. I believe the best thing a parent can give his kid is time. And not just quality time, but big, stinking, lazy, non-productive quantity time. In fact, that's why this book is so badly written. Believe me, you'd be enjoying the experience of reading this book a lot more if I weren't so dedicated to my children.

Which me brings me back to movie violence. Personally I have a fairly low tolerance for movie violence. Especially as a parent. For example, a few years ago, I was concerned that *Bambi* might be too violent for my son, Joe. He was five at the time, and there's the scene where Bambi's mother dies. I took him anyway, but put a lot of thought into what I would tell him.

Sure enough, when the moment came, Joe turned to me and asked, "Where's Bambi's mommy?"

I was prepared. "Well, Bambi's mommy was shot by the hunters. And she's not going to be around anymore. But it's okay, because Bambi's father is going to take care of him, and Bambi's going to be fine. Also, your mom is fine. Hunters will never shoot Mommy. And Mommy is going to be around a long, long time. So don't you worry."

Joe seemed to understand. In fact, he enjoyed the movie so much that we went again the next weekend. And at the same point in the movie a little four-year-old girl in the row in front of us turned to her dad and said, "Where's Bambi's mommy?"

And Joe said, "She's dead."

So I don't worry about Joe.

10

THE INVISIBLE HAND
OF ADAM SMITH

mong Freud's least quoted statements, but to me one of the most comforting, is "The only thing about masturbation to be ashamed of is doing it badly."

Joycelyn Elders knows the power of the subject. When asked whether masturbation should be discussed in sex ed classes, her very reasonable response was immediately caricatured as a proposal to teach jerk-off techniques to schoolchildren. "High school seniors in Little Rock can masturbate at only a fifth-grade level. That is a disgrace!" was the joke we did the next night on SNL.

I don't want to get into the whole sex education (teaching abstinence vs. rolling-condoms-on-a-dildo-in-class) debate. I know I don't buy the Christian Coalition argument that sex education created promiscuity and thus today's alarming rate of illegitimacy. I believe promiscuity grew with the wide availability of the pill and smut like Newt Gingrich's novel *1945*.

I think most people agree that it's a good idea for adoles-

cents to understand how our species reproduces. I recently heard William Bennett say that schools have to treat students as if they're children of God, not mammals in heat. I totally agree. But for those occasions when a 17-year-old child of God happens to become a 17-year-old mammal in heat, I think it's good for the mammal to have some clue about what's going on.

Of course, it's impossible to teach reproduction without discussing sex. And as I think Freud pointed out, sex is kind of a sore point with a lot of people. I knew when I sat down to write this book that I would have to discuss my own sexual history. Ever since Wilt Chamberlain's autobiography, it's become expected. So here goes.

Actually, I have had quite a sex life. Obviously it doesn't compare to Chamberlain, who had over 20,000 sexual encounters in his life (up to his book's first printing). But I have kept track, and I think you're going to be pretty impressed. I have had three hundred and twelve sexual encounters! All with my wife. And we've been married nineteen years. So not bad! Are you with me, fellas?!

Which brings me back to masturbation. And here's the point I wanted to make in the first place. America is a masturbatory society. Just register at any hotel that caters to businessmen, most of whom are angry white men, and check out the movie menu. For every *Forrest Gump* there are twenty *Romancing the Bone*'s. Why? Supply and demand. Adam Smith's "invisible hand," so to speak. Is this good? Absolutely. Because the market unleashes the creative energies of people who create wealth and provide jobs.

Most people don't realize how many jobs are created by one porno film. Of course, we immediately think of the actresses and actors. But what about the technicians who do the lighting and sound? Porno films provide many of the crucial *entry level* jobs that are so important to expanding our work-

force. And how about the fluffer? Don't know about the fluffer? Well, let's see. How do I put this? The fluffer is a woman, usually, who works off camera. Her job is to keep the male actor aroused. And she does this, I am told, orally. Hey. It's a job!

So next time Bob Dole starts bitching about casual sex in movies, ask him one question. How is it possible that he's crisscrossed this great country, stayed in two hundred hotels, and still hasn't seen *Forrest Gump*?

(Mr. Franken is a regular contributor to Juggs *magazine.)*

11
ADVENTURES IN POLITICS
NOVEMBER 8, 1988

BOSTON, MASS., COMEDIAN'S NIGHTMARE: I EMCEE THE DUKAKIS VICTORY CELEBRATION

Ladies and gentlemen . . ." The already very somber crowd grew silent. ". . . I've prepared two kinds of material. One in case we win this thing in a squeaker . . ."

It was about 8:45 P.M. Huge hotel ballroom. Hundreds of Dukakis workers. Men and women, mostly young, but some middle-aged and older, black, white, Democrats of all stripes, who had dropped everything in their lives for weeks, months, maybe a year or more to elect as president of the United States the shortest, swarthiest man ever nominated by a major political party.

By now they all knew he had lost. It wasn't official; the polls hadn't closed anywhere. But at this point we all knew. And I was supposed to entertain them for another four hours or so.

". . . and the other, in case . . . WE WIN BY A LAND-SLIDE!!!"

Gallows humor. No one laughed, except a couple members of the press corps who happened to be paying attention. It

was a massive contingent of print and electronic journalists, now waiting to capture what was becoming a quadrennial ritual, the concession speech of a roundly defeated Democratic presidential nominee.

I decided to go with the conceit that I, the emcee, was the only person in the room who had no idea how badly we were doing. It seemed funny to me. I always love it when the very person who should know something is the only person who doesn't. Like when there's a punt in a football game and the receiver calls for a fair catch on his own one-yard line, and everyone in the stadium assumes he's going to let it go into the end zone so his team (the home team) will get the ball on the twenty. But suddenly everyone realizes that instead he's going to catch the ball. And there's sixty thousand people in the stadium and fifty million at home all thinking the same thought for a split second: "You're on the one-yard line, fuckhead! Let it go!"

See. This is why I'd make a terrible politician. No, not that I used "fuckhead." It's the tortured sports analogy. Any decent politician knows the key to a good sports metaphor is simplicity. When John Kasich described his approach as chairman of the House Budget Committee last spring, he said, "They gave me the bat, and I'm going to swing it. I may strike out, but I could also hit a home run." That's a sports analogy anyone can understand. "It's fourth and goal and we're gonna punch this thing in." I've heard Bob Dole use that. But me, I've taken a situation that occurs in football maybe once every five years and used it to explicate a comic conceit. And one that didn't work, at that.

As the polls closed in the East, the networks started delivering the bad news. Pennsylvania goes for Bush. Ohio goes for Bush. But I would just say things like, "Hey, we won Rhode Island! That's good. As Rhode Island goes, so goes the nation.

Right?! Huh, everybody?!" Blank faces. Well, not blank really. There were a lot of tears.

So I decided to abandon the conceit pretty early in the evening and moved on to old material. This is one I always do at campaign events: "I've been asked by the *(candidate's name)* campaign to announce that the views I express tonight are mine and not necessarily those of the *(candidate's name)* campaign. Okay, now that that's out of the way . . . isn't *(widely respected person)* a *(wildly inappropriate epithet)*?" Thus, when I emceed fund-raisers for Mark Green's '86 Senate race against Al D'Amato, I'd open with: "I've been asked by the Green campaign to announce that the views I express tonight are mine and not necessarily those of the Green campaign. Okay, now that that's out of the way . . . isn't Cardinal O'Connor an asshole?" It would always get a nice laugh, mainly because a lot of Green supporters did think O'Connor was an asshole. Mark kept asking me not to do it, but I always would, and when he took the podium Mark would have to take a minute to emphasize his tremendous regard for the cardinal and his strong ties to the Roman Catholic community in the state of New York.

"The Dukakis campaign has asked me to announce that the views, etc. . . . Okay, now that that's out of the way, isn't George Bush a dink!" Now this gets a big cheer. And I think, "Oh, no! What have I done!?" I'm thinking ABC's taped this and they're going to air it without the disclaimer part, and it's going to look like I just said the newly elected President of the United States was a dink and the Democrats were all cheering. Which is basically what happened, except that the disclaimer part, in my mind, made it a joke, thus mitigating . . . oh, never mind.

Fortunately, Robert Klein had arrived, and I brought him on. Now, I love Robert Klein, and think he's done some of

the classic stand-up routines. Many of which he did that night.

Nobody's laughing. They're just staring at him, and he does his José Feliciano singing the "Star-Spangled Banner" bit. And since Robert is basically dying, I decide that that's a good place to get him off. So I join Robert onstage to suggest that we all sing the "Star-Spangled Banner" as kind of a patriotic gesture to honor America and the free democratic process we've all been privileged to be a part of. Let's show America that Democrats are patriotic, too!

So we sing it, a couple thousand people singing our national anthem, a cappella, which you never hear. And it's really moving. People are weeping, holding each other. Even some of the press are singing. OH SAY DOES THAT STAR-SPANGLED BA-A-A-NER YET WA-AVE? Everybody's got goose bumps. Somehow, now it's all okay. O'ER THE LAND OF THE FREEEEE . . . Lee Atwater and Roger Ailes could walk in at this moment and everyone in the room would hug them . . . AND THE HOME OF THE BRAAAVE!!! The cheer is deafening! And it doesn't matter whether the TV cameras had captured it for America to see. We in that room were all sharing an amazing moment. People were sobbing, flushed with patriotic fervor. It was really something.

Then Robert went into his Pope at Yankee Stadium routine.

The comic high point of the evening was going to be an appearance by my colleague Jon Lovitz. Among the highlights of that SNL season, of any season, was the Bush-Dukakis debate sketch, in which Dana Carvey played his peripatetic George Bush to Jon's emotionally inert Michael Dukakis.

The plan was to announce Dukakis over the P.A. and have

Jon enter to the driving, pounding beat of Neil Diamond's awful song "America," which was, in fact, how the candidate always made his entrance. WE'RE COMING TO AMERICA! TODAY! The song had been chosen to underscore, literally, Dukakis's status as the son of Greek immigrants. And the idea here, as it had been during the campaign, was to pump enough energy into the room to build the excitement of seeing Michael Dukakis (in this case, Jon Lovitz playing Michael Dukakis) to a frenzy. I checked with a young Dukakis staffer to make sure they had the music. He said yeah, and I figured the one thing the Dukakis campaign had to have together was the "America" cue.

It was almost midnight and the polls were closing on the West Coast, so people were expecting Dukakis to make his concession at any moment. Jon was offstage, ready, which is to say in his Dukakis suit, wig, and eyebrows.

I told the staffer to get ready to cue the music and went to center stage and the microphone. "Ladies and gentlemen, it is my distinct honor to introduce the Governor of Massachusetts, the leader of our party, Michael S. Dukakis!"

I could hear the music under the cheers. It was "America," but not the thumping chorus that I and millions of other political junkies had long since grown sick of. It was the *beginning* of the song, which I'd never heard before or since. All I remember is that it has a long, tepid opening followed by a longer, tepid verse that Neil Diamond sort of croons.

Jon and I looked at each other. I signaled for him to wait, and ran over to the staffer. It turned out he had gone out and bought a *CD*, and that's what we were hearing. State of the art. Except that you can't fast-forward a CD, or at least you couldn't on this guy's deck in 1988. The crowd was still cheering, but the music was sucking the energy out of the

room, and as the intro went on and on, people started wondering what was happening. We really had no choice, and Jon made his entrance.

They did get a kick out of seeing Jon, who walked around the stage, smiling, winking, picking out people in the crowd and pointing like he knew them. Mainly, I could see Jon hoping Neil would stop crooning. Jon kept vamping, but the crowd died down before the chorus kicked in.

As flat as his entrance had been, it was pretty much all downhill from there. On the flight up to Boston I had offered to help Jon with his remarks, but he insisted on writing them himself. Jon is a tremendously funny guy, but not a political satirist, and he was really shooting blanks. Some of the jokes were just inappropriate, especially considering that the real Dukakis was going to be out in just a few minutes. The only joke I remember was about how old Barbara Bush looked. "If he did that to Barbara, think what he'll do to the country."

By the time Jon got off, I had only one real remaining fear. That Michael Dukakis would walk on that stage and that before he was able to concede defeat, he'd slip on the collective flop-sweat of Robert Klein, Jon Lovitz, and myself and break his neck.

Jon and I were flown back to New York that night on a very small jet. We had a show that week and had to get back to write for the Wednesday read-through. As Jon and I sat alone in this tiny two-man cabin, I looked out the window down to the lights glowing from the New England towns below. I thought that in a small way we had taken part in American history. I thought about our country and the majesty of our system. And even though I was heartsick by the outcome of the election, I felt that the people had spoken, and, honestly, said a prayer for the man I had jokingly called a dink earlier

that evening. I turned to Jon and saw that he was very upset. "I know," I said, "it's a big disappointment."

"Yeah," he said. "Now fucking Dana gets to play the fucking president for the next four years."

12

PHIL GRAMM, GUN LOVER

I was watching the news last May, and Phil Gramm said something interesting to the NRA convention. He said, "I own more shotguns than I need. But less shotguns than I want."

When I heard that I thought to myself, "Wow. He and I are very different people." His line got a lot of applause, so I guess I'm very different from most of the folks who belong to the NRA. But you know my motto, *Vive la différence!*

I also wondered what exactly he meant by this. For starters I tried to figure out how many shotguns Phil Gramm owns. I guess you'd have to begin by estimating the number of shotguns Phil Gramm thinks he needs. I think he thinks he needs three, one for each domicile. (A home in Texas, an apartment in Washington, and a summer house on Chesapeake Bay.) But remember, he owns *more* than he needs. But less than he wants.

Why would you want more shotguns than you need? Prob-

ably convenience. How many times have you been in the living room, needed the shotgun, and said to yourself, "Nuts, I left the shotgun in the kitchen." I'll bet it happens to Phil Gramm all the time.

Seriously, I guess people collect shotguns. Which is great. I used to collect baseball cards. You know, when I was a kid. The thing about baseball cards is that each one is different; you get a Don Mattingly or a Frank Thomas. Is there that big a difference between shotguns? Somebody enlighten me because I'm operating out of ignorance here.

See, I've never owned a gun. I won't allow one in the house. According to a study in the *New England Journal of Medicine*, guns kept in the home for protection are forty-three times more likely to kill a family member than an assailant. Forty-three! "Hey, honey, I've brought something into the house that's forty-three times more likely to kill one of us than to do us any good." Maybe if the number was only thirty-three, I'd take my chances.

Among my more morbid diversions is collecting stories of tragic gun accidents in the home. There are some common threads. If you do have a gun in the house, here's some really bad advice:

1. *Keep the gun loaded.* When there's an intruder you don't want to be fiddling with bullets. (According to a 1991 Gallup poll more than half of handgun owners with guns in their house said their guns were currently loaded.)

2. *Put the gun in an unlocked drawer.* Who's got time to find a key when Mr. 1-in-43 comes calling?

3. *Rest assured.* Once you teach your kids gun safety, they can show their curious friends the gun while you're at the supermarket.

While I don't have precise figures, the anecdotal evidence leads me to the following conclusions:

- Grandpa is twenty times more likely to be shot by your seven-year-old nephew than by a drug addict trying to steal your VCR. The number goes up to thirty-six if Grandpa is barbecuing in the backyard.

- The odds are slightly better that a neighbor's kid will accidentally blow your kid's face off, than the other way around.

- A bullet fired by a six-year-old through a ceiling is twelve times more likely to lodge in your testicles than any other part of your anatomy. If you're a man, that is.

This, of course, covers *accidental* gun death. In a household with a gun, even more dangerous than the curious child is, of course, the angry spouse. That's really the reason why I won't allow a gun in the house. PMS. Remember that three out of four homicide victims are killed by a spouse, family member, friend, or acquaintance. Which is comforting for all of us who fear random violence.

Now again, I've just been talking about *death* from gunshot wounds. Tragic. But not as damn expensive as the pesky four to six non-fatal gunshot injuries that occur for every fatal shooting and crowd our emergency rooms. Maybe that's why the American Academy of Pediatrics supported the Brady Bill and has called for the ban of handguns and assault weapons.

Gunshot injuries cost 14 billion dollars a year. Who foots the bill? Right now, 80 percent of the cost is paid for by public funds. But I have a good idea. Let's get the money

from people like Phil Gramm. Let's put a little extra tax on every shotgun he doesn't need.

And remember:

> You are three times more likely to shoot a Japanese exchange student who has knocked at your door by mistake than a Swedish exchange student who is trick-or-treating on the wrong night.

13

AFFIRMATIVE ACTION: THE CASE FOR THE MUSHBALL MIDDLE

Jonathan Alter of *Newsweek* recently made the compelling argument that debate on affirmative action has become so polarized that there is no room for those of us in "the mushy middle."

That's right. I said "us." I consider myself a moderate.

See. I hope it's clear to you by now that this book is a *satire* about the breakdown in the civility of public discourse. I'm making fun of meanness in public debate by being mean myself. It's called "irony." Perhaps you've heard of it?

And I know that I've been a little harsh about a few public figures. That's what I'm supposed to do as a satirist. But I want you to know that I admire everyone I'll be making fun of in the book. Except Pat Robertson. He's a lunatic.

And I really don't like Limbaugh. And Pat Buchanan, let's face it, is a racist. Ralph Reed, I have no use for. And Gingrich just plain scares me.

You know what I dislike most about these guys? They're

always so certain. They're always 100 percent sure of what they're saying. Even if it's wrong. It must be a great feeling for a guy like Rush Limbaugh. To be able to sit there and say, "There are more Indians alive today than when Columbus landed," and really believe it.

This is why I like being a Democrat. When we see a complicated, seemingly intractible problem, we have the only really genuine, authentic human reaction you can have: we're confused.

Fortunately, I believe that "confused" is a majority position in this country.

I am not talking about stupid, uninformed confusion. I'm talking about intelligent, over-informed confusion. The kind you get from watching *MacNeil/Lehrer*, C-SPAN, and *Nightline*, listening to three experts from the Cato Institute, four from the Heritage Foundation, two each from the Urban Institute and the Progressive Policy Institute, then reading eleven different newspaper accounts that cite six different polls and four studies. And after all that, you *still* don't know what to think about grazing fees on federal lands.

Affirmative action is an issue that stirs more passion than grazing fees. And it has certainly been hotly debated. On the one hand, those in favor of it believe affirmative action is essential in overcoming the inherently racist nature of our society. I definitely agree with that.

On the other hand, those opposed say that for America to be truly color-blind we must eliminate group entitlements which set one race against another. That also makes sense.

There are horror stories on both sides. You've heard them; you're sick of them. So am I. And it gets even more confusing when the strongest opponents of affirmative action are among its biggest beneficiaries.

Justice Clarence Thomas, for instance, was admitted to

Yale Law School under a 1971 affirmative action plan whose goal was 10 percent minority students in the entering class.

In remarks to his EEOC staff in 1983, Thomas said that affirmative action laws were the best thing that ever happened to him: "But for them, God only knows where I would be today. These laws and their proper application are all that stand between the first seventeen years of my life and the second seventeen years."

Something must have happened to Thomas in his third seventeen years, because the guy really did a 180. I don't know what it was. Maybe a high-tech lynching.

In his concurring opinion in the affirmative action case of *Adarand Constructors v. Pena*:

> There can be no doubt that racial paternalism and its unintended consequences can be as poisonous and pernicious as any other form of discrimination.

A mean person could interpret the change of heart to reflect an "I've got mine" attitude. I'll leave that to a mean African American person.

One mean person who won't say it is Rush Limbaugh. In *The Way Things Ought to Be*, Limbaugh describes Thomas as "a man who has escaped the bonds of poverty by methods other than those prescribed by these civil rights organizations." Not true, but at this point, who's counting? Anyway, Thomas returned the favor two years later, performing the ceremony at Limbaugh's third wedding. I can't think of anything more romantic for a blushing bride than having Clarence Thomas perform your nuptials.

Of course, the first President to apply affirmative action to the Supreme Court was Ronald Reagan, who pledged to appoint a woman during the '80 campaign. When he nominated Sandra Day O'Connor, George Will was not happy:

Reagan dug about as deep as any President ever has into the state judiciary for a nominee. But, then, his sexual criterion excluded about 95% of the law school graduates in the relevant age group.

Will seems to be applying a mathematical formula: that it was nineteen times more likely that a man would be the most qualified nominee. Forgetting that the women admitted to law school at the time were probably twenty times more qualified than the men, Will doesn't seem to understand or accept the value of diversity. Now, I don't know if the fact that Sandra Day O'Connor has two ovaries inherently makes her better able to interpret the law as it affects women. Actually, I'm not sure she has two ovaries. I'll ask my research assistant, Geoff, to look it up. (Sometimes my writing gets ahead of the research.)

While we're waiting for Geoff, I'd like to speak to an affirmative action program which, as a Harvard graduate, I do like. And that is affirmative action for the children of Ivy League grads. Here's how it works. All applicants to Harvard, say, have to meet certain minimum requirements: SAT scores, G.P.A., and (a new one) lack of murder convictions.*

The applicants who meet those requirements are thrown into a pool from which the next year's freshman class is chosen. At this point, they start looking at special abilities. Does the orchestra need an oboe? Does the Sanskrit department need a kid who is actually willing to study Sanskrit? Is there a

---

* Last spring Harvard had to rescind its acceptance of Gina Grant after the college learned she had murdered her abusive mother. Though she had served her time in juvenile prison, Harvard felt that there were other equally deserving applicants on the waiting list who had murdered neither of their parents.

point guard with 1200 on his SAT's who's not good enough to be recruited by Duke or Georgetown?

And: Is the kid a legacy? That is, the child of an alumnus? If so, the kid is in. There are all kinds of good reasons for this. Well, one really. Fund-raising. But as it stands, it's an affirmative action program for one of the most privileged groups in the country: the sons and daughters of people like me.

Now we're told that one of the "poisonous and pernicious" "unintended consequences" of affirmative action is that it taints the real accomplishments of qualified blacks who have earned their place at the table. I'm sure that's true. But I think that's just further evidence of the racism in our culture. All the time I was at Harvard, I never heard a Lowell or a Cabot remark, "I dare say, I despise this godawful legacy policy. It makes me so suspect in the eyes of my classmates."

A small digression. This is an absolutely true story. The first guy I met at Harvard was a legacy. I had flown in from Minneapolis, taken a taxi directly to Harvard Yard, and, lugging my duffel bag and electric Smith Corona, found my freshman dorm. In the entryway was a young man my age, but somehow older. Khakis, polo shirt, tortoiseshell glasses. He extended his hand in a friendly yet proper manner and said, "William Sutherland Strong. I'm from northern New Jersey, but my family moved from Massachusetts."

"When?" I asked.

"In the late eighteenth century."

It took a beat to sink in. I said, "Al Franken. I'm from Minneapolis. But my family moved from Kraków in the early twentieth century."

I returned to Harvard in 1992 to speak to a standing-room-only crowd at the JFK School of Government. The week before, the speaker had been the editor of the only opposition newspaper in El Salvador, and only six people showed up. I

think that was because he had never worked with John Belushi.

Except for the Eddie Murphy years, *Saturday Night Live* has always had a reputation as a white male bastion, and during the Q&A period I was taken to task for it. "Why doesn't the show hire more women and people of color?" At the time we had two very talented African American performers, Ellen Cleghorne and Tim Meadows, and I pointed out that another cast member, Rob Schneider, is half Filipino. Was that of any help?

No. And after I gave what I felt was a sufficiently exhaustive and responsive answer, the questioner pressed further. Finally, as a joke, I said, "Well, another reason, of course, is that minorities just aren't funny." Everyone, including the relentless questioner, laughed.

The next day *The Harvard Crimson* reported that "Mr. Franken said . . . 'minorities just aren't funny.'" No mention of the good-natured irony or the warm wave of laughter.

So, having had someone imply (wrongly) that I'm a racist, and having myself accused (rightly) Pat Buchanan of the same, I think I have some perspective on both sides of this prickly issue.

That's why I was happy when Bill Clinton, the hero of the Mushball Middle and our greatest post-war president, decided to study affirmative action. And when he came down firmly on the "mend it, don't end it" side, it helped me make up my mind. That's what leadership is all about.

Geoff just came back with the research. Both of Justice O'Connor's ovaries are intact.

By the way, Geoff is black.

No, he isn't. He's a white guy from Harvard. But wouldn't it have been a great ending to this if he was?

But he's gay!

No, he isn't.

14

SOMETHING WE CAN ALL GET BEHIND

There was a time when Constitutional amendments did things like free whole races of people. Or enfranchise an entire gender. Now with the American flag-protection amendment it appears that we're really getting down to the short strokes.

So, as long as we're making amendments that create exceptions to the First Amendment, I thought I'd offer up a few of my own. Basically, they would ban certain acts that, I think we can all agree, have been considered protected "speech" for far too long.

Amendment XXIX—makes it a federal offense to take a whiz on the Statue of Liberty.

Amendment XXX—allows states to punish anyone "hocking a loogey" on a reproduction of the Declaration of Independence.

Amendment XXXI—makes it illegal for a tourist visiting the Lincoln Memorial to take a picture of a nude child sitting on Lincoln's lap.

Amendment XXXII—makes it an offense to send that picture through the Internet.

Amendment XXXIII—makes it a felony to walk into the U.S. Capitol and spray that fake Popeil hair paint on the bald spot of the John Quincy Adams statue.

Amendment XXXIV—makes it a high crime to dip a replica of the Washington Monument in a vat of Andres Sarrano's urine.

Amendment XXXV—allows states to prosecute anyone making a jockstrap out of the U.S. Constitution.

Amendment XXXVI—makes it an act of treason to dress up the soldiers of the Iwo Jima Memorial as the Andrews Sisters.

Amendment XXXVII—allows states to prosecute an exotic dancer who picks up United States currency with anything other than her hands.

15

APOCRYPHAL ANECDOTES: THE REPUBLICAN CONTRIBUTION TO PUBLIC DEBATE

Republicans have a very annoying habit of proving political points by telling horror stories that aren't even true to begin with. You know, things like "we should abolish seat belts because I know someone who got strangled by one once."

The master of the apocryphal story was Ronald Reagan, the most successful Republican politician of the last thirty years. Remember Reagan's welfare queen in Chicago? She had bilked the government for $150,000 by applying for benefits using eighty different names, thirty addresses, a dozen social security cards, and four fictional dead husbands.

Attempts to confirm the story yielded only one woman who received $8,000 by using two false names.

Now you might say, "Well, it's a good story, though. It made the point, didn't it?" That's exactly what Reagan's press

secretary said after he learned that another one of Reagan's stories was untrue. This one about England, where "if a criminal carried a gun, even if he didn't use it, he was tried for first-degree murder and hung if he was found guilty." Not true. But wouldn't it be cool if it was!?

Reagan told so many whoppers that the press basically held him to a lower standard. And that's a shame. Because the man felt so strongly about the importance of telling the truth. I know this because he used to tell a great anecdote about telling the truth.

I first ran across the anecdote in an article written by award-winning Reagan biographer Lou Cannon. The story was from his days on his high school varsity football team in Dixon, Illinois. It was during his senior year, and, as Reagan tells it, his team was behind in the last few seconds of the fourth quarter. Just as the final gun went off, Reagan caught a pass in the end zone for the winning touchdown. Only trouble was, Reagan had been offside. So he did the only thing he could. He went to the ref and told him about the infraction. "I told the truth, the penalty was ruled, and Dixon lost the game." The punch line of the story was that none of Reagan's teammates was upset. After all, he told the truth.

Cannon went back to Dixon, and no one could recall the incident. In fact, in the only varsity game in which Reagan played, Dixon lost 24–0. Well, it's a good story though. It made the point.

Reagan, of course, was a B-movie actor. So nobody really expected him to be authoritative on complicated facts and such. But Newt Gingrich, you'll recall, has a Ph.D. in history. That's why it's particularly puzzling when the Speaker of the House turns into the fellow I like to call Bizarro Newt.

See. In Superman's Bizarro World, everything is the opposite of things on Planet Earth. So if you like a hot dog in Bizarro World and would like another one, you would say,

"Me hate hot dog. Me want more, me hate them so much." It's a little confusing, but believe me, so is Bizarro Newt.

Bizarro Newt: "Most people don't know that it's illegal to pray. When they learn that a ten-year-old boy in St. Louis was put in detention for saying grace privately over his lunch, they think that's bizarre. . . ."

Planet Earth: According to the school's superintendent, the boy in St. Louis was *not* disciplined for praying. Prayer is not illegal in school. *Organized* prayer is prohibited.

Bizarro Newt: Gingrich complained in December 1994 that a heart pump that was "invented in Denmark increases by 54 percent the number of people given CPR who get to the hospital with a chance to recover. The Food and Drug Administration makes illegal [a product] that minimizes brain damage, increases the speed of recovery, and saves money."

Planet Earth: The pump was invented in the United States. The Danish company which licensed the pump had yet to apply to the FDA for approval. Initial field tests conducted by the University of California, San Francisco, have "unfortunately showed the pump to be of absolutely no value."

Bizarro Newt: Gingrich claimed, also in December 1994, that 800 babies a year were being left in Dumpsters in Washington, D.C.

Planet Earth: In this case Bizarro Newt was off by 796 babies. The four babies found in Dumpsters in 1994 were rescued and cared for by government bureaucrats.

Bizarro Newt: In February 1995, Bizarro Newt told members of the National Restaurant Association that a federal shelter in Denver had 120 beds and cost $8.8 million a year to operate, while a similar-sized but private shelter in the same area costs only $320,000 a year and saves more lives in the process. Members of the audience gasped, "Oh my God!" and "Wow!"

Planet Earth: The "federal" shelter doesn't exist. What Bizarro Newt was apparently referring to is a rehab clinic run by Arapahoe House, Colorado's largest drug and alcohol treatment program, which operates its multiple clinics and 16 school-based counseling programs at a total cost of $11 million, of which $4.3 million is federal money. The "private shelter" is a homeless shelter which offers some drug counseling but no formal treatment or detoxification program.

Bizarro Newt told the restaurateurs that he wanted to discuss Denver's shelter to show "how totally different our vision of the world is from the welfare state. . . . Twenty-five times as much money to ruin lives. This is why we don't believe the big-spending theory of what liberal compassion is."

In fact, all reliable studies on Planet Earth show that for every dollar spent, good drug rehabs like Arapahoe House save society approximately seven dollars in medical expenses, crime, and lost productivity. They don't "ruin" lives, they save them.

If Newt's apocryphal anecdotes and Reagan's share a certain carefree indifference to the truth, Newt's usually lack the warm personal touch that Reagan could bring to his. That's why my favorite new Republican Apocryphal Horror Story is House majority leader Dick Armey's warm yet tragic tale of Charlie, the semi-retarded janitor.

Armey tells the story often. Charlie, it seems, swept the floors of Wooten Hall, the building where Armey worked as a professor at North Texas State University. Armey took a liking to Charlie and they talked a lot. (That's the warm part.) Well, one day Armey noticed that Charlie was gone. A few months went by before Armey ran into a degraded Charlie on the checkout line, buying his groceries with *food stamps*. "What happened, Charlie?" Charlie told him. The federal government had raised the minimum wage, and the university could no longer afford to pay his salary. (That's the tragic part.) From that moment on, Armey tells his audiences, he swore his undying hostility to the federal minimum wage.

(Here comes the truth part.)

Washington Post reporter David Maraniss spoke to four different professors who also worked at Wooten Hall during that period. None could remember a janitor named Charlie. The current chancellor of the university told Maraniss that, as state employees, university janitors are paid well over the minimum wage, and so Armey's story doesn't make sense. When pressed, Armey changed the tragic, moving story. He said that the head of the university's physical plant ("his name was Dale something") told him Charlie was fired because they could no longer afford him.

Still, there's nothing like a really dumb apocryphal horror story. Republican congressman David McIntosh of Indiana claimed on the House floor and in hearings before the Senate Judiciary Committee that the Consumer Product Safety Commission had issued a guideline requiring that all five-gallon and larger buckets used on worksites be built *with a hole in them* to "avoid the danger of somebody falling face down in the bucket and drowning."

You have to admit. Requiring a hole in a bucket would be really stupid. It would defeat the entire purpose of the bucket! I mean, why have a bucket if you're going to have a hole in

it?! And, let's get real. What hardhat is going to fall face down in a bucket and drown?! Man, the federal government is stupid!

Do I even have to finish this one? Okay. Here goes: The CPSC never issued such a guideline. It did study the issue of small children—not adults, as McIntosh implies—drowning in such buckets (228 died in this manner between 1984 and 1994), but closed the investigation after the bucket industry agreed to put warning labels on the buckets and spend money for an information campaign regarding the problem.

Are there badly written, unnecessary, stupid government regulations? Yes. Are there enough of them that the Republicans don't have to make them up to give interesting examples? Evidently not.

Here's a good one. House Republican whip Tom Delay tells of a dentist who refused to give a child's baby teeth to his parents because the teeth were classified as toxic waste.

I didn't bother to check that one.

Instead I thought I'd spend my time trying to make up my own Democratic apocryphal story. Something really touching and horrible. Here goes.

There's this kid named Jason on my son's Little League team for which I'm the assistant coach. Hell. Let's make me the coach. Jason has Attention Deficit Disorder. No, wait. He's semi-retarded. And we play on a beautiful field that was once a Superfund site. Some corporate polluter had put carcinogens in the groundwater and the EPA forced them to pay for the cleanup, which was a huge success.

Anyway. Jason is semi-retarded. As coach, I've kind of taken him under my wing, and taught him the intricacies of the game. So, one day we're playing a game against a team of bullies. They're a better team, but we're only down by one run in the bottom of the sixth with two outs and the bases loaded. Jason is up and the entire game is on the line. It's the

league championship! And the count is three and two. So Jason gets hit in the head with a pitch. He's fine, because he's wearing a helmet, which is a government regulation. And our team is cheering because that forces in the tying run. Only Jason stops everyone and says his head was in the strike zone, and he should be called out. So the umpire calls him out, but everyone on our team is happy because Jason told the truth. He didn't really; his head wasn't in the strike zone. He just thought it was because he's semi-retarded. But everyone's happy anyway.

So we all go out for hamburgers. I buy because that's the kind of guy I am. Jason's burger is undercooked. It's got the *E. coli* bacteria, because the Republicans deregulated meat inspection, and Jason dies.

I forgot. When he got hit in the head, he was okay, except the shock knocked out two of his baby teeth. And on his deathbed he gave them to his parents and told them to put them under his little sister's pillow so the tooth fairy would give her a quarter.

Unfortunately, she also died from eating an *E. coli* hamburger. As did every kid on the team. And a pregnant woman. And three tourists from Kansas. It was real tragic.

16

THIS BOOK IS NOT PART OF A CONSPIRACY

I just want to assure the reader that this book was not written in the service of some conspiracy to form a one-world government. *Rush Limbaugh Is a Big Fat Idiot and Other Observations* is really meant as an entertainment to provide a few laughs, force my political opinions down your throat, and maybe even get you to think a little bit. But *not* about conspiring to form a one-world government!

There are, I can assure you, no encoded messages anywhere in this book. For example, if you took the fourteenth letter of each page in reverse order, they wouldn't spell out instructions to occupying U.N. soldiers or indicate the sites of future concentration camps for fundamentalist Christians who refuse to surrender their guns in a coming federal crackdown.

That information is already written on the backs of highway signs. Or at least that's what I've been led to believe.

And when I go on my book tour, the order of the cities I visit will be of no special significance. If I spend a couple days near Groom Lake, Nevada, it will be because Delacorte feels I can sell a lot of books there. I will not, and I repeat, *not*, be visiting the defense facility in Groom Lake where scientists and CIA agents are working with six hundred space aliens. If some of the aliens come to the book signing and buy books, I'll sign them. But that's it. Come to think of it, maybe I'll have the aliens sign my copy of *Behold a Pale Horse*, the book by William Cooper, the Worldwide Christian Radio host, who says that President Eisenhower signed a treaty with space aliens in the 1950s allowing humans to be abducted in exchange for technological advice.

If Delacorte hires a black helicopter to fly me around, don't start jumping to conclusions. The logistics of these book tours can be pretty complicated, and sometimes you have to charter your own flights. So let's say I have to get from a signing in Missoula, Montana, to one in Coeur d'Alene, Idaho. My wife doesn't trust those Buddy Holly–Jim Croce puddle jumpers, and a black helicopter manned by Bureau of Alcohol, Tobacco, and Firearms agents might just give her a little more peace of mind.

And if I have really good weather on my tour, it will be just a big coincidence. It will *not* be because I was the beneficiary of government weather-tampering devices, which were designed to starve millions of Americans as part of the new world order's plan to take over the country. Frankly, I didn't know this technology existed before I started the book. Fortunately, I asked my research assistant, Geoff, to watch the Senate militia hearings in June where Robert Fletcher, a Militia of Montana founder, made a very convincing argument to Senator Herbert Kohl of Wisconsin:

> . . . If somebody had told me that equipment even
> existed ten years ago, I would have thought they were
> nuts, sir. And at this point in time, we have all the
> documents to prove it. And if you think that eighty-
> five tornadoes take place in the middle of our growing
> area by simultaneous accident, I'm sorry.

The Militia of Montana, by the way, is the source of a lot of good, solid information. In 1994, for example, the militia's newsletter, "Taking Aim," disclosed that a secret government plan to replace the lower forty-eight states with nine zones was spelled out in an illustration on the back of Kix cereal boxes.

Why Kix? At first I suspected that it was because "Kix are for kids" and that the government knew that kids could never break the code on the back of the box. But then Geoff re-minded me that *Trix* are for kids. So I'm back to square one.

Not to upset anybody, I'd like to give a little credit to other militias. A few months after the Oklahoma City bombing, Commander Norman Olson and Colonel Ray Southwell of the Northern Michigan Regional Militia explained the whole thing. Turns out that a band of rogue CIA and FBI agents working for the Japanese blew up the federal building in re-venge for the Tokyo subway gas attack by U.S. Army agents who were retaliating for the Japanese bugging of White House communications.

Angered by the left-wing, pro-government media's refusal to investigate the theory, Olson and Southwell fired off a fax to news bureaus across the country. Addressed to "COW-ARDS," the fax read: "We have cast pearls of truth before swine. Damn you all!"

Speaking of damnation, I'm very upset with the people at Delacorte. I *begged* them not to put the Universal Product Code on the back of the book. They argued that every retail

item these days has to have the UPC bar code, and I said, "Exactly! That's *why* the UPC is the Mark of the Beast!"

Of course, the Delacorte people *pretended* not to know what I was talking about it. So we had to go through this little charade where I showed them the passage in Revelation: "No man will be able to buy or sell without the Mark of the Beast." And they acted like they had never seen it before. And then I pointed out the passage in Pat Robertson's book *The New World Order*:

> . . . Can any of us doubt the truth expressed in the Book of Revelation that all credit could one day be controlled by a central one-world financial authority and that no one could buy or sell without its approval?

And the charade continued. They acted like I was crazy, and finally I just said, "The man went to Yale!"

Long story short, the back cover bears the Mark of the Beast. I'm sorry.

17
I GET LETTERS

The last time I appeared on C-SPAN I did a call-in show during which I talked about *Saturday Night Live* and political humor for about a half hour. A few days later, I received this letter:

> To the Jew Franken:
>
> I saw you on C-SPAN, and I always knew you were a fag Jew. You fucking faggot. I know you spend all your faggot time on your hands and knees getting fucked in the ass by fellow Jew faggot Barney Frank while you suck off that faggot Gerry Studds.

And I thought to myself, "He could tell all this from one little interview?"

18

ADVENTURES IN POLITICS
DECEMBER 31, 1993

RENAISSANCE WEEKEND. HILTON HEAD. I MEET
WOLF BLITZER AND PLAY TOUCH FOOTBALL WITH
THE PRESIDENT, AND FOOL THE GREATEST MINDS IN
THE COUNTRY WITH "THE PLAY"

I t is a rule of thumb that people like me who write about politics should not hobnob with the people we're writing about.

For example, I have said that President Clinton is, without a doubt, our best post-war president, and, if not for Roosevelt, the greatest of this century. Do I feel this way because I played touch football with him? Maybe.

The occasion was Renaissance Weekend, an annual get-together on Hilton Head Island. Founded fifteen years ago by businessman Phil Lader, the Weekend brings together people of "achievement" for four days of *off the record* exchanges of ideas "in the Renaissance spirit." I emphasize *off the record* because I'm not supposed to be telling you any of this.

The Clintons have been Renaissance regulars. So have peo-

ple like Admiral Bud Zumwalt, Justice Harry Blackmun, Art Buchwald, various corporate CEO's, academes, governors, mayors, and U.S. senators. How did I get invited? Phil was my freshman proctor at Harvard. He had been inviting my family for years, but just the name "*Renaissance* Weekend" had kept me away.

The Weekend has been called "elitist" by many in the press, or at least by those who have never been invited as participants. It's just the kind of crowd Rush Limbaugh would feel most uncomfortable with.

First of all, it's predominantly liberal, with a few token right-wingers like former *Conservative Digest* publisher Richard Viguerie. But more than that, Renaissancers are the wrong type of achievers. If Limbaugh believes in nothing else, he believes that personal success comes from "self-reliance, risk-taking, hard work, and the courage to believe in yourself." None of that counts, however, if you're a liberal. Then you're a socialist who believes success comes from "relying on government handouts and affirmative action." Socialists like Microsoft billionaire Bill Gates come to mind.

For Rush, successful people fall into two basic categories: achievers in the "real world" to be emulated, and pointy-headed elitists to be resented. Thus, in *See, I Told You So* he writes, "Tell me something, friends. If you wanted to become a major-league baseball player, whose advice would you value more—baseball star George Brett's or Donna Shalala's?"* (See bottom of page for answer.)

To be embarrassingly honest, the main reason I decided to spend my New Year's in Hilton Head was the touch football game. I had seen the clips on TV the year before, the young Kennedyesque President-elect frolicking with windswept

* George Brett.

Renaissancers, while the Frankens shivered on 84th and Broadway in the movie line for *Beethoven's 2nd.* So this year, the Frankens accepted.

Sometime in November, with the big Weekend about a month away, I was throwing the football in the park with my eight-year-old, Joe. That's when the play came to me in a flash. It was beautiful!

That night, getting ready for bed, I proudly explained the play to my wife. Franni put down her book. "Honey," she said, "you're not going to play touch football with the President."

"I *might.*"

"I just don't want you to be disappointed." The concern sounded a tad patronizing.

"Honey, you don't understand. It doesn't *matter* whether I play touch football with the President. The point is the beauty of the play. I've designed *the perfect* misdirection play!"

"It's just that I know you, and I don't want you to get your hopes up."

"You're not listening. I *know* this isn't going to happen. It's just the concept, that's all. I just wanted to share the joy of the concept."

"I know." She patted me. "I just don't want you to be disappointed."

The football game was scheduled for Day Three at low tide. About sixty other Renaissancers also wanted to play football with the President, and before he arrived, we were divided into four unwieldy teams, comprised mostly of university presidents, policy wonks, jurists, data processing entrepreneurs, heads of non-profits, journalists, and me. And our kids, some of whom were college age, fast, and tall.

The captain of our team, a well-connected Washington lawyer, had noticed during warm-ups that I had a better arm than anyone from the Brookings Institute, and I humbly ac-

cepted the quarterback duties. As we started playing, sans Bill, it quickly became apparent that there wasn't going to be a lot of scoring. It was a blustery day, but more than that, the game was just chaos. Once I'd get the hike, I was looking at thirty or more people, none of whom I knew except my son and Howard Fineman of *Newsweek*. I completed a few short passes to tall college students and a nifty little toss to the 13-year-old son of an American Enterprise Institute fellow, who had cut across the middle . . . well, now I'm just trying your patience.

Our team was on the sideline when the President arrived, trailed by an entourage of about fifty: Secret Service, the press corps, cameras. Our well-connected captain managed to snare him, and suddenly I found myself in a huddle with the President of the United States. Two things really struck me. The first was that up close he really does look like a Bubba: red-faced, jeans and a sweatshirt, and a gut.

The other was that the President, any President, has to be *in charge*. It's expected of him, and he knows it's expected of him. So now President Clinton was calling the plays, for really no reason other than he's the President. Which was good enough for everyone. We were all thrilled.

Mainly, the President wanted to get the little kids involved. Which is great, except it's no way to move the football. After two quick incompletions, we were facing a third and fifty. Back in the huddle, the President knelt down to draw in the sand, but before he could open his mouth, I said, "I have a play."

Everyone just kind of looked at me. . . . "Mr. President, I'd like to use you as a decoy."

A beat before, ". . . Okay."

We had all been instructed to call him "Mr. President." Some of the Renaissance regulars knew him as "Bill," but everyone was supposed to call him "Mr. President" as in:

"Mr. President, go out ten and cut to the right."

I told everyone else to stay short or block, except for one of the fast, tall college kids, who I told to go deep left. When we got to the scrimmage line, I made an announcement. I shouted, "The President wants everyone to know that whoever blocks a pass intended for the President on this play will get to spend a night in the White House."

The President turned to me and said, "What?!" That got a laugh, and, I think, sold the play. Then he shrugged with another, "Okay."

It couldn't have worked more perfectly. After the snap, the President went out ten and cut to the right sideline. That's when I made the *PUMP FAKE.*

They *ALL* went for it. It was embarrassing really. Fifteen people each thinking the same thing: "Lincoln bedroom." By the time I put the ball in the air, the college kid was, literally, thirty yards behind the defense.

After the touchdown, there was a lot of high-fiving. The President ran to the end zone and hugged the college kid. I ran up for my hug, but didn't get one. That was all right, though. I had played touch football with the greatest president of the twentieth century. And proved my wife wrong.

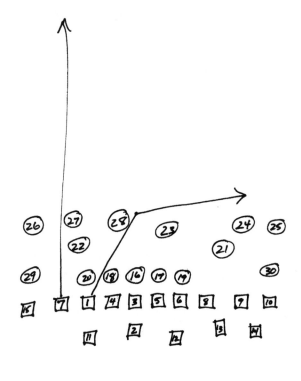

1. President of U.S.   6. Howard Fineman   11. Poverty pimp
2. Me   7. Son of pointy-headed liberal   12. Ira Magaziner
3. Pointy-headed liberal   8. Wacko-feminist
4. Sandal-wearing liberal   9. Enviro-fascist   13. Compassion fascist
5. Eggheaded liberal   10. Daughter of feminazi   14. Pro abortion militant leftist

15. Hollywood filth merchant

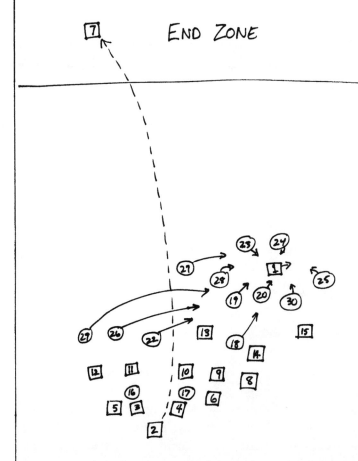

END ZONE

16. Beancurd eater
17. Wolf Blitzer
18. Lawyer
19. Draft dodger
20. Secular humanist
21. Son of enviro-fascist and feminazi
22. Ted Sorensen
23. Militant vegetarian
24. Smooth-talking, Ivy League-educated, Armani-clad class warrior
25. Treehugger
26. Zoe Baird
27. Modern statist
28. Ugly feminist
29. Diabolical Rodhamite
30. Token Conservative Richard Viguerie

19

THE SECRETS OF RENAISSANCE WEEKEND

s I've said, when you accept an invitation to Renaissance, you agree not to reveal anything you see or hear. That way, participants feel they can speak freely in a frank, open manner. But I figured I'd be doing Renaissance Weekend a favor if I lifted some of the shroud of mystery by revealing some of the highlights of my first Renaissance Weekend:

- At a panel discussion entitled "My Favorite Cuts of Veal," Senator Barbara Mikulski got drunk and kneed neo-conservative Ben Wattenberg in the groin.

- At the Renaissance volleyball game, former *Conservative Digest* publisher Richard Viguerie taunted

Justice Harry Blackmun, repeatedly yelling "Show me your serve, baby killer!"

• President Clinton used the four days out of the public eye to undergo a series of painful liposuction procedures.

• At a panel on health care reform Ira Magaziner announced that the comprehensive package would cover people with the willies but not those suffering from the heebie-jeebies.

• Fed Chairman Alan Greenspan was seen leaving dinner sneaking shrimp back to his room.

• At a panel entitled "You're Only as Sick as Your Secrets," Wolf Blitzer admitted that his real name is Leslie Blitzer.

• Zoë Baird screamed at the kitchen help.

20

STOP THIS MAN BEFORE HE KILLS AGAIN

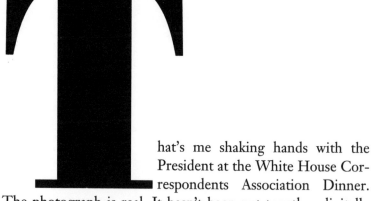

That's me shaking hands with the President at the White House Correspondents Association Dinner. The photograph is real. It hasn't been put together digitally like that *Forrest Gump* footage. It's not a composite. How I wish it were!

Had I known at the time that the man was a murderer, I would never have shaken his hand. I have never *knowingly* shaken the hand of a killer. Once I did a fund-raiser for Pol Pot, but that was before I'd seen *The Killing Fields.*

Unfortunately, I spoke at the Correspondents Association Dinner before I had a chance to see "Bill Clinton's Circle of Power." According to the video, as governor and then as president, Clinton has been connected to the murders of "countless people."

The video has sold over 100,000 copies thanks to regular advertising on Jerry Falwell's *Old Time Gospel Hour.* Which means the information is getting to the right people.

The tape was so successful that its producers, an organization called Citizens for Honest Government, made a sequel called "The Clinton Chronicles," which Falwell promotes as "far more damaging, far more indicting" than the original. Says Falwell:

> . . . Now on this brand-new video exposé, "The Clinton Chronicles," these brave men and women have stepped forward to tell what they know about the dark side of Bill and Hillary Clinton. Even in the face of alleged constant intimidation, threats, physical abuse, and even, some say, mysterious, violent acts of murder.

Basically, the tape tells a sinister tale of murder, adultery, Whitewater, and . . . cocaine:

> An unidentified voice: [Drug smuggler] Barry Seale . . . had to find a state that had a sleazy governor hooked on cocaine, and everybody knew it. Bill Clinton was hooked on cocaine.

> Narrator: Clinton had integrated a number of corrupt cops, judges, and politicians into high-level positions to ensure the continued success of the drug smuggling, money laundering operation.

It gets worse. Much worse. A woman named Linda Ives says her son and a friend witnessed the smuggling and were murdered. But state officials, led by a political appointee of Clinton's, covered it up.

> Ives: I was outraged that protecting a political crony of Clinton's was more important than the fact that two young boys had been murdered.

> Narrator: A number of people approached the police about Don and Kevin's murders and were subsequently murdered themselves.

Wow! We're talking *dozens* of murders. As Florida talk radio host Chuck Harder, who is broadcast on 300 stations, has put it, "The difference between Watergate and Whitewater is a very, very big pile of bodies."

And who are these murder victims? One, obviously, was Vince Foster.

I'm embarrassed to say that for quite a while I bought the party-line "suicide" explanation. Just shows that I've been getting my information from all the wrong sources.

Had I been listening to Rush Limbaugh on March 10th, 1994, I would have heard this:

> Okay, folks, I think I got enough information here to tell you about the contents of this fax that I got. Brace yourselves. . . . What it is is a bit of news which says . . . there's a Washington consulting firm that has

scheduled the release of a report that will appear, it will be published, that claims that Vince Foster was murdered in an apartment owned by Hillary Clinton, and the body was then taken to Fort Marcy Park.

Limbaugh had actually botched it a little. The fax he received had said nothing about a murder and nothing about Hillary's apartment. But the point is still the same. Which is that Vince Foster was murdered in Hillary's apartment.

Had I been watching the *700 Club* around that time I could have heard Pat Robertson say, "Was there a murder of a White House counsel? It looks more and more like that." And more recently, Robertson's guest was James Dale Davidson, chairman of the National Taxpayers' Union, who told *700 Club* viewers that Foster's death was clearly a murder and that top people in the news media know that a cover-up was taking place.

If only I had known all this before I had shaken the Murderer's hand. Come to think of it, I could have used the occasion to say something. After all, there were a lot of top people in the media at the din . . . Wait a minute! Maybe it's good I didn't say anything.

In fact, maybe I shouldn't be writing this.

21

MONETARY POLICY: A TICKING TIME BOMB

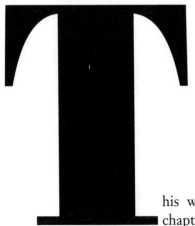his was going to be a hell of a chapter on the danger of monetiz-ing the debt. Geoff did hours and hours of research and tells me the stuff is pretty frightening.

Unfortunately, I just haven't had a chance to look at it. Which is only the first step in writing these little essays. I have to read Geoff's research, then have him explain it to me, then reread it, and *then* try to think of three or four jokes that I can tie together in some lame, half-assed way so I can call the thing an essay. It's hard work. And time-consuming.

But that's what an artist owes his audience. This book is, in a sense, my gift to you the reader. It is a gift of my talent and my dedication. It is a solemn pact, as it were, between you and

me. You keep your side of the bargain by buying the book. I keep my side by investing every fiber of my being into the work.

The thing is, I've got kids. And, sometimes, in life you have to set priorities. It would be nice to invest every fiber of my being in this whole monetary policy thing, whatever it is. But dammit, if this book is about anything, it's about how the family is the building block of a healthy society. And since the book is not about that, I guess it isn't about anything.

Which leaves me free to pitch batting practice for the West Side Little League all-star tournament team. You see, my son, Joe, made the team. In fact, he got the game ball from yesterday's 6–5 victory over Kingsbridge, the Bronx team that usually wins our district. Joe made this amazing throw that nailed the tying run at the plate. Joe got his arm from me. At least the accuracy. Which is why I pitch batting practice. I throw a meatball that any 10-year-old can hit.

The whole tournament has become a real production. Mainly because we keep winning. We now have about fifty-five parents, siblings, and grandparents who come along to the games, after which we eat. My wife is the team parent, so she's on the phone constantly making arrangements for minivans and Gatorade. That's put a lot of pressure on me to be a hands-on parent. Unlike some Republican officeholders I know.

And believe me, monetary policy isn't the only casualty of West Side's post-season juggernaut. If we had been eliminated in the quarterfinals, I would have been able to write a great chapter on campaign finance reform. If it hadn't been for Jake Seltzer's two-run triple against East Harlem in the opening round, you'd know a lot more about our trade deficit. The point is, your loss is my son's gain.

And if we win tomorrow, I probably won't get to the Reagan years. That'd be too bad. Because I think Geoff has some

really good stuff on the subject. Blows Limbaugh right out of the water.

But in the long run, I think the country will reap greater dividends from the added investment in my children, who will grow up to be much happier, more productive members of our society. As opposed to Reagan's kids.* Who, let's be honest, seem kind of screwed up.

---

* In his autobiography, *On the Outside Looking In*, Michael Reagan, the adopted son from Reagan's first marriage to Jane Wyman, tells this story: It's a beautiful June day in 1964. Reagan is the commencement speaker at an exclusive prep school outside Scottsdale, Arizona. Reagan is standing with several of the seniors, who have been invited to pose for pictures with him. He chats up each of the graduates, and to one of the boys says: "My name is Ronald Reagan. What's yours?" The boy says, "I'm your son Mike." "Oh," says Reagan. "I didn't recognize you."

22

THE REAGAN YEARS: RUSH LIMBAUGH IS A BIG FAT LIAR

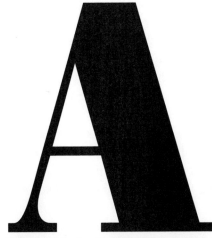s Rush Limbaugh likes to say, "words mean things." Which is why I probably should have called this book *Rush Limbaugh Is a Big Fat Liar*. But that just seemed so confrontational.

Rush lies about a lot of stuff. Some of the lies I don't really hold against him. These are the ones where he's been on the air for an hour or so, and he's really on a roll. He's hunkered down in the booth, probably sweating a lot; he's done a couple Billary jokes, and he's just ranting like there's no tomorrow. He's so far in the zone that he's left objective reality behind and entered this parallel universe where things are true because Rush wants them to be—where the Way Things Ought

to Be is the way things are, even if they aren't. This is the place where Styrofoam becomes biodegradable, Hillary has Vince Foster rubbed out, and cigarettes stop causing cancer.

Other lies bug me a lot. These are the rational, carefully constructed, deliberate lies of a man running a giant propaganda factory dedicated to two things: convincing people who were screwed sideways by Reaganomics that it was actually good for them, and encouraging the people who turned the screws to feel good about themselves.

Reaganomics worked. This is the jewel in Rush's crown of bullshit. This is the big lie—the one he desperately needs the working-class members of his audience to believe. If Reaganomics worked, Rush is a straight-talking champion of the little guy on a populist crusade to take the country back from those pointy-headed liberals who think they know what's good for everybody and are drunk with the power of sending out welfare checks.

If Reaganomics didn't work, Rush is the carnival clown hired to distract the crowd while paramedics carry the mangled bodies from a derailed roller coaster. He does a little juggling, pulls some flowers out of his hat, and when the crowd begins to get a little anxious about the rising body count, he starts shrieking hysterically that this never would have happened if it weren't for those goddam liberal safety inspectors.

So the stakes are pretty high for Rush when it comes to Reaganomics. Which is why he devotes long statistic-riddled chapters in both of his books to proving that Reaganomics not only *didn't* cause the national debt to explode, but *did* result in an era of unprecedented economic growth from which all classes benefited. Especially the poor.

Take this bald assertion, straight from page 128 Of *See, I Told You So:* "don't blame that [the deficit] on Reagan. . . . He tried his best to reduce spending, but every one of his budgets was pronounced 'dead on arrival' by the Democratic

Congress." That's Rush's party line. That Reagan submitted a whole lot of lean, fiscally conservative budgets to the Democrats in Congress, who fattened them up with a bunch of wasteful, "liberal" programs.

Here's a funny thing. In 1985, the midpoint of what Rush calls "full-blown Reaganomics," Reagan submitted a budget of $588 billion to Congress. The budget that Congress sent back for him to sign was $583 billion, five billion dollars smaller than Reagan wanted. Over the eight years of the Reagan presidency, the Gipper asked Congress for $16.1 billion *more* in spending than it passed into law. If Reagan was really "trying his best" to reduce spending, he must have been using some kind of reverse psychology I don't understand.

Either way, Rush has a point when he calls Ronald Reagan "a man to whom we Americans owe a debt that we will never be able to repay."

The second leg of the three-legged coffee table that is the Big Lie About Reaganomics is that Reagan's massive tax cuts were directly responsible for what Limbaugh calls "unprecedented growth and prosperity." This gets to the heart of supply-side economics: the less you tax the rich, the faster the economy will grow.

Take, for example, the fifties. We taxed the shit out of the rich. The top marginal rate was 88 percent. And the economy grew at an annual rate of just over 4 percent. Then look at the eighties. Reagan knocked the top rate down to 28 percent, and the economy grew at a yearly rate of just under 2.5 percent.

So cutting the marginal tax rate didn't give us "unprecedented" growth. What it did give us was "unprecedented" deficits.

But that's not the Way Things Ought to Be. So rather than admit that supply-side economics was kind of a dumb idea, Rush tries to drown his readers in a flood of impressive-sounding statistics, most of which he's twisted like a balloon animal.

Which brings me to the Chart. The Chart is Limbaugh's big attempt to prove the third leg of the Big Lie: that Reagan's economic policies were just as good for the poor as they were for the rich. And maybe even better.

In 725 pages of opinion-barfing spread over two books, only once does Rush consider a point important enough to trot out a visual aid. To prove that "all income groups paid less taxes as a percentage of their income during the Reagan years, but *the poor received the most relief, the middle class the next, and the rich, the least*" (my emphasis), Rush conjures up the Chart.

The Chart purports to use U.S. Census data (actually, they're Congressional Budget Office numbers) to make the argument that the poor received a *540 percent* tax cut during the Reagan years, while the tax cut for the rich was just 7.9 percent.

"What?" say the liberals in the media. "That can't be true."

"But it *is*!" reply the Didiots. "Look! He made a chart!"

Wow! That is pretty convincing. Until you realize the numbers have been cooked like the income statement for Don Corleone's olive oil import business.

First of all, you'll notice that Rush uses the years 1980 and 1992. This is interesting, because the Chart is supposed to be about tax rates "during the Reagan years," while two pages earlier, Rush says, "Reaganomics died in 1990" with George Bush's tax hike. In fact, this is the *only* statistic where Rush defines the Reagan years to include any year after 1989.

Why does he do this? Because including Bush's tax hike makes the size of Reagan's tax break for the rich seem smaller. So why doesn't Rush use 1990? Because it wasn't until the next year that Bush increased the Earned Income Tax Credit for the working poor. Which makes the apparent tax break for the poor seem much larger. So Rush includes the tax hike of 1990 (which he despised) and the increase in the E.I.T.C. of 1991 (which he also despised) in order to create a distorted

REDUCTION OF TAX RATES

Income Quintile	Top Income in Bracket	1980 (% of Income Paid As Taxes)	1992 (% of Income Paid As Taxes)	1992 (% of Taxes Cut)
Poorest 20%	$20,300	-0.5%	-3.2%	-540%
2nd Lowest 20%	$36,800	4.5%	2.8%	-37.8%
Middle 20%	$64,500	7.9%	6.2%	-21.5%
2nd highest 20%	$82,400	11%	8.7%	-20.9%
Richest 20%	....	17.2%	15.6%	-9.3%
Richest 1%	....	23.9%	22%	-7.9%
Source: U.S. Bureau of Census*				

What a dick!

*Actually, these are Congressional Budget Office numbers.

picture of Reaganomics, which he claims was over by 1990 anyway. Those of you who are thinking, "What an incredible hypocrite!" just keep reading. It gets worse.

He leaves out payroll taxes! That's right. He leaves out payroll taxes, the taxes for Social Security and Medicare that come out of your paycheck before you even see it. Now, re- member. Most Americans pay *the majority* of their taxes in payroll taxes. And since payroll taxes only apply to the first $61,000 of income, they are a much bigger burden on the poor than on the rich.

And guess what? While income taxes were going down during the Reagan years, payroll taxes were going up. For the lowest quintile in 1980, payroll taxes were 5.2 percent. By 1989, that number was up to 7.6 percent. The top one percent, on the other hand, paid only 1.5 percent of their income in payroll taxes in 1980. That went up to 1.6 percent by 1989.

So here's what an *honest* chart showing the change in federal tax rates during the Reagan years would look like:

AN <u>HONEST</u> CHART ON TAX RATES DURING THE REAGAN YEARS

Income Quintile	Avg. Income 1989	1980 Total Fed Tax Rate	1989 Total Fed Tax Rate	1989 % of Tax Increase/Cut	1989 Tax Increase Cut in $'s
(1993 Dollars)					
Poorest 20%	8,642	8.1	9.3	+15.0%	+104
2nd Lowest 20%	20,743	15.6	15.7	+0.6%	+21
Middle 20%	33,659	19.8	19.4	-2.0%	-135
2nd highest 20%	49,347	22.9	22.0	-7.6%	-444
Richest 20%	112,700	27.6	25.5	-7.6%	-2367
Richest 1%	576,553	31.9	26.2	-15.0%	-32,864

See? He's a dick

Source: 1992 Green Book, Congressional Budget Office (same as Rush)

So basically, tax rates *rose* for the poor by as much as they *fell* for the rich: 15 percent. And this came during a period when average wages went down, while the incomes of the richest 1 percent more than doubled.

Now let's look at these numbers as bar graphs. (By the way, I think I'm really breaking new ground here. I mean, did you see bar graphs in Jerry Seinfeld's book? In Tim Allen's? Hmmmmm?)

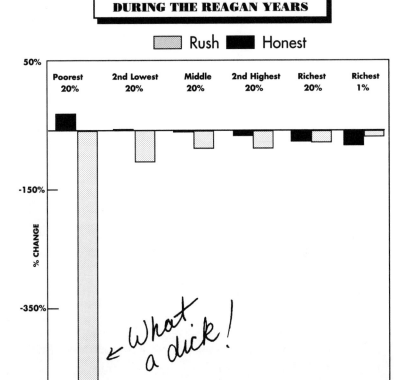

$ CHANGE IN TAX
DURING THE REAGAN YEARS

HONEST BAR GRAPH

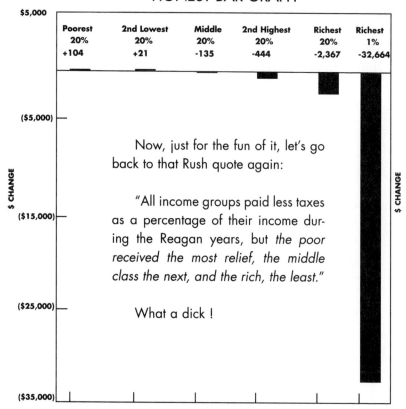

	Poorest 20%	2nd Lowest 20%	Middle 20%	2nd Highest 20%	Richest 20%	Richest 1%
	+104	+21	-135	-444	-2,367	-32,664

$5,000

($5,000)

$ CHANGE

($15,000)

($25,000)

($35,000)

Now, just for the fun of it, let's go back to that Rush quote again:

"All income groups paid less taxes as a percentage of their income during the Reagan years, but *the poor received the most relief, the middle class the next, and the rich, the least.*"

What a dick !

And just for the hell of it, let's add another Rush quote: "Reaganomics did work, and . . . the gap between rich and poor was narrowed rather than expanded during those years."

Now let's listen to an economist, Paul Krugman from Stanford: "The widening of inequality is beyond doubt. It has been as firmly established by evidence as the fact that smoking causes cancer."

Then again, Rush doesn't believe smoking causes cancer, either.

TRACKING A TRICKLE-DOWN DOLLAR

Uncle Sam gives a $1.00 tax break to a Beverly Hills plastic surgeon...

Plastic Surgeon and his wife go to a fancy restaurant and order the foie gras...

Foie gras dollar goes to farmer Jacques who force-feeds his geese in France...

Jacques spends dollar at EuroDisney...

Dollar, along with 200 million others, goes to Michael Eisner...

Eisner takes his wife to dinner. They order the foie gras...

Dollar goes back to Jacques...

Jacques goes back to EuroDisney...

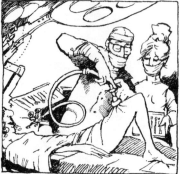

Dollar goes back to Eisner. Takes
Cher to lunch. Cher orders foie gras...

Plastic surgeon performs liposuction
on Cher's thighs...

Fat from Cher's thighs used in celebrity lava lamp.

23
NEWT'S LOOT

I have to confess that techniques I've been employing in this book are taken directly from Gingrich's political action committee, GO-PAC.

GOPAC trains Republican candidates to beat Democrats, providing them with strategies and tactics, audiotapes and videotapes, and the occasional infusion of cash. GOP candidates learn lessons like "Go Negative Early," "Don't Try to Educate," and "Never Back Off." They're told to "use minor details to demonize" their opposition.

Which is why I bring up the first wife, cancer surgery, deadbeat dad stuff as often as possible.

But there's so much more about Newt. Let's start with the money.

Most people know that Gingrich used to teach a course called Renewing American Civilization at a college in Georgia, and that the course was beamed by satellite to about 100 other locations. I say "used to" because he recently dropped it from his roster of activities. I guess he figured that, what with being the Speaker of the House, a shadow presidential candidate, a bestselling author, a cable TV talk show host, and a deadbeat dad, his plate was pretty full.

But what most people *don't* know about the course is that Gingrich financed it by soliciting contributions from various corporations. For example, for $50,000 a corporation could become a "sponsor" and "work directly with the leadership of the Renewing American Civilization Project in the course development process."

It seemed odd to me that a Ph.D. in history would seek the advice of corporate executives in preparing lesson plans. But it seems to have resulted in a real intellectual synergy. The course draws on the works of the Federalists, de Tocqueville, and the marketing department at Hewlett-Packard, which put together a spiffy promotional video that Newt showed his class.

Professor Gingrich also plugs "a very powerful, revolutionary" health insurance plan offered by the Golden Rule Insurance Company of Indiana, which didn't actually give a dime to the course. Instead, it acts as the sole sponsor of Gingrich's cable show on National Empowerment Television, and its executives and employees have donated $117,000 to GOPAC, $42,000 to Gingrich's campaign committee, and over half a million dollars to the Republican party.

Gee, I'd plug a company too, if they'd stuff that kind of money up my bum.

Hmmmm.

24

LEXIS-NEXIS

THE POWERFUL, REVOLUTIONARY
DATABASE TECHNOLOGY

n the last chapter you may have noticed that I cited quite a few facts, statistics, and whatnot. Now, a smart person like yourself might be wondering how I found all this information. Did I go to the library? No. A university research facility? Nope. The fact is, I didn't even have to leave my apartment.

That's right. Thanks to Lexis-Nexis, the powerful, revolutionary database technology, I was able to access literally thousands of different information sources, almost all of which provided documentation of at least one instance of questionable behavior by Newt Gingrich.

Yes, thanks to Lexis-Nexis, my book has entered the Third Wave! And unlike other database companies, many of which are weird, bizarre, and even grotesque, Lexis-Nexis is user-friendly and breathtakingly up-to-date.

Is Lexis-Nexis paying me to say this? It's none of your business. But even if they weren't, I'd still be a satisfied Lexis-Nexis customer.

And while we're talking about state-of-the-art, user-friendly products, I'd like to say a little something on behalf of the good people at Hanes underwear. You know, when you sit in front of a word processor all day attacking right-wing ideologues, it's important that your briefs don't bunch up. Hanes, the underwear of satirists.

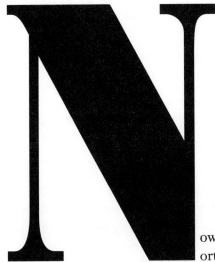

ow that I've paid for my kids' orthodontics, let's get back to Newt, Inc.

Besides GOPAC, there's the tax-exempt Progress and Freedom Foundation, "a non-partisan idea center" which has spent over $600,000 on Newt's course and cable TV show. The think tank gets a lot of its money from pharmaceutical and telecommunications companies. Which explains why a large part of the think tank's agenda is devoted to deregulating telecommunications and ridding America of the FDA. (See "apocryphal heart pump story," page 97.)

Philosophically, the foundation apes a lot of the futuristic mumbo jumbo of Alvin Toffler. As does Newt, who tends to gush when he talks about the Third Wave. Many of us, like Newt, have acknowledged smoking dope and reading Toffler in the early 70s. But after reading Gingrich's bestseller, *To Renew America*, I think Newt's dirty little secret is that he smoked dope and watched *The Jetsons:*

> Imagine a morning in just a decade or so. You wake up to a wall-size, high-definition television showing surf off Maui. (This is my favorite island*—you can pick your own scene.) . . . When you are sick, you sit in your diagnostic chair and communicate with the local health clinic. Sensors take your blood pressure, analyze a blood sample, or do throat cultures.

And when it's time to take Astro out for a walk, you just hop on the space treadmill.

Back to the diagnostic chair:

> The results are quickly relayed to health aides, who make recommendations and prescribe medicine. . . . If you need a specialist, a data bank at your fingertips gives you a range of choices based on cost, reputation, and outcome patterns. . . . Health care has become more flexible and convenient—and less expensive.

Here's my question. If Medicare costs are already spiraling out of control, how exactly is providing every American with a *Blade Runner* diagnostic BarcaLounger going to bring down the cost of health care?

---

* (Gee, I wonder why.)

Also, if company comes over to watch the game, what happens when someone tries to sit in the diagnostic chair? Do you yell: "Don't sit there! It'll give you a throat culture!"

I'm sorry, but if Newt Gingrich thinks our nation's health care problems are going to be solved by the diagnostic chair, then I've got to agree with the Unabomber on this one:

> "Oh," say the technophiles, "science is going to fix all that! We will conquer famine, eliminate psychological suffering, make everybody healthy and happy." Yeah. Sure.

Of course, when we talk about issues like technological development and its role in solving social problems, some pretty fundamental questions come up. Questions about how society can best marshal its limited resources, about the nature of government and its role in contributing to the well-being of its citizens. Unfortunately, the people who are currently deciding the answers to these questions are the same ones who "go negative early" and "never back off."

Which brings us back to GOPAC. Thirty-three members of the House Republican Class of '94 are what a less objective commentator might call "GOPAC Zombies." As such, they are the recipients of large volumes of GOPAC training material and are well versed in "the five key mechanisms of control," one of which is "language."

Fortunately, a copy of the GOPAC memo "Language: A Key Mechanism of Control" has fallen into my hands. According to the memo, it was prepared in response to the "plaintive plea" of candidates across the country: " 'I wish I could speak like Newt.' "

"That takes years of practice," the memo warns. "But, we believe that you could have a significant impact on your cam-

paign and the way you communicate if we help a little. That is why we created this list of words and phrases."

There are two lists, actually. One contains "Optimistic, Positive Governing Words," which the candidate is told to use to "describe your vision for the future of your community (your message)." The other, a list of "Contrasting Words," which the candidate could use to defame, slander, and otherwise impugn his/her opponent.

"The words and phrases are powerful," the memo says. "Read them. Memorize as many as possible."

So for the benefit of any readers who may be considering a run for office, here they are, courtesy of the GOPAC memo "Language A Key Mechanism of Control."

Optimistic Positive Governing Words

Use the list below to help define your campaign and your vision of public service. These words can help give extra power to your message. In addition, these words help develop the positive side of the contrast you should create with your opponent, giving your community something to vote *for*!

share	active(ly)	lead
change	we/us/our	vision
opportunity	candid(ly)	empower(ment)
challenge	humane	citizen
truth	pristine	activist
moral	liberty	dream
courage	principle(d)	freedom
reform	precious	peace
prosperity	care(ing)	rights
children	listen	proud/pride
family	help	preserve

pro-(issue)	eliminate good	protect
flag, children,	time in prison	incentive
environment	strength	hard work
workfare	fair	common sense

Contrasting Words

Often we search hard for words to define our opponents. Sometimes we are hesitant to use contrast. Remember that creating a difference helps you. These are powerful words that can create a clear and easily understood contrast. Apply these to the opponent, their record, proposals, and their party.

decay	radical	corrupt
failure(fail)	devour	insensitive
collapse(ing)	waste	status quo
deeper	corruption	taxes
crisis	incompetent	spend(ing)
destructive	permissive atti-	shame
destroy	tude	disgrace
sick	impose	punish (poor...)
pathetic	self-serving	bizarre
lie	greed	cynicism
liberal	ideological	cheat
they/them	anti-(issue)	steal
"compassion" is	flag, family,	machine
not enough	child, jobs	bosses
traitors	pessimistic	criminal rights
hypocrisy	welfare	red tape

Now, in case you're still a little unclear on how best to make use of these lists, let me offer the following example.

Let's say you're locked in a tight race against Colin Powell. You might want to insert the following into your stump speech: "Colin Powell is a sick, pathetic, corrupt, incompetent, bizarre, selfish traitor whose incompetent, destructive, shallow, cynical, self-serving conduct during the Gulf War was a disgrace." Chances are you'll see a big change in the polls!

Or take an example from Newt's own lips. During the 1990 budget debate in Congress, Newt criticized Democrats involved in the talks as being "sick, pathetic, liberal, incompetent, tax-spending traitors." Sounds like *he* sure memorized the list.

Finally, since these words seem to be so successful for the Republicans, I thought I'd come up with a list of my own. So as a special treat for those of you who wish you could "talk like Al," here's a short list of powerful words and phrases you can use when contrasting your normal, healthy-looking body with Rush Limbaugh's grotesque girth:

fat	porker	lard-ass, lard-
fatso	oinker	butt, tub of lard
fat-ass	piggly wiggly	thunder thighs
fatboy	porcine	obese
meat show	flab(by)	chunkster
waddle	blubber-butt	Ailes-like
wide load	beached whale	balloon butt
hippo	two-ton tessie	cholesterol colony
gutbucket	walrus	fatty fatty two-
enormous	huge	by-four
suet-boy	butterball	elephantine
soo-eeey!	jelly belly	sow

ten pounds of shit in a five-pound bag

26

ADVENTURES IN POLITICS
APRIL 23, 1994

I AM BRILLIANT AT THE WHITE HOUSE
CORRESPONDENTS ASSOCIATION DINNER

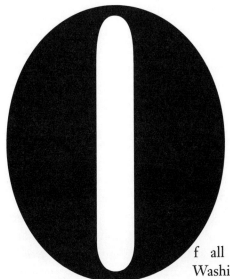

f all the social events in Washington, the annual White House Correspondents Association Dinner is probably the largest. About twenty-five hundred Washingtonians, men and women from the news organizations and their sources, which include congressmen, high-level bureaucrats, administration officials, and Pentagon bigwigs, put on tuxes and gowns for an inside-the-Beltway evening of fun. The only thing comparable that I've been to in Hollywood is the Emmys, although the Hollywood crowd is a lot better-looking.

The highlight of the dinner is supposed to be the entertain-

ment. And over the years they've had the best. Frank Sinatra, Danny Thomas, Jimmy Durante, Fanny Brice, and Danny Kaye all performed for President Truman. During the Eisenhower years they had some tremendous legends: Nat King Cole, Dizzy Gillespie, Bob Hope, James Cagney. Performing for Jack Kennedy were Barbra Streisand, Benny Goodman, and Duke Ellington. In 1969, at President Nixon's request, the entertainment was Disneyland's Golden Horseshoe Revue.

Since 1983, the entertainment has been a comedian—Mark Russell, Rich Little, Jay Leno—on the bill with the President of the United States. I went in 1988 as a guest of the *Washington Post* and saw President Reagan and his favorite comedian, Yakoff Smirnoff. Both were very funny, but Reagan was unbelievably good. The man may have tripled our national debt, but he was a great after-dinner speaker. "I thought the Fourth Estate was one of Walter Annenberg's *homes.*"

It had become my goal after '88 to do the Correspondents dinner. Basically, for a comedian, the gig is comparable to doing a trade show. When a trade group like the scrap metal industry has a convention, they'll hire a comedian to do his act. If the comic can work in a few scrap metal jokes, they go nuts. Only in Washington, the industry is politics. So I imagined doing the White House Correspondents dinner would be like working a scrap metal convention if I knew an awful lot about scrap metal. "I don't want to say Pete Siezmasko is doing a lot of *volume* this year, but Arnie Zimpkin is thinking of moving his operation to *Cleveland!*"

I got a call in March from George Condon, the president of the White House Correspondents Association. George told me that Wolf Blitzer and Andrea Mitchell had reported to him in January that I had been very funny when I spoke at Renaissance Weekend and that I should do this year's dinner. George said that he thought that I would be absolutely *perfect*

for the job, but that he had put off calling me until he had heard back from Garry Shandling. I thanked George for the compliment and tried to guess who had turned him down before Garry.

I was glad that Robin, David, Jerry, Tim, and Garry had better things to do.

Before the dinner, there's a whole bunch of cocktail parties thrown by the various news organizations. The best one is for the dais, which meant I got to have cocktails with the Gores and the Clintons. This is something you'd ordinarily have to pay the Democratic National Committee about $110,000 for, but I didn't enjoy it as much I should have because I was a little nervous. Frankly, I was worried about a couple of jokes.

I got Tipper alone in a corner. "I got this joke about your husband, and my instinct is that it might be over the line. I was wondering if I could run it by you."

She laughed and said, "Okay. Let's hear it."

"Okay. Here's the joke: Vice President Gore continued to show his commitment to the environment by announcing today that he's going to change the policy on the stick up his butt. Instead of replacing the stick every day with a *new* stick, the Vice President will keep the *same* stick up his butt for the rest of the Administration. Evidently, this will save an entire rain forest."

Tipper just kind of looked at me. And then said, "I'd go with your instinct."

The Marine band made me even more nervous. They were behind us on the stage. After the rest of us on the dais had taken our seats, the band played the Gores on with the official vice president's march, which I didn't know existed, and then the President and First Lady entered to "Hail to the Chief." Then they announced the honor guard, which was comprised of servicemen from each branch of the military. Bearing the colors and marching in step down the center aisle, they were a

somber, imposing presence. Watching them, all I could think about were the men and women who died defending our country. Then the Marine band played the national anthem, which everyone sang with patriotic solemnity. "I'm fucked," I thought. This wasn't exactly warming up the crowd. As we sat down, I turned to Tipper, who was next to me, and said, "This is kind of heavy."

She nodded with a knowing "Yeah."

Fortunately, the Marine band and honor guard left, and we ate dinner. I used the time to study my cards and make a monumental decision: whether to do a Nixon joke. Nixon had died the day before, and I was of two minds. On the one hand, it seemed like too significant an event to ignore. On the other, there was the danger of offending everyone and crashing and burning. Fortunately, I have a lot of friends who know Washington. Jonathan Alter of *Newsweek* told me everyone would be *expecting* a Nixon joke, and I'd be crazy not to do one. Norm Ornstein of the American Enterprise Institute said I'd be insane to take the risk.

"Ladies and gentlemen, I'm a little scared tonight. See, I was feeling pretty good a week ago, because I had about twenty minutes of dynamite Nixon material."

That was the joke I decided *not* to do. The whole honor guard thing had spooked me. Instead I started like this:

"Thank you. Thank you very much. First let me just say what a tremendous honor it is to be asked to speak at the White House Correspondents dinner. To be able to perform for the President, the First Lady, the Vice President, Mrs. Gore . . . Wolf Blitzer . . . a dream come true."

That got a nice laugh. Proving my theory that Wolf Blitzer is a funny name. I followed with about thirty minutes of non-Blitzer material. And, I don't know how to say this without seeming self-serving and egotistical, but I *destroyed*. What I

did early on was brilliant, really, laying down the groundwork for the possibly offensive jokes to come:

"Before I go any further, a small caveat. I've never really performed for a Washington crowd like this, and I don't know your sensibilities. Now, there are a couple jokes in here that might be a little risky. So, if I do a joke tonight that offends anyone, if I say something completely out of line, if I make a total jerk of myself, I will simply apologize and move on. I mean, it seems to have worked for Alan Simpson." Big laugh.*

So I went right into a potentially offensive joke:

"I was doing some Washington star-gazing at the pre-dinner cocktail parties. I saw Ed Rollins. I like Ed. Though he does brag a lot. At the party I overheard Ed bragging that while in college he paid a prostitute five hundred dollars to do nothing." Big laugh.

"Now, tonight's dinner is being aired live on C-SPAN. Those of you watching at home might want to flip back and forth to C-SPAN 2, because there's a fascinating panel discussion from the Shorenstein-Barone Center on the Press, entitled 'Constant Self-Reevaluation—Useful Exercise or Giant Wankathon?' I can't wait to see what side Marvin Kalb comes down on. I think Wankathon. Don't you?"

Huge laugh. Now I'm cooking. I go right into:

"By the way, for those of you listening on radio. Seated at the head table are . . . Terrance Hunt of the Associated Press; David Brock of the *American Spectator*; Lani Guinier of Philadelphia, Pennsylvania; the President of the United States; to his left, Zoe Baird of New Haven, Connecticut; Hector and Consuelo Vasquez, Ms. Baird's driver and nanny,

---

* During the previous year, Simpson had been forced to apologize to Nina Totenberg, the women of America, and Peter Arnett. A little inside, but remember, this is a scrap metal convention.

also of New Haven and Tegucigalpa, Honduras; Arkansas state trooper Bobby Fortenberry; to his left, the MacDougals of Little Rock, Arkansas; the First Lady; businessman Nyungen Binh Hac, who I understand is a friend of Ron Brown's, of Ho Chi Minh City and Los Angeles; his wife Mai Kao Hac, and their four children. Admiral Bobby Ray Inman is expected momentarily."

Huge laughs. Rolling laughs. The President's laughing, Hillary is *shaking*. I'm almost embarrassed, frankly, describing how well I did. But it was really something! In fact, you know what? I think it might be less embarrassing if I didn't describe it myself and just let you read some of John Podhoretz's review from the *New York Post*.

> . . . if you happened to be channel-zapping Saturday night and stopped on C-SPAN, you would have seen some dazzling comedy from the man who ought to be the next post-midnight star . . . as his brilliant and utterly fearless monologue proved, he has exactly the hard edge and political sophistication that could make the "Late Late Show with Al Franken" a cultural phenomenon . . . The cleverness of these Beltway barbs was to be expected from the man responsible in part for some of the most brilliant political satire of our time . . .

I mean I was cooking! In comedy terms, I strode the Earth as a colossus.

Go ahead. Read it again.

> . . . if you happened to be channel-zapping Saturday night and stopped on C-SPAN, you would have seen some dazzling comedy from the man who ought to be the next post-midnight star . . . as his brilliant and

utterly fearless monologue proved, he has exactly the hard edge and political sophistication that could make the "Late Late Show with Al Franken" a cultural phenomenon . . . The cleverness of these Beltway barbs was to be expected from the man responsible in part for some of the most brilliant political satire of our time . . .

That. Is a hell of a review!

(The full text of Mr. Podhoretz's review can be found on the Internet via ftp at nypost.com, under the file podhoretz/reviews/sycophantic/franken.)

27

PHIL GRAMM: EVERYBODY'S
FAVORITE BASTARD

o far, every bit of polling evidence seems to suggest that the more people get to know Phil Gramm, the less they like him.

As I write this in August, he's slipped from double to single digits in the national polls and is down to 5 percent in New Hampshire. Talking to Judy Woodruff on CNN's *Inside Politics*, Gramm ascribed his slippage to the statistical inadequacies of the polls themselves. "These polls, you've gotta remember, Judy, have a margin of error of seven points."

Which conceivably could put him at negative 2 percent.

It's not surprising that people aren't taking to him. Gramm himself admits that he sometimes rubs people the wrong way. "I didn't come to Washington to be loved," he likes to say, "and I haven't been disappointed."

That's the bravado of an anti-government budget hawk. But it also exhibits a hint of the sort of self-deprecating humor that voters like so much in their politicians. "I'm going to test whether, in the age of television, someone as ugly as I am can get elected President."*

That's likeable. But consider for a minute that Gramm wasn't referring to mere *physical* ugliness.

Here, after all, is a man who wants to cut food stamps because: "We're the only nation in the world where all our poor people are fat."

Here, too, is a fellow who started off a meeting of his Senate reelection campaign by telling his staff, "I can do any one of your jobs as well as you, but I don't have the time."

During a floor debate on social security, another senator argued that the legislation under consideration would hurt people over 80. Gramm's response: "Most people don't have the luxury of living to be 80 years old, so it's hard for me to feel sorry for them."

And there was the time that an elderly black widow approached Gramm after a speech in Texas. When she told him that his proposals to cut social security and Medicare would make it difficult for people like her to remain independent, Gramm replied, "You haven't thought about a new husband, have you?"

Basically, Gramm is a big jerk.

But I get the feeling that he considers this his biggest strength. Gramm has been counting on his reputation as the

* No.

Senate's Angriest White Male, plus his huge campaign war chest, to carry him to the nomination.

Why isn't it working?

Some say it's because Gramm is the biggest hypocrite in the race. Gramm told the last Republican convention: "In all the world, only in Cuba and North Korea and in the Democratic party in America do we still have organized political groups who believe that the answer to every problem is more government." Yet Gramm himself has lived off the government his entire life. David Segal of the *Washington Monthly* writes:

> The government helped bring him into this world (he was born in a military hospital), funded his upbringing (his father was an army sergeant), paid for him to attend private school (with GI insurance money Gramm's mother received when her husband died), and even picked up the tab for graduate school (thanks to a National Defense Fellowship). After getting his Ph.D., Gramm got a job at Texas A&M, which is state-run, was elected to the House of Representatives, and then to the Senate. In sum, Phil Gramm joined the government rolls the first day of his life and has never left.

And being anti-government hasn't stopped Gramm from backing ridiculously expensive projects like the Superconducting Supercollider that bring federal money back to Texas. "I'm carrying so much pork, I'm beginning to get trichinosis," he once bragged to a local paper.

But I don't think Gramm's lack of physical charisma, his general nastiness, or even his blatant hypocrisy are to blame for his failure to catch on with Republican voters. I think the real problem is his boob fetish.

Bear with me a minute. I can support this.

Let's wade in slowly. When Larry King asked him last March if he'd consider a woman as his running mate, Gramm replied, "Sophia Loren is not a citizen." Okay. So far, so good.

In June, I was watching a CNN report on Gramm in which he discussed his use of the local library as a schoolboy: "We always went there eagerly awaiting the arrival of the next edition of *National Geographic* to look at all those ladies from faraway places who were topless in the magazine." Mighty incriminating. In fact, I could probably rest my case there. But I haven't even played my high card yet.

Much has already been made of Gramm's $7,500 investment in a soft-core porn movie in 1974. First of all, it's worth mentioning that many people call soft core movies "tit" films. But even more damning is the account offered in the *New Republic* by Gramm's former brother-in-law, George Caton, with whom Gramm invested the money.

Caton describes the moment that Gramm's interest in the investment potential of nudie films was first piqued, viewing rushes from the work-in-progress *Truck Stop Women:* "It really got Phil titillated because there was frontal nudity in it." Pow! Really puts the nail in the coffin, don't you think?

So Gramm's got a boob fetish, which is why the religious right doesn't trust him. And without their support, Gramm has no chance of getting the nomination. But that hasn't stopped Gramm from doggedly pursuing his party's nod. So doggedly, in fact, that he's working his poor wife, Wendy, nearly to death.

Mrs. Gramm was hospitalized with heatstroke in July after Rollerblading a hilly fifty-mile leg of the Cycle Across Maryland Tour in sweltering ninety-plus degree heat. According to the Associated Press she had been "combining her love of skating with efforts to boost support for her husband." Most

of the participants rode bikes, but Mrs. Gramm chose to Rollerblade, I guess because it's harder to wave to crowds when you're holding on to handlebars. Also, none of the other participants were scheduled to attend a series of campaign lunches and evening events along the route.

Barbara Bush was never asked to do anything like this.

But if you get beyond the fact that Gramm is ugly, mean, hypocritical, mammario-fetishistic, and drives his wife like a mule, he does have a certain folksy charm. Take, for example, Gramm's hardworking little buddy, Dickey Flatt, a printer from Mexia, Texas. According to Gramm: "Whether you see Dickey Flatt at the PTA or the Boy Scouts or at his church, try as he may he never quite gets that blue ink off the end of his fingers."

Gramm's respect for Dickey Flatt is so great that he's devised a philosophy of governance based on the man. Gramm claims that he won't support any government program which fails the "Dickey Flatt test"; namely, "Is it worth taking money from Dickey Flatt" to pay for the program?

Back in 1994, Gramm-watcher David Segal actually called Dickey to ask whether several programs Gramm had proposed or supported passed the Dickey Flatt test. Dickey's responses ranged from "No, that would not pass the test" to "That is just an *awful* idea, absolutely *awful*."

I'm sure a number of Gramm's proposals would pass the Dickey Flatt test. One of these might be welfare reform, where Gramm has led the charge to get rid of Aid to Families with Dependent Children, make cuts in Medicaid and turn it into a block grant, cut home heating allowances and food stamps, and deny assistance to welfare moms who can't find work. He admitted on *Meet the Press* that there would be some pain: "And I know, when we begin welfare reform, you'll have every horror story imaginable brought up. You can't change this mammoth system without hurting some people."

Gramm seems to be saying that the big challenge in reforming welfare will be to ignore these horror stories of pain and suffering. I agree. In fact, I think the larger challenge here is not just to ignore these stories, but to *laugh* at them.

That's why I've come up with my own Dickey Flatt test. I call it the Stewey Moss test. Stewey's a guy I went to grade school with. Now, just about every third-grade class in America has one kid who thinks it's funny to blow up a frog with a cherry bomb. Stewey was that kid.

I decided to construct a welfare horror story based on the Gramm cuts, but not to print the story unless it passed the Stewey Moss test. That is, unless it made Stewey laugh.

I looked Stewey up. When I reached him at his printing shop in Canadia, Minnesota, I said, "Stewey, do you still derive perverse pleasure from laughing at the misfortune of others?"

"Did Rose Kennedy own a black dress?!" he chuckled. Same old Stewey.

I explained the premise of the Stewey Moss test, and I must say Stewey was flattered and eager to participate.

"Okay," I said. "It's 1997, and the Gramm welfare reform plan has gone into effect. Let's say there's this housewife and she has two little kids, and her husband, who makes about $38,000 a year, suddenly dies."

"That's funny. How did he die?"

"I don't know, Stewey. Maybe a car accident."

"How about some teenager drops a bowling ball off a highway overpass? That's funny."

"Fine. Anyway, the husband had no life insurance, so the wife is left with almost no money. And what she does have is quickly dissipated by mortgage payments."

"Why doesn't she get a job?"

"Well, she does. But there's a lot of unemployment in her area, so the best she can do is a job at a fast-food place."

"Who's taking care of the kids?"

"You're ahead of me. Actually, she can't afford child care, so the kids sort of take care of themselves. So, one day, her little girl gets sick."

"Funny."

"So, the mom stays home from work to take care of her daughter, and she gets fired. And now she's considered an able-bodied adult who refuses to work, so she's ineligible for any cash assistance."

"And this could happen?"

"Yes. Under Gramm's plan."

"Well, then I'm laughin'!"

"Wait. So the girl's really sick, and the mom takes her to the hospital. But it's late November and the state's run out of its block grant for Medicaid. They can't spend any money on Medicaid cases till January, so she's out of luck."

"What's wrong with the kid?"

"We're not sure. In fact, she has something that requires a lot of investigative work. So the mom spends her last four hundred dollars on tests, only to find out they need to do more tests."

"That is fucking hysterical."

"So there's no money, and the bank repossesses the house."

"I'm on the floor."

"Wait, wait. So now she and the kids have to sleep in the car, except that they also repossess the car, so they go to a shelter."

"That's good! A lot of crazies in a shelter!"

"Right. And mom and the kids are totally freaked out. The girl's still sick, and just when they're thinking life couldn't possibly get any worse, the shelter gets closed down for lack of funds."

"Stop, I'm peeing my pants!"

"So, they have to sleep on the street. And there's a cold

snap, so during the night the sick little girl freezes to death. What do you think?"

"I love it. But could the girl be frozen in some kind of weird position?"

"Hmmm. How 'bout she's frozen like Rodin's 'Thinker'?"

"That is fuckin' *hi*larious!"

"So it passes the Stewey Moss test?"

"Absolutely! But one thing. Under the Gramm plan, is there any chance the government might just mow down destitute kids with machine guns?"

"No, Stewey."

"Just asking."

28

FUN WITH NEXIS

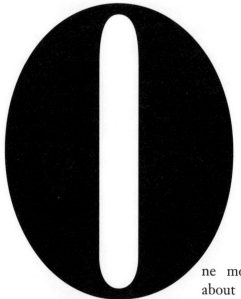

ne more obnoxious thing about Gramm that I didn't cover in the last chapter: he's a famous publicity hog. In fact, he's the absolute worst. And I can prove it too.

Here's how. You've probably heard this joke construction:

The most dangerous place in *(blank)* is between *(blank)* and a camera.

It's used a lot. I first heard it as: "The most dangerous place in Washington is between Phil Gramm and a camera." That

doesn't prove much. Since then I've also heard: "The most dangerous place in the capital is between Newt Gingrich and a camera" and "The most dangerous place in the world is between Alan Dershowitz and a camera."

So I asked Geoff to do a Nexis search. For those readers not familiar with the latest advances in database technology, a Nexis search is something that allows us, at no small expense, to search hundreds of magazines and newspapers for articles which mention a certain person, subject, or key phrase.

For example, let's say you wanted to look up all references to Gingrich's first wife. You would type in: Gingrich AND geometry teacher. Or you might type in: Gingrich AND deadbeat dad. Or: Gingrich AND cancer surgery.

> Gingrich AND geometry teacher yielded 33 stories.
> Gingrich AND deadbeat dad yielded 188 stories.
> Gingrich AND cancer surgery yielded 91 stories.

You get the idea. Well, I wanted to test my theory that it is more dangerous to stand between Phil Gramm and a camera than between anyone else and a camera. So I asked Geoff to perform this search:

> dangerous w/10 [within ten words] between w/15 camera.

Nexis spat out 64 stories, which Geoff went through very painstakingly. The results were fascinating. Most important, they proved me right.

Twenty-three stories had nothing to do with the line: "the most dangerous place to stand is between *(blank)* and a camera."

The remaining 41 stories, however, all contained that joke construction. Here's how it broke down:

Phil Gramm—19

politicians—4

Newt Gingrich—3

congressmen—2

O.J. trial legal experts—2

O.J. lawyers—1

Alan Dershowitz—1

Bill Bennett—1

Jesse Jackson—1

Chuck Schumer—1

Stephen Jones (Tim McVeigh's lawyer)—1

Dallas mayor Steve Bartlett—1

Senators—1

Pat Leahy—1

professional mediator Bill Usery—1

"a certain congressman" (probably Phil Gramm)—1

The evidence clearly indicates that it is at least six times more dangerous to stand between Phil Gramm and a camera than between anybody else and a camera.

A couple of interesting sidelights. As I thought, the joke *was* originally used in reference to Phil Gramm. It first appeared in a 1982 *New York Times* article entitled "Texan Irks Colleagues on Budget."

The Nexis also kicked up a 1994 syndicated column by Molly Ivins in which she writes of Gramm: "I swear to God,

he once nearly trampled me and Marilyn Schwartz of the *Dallas Morning News* to get in front of a lens at the Republican national convention in '88."

So it's not just a clever joke. Apparently, it really *is* dangerous to stand between Phil Gramm and a camera.

This whole exercise was actually a lot of fun. And since we had Nexis up and cranking, I thought we'd just go to town. Really kick out the Nexis jams. It cost me not a few simoleons, but Geoff and I were having a great time. And it was certainly easier than actually sitting down and writing something.

And so we spent the rest of the day typing in search requests:

Packwood AND tongue	336 stories
Gingrich AND grotesque	432
Specter AND hopeless	452
Pat Robertson AND crazy OR nutty OR lunatic	677
Gingrich AND bizarre	992
Limbaugh AND fat	1,084
Buchanan AND racist	1,089
D'Amato AND corruption OR crooked	1,310
Gingrich AND frankly	3,908
Clinton AND sex	33,948
Dole AND mean	53,695
Al Franken AND egomaniac	2

I'm thinking of doing a whole book of these. If you have any good search ideas please send them to the same address listed for the death threats.

29

ARLEN! ARLEN! ARLEN! AND OTHER THOUGHTS ON THE '96 ELECTION

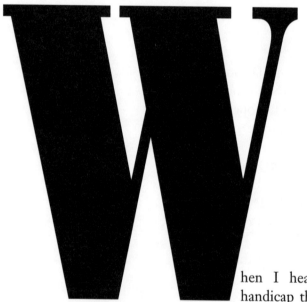

hen I hear pundits handicap the '96 Republican race, I'm always surprised that they leave Arlen Specter out of the first tier of candidates.

He has so much going for him: he's from a big state with a large number of delegates and electoral votes. He's been a U.S. senator for fourteen years. He got a lot of name recognition from the Clarence Thomas hearings, where he attacked Anita Hill for making accusations about sexual harassment.

Speaking of the women's vote, he's pro-choice! And best of all, he's Jewish, with access to a lot of pro-Israel money.

If I were Arlen Specter, I would assign a transition team right now.

But first things first, I guess. Planning his coronation at the Republican convention. I've been trying to envision it since Specter announced his candidacy, and I've decided it will look something like this:

First of all, lots of signs. But they won't say "Specter." Focus groups will show that the name "Specter" scares people. So the signs will read "Arlen." And when Wyoming puts him over the top, there'll be thousands of grassroots Republican loyalists who have worked years just for this moment, all chanting at the top of their lungs, "Arlen!" "Arlen!" "Arlen!"

The theme of the Arlen Convention, as it will come to be known, will be "The Big Tent." Or perhaps, "The Huge Tent." Or maybe, "The Extraordinarily Large Tent." There'll be a big Christian Coalition press conference on the eve of the convention, where Ralph Reed will back off from his threat to oppose any ticket with a pro-abortion nominee. Instead, Reed announces he'll support any Republican ticket that doesn't include a nominee who has actually *performed* an abortion.

I've been giving this a lot of thought. As I see it, there are two possible scenarios that could lead to an Arlen Convention. The first is a plane crash. A 747 carrying Dole, Gramm, Buchanan, and Alexander crashes . . . on top of Newt Gingrich and Colin Powell.

The second is a bus crash. It plays out kind of the same way.

WHAT IN GOD'S NAME IS ARLEN SPECTER THINKING?

REALLY. What is he *thinking*?

Forgetting he's pro-choice in today's Republican party.

Forgetting that the women for whom that would be attractive mostly remember him as the man who accused Anita Hill of committing perjury. Forgetting that he's humorless and pasty-looking. He's Jewish!

See, I've been following the whole Colin Powell phenomenon, and it's led me to one indisputable conclusion: The first Jew to be elected President of the United States will have to be a four-star general.

That gave me the idea of looking for a Jew in the military that we could start grooming for a run at the White House. So I had Geoff do some research. Unfortunately, it turns out that the highest-ranking Jew in the armed forces right now is Comptroller of the Coast Guard.

As I write this, we have no idea of what General Powell will do in '96. Perot showed us in '92 that Americans are yearning for a figure who can rise above the partisan bickering of our two national parties. Someone who can inspire us and move us forward together. Polls show, however, that this time Americans would prefer someone who hasn't claimed that he and a guard dog once fought five mysterious intruders on his front lawn.

Of course, if Powell doesn't run every Republican candidate has the general at the top of his short list for running mate. All except for Alan Keyes. As if Keyes doesn't have enough disadvantages. In addition to being unknown and unemployed, he's the only Republican candidate who might actually *lose* points by putting Colin Powell on the ticket.

I have given a lot of thought to the composition of the '96 Republican ticket. The danger of writing a book like this is that by the time it comes out everything will have changed. In politics a month can be a lifetime, and books take a lot of lead time. You've got to write the book, pose for the cover, then wait. You should know that, as I'm writing this, it is March 1978. So at the risk of looking foolish, here are some thoughts.

Assuming Dole wins the nomination, and there's no reason not to assume that, other than no one in the Republican party seems to really want him . . . assuming he wins the nomination, he has to use the second spot on the ticket to address the age problem. He has to pick someone young enough to represent a different generation and yet experienced enough to take over if, God forbid, Dole only reaches normal U.S. life expectancy.

Dole's been joking about the age issue in his speeches lately: "I'll put Strom Thurmond on the ticket for age balance." Actually, I didn't start worrying about Dole's age until after I heard that joke. Maybe he's lost it.*

By the way, for the record, I like Strom Thurmond because he's the only senator who still refers to a microphone as "the machine."

I think New Jersey governor Christine Whitman would make a good running mate for Dole. True, she's pro-choice and the Christian right already doesn't trust Dole, so they might take a hike. But the Republicans need women, and she's smart and tough. Plus, I have a theory about Christine Whitman that I've never heard anyone else articulate. Here it is: Americans love royalty. No couple represents royalty to Americans more than Prince Charles and Princess Di. Christine Whitman is a dead-on cross between Prince Charles and Princess Di.

So I think Christine Whitman would be a good addition to any ticket. For other vice presidential possibilities, you have to look first to the field of presidential candidates. Since the Eagleton debacle in '72 and the Quayle draft-deer-in-head-

---

* During the Reagan Administration, Dole was present at a ceremony that included every living ex-president. Looking at a tableau of Ford, Carter, and Nixon, Dole said, "There they are: Hear No Evil, See No Evil, and Evil."

lights near-disaster in '88, it's become clear that it's safest to pick someone who's already run for the nomination and lost. That way the media have already, supposedly, investigated the person, and they're afraid to come up with any new bombshells because it would make it look like they didn't do their job during the primaries.

So let's say Gramm wins the nomination. You could have a Gramm-Lugar ticket. Although Lugar is considered unlucky. He announced his candidacy the day of the Oklahoma City bombing. So . . . Gramm-Buchanan. Wow! Or . . . Buchanan-Gramm! No, wait! Buchanan-Dornan!

By the way, I talked to Bob Dornan yesterday. We met a couple years ago on Bill Maher's *Politically Incorrect*, and we talk occasionally. After the White House Correspondents dinner he called me, sounding annoyed: "Someone told me you did a rough joke about me. What was it?"

I told him the joke, which you've read already: "Having Al D'Amato lead an ethics investigation is like getting Bob Dornan to head up a mental health task force."

There was a beat on the other end of the phone, then, "Oh yeah, that's fine."

Anyway, yesterday I told Dornan I was trying to envision an Arlen Specter convention. So I asked if he had any idea what a Dornan convention might look like. I said I thought it would be very militaristic. He said, "Right. We'd have a parade of tanks and an overfly of B-2's."*

Back to vice presidential possibilities (of which Dornan is not realistically one, because he's a crazy homophobe).

Jack Kemp. He's an economic conservative. He ran for

---

* Here's a funny thing I read about Bob in *Newsweek*. Apparently, during his brief career as a fighter pilot, he crashed three jets and a helicopter. I'm not sure how much that cost taxpayers, but I'm pretty certain it's more than he's going to get in presidential matching funds.

president in '88. And he has demonstrated, more than any other Republican, a desire to expand the party to include more blacks and minorities. Which is why no Republicans actually voted for him in '88.

But in a general election, many political observers believe Kemp would attract millions of black votes. Mainly, this is about his support of ideas like empowerment zones and tenant ownership of low-cost housing. But on more than a few occasions, I've heard pundits say that minorities are comfortable with Jack Kemp because he's a former NFL quarterback. As Newt Gingrich once said admiringly, "Jack Kemp has probably showered with more blacks than most Republicans have shaken hands with."

I've heard the same kind of thing said about Bill Bradley, and it always strikes me as odd. But I suppose there's something to it. So as a service to my readers, a short list:

POLITICIANS WHO HAVE SHOWERED WITH BLACKS

Sen. Bill Bradley (D–N.J.)—New York Knicks— showered with Walt Frazier, Willis Reed, and Earl Monroe

Rep. Jim Bunning (R–Ky.)—Philadelphia Phillies— showered with Dick Allen, Curt Flood, and Ferguson Jenkins

Jack Kemp (former Sec. HUD)—Buffalo Bills—showered with Haven Moses and O.J. Simpson

Rep. Steve Largent (R–Okla.)—Seattle Seahawks— showered with John L. Williams, Curt Warner, and Ken Easley

Rep. J.C. Watts (R–Okla.)*—Oklahoma Sooners—
showered with Billy Sims

This is obviously not a complete list. I'm guessing, for example, that Congressman Mel Reynolds has showered with at
least one underage black woman. The point is that if Jack
Kemp had stayed in the league one more year, he could have
also showered with Al Cowlings. That has no relevance to
anything in particular, but it would have made my list more
interesting.

* Is himself black

30

PAT BUCHANAN: NAZI LOVER

In case you've reached this point in the book and are saying to yourself: "Why should I listen to this guy? He doesn't know anything. The only stuff he *pretends* to know comes from his research assistant. *And* he just wasted forty-five seconds of my life, which I will never get back, making me read a list of politicians who have showered with blacks." In case you're saying that to yourself, let me show you a little something from the 1992 year-end issue of *Rolling Stone* magazine:

Comedy Central aired its own live coverage of both conventions alongside the sober networks, with comedian Al Franken anchoring . . . But Comedy Central could get serious, too. Franken sensed—and said —that the ugly tone of Pat Buchanan's speech was a mistake for the Republicans, that it would backfire. It wasn't until days or even weeks later that the traditional pundits called the speech the beginning of the end for the Bush campaign. It was disorienting to watch a comedy broadcast that almost incidentally told more truth and offered more insight than most networks and newspapers and at the same time was so much more comfortable to watch.

Yep. That's right. I was the only one. Not Dan Rather, not Tom Brokaw, not Peter Jennings, not even Cokie Roberts, none of them understood what I, the guy you're doubting, understood: that Pat Buchanan was scaring America and guaranteeing that George Bush would receive the lowest percentage of popular votes of any incumbent president in American history.

Please understand that I called it *during* the speech. See, our Comedy Central convention coverage, which by the way was sponsored by Mentos, was comprised largely of live, simultaneous commentary on the speeches. This requires a quick wit and a commanding knowledge of the broader sweep of world history insofar as it applies to contemporary American politics. Also it's good if you can get an advance copy of the speech and have a small team of writers feeding you lines.

Unfortunately, we didn't get an advance copy of Buchanan's speech. If we had, I could have looked like a genius by predicting that he would make not one, not two, not three, but four attacks on homosexuals.

Maybe I should have expected this from a man who had

once said about AIDS: "The homosexuals have declared war upon nature and nature is exacting an awful retribution." But why *four* attacks? This was, after all, the first prime-time speech of the 1992 Republican convention. America was watching, and America got the message: Pat Buchanan really hates gay people.

But the high point was when Buchanan announced that "there is a religious war going on in our country." I'm sorry, but when you're Jewish and you hear "religious war," you get nervous. We haven't done well in religious wars. At least, not before 1949.

Back to Buchanan's speech. "And in that struggle for the soul of America, Clinton and Clinton are on the other side, and George Bush is on our side." And the Republicans on the floor were screaming with delight. Fists were in the air! It was really something.

So I said, "Is it just me, or is Pat Buchanan making a big mistake? Isn't he just scaring people?" And it *was* just me. Everywhere else on TV, analysts were saying that this was just the kind of "red meat" needed to energize the right and get them working for George Bush. And I was saying, "Wow! Aren't the Bush people upset? This is going to cost them California. And the Rust Belt states of Ohio, Illinois, and Michigan. Why, if Perot decides to reenter the race, I'll bet Bush doesn't get more than 38 percent of the popular vote and only picks up 168 electoral votes to Clinton's 370." Or something like that; I can't remember my exact words.

And so, in keeping with my record of fearless, ahead-of-the-curve punditry, I'd like to make a little prediction right here.

He's going to do it again.

Only this time it will be worse. Because this time the people screaming will be his delegates. In fact, I believe that Pat Buchanan may very well win the nomination. That gives you

some idea how low my regard is for Republican primary voters. I know that's an ad hominem attack on millions of people I've never met. But let me tell you a little about Pat Buchanan.

Where to begin?

First of all, he's the only man running for president who has assaulted a cop. Or at least bragged about it. In his autobiography, *Right from the Beginning*, Buchanan spends a number of pages relishing what was "among the great, dumb deeds of my life." It occurred two weeks before his twenty-first birthday and involved, basically, getting pulled over for speeding, cursing out two police officers, resisting arrest, and then kicking one of them in the ass: "I put a size 10½ cordovan where I thought it might do some good."

As the *New Republic* put it in their 1990 review, "Much of his memoir is a gleeful recounting of brawls, including ones in which he and his brother Hank ganged up on single victims, or 'sucker-punched' guys who deserved it. The book is suffused with a thug's love for combat."

Evidently, Buchanan's love for combat had its limits. After being expelled from college for the assault, he received a 4-F for a bad knee (presumably not the one used to kick the cop's butt), and never served in the military. In case you're concerned, the knee healed nicely, and now Buchanan's daily jogs keep him fit and trim.

Buchanan's beliefs were shaped by his father, William Buchanan, an accountant whose heroes included Joe McCarthy and Francisco Franco. The Buchanans were of Irish and Scotch-Irish ancestry, not Apache as Pat's current "no-immigrant" policy might suggest, and were devout Catholics. "We lived in a world of clarity and absolutes."

One of those absolutes is the belief in the superiority of Christianity. When asked about that earlier this year, Buchanan said, "I believe that Jesus Christ is the son of God and

is actually God and that that is the path to salvation, so quite obviously I believe it's superior to Buddhism and Taoism and other faiths, yes." I'm fine with that, I guess. But, not to be flippant, will someone explain to me how Jesus can be both the *son* of God and also God. Does it have something to do with the Holy Trinity? Help me here; I'm from an inferior religion.

This superiority appears to extend mainly to *white* Christians. As a speechwriter in the Nixon White House, Buchanan was a vehement opponent of integration. In a memo obtained from the Nixon archives, Buchanan called Martin Luther King, Jr., "one of the most divisive men in contemporary history" (remember, this is a memo to *Richard Nixon*), and later wrote the president that "the ship of integration is going down. It's not our ship."

Not surprisingly, Buchanan saw no problem with apartheid, and in another memo to Nixon referred to South Africa's 1960 Sharpeville Massacre, in which sixty-seven blacks were killed, as "whites mistreating a couple of blacks."

In fact, Buchanan admired the white regime in Pretoria so much that after Nixon resigned, he made a bid to become Gerald Ford's Ambassador to South Africa. I don't know why Ford turned him down. It would have been just so *perfect.*

By 1990, Buchanan was still defending apartheid, mocking those who believe "White rule of a Black majority is inherently wrong."

> . . . where did we get that idea? The Founding Fathers did not believe this. They did not give Indians, who were still living a tribal existence, the right to vote us out of North America. When they created the republic, they restricted the franchise to property-owning males, believing that not every man was qualified to rule, nor every people prepared for self-gov-

ernment. If the past 30 years taught us nothing else, it has surely taught us that. To elevate "majority rule" to the level of divine revelation is a heresy of the American idea.

Buchanan has repeatedly expressed disdain for what he called "the one man, one vote Earl Warren system," and once suggested "improving" the Bill of Rights to restrict voting to those who have paid at least $300 in taxes during the previous year. I wonder if there would be an adjustment for inflation on that.

Today, as America's preeminent nativist, Buchanan continues to spout this kind of racist and undemocratic piffle, to borrow a word from George Will. On restricting the immigration of Third World types, Buchanan made this point: "If we had to take a million immigrants in—say, Zulus—next year, or Englishmen, and put them in Virginia, what group would be easier to assimilate?" I think the Englishmen, don't you? But I think the million Zulus would do better than a million Pygmies.

Buchanan's point can be found in his rhetorical question, "Who speaks for the Euro-Americans, who founded the U.S.A. . . . Is it not time to take America back?"

Sure. Let's take it back! How? Buchanan proposes a literal Fortress America erected with border walls and trade barriers. A fierce opponent of NAFTA and GATT, Buchanan blames free trade for the loss of good-paying American jobs. That didn't stop him from buying a Mercedes-Benz and calling American cars "lemons" in 1992. When the Bush campaign criticized him for owning a German car, Buchanan said that his wife made him buy it.

Now, before I get into the Nazi stuff, I have a horrible confession. I've met Pat Buchanan. I spent some time with him over a four-day period. And I liked him very much.

It was during the 1988 Democratic convention in Atlanta, and I was there doing commentary for CNN. And of all the CNN people, Buchanan was the most accessible and unfailingly good-natured and charming. When I told my friends back in New York, I would invariably get a response like: "Yeah, well, Goebbels was charming."

That is so unfair. First of all, Goebbels wasn't charming. He was known as an ill-tempered backbiter.

Also, Goebbels was part of a small group that presided over the most horrible genocide in the history of man. Buchanan, on the other hand, has merely devoted a large part of his career to *defending* people like Goebbels.

Since the early 80s Buchanan has attacked "the hairy-chested Nazi hunters" in the Justice Department's Office of Special Investigations (OSI). "Why not devote those sources to going after organized crime . . . instead of running down 70-year-old camp guards."

John Demjanjuk was one of those 70-year-old camp guards. For years, Buchanan has defended Demjanjuk against charges that he was the infamous Ivan the Terrible of Treblinka and called him "the victim of a greater miscarriage of justice than Alfred Dreyfus." Dreyfus, of course, was guilty of nothing. Buchanan's defense of Demjanjuk was simple. He was a guard at a *different* concentration camp.

> The Soviets took testimony . . . from one Ignat Danilchenko, who said Demjanjuk was a member of his guard platoon at Sobibor . . . Yet at Demjanjuk's trial the witnesses against him all testified he was at Treblinka . . . Can a man be at two places at once?

Good point. What were the chances of someone like Demjanjuk being a guard at *two* camps? I'm guessing that this is why Buchanan supported the "Three Strikes and You're

Out" part of Clinton's crime bill. He thought it meant that to put a Nazi war criminal away, he had to be a guard at three separate camps.

Today Buchanan is fighting Demjanjuk's deportation, even though the former SS volunteer lied on his original visa application. By the way, did you know that to become a citizen of this country, there are different rules for ex-Communists and ex-Nazis? It's true. You can't get citizenship if you've *ever* been a Communist. You can't get citizenship if you were a Nazi *from 1939 to 1945*. It's probably a good policy. I'd trust a guy who became a Nazi in 1946. You know he's not a fair-weather friend.

Buchanan has proven that he, unlike most other politicians, is no fair-weather friend. Particularly if you're an accused former Nazi. But in a way, I trust Pat Buchanan. He is a man who stands by his principles. And the more repugnant and dangerous those principles, the smarter I'm going to look next summer when Pat Buchanan single-handedly scares the country into reelecting Bill Clinton.

31

THE MIDDLE-CLASS
SQUEEZE

his was going to be a fairly
exhaustive chapter on how
life is getting harder and harder for middle-class Americans.
How real wages are going down, how most couples now have
to work at two jobs to make ends meet.

I even had an especially obnoxious Limbaugh quote to start
the thing off. In *The Way Things Ought to Be* he writes: "Why
is it that whenever a corporation fires workers it is never spec-

ulated that the workers might have deserved it?" I've had the same thought about plane crashes.

Unfortunately, I just haven't been able to concentrate this week. See, over the weekend we drove up to my fourteen-year-old daughter's camp. As you already know, the book has suffered considerably because of my commitment to hands-on, always-there-for-you, sensitive-dad parenting. Which is why the Frankens serve as much better role models for the American family than the Doles, the Gingriches, the Reagans, the Wills, or the Wilsons.

Most of the time it's fun. But not this weekend. We drove up to Thomasin's camp to see her in a play. See, it's an arts camp. The kind that liberals send their kids to so they can get in touch with their creative sides.

Well, she got in touch all right. About halfway through the play, this six-foot, sixteen-year-old kid from Long Island with a ponytail planted one right on her lips. And two scenes later she kissed another guy. And then at the end of the play her character died of a drug overdose.

I've been having trouble dealing with it ever since. Frankly, it's been pretty tough to work with the image constantly running through my head of some long-haired punk from Long Island stealing the innocence of my only daughter.

My shrink said this is a normal part of the father-daughter relationship. He suggested I channel my emotions into a chapter on teenage promiscuity, illegitimacy, and AIDS.

That's when I decided to change therapists. The new one says I need to let go of this chapter and move on to something lighter and more fun.

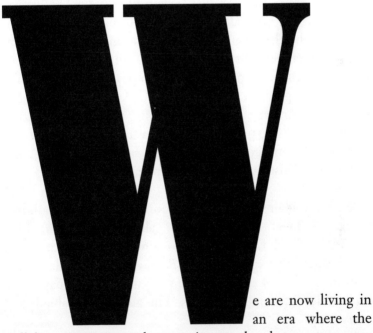

32

RUBBERNECKING ON THE INFOTAINMENT SUPERHIGHWAY

We are now living in an era where the wall between news and entertainment has been eaten away like the cartilage in David Crosby's septum.

That's why the Information Superhighway means different things to different people. To Al Gore it means out-of-work aerospace workers accessing a video classroom to retrain

themselves for the transition from a cold war economy to an information economy. To Clarence Thomas it means 24-hour-a-day pornography.

That's why I think the Information Superhighway should more accurately be called the Infotainment Superhighway. And why all of us who work in the media should be called "infotainers." Dan Rather is an infotainer. Maybe more info than tainer. Connie Chung is about half info, half tainer. Her husband, more tainer than info. Rush Limbaugh is a disinfotainer. (See rest of book.)

More Americans get their news from ABC News than from any other source. At least that's what they say on ABC News, which is where I got all the information for this book.

That's why the Disney–ABC deal had me so worried. You might remember Disney's proposed America Amusement Park in Virginia. Disney was going to pave over a Civil War battlefield to put up a theme park about American history. No irony there. Anyway, the park was going to have an attraction "simulating" the experience of being a slave. I looked into the plans for the attraction, and all I can say is that it is a gross distortion of history to have the Underground Railroad loop the loop.

With the mainstream getting more and more monolithic, thank goodness we've got the alternative media. Like C-SPAN. Which is all info and no tainment. Except that I did see an unexpectedly engrossing *Booknotes* interview last week with the author of the definitive analysis of sliding pay-scales for G-S level federal employees. The guy had visual aids and everything.

Sometimes I worry, though, that on the Infotainment Superhighway, a lot more people are driving on the tainment lanes than the info lanes. Either that or we've always been a nation of idiots. Because I've seen some polling statistics lately that are really scary. For example: Only 64 percent of

U.S. adults know that when it's winter in New York, it's summer in Australia. Only 53 percent know that Arabs and Jews "have been in conflict over Israel." More Americans can name the judge in the O.J. Simpson trial than the Speaker of the House.*

Speaking of the Speaker, during the '94 House race between Tom Foley and George Nethercutt, a third of the voters in their district believed that whoever won would become Speaker of the House.

My favorite, though, comes from a focus group survey done by Mark Mellman, one of the few Washington pollsters who bothered to return my call. When asked what they thought having dinner at their congressman's house would be like, a majority said they thought they would be served by uniformed servants and eat food that they had "never heard of before." Just out of curiosity, I called my congressman and asked him what he'd serve if I went to his house for dinner. He said, "Probably chicken." But who knows? Maybe it would be "chicken fandango" or something.

So I'm worried that a lot of people just aren't really thinking much about things these days. Which is kind of scary, because with all this new technology, there are a lot of big issues out there that aren't being discussed.

For example, there is one aspect of the Infotainment Superhighway that actually frightens me very much. In fact, I'm a little loathe to discuss it publicly. But maybe if it's out in the open, the Senate could hold a hearing on it or something. Because it's a real potential nightmare.

It involves the Internet. No, it's not pornography. It's something much more frightening. And that is the possibility, I think probability, that before long we will be seeing a new

* Lance Ito and Tom Foley

form of terrorism. Mark my words: one of these days you're going to turn on the news and hear some grisly report about a terrorist whom the media will dub "The E-mail Bomber."

Now, I don't know much about the Internet or how it works, but I imagine the E-mail bomber thing would happen this way. Some guy at a university or maybe a big computer company will log up or boot on or whatever. And he'll see a thing saying he has some E-mail. So he'll try to retrieve it, and KABLAM!!!

Pretty frightening, huh? That's why I don't go in for this Internet stuff. Way too dangerous.

33

ANOTHER FEARLESS POLICY
INITIATIVE FROM ME

here are some developments
along the Infotainment Su-
perhighway that I do find encouraging. As the father of two, I
was delighted when the Senate approved a proposal that
would give parents a tool to deal with television violence. The
tool is the v-chip (v for violence), and it would be installed
inside all TV sets 13 inches or larger. A panel would assign

each show a rating, which would then be encoded into the show's signal. Parents could then program their TV's to block out shows that are rated as violent.

The beauty is that the chip now only costs about five dollars, and that price will come down until it costs only cents per TV set. The question is, since we have the technology, why not give parents more options?

That's why I'm proposing a twenty-six-chip system that will *really* give us the tools we need to protect our children:

a-chip: blocks out any program containing the word "asshole."

b-chip: blocks out any program about Leona Helmsley.

c-chip: blocks out any program about Leona Helmsley.

d-chip: blocks out all docudramas.

e-chip: blocks out all programs explaining evolution.

f-chip: blocks out farting.

g-chip: blocks out Geraldo.

h-chip: blocks out all programs portraying whores. (Research shows most people believe "whore" starts with an "h.")

i-chip: blocks out all programs that have ironic content.

j-chip: blocks out Jerry Seinfeld, Ted Koppel, Billy Crystal, Paul Reiser, and me.

k-chip: kickboxing.

l-chip: blocks out all commercials for lawyers.

m-chip: blocks out Madonna.

n-chip: blocks out all news.

o-chip: blocks out all news about O.J. Simpson.

p-chip: either "pornography" or "politicians"—still under consideration.

q-chip: would block out programs with Harvey Fierstein, Barney Frank, and Bob Dornan.

r-chip: blocks out programs in which a woman's bosom is referred to as a "rack."

s-chip: blocks out all sitcoms.

t-chip: would block out all toilet humor, particularly "shit" jokes.

u-chip: blocks out all shows explaining the function of the uterus.

w-chip: blocks out all references to "wetlands."

x-chip: blocks out *The X-Files*.

y-chip: blocks out sex scenes where someone yells "yahoo!"

z-chip: blocks out zombie movies that contain adult language or where the zombies eat people.

34

ADVENTURES IN POLITICS
APRIL 29, 1995

WASHINGTON, D.C. WASHINGTON HILTON, WHITE
HOUSE CORRESPONDENTS ASSOCIATION DINNER.
I CHARM THE SOCKS OFF ARIANNA HUFFINGTON,
MEET NEWT GINGRICH, AND OFFEND AL D'AMATO

onan O'Brien gave me a call.
He had agreed to perform at the White House Correspondents dinner, and he was nervous. Conan said that the woman
from the White House Correspondents Association had told
him that the President was scheduled to speak first. Conan
told her that he was a little apprehensive about speaking af-

ter the President. And she informed him that speaking first had been the President's request, but suggested, "Why don't the two of you work this out between yourselves?"

Conan was nervous because of what had happened a few weeks earlier at the TV and Radio Reporters dinner, where the audience had jeered comedian Bill Maher. Like at the Correspondents dinner, the speaker at the TV and Radio dinner shares the dais with the President. Maher ran afoul of the audience, who felt he crossed the line with jokes like "Phil Gramm is so worried about immigration that he's thinking of deporting his wife." But they were particularly shocked when, discarding a joke, he said something like "fuck this one." In front of the President! A week later Garry Shandling, appearing on Maher's show *Politically Incorrect*, gave Bill some reassurance. "You were part of a long tradition of comedians offending presidents that started when Will Rogers said to FDR, 'Oh, yeah? Well, if you don't think that's funny, you can get out of your chair and blow me.'"

Conan ran through his material. He had a lot of great jokes, including this one: "Evidently, there was quite a disturbance when Pat Buchanan made his announcement for president. Some people jumped onstage and shouted that he was a racist. And those were his supporters!"

There was a joke that referred to a recent shooting incident. Al D'Amato shooting himself in the foot. A few weeks earlier, Senator Pothole had been on the Imus radio show and done an over-the-top Japanese stereotype impression of Judge Ito. It was real Jerry-Lewis-bucktooth-Coke-bottle-glasses stuff, particularly weird since Ito actually has a very strange accent that is not in the least bit Japanese. It created a big flap, and D'Amato had to apologize, but his apology was so weak (an "I'm sorry if anyone was offended" type of thing) that he had to apologize a second time. A couple days later he was rushed to the hospital with heart palpitations, which friends

said had been caused by "stress." Conan's joke was, "The entertainment tonight was either going to be me, or Senator D'Amato doing impressions." I suggested a refinement: ". . . me, or Senator D'Amato doing an impression of a Japanese guy having a heart attack."

Conan felt reassured after we talked. I did, too. I thought he had enough strong material to do very well, but not to do better than I had done.

I had been invited to the dinner by Josette Shiner, managing editor of the *Washington Times*, which most liberals outside the Beltway think of as "the Moonie paper" because it's owned by the Unification Church of the Reverend Sun Young Moon. But the *Times* has become a very well respected conservative paper, and for many in Washington a welcome alternative to the *Post*. Moon, I am told, is very hands-off in the day-to-day operation of the paper. For example, staffers are allowed to marry whomever they choose.

I had met Josette a few months before at the Renaissance Weekend, where we hit it off. See? Conservatives like me. And I like conservatives. As people. I'm a people person. The last night of Renaissance, Josette asked me if I had any questions for Newt. This was January 3rd, and she had an exclusive with Gingrich the next day, his first print interview since the '94 election. So I said, "Yeah. Why don't you ask him if he got the idea of churches filling in for government from his personal experience. From when he was a deadbeat dad, and his ex-wife's church had to take up a collection for his ex-wife and kids." Josette thought she might not have time to ask that.

Instead, she thought she might ask him about a discussion my wife, Franni, and I had had a few days earlier. Newt had called a press conference to announce that he was going to give up his 4.5-million-dollar book advance. I told Franni I

thought he was going to admit he had made an error in judgment. Franni said, "No, he's not that smart."

I said, "No, honey, he's really smart. He's unbelievably smart. He's going to apologize. He's going to say something like, 'It was wrong of me as the newly elected Speaker of the House to take a 4.5-million-dollar advance. It sent the wrong signal. We in Congress are here to serve the people, not line our pockets, and to the extent that I've undermined the public's trust, blah, blah, blah . . .' Something like that."

Franni said, "Well, if he's smart enough to apologize, I'm really scared."

At the press conference Gingrich did announce that he was taking a one dollar advance and a royalty in lieu of the 4.5 million. But instead of apologizing he just sprayed invective like a skunk. "We're about to have the first Republican Congress in forty years, and I did not want to walk in next Wednesday and give the embittered defenders of the old order something that they could run around and yell about." I hate it when my wife is right.

About a week before the Correspondents dinner, we received our tickets along with a seating chart, which had my wife next to the undersecretary of defense and me between Josette and Dr. Ruth Westheimer. When I called to give my wife's regrets (because of Little League, not the undersecretary of defense), Josette's assistant said, "Don't you just love who we put you next to?!" This is one of the curses of being a comedian. They think it's magic to put you next to somebody like Dr. Ruth.

I said, "Well . . . uh, yeah . . ." as diplomatically as possible, while still trying to bring home the point. Which I guess I did.

"Well . . . now that your wife's not coming, we will be rearranging the seating. Is there anyone you see on the chart who you'd like to sit next to?"

"Arianna Huffington."

Arianna (I call her Arianna now) is the wife of Michael Huffington, the oil heir who spent thirty or so million dollars in a losing bid for Dianne Feinstein's Senate seat. The Huffingtons had been the subject of a couple of particularly mean articles in the press. Sidney Blumenthal of the *New Yorker* had called Arianna "the most upwardly mobile Greek since Icarus," and in *Vanity Fair* Maureen Orth accused her of being a New Age cult priestess who yelled at her Mexican help.

Pretty horrible stuff. And I'd get to sit next to her! I called a few people in Washington who might know something about her, including Blumenthal. The consensus was this: When it comes to the Huffingtons, she's the brains of the outfit—and not merely by default.

She was educated at Cambridge University and was the first woman president of the Cambridge Debating Society. Also, she's quite striking, a Greek-born blonde (though not, strictly speaking, a blonde-born Greek), and incredibly charming. She'll do a Pamela Harriman on you. Rivet her attention, gaze into your eyes, make you feel like you're the most enchanting person in the world. Flatter you, laugh at your jokes.

Boy, do I like Arianna Huffington! Man oh man! Dinner was great. Although I can't remember what they served, Arianna was so fascinating. Or really, I was. Mainly I ragged on Newt. A number of people had told me that she had been raising money for his Empowerment Network, so I thought it'd be fun to tear into him. I guess I did it in such a funny and utterly charming way that she didn't take offense. Lines like, "What kind of sleazebag doesn't support his kids?" Witty stuff like that.

Josette, who was joining in when not engaging the undersecretary of defense, would occasionally defend the Speaker. He's made some mistakes, but he's admitted them, that sort of thing. Arianna talked about a TV show she was developing

called *Beat the Press*. The idea was to take on the press, which Arianna felt was getting more cynical and destructive. She said the show was to be produced by Four Point Entertainment, the producers of *American Gladiators*. "Oh, the Tiffany's of TV production," I said. She laughed. It was just delightful.

At one point we were talking about compassion. Arianna heads something called the Center for Effective Compassion. As opposed to ineffective compassion. Way too much of that going around. Republicans think that there has been a "tragedy of American compassion" this century, a phrase borrowed from the book by the same name.* The basic thesis is that liberals' compassion for the underclass had the unintended, or maybe not so unintended, consequence of creating an addiction to dependency and the bureaucracy of the welfare state. I said something about how sad a commentary it is on my generation that we were the ones to coin the phrase "compassion

---

* *The Tragedy of American Compassion* was written by Marvin Olasky with the financial support of the Heritage Foundation. At one point in the book Olasky seeks a "first-hand look at contemporary compassion to the poor," by dressing up like a street person and spending two whole days on the street. He comes away particularly disgusted with the treatment he received at a Congregational church:

> A sweet young volunteer kept putting food down in front of me and asking if I wanted more. Finally I asked, mumbling a bit, "Could I have a Bible?" Puzzled, she tried to figure out what I had said: "Do you want a bagel? A bag?" When I responded, "A Bible," she said, politely but firmly, "I'm sorry, we don't have any Bibles."

For Olansky, this event epitomizes the misguided sense of compassion of modern America. They'll feed your stomach but not your soul. I guess in Olasky's perfect world, a hungry man would walk into a soup kitchen and say, "Could I have a bagel?" And instead he'd receive the King James Bible and a polite but firm, "Not until you've read Second Corinthians."

fatigue." Arianna laughed again and talked about how charitable giving had gone up during the Reagan years. I said, "Yeah, but a lot of that was rich guys giving their hospital a colon cancer machine so it'd have one when they needed it." Arianna laughed.

Between dessert and the entertainment there was enough time to mill around and talk to people. I said hi to Wolf Blitzer, chatted briefly with the Israeli ambassador and then with Kennedy (the MTV VJ, not the bloated senator). Then I left the ballroom to hit the bathroom, and there in the hallway was Arianna standing with Newt.

"Al, you must meet the Speaker!" Now as I said, I'm a people person. So I tried.

"It is an honor to meet the Speaker of the House." It was the best I could do.

"You guys really helped us out at the end of the hundred days," he said with a friendly smile. He was referring to a bit Chris Farley, who played Newt on SNL, had done a few weeks earlier at the Capitol. It was a little surprise that NBC whipped up for the Speaker.

"I had nothing to do with that," I said pointedly. He seemed a little confused.

"It was a real boost. I was caught totally by surprise."

"Yeah, well, I had nothing to do with that." I felt that I made that clear, and I didn't want to be an asshole about it. "But Chris really had a good time, and couldn't talk about anything else for the whole week." Why am I sucking up to this guy? "Could I say something?" He nodded. You're not supposed to talk politics at these things. But how often would I get this chance? "I believe in the market system. I think that, at the end of the day, what you're doing will lead to a situation where the states are forced to compete with each other to drive out their poor by lowering benefits."

"What's wrong with that?" That's what he said. He was serious too.

Then Dennis Hopper walked up. "You, sir, are a great man. You are doing great things." He wasn't talking to me. Newt told Hopper how brilliant his performance was in *Blue Velvet*. How he loved Hopper's *intensity*. I started to feel like I was *in Blue Velvet*.

After Hopper left, Gingrich and I talked about Christina Jeffrey, the woman Gingrich had chosen as House historian. He dropped her like a hot potato when it was disclosed that she had once objected to a course on the Holocaust because it failed to present the Nazi and Ku Klux Klan points of view. He defended her, saying, "She's very anti-Semitic and very anti-racist."

"Can I quote you on that?" I wanted to know. Arianna explained to Newt what he had just said.

"I meant very anti-anti-Semitic." See, I get them mixed up all the time.

Conan did great that night. I was a little disappointed that he used his version of the D'Amato joke, but it got a big laugh.

After dinner, I headed over to what everyone considered the hip party, thrown by *Vanity Fair* magazine. When I walked in, I saw Al D'Amato standing in a corner. That's how hip this party was.

D'Amato's fiancée, former gossip columnist Claudia Cohen, recognized me, and when I approached, she introduced me to the senator. "He's from *Saturday Night Live.*"

He looked a little agitated. "What was that thing about my sistah having sex with a donkey?"

A couple weeks earlier cast member Mark McKinney had done a piece in which Judge Ito responds to D'Amato's impression with an impression of D'Amato's sister having sex with a donkey. "Oh datsa good! Oha I lika dat!"

I said, "Well, you know, I thought it was fair. It was Ito responding to something that you've admitted was a mistake."

"Well, I admit, I did think it was funny," he said, referring to McKinney's piece.

"Then deep down you probably thought it was fair."

"But my sistah?"

I didn't tell him that the NBC censors had made us change it from his mother having sex with a donkey to his sister. In the interest of good taste, I guess. "Okay. Maybe it wasn't fair to your sister. But it was fair to you."

"I don't know. My sistah having sex with a donkey?" Then he went on to say that he really didn't see what was so wrong with what he had done on Imus in the first place. And as long as we were on the general subject, I thought I'd take a little risk.

"I wrote a joke about you for Conan but he didn't use it."

"No, he used it. I thought it was funny."

"Yeah, well, I had a variation. It went, 'The entertainment was either going to be me or Senator D'Amato doing his impression of a Japanese guy having a heart attack.' "

The senator and his fiancée just looked at me.

See, I'm a people person.

35
MORE FUN WITH RUSH
LIMBAUGH'S FACT CHECKER

t's August, and we hadn't heard
from Rush's fact checker, Waylon, since June. Geoff left a
couple messages on his voice mail, but we didn't hear back
until yesterday. And once again, we got it all on tape.

Telephone ring

Geoff: Hello! Rush Limbaugh Is a Big Fat Idiot. How may I direct your call?

Waylon: Oh, I'm sorry. I thought I was calling Empower USA.

Geoff: Oh. You want the conservative think tank across the hall. Hold on a sec, I'll transfer you. *(Pause)* Hello! Empower USA. How may I direct your call?

Waylon: Geoff?

Geoff: Hi, Waylon! Haven't heard from you in a while.

Waylon: Yeah, sorry about that. I've been having a lot of trouble checking my voice mail. I keep forgetting my access code.

Geoff: Have you tried using your birthday?

Waylon: You can't really do that on this system. It only takes numbers.

Geoff: All-righty then . . . Why don't I put Mr. Franken on.

Al: Hi, Waylon! Megadittoes!

Waylon: What?

Al: Never mind. Listen, Waylon, we're preparing our annual report on the environment here at Empower USA, and we

just wanted to run a couple of Rush's comments by you before we publish them as incontrovertible fact.

Waylon: I'm your man.

Al: Okay, let's jump right in. First of all, back in 1991, Rush claimed that Styrofoam was biodegradable and paper wasn't.

Waylon: Right. I remember that. That is . . . uh . . . that's totally wrong.

Al: Oh.

Waylon: Yeah, we caught a lot of flak for that one.

Al: Okay. How about this one? In his book, *See, I Told You So*, Rush writes: "There are more acres of forestland in America today than when Columbus discovered the continent in 1492."

Waylon: Wait. Is that Chapter Fourteen?

Al: Uh-huh.

Waylon: Yeah. Here's the thing. I didn't do Chapter Fourteen. We had a temp in that week, so I just farmed it out.

Al: Really?

Waylon: Yeah, good kid. Didn't have a whole lot on the ball though. Just out of curiosity, *are* there more acres of forestland now than in 1492?

Al: No. Turns out Rush was off by about a quarter of a billion acres.

Waylon: Wow! Don't tell the Sierra Club.

Al: Don't worry. Let me ask you a little something about global warming.

Waylon: Doesn't exist.

Al: Fair enough. But in 1992 Rush said it wouldn't be a big deal if did exist because "Even if the polar ice caps melted, there would be no rise in ocean levels. . . . After all, if you have a glass of water with ice cubes in it, as the ice melts, it simply turns to liquid and the water level in the glass remains the same."

Waylon: Well, that's just common sense.

Al: Except that most of the world's ice is on land.

Waylon: Hold it. You lost me there.

Al: Antarctica. It's a continent, not an ice cube.

Waylon: Your point?

Al: If the ice cap melted, sea level around the world would rise about two hundred feet.

Waylon: Holy cow! We'd all drown!

Al: Calm down, Waylon.

Waylon: Calm down?! I've got a basement apartment!

Geoff: Sorry to jump on. But, Al, James Carville is on line two.

Waylon: James Carville? Isn't he the guy who ran the Dukakis campaign?

Al: Uh, no, Waylon. Actually, he ran the Clinton campaign.

Waylon: The *Clinton* campaign?! Why is he calling Empower USA?!

Al: You know, Waylon, I might as well come clean. There is no Empower USA. We're actually writing a book called *Rush Limbaugh Is a Big Fat Idiot*. . . . Waylon? . . . Waylon?

Waylon: I . . . I feel so violated.

Al: Yeah, well, gotta go. Megadittoes.

Waylon: Yeah, *right*.

36

REPUBLICANS AND ENVIRONMENTAL REGULATION: LIKE MIXING OIL AND WATER. LITERALLY.

I hope you loved that Waylon bit as much as I did. Well, I didn't really. I think I've reached a point in this book where using Rush Limbaugh as a point of departure for discussing a topic has gone from being an amusing device to a sad reminder that millions of Americans are

being lied to every day by an obese millionaire with a repugnant political agenda. But his views on the environment are so god-awful wrong that it would have been a disservice not to include them.

By the way, Rush says that his convictions are spiritual in nature. In *The Way Things Ought to Be*, Rush (or his ghostwriter, anyway) says:

> My views on the environment are rooted in my belief in Creation. . . . I refuse to believe that people, who are themselves the result of Creation, can destroy the most magnificent creation in the entire Universe.

I don't know. If God can allow genocides to occur on a more or less regular basis, if God can stand by while famine ravages large parts of the Third World, if God can permit Sonny Bono to sit on the House Judiciary Committee, why should we figure He's going to get off His Butt to stop Union Carbide from leaking polychlorinated biphenyls into the groundwater underneath Piscataway, New Jersey?

But that probably doesn't concern Rush. If God fails us, there's always the free enterprise system. For example, here's how Rush explains how Cleveland went about cleaning up the Cuyahoga River:

> Take the Cuyahoga River, which caught fire about twenty years ago because it was filled with so much junk and sludge. We set out to clean it up, we rolled up our sleeves and we did it. I'm sure some regulation was used, but the major factor was good old American know-how. . . . The key to cleaning up our environment is unfettered free enterprise.

I've looked into this and it seems that people who actually
live in Ohio have a slightly different interpretation of what
"some regulation" actually means. According to the Cleveland *Plain Dealer* of June 22, 1994, the $1.5 billion cleanup
came about "as a result of federal regulations passed after the
river last burned." (That's the funny thing about the
Cuyahoga. It actually caught fire three times before the federal government finally stepped in.)

But don't take the *Plain Dealer*'s word for it. Listen to what
the *Dayton Daily News* had to say on May 8, 1995: "In 1969,
before the federal government stepped in with its water
pollution controls, the Cuyahoga caught fire as a result of
the industrial waste that clogged it. The Cuyahoga no
longer 'goes smoking through my dreams,' as songwriter
Randy Newman once described it, largely because of the Federal Water Pollution Control Act passed by Congress in
1972."

The Federal Water Pollution Control Act, popularly
known as the Clean Water Act, is currently being rewritten by
the Republican Congress. Not to worry, though. House Republican whip Tom Delay, realizing how complex an overhaul
of our nation's environmental policy might be, was wise
enough to bring in people who "have the expertise" to make
sure that the Clean Water Act will do exactly what they want
it to do.

These people, undeniably "experts" in pollution law, include lobbyists from the chemical, mining, paper, petroleum,
auto, and steel industries. But don't be alarmed. I can't imagine how any group that calls itself the Clean Water Industry
Coalition could possibly have a hand in fouling our nation's
water supply.

Their kindred spirits in the National Endangered Species
Reform Coalition, which includes timber, ranching, mining,

and utility interests,* have been busy improving the Endangered Species Act. All I can say, it's about time. As Rush said, "If the [spotted] owl can't adapt to the superiority of humans, screw it."

But the real E-ticket in Washington lobbying this past year was Project Relief, an all-star team of lobbyists representing 350 different corporate interests that was put together by Tom Delay. Delay, who was a Houston bug exterminator before he became a parliamentarian, has called the EPA "the Gestapo of government." (Which I bet left a lot of people in the ATF feeling unappreciated.)

Delay set up Project Relief to write the House regulatory moratorium bill. As written, the moratorium would prevent the federal government from issuing any more regulations on just about anything. Which in the case of environmental regulations is maybe a good idea. Because after they cut the EPA's enforcement budget in half, the agency won't have the resources to enforce the regulations already on the books.

Delay believes that working hand in hand with business lobbyists is equivalent to Democrats working with labor unions and environmental groups: "Our supporters are no different than theirs. But somehow they have this Christ-like attitude what they are doing [is] protecting the world."

---

* Here's a fun little brainteaser. See if you can match the following special interest groups with their corporate sponsors.

1. National Wetlands Coalition	a. oil drillers, developers, natural gas companies
2. Citizens for Sensible Control of Acid Rain	b. coal and electric companies
3. Global Climate Coalition	c. coal, gas, and oil companies
4. Nevadans for Fair Fuel Economy	d. Detroit automakers

answers: 1,a 2,b 3,c 4,d

Delay's allies don't have the same attitude problem. Project Relief leader-lobbyist Gordon Gooch, who wrote the first draft of the legislation, proudly admits: "I'm not claiming to be a Boy Scout. No question I thought what I was doing was in the best interests of my clients," which include energy and petrochemical companies.

Project Relief is what you might call a dues-paying organization. The dues go directly to members of Congress. From 1989 to 1994, the one hundred and fifteen PACs associated with Project Relief contributed nearly $40 million to various representatives and senators. Last year the top recipient in the House was Newt Gingrich.*

During the debate on regulatory reform, Republicans set up a war room for Project Relief lobbyists in a small office directly off the House floor. As Democrats raised objections to the bill (such as "people will get very sick"), lobbyists with laptops spat out responses for use by Republicans on the floor.

So, in other words, lobbyists aren't just *writing* the bills, they're *debating* them as well. Personally, I think this is good. Because it frees up the members' schedules so they can spend more time fund-raising. In fact, I think government will run a lot more efficiently once we figure out a way to let lobbyists do the voting, too.

Keep in mind that these bills have only passed the House. They have yet to get through the Senate, which is traditionally a more moderate, deliberative body. Unless, of course, some of the senators are running for President.

When Bob Dole took it upon himself to lead the Senate's

---

* See also Gingrich's speech to Perot conference on evils of money in politics, pages 222–223. You'll particularly like the part about our freedom being "bought off in a wave of money."

charge for regulatory reform, he turned to many businesses and lobbyists for, well . . . "advice." And maybe even a little "encouragement."

The final product happened to reflect the regulatory concerns of a lot of Dole-for-President contributors, and was in some ways even more pro-industry than the House bill.

Basically, the Senate bill would require the government to prove through a bureaucratically tortuous process of cost-benefit and risk analysis that any proposed regulation is the cheapest way to protect the public. For example, improved meat inspection by the USDA that could save four thousand lives a year and prevent up to five million illnesses could be nixed, not just because it would cost the meat industry $245 million a year, but because the USDA couldn't prove that it's the "cheapest" way to protect the public.

This whole cost-benefit analysis business is very sticky, because it's hard to put a dollar value on some things. Like human life. At one point in the debate over regulatory reform, Ted Kennedy prepared an amendment which would have set the value of a human life at a minimum of $7.5 million. That probably made the Kopechne family perk up their ears. My guess is that when Congress finally gets down to setting a dollar value on a human life, it'll be closer to the buck ninety-five suggested by the Lawn Jart people.*

Dole's bill probably would have squeaked through the Senate if it weren't for a piece of good luck. Right in the middle of the floor debate, five kids in Tennessee got *E. coli* poisoning from eating bad hamburgers. Fortunately, none of them died, but they got sick enough to kill the bill. Temporarily.

---

* I'm sorry, I got carried away there. The Lawn Jart people never suggested that a human life is only worth $1.95. Everything else in this chapter is true.

Eventually, though, the Republicans will manage to push through a bill deregulating everything from motorcycle helmets to nuclear power plants. And if history's any judge, the results will be a tremendous disaster.

In October of '82, when Ronald Reagan signed the bill deregulating those poor, overburdened savings and loans, he remarked, "I think we hit the jackpot!"

I don't know who the "we" referred to. But with the taxpayer cost of the S&L bailout approaching $200 billion, *somebody* sure hit the jackpot.

37
THE LAW AND ORDER PARTY:
US!

inally. We Democrats are the law and order party. We're for the ATF. The Republicans are for David Koresh, the militias, and guns. That's an oversimplification. But who's got time for a whole long thing?

It's just that we've been taking hits since the 60s on this

issue, and I think we can make some headway if we show that we're on the right side.

I should say right off that I'm just a citizen who's been mugged once. I don't claim to be an authority on crime. For example, I seemed to be the only person I know who didn't follow the O.J. Simpson trial. For a while there, I thought O.J. was the black guy who kidnapped Susan Smith's kids. As I write this, I don't know what the verdict will be. But I will say this about O.J. The man has suffered enough.

Of course, both the O.J. and the Susan Smith cases underline the fact that most murder victims are killed by people they know. And if you believe Newt Gingrich, they also underline the importance of voting Republican.

As Newt put it right before the '94 elections: "I think that the mother killing the two children in South Carolina vividly reminds every American how sick the society is getting and how much we need to change things. . . . The only way you get change is to vote Republican."

I imagine that Susan Smith's stepfather, Beverly Russell, can also attest to "how sick the society is getting." As a member of South Carolina's Republican state executive committee, he's been very actively pushing the Republican agenda for years. Unfortunately, he was also pushing another agenda for quite some time. Russell, who also happened to be a local organizer for the Christian Coalition, has admitted to having molested his stepdaughter Susan from the age of fourteen, as well as to having had consensual sex with her up to two months prior to the death of her children. Russell has made very public expressions of guilt over this. Of course, as far as I know, he's still voting Republican.

But enough about this rather unsettling hypocrisy. Back to violence.

I don't know what makes people violent. Some experts say television. I'm sure it does. But I know that the Nazis didn't

watch a lot of TV, and something tells me the Serbs weren't watching a lot of the *A-Team* during the 70s.

On the other hand, Senator Bill Bradley has quoted this statistic: By the time a kid's eighteen, he'll have seen 26,000 murders on TV. Well, that may seem like a lot, but if you do the math, it comes out to only four per day. So, I don't know what the big deal is.

Other experts say that the rate of violent crime is directly linked to the availability of guns. That's why I'm a big advocate of "gun buy-back" programs. In fact, I have a radical gun buy-back idea that I guarantee would be a huge success. Here's how it works: Hand in a gun, get a free vial of crack.

Of course, that would put more drugs on the street. And that is not good. Last year 78 percent of those arrested in New York City tested positive for cocaine, a drug which makes people very aggressive, and hostile, and violent. That's why heroin would probably be better for the gun buy-back program.

An uncomfortable subject that's not discussed enough is black on black crime. Jesse Jackson had the courage to talk about it in terms that most people can identify with. He said it pains him that when he's walking down the street at night and hears footsteps, he's relieved if it's a white man and not a black man. I know exactly what he means. I was leaving NBC late one night and heard some footsteps. When I turned around, I saw it was Jesse Jackson, and it scared the living daylights out of me!

A couple years ago, the Supreme Court ruled that it was constitutional to give perpetrators of "hate crimes" stiffer penalties than criminals who committed the same crime, only without the hate motive. I'm sympathetic to that. I think hate crimes are despicable. But at least there's a *reason* for the crime. What I fear is *random* acts of violence. I don't know. Something to think about.

One of the largest contributing factors to urban crime is unemployment. Among black teenagers looking for jobs, nearly 40 percent can't find work. I can't understand why anyone would be against midnight basketball, which provides these guys something to do *and* job training. Maybe the Republicans believe this is the kind of social welfare program that attracts undesirable immigrants. I do recall that a lot of the Haitian boat people mentioned they were looking forward to playing midnight basketball.

President Clinton's crime bill paid for a lot of new prisons, and that's good. The question is what to do with these criminals once they're behind bars. I think drug rehab is a good idea, and studies show that it's been a dramatically successful tool in decreasing recidivism. I read Newt Gingrich's chapter in *To Renew America* called "Violent Crime, Freedom from Fear, and the Right to Bear Arms." Nowhere in this, his only chapter on crime, is there any mention of drugs or of domestic violence (unless you count pointing out that Nicole Simpson was killed by a knife and not a gun), but he does touch on Willie Horton and spends quite a bit of space on the need to "eliminate all weight and muscle-building rooms and break down the cult of macho behavior in prison." I agree. My suggestion is to replace weight training with mandatory step-aerobics performed to Ace of Base.

Then there's the death penalty. The Democrats finally won the White House in 1992 because we ran a guy who's pro capital punishment. As governor of Arkansas, Bill Clinton carried out the death penalty many times. He even put a semi-retarded guy away.

Here I am of two minds. I have no moral qualms about executing someone who rapes and murders Kitty Dukakis. That is, as long as we know we have the right guy.

Consider this *New York Times* story from 1985 about a murder trial in Gainesville, Georgia. It appeared under the head-

line RACE AND BLIND JUSTICE BEHIND MIX-UP IN COURT. The key word is "mix-up":

> Here in Hall County last June one man was arrested as a thief and another as a murderer. And last week, when the murder defendant was summoned to stand trial, the other man was produced, and nearly convicted.
>
> . . . Both men are Vietnamese of about the same height and weight, and none of the white participants in the judicial process—not the prosecutor, the sheriff's officers, the defense lawyer, or the witnesses—noticed the difference.

Basically, what happened was this: The county jail was holding two Vietnamese immigrants, neither of whom spoke English. Hen Van Nguyen, age 21, had been arrested for stealing. Nguyen Ngoc Tieu, 27, had been accused of stabbing a woman to death.

Mr. Nguyen was brought to the courthouse to stand trial for theft. A court officer assumed he was Tieu and brought him into another courtroom to stand trial for murder. For a day and a half Nguyen repeated over and over again, "Not me, not me," but that didn't stop several witnesses, including the murder victim's roommate, from identifying him as Mr. Tieu, who was, in fact, sitting three blocks away in jail.

Tieu's court-appointed attorney had interviewed Tieu through an interpreter a few weeks earlier for about an hour ("There wasn't a whole lot to talk about"), but didn't realize that Nguyen wasn't his client. The attorney, sure of a conviction, offered to plead his uncooperative client guilty to a lesser charge.

It all ended as it had started. With a coincidence. A witness

who was there for the theft trial accidently wandered into the wrong courtroom and recognized Mr. Nguyen as the thief.

Former Hall County District Attorney Jeff C. Wayne sort of summed up the whole mix-up this way: "It's like the colored race—most of them look exactly alike."

Again, I have no problem frying a murderer. In some cases I'd even wave the cruel-and-unusual prohibition. But a dead man can't appeal.

Maybe I'm being overly fastidious. I once heard Pat Buchanan's answer to this objection to the death penalty. He said that surgeons lose people on the table all the time. What's the big deal?

38

FAIR MEAN VS. UNFAIR MEAN

hose of us who make our living in what Calvin Trillin calls "the small joke trade" are keeping alive one of America's noblest traditions. By commenting in a humorous way on the events of the day, we bring laughter, and, perhaps, fresh insight to our grateful

readers. Every now and then, however, we come up with something that's just plain mean, having our fun at someone else's expense. And that's fine. That's what high-minded satire like *Rush Limbaugh Is a Big Fat Idiot and Other Observations* is all about.

Now, I am not a mean person. Just ask my kids. But don't ask the guy at the Alamo Rent-a-Car counter that kept me waiting for two and a half hours. And to maintain my own image of myself as a nice person, I have tried to draw a distinction between "fair mean" jokes and "unfair mean" jokes. I can't define the distinction, but like the Supreme Court with pornography, I know it when I see it.

Below are a few mean jokes, some of which you've already read. See if you can tell which are fair and which are unfair.

1. We now live in an era where the wall between news and entertainment has been eaten away like the cartilage in David Crosby's septum.

Fair or Unfair?

2. I'd like a Gingrich-Gramm ticket. That way the president could write the pornography and the vice president could produce it.

Fair or Unfair?

3. Bob Packwood misunderstood the "three strikes and you're out" provision in the crime bill. He thought it was "three strikeouts and you're out."

Fair or Unfair?

4. Packwood used alcoholism as an excuse for his behavior. I say if you're a U.S. senator and you have a

drinking problem, you should just say, "I've done some things I'm not proud of, I've acted in ways not becoming a U.S. senator," and then simply leave it up to the people of Massachusetts.

Fair or Unfair?

5. Sam Donaldson once said on *David Brinkley* that a sketch I wrote "just wasn't funny." I'll tell you what, Sam. You don't make rules about comedy, I won't make rules about hair.

Fair or Unfair?

6. Instead of "with talent on loan from God," Rush Limbaugh should open his show by saying "with fat on loan from the American Beef Council."

Fair or Unfair?

(for answers, turn to next page)

1. Unfair. He mainly freebased.

2. Fair. The first, uncensored version of Gingrich's novel *1945* made me hot. I gave it a six on the peter-meter. Gramm invested $7,500 in a soft-core porn movie. It was never made. But, then again, I don't like him.

3. Fair. But too easy.

4. Unfair. No one has ever *proven* that Ted Kennedy is an alcoholic. Also, two of his brothers were killed by assassins.

5. Extremely fair. His toupee is hideous. And he criticized me.

6. Absolutely fair. You cannot have too many "Rush is fat" jokes. This is only my eighty-third.

And while we're on Limbaugh and the subject of "fair mean" vs. "unfair mean," let's go back to 1993. On his TV show he put up a picture of Socks, the cat, and said, "Did you know there's a White House dog?" Then he put up a picture of 13-year-old Chelsea Clinton. But, you know, she asked for it.

39

ADVENTURES IN POLITICS
AUGUST 12-14, 1995

I ATTEND THE PEROT CONFERENCE IN DALLAS, TALK
TO A LOT OF ANGRY WHITE RETIRED PEOPLE, LISTEN
TO EVERY REPUBLICAN PRESIDENTIAL CANDIDATE,
AND PERSONALLY GET JOHN KASICH TO ADMIT TO
AN ACT OF INTELLECTUAL DISHONESTY.

hen you step off
the plane in Dallas and enter the main terminal, you are
greeted by a huge sign that proudly proclaims: WELCOME TO
DALLAS—WE HAVEN'T HAD AN ASSASSINATION IN OVER THIRTY
YEARS!

Not really. That's just what I was thinking as my cabdriver drove past Dealey Plaza on the way to the Hyatt.

I had come to Dallas for a panderfest. All the declared Republican candidates were scheduled to speak to a gathering of several thousand members of Ross Perot's organization, United We Stand America. I learned later from journalist Gerald Posner that the organization would be called simply "United We Stand" except for the fact that a lesbian group in San Francisco owns the name, and Perot was forced to add the "America."

The Hyatt lobby was filled with excited Perotistas, practically all of them white, most in their sixties or seventies. Jerry Garcia had died a couple of days before, but most of these people were still mourning Lawrence Welk.

In the elevator, a middle-aged woman wearing an orange pantsuit recognized me. "I didn't know you were one of us!"

"Well, I'm not actually." Everyone was staring at me. "But I do agree with a lot of Perot's views."

"Then why aren't you a member?"

"Well, um, he's a little . . . you know." Still staring. "Um . . . you know. He's a little . . ." Help me out here, everybody. "You know . . . a little . . . paranoid. Maybe?"

The rest of the ride was pretty quiet. But I had learned something. Which was to shut up. After all, these were people who cared enough about America to come to Dallas in August at their own expense to try to make a difference. I felt ashamed.

That wore off pretty early the next day. Not that I didn't have fun chatting up a lot of nice folks. It's just that for every friendly, intelligent, concerned idealist, there was an angry, horribly misinformed xenophobe. Sort of Capra on acid.

There was Elaine, a nice enough old lady from North Palm Beach, Florida, and a Buchanan supporter because of his stance on immigration. She told me she lives so close to the

water that "you can practically see the Haitians getting off the boats." Then Elaine leaned in and whispered, "You know which ones because their pants are wet to the knees." She went on about the Haitians' big scam. According to Elaine, the boat people land in Florida, go directly to the Salvation Army, where they stock up on pots and pans and shoes, and then fly back to Haiti to sell them on the black market. Hmmm. I say if you're willing to brave shark-infested waters and third-degree sunburn for the profit margin on a few pairs of used Nikes and some Corning Ware, then more power to you. I mean, *that's* rugged individualism.

Then there was Heather, an "economist" from Citizens for a Sound Economy. She was at a booth beating the drum for Dick Armey's flat tax, an especially popular issue at the conference. Part of the attraction of the flat tax is that I can explain it in one sentence: You take your wages, subtract a personal allowance of $22,700 for a married couple or $14,850 for a single head of household and $5,300 for each dependent, and then pay a flat 17 percent on the difference. That's it.

A friend of mine in Hollywood makes about $3.5 million a year. When I first explained the Armey flat tax to him, he said, "What do I have to do to get this guy elected President?" We estimated that he'd save somewhere in the neighborhood of $600,000.

Heather told me she was for the flat tax because it was progressive. When I disagreed and suggested a Gephardt-like "It's a flat tax because I call it a flat tax" higher rate for people making over $200,000, I got the supply-side response. Heather told me that the greatest economic growth in this country has always been when the marginal tax rate on the top bracket was lowest. I asked Heather what the top marginal rate was during the Eisenhower administration, and she thought a minute and said, "About twenty percent, I think."

Fortunately, the Citizens for a Sound Economy booth had a book that contained the very information we needed. The top rate during the Eisenhower administration was 88 percent. Heather explained, "I'm an economist, not a historian."

And there was the commotion at the Alan Keyes for President booth, where Keyes volunteers showed an exceedingly graphic video of an actual abortion. This violated an agreement that presidential candidates would show only campaign videos. The Keyes people said the abortion video *was* their campaign video, but Perot staff and police came in to close down the booth.

A Keyes campaign worker, who was wearing a T-shirt with an American flag and a cross, started chastising the cops at the top of his lungs, calling their actions "an abomination against the Lord." He was going on and on, and I felt bad for the police, who were being accused of doing the work of Satan, so when the guy stopped for a breath, I shouted something about how the police were doing their jobs. A couple minutes later it was all over, and the guy who had been preaching came up to me and told me he liked my work. Then a friend of his spent ten minutes trying to convert me to Christ.

The presidential candidates weren't speaking until the second day, but Perot was happily emceeing a slate of important, if somewhat dull, political figures. After speeches like Senator Paul Simon's "The Importance of a Strong, Stable Dollar," the little Texan would take the stage with applause-inducing lines like, "Now, didn't that speech hit the bull's-eye?" or "Wasn't that a home run?" or "Was that a world-class presentation or what?"

Pete Petersen, a co-founder of the Concord Coalition, did hit a home run with a very sobering speech about what will happen if we don't reform social security. He was the first speaker to make use of charts, which were projected onto two big video screens, and as such, the first to make a joke about

using charts at a conference hosted by chart enthusiast Ross Perot. I counted eight speakers during the conference who used charts and made the same joke. The last one was Pete Wilson, who seemed utterly bewildered that he didn't get a laugh.

It became apparent very quickly that this was a conservative crowd. Anti-immigration, anti-welfare, anti-tax, anti–big government, anti-U.N., anti–foreign aid, and anti–affirmative action. And, boy, do they hate Clinton! Their welcome for the President's stand-in Mack McLarty was so cold that as he took the stage, you could almost hear his balls shrivel up and recede into his body cavity.

More than anything, the crowd was anti-establishment. So there was a warm response to Jesse Jackson, although I did witness a domestic mini-drama featuring a retiree in a baseball cap who insisted on heckling the Reverend. Every so often the guy would cup his hands around his mouth and yell something while his poor wife sat there mortified. At one point Jackson was decrying the growth of our prison population, and the man yelled out, "Put them in camps!" as his wife buried her face in her hands. I wonder how their car trip home went.

I was really looking forward to Gingrich's speech. The *Vanity Fair* article had just come out. The one in which a former campaign volunteer said that Newt preferred oral sex so he could say he didn't *sleep* with another woman. Which I don't really understand. I mean, I *slept* with the woman sitting next to me on the red-eye down to Dallas.

I was especially interested in how Gingrich would justify his failure to honor his handshake with the President. The one in New Hampshire where they both pledged to form a bipartisan commission on campaign reform. Political reform is at the top of Perot's agenda. And here was Gingrich, perhaps the most egregious offender of the Washington money

game. I mean, lobbyists are now *writing* legislation. So, after winning the crowd over by kissing Perot's ring, Newt had the nerve to say this about money:

> I think this is a topic too serious to play narrow, cheap political games with . . . our freedom as a country and our tradition of over 200 years is too important to let it be bought off in a wave of money from a variety of sources that we don't understand and can't even follow.

And as I watched him on the stage, my hands were clenched in fists of rage. As Don McLean might say, assuming he hates Newt Gingrich as much as he hated Mick Jagger.

But it just got worse. Gingrich went into this obnoxious thing he does about how the Republicans are not cutting Medicare.

> This year Medicare spends $4,800 per senior citizen. Under our plan, over the next seven years, Medicare will spend $6,700 per senior citizen. Now, most of you probably do math well enough that you know if you're at 4,800 here and you're at 6,700 here that's called an increase. Now I want to go real slow here for a minute because we've got a lot of reporters who are listening.

It was really nauseating. He was using his hands: 6,700 up here, 4,800 down there. I kept wondering, "Are these constant dollars?" But people around me were laughing hysterically. He went on:

> Now I don't want to be negative, but you might even have one or two liberals show up who claim that going

from 4,800 to 6,700 is a cut. Now, this is not because they're bad people; this is an early sign of the educational dysfunction which has hit our society.

The crowd laughed, then broke into applause and cheers. No angel born in hell could break that Satan's spell.

But the big hit Friday night was something of a surprise. Bob Novak wrote it this way in the next Monday's *Washington Post*:

> But out of all 36 speakers, the people's choice was somebody few here could have recognized before this weekend, Rep. John Kasich of Ohio, Chairman of the House Budget Committee. . . . Indeed, dozens of admiring Perotites—particularly the younger ones— separately approached Kasich after his speech to praise him and suggest that the presidency lies in his future.

The boyish Kasich, who spoke about his long, heroic, lonely struggle to put the country's fiscal house in order, *did* blow the place away. But he didn't hurt himself any by sucking up to Novak in the Hyatt cocktail lounge later that night.

I was there. At one point Novak asked him who a President Kasich would appoint as Fed Chairman, and Kasich said, "Why you, Bob!" Novak laughed heartily.

We were having a good time. Me, Novak, Kasich, and Margaret Warner. If you're a *MacNeil/Lehrer* fan, as I am, you'll know Margaret as the *Newsweek* reporter who took over for Judy Woodruff as the show's chief Washington correspondent.

At one point Novak was extolling Gingrich's "masterful" speech, and I objected, especially to the patronizing crap about the $4,800 versus the $6,700. So I turned to Kasich:

"By the way, are those constant dollars?"

Margaret jumped in. "It must be constant dollars. They wouldn't be that dishonest."

"Sure they would," I said. Turning back to Kasich, "*Are* those constant dollars?"

"Al . . ." Kasich's voice had a touch of annoyance, "we're *increasing* funding for Medicare."

"But the $4,800 to $6,700, has that been adjusted for inflation?"

"Al, the dollars are going up."

"I just want to know if those are constant dollars."

"Al, we're going from 178 billion to 283 billion." Kasich gave the others an exasperated grin. When will this guy stop?

"Look. Gingrich is going like, 'Hey, you're a *fucking moron* if you can't see that 6,700 is more than 4,800.' I just want to know how big a moron I am. Are those constant dollars?"

A pause. Then. "No, Al, they're not constant dollars."

Kasich slumped in his chair and admitted, "I guess we're being a little intellectually dishonest on this one." And I took a few victory laps around the table.

Margaret was slightly embarrassed and begged me not to repeat the part about her assuming it was constant dollars. I knew she was kidding, however. She's a terrific journalist and knows a good story.

Which brings me to the reason I came to the conference in the first place. Frank Luntz. Frank is Washington's latest *Wunderkind*, a pudgy 33-year-old pollster whose focus-group approach to political research has revolutionized the Republican party's ability to sell itself to the electorate. In fact, Luntz is the guy who produced the GOPAC list of "contrasting words." Which means Frank is evil.

He's also the guy who discovered that more people under thirty believe in UFOs than believe they'll get their social

security. I'd been thinking of putting together a chapter on how stupid people are, so I gave Frank a call.

Luntz is now a consultant to Phil Gramm's campaign. But he had worked for Perot in '92, and suggested I come down for the conference. He told me I could watch him conduct some focus groups of Perot supporters, and that I could even ask some questions. Which gives you some idea how systematic his research is. I asked him if I could be a wiseass, and he said, "Sure. They won't know."

I hooked up with Frank while he was taping a *MacNeil/Lehrer* interview with Margaret "it must be constant dollars" Warner. Part of the interview focused on the Contract with America, which was largely the result of test-marketing by the Luntz Research Company. At one point in the taping, Margaret asked Frank whether the Contract was designed specifically with the Perot people in mind.

Frank answered, "The contract was designed . . ." He stopped himself. As GOPAC's number one celebrity pollster, Frank knows better than anyone that "words and phrases are powerful." And "designed" was a powerfully bad word in this context.

"Well, it's not really designed," he continued, hopelessly thrown. ". . . The contract was effective in convincing . . . don't do that to me."

"What's wrong with saying the contract was designed?" Margaret wanted to know.

". . . Because . . . Because I don't want to say it on camera, that's why."

Margaret let him rephrase his answer, which was some bull about how the Contract demonstrated to the Perot people that a group of elected officials could make a promise and then keep it.

I hung out with Frank on and off for the rest of the weekend, and, of course, actually grew to like him. He's extremely

smart, and his boyish naked ambition is almost endearing. Also, he was a fountain of interesting insights. For example, Frank worked for Pat Buchanan in the '92 primaries, and he told me Buchanan's views were "getting crazier every year." And from the way he discussed Phil Gramm, I gathered that the Gramm campaign strategy at that point had come down pretty much to hoping that Dole gets sick.

Occasionally, I would bother to challenge Frank on something or other and he'd answer, "Do you think you have a really solid grasp on what people are thinking?" Which is a little like Julia Child asking if you think you really know how to make a soufflé.

In fact, Frank pretty much worships at the altar of public opinion. He believes that polling is not just the key to winning elections, but to governing as well. This puts him squarely at odds with Edmund Burke, the eighteenth-century British philosopher who said that a legislator should make decisions based not on the passion of the moment or the whim of the people, but rather on his conscience and best judgment. (I've never read Burke. I heard Cokie Roberts quote him.)

Frank told me that most people who take part in focus groups consider it a "license to whine." And the ten young men and women who bitched and moaned in the Generation X group I witnessed were no exception. They were all college-educated, and their biggest complaint seemed to be that there hadn't been a cushy, high-paying job waiting for them when they graduated.

Frank asked them questions like: "Overall, does Washington help or hinder your achievement of the American dream?" Their answers were bitter denunciations of everything from social security to the Goals 2000 program. David, a 26-year-old from California, suggested that "we let the Catholic Church educate everybody like they used to." I

pointed out that the Catholic Church didn't educate my people. To which he replied, "I mean the Western World."

It turns out that Frank is working on a book about the American dream, so afterwards he asked me what *I* thought the American dream had become. I said, "Well, judging from this group, I'd say it's to have a very well-paying job and to live in an expensive house in a gated community."

A focus group of eleven retirees was more heartening. All of them were excited to be at the conference and were enjoying the speeches. As Bob from California said, "It's what you learn after you know it all that counts."

They all seemed financially comfortable (probably because of the social security "distrust fund" so reviled by their grandchildren), but were concerned with the world they were passing on to their heirs. They worried that the country was being destroyed by partisan bickering. As Myrtle of Florida put it, "I wish people would stop blaming each other for everything." I didn't tell her the title of my book.

The group hated Clinton and held a generally favorable view of the Republican party. Bob felt that they were there to "force the Republicans to do what they promised to do." And most of them didn't want Perot to run for president, wanting him "to be a kingmaker, not a king." But when asked who'd they vote for in a three-way race between Clinton, Dole, and Perot, all but two said Perot. They hated Dole almost as much as Clinton.

Dole knew that when he spoke. Of all the Republican candidates, he was the least craven in tailoring his speech to the Perot crowd. Maybe that's because he knew he wouldn't be fooling anyone. "So I would say right up front, yes, the federal government is big, but the federal government does a lot of good things."

The cold reception just seemed to irk him. At one point he

said, "I am not perfect." Then he couldn't help himself, adding, "Maybe everybody here is."

Dole opened by talking about World War II, and ended by talking about leadership. He seemed to be saying that he deserved the nomination because it was his turn. "I have been tested and I have been tested and I have been tested." But he might as well have been saying, "I have been testy, and I have been testy, and I have been testy."

Phil Gramm fared better. The usual stuff about his momma, Dickey Flatt, and the people in the wagon getting out to help pull the wagon, all that was well received. He added something new, though. His vision. Gramm described what the country would be like on January 1, 2001, the end of his first term and "the first day of the new millenium."

That confused people. Almost everyone thinks the first day of the new millenium will be January 1, 2000. But they're wrong. Gramm is right. The first year of the first century was the year one, not the year zero, so the first year of the new millenium will be 2001, not 2000. I've been trying to explain this to people for years, but no one will listen. On New Year's Eve, December 31, 1999, I'll be there in Times Square, along with Phil Gramm and maybe George Will and perhaps Dick Cavett, telling people to calm down. A thankless job, but someone will have to do it.

Alan Keyes brought the crowd to its feet with his highly charged speech. Well, performance, really. I found it particularly disturbing, not so much for its content, which was disturbing enough (abortion, abortion, abortion), but for its canned emotion. See, I'd seen the speech before on C-SPAN. Now, it's one thing to give your standard stump speech over and over, but when it involves thrashing and sweating and dramatic pauses which signify that you've been overcome with emotion, and those pauses always appear at the same exact

point in the speech, it's time to apply for your actor's equity card.

Arlen Specter, on the other hand, urged that abortion be taken "off the political table" and won an ovation, which isn't easy when most of the audience is walking out of the room.

Richard Lugar did himself no good whatsoever by concentrating on foreign policy, and Bob Dornan spent about 80 percent of his time ranting about all things military, at one point reminding us that it took four years to thrash "the Krauts." He did leave the battlefield long enough to call Bill Clinton "the most corrupt person to sit in the Oval Office in two hundred years."

Pete Wilson tried to pull a cheap standing O at the end of his speech by exhorting the crowd: "If you want to take back our government, stand up!" The crowd knew it was a ploy for the benefit of the TV cameras and resented it. But they also wanted to take back their government, so they stood up quickly and then sat down as fast as possible.

Lamar Alexander. What can I say about Lamar Alexander? Lamar, give it up.

Pat Buchanan stole the show. I counted six standing ovations, although it's hard to count when you're cowering under your seat. Like Dornan, Buchanan gave us a martial tour of American history, touching on Lexington and Concord, Paul Revere's ride, Robert E. Lee, Little Big Horn, Pearl Harbor, the Bataan Death March, Corregidor, Midway, the Coral Sea, Okinawa, Iwo Jima, his uncle losing a leg in the "European Theater of Operations," Vietnam, the Marine barracks in Beirut, and what he referred to as "that so-called friendly fire incident in Iraq." This from a guy who was 4-F.

Buchanan was almost totally in sync with the Perot crowd and drew his biggest ovations on their red meat issues. On NAFTA and the Mexican bailout: "Politicians of both parties sold us out up in Washington, D.C. They took Citibank and

Chase Manhattan and J.P. Morgan and Goldman Sachs off the hook, and they put us on. Well, I'll tell you this, you've got my word, when I get to the White House, NAFTA will be canceled!"

International bankers caught it on the chin a few times, along with the U.N.: "So I want to say today to all the globalists up there in Tokyo and New York and Paris, when I raise my hand to take that oath of office, your new world order comes crashing down!"

On immigration: "I will build a security fence and we will seal the border of this country cold!"

On dress codes: "We don't need some character in the Department of Education in sandals and beads telling us how America's children should be educated."

Buchanan ended his speech with a Freudian slip. He meant to say, "We'll take back my party, and then together we're going up the federal road, and we'll take back Washington, D.C., and we will take America back to the things we believe in." He messed up just one word. So it came out: "we'll take *black* Washington, D.C." I swear. I saw it again later on *Mac-Neil/Lehrer*.

When Buchanan finished the speech, emcee Perot brought Buchanan's wife, Shelley, to the podium. "Can we agree on one thing? This guy married way over his head, didn't he?"

Now it was Perot's turn. He thanked his people for not being morning glories. "Remember, morning glories wilt by noon." He told his people that they were responsible for the Republican '94 victory. He complained that the Republicans had pilfered the Contract with America:

> And that came right out of the back of one of our
> books. . . . Again and again, people have come to
> me and said, "Weren't you offended by the fact that

they took . . . ?" And I said, no, no. That's the nicest compliment they could pay us.

Then he demanded another Contract. For campaign finance reform. ". . . and let's make all these government reforms in the next hundred days and give it to the American people as a Christmas present in 1995. Right?"

The implication was clear. I'll form a third party if Congress doesn't pass political reform in the next hundred days. Sooner, if Colin Powell sells a lot of books in September and starts to upstage me.

The irony, of course, is that Perot's is easily the most autocratic, least democratic organization in the country. And any candidate who gets the nomination of the Independence party or the Reform party or whatever it's called will really be getting the nomination of "The Lunatic Who Dropped Out Because the Republicans Were Going to Disrupt His Daughter's Wedding" party.

I'm guessing Lowell Weicker.

40

THE URGENT NEED FOR HEALTH CARE REFORM

t was my original intention that this piece would be the linchpin of my book, much as health care reform was meant to be the linchpin of the first Clinton Administration.

My initial plan was to overwhelm you with facts, figures, and unassailable logic that would all lead to one inescapable conclusion: namely, that America urgently needs to adopt all of Ira Magaziner's proposals for a system of universal health coverage based on the principles of managed competition.

Unfortunately, we've run into a little difficulty here at *Rush Limbaugh Is a Big Fat Idiot*. It seems that my researcher, Geoff, is sick. Which has led to something of a bottleneck in the production of facts, figures, and unassailable logic.

So we . . . I mean "I" (he's really sick) have had to change tack. Instead of a rational argument in favor of health care reform, I've decided to take a cue from the congressional Republicans and prove my point anecdotally.

Which brings me back to Geoff's illness. Right now he is lying in St. Luke's with a shunt draining neural fluid from the lining of his brain. But don't worry. The doctors say that's under control. Apparently the head injury isn't as bad as it looks.

The real worry is the Lyme disease, which may have entered its irreversible phase.

Let me back up. I don't pay Geoff much. Basically, I pay him the going rate for researchers. Which, believe me, is a joke. So Geoff can't exactly afford his own health insurance. And since he's only a temporary employee, Lord knows I'm not going to pick up the tab.

Which is exactly why we need government-mandated universal health insurance.

You see, if Geoff had had health coverage, he would have gone to a doctor right after he was bitten by the tick. Or at least as soon as he developed the rash and fever.

We think the tick was a deer tick. They're pretty prevalent around my son's day camp up in Westchester. It was funny hat day, and my boy had left his funny hat at home. So, I sent

Geoff up to the camp with it, and he came back with Lyme disease.

It's actually a very treatable disease. If you catch it in the early phase, before the heart palpitations and fainting spells set in. It's like Ira Magaziner says: A lot of unnecessary medical costs are incurred because people don't seek treatment until they're really sick.

That is so true! Had Geoff seen a doctor when he was only running a 102 degree fever, a simple course of antibiotics would have done the trick. But when he asked me if I knew any good doctors, I couldn't think of a single one in his price range.

So Geoff stuck it out. The fever came and went. The rash pretty much stayed with him from the get-go, but we thought it was an allergic reaction to the laundry detergent he had been using, so we ignored it. Likewise, the arthritic condition of his hands, which we chalked up to carpal tunnel syndrome. See, he had been doing a lot of typing. You know, mainly research stuff. Well, actually, he *wrote* pages 76 to 124 while I was summering in Maine. I don't know why I'm telling you this.

When I got back from Maine, I noticed that his performance was getting a little spotty. Some of the research seemed kind of suspect. I don't think Richard Lugar was ever married to Elizabeth Taylor. And I'm *sure* Dick Armey never played third base for the Astros.

Then it happened. Geoff had been having dizzy spells for a while, but he'd never actually fainted until one day when I was out for a long lunch with my publicist. When I left, Geoff was doing a Nexis search on Limbaugh's third wife, and when I returned he was lying on the floor passed out cold. At first I was pretty ticked off, because he'd left the Nexis connection running and they charge by the minute.

The emergency room was a zoo. There were something

like six or eight head injuries ahead of Geoff's, so we had to wait for hours. Finally, when they got to him, the doctors put him through all kinds of tests, including a CAT scan, and determined that Geoff had suffered a cranial hematoma when he hit his head on the desk or floor after he passed out.

It wasn't until he'd been in the hospital a couple days that they figured out he had fainted because of the Lyme disease. So now even though the doctors think Geoff will only need the shunt for a few more days, they're worried about possible Lyme-related heart failure. Which means Geoff may be in the hospital for weeks.

All of which you're paying for in two ways. One, this book is not nearly as well researched as it should be. And second, since Geoff doesn't have insurance, the hospital is passing on the entire expense, now approaching six figures, to your insurance company and mine. This is why you pay seven dollars for an aspirin when you get it in the hospital: because employers like me aren't required to cover employees like Geoff. It's an outrage!

And it's all the fault of the Republicans in Congress. All two hundred and . . . whatever, of them. Especially that guy, you know, the one who made that speech about how he didn't want his mom going to some government bureaucrat if she got sick. You know the guy. I could find out his name if I could just get this damn Nexis thing to work.

41
THE CRITICAL NEED FOR LEGAL REFORM

t's been a tumultuous couple of weeks here at *Rush Limbaugh Is a Big Fat Idiot and Other Observations*. First, Geoff got out of the hospital. And he's made a miraculous recovery.

Now that we've settled the lawsuit.

When Geoff first returned to work, everything was fine. Except that one of us seemed a little bitter. Since I felt that we had covered health care, I decided to move on to the issue of legal reform.

You see, I'd always intended to put a chapter in the book about how we *don't* need legal reform. I've always felt that as cumbersome and unwieldy as our legal system is, we need to preserve the right of the little guy to seek redress for any injustice he may suffer at the hands of faceless corporate behemoths.

That was before I realized that in the eyes of the state of New York, I am, in fact, a faceless corporate behemoth. But I'm getting ahead of myself.

When I told Geoff to do some research on legal reform, the first thing he did was to phone an organization called the Center for Legal Reform. The guy he talked to gave Geoff the usual arguments about frivolous lawsuits and ridiculously high awards for silly things like "pain and suffering." This struck me as very sloppy research, because what I really wanted were the arguments *against* legal reform. And I guess I came down a little hard on him.

I told him to call the American Trial Lawyers Association and then went out for a long lunch with my new publicist. When I returned, Geoff had a big smile on his face for the first time since he developed his rash.

Some shyster at the American Trial Lawyers Association had told Geoff that the whole Lyme disease thing was actionable and that he'd be happy to take the case for a third of the future settlement.

First I thought Geoff was bluffing. So I laughed at him. Which he tape recorded. Ultimately, my lawyer figures, that recording cost me about . . . well, I'm not allowed to discuss

the terms of the settlement. Let's just say I chortled away about two years of tuition at a very good private college.

It was two days after what both parties now call "the laughing incident" that my lawyer received the letter from Geoff's new "counsel." In addition to restitution for his ongoing medical expenses, Geoff was seeking damages for pain and suffering, lost wages (I didn't pay him for the days he was in the hospital), incapacitation, irreparable emotional injury, and something called "loss of consortium," which I understand had something to do with his girlfriend. He also sought compensatory damages on the grounds that I had grossly deflated his ego.

Worse still, he was threatening a civil rights action against me, claiming that he was a member of a minority group (Generation X) which has been discriminated against by the Baby Boomers, of which I am a member.

Once I realized that Geoff was playing hardball, I fired him. But the next day he showed up for work with a court order which said I was legally prohibited from dismissing him while the case was still pending. In addition, he got a special injunction seeking additional monetary damages on the grounds that my attempt to fire him was retaliatory and constituted an attempt to prevent him from exercising his constitutionally protected right to sue me.

So Geoff continued to work for me. Sort of. Because his lawsuit was work-related, he was entitled to spend all of his time on Nexis doing legal research for his case against me. The cost of which he billed to me, in addition to time-and-a-half for overtime.

Work on the book ground to a halt once the court required me to comply with discovery requests made by Geoff's lawyer. I had to hand over all my papers, including my financial records, my diary, even my video rental records, which were very embarrassing. As were the numerous depositions, includ-

ing one six-hour session which was devoted entirely to an argument I once had with a guy from Alamo Rent-a-car.

My lawyer kept assuring me that we had them cold on the civil rights complaint, ego deflation, and loss of consortium, and that we'd probably win everything else. Unless someone on the jury had ever had a problem with an employer.

Of course, my lawyer had also assured me that the other side would come down from its original settlement demand. Instead, as the days dragged on, the number multiplied like bacteria in an unflushed toilet.

By this time the aggravation and uncertainty were beginning to take their toll. Plus the deadline for the book was approaching, and Geoff hadn't written a line in weeks.

Finally, I caved. As I've indicated, I am not free to discuss the precise terms of the settlement. Let's just say that I have more mortgages now than when I started the book. Also, you'll notice that the next chapter is written by Geoff, who appears to have an ax to grind. All I can say is I have a new respect for the efforts of the Republican leadership in Congress to bring some common sense back to our legal system before it careens out of control and destroys us all!

One last thing. If you guys could make whatever you do retroactive, I'd appreciate it.

<h1 align="center">42</h1>

THE DESPERATE NEED FOR ENTITLEMENT REFORM

OR MY GENERATION IS HOPELESSLY SCREWED
BY GEOFF RODKEY, RESEARCH ASSISTANT

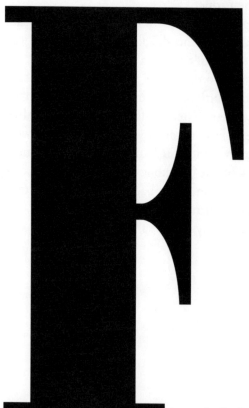

irst of all, I would like to thank my attorney for negotiating the terms of the agreement under which I have been allowed to air my grievances against Mr.

Franken. Since my ongoing medical expenses are likely to consume most of the financial settlement, I consider this chapter my only real compensation for the cruelty to which I have been subjected at the hands of this man.

I could, and perhaps may, write an entire book on the depth of Mr. Franken's self-centeredness. His shameless self-promotion knows no moral or ideological bounds. In Mr. Franken's universe, a fifteen-minute phone conversation with Arianna Huffington, during which the phrases "Greek goddess" and "preeminent social thinker of our time" pass his lips repeatedly, may well be followed by a series of plaintive calls to the White House social office in a pathetic attempt to wheedle an invitation to a dinner honoring Marian Wright Edelman.

While this may sound amusing, I can assure you that watching it at close range, day in and day out, is not. Neither is being forced to watch the videotape of the West Side–Kingsbridge Little League game in its entirety, twice daily, for six consecutive weeks. There is a school of thought which asserts that parenting is the ultimate form of narcissism. Having observed the inner dynamics of the Franken family, I find myself in full agreement.

But I have far too much self-respect to spend the balance of this chapter engaged in the sort of ad hominem attacks which Mr. Franken employs to mask his near-total lack of political insight. Besides which, I have bigger fish to fry.

It occurs to me that Mr. Franken's relentless self-absorption is symptomatic of his entire generation of Baby Boomers. Likewise, the atrocities which I have personally suffered at his hands are destined to be inflicted wholesale upon my entire generation in the not-too-distant future. I am talking about the looming crisis in the social security system.

The economic facts on this point are appalling. The federal government is currently engaged in a massive transfer of

wealth from the young (me) to the old (Mr. Franken's mother). Contrary to the AARP-inspired propaganda that retirees only get out of the social security system what they put in, the average one-earner couple retiring this year will eventually receive a quarter of a million dollars *more* in present dollars than they contributed.

This national Ponzi scheme is currently scheduled to implode in a spectacular fiscal nightmare right about the time Mr. Franken retires. When I first explained this to him, he shrugged it off and suggested that my time would be better spent researching synonyms for the word "fat."

At first I assumed that Mr. Franken simply did not grasp the contours of the issue. Here, after all, is a man who to this day believes that the Education Department's Goals 2000 program actually has something to do with World Cup soccer. So I carefully explained that unfunded liabilities in the social security system already amount to about nine trillion dollars, a sum which is almost twice that of the current national debt.

Mr. Franken pondered this, then asked me to make a graph comparing that number to Rush Limbaugh's weight in pounds. When I informed him that such a graph, if scaled at one hundred pound/dollars per inch, would be over a million miles high, he dismissed the idea as impractical and recued the videotape of his son's game-winning throw against Kingsbridge.

Undeterred, I pointed out that if the social security problem were left to fester, his son's generation would face a lifetime tax rate of 84 percent. At this point Mr. Franken paused the videotape and, in a rare moment of intellectual honesty, admitted to me the reason he has refused to address the social security crisis in his book.

Mr. Franken, it turns out, is deathly afraid that if we reform the social security system, his mother will have to move in

with him. It is exactly this fear that has led some eighty million Baby Boomers to make a Faustian pact with their political leaders to lay waste to our nation in exchange for another twenty years of relative peace.

This is in direct contrast to my generation. Most of us can't afford to leave home to begin with. And by the time we manage to get jobs that pay us well enough to strike out on our own, the Baby Boomers in the federal government will raise payroll taxes again, beating us back into our parents' basements with our spouses and children in tow.

By then the inevitable crisis will be upon us. Already denied the opportunity to own our own homes or send our children to college, what meager financial reserves we do have will be wiped out in the inevitable hyperinflation that will result when the government is forced to monetize the debt. Those of us who do not starve to death will die of easily preventable diseases because we *still* won't be able to afford health insurance.

The only alternative to this apocalyptic scenario is generational warfare. On this point let there be no mistake: in any conflict which pits Generation X against either the baby boomers or their parents, *we will lose*. We are poorly educated, Nintendo-addicted children of divorce, intermingled with the occasional crack baby. Those of us who haven't been lulled into a state of mild hypnosis by the Fox Network are mostly busying ourselves with discovering new and different parts of our bodies to pierce. And our generational representation in Congress is limited to Patrick Kennedy.

Collectively, our only hope is that the baby boomers experience some sort of spiritual awakening—or at least a modicum of shame—that leads them to shoulder their part of the burden before it crushes us completely. If the track record of the "Me Generation" is any indication, this will not happen.

As for myself, I am possessed of the clarity of mind which

only a near-death experience can provide. Consequently, I am well equipped to weather the coming "time of troubles" (to borrow a phrase from Pat Robertson) with serenity and resignation. For that, I have Mr. Franken to thank.

(Mr. Rodkey died of complications from Lyme disease in October 1995. He was 24.)

43

BILL CLINTON: GREATEST PRESIDENT OF THE TWENTIETH CENTURY

s you may
have noticed, I haven't spent a lot of time talking about the

Democrats. That's because we're in such good shape. We currently have the White House, the governorships of several middle-sized states, and a real shot at keeping the Republicans below a filibuster-proof sixty seats in the Senate.

I can't wait until August. We Democrats are going to have one rollicking good time in Chicago. Of course, there'll be some intraparty squabbles between competing factions. Hey, we're Democrats! We've got a big tent. And if we want to hold together that 43 percent of the electorate that voted the Big D last time, we're going to have smooth over the rough edges in our coalition of dispirited liberals, confused moderates, government employees, working-class gays, the voting poor, and the nostalgic elderly. Oh yeah, plus labor.

And who better to forge these disparate elements into a galvanized bloc of electoral steel than the Man from Hope? The man whom I like to call: The Greatest President of the Twentieth Century.

I know you're thinking, "Wait a minute, Al. Franklin Roosevelt was the greatest president of the century." And I suppose an argument *could* be made for FDR. Or Truman, I guess. Or Wilson, Kennedy, or Johnson. Or the other Roosevelt, if you're a Republican. Or Reagan, if you're a fucking idiot.

Well, I think it's time someone made the case for Bill Clinton. In fact, I believe one of the reasons we lost control of Congress in '94 was that he hasn't received anywhere near the credit he deserves.

Admittedly, some of that is his fault. Sometimes he gets off message. For example, in '93 he was off message for pretty much the whole year. And in large parts of '94. Whitewater was a big distraction. And they really ambushed us with that midnight basketball thing.

By mid-'95, though, he was right on message, delivering a balanced budget proposal against the wishes of just about every Democrat in Congress. But like I said, we've got a big tent, and you have to expect a little grousing sometimes.

That's why it's particularly important for someone to cut through all the political hype and set the record straight. Why me? Well, for one thing, I really want to get invited to dinner at the White House. And once this book comes out, the chances of my eating with a Republican president are going to be pretty slim.

So here goes. Bill Clinton, greatest twentieth-century President.

First things first. Gays in the military. Right out of the gate, Clinton proved he was willing to offend tens of millions of Americans to honor a commitment on an issue of relatively little consequence to our nation's future. Then he backpedaled, proving he's no straightjacketed ideologue.

Honoring another campaign commitment—to choose a Cabinet that "looked like America"—Clinton stocked his administration with an adulterous Hispanic, a couple of mildly crooked black guys, a six-foot-one woman whose mother used to wrestle alligators, and a four-foot-tall Jewish guy. Which doesn't look like America at all, but it's an exceptional model of diversity.

In a brilliant political maneuver, for which he's never received credit, Clinton used the nomination process as a tool to open a national dialogue on a festering social problem. I think I speak for every American when I say we're all much more aware of the problem of yuppies who don't pay social security for their domestic help than we were during the "hear-no-evil, see-no-evil" Bush administration.

Meanwhile, America was falling in love with the Clintons. Hillary's hairstyles were aped by women across the country. Journalists of all stripes swooned during Bill's press conferences. Huge popular demand coaxed a bashful First Brother Roger out of his shell to record an album of soulful R&B croonings. And millions of kids across America begged their parents to send them to private school just like Chelsea.

Having conquered the hearts and minds of the country, Clinton set out to conquer Capitol Hill. Working with such bold visionaries as Dick Gephardt, Tom Foley, and Dan Rostenkowski in the House, as well as the gritty, take-no-prisoners George Mitchell in the Senate, Clinton pushed the 1993 Deficit Reduction Act through Congress by rallying a sizeable majority of his own party around the flag of slightly smaller government. Fifty senators and 218 Representatives marched in lockstep, providing a comfortable margin of one vote in the House and giving Vice President Gore the Constitutionally protected honor of breaking the tie in the Senate.

As the deficit plummeted to $161 billion a year, the Clinton juggernaut rolled on like a panzer through France: Family Leave. Americorps. Reinventing Government. Expansion of Head Start. The School-to-Work Program. NAFTA. GATT. The Brady Bill. The Assault Weapons Ban. The Crime Bill. A cease-fire in Northern Ireland. Democracy in Haiti. Peace in the Middle East. Six million new jobs. And both inflation and unemployment at near-record lows.

Jesus Christ. This guy really *is* a good President. And I was going to spend the rest of this chapter being sarcastic. There's a real irony at work here. I mean, here I was trying to write a scathing piece on Clinton, and at a certain point it just became impossible.

Wow. This kind of thing never happened when I was writing the Phil Gramm chapter.

And you know who else is really great? Hillary.

(The White House social office can reach Mr. Franken via Delacorte Press.)

44

ADVENTURES IN POLITICS
SEPTEMBER 9, 1995

Washington Hilton
I Attend the Christian Coalition "Road to Victory" Conference and Become Ill

f the Road to Victory Conference convinced me of anything, it's that I wouldn't make a good

journalist. A journalist's job is to observe and report. I observed and got a migraine.

I'd decided to go because the rise of the Christian Coalition amounts to one of the most astounding political stories of the last decade. Its founder, televangelist Pat Robertson, built the 1.6 million–strong coalition out of the ashes—or, really, the mailing lists—of his failed 1988 presidential campaign. Under the leadership of Robertson and made-for-TV Boy Wonder Ralph Reed, the coalition is now the single largest political action group in America and effectively controls the Republican party in at least twelve states, including Texas and Florida.

And six years ago the organization didn't even exist. Robertson and Reed have somehow managed to convert a group of Americans whose previous organized political activity was pretty much limited to picketing Ozzy Osbourne concerts into a force that now runs school boards and legislatures all over the country. And now they were getting together for their annual blowout, and all the Republican presidential candidates (all the pro-life ones anyway) had signed on for the opportunity to snuggle up.

Unfortunately, I wound up missing a lot of the snuggling, because, basically, after a couple hours I had to lie down. In a dark, quiet room. So if my report is a little sketchy, please cut me some slack.

Pat Robertson—Founder, Leader, Lunatic

The person I really wanted to hear speak was Robertson, because I had done a lot of research on the guy. Research that, frankly, made me nervous. For example, I learned that Pat Robertson believes that a satanic conspiracy led by Jews has threatened the world for centuries.

Now I know you might be thinking: C'mon, Robertson's

not a *nut*! He's a businessman, a reverend, a graduate of Yale Law School. Yeah, I guess you're right. I mean faith healing, that's pretty mainstream:

> There's a woman named Marcia who's got cancer of the throat and the Lord has just healed you . . . someone else who has a lung fungus has just been healed by God's power. . . . A hernia has been healed. If you're wearing a truss you can take it off. It's gone! Several people are being healed of hemorrhoids and varicose veins . . . in the center section here, somebody's just been healed of an ulcer.

That's from the *700 Club*, where faith healing has been a regular feature. Kind of like Stupid Pet Tricks.

OK, you might say. So he's a little fervent. Maybe even a nut. But what about this satanic conspiracy stuff? C'mon, Al. Be fair.

> It may well be that men of goodwill like Woodrow Wilson, Jimmy Carter, and George Bush, who sincerely want a larger community of nations living at peace in our world, are in reality unknowingly and unwittingly carrying out the mission and mouthing the phrases of a tightly knit cabal whose goal is nothing less than a new order for the human race under the domination of Lucifer and his followers.

That's from Robertson's 1991 book, *The New World Order*, the paperback edition of which begins with a couple pages' worth of quotes in praise of the book. Somewhat mysteriously, all of them are anonymous, including my favorite: "I hardly ever read or even finish a book . . . I finished this one."

Well, I also hardly ever read or finish a book, but Geoff read *The New World Order* and highlighted some of the better passages with a yellow marker. I had trouble reading the yellow and had Geoff reunderline with a green marker. And I must say, after reading the greenish yellow stuff, I was a bit unsettled.

> It is reported in Frankfurt, Jews for the first time were admitted to the order of Freemasons. If indeed members of the Rothschild family or their close associates were polluted by the occultism of Weishaupt's Illuminated Freemasonry, we may have discovered the link between the occult and the world of high finance.

Actually, this was good to know. See, I've been looking for the link between the occult and the world of high finance for years, and wouldn't you know it, the missing link is a Jew. Uncle Baron. (I wish!)

Continuing on, I discovered that this secret cabal of Jewish bankers (usually referred to as "Europeans" or "Germans") had its hand in the "satanic carnage" of the French Revolution, the Civil War, Bolshevism, the Cold War, and most recently the Gulf War. And God help those who tried to stop them.

> There is no hard evidence to prove it, but it is my belief that John Wilkes Booth, the man who assassinated Lincoln, was in the employ of the European bankers who wanted to nip this American populist experiment in the bud.

In other words, we Jews didn't just kill Christ, we killed Lincoln. Of course, Robertson admits he has "no hard evidence," and, in fact, he has little proof of anything.

That's why the book is written in an annoying "can it be that . . . ?" style. . . .

> **Can it be** that the phrase "the new world order" means something entirely different to the inner circle of a secret society than it does to the ordinary person. . . ?

> . . . **is there not a possibility** that the Wall Street bankers . . . enthusiastically financed Bolshevism . . . for the purpose of saddling the potentially rich Soviet Union with a totally wasteful and inefficient system that in turn would force the Soviets to be dependent on Western bankers for their survival?

> **Is it possible** that the Gulf War was, in fact, a setup?

> Before the war [WWI], monarchies held sway. After the war, socialism and high finance held sway. **Was it planned that way or was it merely** an "accident" of history?

> **Can it be** that the leader of American's most powerful grass-roots political movement is a raving lunatic? **Is there not a possibility** that Robertson himself is Satan and that the members of the Christian Coalition are, in fact, his unwitting dupes? **Is it possible** that the Republican party is in the thrall of Lucifer? **Was it planned that way or was it merely** an "accident" of history?* (See bottom of page for answers.)

* yes, no, yes, "accident of history"

By now I know some of you are thinking: "Wait a minute. Robertson is a supporter of Israel. He can't be anti-Semitic!"

Let's take this one step at a time. I have not said that Robertson was anti-Semitic. I said only that he was a lunatic who thinks that a satanic conspiracy led by Jews has threatened the world for centuries.

Robertson *is* a big supporter of Israel. And if you read his interpretation of prophecy as put forth in his 1990 book *The Last Millenium*, you'll learn why. According to Robertson, Israel must exist so that when Armageddon rolls around, it can get wiped off the face of the Earth. At that point, says Robertson, "the Jews will cry out to the one they have so long rejected."

In a way, Robertson's words would prove prophetic. Two hours into the Road to Victory Conference, I was moaning, "Jesus! Have I got a headache!"

THE CONFERENCE—RALPH REED, EMCEE

Unless you make it a point to catch the *700 Club*, you don't see much of Pat Robertson these days. That's because the spokesman of the Christian Coalition is now its baby-faced executive director Ralph Reed. Reed is a self-professed practitioner of "stealth" politics.* "Every moment you disguise your position and your truth from the enemy," he has said.

But since the press was covering this event, the Ralph Reed who opened the Road to Victory Conference presented the

---

* Basically, these "stealth" tactics include "voters' guides," which are mailed out containing misleading information about opposition candidates; telephone smear campaigns; anonymous flyers which demonize opponents. That sort of thing.

moderate, "healing" face of the Christian Coalition. That was frightening enough.

Celebrating the progress that had been made since the last conference, Reed boasted: "Howard Metzenbaum (BOOS FROM THE CROWD), one of our favorite members of the U.S. Senate, has been replaced by a pro-family, pro-life *Roman Catholic* (CHEERS), Mike Dewine." That's when the veins in my head started contracting.

Then he reminded the crowd that "we bear the name of He at which every knee shall bow and every tongue shall confess." By now my head had started throbbing.

Speaking of tongues, Reed urged participants in the conference to refrain from "violence of the tongue." Two minutes later, he engaged in a little tongue-violence himself, telling a bald-faced lie about Joycelyn Elders. Ralph claimed she had "called for the legalization of drugs," which is just plain false.

How Big a Nut Is He?

"The feminist agenda . . . is not about equal rights for women. It is about a socialist, anti-family political movement that encourages women to leave their husbands, kill their children, practice witchcraft and become lesbians."

Pat Robertson, fund-raising letter to Iowans

Reed also touched on the subject of my book. Noting that Mario Cuomo is now a talk-show host, Reed joked, "I know Rush Limbaugh. Rush Limbaugh is a friend of mine, and you, sir, are no Rush Limbaugh." The crowd loved that one, especially the tow-headed 14-year-old Christian Coalition kid who, when he saw me on the edge of the crowd, rushed up to have his picture taken. I guess because I'm on TV. And I'm pretty sure he didn't know my poli-

tics. As he shook my hand, I got a very nervous feeling that his parents would burn the picture once this book comes out.

Reed, it turns out, is also a fan. Or at least he says so. Remember, he believes in "stealth" politics, so he might have just been "coming in under my radar screen." At one point, I tried to buttonhole Reed to see if we could talk. He saw me as he was coming offstage, smiled, and extended his hand. "Al," he said exuberantly, "I'm a big fan. What's the name of that character with the yellow sweater?"

"Stuart Smalley," I said, shaking his hand.

"I love him!"

I shouldn't have been surprised. As evangelical Christians go, Reed is very well versed in popular culture. In fact, a 1994 *People* magazine profile began with Reed extolling the virtues of John and Paul:

> *Sgt. Pepper* was one of the most significant albums in the history of rock and roll. Lennon was a dark and troubled genius, and the Beatles elevated rock music to a kind of art form.

When I read that, my first thought was that Reed is just a real big Beatles fan. But then I remembered what Reed has said about his approach to politics:

> It's like guerrilla welfare. . . . You've got two choices: You can wear cammies and shimmy along on your belly, or you can put on a red coat and stand up for everyone to see. It comes down to whether you want to be the British Army in the Revolutionary War or the Vietcong. History tells us which tactic was more effective.

This got me thinking that maybe Reed's hipster knowledge of popular culture had been a bit of camouflage, designed to lull the Baby-Boomer *People* reporter into letting his guard down.

How far can something like this go? Imagine Reed in a Florida condo complex trying to win over a crowd of elderly Jews. "Hackett was the master of the heartburn joke, whereas Rickles is still the consummate practitioner of the ethnic putdown. Yet at the end of the evening, Rickles makes it clear that he loves everyone and is just kidding."

Or suppose Reed wanted to sway a group of Harlem teenagers. "Public Enemy are more than just a fly posse. *Fear of a Black Planet* is a political manifesto, boyee. Chuck D is a prophet of rage, knowutImsayin'?"

But I digress.

Reed agreed to give me a five-minute interview and suggested I speak with his press secretary, Mike Russell. I found Russell, who also told me he was a big fan. He told me to call him in a few days to set up the interview. I called. Many times. He never called back. Frankly, I don't think that's very Christian. Then again, if I were him, *I* wouldn't call me.

I reentered the hall to hear Reed introduce Newt. "Newt Gingrich was pro-family before pro-family was cool." I tried to figure out if that meant being pro-family became cool *before* or *after* Newt got those blow jobs from the wife of a fellow college professor.

This was interesting. How would Newt address the oral revelations in the recently published *Vanity Fair* article in front of the Christian Coalition? As it turned out, he did it the usual way. By attacking liberals:

> A number of liberals, particularly columnists and reporters, start with two standards, and these are their two standards: A number of Republican candidates for

president . . . and I'm not one but I fit because I'm a national leader . . . who say they're pro-family are divorced. "Hah! We know what that means. So what right do they have?" Now, they have a second standard: People like Jesse Helms have been married too long to understand the problems of modern America. (BIG LAUGH) . . . So the only people you should listen to are social therapists who do not believe in God and who will tell you that you should simply relax and accept your decay and your depravity because it's the most you've got. (HUGE APPLAUSE)

Yes. That's us liberals, all right. When we're not attacking Jesse Helms for being married too long, we're paying our atheist therapists to tell us to accept our depravity.

I had a whole day of this stuff. I heard speakers from the podium refer to people like me as "lewd leftists," call liberals "corrupt and licentious," and say that "liberalism had made a pact with the devil." Also, it seems that the Prophet Isaiah had a real beef with the Great Society, saying all liberals were "vile. And they hate the poor."

I walked into a smaller "breakout session" on the 104th Congress, where one Christian referred to the President as "a scumbag," the First Lady as a "scumbagette," and their daughter as a "scumbagger."

Then there's abortion. Here's something I'll bet you didn't know. According to one speaker, "Of the four women listed in the genealogy of Jesus Christ . . . one [was] a product of rape and one a product of incest." Good thing for Western civilization that *Roe v. Wade* didn't take effect two thousand years earlier.

I heard a lot about prayer in school. Right now, the Coalition is pushing for the Religious Equality Amendment, which would allow "voluntary, student and citizen-initiated free

speech in noncompulsory settings such as courthouse lawns, high school graduation ceremonies, and sports events." I think this means you could have a homecoming float with the nativity scene on it, but I'm not sure. I'm pretty certain, though, that if the Blessed Mother had pom-poms, it would spoil the whole thing for everybody.

By now you may be thinking that I'm showing an anti-Christian bias. Nonsense! Need I remind you that I *married* a Roman Catholic, whom I met in college, despoiled, and then convinced to renounce the Pope? So give me a break.

Convicted felons were invited to speak. Former Nixon aide Chuck "Let's firebomb the Brookings Institute" Colson, who found Christ in prison, not only spoke but, if I heard correctly, was the recipient of this year's Layman of the Year Award. I think that's fine. I'm all for redemption. But I'd be pissed if I had been Layman of the Year runner-up.

Ollie North spoke about the importance of electing local officials. And the Coalition has had tremendous success recently in taking over local school boards. All part of its attempt to rid curricula of "politically correct" liberal ideas like, say, evolution.

In fact, Creationism rou-

> ### *Hey Gals, Check This Out!*
>
> "You know who's pushing [abortion]. You saw some of those women out there. I mean those women aren't ever going to have a baby by anybody. I mean, these are primarily lesbians, and lesbians don't have babies. And it's the one thing a mother has—that a lesbian can never have—is this femininity, and they can never achieve that. And so, in order to level the field, they say, "Hey, let you abort your baby so you'll be like us, because we don't have them.' "
>
> Pat Robertson,
> *700 Club*

tinely won enthusiastic applause at the conference. I asked a nice 40-year-old woman named Pat from Florida about her views on the subject. She told me that God created man in his own image ten thousand years ago, not four billion, as those godless "experts" at universities believe. "Ten thousand?" I asked.

"Ten thousand." She nodded.

I asked her if she had seen *Jurassic Park*. She said that she had and that her entire family loved it. I tried to explain to her that she had to choose. Either *Jurassic Park* or Creationism. You can't have both.

Pat didn't seem to get my point. But she was very nice, noticed I was ill, and wordlessly led me by the hand to her hotel room, where we spent an evening of unbridled passion.

Okay, that last part is just not true. What I actually did was go over to the American Enterprise Institute and take a nap on Norm Ornstein's couch.

So I missed Pat Robertson's speech. I learned later I would have been disappointed. He made no mention of any centuries-old satanic plots and, other than a passing reference to possibly repealing some of the sixties civil rights legislation, said nothing that could be construed as insane, apocalyptic, or even vaguely anti-Semitic.

I missed most of the presidential candidates, too. But I understand that most of them gave their standard stump speeches, only with a lot more references to fetuses.

In fact, I missed so many of the speeches that I've decided to ask the Christian Coalition for a partial refund on the $40 registration fee. Which I'm going to do as soon as Ralph Reed calls me back. Of course, I figure the chances of that are about as good as the chances of an unrepentant Jew surviving the Apocalypse.

(Send anti-Semitic hate mail to Delacorte Press, attn: Jewish Media Conspirators.)

45
EPILOGUE:
A TIME FOR HEALING

By the next day my

headache had disappeared. And yet, as I flew back to New York, I felt overwhelmed by a disquieting spiritual emptiness. In a way, I envied the absolute moral certainty of the people I met at the Road to Victory Conference. Sure, a lot of them were sanctimonious zealots. But some of them had seemed very nice. One or two had even offered to pray for me. And now it was my intention to make them objects of my ridicule.

I thought about what Ralph Reed had said about "violence of the tongue." Yes, Reed had been hypocritical about that himself, but it was Christ who said on the cross: "Forgive them, Father, for they know not what they do." Then I remembered that Reed knows exactly what he's doing and got mad all over again.

But I began to think about this book in terms of that phrase: Violence of the tongue. Is that what *Rush Limbaugh Is a Big Fat Idiot and Other Observations* had become? Is that what I was giving my readers? Don't I owe you more? Don't I owe America more?

I thought back to the Americans I had met at the Perot conference. Some of them were crackpots, sure. But I thought about Hank from Michigan, a retired autoworker who was worried about jobs moving overseas. I thought about Louise from Washington state, who was scared for her children because wages for non–college graduates have fallen 20 percent in the last twenty years. I thought about Gayle from Texas, who thought that members of the Bilderbergs, the Council on Foreign Relations, the Trilateral Commission, and the Skull and Bones Society were involved in a worldwide conspiracy.

I opened my briefcase and pulled out a stack of Frank Luntz's research. Most Americans think we're on the wrong track. Americans are working harder and longer for less. If there are two parents in a household (which is getting rarer and rarer), chances are they're both working. Sometimes at

two jobs each. And they're spending less and less time with their kids.

We are all living in a wildly more complicated world than we were born into. And at the same time the trust in our institutions, in government, in family, in individuals, is eroding. And lack of trust creates fear, and fear creates anger.

I thought about how our political system appeals to the worst, not the best, in us. Not to the goodness of America. And again I thought about this book.

Maybe, I thought, maybe *I'm* on the wrong track. Yes, someone needs to take on demagogues like Limbaugh and Gingrich and Robertson. But maybe I'm doing my country a disservice. Maybe I'm sowing the very seeds of distrust that I so decry.

Perhaps, I thought, I should throw away the 200-plus pages of cheap, tawdry, mean-spirited (yet accurate) bile, and start over on a book whose humor heals rather than wounds.

Then, as we flew over Manhattan, I happened to look down and catch a glimpse of the Delacorte building, and it occurred to me that my book was due in a week.

Then we flew over my daughter's private school. And then my son's orthodontist. Followed by the bank that holds the mortgage on my apartment.

And as the plane turned and banked its wings, a stream of light pierced the window, bathing my face in the orange glow of the sun setting over the American continent. And I thought to myself, "You know, Rush Limbaugh *is* a big fat idiot."

THE END

INDEX

ACKNOWLEDGMENTS

This is my second book. The first book, *I'm Good Enough, I'm Smart Enough, and Doggone It, People Like Me* (Dell, $9.95), was a work of fiction. Basically I just made things up. Which meant I didn't have all that many people to thank. The foundation of this book, however, is hard, factual information. And that means I had the help of a lot of people who know things.

My research assistant, Geoff Rodkey, was responsible for pulling together the information in a way that was useful to me and, hopefully, entertaining to you. This meant culling the newspapers, reading books by people like Rush Limbaugh and Pat Robertson, and nagging people at think tanks. As the process of writing the book progressed, Geoff became more and more indispensable, not just as a researcher, but as a source of humor, inspiration, and good sound judgment. And more than occasionally, he cleaned up my prose.

On that score, bad stuff that got past Geoff did not get past the keen eye of my editor, Leslie Schnur. Despite being pregnant with twins, Leslie worked tirelessly and gave me constant encouragement, mainly so I'd finish on time.

My agent, Jonathon Lazear, also gave me a tremendous amount of encouragement, and not just in the form of the sizable advance he negotiated.

Jonathon's wife, Wendy, was among the friends who read that manuscript as I was writing it. I apologize to Wendy and to David Mandel, Hazel Lichterman, and Melissa Mathis for my neediness, but thanks to all of you for spending so much time with me on the phone.

And special thanks to Norman Ornstein of the American Enterprise Institute, who spent the most time on the phone with me, fulfilling the triple function of friend, reader, and think-tank expert.

Which brings me back to the people who know things. They include Thomas Mann of the Brookings Institute, Brian Blackstone of the Competitiveness Policy Council, Jonathan Alter and Howard Fineman of *Newsweek*, John Camp of CNN, Steve Talbot of *Frontline*, Peter Boyer of *The New Yorker*, Ben Jones, Steve Jost, Dave Mizner of People for the American Way, Diane Colasanto of Princeton Survey Research, Brian Johnson from the Council on Environmental Quality, Kathleen Hall Jamieson of the Annenberg School for Communications, Mark Mellman of Mellman and Lazarus, and Kenan Block of the *MacNeil/Lehrer NewsHour*.

I had lunch with James Carville, who told me I could call his researcher Lowell Weiss for assistance. I did. A lot.

My friend Wendell Willkie II gave me the benefit of his expertise on tort reform. My pal Lawrence O'Donnell, likewise, on welfare. All my information on Lyme disease came from my friend-since-junior-high Dr. David Griffin.

James Retter gave me insight into Rush Limbaugh, as did Warren Hudson. Dan Bateman helped conceptualize the bar graphs for the Reagan Years chapter. Dick Benson and John Drony, two Vietnam vets, consulted on "Operation Chickenhawk."

William Bramhall's illustrations are the perfect complement for that piece. I thank him for his artistry.

Kristin Kiser from Delacorte was terrific to work with on the mechanics of the book. For that matter, everyone at Delacorte has treated me with far more respect than I deserve.

Then there are the Conservatives whose kindnesses I took advantage of: Frank Luntz, Josette Shiner, Arianna Huffington, George Will, Richard Viguerie, John Kasich, Bob

Dornan. None of them knew the title of the book when they agreed to cooperate with me. I think I did tell Ben Stein the title. Also, a hearty megadittoes to those Conservatives who didn't call me back.

And finally, I want to thank my family. My kids, Thomasin and Joe, whose dedication to social justice is ever inspiring. Well, that's not actually true. But they're good kids.

And mostly, to my wife, Franni. Who, believe me, has *tremendous* patience. Honey, thanks.

Al Franken is best known for his Emmy award-winning work on *Saturday Night Live.* He is the author of *I'm Good Enough, I'm Smart Enough, and Doggone It, People Like Me!* and co-author of the hit movie *When a Man Loves a Woman.* He also wrote and starred in the motion picture *Stuart Saves His Family.* He lives in New York City with his wife and two children.